PREPARE!

An Ecumenical
Music and Worship Planner

2025–2026

David L. Bone
and
Mary Scifres

Abingdon Press
Nashville

PREPARE! AN ECUMENICAL MUSIC AND WORSHIP PLANNER 2025–2026

ISBN 978-1-7910-2698-1

MANUFACTURED IN CHINA

Do you have the book you need?
We want you to have the best planner,
designed to meet your specific needs.
How do you know if you have
the right resource?
Simply complete this one-question quiz:

Do you lead worship in a United Methodist congregation?

Yes.

Use *The United Methodist Music and Worship Planner, 2025–2026* (ISBN: 9781791026936)

No.

Use *Prepare! An Ecumenical Music and Worship Planner, 2025–2026* (ISBN: 9781791026981)

To order these resources, call Cokesbury toll-free at 1-877-877-8674, or shop online at www.cokesbury.com.

Do you find yourself rushing at the last minute to order your new planner? Subscribe today and receive your new *The United Methodist Music and Worship Planner* or *Prepare! An Ecumenical Music and Worship Planner* automatically next year and every year. Call toll-free 1-800-672-1789 to request subscription.

Using *Prepare!*

How We Organize the Resource Lists

Prepare! is designed to give you as many ideas as possible about a given worship service. Use it along with a worship plan notebook that you create, a copy of your church's hymnal, and other supplements you use such as *The Faith We Sing* or *Worship & Song*. Features of *Prepare!* include:

- NEW THIS YEAR! THREE new primary hymnals have been added to the references: *Our Great Redeemer's Praise, Songs of Zion,* and *Zion Still Sings.*
- CONTINUED FEATURES!
  - Two versions of the lectionary scriptures are now found for each worship entry. Scriptures on the left-hand columns come from the New Revised Standard Version Updated Edition of the Bible and scriptures on the right-hand columns come from the Common English Bible Version. Where available, we have added psalter numbers from the *UM Hymnal.*
  - Many new hymn, song, and other suggestions have been added, all marked with a + symbol.
  - With the expanded scripture format, we've been able to expand the suggestion lists and add some "white space" for your own notes as you plan.
  - There is a new short section of **Other Hymn Resources**. These are items from other hymnals that may be of interest to you. With proper licensing, these can be projected or printed for your congregation. Most of these have been published since the publication of our United Methodist resources. See the "Hymn Resources" list on page 7 for the key to these other hymnals.
  - The Contemporary and Modern Suggestions continue to include the **CCLI number** from https://songselect.ccli.com, but this year the Primary Hymns and Songs for the Day list includes these as well. Additionally, we've also added numbers from **OneLicense.net** in both lists to expand your access to songs beyond the hymnals in your library. These licensing numbers are used universally by musicians who subscribe to either or both of these services. Each year, we'll continue building in more and more of those licensing numbers to ease your planning process and expand your repertoire. NOTE: Assigning these numbers is an inexact science, and depending on your use, another number may be the most accurate.
  - We've combined our suggestions for vocal musical offerings (anthems, solos, and duets) into one category **Solo/Ensemble Suggestions**. We hope this will encourage you to think beyond specific categories. Could this anthem be sung as a solo? Could this solo work as a unison anthem or praise band offering? Could this melody inspire a prelude or postlude? Or do I have that title in a different arrangement in my files?
  - Most **anthems** suggested in the **Solo/Ensemble** lists include a link to the publisher's online version of the anthem, which often includes recordings. Simply enter the http://bit.ly/... link in your browser to reach the appropriate page.
  - There is a **Hymn Anthem** arrangement for each entry. These are primarily designed to help smaller ensembles sing anthems directly from the hymnal. These may also be used as solos or creative ways to introduce a hymn or sing it congregationally.
- Each week **Primary Hymns and Songs for the Day** are suggested first. These suggestions include various helps for singing the hymns. These hymns and songs have the closest relationship to the scriptures and are widely known. The lengthier lists of **Additional Hymn Suggestions** and **Additional Contemporary and Modern Suggestions** will add variety to your musical selections.
- The musical suggestions are chosen to suggest a wide variety of styles.
- Each item is referenced to scripture or occasion.
- **Opening (O)** and **Closing (C)** hymns are suggested for each worship service.
- At least one **Communion (Comm.)** hymn is recommended for the first Sunday of each month and liturgical season. When appropriate, Communion hymns related to the scriptures are noted on other days as well.
- **Additional Contemporary and Modern Suggestions** include not only praise choruses but also global and ethnic music, folk music, and meditative music from traditions such as Taizé. Information about resources referenced in this section can be found on page 7. Please note that contemporary songs may also be listed under **Additional Hymn Suggestions, Solo/Ensemble Suggestions,** or **Other Suggestions**.
  - **One word of advice:** Be sure to consult all the music suggestions regardless of the type of service you are planning. In the changing world of worship, no one style defines a song or a worship service. Many items appropriate for contemporary and emergent styles are listed under the **Additional Hymn Suggestions**, and many resources for traditional and blended services can be found in the **Additional Contemporary and Modern Suggestions** list. **Solo/Ensemble Suggestions** and **Other Suggestions** may be appropriate for congregational use as well. Don't let the "category" deter you from using any item that will enhance your worship service. We recommend that worship planners consult all lists when choosing music.
- **Vocal Solos** and **Anthems** provide ideas for vocal music "performance" offerings, and may also inspire ideas for additional congregational selections.
- The recommended **vocal solos** are taken from a group of ten collections that range from contemporary settings of hymn texts and praise choruses to spirituals to well-known classics (see p. 7). Augment these suggestions from your own library. The recommended anthems include new works as well as generally known

works that are already in many church choral libraries. This year, these suggestions lean toward easier and less complicated anthems as many post-pandemic choirs are smaller. Likewise, many anthem suggestions are taken from the three volumes of the Augsburg Easy Choirbook (AEC) series. Your understanding of the week's theme along with study of scripture and hymn texts will lead you to music in your repertoire that corresponds to the day's message.

- **Other Suggestions** also include words for worship, suggestions for choral introits and sung benedictions, and ideas for musical responses related to the spoken liturgy.
- Suggestions for **Visuals** are offered for each service. See the article "Visuals in Worship" (p. 6) for discussion of these suggestions. Visual ideas are found in the **Other Suggestions** lists. They have been compiled by Ashley M. Calhoun and supplemented by our authors. Ashley is known for his inventive use of "found" items in creating visual worship settings. Worship committees, visual artists, dancers, and altar guilds can use these ideas to create their own unique worship centers, altarpieces, banners, and dance images. Screen visual artists can use these themes to select appropriate background and theme screens for worship.
- **Themes** for the day are listed in the Other Suggestions and found in the **Theme Index** (see p. 262). These tools will help with thematic planning when a community is following a thematic/sermon series rather than the Lectionary.
- A two-year, at-a-glance **2025–2026 Calendar** follows the **Worship Planning Sheets** (see p. 272). It includes a note on the lectionary years covered in this edition of *Prepare!*
- *Prepare!* uses the *Revised Common Lectionary.* From the Second Sunday after Pentecost to Christ the King Sunday, the lectionary includes two patterns of readings. One pattern includes semi-continuous readings from the Hebrew Scriptures, Epistles, and Gospels. These readings are not necessarily related but allow for a sequential experience of the biblical narrative. **This is the pattern used to determine the scripture texts included in *Prepare!*** It is the pattern followed by most users of the hymnals referenced. In the second pattern, the Hebrew scripture is chosen to relate to the Gospel passage. This pattern is used primarily in traditions where Communion is celebrated at every service of worship. These **Alternate Lections** may be found in *The Revised Common Lectionary* (Abingdon Press, 1992) or online at http://lectionary.library.vanderbilt.edu/. Worship planners may certainly choose to follow the pattern that best serves the needs and traditions of your church. Neither pattern is necessarily better than the other; they are simply different ways of offering scripture in the worship setting over a three-year cycle in the church.

Planning Worship with These Resources

When planning any worship service, it is always best to start with the scripture and let it guide your thoughts and plans. It is also helpful if a specific theme arising from the texts is chosen as a focal point for your planning. If your church is not using the *Revised Common Lectionary* but you do know what the scripture text or theme will be for a service, look up that text in the **Scripture Index** on page 263 or look up the theme in the **Theme Index** on page 262.

As you read and study the scripture passages, read the full list of suggested music, to inspire not just hymn selections, but also anthems, solos, or keyboard selections. It is wise to mark your hymnal with the dates individual hymns are sung to avoid singing some too frequently. The **Hymn Enhancement Resources** (see p. 7) can enhance congregational singing but should be used sparingly.

Use a three-ring binder to organize your plans. For each service of worship, include a copy of one of the **Worship Planning Sheets** found on pages 266–268 (or design your own!) along with blank paper for listing further ideas. Do not simply "fill in the blanks" for each service, but use the Planning Sheet to guide your work.

Use the suggestions in *Prepare!* along with your own page of ideas to begin making decisions about worship. Will the choir sing a "Call to Worship"? Can a hymn verse serve as a prayer response? Can a particular anthem or vocal solo give direction to the sermon? What prayers will be used?

Once your decisions are made, complete the **Worship Planning Sheet**. Make a separate list of tasks related to that service. Planning worship is an awesome responsibility, but one that can be accomplished with an organized effort along with spiritual guidance.

Can the Lectionary Still Liberate?

Reasons to Keep Using the *Revised Common Lectionary* in Worship Planning

Mary Scifres

The question arises for worship leaders and ordained ministers, "How does one prepare worship services that allow the flexibility necessary for the work of the Holy Spirit while also ordering the life of prayer and meditation to encourage disciplined growth?" Even in a world enamored with theme-based planning, new lectionaries like *Seasons of Creation* and the *Narrative Lectionary*, the *Revised Common Lectionary* can be one of the best liberators for organizing and designing creative, meaningful worship. Although my writing partner David Bone and I use many resources in our creative planning and respect the diversity of resources available, we still see the lectionary as a helpful tool on which to base inspired worship planning to encourage growth in the life of the church. Even theme-based worship is easily created from lectionary-based worship, as you can see from our addition of **Theme Ideas** to our weekly **Other Suggestions** in this volume.

Attempting to coordinate the message of the musical selections, the visual images, the words of worship with the message of the pulpit is a time-consuming and important task for church staff and worship leaders. Time and again, we hear from worship leaders who discover that lectionary use frees them for creative design time that otherwise would need to be spent in coordination meetings and individualized research. Church musicians, artists, laypersons, worship coordinators, and pastors give many hours each week to plan worship services that proclaim the Word, strengthen and challenge the community, and deepen the participants' faith. Ordained and diaconal ministers face the challenge of writing and choosing texts, prayers, and sermons for worship each week; musicians select, plan, and rehearse a variety of vocal and instrumental music to enhance and facilitate the worship experience of the churches they serve; and church artists and lay worship leaders pursue means of leading worship, preparing the sanctuary for worship, designing additional creative elements, and devising other aspects of the worshiping experience.

The preacher can ease this task significantly by utilizing the *Revised Common Lectionary* and communicating on a regular basis with other church worship leaders regarding worship service needs. A church can find both freedom and unity when the pastoral leadership uses this lectionary as the basis for planning worship and its individual aspects (sermon, hymns, anthems, prayers) without exalting it to a level of sole importance. First, lectionary use prevents the abusive appeal to a limited number of scriptures and topics, toward which some preachers are tempted. Regarding the concern for local needs, the lectionary can provide a means for integrating such needs into the worship service by relating scriptural messages to the current needs and situation of the community. While interpreting the lections for worship, both planners and preachers can find ways of exploring the historical meanings of the texts and bringing such historical understandings into the present.

Second, the pedagogical advantage of using the lectionary to acquaint Christians with the broad tradition of which we are a part can deepen worship and learning experiences of the community of faith. As pastors in the twenty-first century face growing concern regarding the types of "burn out" that result from remaining static in a setting that has become routine instead of a challenge, following the lectionary cycle can open up opportunities for growth and support in a number of ways. Being forced to grapple with difficult texts in addition to familiar passages enlivens the mind and encourages the preacher to look to new exegetical resources and homiletic aids. Support can also come from an ecumenical community of pastors in one's city or county who are studying the same text during the cycle. Study groups within the local church can wrestle with the lectionary scriptures, growing their biblical and theological knowledge in the process.

Likewise, church musicians who wade through piles of contemporary and classical music every season to choose the anthems, organ selections, hymns, responsive psalms, and other musical contributions to the worship service can find a common guide to that selection when the lectionary is used. In the local church, the musician finds the opportunity to be a minister of music and Word when the lections provide the core of the worship service. In a time when the shortage of church musicians affects many churches, a church musician may be able to serve several churches and utilize the same musical selections in each setting. If a church musician, called to full-time ministry of music, can be employed by two or three local congregations who agree to use the same anthems and hymns each week and to schedule worship services at different times, both musician and congregation can benefit from this new approach to music ministry that supports full-time service and receives music of high quality. The possibilities for providing equitable salaries for ministers of music as well as nurturing several local church communities through Spirit-filled, well-performed music are enhanced when the unifying elements of ecumenical cooperation and common lections are available.

In terms of teaching, the lectionary can provide a helpful method of coordinating the community worship experience of Sunday morning with all of the other events—church school, weekly Bible study groups, prayer and devotional groups, music rehearsals, singing and praise gatherings, and other small groups—in the life of the church. Small groups, which sometimes seem to go off in their own directions, away from the Sunday morning community, would more easily feel a part of the fold with the integrative element of the lectionary. And the educational system of the church, which so often leaves teachers and students feeling excluded and separated from the worshiping body, can find inclusion in the integrative element of the lectionary. Children sit through sermons and find meaning in mysterious hymns much more easily when the basic scriptural text has been heard and discussed in church school prior to worship or explored in church school after worship!

Overall, lectionary use can provide an integrative and unifying element to the entire life of the church, when used in its various dimensions through curriculum, worship resources, music selections, and local cooperative church events. Where proclamation of the Word is central, that Word can and should be the integrative element of a holistic worship service. In churches that seek to reach people with a message that is unified thematically, lectionary use provides a scriptural base that all planners know well in advance and can utilize when choosing and developing the themes or topics for the Sundays of any given season. When the lectionary is used in this way, choirs or music teams have adequate time to rehearse appropriate music, liturgists or worship facilitators have sufficient time to write or find liturgy and prayers for the service, and other church artists (actors, dancers, composers, visual artists, banner makers, arts guilds, and screen programmers) may plan and prepare their contributions to the service and the season.

Frequent lectionary use need not limit other options during the year. When preaching pastors are called to address a pressing congregational or community issue, lectionary scriptures can provide a starting point to keep the conversation biblically based in worship. When the Spirit calls a preacher or worship team to focus in a different direction, taking a short or even seasonal break from lectionary use is another option. When a sermon series or a church theme pulls worship designers toward different scriptures, the vast indices in lectionary resources can help you reference scriptures even when used on non-lectionary schedules. Even as a preacher who is led by the Spirit, I find myself returning to the *Revised Common Lectionary* to ease the burden on my staff and create a cohesive conversation as we plan not only worship but also the focused life and ministry of the churches we serve.

With this book, we invite your congregation and its worship leaders to begin the process of integrating your various aspects of worship planning by means of the *Revised Common Lectionary*. As thematic ideas begin to emerge in each week's worship service and as the various scriptures provide diverse bases for worship planning, we hope that you will find worship becoming an increasingly growth-filled and exciting aspect of your congregation's life.

Mary Scifres
admin@maryscifres.com
www.maryscifres.com

Visuals in Worship

Ashley M. Calhoun

The suggestions for visuals in this planner are meant to help worship leaders use objects and images to increase the impact of the gospel on a people who are increasingly visually oriented. These suggestions can be incorporated into many visual elements: hanging and processional banners, worship settings (whether on the altar or in the chancel or narthex), worship folder covers, and bulletin boards. The ideas can also be used to suggest ways to use classical and contemporary works of art, sculpture, needlework, and photography in worship services.

With more churches incorporating screens and video walls into their worship spaces, there is tremendous potential for the use of still or moving imagery. Also, interpretive movement and drama can be very strong in visual impact.

The visual suggestions in this *Planner* have several characteristics:

- The suggestions are not meant to give detailed plans but to spark your imagination and creativity.
- Some are drawn literally from the lessons; others are thematic.
- The suggestions are organized by reference to the lectionary passages:

  O Old Testament or Easter season, Acts reading
  P Psalm reading or Canticle
  E Epistle or New Testament reading
  G Gospel reading

- Chapter and verse numbers are sometimes given to indicate actual phrases in the scripture passage that can serve as visual elements.
- Themes such as forgiveness, love, or rejoicing are offered to encourage creative use of video and photographic images of people engaged in demonstrating those themes.

So much about worship is visual and intended to strengthen the proclamation of the gospel. The worship space is filled with visual elements that send a message. The church year is a treasure trove of color, texture, symbolism, and visual imagery. Special Sundays and special days in the cultural and denominational calendars also offer opportunities for visual expression. Evaluate the visual aspects of your worship services and find ways to enhance the worship experience with thoughtful, intentional use of visual elements and images.

RESOURCE KEY

C — *Chalice Hymnal.* St. Louis: Chalice Press, 1996. ISBN: 9780827280359.

CG — *Celebrating Grace Hymnal.* Macon: Celebrating Grace, 2010. ISBN: 9781936151103.

E — *The Hymnal 1982.* New York: The Church Hymnal Corporation, 1985. ISBN: 9780898691214.

EL — *Evangelical Lutheran Worship.* Minneapolis: Augsburg Fortress, 2006. ISBN: 9780806656182.

G — *Glory to God: The Presbyterian Hymnal.* Louisville: Presbyterian Publishing Corporation, 2013. ISBN: 9780664238971.

GR — *Our Great Redeemer's Praise.* Franklin, Tennessee: Seedbed Publishing, 2022. ISBN 9781628249729.

N — *The New Century Hymnal.* Cleveland, OH: The Pilgrim Press, 1995. ISBN: 9780829810509.

P — *The Presbyterian Hymnal.* Louisville: Westminster/John Knox Press, 1990. ISBN: 9780664100971.

S — *The Faith We Sing.* Nashville: Abingdon Press, 2000. ISBN: 9780687090549 (Pew edition).

SA — *The Song Book of the Salvation Army.* London: The Salvation Army, 2015. ISBN: 9780854129447.

SH — *Santo, Santo, Santo.* Chicago: GIA Publications, Inc., 2019. ISBN: 9781622773961.

UM — *The United Methodist Hymnal. Nashville:* The United Methodist Publishing House, 1989. ISBN: 9780687431328.

VU — *Voice United.* Etobicoke, Ontario, Canada: The United Church Publishing House, 1996. ISBN: 9781551340173.

WS — *Worship & Song.* Nashville: Abingdon Press, 2011. Accompaniment, singer, guitar, and planning editions available. ISBN: 9781426709937 (Pew edition).

WSL — *Worship & Song Leader's Edition.* Nashville: Abingdon Press, 2011. ISBN: 9781426709944 (Leader's edition). NOTE: The resources WSL1–WSL222 refer to the written words for worship (prayers, litanies, benedictions) available in worship resource editions of *Worship & Song.*

Z — *Songs of Zion.* Nashville: Abingdon Press, 1981, 1982. ISBN: 0687391202.

ZS — *Zion Still Sings.* Nashville: Abingdon Press, 2007. ISBN: 9780689335275.

HYMN RESOURCES

S-1 — Smith, Gary Alan, ed. *The United Methodist Hymnal: Music Supplement.* Nashville: Abingdon Press, 1991. ISBN: 9780687431472.

S-2 — Bennett, Robert C., ed. *The United Methodist Hymnal: Music Supplement II.* Nashville: Abingdon Press, 1993. ISBN: 9780687430130.

H-3 — Hopson, Hal H. *The Creative Church Musician Series.* Carol Stream, IL: Hope Publishing Co.
Hbl Vol. 1. *The Creative Use of Handbells in Worship. 1997.* Hope Publishing #1956.
Chr Vol. 2. *The Creative Use of Choirs in Worship. 1999.* Hope Publishing #8013.
Desc *The Creative Use of Descants in Worship. 1999.* Hope Publishing #8018.
Org *The Creative Use of the Organ in Worship. 1997.* Hope Publishing #8070.

CONTEMPORARY SOLOS
See Vocal Solo suggestions from V-3, V-5, and V-9 volumes.

LICENSING NUMBERS
Following the title of many suggestions, you'll find licensing numbers from CCLI SongSelect or OneLicense.

CCLI — License number from songselect.ccli.com
Ex.: "Fairest Lord Jesus" **27800**

OneLicense — License number from onelicense.net
Ex.: "Arise, Your Light Is Come" **OL-07293**

PD — Text and Tune are in the Public Domain and both may be printed and/or projected. NOTE: Usually it is the melody line only that is in the Public Domain. The harmonization may be copyrighted.
Ex.: "Are Ye Able" **(PD)**

PD-TO — Text Only is in the Public Domain. The text may be printed or projected, but not the music.
Ex.: "Rule of Life" **(PD-TO)**

VOCAL SUGGESTION RESOURCES

V-1 — Pote, Allen. *A Song of Joy.* Carol Stream, IL: Hope Publishing, 2003. Cokesbury Ord. #505068.

V-2 — Handel, George Frederick. *Messiah.* Various editions available.

V-3 — Hayes, Mark. *The Mark Hayes Vocal Solo Collection*
V-3 (1) *Ten Spirituals for Solo Voice.* Van Nuys, CA: Alfred Music Publishing, 2007. ISBN: 9780882848808.
V-3 (2) *Seven Praise and Worship Songs for Solo Voice.* Van Nuys, CA: Alfred Music Publishing, 2010. ISBN: 9780739037249.
V-3 (3) *Ten Hymns and Gospel Songs for Solo Voice.* ISBN: 9780739006979.
V-3 (4) *The Best of Mark Hayes for Solo Voice.* Van Nuys, CA: Alfred Music Publishing, 2013. ISBN: 9780739067161.
V-3 (5) *Seven Psalms and Spiritual Songs for Solo Voice.* Van Nuys, CA: Alfred Music Publishing, 2009. ISBN: 9780739034927.

V-4 — Scott, K. Lee. *Sing a Song of Joy.* Minneapolis, MN: Augsburg Fortress, 1989. ISBN: 9780800647889, (*Medium High Voice*) ISBN: 9780800647889, (*Medium Low Voice*) ISBN: 9780800652821.

V-5 — Various Editors. *With All My Heart: Contemporary Vocal Solos.* Minneapolis, MN: Augsburg Fortress, 2004.
V-5 (1) *Volume 1: Autumn and Winter.* ISBN: 9780800676841.
V-5 (2) *Volume 2: Spring and Summer.* ISBN: 9780800676858.
V-5 (3) *Volume 3: Baptisms, Weddings, Funerals.* ISBN: 9780800679460.

V-6 — Walters, Richard, Arr. *Hymn Classics: Concert Arrangements of Traditional Hymns for Voice and Piano.* Milwaukee, WI: Hal Leonard Publishing, 1993. ISBN: 9780793560080. *High Voice:* Cokesbury Ord. #811290. *Low Voice:* Cokesbury Ord. #811233.

V-7 — Duncan IV, Norah, Arr. *Give Me Jesus: Sacred Spirituals.* Chicago: GIA Publications, Inc., 2021.

V-8 — Wilson, John F., Don Doig, and Jack Schrader, eds. *Everything for the Church Soloist.* Carol Stream, IL: Hope Publishing Company, 1980. Cokesbury Ord. #810103.

V-9 — Various Artists. *Top Christian Hits of 2020–2021: 21 Powerful Songs Arranged for Piano/Vocal/Guitar.* Milwaukee, WI: Hal Leonard Publishing, 2021. ISBN: 9781705133460.

V-10 — Hayes, Mark et al. *From the Manger to the Cross—Seasonal Solos for Medium Voice.* Dayton, OH: The Lorenz Corporation, 2006. Cokesbury Ord. #526369.

New Revised Standard Version Updated Edition (NRSVue)

Jeremiah 18:1-11

1The word that came to Jeremiah from the LORD: 2“Come,
go down to the potter’s house, and there I will let you hear my
words.” 3So I went down to the potter’s house, and there he
was working at his wheel. 4The vessel he was making of clay was
spoiled in the potter’s hand, and he reworked it into another
vessel, as seemed good to him.

5Then the word of the LORD came to me: 6Can I not do with
you, O house of Israel, just as this potter has done? says the
LORD. Just like the clay in the potter’s hand, so are you in my
hand, O house of Israel. 7At one moment I may declare concerning a nation or a kingdom that I will pluck up and break
down and destroy it, 8but if that nation, concerning which I have
spoken, turns from its evil, I will change my mind about the
disaster that I intended to bring on it. 9And at another moment
I may declare concerning a nation or a kingdom that I will build
and plant it, 10but if it does evil in my sight, not listening to my
voice, then I will change my mind about the good that I had
intended to do to it. 11Now, therefore, say to the people of Judah
and the inhabitants of Jerusalem: Thus says the LORD: Look, I
am a potter shaping evil against you and devising a plan against
you. Turn now, all of you, from your evil way, and amend your
ways and your doings.

Psalm 139:1-6, 13-18 (G28/29, N715, P248, UM854)

1O LORD, you have searched me and known me.
2You know when I sit down and when I rise up;
you discern my thoughts from far away.
3You search out my path and my lying down
and are acquainted with all my ways.
4Even before a word is on my tongue,
O LORD, you know it completely.
5You hem me in, behind and before,
and lay your hand upon me.
6Such knowledge is too wonderful for me;
it is so high that I cannot attain it.
. . . .
13For it was you who formed my inward parts;
you knit me together in my mother’s womb.
14I praise you, for I am fearfully and wonderfully made.
Wonderful are your works;
that I know very well.
15 My frame was not hidden from you,
when I was being made in secret,
intricately woven in the depths of the earth.
16Your eyes beheld my unformed substance.
In your book were written
all the days that were formed for me,
when none of them as yet existed.
17How weighty to me are your thoughts, O God!
How vast is the sum of them!
18I try to count them—they are more than the sand;
I come to the end—I am still with you.

Common English Bible (CEB)

Jeremiah 18:1-11

1Jeremiah received the LORD’s word: 2Go down to the potter’s
house, and I’ll give you instructions about what to do there. 3So I
went down to the potter’s house; he was working on the potter’s
wheel. 4But the piece he was making was flawed while still in his
hands, so the potter started on another, as seemed best to him.
5Then the LORD’s word came to me: 6House of Israel, can’t I
deal with you like this potter, declares the LORD? Like clay in the
potter’s hand, so are you in mine, house of Israel! 7At any time I
may announce that I will dig up, pull down, and destroy a nation
or kingdom; 8but if that nation I warned turns from its evil, then
I’ll relent and not carry out the harm I intended for it. 9At the
same time, I may announce that I will build and plant a nation
or kingdom; 10but if that nation displeases and disobeys me, then
I’ll relent and not carry out the good I intended for it. 11Now
say to the people of Judah and those living in Jerusalem: This is
what the LORD says: I am a potter preparing a disaster for you;
I’m working out a plan against you. So each one of you, turn
from your evil ways; reform your ways and your actions.

Psalm 139:1-6, 13-18 (G28/29, N715, P248, UM854)

1LORD, you have examined me.
You know me.
2You know when I sit down and when I stand up.
Even from far away, you comprehend my plans.
3You study my traveling and resting.
You are thoroughly familiar with all my ways.
4There isn’t a word on my tongue, LORD,
that you don’t already know completely.
5You surround me—front and back.
You put your hand on me.
6That kind of knowledge is too much for me;
it’s so high above me that I can’t fathom it.
. . . .
13You are the one who created my innermost parts;
you knit me together while I was still in my mother’s womb.
14I give thanks to you that I was marvelously set apart.
Your works are wonderful—I know that very well.
15My bones weren’t hidden from you
when I was being put together in a secret place,
when I was being woven together in the deep parts of the
earth.
16Your eyes saw my embryo,
and on your scroll every day was written what was being
formed for me,
before any one of them had yet happened.
17God, your plans are incomprehensible to me!
Their total number is countless!
18If I tried to count them—they outnumber grains of sand!
If I came to the very end—I’d still be with you.

New Revised Standard Version Updated Edition (NRSVue)

Philemon 1-21

1Paul, a prisoner of Christ Jesus, and Timothy our brother,

To our beloved coworker Philemon, 2to our sister Apphia, to our fellow soldier Archippus, and to the church in your house:

3Grace to you and peace from God our Father and the Lord Jesus Christ.

4I thank my God always when I mention you in my prayers, 5because I hear of your love for all the saints and your faith toward the Lord Jesus. 6I pray that the partnership of your faith may become effective as you comprehend all the good that we may share in Christ. 7I have indeed received much joy and encouragement from your love, because the hearts of the saints have been refreshed through you, my brother.

8For this reason, though I am more than bold enough in Christ to command you to do the right thing, 9yet I would rather appeal to you on the basis of love—and I, Paul, do this as an old man and now also as a prisoner of Christ Jesus. 10I am appealing to you for my child, Onesimus, whose father I have become during my imprisonment. 11Formerly he was useless to you, but now he is indeed useful to you and to me. 12I am sending him, that is, my own heart, back to you. 13I wanted to keep him with me so that he might minister to me in your place during my imprisonment for the gospel, 14but I preferred to do nothing without your consent in order that your good deed might be voluntary and not something forced. 15Perhaps this is the reason he was separated from you for a while, so that you might have him back for the long term, 16no longer as a slave but more than a slave, a beloved brother—especially to me but how much more to you, both in the flesh and in the Lord.

17So if you consider me your partner, welcome him as you would welcome me. 18If he has wronged you in any way or owes you anything, charge that to me. 19I, Paul, am writing this with my own hand: I will repay it. I say nothing about your owing me even your own self. 20Yes, brother, let me have this benefit from you in the Lord! Refresh my heart in Christ. 21Confident of your obedience, I am writing to you, knowing that you will do even more than I ask.

Luke 14:25-33

25Now large crowds were traveling with him, and he turned and said to them, 26"Whoever comes to me and does not hate father and mother, wife and children, brothers and sisters, yes, and even life itself, cannot be my disciple. 27Whoever does not carry the cross and follow me cannot be my disciple. 28For which of you, intending to build a tower, does not first sit down and estimate the cost, to see whether he has enough to complete it? 29Otherwise, when he has laid a foundation and is not able to finish, all who see it will begin to ridicule him, 30saying, 'This fellow began to build and was not able to finish.' 31Or what king, going out to wage war against another king, will not sit down first and consider whether he is able with ten thousand to oppose the one who comes against him with twenty thousand? 32If he cannot, then while the other is still far away, he sends a delegation and asks for the terms of peace. 33So therefore, none of you can become my disciple if you do not give up all your possessions."

Common English Bible (CEB)

Philemon 1-21

1From Paul, who is a prisoner for the cause of Christ Jesus, and our brother Timothy.

To Philemon our dearly loved coworker, 2Apphia our sister, Archippus our fellow soldier, and the church that meets in your house.

3May the grace and peace from God our Father and the Lord Jesus Christ be with you.

4Philemon, I thank my God every time I mention you in my prayers 5because I've heard of your love and faithfulness, which you have both for the Lord Jesus and for all God's people. 6I pray that your partnership in the faith might become effective by an understanding of all that is good among us in Christ. 7I have great joy and encouragement because of your love, since the hearts of God's people are refreshed by your actions, my brother.

8Therefore, though I have enough confidence in Christ to command you to do the right thing, 9I would rather appeal to you through love. I, Paul—an old man, and now also a prisoner for Christ Jesus—10appeal to you for my child Onesimus. I became his father in the faith during my time in prison. 11He was useless to you before, but now he is useful to both of us. 12I'm sending him back to you, which is like sending you my own heart. 13I considered keeping him with me so that he might serve me in your place during my time in prison because of the gospel. 14However, I didn't want to do anything without your consent so that your act of kindness would occur willingly and not under pressure. 15Maybe this is the reason that Onesimus was separated from you for a while so that you might have him back forever—16no longer as a slave but more than a slave—that is, as a dearly loved brother. He is especially a dearly loved brother to me. How much more can he become a brother to you, personally and spiritually in the Lord!

17So, if you really consider me a partner, welcome Onesimus as if you were welcoming me. 18If he has harmed you in any way or owes you money, charge it to my account. 19I, Paul, will pay it back to you (I'm writing this with my own hand). Of course, I won't mention that you owe me your life.

20Yes, brother, I want this favor from you in the Lord! Refresh my heart in Christ. 21I'm writing to you, confident of your obedience and knowing that you will do more than what I ask.

Luke 14:25-33

25Large crowds were traveling with Jesus. Turning to them, he said, 26"Whoever comes to me and doesn't hate father and mother, spouse and children, and brothers and sisters—yes, even one's own life—cannot be my disciple. 27Whoever doesn't carry their own cross and follow me cannot be my disciple.

28"If one of you wanted to build a tower, wouldn't you first sit down and calculate the cost, to determine whether you have enough money to complete it? 29Otherwise, when you have laid the foundation but couldn't finish the tower, all who see it will begin to belittle you. 30They will say, 'Here's the person who began construction and couldn't complete it!' 31Or what king would go to war against another king without first sitting down to consider whether his ten thousand soldiers could go up against the twenty thousand coming against him? 32And if he didn't think he could win, he would send a representative to discuss terms of peace while his enemy was still a long way off. 33In the same way, none of you who are unwilling to give up all of your possessions can be my disciple."

Primary Hymns and Songs for the Day
"Take Up Thy Cross" 2154808 (Luke) (O)
E675, EL667, G718, P393
H-3 Chr-178
GR220, UM415 (PD)
H-3 Chr-178, 180; Org-44
S-1 #141-143 Various treatments
N204
H-3 Chr-178; Org-27
S-2 #48-49. Desc. and harm.
L398, SH605, VU561
"Change My Heart, O God" 1565 (Jer)
EL801, G695, S2152, SH507, ZS178
"I Was There to Hear Your Borning Cry" (Pss, Baptism)
C75, EL732, G488, N351, S2051, VU644
"Help Us Accept Each Other" 133756 (Phlm)
C487, G754, N388, P358, UM560
"In the Cross of Christ I Glory" 36499 (Phlm, Luke)
C207, CG183, E441/E442, EL324, G213, GR239, N193, P84, UM295 (PD)
H-3 Hbl-72; Chr-113; Desc-89; Org-119
S-1 #276-277. Harmonization with descant
"When I Survey the Wondrous Cross" 27893 (Phlm, Luke)
C195, CG186, EL803, G223, GR221, N224, P101, SH163/164, UM298 (PD)
H-3 Hbl-6, 102; Chr-213; Desc-49; Org-49
S-1 #155. Descant
"When I Survey the Wondrous Cross" 721333 (Phlm, Luke)
E474, G224, P100, UM299 (PD), VU149 (Fr.)
H-3 Hbl-47; Chr-214; Desc-90; Org-127
S-1 #288. Transposition to E-flat major
"I Have Decided to Follow Jesus" (Luke)
C344, CG497, GR603, S2129, SH610
"Have Thine Own Way, Lord" (Jer, Luke) (C)
C588, CG493, GR343. SH626, UM382 (PD)
S-2 #2. Instrumental descant

Additional Hymn Suggestions
+"O God, as with a Potter's Hand" (Jer)
N550
"Spirit of the Living God" 23488 (Jer)
C259, CG233, G288, GR299, N283, P322, SH555, UM393, VU376, Z226, S-1 #212 Vocal desc. idea
"My Lord, What a Morning" (PD-TO) (Jer)
C708, EL438, G352, P449, SH356, UM719, VU708, Z145
"God the Sculptor of the Mountains" (Jer, Pss)
EL736, G5, S2060
"Go Down, Moses" (Phlm)
C663, E648, G52, GR403, N572, P334, SH28, UM448, Z112 (PD), Z212
"Where Charity and Love Prevail" 40313 (Phlm)
CG264, E581, EL359, G316, N396, SH271, UM549
"Awake, O Sleeper" (Phlm)
E547, EL452, GR390, UM551, VU566
"In Christ There Is No East or West" 2608952 (UMH only St. 3 OL-13651) (Phlm)
C687, CG273, E529, EL650 (PD), G317/318, GR392, N394/395, P439/440, UM548, VU606, Z65 (PD)
"Since Jesus Came into My Heart" (Phlm)
CG614, GR552, S2140
"Over My Head" (Phlm)
N514, S2148 (PD-TO), Z167
"Together We Serve" (Phlm)
G767, S2175
"Called as Partners in Christ's Service" (Phlm)
C453, G761, N495, P343
"A Place at the Table" (Phlm, Comm.)
G769, WS3149
+"Lift High the Cross" 5169 (Luke)
C108, CG415, E473, EL660, G826, GR226, N198, P371, SH162, UM159, VU151
+"Rejoice, Ye Pure in Heart" (Luke)
C15, CG312, E556/557, EL873/874, G804, GR62, N55/71, P145/146, UM160/161
"Where He Leads Me" (Luke)
C346, GR516, UM338 (PD), Z42
"Must Jesus Bear the Cross Alone" (Luke)
CG505, GR598, UM424 (PD)
"More Love to Thee, O Christ" 36750 (Luke)
See especially stanza 2.
C527, CG365, G828, GR588, N456, P359, UM453 (PD)
"Am I a Soldier of the Cross" 115145 (Luke)
CG632, GR600, UM511 (PD)
"And Are We Yet Alive" (Luke) (O)
GR386, UM553 (PD)
"This Little Light of Mine" 5305434, OL-22794 (Luke)
N525, UM585, Z132 (*See also* EL677, N524, SH257)
"For the Bread Which You Have Broken" (Luke, Comm.)
C411, E340/341, EL494, G516, P508/509, UM614/615, VU470
"Swiftly Pass the Clouds of Glory" (Luke)
G190, P73, S2102
"O How He Loves You and Me" 15850 (Luke)
CG600, S2108, SH535, ZS208
"Living for Jesus" (Luke)
C610, GR595, S2149

Additional Contemporary and Modern Suggestions
"Praise You" 863806 (Jer, Stewardship)
S2003, ZS170
"Water, River, Spirit, Grace" OL-126179 (Jer, Baptism)
C366, N169, S2253
+"Beautiful Things" 5665521 (Jer)
+"Called Me Higher" 5887880 (Jer)
+"New Wine" 7102397 (Jer, Luke)
+"Freedom in the Spirit" 7127886 (Jer, Phlm)
"The Potter's Hand" 2449771 (Jer, Pss, Stewardship)
"Oh, I Know the Lord's Laid His Hands on Me" (PD) (Pss)
S2139 (PD), Z166
"How Great Is Our God" 4348399 (Pss)
CG322, GR31, SH458, WS3003
"How Great You Are" 6271677 (Pss)
WS3015
"He Knows My Name" 2151368 (Pss)
"These Hands" 3251827 (Pss, Stewardship)
+"Wonderfully Made" 5768239 (Pss)
+"Come to the Table" 7130008 (Pss, Comm.)
"Freedom in the Spirit" 7127886 (Pss, Phlm)
+"We'll All Be Free" No SS (Phlm)
https://bit.ly/BeFreeGungor
+"Chain Breaker" 7060031 (Phlm)
+"Freedom" 7078151 (Phlm)
+"Amazing Grace" ("My Chains Are Gone") 4768151 (Phlm)
GR574, WS3104
+"If You Believe and I Believe" 3273104 (Phlm)
WS3121
"Cry of My Heart" 844980 (Luke)
S2165
"*Somlandela*" ("We Will Follow") (PD-TO) (Luke)
WS3160
"Let It Be Said of Us" 1855882 (Luke)
"Every Move I Make" 1595726 (Luke)
"Everyday" 2798154 (Luke)
"One Way" 4222082 (Luke)
"Take Up Our Cross" 5358955 (Luke)

Solo/Ensemble Suggestions

"Have Thine Own Way, Lord!" (Jer)
V-8 p. 191
+"God Will Make a Way" (with "He Leadeth Me")
V-3 (2) p. 9
"Sing a Song of Joy" (Pss)
V-4 p. 2
"Borning Cry" (Pss, Baptism)
V-5 (1) p. 10
"Lead Me to Calvary" (Luke)
V-8 p. 226
+"O Lord, You Know Me Completely" (Pss)
Hal H. Hopson; Choristers Guild CGA-833
Unison/2-part, keyboard (https://bit.ly/CGA-833)
"The Image of God" (Pss)
Craig Courtney; Beckenhorst BP2054
SATB, piano, opt. C-instrument (https://bit.ly/BP2054)

+Hymn Anthem

"My Lord, What a Morning" (PD-TO) (Jer)
C708, EL438, G352, P449, SH356, UM719, VU708, Z145

This anthem is best sung *a cappella*, but may be lightly accompanied. If used, the keyboard would play the hymnal setting throughout.

Introduction: (if accompanied) Keyboard plays final phrase of refrain, "when the stars begin to fall."

Refrain: Choir sings refrain in four parts as directed.

Stanza 1: Female soloist sings first line of stanza, faster and in a declamatory style. Choir joins soloist on second line of stanza, singing four parts, ending with a great deal of *ritard.*

Refrain: As before, choir singing four parts.

Stanza 2: Male soloist sings first line of stanza, slower and in a mournful style. Choir joins soloist on second line of stanza, singing four parts, with a great deal of *ritard* at end.

Refrain: Choir sings four parts again, but on an "ooh" vowel. A soloist may be selected to sing the text.

Stanza 3: All voices, unison sing the first line of the stanza, in faster declamatory style as in stanza 1. Choir sings four-parts on the second line, with less *ritard* at end.

Refrain: Choir sings four parts as before, with text. Two sopranos are selected to sing the alto and tenor parts one octave higher than written, creating two seemingly improvised descants. End very quietly.

Other Suggestions

Visuals:
- **O** Potter's wheel/clay, hands/clay, building, planting
- **P** Sitting/standing, open mouth, hand on shoulder
- **E** Letter, old man writing. manacles, heart
- **G** Carrying crosses, tower, calculator, document, dove

+Introit: S2101, stanza 4. "Two Fishermen" (Jer, Luke)

Opening Prayer: N826 (Jer) or C771 (Pss)

Prayer: C262. You Are the Work of God (Jer)

Create a choral medley or praise band song set, using the traditional "How Great Thou Art" 14181and the newer "How Great You Are." 6271677

Blessing: WSL158. "Here in this sanctuary" (Phlm, Luke)

Sung Benediction: "Let the Peace of God Reign" 1839987 (Phlm)

Alternate Lessons (see page 4): Deut 30:15-20, Ps 1

Theme Ideas: Cross, Discipleship / Following God, Inclusion, Sin and Forgiveness, Welcome

Notes

NRSVue

Jeremiah 4:11-12, 22-28

[11]At that time it will be said to this people and to Jerusalem:
A hot wind comes from me out of the bare heights in the desert
toward the daughter of my people, not to winnow or cleanse,
[12]a wind too strong for that. Now it is I who speak in judgment
against them.

. . . .

[22]"For my people are foolish;
they do not know me;
they are stupid children;
they have no understanding.
They are skilled in doing evil
but do not know how to do good."
[23]I looked on the earth, and it was complete chaos,
and to the heavens, and they had no light.
[24]I looked on the mountains, and they were quaking,
and all the hills moved to and fro.
[25]I looked, and there was no one at all,
and all the birds of the air had fled.
[26]I looked, and the fruitful land was a desert,
and all its cities were laid in ruins
before the LORD, before his fierce anger.
[27]For thus says the LORD: The whole land shall be a desolation, yet I will not make a full end.
[28]Because of this the earth shall mourn
and the heavens above grow black;
for I have spoken; I have purposed;
I have not relented, nor will I turn back.

Psalm 14 (G335, N626, SH26, UM746)

[1]Fools say in their hearts, "There is no God."
They are corrupt; they do abominable deeds;
there is no one who does good.
[2]The LORD looks down from heaven on humankind
to see if there are any who are wise,
who seek after God.
[3]They have all gone astray, they are all alike perverse;
there is no one who does good,
no, not one.
[4]Have they no knowledge, all the evildoers
who eat up my people as they eat bread
and do not call upon the LORD?
[5]There they shall be in great terror,
for God is with the company of the righteous.
[6]You would confound the plans of the poor,
but the LORD is their refuge.
[7]O that deliverance for Israel would come from Zion!
When the LORD restores the fortunes of his people,
Jacob will rejoice; Israel will be glad.

CEB

Jeremiah 4:11-12, 22-28

[11]At that time, this people and Jerusalem will be told:
A blistering wind from the bare heights;
it rages in the desert toward my people,
not merely to winnow or cleanse.
[12] This wind is too devastating for that.
Now I, even I, will pronounce
my sentence against them. . . .

. . . .

[22]My people are foolish.
They don't even know me!
They are thoughtless children
without understanding;
they are skilled at doing wrong,
inept at doing right.
[23]I looked at the earth,
and it was without shape or form;
at the heavens
and there was no light.
[24]I looked at the mountains
and they were quaking;
all the hills were rocking back and forth.
[25]I looked and there was no one left;
every bird in the sky had taken flight.
[26]I looked and the fertile land was a desert;
all its towns were in ruins
before the LORD,
before his fury.
[27]The LORD proclaims:
The whole earth
will become a desolation,
but I will not destroy it completely.
[28]Therefore, the earth will grieve
and the heavens grow dark
because I have declared my plan
and will neither change my mind
nor cancel the plan.

Psalm 14 (G335, N626, SH26, UM746)

[1]Fools say in their hearts, There is no God.
They are corrupt and do evil things;
not one of them does anything good.
[2]The LORD looks down from heaven on humans
to see if anyone is wise,
to see if anyone seeks God,
[3] but all of them have turned bad.
Everyone is corrupt.
No one does good—
not even one person!
[4]Are they dumb, all these evildoers,
devouring my people
like they are eating bread
but never calling on the LORD?
[5]Count on it: they will be in utter panic
because God is with the righteous generation.
[6]You evildoers may humiliate
the plans of those who suffer,
but the LORD is their refuge.
[7]Let Israel's salvation come out of Zion!
When the LORD changes
his people's circumstances for the better,
Jacob will rejoice;
Israel will celebrate!

NRSVue

1 Timothy 1:12-17

12I am grateful to Christ Jesus our Lord, who has strengthened
me, because he considered me faithful and appointed me to his
service, 13even though I was formerly a blasphemer, a persecutor,
and a man of violence. But I received mercy because I had acted
ignorantly in unbelief, 14and the grace of our Lord overflowed
for me with the faith and love that are in Christ Jesus. 15The saying is sure and worthy of full acceptance: that Christ Jesus came
into the world to save sinners—of whom I am the foremost.
16But for that very reason I received mercy, so that in me, as the
foremost, Jesus Christ might display the utmost patience as an
example to those who would come to believe in him for eternal
life. 17To the King of the ages, immortal, invisible, the only God,
be honor and glory forever and ever. Amen.

Luke 15:1-10

1Now all the tax collectors and sinners were coming near to
listen to him. 2And the Pharisees and the scribes were grumbling
and saying, "This fellow welcomes sinners and eats with them."
3So he told them this parable: 4"Which one of you, having a hundred sheep and losing one of them, does not leave the ninety-
nine in the wilderness and go after the one that is lost until he
finds it? 5And when he has found it, he lays it on his shoulders
and rejoices. 6And when he comes home, he calls together his
friends and neighbors, saying to them, 'Rejoice with me, for I
have found my lost sheep.' 7Just so, I tell you, there will be more
joy in heaven over one sinner who repents than over ninety-nine
righteous persons who need no repentance. 8"Or what woman
having ten silver coins, if she loses one of them, does not light
a lamp, sweep the house, and search carefully until she finds it?
9And when she has found it, she calls together her friends and
neighbors, saying, 'Rejoice with me, for I have found the coin
that I had lost.' 10Just so, I tell you, there is joy in the presence of
the angels of God over one sinner who repents."

CEB

1 Timothy 1:12-17

12I thank Christ Jesus our Lord, who has given me strength
because he considered me faithful. So he appointed me to
ministry 13even though I used to speak against him, attack his
people, and I was proud. But I was shown mercy because I acted
in ignorance and without faith. 14Our Lord's favor poured all
over me along with the faithfulness and love that are in Christ
Jesus. 15This saying is reliable and deserves full acceptance:
"Christ Jesus came into the world to save sinners"—and I'm the
biggest sinner of all. 16But this is why I was shown mercy, so that
Christ Jesus could show his endless patience to me first of all. So
I'm an example for those who are going to believe in him for
eternal life. 17Now to the king of the ages, to the immortal, invisible, and only God, may honor and glory be given to him forever
and always! Amen.

Luke 15:1-10

1All the tax collectors and sinners were gathering around
Jesus to listen to him. 2The Pharisees and legal experts were
grumbling, saying, "This man welcomes sinners and eats with
them."

3Jesus told them this parable: 4"Suppose someone among you
had one hundred sheep and lost one of them. Wouldn't he leave
the other ninety-nine in the pasture and search for the lost one
until he finds it? 5And when he finds it, he is thrilled and places
it on his shoulders. 6When he arrives home, he calls together
his friends and neighbors, saying to them, 'Celebrate with me
because I've found my lost sheep.' 7In the same way, I tell you,
there will be more joy in heaven over one sinner who changes
both heart and life than over ninety-nine righteous people who
have no need to change their hearts and lives.

8"Or what woman, if she owns ten silver coins and loses one
of them, won't light a lamp and sweep the house, searching her
home carefully until she finds it? 9When she finds it, she calls
together her friends and neighbors, saying, 'Celebrate with me
because I've found my lost coin.' 10In the same way, I tell you, joy
breaks out in the presence of God's angels over one sinner who
changes both heart and life."

Primary Hymns and Songs for the Day

"Immortal, Invisible, God Only Wise" 124466 (1 Tim) (O)
C66, CG58, E423, EL834, G12, GR7, N1, P263, UM103 (PD), VU264 (*See also* ZS4)
H-3 Hbl-15, 71; Chr-65; Desc-93; Org-135
S-1 #300. Harm.

+"O for a Closer Walk with God" (Jer)
CG679, E684, G739, GR327, N450, P396

"My Lord, What a Morning" (PD-TO) (Jer, Pss, Luke)
C708, EL438, G352, P449, SH356, UM719, VU708, Z145

"Amazing Grace" 22025 (Pss, 1 Tim, Luke)
C546, CG587, E671, EL779, G649, GR572, N547/548, P280, SH523, UM378 (PD), VU266 (Fr.), Z211
H-3 Hbl-14, 46; Chr-27; Desc-14; Org-4
S-2 #5-7. Various treatments
V-8 p. 56. Vocal Solo

"Praise, My Soul, the King of Heaven" 800443 (1 Tim)
C23, CG337, E410, EL864/865, G619/620, GR22, P478/479, SH418, UM66 (PD), VU240
H-3 Hbl-88; Chr-162; Desc-67; Org-75
S-1 #205. Harmonization
#206. Descant

"Grace Alone" 2335524 (1 Tim)
CG43, S2162, ZS100

"To God Be the Glory" (1 Tim) (C)
C72, CG349, G634, GR531, P485, SH545, UM98 (PD)

Additional Hymn Suggestions

+"It's Me, It's Me, O Lord" (Jer)
C579, GR444, N519, UM352, Z110 (PD), ZS149

"La Palabra Del Señor Es Recta" ("Righteous and Just Is the Word of Our Lord") (Jer, Pss)
G40, UM107, SH4

"Steal Away to Jesus" (Jer, Pss, Luke)
C644, G358 (PD), GR631, N599, UM704, Z134

"O Day of God, Draw Nigh" (PD) (Jer, Pss)
C700, E601, N611, P452, UM730 (PD), VU688/689 (Fr.)

"Hope of the World" 643002 (1 Tim)
C538, E472, G734, N46, P360, UM178, VU215

"Alas! and Did My Savior Bleed" 29499 (1 Tim)
C204, CG182/595, EL337, G212, GR231/564, N199/200, P78, UM294/359, SH172/173, Z8, ZS67

"And Can It Be that I Should Gain" 25280 (1 Tim)
CG605, GR569, SH540, UM363 (PD)

"My Hope Is Built" (PD) (1 Tim)
C537, CG590, EL596/597, G353, GR102, N403, P379, SH324, UM368 (PD), ZS182

"I Stand Amazed in the Presence" (1 Tim)
CG576, GR122, SH537, UM371 (PD)

"Gloria a Dios" ("Glory to God") (PD) (1 Tim)
CG320, EL164, G585, S2033, SH381

"There Are Some Things I May Not Know" (1 Tim)
N405, S2147, Z201 (PD), ZS172

"Come, Thou Fount of Every Blessing" (1 Tim, Luke)
C16, CG295, E686, EL807, G475, GR37, N459, P356, SH394, UM400 (PD), VU559

+"The King of Love, My Shepherd Is" (Luke)
CG64, E645/646, EL502, G802, GR90, N248, P171, SH359, UM138 (PD), VU273

+"Softly and Tenderly Jesus Is Calling" (Luke)
C340, CG474, EL608 (PD), G418, GR504, N449, SH601, UM348

"Just as I Am, Without One Plea" 1039000 (Luke)
C339, CG500, E693, EL592, G442, GR509, N207, P370, SH500, UM357 (PD), VU508, Z208

"Savior, Like a Shepherd Lead Us" 24078 (Luke)
C558, CG405, EL789, G187, GR130, N252, P387, SH538, UM381 (PD)

+"Prayer Is the Soul's Sincere Desire" (Luke)
CG391, GR438, N508, UM492

"Come, We That Love the Lord" 84159 (Luke)
CG549, E392, GR38, N379, UM732, VU715

"Marching to Zion" 144398 (Luke)
C707, CG550, EL625, GR626, N382, UM733, VU714, Z3

"Bring Many Names" (Luke)
C10, G760, N11, S2047, VU268

"I'm So Glad Jesus Lifted Me" (PD) (Luke)
C529, EL860 (PD), N474, S2151

"Lord of All Hopefulness" 5579875 (Luke)
CG678, E482, EL765, G683, S2197, SH464

+"Fill My Cup, Lord" 15946 (Luke)
C351, UM641 *(refrain only)*, WS3093

"A Woman and a Coin" (Luke)
C74, G173, VU360

"Heaven Is Singing for Joy" *("El cielo canta alegría")* (Luke)
G382, EL664, SH13, VU230

Additional Contemporary and Modern Suggestions

+"Thou Art Worthy" 14789 (Jer, 1 Tim)
C114, S2041

"Mighty to Save" 4591782 (Jer, Luke, Pss)
WS3038

"Amazing Grace" ("My Chains Are Gone") 4768151 (Pss, 1 Tim)
GR574, WS3104

"My Tribute" 11218 (1 Tim)
C39, CG574, GR580, N14, SH434, UM99; V-8 p. 5. Vocal Solo

"Something Beautiful" 18060 (1 Tim)
UM394

"God Is Good All the Time" 1729073 (1 Tim)

"There Is Joy in the Lord" 1184209 (1 Tim)

"Forevermore" 5466830 (1 Tim)

"Sing Alleluia to the Lord" 26272 (1 Tim, Comm.)
C32, S2258, SH685

"Here Is Bread, Here Is Wine" 983717 (1 Tim, Comm.)
EL483, S2266

"God Is So Good" 4956994 (1 Tim, Luke)
G658, GR52, S2056, SH461, Z231

"Grace Like Rain" 3689877 (1 Tim, Luke)

+"Who You Say I Am" 7102401 (1 Tim, Luke)

+"Won't Stop Now" 7111932 (1 Tim, Luke)

+"All the Poor and Powerless" 5881130 (1 Tim, Luke)

+"Never Runs Out" 7193998 (1 Tim, Luke)

+"No Outsiders" 7101035 (1 Tim, Luke)

+"Here at the Cross" 7046292 (1 Tim, Luke)

+"His Mercy Is More" 7065053 (1 Tim, Luke)

+"Love Moves You" ("Love Alone") 5775514 (1 Tim, Luke)

+"Beautiful Things" 5665521 (Luke)

+"Head to the Heart" 7047283 (Luke)

+"The Kingdom Is Yours" 7109354 (Luke)

+"The King of Love My Shepherd Is" 7023979 (Luke)

+"Better Than A Hallelujah" 5622564 (Luke)

"That's Why We Praise Him" 2668576 (Luke)

"You Are My All in All" 825356 (Luke)
CG571, G519, SH335, WS3040, ZS184

"You Are My King" ("Amazing Love") 2456623 (Luke)
SH539, WS3102

"Take, O Take Me as I Am" 4562041 (Luke)
EL814, G698, SH620, WS3119

"Here at the Cross" 7046292 (Luke)

"I Come to the Cross" 1965249 (Luke)

"When It's All Been Said and Done" 2788353 (Luke)

Solo/Ensemble Suggestions

"Strength to My Soul" (1 Tim, Luke)
V-8 p. 352

"Love Moved First" 7121825 (1 Tim, Luke)
V-9 p. 56

"God, Our Ever Faithful Shepherd" (Luke)
V-4 p. 15
+"Softly and Tenderly" (Luke)
V-5(3) p. 52
+"Shepherd of Love" (Luke)
V-8 p. 142
+"Grace Alone" (1 Tim)
Arr. Molly Ijames; Hope C6094
SATB, piano (https://bit.ly/C6094)
+"Come to the Table" (1 Tim, Luke)
Arr. David Angerman; Hal Leonard HL-00284659
SATB, piano (https://bit.ly/HL284659)

+Hymn Anthem

"Come, Thou Fount of Every Blessing" (1 Tim, Luke)
C16, CG295, E686, EL807, G475, GR37, N459, P356, SH394, UM400 (PD), VU559

Each stanza of this hymn is divided into four distinct phrases. The melodies of the first, second and fourth phrases are exactly alike.

Introduction: Keyboard plays bass part, phrase 1. (May be omitted if sung *a cappella*.)

Stanza 1: Basses sing their part on phrase 1. Tenors join on phrase 2 singing melody, basses continue singing their part. Phrase 3: Sopranos sing melody, tenors and basses sing their parts. Phrase 4: All voices in four parts. The entire stanza is sung in a lilting manner, singing the eighth notes on the third beat of each measure in a slightly detached manner. (Option: T/B sing phrases 1, 2, and 4; S/A sing phrase 3. Keyboard plays full setting.)

Stanza 2: Four part singing, legato. Begin *forte* and strong. Begin to slow the tempo at the end of phrase 2 and hold the word "home." Continue through phrase 3, softly and slowly. Add to the vocal texture by having some T/B sing the soprano and alto parts down one octave and some S/A sing the bass and tenor parts up one octave. *Molto ritard* the end of this phrase. While the choir holds the word "God," a soloist sings phrase 4. Choir cuts off when soloist reaches "danger." (Option: Choir sings either melody or soprano and bass parts. Keyboard plays full setting.)

Stanza 3: Return to a full, vibrant sound. Some sopranos may sing the descant, S-1, #244. Some choir members may improvise a part. Allow this stanza to have a somewhat unrestrained character, bordering on over-singing. (Option: Accompany unison singing with full setting.)

Ending: Repeat stanza 1 as directed above. *Ritard* and *decrescendo* the last notes.

Other Suggestions

Visuals:
O Desert, wind, mountains, earthquake, birds, ruins, mourning, darkness
P Stray sheep, eating bread, Ps. 14:6, poor, joy
E Christ, 1 Tim 1:15, Paul, glory, crown
G One sheep, Jesus carrying lost sheep, ten coins, lamp, broom, woman rejoicing, one coin

Introit: C583, CG403, EL768, G740, S2214, SH582, ZS173. "Lead Me, Guide Me" (Luke)
Opening Prayer: N830 (2 Tim) and Confession: N838 (Pss)
Prayer: UM535. A Refuge amid Distraction (Pss)
Affirmation of Faith: WSL76 or UM889 (1 Tim)
Benediction: WSL159. "Sisters and brothers" (Luke)
Alternate Lessons (see page 4): Exod. 32:7-14, Ps. 51:1-10
Theme Ideas: God: Shepherd, Grace, Redemption / Salvation, Sin and Forgiveness

Notes

NRSVue

Jeremiah 8:18–9:1
18My joy is gone; grief is upon me;
my heart is sick.
19Listen! The cry of the daughter of my people
from far and wide in the land:
"Is the LORD not in Zion?
Is her King not in her?"
("Why have they provoked me to anger with their images,
with their foreign idols?")
20"The harvest is past, the summer is ended,
and we are not saved."
21For the brokenness of the daughter of my people I am broken,
I mourn, and horror has seized me.
22Is there no balm in Gilead?
Is there no physician there?
Why then has the health of the daughter of my people
not been restored?
9 O that my head were a spring of water
and my eyes a fountain of tears,
so that I might weep day and night
for the slain of the daughter of my people!

Psalm 79:1-9 (G430, N671)
1O God, the nations have come into your inheritance;
they have defiled your holy temple;
they have laid Jerusalem in ruins.
2They have given the bodies of your servants
to the birds of the air for food,
the flesh of your faithful to the wild animals of the earth.
3They have poured out their blood like water
all around Jerusalem,
and there was no one to bury them.
4We have become a taunt to our neighbors,
mocked and derided by those around us.
5How long, O LORD? Will you be angry forever?
Will your jealous wrath burn like fire?
6Pour out your anger on the nations
that do not know you
and on the kingdoms
that do not call on your name.
7For they have devoured Jacob
and laid waste his habitation.
8Do not remember against us the iniquities of our ancestors;
let your compassion come speedily to meet us,
for we are brought very low.
9Help us, O God of our salvation,
for the glory of your name;
deliver us, and forgive our sins,
for your name's sake.

CEB

Jeremiah 8:18–9:1
18No healing,
only grief;
my heart is broken.
19Listen to the weeping of my people
all across the land:
"Isn't the LORD in Zion?
Is her king no longer there?"
Why then did they anger me
with their images,
with pointless foreign gods?
20"The harvest is past,
the summer has ended,
yet we aren't saved."
21Because my people are crushed,
I am crushed;
darkness and despair overwhelm me.
22Is there no balm in Gilead?
Is there no physician there?
Why then have my people
not been restored to health?
9 If only my head were a spring of water
and my eyes a fountain of tears,
I would weep day and night
for the wounds of my people.

Psalm 79:1-9 (G430, N671)
1The nations have come into your inheritance, God!
They've defiled your holy temple.
They've made Jerusalem a bunch of ruins.
2They've left your servants' bodies
as food for the birds;
they've left the flesh of your faithful
to the wild animals of the earth.
3They've poured out the blood of the faithful
like water all around Jerusalem,
and there's no one left to bury them.
4We've become a joke to our neighbors,
nothing but objects of ridicule
and disapproval to those around us.
5How long will you rage, LORD? Forever?
How long will your anger burn like fire?
6Pour out your wrath on the nations
who don't know you,
on the kingdoms
that haven't called on your name.
7They've devoured Jacob
and demolished his pasture.
8Don't remember the iniquities of past generations;
let your compassion hurry to meet us
because we've been brought so low.
9God of our salvation, help us
for the glory of your name!
Deliver us and cover our sins
for the sake of your name!

NRSVue

1 Timothy 2:1-7

[1]First of all, then, I urge that supplications, prayers, intercessions, and thanksgivings be made for everyone, [2]for kings and all who are in high positions, so that we may lead a quiet and peaceable life in all godliness and dignity. [3]This is right and acceptable before God our Savior, [4]who desires everyone to be saved and to come to the knowledge of the truth. [5]For

there is one God;
there is also one mediator between God and humankind,
Christ Jesus, himself human,
6 who gave himself a ransom for all
—this was attested at the right time. [7]For this I was appointed a herald and an apostle (I am telling the truth; I am not lying), a teacher of the gentiles in faith and truth.

Luke 16:1-13

[1]Then Jesus said to the disciples, "There was a rich man who had a manager, and charges were brought to him that this man was squandering his property. [2]So he summoned him and said to him, 'What is this that I hear about you? Give me an accounting of your management because you cannot be my manager any longer.' [3]Then the manager said to himself, 'What will I do, now that my master is taking the position away from me? I am not strong enough to dig, and I am ashamed to beg. [4]I have decided what to do so that, when I am dismissed as manager, people may welcome me into their homes.' [5]So, summoning his master's debtors one by one, he asked the first, 'How much do you owe my master?' [6]He answered, 'A hundred jugs of olive oil.' He said to him, 'Take your bill, sit down quickly, and make it fifty.' [7]Then he asked another, 'And how much do you owe?' He replied, 'A hundred containers of wheat.' He said to him, 'Take your bill and make it eighty.' [8]And his master commended the dishonest manager because he had acted shrewdly; for the children of this age are more shrewd in dealing with their own generation than are the children of light. [9]And I tell you, make friends for yourselves by means of dishonest wealth so that when it is gone, they may welcome you into the eternal homes.

[10]"Whoever is faithful in a very little is faithful also in much; and whoever is dishonest in a very little is dishonest also in much. [11]If, then, you have not been faithful with the dishonest wealth, who will entrust to you the true riches? [12]And if you have not been faithful with what belongs to another, who will give you what is your own? [13]No slave can serve two masters; for a slave will either hate the one and love the other or be devoted to the one and despise the other. You cannot serve God and wealth."

CEB

1 Timothy 2:1-7

[1]First of all, then, I ask that requests, prayers, petitions, and thanksgiving be made for all people. [2]Pray for kings and everyone who is in authority so that we can live a quiet and peaceful life in complete godliness and dignity. [3]This is right and it pleases God our savior, [4]who wants all people to be saved and to come to a knowledge of the truth. [5]There is one God and one mediator between God and humanity, the human Christ Jesus, [6]who gave himself as a payment to set all people free. This was a testimony that was given at the right time. [7]I was appointed to be a preacher and apostle of this testimony—I'm telling the truth and I'm not lying! I'm a teacher of the Gentiles in faith and truth.

Luke 16:1-13

[1]Jesus also said to the disciples, "A certain rich man heard that his household manager was wasting his estate. [2]He called the manager in and said to him, 'What is this I hear about you? Give me a report of your administration because you can no longer serve as my manager.'

[3]"The household manager said to himself, What will I do now that my master is firing me as his manager? I'm not strong enough to dig and too proud to beg. [4]I know what I'll do so that, when I am removed from my management position, people will welcome me into their houses.

[5]"One by one, the manager sent for each person who owed his master money. He said to the first, 'How much do you owe my master?' [6]He said, 'Nine hundred gallons of olive oil.' The manager said to him, 'Take your contract, sit down quickly, and write four hundred fifty gallons.' [7]Then the manager said to another, 'How much do you owe?' He said, 'One thousand bushels of wheat.' He said, 'Take your contract and write eight hundred.'

[8]"The master commended the dishonest manager because he acted cleverly. People who belong to this world are more clever in dealing with their peers than are people who belong to the light. [9]I tell you, use worldly wealth to make friends for yourselves so that when it's gone, you will be welcomed into the eternal homes.

[10]"Whoever is faithful with little is also faithful with much, and the one who is dishonest with little is also dishonest with much. [11]If you haven't been faithful with worldly wealth, who will trust you with true riches? [12]If you haven't been faithful with someone else's property, who will give you your own? [13]No household servant can serve two masters. Either you will hate the one and love the other, or you will be loyal to the one and have contempt for the other. You cannot serve God and wealth."

Primary Hymns and Songs for the Day

"O Master, Let Me Walk with Thee" (Jer) (O)
C602, CG660, E659/E660, EL818, G738, GR596, N503, P357, SH612, UM430 (PD), VU560
H-3 Hbl-81; Chr-147; Desc-74; Org-87
S-2 #118. Descant

"There Is a Balm in Gilead" (Jer)
C501, CG74, E676, EL614 (PD), G792, GR350, N553, P394, SH340, UM375, VU612, Z123, ZS114
S-2 #21. Desc.

"How Long, O Lord" 3317053 (Pss)
G777, S2209

"We Believe in One True God" (PD) (1 Tim)
GR26, P137 (PD), UM85
S-1 #278-279. Harms.

"O-So-So" ("Come Now, O Prince of Peace") OL-AF20201411 (1 Tim)
EL247, G103, S2232, SH235

"Take, O Take Me as I Am" 4562041 (Luke)
EL814, G698, SH620, WS3119

"Forth in Thy Name, O Lord" (Luke) (C)
GR685, UM438 (PD), VU416
H-3 Hbl-29, 57, 58; Chr-117; Desc-31; Org-31
S-1 #100-103. Various treatments.

Additional Hymn Suggestions

"Jesus, Lover of My Soul" (Jer)
C542, CG406, E699, G440, GR120, N546, P303, SH542/543, UM479, VU669

"O Love That Wilt Not Let Me Go" (Jer)
C540, CG631, G833, GR92, N485, P384, SH314, UM480 (PD), VU658

"Lord of All Hopefulness" 5579875 (Jer)
CG678, E482, EL765, G683, S2197, SH464

"Why Stand So Far Away, My God" (Jer, Pss)
C671, G786, S2180

"O for a Closer Walk with God" (Jer, Pss)
CG679, E684, G739, GR327, N450, P396

+"Hear My Prayer, O God" (Jer, Pss)
G782, WS3131

"Forgive Our Sins as We Forgive" (Jer, Pss)
CG694, E674, EL605, G444, GR442, P347, SH504, UM390, VU364

"I Want a Principle Within" (Jer, Pss)
See especially stanza 3.
GR313, UM410 (PD)

"O Thou, in Whose Presence" (Jer, Pss)
GR58 (PD), UM518

"Dear Lord and Father of Mankind" 106185 (Jer, Pss, Luke)
(Alternate Text: "Dear God, Embracing Humankind")
C594, CG413, E652/563, G169, GR499, N502, P345, UM358 (PD), VU608

"I Love the Lord" 1168957 (Jer, Pss, Luke)
CG613, G799, P362, N511, SH343, VU617, WS3142, ZS176

+"Breath of God, Breath of Peace" OL-99430 (Jer, Pss, 1 Tim)
WS3145

"For the Healing of the Nations" 1510804 (Jer, 1 Tim)
C668, CG698, G346, N576, UM428, VU678

+"Let There Be Peace on Earth" (Jer, 1 Tim)
C677, UM431

"What Does the Lord Require of You" 456859 (Jer, Luke)
C661, CG690, G70, S2174, VU701

"Purify My Heart" 1314323 (Jer, Luke)

"All Who Love and Serve Your City" 1277415 (Pss, Luke)
C670, CG674, E570/E571, EL724, G351, P413, UM433

+"O God of Every Nation" (1 Tim)
C680, CG46, E607, EL713, G756, P289, UM435, VU677

"This Is My Song" (1 Tim)
C722, CG697, EL887, G340, N591, UM437

"To God Be the Glory" (1 Tim)
C72, CG349, G634, GR531, P485, SH545, UM98 (PD)

"Make Me a Channel of Your Peace" OL-80478 (1 Tim)
G753, S2171, SH616 VU684

"Make Me a Channel of Your Peace" 6399315 (1 Tim)

"Baptized in Water" 5853694 (1 Tim, Baptism)
CG449, E294, EL456, G482, P492, S2248, SH666

"Take My Life, and Let It Be" 1390 (1 Tim, Luke)
C609, CG490, E707, EL583/EL685, G697, GR586, P391, N448, SH627/628, UM399 (PD), VU506

"Jesús Es Mi Rey Soberano" ("O Jesus, My King and My Sovereign") (Luke)
C109, P157, SH211, UM180

"I Want to Walk as a Child of the Light" (Luke)
CG96, E490, EL815, G377, GR216, SH352, UM206

"I Surrender All" (Luke)
CG499, SH619, GR607, UM354, Z67 (PD)

"Nothing Between" (Luke)
GR339, UM373 (PD), Z21, ZS71

"Jesus Calls Us" 68900 (Luke)
C337, CG486, E549/550, EL696, G720, GR520, N171/172, SH604, UM398, VU562

"What Does the Lord Require" 287413 (Luke)
C659, E605, P405, UM441

"More Love to Thee, O Christ" 36750 (Luke)
C527, CG365, G828, GR588, N456, P359, UM453 (PD)

"Living for Jesus" (Luke)
C610, GR595, S2149

"I'm Gonna Live So God Can Use Me" (Luke)
C614, G700, GR615, P369, S2153, SH632, VU575

+"Here Am I" (Luke)
C654, S2178

"Somebody's Knockin' at Your Door" (PD-TO) (Luke)
G728, P382, SH597, WS3095 (PD-TO), Z154

"We Give Thee but Thine Own" 3922369 (Luke)
C382, EL686, G708, N785, P428, SH643, VU543

Additional Contemporary and Modern Suggestions

"Hear Us from Heaven" 4455392 (Jer, Pss)
+"Better Than A Hallelujah" 5622564 (Jer, Pss)
+"Daughters of Zion" 7133716 (Jer, Pss, Luke)
+"Let Justice Roll" ("Like a River") 4974842 (Jer, Pss, Luke)
+"How Shall I Come Before the Lord" (Jer, Luke)
WS3124
+"As It Is in Heaven" 4669748 (1 Tim)
"Jesus Messiah" 5183443 (1 Tim)
+"Give Thanks" 20285 (1 Tim)
C528, CG373, G647, S2036, SH489, ZS127
"Jesus, Name above All Names" 21291 (1 Tim)
S2071, ZS27
"Praise You" 863806 (Luke, Praise)
S2003, ZS170
"Make Me a Servant" 33131 (Luke)
CG651, S2176
"Seek Ye First" 1352 (Luke)
C354, CG436, E711, G175, GR341, P333, SH126, UM405, VU356
"Knowing You" 1045238 (Luke)
"Take This Life" 2563365 (Luke, Stewardship)
"These Hands" 3251827 (Luke, Stewardship)
"Be Glorified" 2732646 (2 Thess)
"Lord, Be Glorified" 26368 (Luke, Stewardship)
EL744, G468, S2150, SH420

Solo/Ensemble Suggestions
"There Is a Balm in Gilead" (Jer)
V-3 (1) p. 29
+"I Couldn't Hear Nobody Pray" (Jer, Pss)
V-7 p. 40/43
+"If My People Will Pray" (Jer, Pss, 1 Tim)
V-8 p. 66
"Take My Life" (1 Tim, Luke, Stewardship)
V-8 p. 262
"Seek First" (Luke)
V-8 p. 145
"Prayer for Today" (Jer)
Margaret Tucker; Choristers Guild CGA855
SATB, keyboard, opt. flute (https://bit.ly/CG-855)
"Love, Come Down" (Jer)
Karen Marrolli; MorningStar MSM-50-4844
SATB, piano (https://bit.ly/MSM-50-4844)

+Hymn Anthem
"O Thou, in Whose Presence" 271864 (Jer, Pss)
GR58 (PD), UM518
Purchasers of this book may photocopy UM518 for one-time use by their choir in performing this anthem. Other uses require permission.
Perform this anthem at a fast, dance-like tempo ([half note] = 100, with two pulses per bar). Stress the first pulse in each measure. Use instrument parts below or alternate suggestions.
Introduction: Bass metallophone (whole note open 5th, C & G) and tambourine (improvised) play four measures. (In absence of metallophone, organ plays notes 8ve lower than written.) *Mezzo forte.*
Stanza 1: S/A sing the melody in a lilting manner. Accompany with tambourine and metallophone (or organ). T/B hum the metallophone pitches, creating a drone. *Mezzo forte.*
Stanza 2: T/B sing the melody and S/A hum the drone. Accompany metallophone (or organ). *Mezzo forte.*
Stanza 3: This stanza is twice as slow as before (quarter note becomes half note) and softer. Perform in a 2-4 part round assigning singers to each group. Groups begin two measures apart. *A cappella. Mezzo piano.*
Stanza 4: Return to the original tempo and dynamic. All voices, unison. Accompany with tambourine, drum (on the first beat of each measure) and triangle (on the 3rd beat of each measure). *Mezzo forte.*
Stanza 5: All voices sing the melody. Some S/T sing a descant, maybe the alto part up one octave. Accompany with all instruments. *Forte.*

Other Suggestions
Visuals:
O Grief, heart, reaching, harvest, poor, heal, spring
P Ruins, blood, fire, Ps. 79:9
E Praying hands, judge, hand of God, Christ, cross
G Ledger, shovel, tin cup, 100/50, oil, wheat, 100/80, darkness/light, symbols of wealth
A stewardship focus relates well to today's Luke reading.
Opening Prayer: UM677. Listen, Lord (Jer, Pss)
+Sung Prayer: S2201. "Prayers of the People" (1 Tim)
+Prayer: UM429. For Our Country (1 Tim)
Prayer: N851. Guidance (Jer)
Prayer: N854 or N863 (Pss)
Prayer: WSL205. "Loving God, we spend so much time" (Luke)
Offertory Prayer: WSL146 or WSL147 (Luke)
Response: UM588. "All Things Come of Thee" (Luke)
Alternate Lessons (see page 4): Amos 8:4-7, Ps. 113
Theme Ideas: Faithfulness, Grief, Lament, Prayer, Stewardship

Notes

NRSVue

Jeremiah 32:1-3a, 6-15

1The word that came to Jeremiah from the LORD in the tenth year of King Zedekiah of Judah, which was the eighteenth year of Nebuchadrezzar. 2At that time the army of the king of Babylon was besieging Jerusalem, and the prophet Jeremiah was confined in the court of the guard that was in the palace of the king of Judah, 3awhere King Zedekiah of Judah had confined him. . . .

6Jeremiah said, "The word of the LORD came to me: 7Hanamel son of your uncle Shallum is going to come to you and say, 'Buy my field that is at Anathoth, for the right of redemption by purchase is yours.' " 8Then my cousin Hanamel came to me in the court of the guard, in accordance with the word of the LORD, and said to me, "Buy my field that is at Anathoth in the land of Benjamin, for the right of possession and redemption is yours; buy it for yourself." Then I knew that this was the word of the LORD.

9And I bought the field at Anathoth from my cousin Hanamel and weighed out the silver to him, seventeen shekels of silver. 10I signed the deed, sealed it, got witnesses, and weighed the silver on scales. 11Then I took the sealed deed of purchase containing the terms and conditions and the open copy, 12and I gave the deed of purchase to Baruch son of Neriah son of Mahseiah, in the presence of my cousin Hanamel, in the presence of the witnesses who signed the deed of purchase, and in the presence of all the Judeans who were sitting in the court of the guard. 13In their presence I charged Baruch, saying, 14"Thus says the LORD of hosts, the God of Israel: Take these deeds, both this sealed deed of purchase and this open deed, and put them in an earthenware jar, in order that they may last for a long time. 15For thus says the LORD of hosts, the God of Israel: Houses and fields and vineyards shall again be bought in this land.

Psalm 91:1-6, 14-16 (G43/168, N681, P212, UM810)

1You who live in the shelter of the Most High,
who abide in the shadow of the Almighty,
2will say to the LORD, "My refuge and my fortress;
my God, in whom I trust."
3For he will deliver you from the snare of the hunter
and from the deadly pestilence;
4he will cover you with his pinions,
and under his wings you will find refuge;
his faithfulness is a shield and defense.
5You will not fear the terror of the night
or the arrow that flies by day
6or the pestilence that stalks in darkness
or the destruction that wastes at noonday.
. . . .
14Those who love me, I will deliver;
I will protect those who know my name.
15When they call to me, I will answer them;
I will be with them in trouble;
I will rescue them and honor them.
16With long life I will satisfy them
and show them my salvation.

CEB

Jeremiah 32:1-3a, 6-15

1Jeremiah received the LORD's word in the tenth year of Judah's King Zedekiah, which was the eighteenth year of Nebuchadnezzar's rule. 2At that time, the army of the Babylonian king had surrounded Jerusalem, and the prophet Jeremiah was confined to the prison quarters in the palace of Judah's king. 3aJudah's King Zedekiah had Jeremiah sent there after questioning him. . . .

6Jeremiah said, The LORD's word came to me: 7Your cousin Hanamel, Shallum's son, is on his way to see you; and when he arrives, he will tell you: "Buy my field in Anathoth, for by law you are next in line to purchase it." 8And just as the LORD had said, my cousin Hanamel showed up at the prison quarters and told me, "Buy my field in Anathoth in the land of Benjamin, for you are next in line and have a family obligation to purchase it." Then I was sure this was the LORD's doing.

9So I bought the field in Anathoth from my cousin Hanamel, and weighed out for him seventeen shekels of silver. 10I signed the deed, sealed it, had it witnessed, and weighed out the silver on the scales. 11Then I took the deed of purchase—the sealed copy, with its terms and conditions, and the unsealed copy—12and gave it to Baruch, Neriah's son and Mahseiah's grandson, before my cousin Hanamel and the witnesses named in the deed, as well as before all the Judeans who were present in the prison quarters. 13I charged Baruch before all of them: 14"The LORD of heavenly forces, the God of Israel, proclaims: Take these documents—this sealed deed of purchase along with the unsealed one—and put them into a clay container so they will last a long time. 15The LORD of heavenly forces, the God of Israel, proclaims: Houses, fields, and vineyards will again be bought in this land."

Psalm 91:1-6, 14-16 (G43/168, N681, P212, UM810)

1Living in the Most High's shelter,
camping in the Almighty's shade,
2I say to the LORD, "You are my refuge, my stronghold!
You are my God—the one I trust!"
3God will save you from the hunter's trap
And from deadly sickness.
4God will protect you with his pinions;
You'll find refuge under his wings.
His faithfulness is a protective shield.
5Don't be afraid of terrors at night,
Arrows that fly in daylight,
6 Or sickness that prowls in the dark,
Destruction that ravages at noontime.
. . . .
14God says, "Because you are devoted to me,
I'll rescue you.
I'll protect you because you know my name.
15Whenever you cry out to me, I'll answer.
I'll be with you in troubling times.
I'll save you and glorify you.
16 I'll fill you full with old age.
I'll show you my salvation."

NRSVue

1 Timothy 6:6-19

[6]Of course, there is great gain in godliness combined with contentment, [7]for we brought nothing into the world, so that we can take nothing out of it, [8]but if we have food and clothing, we will be content with these. [9]But those who want to be rich fall into temptation and are trapped by many senseless and harmful desires that plunge people into ruin and destruction. [10]For the love of money is a root of all kinds of evil, and in their eagerness to be rich some have wandered away from the faith and pierced themselves with many pains.

[11]But as for you, man of God, shun all this; pursue righteousness, godliness, faith, love, endurance, gentleness. [12]Fight the good fight of the faith; take hold of the eternal life to which you were called and for which you made the good confession in the presence of many witnesses. [13]In the presence of God, who gives life to all things, and of Christ Jesus, who in his testimony before Pontius Pilate made the good confession, I charge you [14]to keep the commandment without spot or blame until the manifestation of our Lord Jesus Christ, [15]which he will bring about at the right time—he who is the blessed and only Sovereign, the King of kings and Lord of lords. [16]It is he alone who has immortality and dwells in unapproachable light, whom no one has ever seen or can see; to him be honor and eternal dominion. Amen.

[17]As for those who in the present age are rich, command them not to be haughty or to set their hopes on the uncertainty of riches but rather on God, who richly provides us with everything for our enjoyment. [18]They are to do good, to be rich in good works, generous, and ready to share, [19]thus storing up for themselves the treasure of a good foundation for the future, so that they may take hold of the life that really is life.

Luke 16:19-31

[19]"There was a rich man who was dressed in purple and fine linen and who feasted sumptuously every day. [20]And at his gate lay a poor man named Lazarus, covered with sores, [21]who longed to satisfy his hunger with what fell from the rich man's table; even the dogs would come and lick his sores. [22]The poor man died and was carried away by the angels to be with Abraham. The rich man also died and was buried. [23]In Hades, where he was being tormented, he lifted up his eyes and saw Abraham far away with Lazarus by his side. [24]He called out, 'Father Abraham, have mercy on me, and send Lazarus to dip the tip of his finger in water and cool my tongue, for I am in agony in these flames.' [25]But Abraham said, 'Child, remember that during your lifetime you received your good things and Lazarus in like manner evil things, but now he is comforted here, and you are in agony. [26]Besides all this, between you and us a great chasm has been fixed, so that those who might want to pass from here to you cannot do so, and no one can cross from there to us.' [27]He said, 'Then I beg you, father, to send him to my father's house—[28]for I have five brothers—that he may warn them, so that they will not also come into this place of torment.' [29]Abraham replied, 'They have Moses and the prophets; they should listen to them.' [30]He said, 'No, father Abraham, but if someone from the dead goes to them, they will repent.' [31]He said to him, 'If they do not listen to Moses and the prophets, neither will they be convinced even if someone rises from the dead.'"

CEB

1 Timothy 6:6-19

[6]Actually, godliness is a great source of profit when it is combined with being happy with what you already have. [7]We didn't bring anything into the world and so we can't take anything out of it: [8]we'll be happy with food and clothing. [9]But people who are trying to get rich fall into temptation. They are trapped by many stupid and harmful passions that plunge people into ruin and destruction. [10]The love of money is the root of all kinds of evil. Some have wandered away from the faith and have impaled themselves with a lot of pain because they made money their goal.

[11]But as for you, man of God, run away from all these things. Instead, pursue righteousness, holy living, faithfulness, love, endurance, and gentleness. [12]Compete in the good fight of faith. Grab hold of eternal life—you were called to it, and you made a good confession of it in the presence of many witnesses. [13]I command you in the presence of God, who gives life to all things, and Christ Jesus, who made the good confession when testifying before Pontius Pilate. [14]Obey this order without fault or failure until the appearance of our Lord Jesus Christ. [15]The timing of this appearance is revealed by God alone, who is the blessed and only master, the King of kings and Lord of lords. [16]He alone has immortality and lives in light that no one can come near. No human being has ever seen or is able to see him. Honor and eternal power belong to him. Amen.

[17]Tell people who are rich at this time not to become egotistical and not to place their hope on their finances, which are uncertain. Instead, they need to hope in God, who richly provides everything for our enjoyment. [18]Tell them to do good, to be rich in the good things they do, to be generous, and to share with others. [19]When they do these things, they will save a treasure for themselves that is a good foundation for the future. That way they can take hold of what is truly life.

Luke 16:19-31

[19]"There was a certain rich man who clothed himself in purple and fine linen, and who feasted luxuriously every day. [20]At his gate lay a certain poor man named Lazarus who was covered with sores. [21]Lazarus longed to eat the crumbs that fell from the rich man's table. Instead, dogs would come and lick his sores.

[22]"The poor man died and was carried by angels to Abraham's side. The rich man also died and was buried. [23]While being tormented in the place of the dead, he looked up and saw Abraham at a distance with Lazarus at his side. [24]He shouted, 'Father Abraham, have mercy on me. Send Lazarus to dip the tip of his finger in water and cool my tongue because I'm suffering in this flame.' [25]But Abraham said, 'Child, remember that during your lifetime you received good things whereas Lazarus received terrible things. Now Lazarus is being comforted and you are in great pain. [26]Moreover, a great crevasse has been fixed between us and you. Those who wish to cross over from here to you cannot. Neither can anyone cross from there to us.'

[27]"The rich man said, 'Then I beg you, Father, send Lazarus to my father's house. [28]I have five brothers. He needs to warn them so that they don't come to this place of agony.' [29]Abraham replied, 'They have Moses and the Prophets. They must listen to them.' [30]The rich man said, 'No, Father Abraham! But if someone from the dead goes to them, they will change their hearts and lives.' [31]Abraham said, 'If they don't listen to Moses and the Prophets, then neither will they be persuaded if someone rises from the dead.'"

Primary Hymns and Songs for the Day

"Ye Servants of God" 90765 (1 Tim) (O)
C110, CG420, E535, EL825 (PD), G299, GR40, N305, P477, UM181 (PD), VU342
H-3 Hbl-90, 105; Chr-221; Desc-49; Org-51
S-2 #71-74. Introduction and harmonizations
"On Eagle's Wings" OL-80468 (Pss)
C77, CG51, EL787, G43, N775, SH318, UM143, VU807/VU808, S-2 #143. Stanzas for soloist
S-2 #143 Stanzas for soloist
"God Will Take Care of You" 93645 (Pss, 1 Tim)
GR358, N460, SH289, UM130 (PD)
"Give Thanks" 20285 (Luke)
C528, CG373, G647, S2036, SH489, ZS127
"A Charge to Keep I Have" 118850 (1 Tim) (C)
CG623, GR456, SH634, UM413 (PD)
S-1 #46. Choral Harm.

Additional Hymn Suggestions

"Hope of the World" 643002 (Jer)
C538, E472, G734, N46, P360, UM178, VU215
"O Day of Peace That Dimly Shines" (Jer)
C711, E597, EL711, G373, P450, UM729, VU682
"Eternal Father, Strong to Save" (Jer)
C85, CG14, E608, EL756, G8, P562 (PD), S2191, VU659
"O Thou, in Whose Presence" (Jer, Pss)
GR58 (PD), UM518
"What Does the Lord Require of You" 456859 (Jer, Luke)
C661, CG690, G70, S2174, VU701
"It Is Well with My Soul" 25376 (Pss)
C561, CG573, EL785, G840, GR344, N438, SH305, UM377 (PD), Z20
"We Sing to You, O God" 2192729 (Pss)
EL791, N9, S2001
"O Holy Spirit, Root of Life" (Pss)
C251, EL399, N57, S2121, VU379
"Blessed Quietness" (Pss)
C267, CG244, N284 (PD), S2142, Z206
"El que habita al abrigo de Dios" ("Those Who Dwell in the Shelter of God") (Pss)
SH49
"Escogido fui de Dios" ("From Before the Dawn of Time") (Pss)
SH61
"Immortal, Invisible, God Only Wise" 124466 (1 Tim)
C66, CG58, E423, EL834, G12, GR7, N1, P263, UM103 (PD), VU264 (*See also* ZS4)
"Rejoice, Ye Pure in Heart" (Phil)
C15, CG312, E556/557, EL873/874, G804, GR62, N55/71, P145/146, UM160/161
"Take My Life, and Let It Be" 1390 (1 Tim)
C609, CG490, E707, EL583/EL685, G697, GR586, P391, N448, SH627/628, UM399 (PD), VU506
"Stand Up, Stand Up for Jesus" (1 Tim)
C613, CG639, E561, GR477, UM514 (PD)
"He Is King of Kings" (1 Tim)
G273, P153
"We Give Thee but Thine Own" 3922369 (1 Tim)
C382, EL686, G708, N785, P428, SH643, VU543
"Fight the Good Fight" (1 Tim)
E552, G846, GR473, P307 (PD), VU674
"Fairest Lord Jesus" 27800 (1 Tim, Luke)
C97, CG159, E383/384, EL838, G630, GR113, N44, P306, SH7, UM189 (PD), VU341
"I Sing a Song of the Saints of God" (1 Tim, Luke)
E293, G730, GR482, N295, P364, UM712 (PD)
"Pues Si Vivimos" ("When We Are Living") 4968810 (1 Tim, Luke)
C536, CG265, EL639, G822, N499, P400, SH299, UM356, VU581
"Where Cross the Crowded Ways of Life" 2961345 (Luke)
C665, CG657, E609, EL719, G343, N543, P408, UM427 (PD), VU681
"Cuando el Pobre" ("When the Poor Ones") OL-97385 (Luke)
C662, EL725, G762, P407, SH240, UM434, VU702
"The Church of Christ, in Every Age" (Luke)
C475, EL729, G320, N306, P421, UM589, VU601
+"Blessed Jesus, at Thy Word" (Luke)
E440, EL520, G395, N74, P454, UM596 (PD), VU500
"God Be with You till We Meet Again" (Luke)
C434, CG523, EL536, G541, GR688, N81, UM672 (PD), VU422, Z37
"God Be with You Till We Meet Again" (Luke)
G542, P540, UM673 (PD), VU423
+"God Be with You" (Luke)
C435, N809, Z203, ZS215
+"Why Stand So Far Away, My God?" (Luke)
C671, G786, S2180
+"Touch the Earth Lightly" (Luke)
C693, EL739, G713, N569, VU307, WS3129

Additional Contemporary and Modern Suggestions

"I Have a Hope" 5087587 (Jer)
"Song of Hope" ("Heaven Come Down") 5111477 (Jer)
+"No Outsiders" 7101035 (Pss)
"I Will Call upon the Lord" 11263 (Pss)
G621, S2002
"You Are My Hiding Place" 21442 (Pss)
C554, S2055, SH46
"Nada Te Turbe" ("Nothing Can Trouble") OL-00128 (Pss)
CG73, G820, N772, S2054, SH292, VU290
"I've Got Peace Like a River" (PD) (Pss)
C530, G623, N478, P368, S2145, SH276, VU577
"Everlasting God" 4556538 (Pss)
WS3021
"Still" 3940963 (Pss)
WS3134
"This is My Story" 7046375 (Pss)
"Who Can Satisfy My Soul Like You?" 208492 (Pss)
"I Stand Amazed" 769450 (Pss)
"All Things Are Possible" 2245140 (Pss)
"Eagle's Wings" 2478168 (Pss)
"Came to My Rescue" 4705190 (Pss)
"Crown Him King of Kings" 206009 (1 Tim)
"All Hail King Jesus" 12877 (1 Tim)
S2069, ZS53
"King of Kings" 23952 (1 Tim)
S2075, VU167
"We Will Glorify the King of Kings" 19038 (1 Tim)
CG360, S2087
"He Who Began a Good Work in You" 15238 (1 Tim)
S2163, ZS98
"More Like You" 2145051 (1 Tim)
S2167
"Majesty" 1527 (1 Tim)
CG346, GR63, SH212, UM176
"Worthy, You Are Worthy" 17384 (1 Tim)
"Worthy" 2646749 (1 Tim)
"Forevermore" 5466830 (1 Tim)
"I Will Boast" 4662350 (1 Tim, Luke)
"When It's All Been Said and Done" 2788353 (1 Tim, Luke)
+"My Worth Is Not in What I Own" 7024758 (1 Tim, Luke)
+"From Ashes to Beauty" 5288953 (1 Tim, Luke)
+"Fill My Cup, Lord" 15946 (1 Tim, Luke)
C351, UM641 *(refrain only)*, WS3093
"You Are My All in All" 825356 (1 Tim, Luke)
CG571, G519, SH335, WS3040, ZS184

"Jesus, Remember Me" OL-00122 (Luke)
C569, CG393, EL616, G227, P599, SH175, UM488, VU148
"Today" 5775617 (Luke)
+"Let the River Flow" 1686824 (Luke)

Solo/Ensemble Suggestions
+"My Heart Is Steadfast" (Pss)
V-5(2) p. 40
"On Eagle's Wings" (Pss)
V-3 (3) p. 4
V-3 (2) p. 2
+"Refuge and Strength" (Pss)
V-3 (5) p. 14
+"I Know Where I'm Going" (1 Tim, Luke)
V-8 p. 328
+"Graves Into Gardens" (1 Tim, Luke)
V-9 p. 15
+"The Church of Christ in Every Age" (Luke)
Arr. David M. Cherwien; Augsburg 9781506495392
SATB, organ, C-instrument (https://bit.ly/Aug-95392)
"Poor Man Lazarus" (Luke)
arr. Jester Hairston; Bourne 2653-7
SATB a cappella (https://bit.ly/2653-7-Lazarus)

+Hymn Anthem
"Thy Holy Wings, O Savior" OL-25950, OL-02378 (Pss)
EL613, UM502
Introduction: S-1, #49. Flute parts could be played on organ or synthesizer. Alternate: play the last 4 measures on keyboard.
Stanza 1: T/B only on systems 1-2. S/A join on system 3, but all voices continue to sing melody only. All voices on system 4. Accompany with bass clef only of S-1, #48 on piano, or improvise a simple folk accompaniment.
Interlude: Piano plays S-1, #48. One or both flutes play S-1, #47 (descant). Choir softly sings the melody on "oo" vowel. Very gentle. Let the descant soar above and predominate.
Stanza 2: All voices begin on melody, go to parts on system 3, return to melody on system 4. Piano and one flute play S-1, #47 and #48.
Ending: Piano plays S-1, #48, bass clef only. Flutes play melody. Choir sings melody on "oo" vowel. You may invite the congregation to join the choir in this ending.

Other Suggestions
Visuals:
O War, field, scales, earthen jar, house
P Shadow, refuge, fort, eagle, snare, shield/arrow
E Newborn, coffin, money, 1 Tim. 6:11b, Jesus/Pilot, cross/crown, generosity, treasure
G Purple robe/linen, feast, sores, dogs, five men, angels, flames, water, Bible open to Exodus
Stewardship emphasis relates to New Testament lessons today.
+Call to Prayer: EL406, G281, S2118. "Holy Spirit, Come to Us" (Pss)
Prayer: N863. Justice (Jer, Luke)
Prayer for Healing: WSL204. "God of compassion" (Luke)
Prayer of Confession: WSL92 or WSL93 (Luke)
Response: C299, G576, S2277. "Lord, Have Mercy" (Luke)
Offertory Prayer: WSL104. "O God, may our use of money" (Luke)
Communion Prayer: C774 (Luke)
Alternate Lessons (see page 4): Amos 6:1a, 4-7, Ps.146
Theme Ideas: God: Providence / God our Help, Hope, Stewardship

Notes

NRSVue

Lamentations 1:1-6

1How lonely sits the city
that once was full of people!
How like a widow she has become,
she that was great among the nations!
She that was a princess among the provinces
has become a subject to forced labor.
2She weeps bitterly in the night,
with tears on her cheeks;
among all her lovers,
she has no one to comfort her;
all her friends have dealt treacherously with her;
they have become her enemies.
3Judah has gone into exile with suffering
and hard servitude;
she lives now among the nations;
she finds no resting place;
her pursuers have all overtaken her
in the midst of her distress.
4The roads to Zion mourn,
for no one comes to the festivals;
all her gates are desolate;
her priests groan;
her young girls grieve,
and her lot is bitter.
5Her foes have become the masters;
her enemies prosper
because the Lord has made her suffer
for the multitude of her transgressions;
her children have gone away,
captives before the foe.
6From daughter Zion has departed
all her majesty.
Her princes have become like stags
that find no pasture;
they fled without strength
before the pursuer.

Psalm 137 (G72/784, N713, P246, UM852)

1By the rivers of Babylon—
there we sat down, and there we wept
when we remembered Zion.
2On the willows there
we hung up our harps.
3For there our captors
asked us for songs,
and our tormentors asked for mirth, saying,
"Sing us one of the songs of Zion!"
4How could we sing the Lord's song
in a foreign land?
5If I forget you, O Jerusalem,
let my right hand wither!
6Let my tongue cling to the roof of my mouth,
if I do not remember you,
if I do not set Jerusalem
above my highest joy.
7Remember, O Lord, against the Edomites
the day of Jerusalem's fall,
how they said, "Tear it down! Tear it down!
Down to its foundations!"
8O daughter Babylon, you devastator!
Happy shall they be who pay you back
what you have done to us!
9Happy shall they be who take your little ones
and dash them against the rock!

CEB

Lamentations 1:1-6

1Oh, no!
She sits alone,
the city that was once full of people.
Once great among nations,
she has become like a widow.
Once a queen over provinces,
she has become a slave.
2She weeps bitterly in the night,
her tears on her cheek.
None of her lovers comfort her.
All her friends lied to her;
they have become her enemies.
3Judah was exiled after suffering
and hard service.
She lives among the nations;
she finds no rest.
All who were chasing her caught her—
right in the middle of her distress.
4Zion's roads are in mourning;
no one comes to the festivals.
All her gates are deserted.
Her priests are groaning,
her young women grieving. She is bitter.
5Her adversaries have become rulers;
her enemies relax.
Certainly the Lord caused her grief
because of her many wrong acts.
Her children have gone away,
captive before the enemy.
6Daughter Zion lost all her glory.
Her officials are like deer
that can't find pasture.
They have gone away, frail,
before the hunter.

Psalm 137 (G72/784, N713, P246, UM852)

1Alongside Babylon's streams,
there we sat down,
crying because we remembered Zion.
2We hung our lyres up
in the trees there
3 because that's where our captors asked us to sing;
our tormentors requested songs of joy:
"Sing us a song about Zion!" they said.
4But how could we possibly sing
the Lord's song on foreign soil?
5Jerusalem! If I forget you,
let my strong hand wither!
6Let my tongue stick to the roof of my mouth
if I don't remember you,
if I don't make Jerusalem my greatest joy.
7Lord, remember what the Edomites did
on Jerusalem's dark day:
"Rip it down, rip it down!
All the way to its foundations!" they yelled.
8Daughter Babylon, you destroyer,
a blessing on the one who pays you back
the very deed you did to us!
9 A blessing on the one who seizes your children
and smashes them against the rock!

NRSVue

2 Timothy 1:1-14

[1]Paul, an apostle of Christ Jesus by the will of God, for the sake of the promise of life that is in Christ Jesus,

[2]To Timothy, my beloved child:

Grace, mercy, and peace from God the Father and Christ Jesus our Lord.

[3]I am grateful to God—whom I worship with a clear conscience, as my ancestors did—when I remember you constantly in my prayers night and day. [4]Recalling your tears, I long to see you so that I may be filled with joy. [5]I am reminded of your sincere faith, a faith that lived first in your grandmother Lois and your mother Eunice and now, I am sure, lives in you. [6]For this reason I remind you to rekindle the gift of God that is within you through the laying on of my hands, [7]for God did not give us a spirit of cowardice but rather a spirit of power and of love and of self-discipline.

[8]Do not be ashamed, then, of the testimony about our Lord or of me his prisoner, but join with me in suffering for the gospel, in the power of God, [9]who saved us and called us with a holy calling, not according to our works but according to his own purpose and grace, and this grace was given to us in Christ Jesus before the ages began, [10]but it has now been revealed through the appearing of our Savior Jesus Christ, who abolished death and brought life and immortality to light through the gospel. [11]For this gospel I was appointed a herald and an apostle and a teacher, [12]and for this reason I suffer as I do. But I am not ashamed, for I know the one in whom I have put my trust, and I am sure that he is able to guard the deposit I have entrusted to him. [13]Hold to the standard of sound teaching that you have heard from me, in the faith and love that are in Christ Jesus. [14]Guard the good deposit entrusted to you, with the help of the Holy Spirit living in us.

Luke 17:5-10

[5]The apostles said to the Lord, "Increase our faith!" [6]The Lord replied, "If you had faith the size of a mustard seed, you could say to this mulberry tree, 'Be uprooted and planted in the sea,' and it would obey you.

[7]"Who among you would say to your slave who has just come in from plowing or tending sheep in the field, 'Come here at once and take your place at the table'? [8]Would you not rather say to him, 'Prepare supper for me; put on your apron and serve me while I eat and drink; later you may eat and drink'? [9]Do you thank the slave for doing what was commanded? [10]So you also, when you have done all that you were ordered to do, say, 'We are worthless slaves; we have done only what we ought to have done!'"

CEB

2 Timothy 1:1-14

[1]From Paul, an apostle of Christ Jesus by God's will, to promote the promise of life that is in Christ Jesus.

[2]To Timothy, my dear child.

Grace, mercy, and peace from God the Father and Christ Jesus our Lord.

[3]I'm grateful to God, whom I serve with a good conscience as my ancestors did. I constantly remember you in my prayers day and night. [4]When I remember your tears, I long to see you so that I can be filled with happiness. [5]I'm reminded of your authentic faith, which first lived in your grandmother Lois and your mother Eunice. I'm sure that this faith is also inside you. [6]Because of this, I'm reminding you to revive God's gift that is in you through the laying on of my hands. [7]God didn't give us a spirit that is timid but one that is powerful, loving, and self-controlled.

[8]So don't be ashamed of the testimony about the Lord or of me, his prisoner. Instead, share the suffering for the good news, depending on God's power. [9]God is the one who saved and called us with a holy calling. This wasn't based on what we have done, but it was based on his own purpose and grace that he gave us in Christ Jesus before time began. [10]Now his grace is revealed through the appearance of our savior, Christ Jesus. He destroyed death and brought life and immortality into clear focus through the good news. [11]I was appointed a messenger, apostle, and teacher of this good news. [12]This is also why I'm suffering the way I do, but I'm not ashamed. I know the one in whom I've placed my trust. I'm convinced that God is powerful enough to protect what he has placed in my trust until that day. [13]Hold on to the pattern of sound teaching that you heard from me with the faith and love that are in Christ Jesus. [14]Protect this good thing that has been placed in your trust through the Holy Spirit who lives in us.

Luke 17:5-10

[5]The apostles said to the Lord, "Increase our faith!"

[6]The Lord replied, "If you had faith the size of a mustard seed, you could say to this mulberry tree, 'Be uprooted and planted in the sea,' and it would obey you.

[7]"Would any of you say to your servant, who had just come in from the field after plowing or tending sheep, 'Come! Sit down for dinner'? [8]Wouldn't you say instead, 'Fix my dinner. Put on the clothes of a table servant and wait on me while I eat and drink. After that, you can eat and drink'? [9]You won't thank the servant because the servant did what you asked, will you? [10]In the same way, when you have done everything required of you, you should say, 'We servants deserve no special praise. We have only done our duty.'"

Primary Hymns and Songs for the Day
"Standing on the Promises" (2 Tim) (O)
C552, CG625, G838, GR434, SH45, UM374 (PD)
H-3 Chr-177; Org-117
"By the Babylonian Rivers" (Pss)
G72, P246, S2217, VU859
"By the Waters of Babylon" (Pss)
G784, P245, VU858b
"I Know Whom I Have Believed" (2 Tim)
CG588, GR571, SH529, UM714 (PD)
"Oh, I Know the Lord's Laid His Hands on Me" (PD) (2 Tim)
S2139 (PD), Z166
"I Bind unto Myself Today" (2 Tim)
E370, EL450 (PD), G6, VU317
"One Bread, One Body" OL-80673 (World Comm.)
C393, EL496, G530, SH678, UM620, VU467
H-3 Chr-156
"Forth in Thy Name, O Lord" (1 Tim, Luke) (C)
GR685, UM438 (PD), VU416
H-3 Hbl-29, 57, 58; Chr-117; Desc-31; Org-31
S-1 #100-103. Various treatments.

Additional Hymn Suggestions
"It's Me, It's Me, O Lord" (Lam)
C579, GR444, N519, UM352, Z110 (PD), ZS149
"My Song Is Love Unknown" 2399704 (Lam, 2 Cor)
E458, EL343, G209, N222, P76, S2083, VU143
"In the Midst of New Dimensions" (Lam, Pss, World Comm.)
C458, G315, N391, S2238
"I Love Thy Kingdom, Lord" (Pss, 2 Tim)
C274, CG262, G310, GR396, N312, P441, UM540 (PD)
"Take My Life, and Let It Be" 1390 (2 Tim)
C609, CG490, E707, EL583/EL685, G697, GR586, P391, N448, SH627/628, UM399 (PD), VU506
"Holy Spirit, Truth Divine" 300431 (2 Tim)
C241, EL398, GR320, N63, P321, UM465, VU368
"God of Grace and God of Glory" 43107 (2 Tim)
C464, CG285, E594/595, EL705, G307, GR45, N436, P420, SH250, UM577, VU686
"I Come with Joy" (2 Tim, World Comm.)
C420, CG456, E304, EL482, G515, N349, P507, SH682, UM617, VU477
"Draw Us in the Spirit's Tether" (2 Tim, Comm.)
C392, EL470, G529, N337, P504, UM632, VU479
"In the Singing" (2 Tim, Comm.)
EL466, G533, S2255
"Here Is Bread, Here Is Wine" 983717 (2 Tim, Comm.)
EL483, S2266
"Take, O Take Me as I Am" 4562041 (2 Tim)
EL814, G698, SH620, WS3119
"Give Me Jesus" (PD-TO) (2 Tim)
CG546, EL770, N409, SH306, WS3140, Z165, ZS84
+"Great Is Thy Faithfulness" 18723 (2 Tim, Luke)
C86, CG48, EL733, G39, GR44, N423, P276, SH48, UM140, VU288
+"I Will Trust in the Lord" (2 Tim, Luke)
N416, UM464, Z14 (PD-TO)
+"Through It All" 18211 (2 Tim, Luke)
C555, GR384, UM507
"By Gracious Powers" (2 Tim, Luke)
E695/696, EL626, G818, N413, P342, UM517
+"My Life Flows On" (2 Tim, Luke)
C619, CG592, EL763, G821, N476, S2212, VU716
"All Who Love and Serve Your City" 1277415 (Luke)
C670, CG674, E570/E571, EL724, G351, P413, UM433
"Give Me the Faith Which Can Remove" (Luke)
GR583, UM650 (PD)
+"There Are Some Things I May Not Know" ("Yes, God Is Real") (Luke)
N405, S2147, Z201 (PD), ZS172
"We Walk by Faith" 2591911 (Luke)
CG634, E209, EL635, G817, N256, P399, S2196, SH660
"Lord, When I Came into This Life" (Luke)
N354, G691, P522
"Bread of the World" (World Comm.)
C387, E301, G499, GR412, N346, P502, UM624, VU461
"In Unity We Lift Our Song" (World Comm.)
CG563, S2221
+"Peace for the Children" (World Comm.)
WS3125
"A Place at the Table" (World Comm.)
G769, WS3149
"One Is the Body" 1099301 (World Comm.)
WS3156
+"You Feed Us, Gentle Savior" (World Comm.)
WS3169

Additional Contemporary and Modern Suggestions
"I Have a Hope" 5087587 (Lam, Pss)
+"Let Justice Roll" ("Like a River") 4974842 (Lam, Pss)
+"Daughters of Zion" 7133716 (Lam, Pss)
+"Better Than A Hallelujah" 5622564 (Lam, Pss)
"Someone Asked the Question" 1640279 (Pss)
N523, S2144
"Come to the Table of Grace" 7034746 (Pss, 2 Tim, Comm.)
G507, WS3168
"He Who Began a Good Work in You" 15238 (2 Tim)
S2163, ZS98
"Cry of My Heart" 844980 (2 Tim)
S2165
"He Is Able" 115420 (2 Tim)
"These Hands" 3251827 (2 Tim)
"Grace Like Rain" 3689877 (2 Tim)
+"Presence" 7116947 (2 Tim, World Comm.)
"Sing Alleluia to the Lord" 26272 (2 Tim, Comm.)
C32, S2258, SH685
+"Great Things" 7111321 (2 Tim, Luke)
+"Promises" 7149439 (2 Tim, Luke)
+"Who You Say You Are" 7130503 (2 Tim, Luke)
+"Do It Again" 7067555 (Luke)
+"Made a Way" 7071768 (Luke)
"If You Believe and I Believe" 3273104 (Luke)
WS3121
"Make Us One" 695737 (World Comm.)
S2224, ZS93
"Bind Us Together" 1228 (World Comm.)
S2226
"Draw the Circle Wide" OL-117657 / OL-101422 (World Comm.)
WS3154

Solo/Ensemble Suggestions
+"Nobody Knows the Trouble I've Seen" (Lam, Pss)
V-7 p. 64/68
"Patiently Have I Waited for the Lord" (2 Tim)
V-4 p. 24
+"Great Is Thy Faithfulness" (2 Tim, Luke)
V-8 p. 48
+"Famous For" ("I Believe") (Luke)
V-9 p. 22
"One Bread, One Body" (World Comm.)
V-3 (2) p. 40
"The Body of the Lord" (World Comm.)
V-8 p. 344

+*"O sacrum convivium"* (World Comm.)
Francisco J. Carbonell; MorningStar MSM-50-2668
SATB, *a cappella* (https://bit.ly/MSM-2668)
+"One Bread, One Body" (World Comm.)
Arr. Mark Hayes; Jubilate
SATB, piano 00-19880 (https://bit.ly/00-19880)
Unison/2-part mixed 00-19882

+Hymn Anthem
"God of Grace and God of Glory" 43107 (2 Tim)
C464, CG285, E594, EL705, G307, GR45, N436, P420, SH250, UM577
No introduction.
Stanza 1: T/B only. A man with a full voice begins the stanza. Another man joins at the second phrase ("Crown thine ancient . . ."). Other T/B join one by one through this phrase. At "Grant us wisdom," all T/B sing. Tenors sing melody, basses sing bass part, and baritones sing alto part one octave lower than written. *Mezzo forte.* This will be most effective *a cappella*, but can be accompanied. A men's trio might also be used instead of the entire section.
Stanza 2: Same soloist begins Stanza 2 and sings first 2 phrases. Keyboard accompanies playing only the bass part. Full choir joins at "Grant us wisdom," singing parts or unison, *mezzo forte.* Keyboard then accompanies with the full hymnal setting.
Stanza 3: All voices unison. Keyboard plays S-1, #77 or another harmonization. Remain *mezzo piano* until "Grant us wisdom." There, begin crescendo, reaching *mezzo forte* by the first "kingdom's goal."
Stanza 4: All voices unison or singing parts. Some sopranos or tenors may sing a descant such as S-1, #76. Keyboard accompanies with full hymnal setting.

Other Suggestions
Visuals: Flags, nationalities, breads
O Empty city, widow, tiara/chains, weeping, stag
P River, sitting/weeping, harp on willow
E Letter, praying hands, tears/joy, women, flame, risen Christ, trumpet, treasure, Spirit
G Mustard/mulberry trees, sea, plow, sheep, table/meal, chain/manacles
Opening Prayer: N830 (2 Tim)
Reading: C412. The Miracle of Communion (World Comm.)
Prayer: N848 (World Comm.)
Opening Prayer: WSL67. "Jesus Christ, Lord" (World Comm.)
Prayer: WSL151. "O God, we are so grateful" (2 Tim)
Prayer: UM412 or UM564 (World Comm.)
Litany: UM556. Litany for Christian Unity (World Comm.)
Offertory Prayer: WSL151. "O God" (World Comm.)
Call to Communion: UM621. "Be Present at Our Table, Lord" (World Comm.)
Communion Prayers: C774 (World Comm.)
+Communion Song: Alternate between the verses of "For the Bread Which You Have Broken" (UM614) and "Alleluia" (C106, N765, SH699, UM186). An ensemble/choir might sing the verses with the congregation joining in the "Alleluia."
Communion Response: N786 or N787 (World Comm.)
Blessing: WSL40. "May the Spirit of God" (2 Tim)
Blessing: N875 (2 Tim)
Sung Benediction: "Let the Peace of God Reign" 1839987 (2 Tim)
Alternate Lessons (see page 4): Hab. 1:1-4, 2:1-4, Ps. 37:1-9
Theme Ideas: Call of God, Communion, Faith, Faithfulness, Grief, Lament

Notes

NRSVue

Jeremiah 29:1, 4-7

1 These are the words of the letter that the prophet Jeremiah
sent from Jerusalem to the remaining elders among the exiles
and to the priests, the prophets, and all the people whom Nebuchadnezzar had taken into exile from Jerusalem to Babylon. . . .
4 Thus says the LORD of hosts, the God of Israel, to all the exiles
whom I have sent into exile from Jerusalem to Babylon: 5 Build
houses and live in them; plant gardens and eat what they produce. 6 Take wives and have sons and daughters; take wives for
your sons, and give your daughters in marriage, that they may
bear sons and daughters; multiply there, and do not decrease.
7 But seek the welfare of the city where I have sent you into exile,
and pray to the LORD on its behalf, for in its welfare you will find
your welfare.

Psalm 66:1-12 (G54, N662)

1 Make a joyful noise to God, all the earth;
 2 sing the glory of his name;
 give to him glorious praise.
3 Say to God, "How awesome are your deeds!
 Because of your great power, your enemies cringe before you.
4 All the earth worships you;
 they sing praises to you,
 sing praises to your name." *[Selah]*
5 Come and see what God has done:
 he is awesome in his deeds among mortals.
6 He turned the sea into dry land;
 they passed through the river on foot.
There we rejoiced in him,
 7 who rules by his might forever,
whose eyes keep watch on the nations—
 let the rebellious not exalt themselves. *[Selah]*
8 Bless our God, O peoples;
 let the sound of his praise be heard,
9 who has kept us among the living
 and has not let our feet slip.
10 For you, O God, have tested us;
 you have tried us as silver is tried.
11 You brought us into the net;
 you laid burdens on our backs;
12 you let people ride over our heads;
 we went through fire and through water;
yet you have brought us out to a spacious place.

CEB

Jeremiah 29:1, 4-7

1 The prophet Jeremiah sent a letter from Jerusalem to the few
surviving elders among the exiles, to the priests and the prophets, and to all the people Nebuchadnezzar had taken to Babylon
from Jerusalem. . . .

4 The LORD of heavenly forces, the God of Israel, proclaims
to all the exiles I have carried off from Jerusalem to Babylon:
5 Build houses and settle down; cultivate gardens and eat what
they produce. 6 Get married and have children; then help your
sons find wives and your daughters find husbands in order that
they too may have children. Increase in number there so that
you don't dwindle away. 7 Promote the welfare of the city where
I have sent you into exile. Pray to the LORD for it, because your
future depends on its welfare.

Psalm 66:1-12 (G54, N662)

1 Shout joyfully to God, all the earth!
2 Sing praises to the glory of God's name!
 Make glorious his praise!
3 Say to God:
 "How awesome are your works!
 Because of your great strength,
 your enemies cringe before you.
4 All the earth worships you,
 sings praises to you,
 sings praises to your name!" *[Selah]*
5 Come and see God's deeds;
 his works for human beings are awesome:
6 He turned the sea into dry land
 so they could cross the river on foot.
 Right there we rejoiced in him!
7 God rules with power forever;
 keeps a good eye on the nations.
 So don't let the rebellious exalt themselves. *[Selah]*
8 All you nations, bless our God!
 Let the sound of his praise be heard!
9 God preserved us among the living;
 he didn't let our feet slip a bit.
10 But you, God, have tested us—
 you've refined us like silver,
11 trapped us in a net,
 laid burdens on our backs,
12 let other people run right over our heads—
 we've been through fire and water.
But you brought us out to freedom!

NRSVue

2 Timothy 2:8-15

8Remember Jesus Christ, raised from the dead, a descendant
of David—that is my gospel, 9for which I suffer hardship, even
to the point of being chained like a criminal. But the word of
God is not chained. 10Therefore I endure everything for the sake
of the elect, so that they may also obtain the salvation that is in
Christ Jesus, with eternal glory. 11The saying is sure:
If we have died with him, we will also live with him;
12 if we endure, we will also reign with him;
if we deny him, he will also deny us;
13 if we are faithless, he remains faithful—
for he cannot deny himself.
14Remind them of this, and warn them before the Lord that
they are to avoid wrangling over words, which does no good
but only ruins those who are listening. 15Do your best to present
yourself to God as one approved by him, a worker who has no
need to be ashamed, rightly explaining the word of truth.

Luke 17:11-19

11On the way to Jerusalem Jesus was going through the region
between Samaria and Galilee. 12As he entered a village, ten men
with a skin disease approached him. Keeping their distance,
13they called out, saying, "Jesus, Master, have mercy on us!"
14When he saw them, he said to them, "Go and show yourselves
to the priests." And as they went, they were made clean. 15Then
one of them, when he saw that he was healed, turned back,
praising God with a loud voice. 16He prostrated himself at Jesus's
feet and thanked him. And he was a Samaritan. 17Then Jesus
asked, "Were not ten made clean? So where are the other nine?
18Did none of them return to give glory to God except this
foreigner?" 19Then he said to him, "Get up and go on your way;
your faith has made you well."

CEB

2 Timothy 2:8-15

8Remember Jesus Christ, who was raised from the dead and
descended from David. This is my good news. 9This is the reason
I'm suffering to the point that I'm in prison like a common
criminal. But God's word cannot be imprisoned. 10This is why I
endure everything for the sake of those who are chosen by God
so that they too may experience salvation in Christ Jesus with
eternal glory. 11This saying is reliable:
"If we have died together, we will also live together.
12 If we endure, we will also rule together.
If we deny him, he will also deny us.
13 If we are disloyal, he stays faithful"
because he can't be anything else than what he is.
14Remind them of these things and warn them in the sight of
God not to engage in battles over words that aren't helpful and
only destroy those who hear them. 15Make an effort to present
yourself to God as a tried-and-true worker, who doesn't need
to be ashamed but is one who interprets the message of truth
correctly.

Luke 17:11-19

11On the way to Jerusalem, Jesus traveled along the border
between Samaria and Galilee. 12As he entered a village, ten men
with skin diseases approached him. Keeping their distance from
him, 13they raised their voices and said, "Jesus, Master, show us
mercy!"
14When Jesus saw them, he said, "Go, show yourselves to the
priests." As they left, they were cleansed. 15One of them, when
he saw that he had been healed, returned and praised God with
a loud voice. 16He fell on his face at Jesus' feet and thanked
him. He was a Samaritan. 17Jesus replied, "Weren't ten cleansed?
Where are the other nine? 18No one returned to praise God
except this foreigner?" 19Then Jesus said to him, "Get up and go.
Your faith has healed you."

Primary Hymns and Songs for the Day
"Great Is Thy Faithfulness" 18723 (Jer, Pss, Luke) (O)
C86, CG48, EL733, G39, GR44, N423, P276, SH48, UM140, VU288
H-3 Chr-87; Desc-39; Org-39
S-2 #59. Piano arrangement
"When God Restored Our Common Life" OL-00642 (Jer, Pss)
G74, S2182
H-3 Chr-139; Desc-90; Org-123
"O Christ, the Healer" 1730268 (Luke)
C503. EL610, G793, N175, P380, UM265
"An Outcast among Outcasts" (Luke)
N201, S2104
H-3 Hbl-80; Chr-142; Desc-69; Org-78
S-1 #215. Harm.
"Give Thanks" 20285 (Luke)
C528, CG373, G647, S2036, SH489, ZS127
"O For a Thousand Tongues to Sing" 1369 (Luke) (C)
C5, CG332, E493, EL886, G610, GR1, N42, P466, SH439, UM57 (PD), VU326 (*See also* WS3001)
H-3 Hbl-79; Chr-142; Desc-17; Org-12
S-1 #33-38. Various Treatments
"All Who Love and Serve Your City" 1277415 (Jer) (C)
C670, CG674, E570/E571, EL724, G351, P413, UM433
H-3 Chr-26, 65; Org-19
S-1 #62. Desc.
"O Jesus, I Have Promised" 40454 (2 Tim) (C)
C612, E655, EL810, G724/725, GR592, N493, P388/389, SH623, UM396 (PD), VU120
S-2 #9. Descant

Additional Hymn Suggestions
"Lift Every Voice and Sing" 7071034 (Jer, Pss)
C631, CG638, E599, EL841, G339, GR408, N593, P563, SH36, UM519, Z32 (PD), Z210, ZS113
"Heleluyan" (Pss)
EL171, G642, P595, UM78
"Joyful, Joyful, We Adore Thee" (Pss, 2 Tim)
C2, CG310, E376, EL836, G611, GR8, N4, P464, SH390, UM89 (PD), VU232
"I'll Praise My Maker While I've Breath" (Pss, Luke)
C20, CG336, E429 (PD), G806, GR17, P253, UM60, VU867
"Praise, My Soul, the King of Heaven" 800443 (Pss, Luke)
C23, CG337, E410, EL864/865, G619/620, GR22, P478/479, SH418, UM66 (PD), VU240
"All People That on Earth Do Dwell" (Pss, Luke)
C18, CG331, E377/378, EL883, G385, GR662, N7, P220, SH416, UM75 (PD), VU822 (Fr.)
"How Clear Is Our Vocation, Lord" (2 Tim)
EL580, G432, P419, VU504
"God, Whose Giving Knows No Ending" (2 Tim)
C606, CG671, G716, N565, P422
"Jesus, the Very Thought of Thee" (2 Tim)
C102, CG386, E642, EL754, G629, GR127, N507, P310, UM175 (PD)
"In the Cross of Christ I Glory" 36499 (2 Tim)
C207, CG183, E441/E442, EL324, G213, GR239, N193, P84, UM295 (PD)
"Pues Si Vivimos" ("When We Are Living") 4968810 (2 Tim)
C536, CG265, EL639, G822, N499, P400, SH299, UM356, VU581
"Take Up Thy Cross" 2154808 (2 Tim)
E675, EL667, G718, GR220, N204, P393, SH605, UM415, VU561
"Lord, Speak to Me" 2769286 (2 Tim)
CG503, EL676, G722, GR439, N531, P426, SH557, UM463 (PD), VU589
+"Blest Be the Tie that Binds" 7106572 (2 Tim)
C433, CG267, EL656, G306, GR405, N393, P438, SH701, UM557 (PD), VU602
"We Know That Christ Is Raised" OL-40344 (2 Tim, Baptism)
E296, EL449, G485, P495, UM610, VU448
+"Make Me a Channel of Your Peace" OL-80478 (2 Tim)
G753, S2171, SH616 VU684
+"Healer of Our Every Ill" OL-00115 (2 Tim, Luke)
C506, EL612, G795, S2213, SH339, VU619
+"Through It All" 18211 (2 Tim, Luke)
C555, GR384, UM507
"Lord of the Dance" 78529 (Luke)
G157, P302, UM261, VU352
"Heal Me, Hands of Jesus" (Luke)
C504, CG541, UM262, VU621
"We Cannot Measure How You Heal" 4751065 (Luke)
CG540, G797, SH341, VU613, WS3139
"Ten Lepers Facing Constant Scorn" (Luke)
G179
"Live Into Hope" (Luke)
G772, P332, VU699

Additional Contemporary and Modern Suggestions
"Canto de Esperanza" ("Song of Hope") 5193990 (Jer)
G765, P432, S2186, SH721, VU424
"Your Grace Is Enough" 4477026 (Jer, Pss, Luke)
WS3106
"Awesome God" 41099 (Pss)
G616, S2040, ZS7
"Awesome Power" 159338 (Pss)
"Come Just As You Are" 1189479 (Pss)
"Refiner's Fire" 426298 (Pss)
+"Sing, Sing, Sing" 5114065 (Pss)
+"Your Spirit" 7091513 (Pss)
+"Alpha and Omega" 4654148 (Pss)
ZS221
+"Made a Way" 7071768 (Pss)
+"Behold Him" 7133698 (Pss, Luke)
+"The Kingdom Is Yours" 7109354 (2 Tim)
+"Make Me a Channel of Your Peace" 6399315 (2 Tim)
+"Words" 6437497 (2 Tim)
"I Am Crucified with Christ" 2652874 (2 Tim)
"All Hail King Jesus" 12877 (2 Tim)
S2069, ZS53
+"He Who Began a Good Work in You" 15238 (2 Tim)
S2163, ZS98
+"Guide My Feet" OL-LMGM2537 (2 Tim)
CG637, G741, GR326, N497, P354, S2208, SH54, ZS141
+"Trading My Sorrows" 2574653 (2 Tim, Luke)
WS3108
"Through It All" 18211 (2 Tim, Luke)
C555, GR384, UM507
"Thank You, Lord" 865000 (Luke)
C531, SH496, UM84, Z228
"Oh Lord, You're Beautiful" 14514 (Luke)
S2064
"Tino tenda, Jesu" ("Thank You, Jesus") OL-94999 (Luke)
S2081
"I'm So Glad Jesus Lifted Me" (PD) (Luke)
C529, EL860 (PD), N474, S2151
"People Need the Lord" 18084 (Luke)
S2244
"I Thank You, Jesus" OL-87176 (Luke)
C116, N41, WS3037, ZS124
"Grateful" 7023348 (Luke)
"You Hear" 6005063 (Luke)
+"Great Are You Lord" 6460220 (Luke)

Solo/Ensemble Suggestions

"Bright and Beautiful" (Pss, Luke)
V-3 (3) p. 10
+"O For a Thousand Tongues to Sing" (Pss, Luke)
V-1 p. 32
V-6 p. 28
"I Just Came to Praise the Lord" (Luke)
V-8 p. 294
+"O Jesus, I Have Promised" (2 Tim)
Arr. Thomas Keesecker; Augsburg 9781506495323
SATB, piano (https://bit.ly/Aug-95323)
+"Speak, Lord"
Tom Trenney; MorningStar
2-part Mixed, piano 50-7981 (https://bit.ly/MWM-50-7082)
SATB, piano 50-7982 (https://bit.ly/MSM-50-7982)

+Hymn Anthem

"God of the Sparrow, God of the Whale" (Luke)
C70, EL740, G22, N32, P272, UM122, VU229

Explore this text first by shairing it with the choir printed as a poem, not wrtten within the musical score. The author's intent is much clearer when seen poetically.

This anthem should be sung like a folksong, in one beat to the measure. Adapt these accompaniment suggestions as needed. Handbells may also be used by creating a part from the notes in the bass cleff of the hymnal accompaniment.

Introduction: Keyboard plays two measure introduction as in hymnal (N32, UM122). *Mezzo forte.*

Stanza 1: All voices, unison. *Mezzo forte.*

Stanza 2: T/B sing melody Accompany with keyboard or handbells. *Mezzo forte.*

Stanza 3: S/A sing melody. Finger cymbals play on the first beat of each measure. *Mezzo forte.*

Stanza 4:
Option 1: A small mixed emsemble (duet, trio) sings this stanza.
Option 2: Sopranos (or a soloist) sing the melody. A/T/B hum the other accompanimental notes. *A cappella* or acompanied. *Mezzo piano.*

Stanza 5: Soloist sings melody. Handbells play handbell part. *Mezzo forte.*

Stanza 6: All voices, unison. Finger cymbals and handbells play as before. Three- and five-octave choirs should ring the part in all possible octaves. The text requires a rather dramatic *ritard* at the close of this stanza. *Mezzo forte* with *molto ritard* at end.

Other Suggestions

Visuals:
O Letter, houses, garden, marriage, prayer/chain
P Praise, nations, awe, sea/desert, river, feet, refining, net, full backpack, fire/water, open space
E Christus Rex, chain, open manacles, cross
G Lepers, one prostrate, feet, praise, walking

Introit: WS3047, st. 3. "God Almighty, We Are Waiting" (Jer)
Greeting or Litany: WSL158. "Here in this sanctuary" (Jer)
Response: C299, EL152, G576, S2275, S2277, WS3133. "Lord, Have Mercy" (Luke)
Prayer: C549. Thoughtful Silence (2 Tim)
Offertory Prayer: WSL142. "Heavenly Father, each day we witness" (Luke)
Prayer of Thanksgiving: N859. Thankfulness and Hope (Luke)
Closing Prayer: WSL171. "Thank you, God" (Jer, Comm.)
Alternate Lessons (see page 4): 2 Kgs. 5:1-3, 7-15c; Ps. 111
Theme Ideas: Faithfulness, Healing, Joy, Peace, Unity, Praise, Thanksgiving / Gratitude

Notes

NRSVue

Jeremiah 31:27-34

27The days are surely coming, says the LORD, when I will sow
the house of Israel and the house of Judah with the seed of
humans and the seed of animals. 28And just as I have watched
over them to pluck up and break down, to overthrow, destroy,
and bring evil, so I will watch over them to build and to plant,
says the LORD. 29In those days they shall no longer say:
"The parents have eaten sour grapes,
and the children's teeth are set on edge."
30But all shall die for their own sins; the teeth of the one who
eats sour grapes shall be set on edge.
31The days are surely coming, says the LORD, when I will make
a new covenant with the house of Israel and the house of Judah.
32It will not be like the covenant that I made with their ancestors
when I took them by the hand to bring them out of the land of
Egypt—a covenant that they broke, though I was their husband,
says the LORD. 33But this is the covenant that I will make with the
house of Israel after those days, says the LORD: I will put my law
within them, and I will write it on their hearts; and I will be their
God, and they shall be my people. 34No longer shall they teach
one another, or say to each other, "Know the LORD," for they
shall all know me, from the least of them to the greatest, says the
LORD, for I will forgive their iniquity and remember their sin no
more.

Psalm 119:97-104 (G64, N701, UM840)

97Oh, how I love your law!
It is my meditation all day long.
98Your commandment makes me wiser than my enemies,
for it is always with me.
99I have more understanding than all my teachers,
for your decrees are my meditation.
100I understand more than the aged,
for I keep your precepts.
101I hold back my feet from every evil way,
in order to keep your word.
102I do not turn away from your ordinances,
for you have taught me.
103How sweet are your words to my taste,
sweeter than honey to my mouth!
104Through your precepts I get understanding;
therefore I hate every false way.

CEB

Jeremiah 31:27-34

27The time is coming, declares the LORD, when I will plant
seeds in Israel and Judah, and both people and animals will
spring up. 28Just as I watched over them to dig up and pull down,
to overthrow, destroy, and bring harm, so I will watch over them
to build and plant, declares the LORD. 29In those days, people
will no longer say:
Sour grapes eaten by parents
leave a bitter taste
in the mouths of their children.
30 Because everyone will die
for their own sins:
whoever eats sour grapes
will have a bitter taste
in their own mouths.
31The time is coming, declares the LORD, when I will make a
new covenant with the people of Israel and Judah. 32It won't be
like the covenant I made with their ancestors when I took them
by the hand to lead them out of the land of Egypt. They broke
that covenant with me even though I was their husband, declares
the LORD. 33No, this is the covenant that I will make with the
people of Israel after that time, declares the LORD. I will put my
Instructions within them and engrave them on their hearts. I will
be their God, and they will be my people. 34They will no longer
need to teach each other to say, "Know the LORD!" because they
will all know me, from the least of them to the greatest, declares
the LORD; for I will forgive their wrongdoing and never again
remember their sins.

Psalm 119:97-104 (G64, N701, UM840)

97I love your Instruction!
I think about it constantly.
98Your commandment makes me wiser than my enemies
because it is always with me.
99I have greater insight than all my teachers
because I contemplate your laws.
100I have more understanding than the elders
because I guard your precepts.
101I haven't set my feet on any evil path
so I can make sure to keep your word.
102I haven't deviated from any of your rules
because you are the one who has taught me.
103Your word is so pleasing to my taste buds—
it's sweeter than honey in my mouth!
104I'm studying your precepts—
that's why I hate every false path.

NRSVue

2 Timothy 3:14–4:5

14But as for you, continue in what you have learned and firmly believed, knowing from whom you learned it 15and how from childhood you have known sacred writings that are able to instruct you for salvation through faith in Christ Jesus. 16All scripture is inspired by God and is useful for teaching, for reproof, for correction, and for training in righteousness, 17so that the person of God may be proficient, equipped for every good work.

4 In the presence of God and of Christ Jesus, who is to judge the living and the dead, and in view of his appearing and his kingdom, I solemnly urge you: 2proclaim the message; be persistent whether the time is favorable or unfavorable; convince, rebuke, and encourage with the utmost patience in teaching. 3For the time is coming when people will not put up with sound teaching but, having their ears tickled, they will accumulate for themselves teachers to suit their own desires 4and will turn away from listening to the truth and wander away to myths. 5As for you, be sober in everything, endure suffering, do the work of an evangelist, carry out your ministry fully.

Luke 18:1-8

1Then Jesus told them a parable about their need to pray always and not to lose heart. 2He said, "In a certain city there was a judge who neither feared God nor had respect for people. 3In that city there was a widow who kept coming to him and saying, 'Grant me justice against my accuser.' 4For a while he refused, but later he said to himself, 'Though I have no fear of God and no respect for anyone, 5yet because this widow keeps bothering me, I will grant her justice, so that she may not wear me out by continually coming.'" 6And the Lord said, "Listen to what the unjust judge says. 7And will not God grant justice to his chosen ones who cry to him day and night? Will he delay long in helping them? 8I tell you, he will quickly grant justice to them. And yet, when the Son of Man comes, will he find faith on earth?"

CEB

2 Timothy 3:14–4:5

14But you must continue with the things you have learned and found convincing. You know who taught you. 15Since childhood you have known the holy scriptures that help you to be wise in a way that leads to salvation through faith that is in Christ Jesus. 16Every scripture is inspired by God and is useful for teaching, for showing mistakes, for correcting, and for training character, 17so that the person who belongs to God can be equipped to do everything that is good.

4 I'm giving you this commission in the presence of God and of Christ Jesus, who is coming to judge the living and the dead, and by his appearance and his kingdom. 2Preach the word. Be ready to do it whether it is convenient or inconvenient. Correct, confront, and encourage with patience and instruction. 3There will come a time when people will not tolerate sound teaching. They will collect teachers who say what they want to hear because they are self-centered. 4They will turn their back on the truth and turn to myths. 5But you must keep control of yourself in all circumstances. Endure suffering, do the work of a preacher of the good news, and carry out your service fully.

Luke 18:1-8

1Jesus was telling them a parable about their need to pray continuously and not to be discouraged. 2He said, "In a certain city there was a judge who neither feared God nor respected people. 3In that city there was a widow who kept coming to him, asking, 'Give me justice in this case against my adversary.' 4For a while he refused but finally said to himself, I don't fear God or respect people, 5but I will give this widow justice because she keeps bothering me. Otherwise, there will be no end to her coming here and embarrassing me." 6The Lord said, "Listen to what the unjust judge says. 7Won't God provide justice to his chosen people who cry out to him day and night? Will he be slow to help them? 8I tell you, he will give them justice quickly. But when the Human One comes, will he find faithfulness on earth?"

Primary Hymns and Songs for the Day

"Love Divine, All Loves Excelling" 40306 (Jer) (O)
C517, CG281, E657, EL631, G366, GR88, N43, P376, SH353/354, UM384 (PD), VU333
H-3 Chr-134; Desc-18; Org-13
S-1 #41-42. Desc. and harm.
"Here I Am, Lord" OL-80670 (Jer)
C452, CG482, EL574, G69, GR589, P525, SH608, UM593, VU509
H-3 Chr-97; Org-54
"Change My Heart, O God" 1565 (Jer)
EL801, G695, S2152, SH507, ZS178
"Spirit of God, Descend upon My Heart" 2083 (Jer, Luke)
C265, CG243, EL800, G688, GR294, N290, P326, SH277, UM500 (PD), VU378
"Thy Word Is a Lamp" 14301 (Pss, 2 Tim)
C326, CG38, G458, UM601
"It's Me, It's Me, O Lord" (Luke)
C579, GR444, N519, UM352, Z110 (PD), ZS149
H-3 Chr-177
"Seek Ye First" 1352 (Luke)
C354, CG436, E711, G175, GR341, P333, SH126, UM405, VU356
"Lord, Listen to Your Children Praying" 22829 (Luke)
C305, CG389, G469, S2193, SH577, VU400, ZS156
"Lord, Speak to Me" 2769286 (2 Tim, Luke) (C)
CG503, EL676, G722, GR439, N531, P426, SH557, UM463 (PD), VU589

Additional Hymn Suggestions

"This Is a Day of New Beginnings" 231043 (Jer)
C518, N417, UM383
"O Come and Dwell in Me" (Jer)
GR298, UM388 (PD)
"O Love That Wilt Not Let Me Go" (Jer)
C540, CG631, G833, GR92, N485, P384, SH314, UM480 (PD), VU658
"Come, Let Us Use the Grace Divine" (Jer)
GR413, UM606 (PD)
"O Day of Peace That Dimly Shines" (Jer)
C711, E597, EL711, G373, P450, UM729, VU682
"God the Sculptor of the Mountains" (Jer)
EL736, G5, S2060
"Wonder of Wonders" (Jer, Baptism)
C378, G489, N328, P499, S2247
+"Fill Us with Your Love, O Lord" OL-87676 (Jer)
WS3005
"Living Spirit, Holy Fire" OL-57648 (Jer)
WS3109
"Holy Spirit, Truth Divine" 300431 (Jer, 2 Tim, Luke)
C241, EL398, GR320, N63, P321, UM465, VU368
"O Thou Who Camest from Above" (Jer, Luke)
E704, GR308, UM501 (PD)
"Blessed Jesus, at Thy Word" (Jer, Pss, 2 Tim)
E440, EL520, G395, N74, P454, UM596 (PD), VU500
+"Come, Holy Ghost, Our Hearts Inspire" (Jer, Pss, 2 Tim)
GR291, UM603 (PD)
"Covenant Prayer" (Jer, Pss, 2 Tim)
WS3115 (*See also* UM607)
"Wonderful Words of Life" 47392 (Pss, 2 Tim)
C323, CG163, GR429, N319, SH549, UM600 (PD)
"O Lord, May Church and Home Combine" (Pss)
CG684, UM695
"O Master, Let Me Walk with Thee" 158243 (Pss, 2 Tim)
C602, CG660, E659/E660, EL818, G738, GR596, N503, P357, SH612, UM430 (PD), VU560
"O Word of God Incarnate" 2786410 (Pss, 2 Tim)
C322, E632, EL514, G459, GR1126, N315, P327, UM598 (PD), VU499
"Immortal, Invisible, God Only Wise" 124466 (2 Tim)
C66, CG58, E423, EL834, G12, GR7, N1, P263, UM103 (PD), VU264 (*See also* ZS4)
"Through It All" 18211 (2 Tim)
C555, GR384, UM507
"Lord, You Give the Great Commission" 230673 (2 Tim) (C)
C459, CG651/CG653, E528, EL579, G298, GR463, P429, S2176, UM584, VU512
"I Know Whom I Have Believed" (2 Tim)
CG588, GR571, SH529, UM714 (PD)
"Praise the Source of Faith and Learning" 3422034 (2 Tim)
N411, S2004
"Deep in the Shadows of the Past" (2 Tim)
G50, N320, P330, S2246
"Lord of All Good" (2 Tim)
G711, P375, VU539
"Break Thou the Bread of Life" (2 Tim, Comm.)
C321, CG35, EL515, G460, GR430, N321, P329, SH552, UM599 (PD), VU501
"Be Thou My Vision" 5021907 (Luke)
C595, CG71, E488, EL793, G450, GR49, N451, P339, SH640, UM451, VU642
"Not So in Haste, My Heart" (Luke)
UM455 (PD)
"I Will Trust in the Lord" (Luke)
N416, UM464, Z14 (PD-TO)
"What a Friend We Have in Jesus" (Luke)
C585, CG409, EL742, G465, GR116, N506, P403, SH585/586, UM526 (PD), VU661
"The Lord's Prayer" OL-88798 (Luke)
C307-C310, G464, GR441, P589, S2278, SH595, UM271, WS3068/3069/3071
"Hear My Prayer, O God" (Luke)
G782, WS3131
"Give Me Jesus" (PD-TO) (Luke)
CG546, EL770, N409, SH306, WS3140, Z165, ZS84

Additional Contemporary and Modern Suggestions

"Please Enter My Heart, Hosanna" 2485371 (Jer)
S2154
+"Beautiful Things" 5665521 (Jer)
+"Called Me Higher" 5887880 (Jer)
+"New Wine" 7102397 (Jer)
"Refresh My Heart" 917518 (Jer)
"The Potter's Hand" 2449771 (Jer)
"You Have Saved Us" 5548514 (Jer)
"Knowing You" 1045238 (Pss)
"Holy and Anointed One" 164361 (Pss)
"In the Secret" 1810119 (Pss)
"Show Me Your Ways" 1675024 (Pss)
"Breathe" 1874117 (Pss)
WS3112, ZS47
"More Precious than Silver" 11335 (Pss)
S2065
"As the Deer" 1431 (Pss)
CG49, G626/G778, S2025, VU766
"To Know You More" 1767420 (Pss)
S2161
"Cry of My Heart" 844980 (Pss)
S2165
"Ancient Words" 2986399 (Pss, 2 Tim)
"He Who Began a Good Work in You" 15238 (2 Tim)
S2163, ZS98

"Lord, Listen to Your Children" 659072 (Luke)
EL752, S2207
"The Lord's Prayer" OL-82690 (Luke)
WS3069

Solo/Ensemble Suggestions

"God Will Make a Way" (with "He Leadeth Me") (Jer)
V-3 (2) p. 9
+"Turn My Heart to You" (Jer)
V-5(2) p. 14
+"How I Love Your Word" (Pss)
V-3 (5) p. 9
+"If My People Will Pray" (Luke)
V-8 p. 66
"Lord, Listen to Your Children" (Luke)
V-8 p. 168
+"Seek Ye First" (Jer, Luke)
Arr. Douglas Wagner; Hope C5196
SAB, piano (https://bit.ly/C-5196)
+"Come to Zion" (Luke)
Kevin Siegfried; MorningStar MSM-50-9344
SATB, *a cappella* (https://bit.ly/MSM-9344)

+Hymn Anthem

"This Is a Day of New Beginnings" 231043 (Jer)
C518, N417, UM383
Introduction: Keyboard (piano) plays first two systems, melody only.
Stanza 1: Male soloist sings melody. Keyboard plays everything except melody notes. Play all notes in last three measures.
Stanza 2: S/A sing melody only, mezzo forte. Keyboard plays full accompaniment.
Stanza 3: All voices, mezzo forte. Keyboard plays only first chord of each measure with strong, constant pulse.
Stanza 5: All voices, forte. Accompaniment plays full accompaniment, forte. Use last ending.

Other Suggestions

Visuals:
O Sowing seeds, destruction, build/plant, torn document, Jer. 31:33b, heart, all ages, eraser
P Bible, meditation, feet, Ps. 119:103, honey
E Child, Bible, Christ, teacher, 2 Tim. 3:16, tools, gavel
G Prayer, gavel, scales of justice, woman pleading
Introit: WS3047, st. 3. "God Almighty, We Are Waiting" (Jer)
Prayer of Confession: UM597. For the Spirit of Truth (2 Tim)
Prayer Response: CG399, EL751, G471, S2200, SH311/517. "O Lord, Hear My Prayer" (Luke)
Prayer: UM392 (Jer, Pss)
Prayer: S2201. "Prayers of the People" (Luke)
Prayer of Preparation: WSL75 or UM602 (2 Tim)
Alternate Lessons (see page 4): Gen.32:22-31, Ps. 121
Theme Ideas: Covenant, God: Wisdom, God: Word of God, Hope, Love, Prayer

Notes

NRSVue

Joel 2:23-32

23O children of Zion, be glad
and rejoice in the LORD your God,
for he has given the early rain for your vindication;
he has poured down for you abundant rain,
the early and the later rain, as before.
24The threshing floors shall be full of grain;
the vats shall overflow with wine and oil.
25I will repay you for the years
that the swarming locust has eaten,
the hopper, the destroyer, and the cutter,
my great army that I sent against you.
26You shall eat in plenty and be satisfied
and praise the name of the LORD your God,
who has dealt wondrously with you.
And my people shall never again be put to shame.
27You shall know that I am in the midst of Israel
and that I, the LORD, am your God and there is no other.
And my people shall never again be put to shame.
28 Then afterward
I will pour out my spirit on all flesh;
your sons and your daughters shall prophesy,
your old men shall dream dreams,
and your young men shall see visions.
29Even on the male and female slaves,
in those days I will pour out my spirit.
30I will show portents in the heavens and on the earth, blood
and fire and columns of smoke. 31The sun shall be turned to
darkness and the moon to blood, before the great and terrible
day of the LORD comes. 32Then everyone who calls on the name
of the LORD shall be saved, for in Mount Zion and in Jerusalem there shall be those who escape, as the LORD has said, and
among the survivors shall be those whom the LORD calls.

Psalm 65 (G38, N661, P200/201, SH492, UM789)

1Praise is due to you,
O God, in Zion,
and to you shall vows be performed,
2 O you who answer prayer!
To you all flesh shall come.
3When deeds of iniquity overwhelm us,
you forgive our transgressions.
4Happy are those whom you choose and bring near
to live in your courts.
We shall be satisfied with the goodness of your house,
your holy temple.
5By awesome deeds you answer us with deliverance,
O God of our salvation;
you are the hope of all the ends of the earth
and of the farthest seas.
6By your strength you established the mountains;
you are girded with might.
7You silence the roaring of the seas,
the roaring of their waves,
the tumult of the peoples.
8Those who live at earth's farthest bounds are awed by your
signs;
you make the gateways of the morning and the evening shout
for joy.
9You visit the earth and water it;
you greatly enrich it;
the river of God is full of water;
you provide the people with grain,
for so you have prepared it.

CEB

Joel 2:23-32

23Children of Zion,
rejoice and be glad in the LORD your God,
because he will give you the early rain as a sign of
righteousness;
he will pour down abundant rain for you,
the early and the late rain, as before.
24The threshing floors will be full of grain;
the vats will overflow with new wine and fresh oil.
25I will repay you for the years
that the cutting locust,
the swarming locust, the hopping locust, and the devouring
locust have eaten—
my great army, which I sent against you.
26You will eat abundantly and be satisfied,
and you will praise the name of the LORD your God,
who has done wonders for you;
and my people will never again be put to shame.
27You will know that I am in the midst of Israel,
and that I am the LORD your God—no other exists;
never again will my people be put to shame.
28After that I will pour out my spirit upon everyone;
your sons and your daughters will prophesy,
your old men will dream dreams,
and your young men will see visions.
29In those days, I will also pour out my
spirit on the male and female slaves.
30I will give signs in the heavens and on the earth—blood and
fire and columns of smoke. 31The sun will be turned to darkness,
and the moon to blood before the great and dreadful day of
the LORD comes. 32But everyone who calls on the LORD's name
will be saved; for on Mount Zion and in Jerusalem there will be
security, as the LORD has promised; and in Jerusalem, the LORD
will summon those who survive.

Psalm 65 (G38, N661, P200/201, SH492, UM789)

1God of Zion, to you even silence is praise.
Promises made to you are kept—
2 you listen to prayer—
and all living things come to you.
3When wrongdoings become too much for me,
you forgive our sins.
4How happy is the one you choose to bring close,
the one who lives in your courtyards!
We are filled full by the goodness of your house,
by the holiness of your temple.
5In righteousness you answer us,
by your awesome deeds,
God of our salvation—
you, who are the security
of all the far edges of the earth,
even the distant seas;
6 you establish the mountains by your strength;
you are dressed in raw power;
7 you calm the roaring seas;
calm the roaring waves,
calm the noise of the nations.
8Those who dwell on the far edges
stand in awe of your acts.
You make the gateways
of morning and evening sing for joy.
9You visit the earth and make it abundant,
enriching it greatly
by God's stream, full of water.
You provide people with grain
because that is what you've decided.

NRSVue

Psalm 65 (continued)
10You water its furrows abundantly,
settling its ridges,
softening it with showers,
and blessing its growth.
11You crown the year with your bounty;
your wagon tracks overflow with richness.
12The pastures of the wilderness overflow;
the hills gird themselves with joy;
13the meadows clothe themselves with flocks;
the valleys deck themselves with grain;
they shout and sing together for joy.

---

2 Timothy 4:6-8, 16-18
6As for me, I am already being poured out as a libation, and
the time of my departure has come. 7I have fought the good
fight; I have finished the race; I have kept the faith. 8From now
on there is reserved for me the crown of righteousness, which
the Lord, the righteous judge, will give me on that day, and not
only to me but also to all who have longed for his appearing. . . .
16At my first defense no one came to my support, but all
deserted me. May it not be counted against them! 17But the Lord
stood by me and gave me strength, so that through me the message might be fully proclaimed and all the gentiles might hear it.
So I was rescued from the lion's mouth. 18The Lord will rescue
me from every evil attack and save me for his heavenly kingdom.
To him be the glory forever and ever. Amen.

Luke 18:9-14
9He also told this parable to some who trusted in themselves
that they were righteous and regarded others with contempt:
10"Two men went up to the temple to pray, one a Pharisee and
the other a tax collector. 11The Pharisee, standing by himself,
was praying thus, 'God, I thank you that I am not like other
people: thieves, rogues, adulterers, or even like this tax collector.
12I fast twice a week; I give a tenth of all my income.' 13But the
tax collector, standing far off, would not even lift up his eyes to
heaven but was beating his breast and saying, 'God, be merciful
to me, a sinner!' 14I tell you, this man went down to his home
justified rather than the other, for all who exalt themselves will
be humbled, but all who humble themselves will be exalted."

CEB

Psalm 65 (continued)
10Drenching the earth's furrows,
leveling its ridges,
you soften it with rain showers;
you bless its growth.
11You crown the year with your goodness;
your paths overflow with rich food.
12Even the desert pastures drip with it,
and the hills are dressed in pure joy.
13The meadowlands are covered with flocks,
the valleys decked out in grain—
they shout for joy;
they break out in song!

---

2 Timothy 4:6-8, 16-18
6I'm already being poured out like a sacrifice to God, and the
time of my death is near. 7I have fought the good fight, finished
the race, and kept the faith. 8At last the champion's wreath that
is awarded for righteousness is waiting for me. The Lord, who
is the righteous judge, is going to give it to me on that day. He's
giving it not only to me but also to all those who have set their
heart on waiting for his appearance. . . .
16No one took my side at my first court hearing. Everyone
deserted me. I hope that God doesn't hold it against them! 17But
the Lord stood by me and gave me strength, so that the entire
message would be preached through me and so all the nations
could hear it. I was also rescued from the lion's mouth! 18The
Lord will rescue me from every evil action and will save me for
his heavenly kingdom. To him be the glory forever and always.
Amen.

Luke 18:9-14
9Jesus told this parable to certain people who had convinced
themselves that they were righteous and who looked on everyone else with disgust. 10"Two people went up to the temple to
pray. One was a Pharisee and the other a tax collector. 11The
Pharisee stood and prayed about himself with these words, 'God,
I thank you that I'm not like everyone else—crooks, evildoers,
adulterers—or even like this tax collector. 12I fast twice a week.
I give a tenth of everything I receive.' 13But the tax collector
stood at a distance. He wouldn't even lift his eyes to look toward
heaven. Rather, he struck his chest and said, 'God, show mercy
to me, a sinner.' 14I tell you, this person went down to his home
justified rather than the Pharisee. All who lift themselves up
will be brought low, and those who make themselves low will be
lifted up."

Primary Hymns and Songs for the Day

"I Sing the Almighty Power of God" 738058 (Joel, Pss) (O)
C64, G32, N12, P288 (PD), SH15
H-3 Hbl-16, 22, 68; Chr-101; Desc-37
S-1 #115. Harmonization
CG19, E398, GR4, UM152 (PD)
H-3 Hbl-44; Chr-21; Desc-40; Org-40
S-1 #131-132. Introduction and descant
VU231 (PD)
"Now Praise the Hidden God of Love" (Joel, Pss, 2 Tim)
P402, S2027
H-3 Chr-200; Org-45
"The Trees of the Field" 20546 (Pss) (C)
G80, S2279, VU884
"Guide My Feet" OL-LMGM2537 (2 Tim) (O)
CG637, G741, GR326, N497, P354, S2208, SH54, ZS141
H-3 Hbl-66; Chr-89
"We've Come This Far by Faith" (2 Tim)
C533, EL633, G656, SH58, Z192
"Just As I Am, Without One Plea" 1039000 (1 Tim, Luke)
C339, CG500, E693, EL592, G442, GR509, N207, P370, SH500, UM357 (PD), VU508, Z208
H-3 Chr-120; Org-186
"Humble Thyself in the Sight of the Lord" 26564 (Luke)
S2131
"Lord, I Want to Be a Christian" 3184437 (Luke) (C)
C589, CG507, G729, GR611, N454, P372 (PD), SH621, UM402, Z76 (PD-TO)
H-3 Chr-130

Additional Hymn Suggestions

"A Mighty Fortress Is Our God" 42964 (Reformation) (O)
C65, CG418, E687/688, EL503/504/505, G275, GR35, N439/440, P259/260, SH651, UM110 (PD), VU261/262/263
"Be Thou My Vision" 5021907 (Joel)
C595, CG71, E488, EL793, G450, GR49, N451, P339, SH640, UM451, VU642
"Spirit of God, Descend upon My Heart" 2083 (Joel)
C265, CG243, EL800, G688, GR294, N290, P326, SH277, UM500 (PD), VU378
"Wind Who Makes All Winds That Blow" (Joel)
C236, CG226, N271, P131, UM538, VU196
"Come, Holy Ghost, Our Souls Inspire" (Joel)
E503/504, N268, G278, P125, UM651, VU201
"O Day of Peace That Dimly Shines" (Joel)
C711, E597, EL711, G373, P450, UM729, VU682
"Spirit, Spirit of Gentleness" (Joel)
C249, EL396, G291, N286, P319, S2120, VU375 (Fr.)
"Lead On, O Cloud of Presence" (Joel)
C633, S2234, VU421
"How Great Thou Art" 14181 (Pss, Luke)
C33, CG323, EL856, G625, GR32, N35, P467, SH14, UM77, VU238 (Fr.)
"Fight the Good Fight" (2 Tim)
E552, G846, GR473, P307 (PD), VU674
"He Leadeth Me" (2 Tim)
C545, CG68, GR73, SH304, UM128 (PD), VU657
"Leaning on the Everlasting Arms" (2 Tim)
C560, CG640, EL774, G837, GR61, N471, UM133, Z53
"Through It All" 18211 (2 Tim)
C555, GR384, UM507
"Jesus, Lover of My Soul" (2 Tim, Luke)
C542, CG406, E699, G440, GR120, N546, P303, SH542/543, UM479, VU669
"Before I Take the Body of My Lord" (Luke, Comm.)
C391, G428, VU462
"There's a Wideness in God's Mercy" 3063417 (Luke)
C73, CG41, E469/470, EL587/588, G435, GR64, N23, P298, SH526, UM121, VU271
"Pass Me Not, O Gentle Savior" 41594 (Luke)
GR527, N551, UM351 (PD), VU665
"Depth of Mercy" 1320726 (Luke)
GR234, UM355, WS3097
"Have Thine Own Way, Lord" (Luke)
C588, CG493, GR343. SH626, UM382 (PD)
"I Am Thine, O Lord" (Luke)
C601, CG504, GR591, N455, UM419 (PD)
"The Lily of the Valley" (Luke)
CG624, GR142, S2062
"Perdón, Señor" ("Forgive Us, Lord") 3409466 (Luke)
G431, S2134, SH505
"Gather Us In" OL-00031 (Luke)
C284, EL532, G401, S2236, SH393
"Love Lifted Me" (Luke)
CG618, GR89, WS3101, Z71 (PD)
+"Confession" (Luke)
WS3138

Additional Contemporary and Modern Suggestions

"I Will Call upon the Lord" 11263 (Joel)
G621, S2002
"Open Our Eyes, Lord" 1572 (Joel)
CG392, S2086, SH562
"Open the Eyes of My Heart" 2298355 (Joel)
G452, SH378, WS3008
"The Power of Your Love" 917491 (Joel)
+"Your Spirit" 7091513 (Joel)
+"Freedom" 7078151 (Joel)
+"Springtime" 7146308 (Joel)
+"From Ashes to Beauty" 5288953 (Joel, Luke)
"Shout to the Lord" 1406918 (Pss)
CG348, EL821, GR124, S2074, SH426, ZS15
"Awesome God" 41099 (Pss)
G616, S2040, ZS7
"How Great Is Our God" 4348399 (Pss)
CG322, GR31, SH458, WS3003
"The Battle Belongs to the Lord" 21583 (2 Tim)
"He Who Began a Good Work in You" 15238 (2 Tim)
S2163, ZS98
+"In the Secret" 1810119 (2 Tim)
"Let It Be Said of Us" 1855882 (2 Tim)
"Good to Me" 313480 (2 Tim)
"I Will Never Be (the Same Again)" 1874911 (2 Tim, Luke)
"I Will Boast" 4662350 (2 Tim, Luke)
"Came to My Rescue" 4705190 (2 Tim, Luke)
"Grace Alone" 2335524 (2 Tim, Luke)
CG43, S2162, ZS100
"I'm So Glad Jesus Lifted Me" (PD) (Luke)
C529, EL860 (PD), N474, S2151
"Hungry" ("Falling on My Knees") 2650364 (Luke)
WS3099
"Take, O Take Me as I Am" 4562041 (Luke)
EL814, G698, SH620, WS3119
+"God Is Love" 7136019 (Luke)
+"Head to the Heart" 7047283 (Luke)
+"His Mercy Is More" 7065053 (Luke)
+"Here at the Cross" 7046292 (Luke)

Solo/Ensemble Suggestions

"Rejoice Greatly, O Daughter of Zion" (Joel)
V-2
Spirit of God" (Joel)
V-8 p. 170

+"Where Shall My Wondering Soul Begin?" (Luke)
V-1 p. 59
+"What a Fellowship" (2 Tim)
Arr. David M. Cherwien; MorningStar MSM-50-0600
SAB, piano (https://bit.ly/M-0600)
"O, My God, Bestow Thy Tender Mercy" (Luke)
Pergolesi/Hopson; Carl Fischer CM7974
2-part mixed, keyboard (https://bit.ly/CM-7974)

+Hymn Anthem
"When Our Confidence Is Shaken" (2 Tim)
C534, UM505 (Text: 3109072 or OL-02933. Melody: Public Domain)
The arrangement moves from the quietness of our uncertainty to the grandeur of our knowledge of God's love for us. Keyboard (organ) plays the hymnal setting throughout, increasing intensity and dynamics from stanza to stanza. The last stanza should be full with the pedal strongly playing the bass part. Pianists can double the bass part in the left hand for this full effect. Tempo should not rush the eighth notes, but should move along, about MM = 80.
Introduction: Last four measures, *mezzo piano.*
Stanza 1: All voices, sing four-parts (or unison). *Mezzo piano.*
Stanza 2: Measure 1: T/B sing the melody
Measures 2-4: Tenors sing melody, basses sing bass part (or melody).
Measures 5-8: S/A sing melody.
Measures 9-10: T/B sing melody.
Measures 11-12: Tenors sing melody, basses sing bass part (or melody).
Stanza 3: Tenors (and some basses) sing the melody. Basses sing their part (or melody). Some sopranos sing the tenor part up one octave. Altos sing their part. Be sure that the melody predominates.
Interlude: Last four measures.
Stanza 4: Tenors and altos sing melody. Basses sing their part with strength and breadth. Sopranos sing the alto part up one octave as a descant. (This stanza may also be sung by all voices, unison.) *Fortissimo,* a little slower than the other verses. (You may wish to have some tenors sing the tenor part).

Other Suggestions
Visuals:
O Rain, thresh/grain, wine/oil, locusts, plenty, people, manacles, blood/fire/smoke, eclipse, red moon
P Praise, worship, sea/mountain, storm/calm, sunrise/set, rain, river, harvest/wagon tracks, hills, flocks
E Spilled wine, boxing gloves, open Bible, scales
G Two men (proud/humble), hands (raised/beating chest), Luke 18:14b
Reformation Sunday: Luther, reformers, 95 theses
Introit: WS3046. "Come, O Redeemer, Come" (Luke)
Opening Prayer: WSL37. "Holy Spirit, rain down" (Joel)
Call to Confession: N833 (Luke)
Prayer of Confession: N834 or C772 (Luke)
+Sung Confession: WS3138. "Confession" (Luke)
Prayer: WSL38 (Joel)
Prayer: UM401. For Holiness of Heart (Luke)
Response: S2275 or S2277. "Lord, Have Mercy" (Luke)
Prayer: WSL190. "Make my life a libation" *("Haz de mi vida un sacrificio")* (2 Tim)
Sung Benediction: "Let the Peace of God Reign" 1839987 (2 Tim)
Alternate Lessons (see page 4): Jer. 14:7-10, 19-22; Ps. 84:1-7
Theme Ideas: Discipleship / Following God, Faithfulness, Holy Spirit, Humility, Joy, Praise

Notes

NRSVue

Daniel 7:1-3, 15-18

1In the first year of King Belshazzar of Babylon, Daniel had a
dream and visions of his head as he lay in bed. Then he wrote
down the dream: 2I, Daniel, saw in my vision by night the four
winds of heaven stirring up the great sea, 3and four great beasts
came up out of the sea, different from one another. . . .

15As for me, Daniel, my spirit was troubled within me, and the
visions of my head terrified me. 16I approached one of the attendants to ask him the truth concerning all this. So he said that he
would disclose to me the interpretation of the matter: 17"As for
these four great beasts, four kings shall arise out of the earth.
18But the holy ones of the Most High shall receive the kingdom
and possess the kingdom forever—forever and ever."

Psalm 149 (G550, N722, P257)

1Praise the Lord!
Sing to the Lord a new song,
his praise in the assembly of the faithful.
2Let Israel be glad in its Maker;
let the children of Zion rejoice in their King.
3Let them praise his name with dancing,
making melody to him with tambourine and lyre.
4For the Lord takes pleasure in his people;
he adorns the humble with victory.
5Let the faithful exult in glory;
let them sing for joy on their couches.
6Let the high praises of God be in their throats
and two-edged swords in their hands,
7to execute vengeance on the nations
and punishment on the peoples,
8to bind their kings with fetters
and their nobles with chains of iron,
9to execute on them the judgment decreed.
This is glory for all his faithful ones.
Praise the Lord!

CEB

Daniel 7:1-3, 15-18

1In the first year of Babylon's King Belshazzar, Daniel had a
dream—a vision in his head as he lay on his bed. He wrote the
dream down. Here is the beginning of the account:

2I am Daniel. In the vision I had during the night I saw the
four winds of heaven churning the great sea. 3Four giant beasts
emerged from the sea, each different from the others. . . .

15Now this caused me, Daniel, to worry. My visions disturbed
me greatly. 16So I went to one of the servants who was standing
ready nearby. I asked him for the truth about all this.

He spoke to me and explained to me the meaning of these
things. 17"These four giant beasts are four kings that will rise up
from the earth, 18but the holy ones of the Most High will receive
the kingship. They will hold the kingship securely forever and
always."

Psalm 149 (G550, N722, P257)

1Praise the Lord!
Sing to the Lord a new song;
sing God's praise in the assembly of the faithful!
2Let Israel celebrate its maker;
let Zion's children rejoice in their king!
3Let them praise God's name with dance;
let them sing God's praise with the drum and lyre!
4Because the Lord is pleased with his people,
God will beautify the poor with saving help.
5Let the faithful celebrate with glory;
let them shout for joy on their beds.
6Let the high praises of God be in their mouths
and a double-edged sword in their hands,
7 to get revenge against the nations
and punishment on the peoples,
8 binding their rulers in chains
and their officials in iron shackles,
9 achieving the justice
written against them.
That will be an honor for all God's faithful people.
Praise the Lord!

NRSVue

Ephesians 1:11-23

[11]In Christ we have also obtained an inheritance, having been
destined according to the purpose of him who accomplishes all
things according to his counsel and will, [12]so that we, who were
the first to set our hope on Christ, might live for the praise of
his glory. [13]In him you also, when you had heard the word of
truth, the gospel of your salvation, and had believed in him,
were marked with the seal of the promised Holy Spirit; [14]this is
the pledge of our inheritance toward redemption as God's own
people, to the praise of his glory.

[15]I have heard of your faith in the Lord Jesus and your love
toward all the saints, and for this reason [16]I do not cease to give
thanks for you as I remember you in my prayers, [17]that the God
of our Lord Jesus Christ, the Father of glory, may give you a
spirit of wisdom and revelation as you come to know him, [18]so
that, with the eyes of your heart enlightened, you may perceive
what is the hope to which he has called you, what are the riches
of his glorious inheritance among the saints, [19]and what is the
immeasurable greatness of his power for us who believe, according to the working of his great power. [20]God put this power to
work in Christ when he raised him from the dead and seated
him at his right hand in the heavenly places, [21]far above all rule
and authority and power and dominion and above every name
that is named, not only in this age but also in the age to come.
[22]And he has put all things under his feet and has made him the
head over all things for the church, [23]which is his body, the fullness of him who fills all in all.

Luke 6:20-31

[20]Then he looked up at his disciples and said:
"Blessed are you who are poor,
for yours is the kingdom of God.
[21]"Blessed are you who are hungry now,
for you will be filled.
"Blessed are you who weep now,
for you will laugh.

[22]"Blessed are you when people hate you and when they
exclude you, revile you, and defame you on account of the Son
of Man. [23]Rejoice on that day and leap for joy, for surely your
reward is great in heaven, for that is how their ancestors treated
the prophets.
[24]"But woe to you who are rich,
for you have received your consolation.
[25]"Woe to you who are full now,
for you will be hungry.
"Woe to you who are laughing now,
for you will mourn and weep.

[26]"Woe to you when all speak well of you, for that is how their
ancestors treated the false prophets.

[27]"But I say to you who are listening: Love your enemies; do
good to those who hate you; [28]bless those who curse you; pray
for those who mistreat you. [29]If anyone strikes you on the cheek,
offer the other also, and from anyone who takes away your coat
do not withhold even your shirt.[30]Give to everyone who asks of
you, and if anyone takes away what is yours, do not ask for it
back again. [31]Do to others as you would have them do to you."

CEB

Ephesians 1:11-23

[11]We have also received an inheritance in Christ. We were
destined by the plan of God, who accomplishes everything
according to his design. [12]We are called to be an honor to God's
glory because we were the first to hope in Christ. [13]You too heard
the word of truth in Christ, which is the good news of your salvation. You were sealed with the promised Holy Spirit because you
believed in Christ. [14]The Holy Spirit is the down payment on our
inheritance, which is applied toward our redemption as God's
own people, resulting in the honor of God's glory.

[15]Since I heard about your faith in the Lord Jesus and your
love for all God's people, this is the reason that [16]I don't stop giving thanks to God for you when I remember you in my prayers.
[17]I pray that the God of our Lord Jesus Christ, the Father of
glory, will give you a spirit of wisdom and revelation that makes
God known to you. [18]I pray that the eyes of your heart will have
enough light to see what is the hope of God's call, what is the
richness of God's glorious inheritance among believers, [19]and
what is the overwhelming greatness of God's power that is working among us believers. This power is conferred by the energy
of God's powerful strength. [20]God's power was at work in Christ
when God raised him from the dead and sat him at God's right
side in the heavens, [21]far above every ruler and authority and
power and angelic power, any power that might be named not
only now but in the future. [22]God put everything under Christ's
feet and made him head of everything in the church, [23]which is
his body. His body, the church, is the fullness of Christ, who fills
everything in every way.

Luke 6:20-31

[20]Jesus raised his eyes to his disciples and said:
"Happy are you who are poor,
because God's kingdom is yours.
[21]Happy are you who hunger now,
because you will be satisfied.
Happy are you who weep now,
because you will laugh.

[22]Happy are you when people hate you, reject you, insult you,
and condemn your name as evil because of the Human One.
[23]Rejoice when that happens! Leap for joy because you have a
great reward in heaven. Their ancestors did the same things to
the prophets.
[24]But how terrible for you who are rich,
because you have already received your comfort.
[25]How terrible for you who have plenty now,
because you will be hungry.
How terrible for you who laugh now,
because you will mourn and weep.
[26]How terrible for you when all speak well of you.
Their ancestors did the same things to the false prophets.

[27]But I say to you who are willing to hear: Love your enemies.
Do good to those who hate you. [28]Bless those who curse you.
Pray for those who mistreat you. [29]If someone slaps you on the
cheek, offer the other one as well. If someone takes your coat,
don't withhold your shirt either. [30]Give to everyone who asks
and don't demand your things back from those who take them.
[31]Treat people in the same way that you want them to treat you."

Primary Hymns and Songs for the Day
"Come, Thou Almighty King" 29073 (Dan) (O)
C27, CG2, E365, EL408, G2, GR27, N275, P139, SH388, UM61 (PD), VU314
H-3 Hbl-28, 49, 53; Chr-56; Desc-57; Org-63
S-1 #185-186. Desc. and harm.
"My Hope Is Built" (PD) (Eph)
C537, CG590, EL596/597, G353, GR102, N403, P379, SH324, UM368 (PD), ZS182
H-3 Chr-191
S-2 #171-172. Trumpet and vocal desc.
"Kum Ba Yah" 2749763 (Luke)
C561/590, G472 (PD), P338, UM494, Z139
"I Sing a Song of the Saints of God" (All Saints)
E293, G730, GR482, N295, P364, UM712 (PD)
"For All the Saints" 90590 (Dan, Eph) (C)
C637, CG567, E287, EL422, G326, GR480, N299, P526, SH231, UM711 (PD), VU705
H-3 Hbl-58; Chr-65; Org-152
S-1 #314-318. Various treatments

Additional Hymn Suggestions
"Immortal, Invisible, God Only Wise" 124466 (Dan) (O)
C66, CG58, E423, EL834, G12, GR7, N1, P263, UM103 (PD), VU264 (*See also* ZS4)
"The God of Abraham Praise" 484742 (Dan)
C24, CG45, E401, EL831, G49, GR16, N24, P488, SH50, UM116 (PD), VU255
"Give Thanks for Those Whose Faith Is Firm" (Dan)
EL428, G731
"Cantad al Señor" ("O Sing to the Lord") (Pss)
CG328, EL822, G637, P472, SH429, VU241
"Praise to the Lord, the Almighty" 785135 (Dan, Pss) (O)
C25, CG319, E390, EL858 (PD)/859, G35, GR3, N22, P482, SH453, UM139, VU220 (Fr.) and VU221
"All People That on Earth Do Dwell" (Pss)
C18, CG331, E377/378, EL883, G385, GR662, N7, P220, SH416, UM75 (PD), VU822 (Fr.)
"Cantemos al Señor" ("Let's Sing unto the Lord") (Pss)
C60, EL555, G669, N39, SH432, UM149
"Open My Eyes, That I May See" 68003 (Pss, Eph)
C586, CG395, G451, GR311, P324, SH583, UM454, VU371
"Holy, Holy, Holy! Lord God Almighty" 1156 (Eph)
C4, CG1, E362, EL413, G1, GR23, N277, P138, SH450, UM64/65, VU315
"Holy God, We Praise Thy Name" 114555 (Eph)
CG9, E366, EL414 (PD), G4, GR2, N276, P460, SH431, UM79, VU894 (Fr.)
"At the Name of Jesus" (Eph)
CG424, E435, EL416, G264, GR105, P148, SH657, UM168, VU335
"Hope of the World" 643002 (Eph)
C538, E472, G734, N46, P360, UM178, VU215
"Come, Let Us Join Our Friends Above" (Eph)
GR479, UM709 (PD)
"There Are Some Things I May Not Know" (Eph)
N405, S2147, Z201 (PD), ZS172
"Life-Giving Bread" (Eph, Comm.)
S2261
"Come, Share the Lord" (Eph, Comm.)
C408, CG459, G510, S2269, VU469
"Take, O Take Me as I Am" 4562041 (Eph)
EL814, G698, SH620, WS3119
"Give Me Jesus" (PD-TO) (Eph, All Saints)
CG546, EL770, N409, SH306, WS3140, Z165, ZS84
+"One Is the Body" 1099301 (Eph)
WS3156
"If Thou But Suffer God to Guide Thee" 564215 (Eph, Luke)
C565, CG76, E635, EL769, G816, GR75, N410, P282, SH326, UM142 (PD), VU285 (Fr.) and VU286
"Lift Every Voice and Sing" 7071034 (Eph, Luke)
C631, CG638, E599, EL841, G339, GR408, N593, P563, SH36, UM519, Z32 (PD), Z210, ZS113
"Faith of Our Fathers" 7029079 (Eph, Luke)
C635, CG645, EL812/813, N381, UM710 (PD), VU580
"Lord, I Want to be a Christian" 3184437 (Luke, All Saints)
C589, CG507, G729, GR611, N454, P372 (PD), SH621, UM402, Z76 (PD-TO)
"Nobody Knows the Trouble I See" (Luke)
UM520, Z170 (PD)
"How Firm a Foundation" 107816 (Luke)
C618, CG425, E636, EL796, G463, GR46, N407, P361, SH291, UM529 (PD), VU660
"Come Sunday" (Luke)
N602, UM728
"Santo" ("Holy") (Luke)
EL762, G594, SH39, S2019
"Goodness Is Stronger than Evil" OL-02636 (Luke)
EL721, G750, S2219
"How Lovely, Lord, How Lovely" (All Saints)
C285, CG50, G402, P207, S2042, VU801
"In Unity We Lift Our Song" (All Saints)
CG563, S2221
"Deep in the Shadows of the Past" (All Saints)
G50, N320, P330, S2246
"As We Gather at Your Table" (All Saints, Comm.)
EL522, N332, S2268, SH411, VU457
+"For the Bread Which You Have Broken" (All Saints, Comm.)
C411, E340/341, EL494, G516, P508/509, UM614/615, VU470
"Rejoice in God's Saints" (All Saints)
C476, EL418, G732, UM708
"By All Your Saints Still Striving" (All Saints)
EL420/421, G325

Additional Contemporary and Modern Suggestions
"There's Something About That Name" 14064 (Dan)
C115, GR124, UM171
+"Is He Worthy?" 7108951 (Dan)
+"Behold Him" 7133698 (Dan, Pss, Eph)
"I Could Sing of Your Love Forever" 1043199 (Pss)
"Clap Your Hands" 806674 (Pss)
S2028, ZS10
"Someone Asked the Question" 1640279 (Pss, All Saints)
N523, S2144
"I Will Enter His Gates" 1493 (Pss)
S2270
"Sing Unto the Lord a New Song" 571215 (Pss)
"I Will Celebrate" 21239 (Pss)
"Let Everything That Has Breath" 2430979 (Pss)
"Song of Hope" ("Heaven Come Down") 5111477 (Eph)
+"Above All" 2672885 (Eph)
V-3 (2), p. 17. Vocal Solo
"He Who Began a Good Work in You" 15238 (Eph)
S2163, ZS98
"Open the Eyes of My Heart" 2298355 (Eph)
G452, SH378, WS3008
+"In Christ Alone" 3350395 (Eph)
CG569, GR106, SH656, WS3105
"Forever" 3148428 (Eph)
CG53, WS3023
"Give Thanks" 20285 (Luke)
C528, CG373, G647, S2036, SH489, ZS127

"Foundation" 706151 (Luke)
"We Fall Down" 2437367 (All Saints)
G368, WS3187
"Go in Peace" 451022 (All Saints)

Solo/Ensemble Suggestions

+"Sing a Song of Joy" (Pss)
V-4 p. 2
+"You Keep Hope Alive" (Luke)
V-9 p. 132
"Deep River" (All Saints)
V-3 (1) p. 4
"In Bright Mansions Above" (All Saints)
V-4 p. 39
"Borning Cry" (All Saints, Memorial)
V-5 (1) p. 10
"As We Gather at Your Table" (Comm.)
K. Lee Scott; AEC-2 p. 12 and Augsburg 0-8006-7808-7
SAB, organ (https://bit.ly/7808-7)
"By All Your Saints Still Striving" (All Saints)
arr. Joel Martinson; AEC-2 p. 23
SATB, organ (https://bit.ly/AEC-2)

+Hymn Anthem

"I Sing a Song of the Saints of God" (All Saints)
E293, G730, GR482, N295, P364, UM712 (PD)
Stanza 1: A soloist sings with guitar (or improvised piano) accompaniment. Use a folk, storytelling style of singing.
Stanza 2: All voices lightly sing melody. Continue guitar (or piano) accompaniment.
Interlude: Accompaniment continues. Leader and congregation read UM713, "All Saints," (or another appropriate prayer) in unison. Choir may sing melody on "oo" vowel as congregation reads or may read with them.
Stanza 3: All voices (with congregation) sing this stanza. Add organ or piano to the guitar for fullness, but keep the overall sound simple.

Other Suggestions

These scriptures and ideas may be used on Nov. 2 as All Saints Sunday. Daylight Savings Time ends Nov. 2.
Visuals: Pictures of deceased members
O Storm, bed, dreamscape, 4 beasts, 4 crowns, terror
P Praise, new song, assembly, dance, instruments
E Will, Christ, Bible, seal, flames/dove, jewelry box
G Feeding/poor, smile through tears, leaping, prayer, turned cheek, shirt/coat, giving, warning
Greeting: C825 (Luke)
Affirmation of Faith: WSL83 (Luke, All Saints)
Prayer: UM713 or WSL44 (All Saints)
Prayer: WSL200. "Show us, good Lord" (Luke)
+Sung Lord's Prayer: "As It Is in Heaven" 4669748 (Pss)
Canticle: UM652. "Canticle of Remembrance" (Eph)
Litany for Reading Names: WSL45 (All Saints)
Litany: C488 or WSL49 (Luke, All Saints)
Offering Prayer: WSL129. "Blessed one, we discover" (Luke)
Response: WS3010. "Sing of the Lord's Goodness" (Pss, All Saints)
Closing Prayer: WSL46. "May God, who has given" (All Saints)
Benediction: WSL167. "Go! Never stop going out" (Matt)
Theme Ideas: Beatitudes/Blessings, Hope, Praise, Saints

Notes

NRSVue

Habakkuk 1:1-4; 2:1-4

[1]The oracle that the prophet Habakkuk saw.
[2]O LORD, how long shall I cry for help,
and you will not listen?
Or cry to you "Violence!"
and you will not save?
[3]Why do you make me see wrongdoing
and look at trouble?
Destruction and violence are before me;
strife and contention arise.
[4]So the law becomes slack,
and justice never prevails.
The wicked surround the righteous;
therefore judgment comes forth perverted.
. . . .
2 I will stand at my watchpost
and station myself on the rampart;
I will keep watch to see what he will say to me
and what he will answer concerning my complaint.
[2]Then the LORD answered me and said:
Write the vision;
make it plain on tablets,
so that a runner may read it.
[3]For there is still a vision for the appointed time;
it speaks of the end and does not lie.
If it seems to tarry, wait for it;
it will surely come; it will not delay.
[4]Look at the proud!
Their spirit is not right in them,
but the righteous live by their faithfulness.

Psalm 119:137-144 (G64, N701, UM840)

[137]You are righteous, O LORD,
and your judgments are right.
[138]You have appointed your decrees in righteousness
and in all faithfulness.
[139]My zeal consumes me
because my foes forget your words.
[140]Your promise is well tried,
and your servant loves it.
[141]I am small and despised,
yet I do not forget your precepts.
[142]Your righteousness is an everlasting righteousness,
and your law is the truth.
[143]Trouble and anguish have come upon me,
but your commandments are my delight.
[144]Your decrees are righteous forever;
give me understanding that I may live.

CEB

Habakkuk 1:1-4; 2:1-4

[1]The oracle that Habakkuk the prophet saw.
[2]LORD, how long will I call for help and you not listen?
I cry out to you, "Violence!"
but you don't deliver us.
[3]Why do you show me injustice and look at anguish
so that devastation and violence are before me?
There is strife, and conflict abounds.
4 The Instruction is ineffective;
justice does not endure because the wicked
surround the righteous.
Justice becomes warped.
. . . .
2 I will take my post;
I will position myself on the fortress.
I will keep watch to see what the Lord says to me
and how he will respond to my complaint.
[2]Then the LORD answered me and said,
Write a vision, and make it plain upon a tablet
so that a runner can read it.
3 There is still a vision for the appointed time;
it testifies to the end;
it does not deceive.
If it delays, wait for it;
for it is surely coming;
it will not be late.
4 Some people's desires are truly audacious;
they don't do the right thing.
But the righteous person will live honestly.

Psalm 119:137-144 (G64, N701, UM840)

[137]LORD, you are righteous,
and your rules are right.
[138]The laws you commanded are righteous,
completely trustworthy.
[139]Anger consumes me
because my enemies have forgotten what you've said.
[140]Your word has been tried and tested;
your servant loves your word!
[141]I'm insignificant and unpopular,
but I don't forget your precepts.
[142]Your righteousness lasts forever!
Your Instruction is true!
[143]Stress and strain have caught up with me,
but your commandments are my joy!
[144]Your laws are righteous forever.
Help me understand so I can live!

NRSVue

2 Thessalonians 1:1-4, 11-12

1Paul, Silvanus, and Timothy,
To the church of the Thessalonians in God our Father and
the Lord Jesus Christ:
2Grace to you and peace from God the Father and the Lord
Jesus Christ.
3We must always give thanks to God for you, brothers and sisters, as is right, because your faith is growing abundantly and the
love of every one of you for one another is increasing. 4There-
fore we ourselves boast of you among the churches of God for
your steadfastness and faith during all your persecutions and the
afflictions that you are enduring. . . .
11To this end we always pray for you, asking that our God will
make you worthy of his call and will fulfill by his power every
good resolve and work of faith, 12so that the name of our Lord
Jesus may be glorified in you and you in him, according to the
grace of our God and the Lord Jesus Christ.

Luke 19:1-10

1He entered Jericho and was passing through it. 2A man was
there named Zacchaeus; he was a chief tax collector and was
rich. 3He was trying to see who Jesus was, but on account of
the crowd he could not, because he was short in stature. 4So he
ran ahead and climbed a sycamore tree to see him, because he
was going to pass that way. 5When Jesus came to the place, he
looked up and said to him, "Zacchaeus, hurry and come down,
for I must stay at your house today." 6So he hurried down and
was happy to welcome him. 7All who saw it began to grumble
and said, "He has gone to be the guest of one who is a sinner."
8Zacchaeus stood there and said to the Lord, "Look, half of my
possessions, Lord, I will give to the poor, and if I have defrauded
anyone of anything, I will pay back four times as much." 9Then
Jesus said to him, "Today salvation has come to this house,
because he, too, is a son of Abraham. 10For the Son of Man came
to seek out and to save the lost."

CEB

2 Thessalonians 1:1-4, 11-12

1From Paul, Silvanus, and Timothy:
To the church of the Thessalonians, which is in God our
Father, and in the Lord Jesus Christ.
2Grace and peace to all of you from God our Father and the
Lord Jesus Christ.
3Brothers and sisters, we must always thank God for you.
This is only right because your faithfulness is growing by leaps
and bounds, and the love that all of you have for each other is
increasing. 4That's why we ourselves are bragging about you in
God's churches. We tell about your endurance and faithfulness
in all the harassments and trouble that you have put up with. . . .
11We are constantly praying for you for this: that our God will
make you worthy of his calling and accomplish every good desire
and faithful work by his power. 12Then the name of our Lord
Jesus will be honored by you, and you will be honored by him,
consistent with the grace of our God and the Lord Jesus Christ.

Luke 19:1-10

1Jesus entered Jericho and was passing through town. 2A man
there named Zacchaeus, a ruler among tax collectors, was rich.
3He was trying to see who Jesus was, but, being a short man, he
couldn't because of the crowd. 4So he ran ahead and climbed up
a sycamore tree so he could see Jesus, who was about to pass that
way.5When Jesus came to that spot, he looked up and said, "Zacchaeus, come down at once. I must stay in your home today." 6So
Zacchaeus came down at once, happy to welcome Jesus.
7Everyone who saw this grumbled, saying, "He has gone to be
the guest of a sinner."
8Zacchaeus stopped and said to the Lord, "Look, Lord, I give
half of my possessions to the poor. And if I have cheated anyone,
I repay them four times as much."
9Jesus said to him, "Today, salvation has come to this household because he too is a son of Abraham. 10The Human One
came to seek and save the lost."

Primary Hymns and Songs for the Day

"O God of Every Nation" (Hab) (O)
C680, CG46, E607, EL713, G756, P289, UM435, VU677
H-3 Chr-63, 145; Org-102
"Be Thou My Vision" 5021907 (Hab)
C595, CG71, E488, EL793, G450, GR49, N451, P339, SH640, UM451, VU642
H-3 Hbl-15, 48; Chr-36; Org-153
S-1 #319. Arr. for organ/voices in canon
"Lord, Be Glorified" (2 Thess)
EL744, G468, S2150, SH420
"Rescue the Perishing" 34549 (Luke)
CG480, GR457, UM591 (PD)
"I Am Thine, O Lord" (Luke) (C)
C601, CG504, GR591, N455, UM419 (PD)

Additional Hymn Suggestions

"Be Still, My Soul" (Hab)
C566, CG57, G819, GR346, N488, SH330, UM534, VU652
"Let All Mortal Flesh Keep Silence" (Hab)
C124, CG81, E324, EL490, G347, GR169, N345, P5, UM626 (PD), VU473 (Fr.)
"O Day of God, Draw Nigh" (PD) (Hab)
C700, E601, N611, P452, UM730 (PD), VU688/689 (Fr.)
"O Holy City, Seen of John" (PD-TO) (Hab)
E582/583, G374, N613, P453, UM726, VU709
"O What Their Joy and Their Glory Must Be" (PD) (Hab)
E623, N385, UM727 (PD)
"The Lily of the Valley" (Hab)
CG624, GR142, S2062
"We'll Understand It Better By and By" (Hab, 2 Thess)
GR370, N444, UM525 (PD), Z55, ZS168
"I Love Thy Kingdom, Lord" (2 Thess)
C274, CG262, G310, GR396, N312, P441, UM540 (PD)
"Blest Be the Tie that Binds" 7106572 (2 Thess)
C433, CG267, EL656, G306, GR405, N393, P438, SH701, UM557 (PD), VU602
"How Blest Are They Who Trust in Christ" (2 Thess)
C646, N365, UM654
"Stand Up and Bless the Lord" 86652 (2 Thess)
CG299, GR39, P491, UM662 (PD)
"O Jesus, I Have Promised" 40454 (2 Thess, Luke)
C612, E655, EL810, G724/725, GR592, N493, P388/389, SH623, UM396 (PD), VU120
"Lord Jesus, Think on Me" (Luke)
E641, EL599 (PD), G417, GR493, P301, VU607
"Heal Me, Hands of Jesus" (Luke)
C504, CG541, UM262, VU621
"Come, Sinners, to the Gospel Feast" 4047140 (Luke)
GR409, UM339 (PD)
"Come, Ye Sinners, Poor and Needy" (Luke)
CG471, G415, GR502, UM340, ZS186
+"He Touched Me" (Luke)
C564, GR578, UM367, Z72
+"Nothing Between" (Luke)
GR339, UM373 (PD), Z21, ZS71
"Amazing Grace" 22025 (Luke)
C546, CG587, E671, EL779, G649, GR572, N547/548, P280, SH523, UM378 (PD), VU266 (Fr.), Z211
+"Savior, Like a Shepherd Lead Us" 24078 (Luke)
C558, CG405, EL789, G187, GR130, N252, P387, SH538, UM381 (PD)
"Have Thine Own Way, Lord" (Luke, Stewardship)
C588, CG493, GR343. SH626, UM382 (PD)
"This Is a Day of New Beginnings" 231043 (Luke, Comm.)
C518, N417, UM383
"Come, O Thou Traveler Unknown" (Luke)
E638/639, GR577, SH24, UM386
"Jesus Calls Us" 68900 (Luke)
C337, CG486, E549/550, EL696, G720, GR520, N171/172, SH604, UM398, VU562
"Take My Life, and Let It Be" 1390 (Luke, Stewardship)
C609, CG490, E707, EL583/EL685, G697, GR586, P391, N448, SH627/628, UM399 (PD), VU506
"Cuando el Pobre" ("When the Poor Ones") OL-97385 (Luke)
C662, EL725, G762, P407, SH240, UM434, VU702
"I Come with Joy" (Luke, Comm.)
C420, CG456, E304, EL482, G515, N349, P507, SH682, UM617, VU477
"The Summons" ("Will You Come and Follow Me") 4668756 (Luke)
CG473, EL798, G726, S2130, SH598, VU567
"Living for Jesus" (Luke)
C610, GR595, S2149
"When God Restored Our Common Life" OL-00642 (Luke)
G74, S2182
"Somebody's Knockin' at Your Door" (PD-TO) (Luke)
G728, P382, SH597, WS3095 (PD-TO), Z154
+"Living Spirit, Holy Fire" OL-57648 (Luke)
WS3109
"Jesus, You Are the New Day" OL-13732 (Luke)
WS3143
"Jesús está pasando por aquí" ("Jesus Is Passing By") (Luke)
SH120
+"We Give Thee but Thine Own" 3922369 (Luke)
C382, EL686, G708, N785, P428, SH643, VU543

Additional Contemporary and Modern Suggestions

"Until Jesus Comes" (Hab)
WS3050
"Hungry" ("Falling on My Knees") 2650364 (Hab, Pss, Luke)
WS3099
"Thy Word Is a Lamp" 14301 (Pss)
C326, CG38, G458, UM601
"To Know You More" 1767420 (Pss)
S2161
"Breathe" 1874117 (Pss)
WS3112, ZS47
"Knowing You" 1045238 (Pss)
"In the Secret" 1810119 (Pss)
"I Could Sing of Your Love Forever" 1043199 (Pss)
"Show Me Your Ways" 1675024 (Pss)
"Ancient Words" 2986399 (Pss)
"He Who Began a Good Work in You" 15238 (2 Thess)
S2163, ZS98
"Lord, Be Glorified" 26368 (2 Thess)
EL744, G468, S2150, SH420
"Be Glorified" 429226 (2 Thess)
"Be Glorified" 2732646 (2 Thess)
"Take My Life" 1617154 (2 Thess, Luke)
+"All the Poor and Powerless" 5881130 (2 Thess, Luke)
+"Behold Him" 7133698 (2 Thess, Luke)
"Give Thanks" 20285 (2 Thess, Luke)
C528, CG373, G647, S2036, SH489, ZS127
"I'm So Glad Jesus Lifted Me" (PD) (Luke)
C529, EL860 (PD), N474, S2151
"Something Beautiful" 18060 (Luke)
UM394
"Across the Lands" 3709898 (Luke)
SH654, WS3032
"Shout to the North" 1562261 (Luke)
G319, WS3042
"Amazing Grace" ("My Chains Are Gone") 4768151 (Luke)
GR574, WS3104
"We Fall Down" 2437367 (Luke, All Saints)
G368, WS3187

"I Will Never Be (the Same Again)" 1874911 (Luke)
"Everyday" 2798154 (Luke)
"Salvation Is Here" 4451327 (Luke)
"Grace Like Rain" 3689877 (Luke)
+"Better Than A Hallelujah" 5622564 (Luke)
+"His Mercy Is More" 7065053 (Luke)
+"Let Justice Roll" ("Like a River") 4974842 (Luke)
+"The Kingdom Is Yours" 7109354 (Luke)

Solo/Ensemble Suggestions
"Be Thou My Vision" (Hab)
V-6 p. 13
+"How I Love Your Word" (Pss)
V-3 (5) p. 9
+"Here's One" (Luke)
V-7 p. 32/36
"Be Thou My Vision" (Hab)
arr. Marie Pooler; AEC-1 p. 9
Unison, keyboard (https://bit.ly/AEC-1-9-SATB)
+"Come, Ye Sinners, Poor and Needy" (Luke)
Arr. Keith Christopher; Lorenz 10/4493L
SATB, piano, opt. percussion (https://bit.ly/4493L)

+Hymn Anthem
"Be Thou My Vision" 5021907 (Hab)
C595, CG71, E488, EL793, G450, GR49, N451, P339, SH640, UM451, VU642
This arrangement uses a recurring flute line that can be fashioned from the non-melody notes (alto) in the treble clef, played two octaves higher. It may also be played by a violin, oboe, electronic keyboard, or other treble instrument. Organ (or piano) provides the rest of the accompaniment. The voices always sing the melody.
Introduction: Flute part alone, freely.
Stanza 1: Treble voices, *piano.* Organ plays non-melody notes only, treble and bass clef.
Stanza 2: All voices, *mezzo piano.* Organ plays full accompaniment.
Interlude: All voices "oo" on melody. Organ plays S-1, #319 (delete last measure with fermata) and flute plays its part.
Stanza 3: Voices sing melody in canon as in S-1, #319. Organ plays S-1, #319. Flute plays its part. (Flute may double the upper part of the organ part in the last 5 measures.)

Other Suggestions
The scriptures and service ideas from Nov. 1 may be used today as All Saints Sunday.
Daylight Savings Time ends today.
Visuals:
O Praying hands, overturned scales, tower, tablets
P Open Bible, ten commandments
E Letter, embrace, love, persecution, prayer
G Tax form, small man (running, climbing tree), 1/2, 4x, Jesus, Luke 19:9a
+Introit: WS3047, st. 3 "God Almighty, We Are Waiting" (Hab)
Greeting: WSL22. "From Bethlehem to Nazareth" (Luke)
Opening Prayer: WSL15. "O God, you delight not" (Luke)
Prayer of Confession: WSL189 (Luke)
Closing Prayer: WSL163. "From where we are are" (Luke)
Sung Benediction: "Let the Peace of God Reign" 1839987 (2 Thess)
Alternate Lessons (see page 4): Isa. 1:10-18, Ps. 32:1-7
Theme Ideas: Discipleship / Following God, Faithfulness, Lament, Repentance, Stewardship, Vision, Waiting

Notes

NRSVue

Haggai 1:15b–2:9

15In the second year of King Darius,
2 in the seventh month, on the twenty-first day of the month,
the word of the LORD came by the prophet Haggai, saying:
2“Speak now to Zerubbabel son of Shealtiel, governor of Judah,
and to Joshua son of Jehozadak, the high priest, and to the
remnant of the people, and say: 3Who is left among you who saw
this house in its former glory? How does it look to you now? Is it
not in your sight as nothing? 4Yet now take courage, O Zerubbabel, says the LORD; take courage, O Joshua, son of Jehozadak,
the high priest; take courage, all you people of the land, says the
LORD; work, for I am with you, says the LORD of hosts, 5accord-
ing to the promise that I made you when you came out of Egypt.
My spirit abides among you; do not fear. 6For thus says the LORD
of hosts: Once again, in a little while, I will shake the heavens
and the earth and the sea and the dry land, 7and I will shake all
the nations, so that the treasure of all nations will come, and I
will fill this house with splendor, says the LORD of hosts. 8The
silver is mine, and the gold is mine, says the LORD of hosts. 9The
latter splendor of this house shall be greater than the former,
says the LORD of hosts, and in this place I will give prosperity,
says the LORD of hosts.”

Psalm 145:1-5, 17-21 (G42/270/622, N718, P251/252, UM857)

1I will extol you, my God and King,
and bless your name forever and ever.
2Every day I will bless you
and praise your name forever and ever.
3Great is the LORD and greatly to be praised;
his greatness is unsearchable.
4One generation shall extol your works to another
and shall declare your mighty acts.
5They will recount the glorious splendor of your majesty,
and on your wondrous works I will meditate.

. . . .

17The LORD is just in all his ways
and kind in all his doings.
18The LORD is near to all who call on him,
to all who call on him in truth.
19He fulfills the desire of all who fear him;
he also hears their cry and saves them.
20The LORD watches over all who love him,
but all the wicked he will destroy.
21My mouth will speak the praise of the LORD,
and all flesh will bless his holy name forever and ever.

CEB

Haggai 1:15b–2:9

15b[I]n the second year of Darius the king.
2 On the twenty-first day of the seventh month, the LORD’s
word came through Haggai the prophet: 2Say to Judah’s Governor Zerubbabel, Shealtiel’s son, and to the Chief Priest Joshua,
Jehozadak’s son, and to the rest of the people:

3 Who among you is left who saw this house in its former glory?
How does it look to you now?
Doesn’t it appear as nothing to you?
4 So now, be strong, Zerubbabel, says the LORD.
Be strong, High Priest Joshua, Jehozadak’s son,
and be strong, all you people of the land, says the LORD.
Work, for I am with you, says the LORD of heavenly forces.
5 As with our agreement when you came out of Egypt,
my spirit stands in your midst.
Don’t fear.
6 This is what the LORD of heavenly forces says:
In just a little while, I will make the heavens, the earth, the sea, and the dry land quake.
7 I will make all the nations quake.
The wealth of all the nations will come.
I will fill this house with glory, says the LORD of heavenly forces.
8 The silver and the gold belong to me, says the LORD of heavenly forces.
9 This house will be more glorious than its predecessor, says the LORD of heavenly forces.
I will provide prosperity in this place, says the LORD of heavenly forces.

Psalm 145:1-5, 17-21 (G42/270/622, N718, P251/252, UM857)

1I will lift you up high, my God, the true king.
I will bless your name forever and always.
2I will bless you every day.
I will praise your name forever and always.
3The LORD is great and so worthy of praise!
God’s greatness can’t be grasped.
4One generation will praise your works to the next one,
proclaiming your mighty acts.
5They will talk all about the glorious splendor of your majesty;
I will contemplate your wondrous works.

. . . .

17The LORD is righteous in all his ways,
faithful in all his deeds.
18The LORD is close to everyone who calls out to him,
to all who call out to him sincerely.
19God shows favor to those who honor him,
listening to their cries for help and saving them.
20The LORD protects all who love him,
but he destroys every wicked person.
21My mouth will proclaim the LORD’s praise,
and every living thing will bless God’s holy name forever and always.

NRSVue

2 Thessalonians 2:1-5, 13-17

1As to the coming of our Lord Jesus Christ and our being
gathered together to him, we beg you, brothers and sisters, 2not
to be quickly shaken in mind or alarmed, either by spirit or by
word or by letter, as though from us, to the effect that the day
of the Lord is already here. 3Let no one deceive you in any way,
for that day will not come unless the rebellion comes first and
the lawless one is revealed, the one destined for destruction. 4He
opposes and exalts himself above every so-called god or object of
worship, so that he takes his seat in the temple of God, declaring
himself to be God. 5Do you not remember that I told you these
things when I was still with you? . . .

13But we must always give thanks to God for you, brothers
and sisters beloved by the Lord, because God chose you as the
first fruits for salvation through sanctification by the Spirit and
through belief in the truth. 14For this purpose he called you
through our gospel, so that you may obtain the glory of our
Lord Jesus Christ. 15So then, brothers and sisters, stand firm and
hold fast to the traditions that you were taught by us, either by
word of mouth or by our letter.

16Now may our Lord Jesus Christ himself and God our Father,
who loved us and through grace gave us eternal comfort and
good hope, 17comfort your hearts and strengthen them in every
good work and word.

Luke 20:27-38

27Some Sadducees, those who say there is no resurrection,
came to him 28and asked him a question, "Teacher, Moses wrote
for us that if a man's brother dies leaving a wife but no children,
the man shall marry the widow and raise up children for his
brother. 29Now there were seven brothers; the first married a
woman and died childless; 30then the second 31and the third
married her, and so in the same way all seven died childless.
32Finally the woman also died. 33In the resurrection, therefore,
whose wife will the woman be? For the seven had married her."

34Jesus said to them, "Those who belong to this age marry and
are given in marriage, 35but those who are considered worthy of
a place in that age and in the resurrection from the dead neither marry nor are given in marriage. 36Indeed, they cannot die
anymore, because they are like angels and are children of God,
being children of the resurrection. 37And the fact that the dead
are raised Moses himself showed, in the story about the bush,
where he speaks of the Lord as the God of Abraham, the God of
Isaac, and the God of Jacob. 38Now he is God not of the dead but
of the living, for to him all of them are alive."

CEB

2 Thessalonians 2:1-5, 13-17

1Brothers and sisters, we have a request for you concerning our Lord Jesus Christ's coming and when we are gathered
together to be with him. 2We don't want you to be easily con-
fused in your mind or upset if you hear that the day of the Lord
is already here, whether you hear it through some spirit, a message, or a letter supposedly from us. 3Don't let anyone deceive
you in any way. That day won't come unless the rebellion comes
first and the person who is lawless is revealed, who is headed for
destruction. 4He is the opponent of every so-called god or object
of worship and promotes himself over them. So he sits in God's
temple, displaying himself to show that he is God. 5You remember that I used to tell you these things while I was with you, don't
you? . . .

13But we always must thank God for you, brothers and sisters
who are loved by God. This is because he chose you from the
beginning to be the first crop of the harvest. This brought salvation, through your dedication to God by the Spirit and through
your belief in the truth. 14God called all of you through our
good news so you could possess the honor of our Lord Jesus
Christ. 15So then, brothers and sisters, stand firm and hold on to
the traditions we taught you, whether we taught you in person
or through our letter. 16Our Lord Jesus Christ himself and God
our Father loved us and through grace gave us eternal comfort
and a good hope. 17May he encourage your hearts and give you
strength in every good thing you do or say.

Luke 20:27-38

27Some Sadducees, who deny that there's a resurrection, came
to Jesus and asked, 28"Teacher, Moses wrote for us that *if a man's
brother dies* leaving a widow *but no children, the brother must marry
the widow and raise up children for his brother.* 29Now there were
seven brothers. The first man married a woman and then died
childless. 30The second 31and then the third brother married her.
Eventually all seven married her, and they all died without leaving any children. 32Finally, the woman died too. 33In the resurrection, whose wife will she be? All seven were married to her."

34Jesus said to them, "People who belong to this age marry
and are given in marriage. 35But those who are considered worthy to participate in that age, that is, in the age of the resurrection from the dead, won't marry nor will they be given in marriage. 36They can no longer die, because they are like angels and
are God's children since they share in the resurrection. 37Even
Moses demonstrated that the dead are raised—in the passage
about the burning bush, when he speaks of the Lord as *the God of
Abraham, the God of Isaac, and the God of Jacob.* 38He isn't the God
of the dead but of the living. To him they all are alive."

Primary Hymns and Songs for the Day

"Come, Ye Faithful, Raise the Strain" 355929 (2 Thess, Luke) (O)
C215, CG218, E199, G234, GR253, N230, P115, UM315 (PD)
H-3 Hbl-53; Chr-57; Desc-94; Org-141
S-2 #161. Descant
E200, EL363, P114 (PD), VU165
"God Is Here" 223549 (2 Thess, Luke) (O)
C280, CG298, EL526, G409, GR393, N70, P461, UM660, VU389
H-3 Hbl-61; Chr-132; Org-2
S-1 #4-5. Instrumental and vocal descants
"Great Is the Lord" 1149 (Pss)
CG325, G614, S2022, SH459
"I Love the Lord" 1168957 (Pss)
CG613, G799, P362, N511, SH343, VU617, WS3142, ZS176
"O Master, Let Me Walk with Thee" 158243 (2 Thess)
C602, CG660, E659/660, EL818, G738, GR596, N503, P357, SH612, UM430 (PD), VU560
H-3 Hbl-81; Chr-147; Desc-74; Org-87
S-2 #118. Descant
"Pues Si Vivimos" ("When We Are Living") 4968810 (Luke)
C536, CG265, EL639, G822, N499, P400, SH299, UM356, VU581
"Thine Be the Glory" (Luke) (C)
C218, CG222, EL376, G238, GR255, N253, P122, SH192, UM308, VU173 (Fr.)
H-3 Hbl-98; Chr-195; Desc-59
S-1 #190. Arrangement
S-2 #95. Various treatments and harmonizations

Additional Hymn Suggestions

"Come, Thou Long-Expected Jesus" 31999 (Hag) (O)
C125, CG83, E66, EL254, G82/83, GR163, N122, P1/2, SH64, UM196 (PD), VU2
"Jesus, Joy of Our Desiring" (Hag)
GR129, UM644 (PD), VU328
"Glorious Things of Thee Are Spoken" 99371 (Hag)
C709, CG282, E522/523, EL647, G81, GR395, N307, P446, UM731 (PD)
"Immortal, Invisible, God Only Wise" 124466 (Hag, Luke) (O)
C66, CG58, E423, EL834, G12, GR7, N1, P263, UM103 (PD), VU264 (*See also* ZS4)
"Standing on the Promises" (Hag, Luke)
C552, CG625, G838, GR434, SH45, UM374 (PD)
"God of the Ages" (Hag, Luke)
C725, CG62, E718, G331, GR59, N592, P262, UM698 (PD)
"My Lord, What a Morning" (PD-TO) (Hag, 2 Thess)
C708, EL438, G352, P449, SH356, UM719, VU708, Z145
"O God, Our Help in Ages Past" 43152 (Hag, Pss) (C)
C67, CG566, E680, EL632, G687, GR15, N25, P210, SH41, UM117 (PD), VU806
"Sing Praise to God Who Reigns Above" 7061649 (Pss, 2 Thess, Luke)
C6, CG315, E408, EL871, G645, GR5, N6, P483, UM126 (PD), VU216
"Let All Things Now Living" 171701 (Pss, Luke)
C717, CG379, EL881, G37, GR636, P554, S2008, SH23, VU242
"Now Thank We All Our God" 86638 (2 Thess)
C715, CG371, E396/397, EL839/840, G643, GR84, N419, P555, SH485, UM102 (PD), VU236 (Fr.)
"Holy God, We Praise Thy Name" 114555 (2 Thess)
CG9, E366, EL414 (PD), G4, GR2, N276, P460, SH431, UM79, VU894 (Fr.)
"Close to Thee" (2 Thess)
GR335, UM407 (PD), Z7
"Jesus, Lover of My Soul" (2 Thess)
C542, CG406, E699, G440, GR120, N546, P303, SH542/543, UM479, VU669
"O Love That Wilt Not Let Me Go" (2 Thess)
C540, CG631, G833, GR92, N485, P384, SH314, UM480 (PD), VU658
"How Firm a Foundation" 107816 (2 Thess)
C618, CG425, E636, EL796, G463, GR46, N407, P361, SH291, UM529 (PD), VU660
"I Want Jesus to Walk with Me" (2 Thess)
C627, CG635, EL325, G775, GR368, N490, P363, SH135, UM521 (PD-TO), Z95, ZS69
"Faith of Our Fathers" 7029079 (2 Thess)
C635, CG645, EL812/813, N381, UM710 (PD), VU580
"Loving Spirit" 3379424 (2 Thess)
C244, EL397, G293, P323, S2123, VU387
"In the Singing" (2 Thess, Comm.)
EL466, G533, S2255
"Living for Jesus" (2 Thess, Luke)
C610, GR595, S2149
"The God of Abraham Praise" 484742 (Luke)
C24, CG45, E401, EL831, G49, GR16, N24, P488, SH50, UM116 (PD), VU255
"Children of the Heavenly Father" (Luke)
CG69, EL781, GR56, N487, SH42, UM141
"Sing with All the Saints of Glory" 457573 (Luke)
EL426, GR258, SH197, UM702 (PD)
"Praise the Source of Faith and Learning" 3422034 (Luke)
N411, S2004
"Sent Forth by God's Blessing" OL-40362 (Luke) (C)
CG519, EL547, N76, SH715, UM664, VU481

Additional Contemporary and Modern Suggestions

"Hosanna" 4785835 (Hag)
SH361, WS3188
"Famous One" 3599431 (Hag, Pss)
"Be Bold, Be Strong" 58563 (Hag)
"Waiting Here for You" 5925663 (Hag, Pss, 2 Thess)
"Today Is the Day" 5200924 (Hagg, 2 Thess)
+"Nothing to Fear" 7133723 (Hagg, 2 Thess)
+"Good Grace" 7122177 (Hag, 2 Thess)
+"Stand in Your Love" 7107821 (Hag, 2 Thess, Luke)
+"You Keep Hope Alive" 7125876 (Hag, 2 Thess, Luke)
+"Every Praise" 6623483 (Pss)
+"Goodness of God" 7117726 (Pss)
+"So Will I" ("100 Billion X") 7084123 (Pss)
+"Blessed Be the Name" 34525 (Pss)
CG350, GR67, UM63
"He Is Exalted" 17827 (Pss)
CG342, S2070, SH423
"Laudate Dominum" ("Sing, Praise") OL-00123 (Pss)
G635, WS3007
"God Is Good All the Time" OL-88288 (Pss)
WS3026, ZS18
"God Is Good All the Time" 1729073 (Pss)
"You Are Good" 3383788 (Pss)
SH455, WS3014
"I Extol You" 18307 (Pss)
"I Will Celebrate" 21239 (Pss)
"Awesome Is the Lord Most High" 4674159 (Pss)
"Lord, I Lift Your Name on High" 117947 (Pss, Luke)
CG606, EL857, S2088, SH205
"Lord, Be Glorified" 26368 (2 Thess)
EL744, G468, S2150, SH420
"Give Thanks" 20285 (2 Thess)
C528, CG373, G647, S2036, SH489, ZS127
"Sing Alleluia to the Lord" 26272 (2 Thess, Comm.)
C32, S2258, SH685

"Here Is Bread, Here Is Wine" 983717 (2 Thess, Comm.)
EL483, S2266
"Wait for the Lord" OL- 00172 (2 Thess)
CG644, EL262, G90, SH580, VU22, WS3049
"Grace Like Rain" 3689877 (2 Thess)
"Foundation" 706151 (2 Thess)
+"Springtime" 7146308 (2 Thess)
"Spirit of the Living God" 23488 (2 Thess, Luke)
C259, CG233, G288, GR299, N283, P322, SH555, UM393, VU376, Z226, S-1 #212 Vocal desc. idea
"God Is Speaking" 5357444 (Luke)
WS3025
"Alive Forever, Amen" 4190176 (Luke)

Solo/Ensemble Suggestions

"Thus Saith the Lord" (Hag)
V-2
+"Prepare the Way of the Lord" (Hag)
V-3 (5) p. 30
"Come, Thou Long-Expected Jesus" (Hag)
V-3(3) p. 50
V-10 p. 11
"Patiently Have I Waited for the Lord" (Hag, 2 Thess)
V-4 p. 24
"Redeeming Grace" (2 Thess)
V-4 p. 47
"Great Is the Lord" (Pss)
Rosephanye Powell; Gentry 00145523
SATB, percussion (https://bit.ly/G-45523)
+"We Belong To Christ" (Luke)
Arr. Emily Lund; Hope C6096
SATB, piano, opt. oboe (https://bit.ly/C-6096)

+Hymn Anthem

"Let All the World in Every Corner Sing" OL-FBC-A017367 (Pss)
E402, G636, P468, UM93
You may wish to invite the congregation to sing the final antiphon or unison section. Sing with power and vigor.
Introduction: Keyboard (organ) plays the antiphon (first 6 measures) once. *Mezzo forte.*
Antiphon: All voices, unison. *Mezzo forte.*
Stanza 1: SATB or S/A singing melody. *Mezzo forte.*
Antiphon: All voices, unison. *Mezzo forte.*
Stanza 1: SATB or T/B singing melody. *Mezzo forte.*
Antiphon: All voices (including congregation), unison. *Fortissimo* with *ritard* at end.

Other Suggestions

Visuals:
O Church in ruins/restored, Exodus, quake, sea/desert
P Crown, teach/learn, light, natural wonders, praise
E Second Coming, fruit, preaching, letter, 2 Thess. 2:16-17
G Coffin, wedding, seven brothers, bride, resurrection, children in white robes, burning bush, Luke 20:38a
Opening Prayer: N831 (Hag, Pss)
Affirmation of Faith: WSL82. "We are children" (2 Thess, Luke)
Prayer: UM721. Christ the King (Hag, 2 Thess)
Blessing: N872 (Hag) or C776 (2 Thess)
Alternate Lessons (see page 4): Job 19:23-27a, Ps. 17:1-9
Theme Ideas: Courage, Faithfulness, God: Faithfulness, Resurrection, Saints, Waiting

Notes

NRSVue

Isaiah 65:17-25

[17]For I am about to create new heavens
and a new earth;
the former things shall not be remembered
or come to mind.
[18]But be glad and rejoice forever
in what I am creating,
for I am about to create Jerusalem as a joy
and its people as a delight.
[19]I will rejoice in Jerusalem
and delight in my people;
no more shall the sound of weeping be heard in it
or the cry of distress.
[20]No more shall there be in it
an infant that lives but a few days
or an old person who does not live out a lifetime,
for one who dies at a hundred years will be considered a youth,
and one who falls short of a hundred will be considered
accursed.
[21]They shall build houses and inhabit them;
they shall plant vineyards and eat their fruit.
[22]They shall not build and another inhabit;
they shall not plant and another eat,
for like the days of a tree shall the days of my people be,
and my chosen shall long enjoy the work of their hands.
[23]They shall not labor in vain
or bear children for calamity,
for they shall be offspring blessed by the LORD—
and their descendants as well.
[24]Before they call I will answer,
while they are yet speaking I will hear.
[25]The wolf and the lamb shall feed together;
the lion shall eat straw like the ox,
but the serpent—its food shall be dust!
They shall not hurt or destroy
on all my holy mountain,
says the LORD.

Isaiah 12

[1]You will say on that day:
"I will give thanks to you, O LORD,
for though you were angry with me,
your anger turned away,
and you comforted me.
[2]Surely God is my salvation;
I will trust and will not be afraid,
for the LORD is my strength and my might;
he has become my salvation."
[3]With joy you will draw water from the wells of salvation. [4]And
you will say on that day:
"Give thanks to the LORD;
call on his name;
make known his deeds among the nations;
proclaim that his name is exalted.
[5]Sing praises to the LORD, for he has done gloriously;
let this be known in all the earth.
[6]Shout aloud and sing for joy, O royal Zion,
for great in your midst is the Holy One of Israel."

CEB

Isaiah 65:17-25

[17]Look! I'm creating
a new heaven and a new earth:
past events won't be remembered;
they won't come to mind.
[18]Be glad and rejoice forever
in what I'm creating,
because I'm creating Jerusalem as a joy
and her people as a source of gladness.
[19]I will rejoice in Jerusalem
and be glad about my people.
No one will ever hear the sound
of weeping or crying in it again.
[20]No more will babies live only a few days,
or the old fail to live out their days.
The one who dies at a hundred
will be like a young person,
and the one falling short of a hundred
will seem cursed.
[21]They will build houses and live in them;
they will plant vineyards
and eat their fruit.
[22]They won't build for others to live in,
nor plant for others to eat.
Like the days of a tree
will be the days of my people;
my chosen will make full use
of their handiwork.
[23]They won't labor in vain,
nor bear children to a world of horrors,
because they will be people
blessed by the LORD,
they along with their descendants.
[24]Before they call, I will answer;
while they are still speaking, I will hear.
[25]Wolf and lamb will graze together,
and the lion will eat straw like the ox,
but the snake—its food will be dust.
They won't hurt or destroy
at any place on my holy mountain,
says the LORD.

Isaiah 12

[1]You will say on that day:
"I thank you, LORD.
Though you were angry with me,
your anger turned away and you comforted me.
[2]God is indeed my salvation;
I will trust and won't be afraid.
Yah, the LORD, is my strength and my shield;
he has become my salvation."
[3]You will draw water with joy from the springs of salvation.
[4]And you will say on that day:
"Thank the LORD; call on God's name;
proclaim God's deeds among the peoples;
declare that God's name is exalted.
[5]Sing to the LORD, who has done glorious things;
proclaim this throughout all the earth."
[6]Shout and sing for joy, city of Zion,
because the holy one of Israel is great among you.

NRSVue

2 Thessalonians 3:6-13

[6]Now we command you, brothers and sisters, in the name of our Lord Jesus Christ, to keep away from every brother or sister living irresponsibly and not according to the tradition that they received from us. [7]For you yourselves know how you ought to imitate us; we were not irresponsible when we were with you, [8]and we did not eat anyone's bread without paying for it, but with toil and labor we worked night and day so that we might not burden any of you. [9]This was not because we do not have that right but in order to give you an example to imitate. [10]For even when we were with you, we gave you this command: anyone unwilling to work should not eat. [11]For we hear that some of you are living irresponsibly, mere busybodies, not doing any work. [12]Now such persons we command and exhort in the Lord Jesus Christ to do their work quietly and to earn their own living. [13]Brothers and sisters, do not be weary in doing what is right.

Luke 21:5-19

[5]When some were speaking about the temple, how it was adorned with beautiful stones and gifts dedicated to God, he said, [6]"As for these things that you see, the days will come when not one stone will be left upon another; all will be thrown down."

[7]They asked him, "Teacher, when will this be, and what will be the sign that this is about to take place?" [8]And he said, "Beware that you are not led astray, for many will come in my name and say, 'I am he!' and, 'The time is near!' Do not go after them.

[9]"When you hear of wars and insurrections, do not be terrified, for these things must take place first, but the end will not follow immediately." [10]Then he said to them, "Nation will rise against nation and kingdom against kingdom; [11]there will be great earthquakes and in various places famines and plagues, and there will be dreadful portents and great signs from heaven.

[12]"But before all this occurs, they will arrest you and persecute you; they will hand you over to synagogues and prisons, and you will be brought before kings and governors because of my name. [13]This will give you an opportunity to testify. [14]So make up your minds not to prepare your defense in advance, [15]for I will give you words and a wisdom that none of your opponents will be able to withstand or contradict. [16]You will be betrayed even by parents and siblings, by relatives and friends, and they will put some of you to death. [17]You will be hated by all because of my name. [18]But not a hair of your head will perish. [19]By your endurance you will gain your souls."

CEB

2 Thessalonians 3:6-13

[6]Brothers and sisters, we command you in the name of our Lord Jesus Christ to stay away from every brother or sister who lives an undisciplined life that is not in line with the traditions that you received from us. [7]You yourselves know how you need to imitate us because we were not undisciplined when we were with you. [8]We didn't eat anyone's food without paying for it. Instead, we worked night and day with effort and hard work so that we would not impose on you. [9]We did this to give you an example to imitate, not because we didn't have a right to insist on financial support. [10]Even when we were with you we were giving you this command: "If anyone doesn't want to work, they shouldn't eat." [11]We hear that some of you are living an undisciplined life. They aren't working, but they are meddling in other people's business. [12]By the Lord Jesus Christ, we command and encourage such people to work quietly and put their own food on the table. [13]Brothers and sisters, don't get discouraged in doing what is right.

Luke 21:5-19

[5]Some people were talking about the temple, how it was decorated with beautiful stones and ornaments dedicated to God. Jesus said, [6]"As for the things you are admiring, the time is coming when not even one stone will be left upon another. All will be demolished."

[7]They asked him, "Teacher, when will these things happen? What sign will show that these things are about to happen?"

[8]Jesus said, "Watch out that you aren't deceived. Many will come in my name, saying, 'I'm the one!' and 'It's time!' Don't follow them. [9]When you hear of wars and rebellions, don't be alarmed. These things must happen first, but the end won't happen immediately."

[10]Then Jesus said to them, "Nations and kingdoms will fight against each other. [11]There will be great earthquakes and wide-scale food shortages and epidemics. There will also be terrifying sights and great signs in the sky. [12]But before all this occurs, they will take you into custody and harass you because of your faith. They will hand you over to synagogues and prisons, and you will be brought before kings and governors because of my name. [13]This will provide you with an opportunity to testify. [14]Make up your minds not to prepare your defense in advance. [15]I'll give you words and wisdom that none of your opponents will be able to counter or contradict. [16]You will be betrayed by your parents, brothers and sisters, relatives, and friends. They will execute some of you. [17]Everyone will hate you because of my name. [18]Still, not a hair on your heads will be lost. [19]By holding fast, you will gain your lives."

Primary Hymns and Songs for the Day
"Sing Praise to God Who Reigns Above" 7061649 (Isa 12) (O)
C6, CG315, E408, EL871, G645, GR5, N6, P483, UM126 (PD), VU216
H-3 Hbl-92; Chr-22, 126, 173; Desc-76; Org-91
S-1 #237. Descant
"Joy in the Morning" 112887 (Isa 65) (O)
S2284
"O Day of Peace That Dimly Shines" (Isa 65, Luke)
C711, E597, EL711, G373, P450, UM729, VU682
"The First Song of Isaiah" 196023 (Isa 12)
G71, S2030
+"Come, Let Us Dream" (Isa)
WS3157
"Soon and Very Soon" 11249 (2 Thess, Luke)
CG562, EL439, G384, GR629, SH357, UM706, Z198, ZS136
S-2 #187. Piano arrangement
"My Lord, What a Morning" (PD-TO) (Luke)
C708, EL438, G352, P449, SH356, UM719, VU708, Z145
"O Master, Let Me Walk with Thee" 158243 (Luke) (C)
C602, CG660, E659/E660, EL818, G738, GR596, N503, P357, SH612, UM430 (PD), VU560
"Forth in Thy Name, O Lord" (2 Thess) (C)
GR685, UM438 (PD), VU416
H-3 Hbl-29, 57, 58; Chr-117; Desc-31; Org-31
S-1 #100-103. Various treatments.

Additional Hymn Suggestions
"This Is a Day of New Beginnings" 231043 (Isa 65)
C518, N417, UM383
"O What Their Joy and Their Glory Must Be" (PD) (Isa 65)
E623, N385, UM727 (PD)
"Joy Comes with the Dawn" OL-117798 (Isa 65)
S2210, VU166
"I'll Fly Away" (Isa 65)
N595, S2282, Z183
"Isaiah the Prophet Has Written of Old" (Isa 65)
G77, N108, P337, VU680
"For the Healing of the Nations" 1510804 (Isa, 2 Thess, Luke)
C668, CG698, G346, N576, UM428, VU678
"On Jordan's Stormy Banks I Stand" (Isa 65, Luke)
CG556, EL437, GR623, N598, SH368, UM724 (PD), Z54
"Come, We That Love the Lord" 84159 (Isa 65, Luke)
CG549, E392, GR38, N379, UM732, VU715
"Marching to Zion" 144398 (Isa 65, Luke) (O)
C707, CG550, EL625, GR626, N382, UM733, VU714, Z3
"I Want a Principle Within" (2 Thess)
GR313, UM410 (PD)
"Christ, from Whom All Blessings Flow" (2 Thess)
GR399, UM550 (PD)
"Together We Serve" (2 Thess)
G767, S2175
"You, Lord, Are Both Lamb and Shepherd" (2 Thess)
G274, SH210, VU210. WS3043
"Go to the World" (2 Thess)
CG481, G295, SH720, VU420, WS3158
"Come, Labor On" (2 Thess)
E541, G719, N532, P415
"Today We All Are Called to Be Disciples" (2 Thess)
G757, P434, VU507
"Called as Partners in Christ's Service" (2 Thess)
C453, G761, N495, P343
"It Is Well with My Soul" 25376 (2 Thess, Luke)
C561, CG573, EL785, G840, GR344, N438, SH305, UM377 (PD), Z20
"A Charge to Keep I Have" 118850 (2 Thess, Luke)
CG623, GR456, SH634, UM413 (PD)
"All Who Love and Serve Your City" 1277415 (2 Thess, Luke)
C670, CG674, E570/E571, EL724, G351, P413, UM433
"I Want to Be Ready" (2 Thess, Luke)
N616, UM722 (PD-TO), Z151
"Blessed Quietness" (2 Thess, Luke)
C267, CG244, N284 (PD), S2142, Z206
"Bring Forth the Kingdom" (2 Thess, Luke)
N181, S2190, SH130
"My Hope Is Built" (PD) (Luke)
C537, CG590, EL596/597, G353, GR102, N403, P379, SH324, UM368 (PD), ZS182
"Where Cross the Crowded Ways of Life" 2961345 (Luke)
C665, CG657, E609, EL719, G343, N543, P408, UM427 (PD), VU681
"Lord, Speak to Me" 2769286 (Luke)
CG503, EL676, G722, GR439, N531, P426, SH557, UM463 (PD), VU589
"Come, Ye Thankful People, Come" 50200 (Luke)
C718, CG372, E290, EL693, G367, GR83, N422, P551, SH355, UM694 (PD), VU516
"Mine Eyes Have Seen the Glory" (Luke)
C705, CG439, EL890, G354, GR283, N610, UM717 (PD), Z24/213
"O Day of God, Draw Nigh" (PD) (Luke) (C)
C700, E601, N611, P452, UM730 (PD), VU688/689 (Fr.)

Additional Contemporary and Modern Suggestions
"I Will Enter His Gates" 1493 (Isa 65) (O)
S2270
"There's Something About That Name" 14064 (Isa 65)
C115, GR124, UM171
+"Let Justice Roll" ("Like a River") 4974842 (Isa 65)
+"The Kingdom Is Yours" 7109354 (Isa 65, Isa 12)
"Forever" 3148428 (Isa 65, Isa 12)
CG53, WS3023
"Someone Asked the Question" 1640279 (Isa 65, Isa 12)
N523, S2144
"Hear our Praises" 2543402 (Isa 65, Isa 12)
"Give Thanks" 20285 (Isa 12)
C528, CG373, G647, S2036, SH489, ZS127
"He Is Exalted" 17827 (Isa 12)
CG342, S2070, SH423
"Shout to the Lord" 1406918 (Isa 12)
CG348, EL821, GR124, S2074, SH426, ZS15
"In the Lord I'll Be Ever Thankful" OL-00118 (Isa 12)
G654, S2195, SH316
"You Are My All in All" 825356 (Isa 12)
CG571, G519, SH335, WS3040, ZS184
"I Exalt You" 17803 (Isa 12)
"Be Exalted, O God" ("I Will Give Thanks") 21112 (Isa 12)
"God Is the Strength of My Heart" 80919 (Isa 12)
"Good to Me" 313480 (Isa 12)
"I See the Lord" 1406176 (Isa 12, Luke)
"Rule of Life" (PD-TO) (2 Thess)
WS3117, ZS95
"Freedom Is Coming" 4194244 (Luke)
G359, S2192, SH29, ZS110
"O Freedom" OL-68414 (Luke)
S2194 (PD-TO), Z102, ZS109
+"Until Jesus Comes" (Luke)
WS3050
"Hosanna" 4785835 (Luke)
SH361, WS3188
"The Battle Belongs to the Lord" 21583 (Luke)
"This Kingdom" 1650898 (Luke)
"Did You Feel the Mountains Tremble?" 1097028 (Luke)

Solo/Ensemble Suggestions
+"Make a Joyful Noise" (Isa)
V-3 (5) p. 44
"Turn My Heart to You" (Isa, 2 Thess)
V-5 (2) p. 14
"I'm Goin' Home" (Isa, Luke)
V-8 p. 325
"It Is Well with My Soul" (2 Thess, Luke)
V-5 (2) p. 35
"My Lord, What a Mornin'" (Luke)
V-3 (1) p. 39
V-3 (4) p. 32
+"See a Victory" (Luke)
V-9 p. 88
+"A New Jerusalem Arise" (Isa 65)
Kyle Pederson; Beckenhorst BP2272
SATB, piano, opt. instruments (https://bit.ly/BP-2272)
+"Sing Praise to God Who Reigns Above" (Isa 12)
Arr. Richard A. Williamson; Augsburg 9781506495378
2-part mixed, keyboard (https://bit.ly/Aug-95378)

+Hymn Anthem
"All Who Love and Serve Your City" 1277415 (2 Thess, Luke)
C670, CG674, E570/E571, EL724, G351, P413, UM433
This folk melody may be sung in a folk style by the soloists, with glides and scoops between some notes.
Introduction: Chimes (A flat, D flat) (or handbells, tone bars) play four dotted half notes. Continue this pattern throughout stanza 1.
Stanza 1: Woman soloist singing in a folk style. Bells continue.
Stanza 2: All S/A sing melody. Keyboard (organ) plays full setting. *Mezzo forte.*
Stanza 3: Tenor soloist sings a descant (S-1, #62) in a folk style. Accompany with full setting. *Mezzo forte.*
Stanza 4: All T/B sing melody. Bells play as in stanza 1. *Forte,* with strength.
Stanza 5: All voices, *forte.* A/B sing melody, S/T sing a descant (S-1, #62). Keyboard plays full setting. Continue chimes if desired.

Other Suggestions
Visuals:
O Space/earth, joy, building, grapes, work, wolf/lamb
P Worship, anger/comfort, arm, water/well, joy
E Idleness, bread, work, food
G Temple, toppled rock, Jesus, war, whip/chain, betrayal, hair
Introit: WS3047, st. 2. "God Almighty, We Are Waiting" (Isa) WS3047
Canticle: UM734. "Canticle of Hope" (Isa, Luke)
Confession: WSL90. "You asked for my hands" (2 Thess)
Prayer: UM409. For Grace to Labor (2 Thess)
Prayer: UM705. For Direction (2 Thess)
Prayer: N857. Renewal of Mission (Isa)
Prayer: N856. Eternal Life (Luke)
Alternate Lessons (see page 4): Mal. 4:1-2a, Ps. 98
Theme Ideas: Endurance, God: Kingdom of God, New Creation, Thanksgiving / Gratitude

Notes

NRSVue

Jeremiah 23:1-6

[1]Woe to the shepherds who destroy and scatter the sheep of
my pasture! says the LORD. [2]Therefore thus says the LORD, the
God of Israel, concerning the shepherds who shepherd my people: It is you who have scattered my flock and have driven them
away, and you have not attended to them. So I will attend to you
for your evil doings, says the LORD. [3]Then I myself will gather
the remnant of my flock out of all the lands where I have driven
them, and I will bring them back to their fold, and they shall be
fruitful and multiply. [4]I will raise up shepherds over them who
will shepherd them, and they shall no longer fear longer or be
dismayed, nor shall any be missing, says the LORD.

[5]The days are surely coming, says the LORD, when I will raise
up for David a righteous Branch, and he shall reign as king and
deal wisely and shall execute justice and righteousness in the
land. [6]In his days Judah will be saved, and Israel will live in safety.
And this is the name by which he will be called: "The LORD is
our righteousness."

Luke 1:68-79

[68]"Blessed be the Lord God of Israel,
for he has looked favorably on his people and redeemed
them.
[69]He has raised up a mighty savior for us
in the house of his child David,
[70]as he spoke through the mouth of his holy prophets from of
old,
71 that we would be saved from our enemies and from the hand
of all who hate us.
[72]Thus he has shown the mercy promised to our ancestors
and has remembered his holy covenant,
[73]the oath that he swore to our ancestor Abraham,
to grant us
[74]that we, being rescued from the hands of our enemies,
might serve him without fear,
[75]in holiness and righteousness
in his presence all our days.
[76]And you, child, will be called the prophet of the Most High;
for you will go before the Lord to prepare his ways,
[77]to give his people knowledge of salvation
by the forgiveness of their sins.
[78]Because of the tender mercy of our God,
the dawn from on high will break upon us,
[79]to shine upon those who sit in darkness and in the shadow of
death,
to guide our feet into the way of peace."

CEB

Jeremiah 23:1-6

[1]Watch out, you shepherds who destroy and scatter the sheep
of my pasture, declares the LORD. [2]This is what the LORD, the
God of Israel, proclaims about the shepherds who "tend to" my
people: You are the ones who have scattered my flock and driven
them away. You haven't attended to their needs, so I will take
revenge on you for the terrible things you have done to them,
declares the LORD. [3]I myself will gather the few remaining sheep
from all the countries where I have driven them. I will bring
them back to their pasture, and they will be fruitful and multiply.
[4]I will place over them shepherds who care for them. Then they
will no longer be afraid or dread harm, nor will any be missing,
declares the LORD.

[5]The time is coming, declares the LORD, when I will raise up
a righteous descendant from David's line, and he will rule as a
wise king. He will do what is just and right in the land. [6]During
his lifetime, Judah will be saved and Israel will live in safety. And
his name will be The LORD is Our Righteousness.

Luke 1:68-79

[68]"Bless the Lord God of Israel
because he has come to help and has delivered his people.
[69]He has raised up a mighty savior for us in his servant David's
house,
[70]just as he said through the mouths of his holy prophets long
ago.
[71]He has brought salvation from our enemies
and from the power of all those who hate us.
[72]He has shown the mercy promised to our ancestors,
and remembered his holy covenant,
73 the solemn pledge he made to our ancestor Abraham.
He has granted [74]that we would be rescued
from the power of our enemies
so that we could serve him without fear,
75 in holiness and righteousness in God's eyes,
for as long as we live.
[76]You, child, will be called a prophet of the Most High,
for you will go before the Lord to prepare his way.
[77]You will tell his people how to be saved
through the forgiveness of their sins.
[78]Because of our God's deep compassion,
the dawn from heaven will break upon us,
79 to give light to those who are sitting in darkness
and in the shadow of death,
to guide us on the path of peace."

NRSVue

Colossians 1:11-20

11May you be made strong with all the strength that comes
from his glorious power, so that you may have all endurance
patience, joyfully 12giving thanks to the Father, who has enabled
you to share in the inheritance of the saints in the light. 13He has
rescued us from the power of darkness and transferred us into
the kingdom of his beloved Son, 14in whom we have redemption,
the forgiveness of sins.

15He is the image of the invisible God, the firstborn of all
creation, 16for in him all things in heaven and on earth were
created, things visible and invisible, whether thrones or domin-
ions or rulers or powers—all things have been created through
him and for him. 17He himself is before all things, and in him all
things hold together. 18He is the head of the body, the church;
he is the beginning, the firstborn from the dead, so that he
might come to have first place in everything. 19For in him all the
fullness of God was pleased to dwell, 20and through him God was
pleased to reconcile to himself all things, whether on earth or in
heaven, by making peace through the blood of his cross.

Luke 23:33-43

33When they came to the place that is called The Skull, they
crucified Jesus there with the criminals, one on his right and
one on his left. 34Then Jesus said, "Father, forgive them, for they
do not know what they are doing." And they cast lots to divide
his clothing. 35And the people stood by watching, but the leaders
scoffed at him, saying, "He saved others; let him save himself if
he is the Messiah of God, his chosen one!" 36The soldiers also
mocked him, coming up and offering him sour wine 37and saying, "If you are the King of the Jews, save yourself!" 38There was
also an inscription over him, "This is the King of the Jews."

39One of the criminals who were hanged there kept deriding
him and saying, "Are you not the Messiah? Save yourself and us!"
40But the other rebuked him, saying, "Do you not fear God, since
you are under the same sentence of condemnation? 41And we
indeed have been condemned justly, for we are getting what we
deserve for our deeds, but this man has done nothing wrong."
42Then he said, "Jesus, remember me when you come into your
kingdom." 43He replied, "Truly I tell you, today you will be with
me in Paradise."

CEB

Colossians 1:11-20

11by being strengthened through his glorious might so that
you endure everything and have patience; 12and by giving thanks
with joy to the Father. He made it so you could take part in the
inheritance, in light granted to God's holy people. 13He rescued
us from the control of darkness and transferred us into the
kingdom of the Son he loves. 14He set us free through the Son
and forgave our sins.

15 The Son is the image of the invisible God,
    the one who is first over all creation,
16 Because all things were created by him:
    both in the heavens and on the earth,
    the things that are visible and the things that are invisible.
    Whether they are thrones or powers,
    or rulers or authorities,
    all things were created through him and for him.
17 He existed before all things,
    and all things are held together in him.
18 He is the head of the body, the church,
who is the beginning,
    the one who is firstborn from among the dead
    so that he might occupy the first place in everything.
19 Because all the fullness of God was pleased to live in him,
20 and he reconciled all things to himself through him—
    whether things on earth or in the heavens.
    He brought peace through the blood of his cross.

Luke 23:33-43

33When they arrived at the place called The Skull, they crucified him, along with the criminals, one on his right and the
other on his left. 34Jesus said, "Father, forgive them, for they
don't know what they're doing." They drew lots as a way of dividing up his clothing.

35The people were standing around watching, but the leaders
sneered at him, saying, "He saved others. Let him save himself if
he really is the Christ sent from God, the chosen one."

36The soldiers also mocked him. They came up to him offering him sour wine 37and saying, "If you really are the king of the
Jews, save yourself." 38Above his head was a notice of the formal
charge against him. It read "This is the king of the Jews."

39One of the criminals hanging next to Jesus insulted him,
"Aren't you the Christ? Save yourself and us!"

40Responding, the other criminal spoke harshly to him, "Don't
you fear God, seeing that you've also been sentenced to die?
41We are rightly condemned, for we are receiving the appropriate sentence for what we did. But this man has done nothing
wrong." 42Then he said, "Jesus, remember me when you come
into your kingdom."

43Jesus replied, "I assure you that today you will be with me in
paradise."

Primary Hymns and Songs for the Day

"Crown Him with Many Crowns" (Christ the King) (O)
C234, CG223. E494, EL855, G268, GR278, N301, P151, SH208, UM327 (PD), VU211
"Blessed Be the God of Israel" 860627 (Luke 1)
C135, CG88, E444, EL250/552, G109, P602, UM209, VU901
"Jesus, Remember Me" OL-00122 (Luke)
C569, CG393, EL616, G227, P599, SH175, UM488, VU148
"Jesus Shall Reign" 1510 (Christ the King) (C)
C95, CG158, E544, EL434, G265, GR282, N300, P423, SH209, UM157 (PD), VU330
H-3 Hbl-29, 57, 58; Chr-117; Desc-31; Org-31
S-1 #100-103. Various treatments.

Additional Hymn Suggestions

"How Great Thou Art" 14181 (Jer)
C33, CG323, EL856, G625, GR32, N35, P467, SH14, UM77, VU238 (Fr.)
"How Firm a Foundation" 107816 (Jer)
C618, CG425, E636, EL796, G463, GR46, N407, P361, SH291, UM529 (PD), VU660
"O Worship the King" (Luke 1)
C17, CG52, E388, EL842, G41, GR11, N26, P476, SH255, UM73 (PD), VU235
"You, Lord, Are Both Lamb and Shepherd" (Luke 1, Col)
G274, SH210, VU210, WS3043
"Immortal, Invisible, God Only Wise" 124466 (Col) (O)
C66, CG58, E423, EL834, G12, GR7, N1, P263, UM103 (PD), VU264 (*See also* ZS4)
"Holy God, We Praise Thy Name" 114555 (Col)
CG9, E366, EL414 (PD), G4, GR2, N276, P460, SH431, UM79, VU894 (Fr.)
"To God Be the Glory" (Col)
C72, CG349, G634, GR531, P485, SH545, UM98 (PD)
"In the Cross of Christ I Glory" 36499 (Col)
C207, CG183, E441/442, EL324, G213, GR239, N193, P84, UM295 (PD)
"God of Grace and God of Glory" 43107 (Col)
C464, CG285, E594/595, EL705, G307, GR45, N436, P420, SH250, UM577, VU686
"Come, Share the Lord" (Col, Comm.)
C408, CG459, G510, S2269, VU469
"Blessed Quietness" (Col, Luke 23)
C267, CG244, N284 (PD), S2142, Z206
"Beneath the Cross of Jesus" (Col, Luke 23)
C197, CG184, E498, EL338, G216, GR248, N190, P92, SH166, UM297 (PD), VU135
"Jesus, Keep Me Near the Cross" (Col, Luke 23)
C587, CG642, EL335, GR241, N197, UM301 (PD), VU142, Z19
"Victory in Jesus" (Col, Luke 23)
CG627, GR119, UM370
"When Jesus Wept" (Luke 23)
C199, E715, G194, N192, P312, S2106, VU146
+"All Praise to Thee, for Thou, O King Divine" (Christ the King)
CG352, E477, GR281, UM166, VU327
"Jesús Es Mi Rey Soberano" ("O Jesus, My King and My Sovereign") (Christ the King)
C109, P157, SH211, UM180
"Ye Servants of God" 90765 (Christ the King)
C110, CG420, E535, EL825 (PD), G299, GR40, N305, P477, UM181 (PD), VU342
+"Hail to the Lord's Anointed" (PD) (Christ the King)
C140, CG98, E616, EL311, G149, GR165, N104, P205, SH112, UM203, VU30
+"Lead On, O King Eternal" (Christ the King)
C632, CG63, E555, EL805, G269, GR478, N573, P447/448, UM580
"Rejoice, the Lord Is King" 36592 (Christ the King)
C699, CG215, E481, EL430, G363, GR277, N303, P155, SH213, UM715/716, VU213

Additional Contemporary and Modern Suggestions

"Foundation" 706151 (Jer)
"I Have a Hope" 5087587 (Jer, Luke 1)
+"Let Justice Roll" ("Like a River") 4974842 (Jer, Luke 1, Christ the King)
+"The Kingdom Is Yours" 7109354 (Jer, Luke 1, Col, Luke 23, Christ the King)
+"Daughters of Zion" 7133716 (Jer, Luke 23, Christ the King)
"Siyahamba" ("We Are Marching") 1321512 (Luke 1)
C442, CG155, EL866, G853, N526, S2235-ab, SH717, VU646, ZS111
"Shine, Jesus, Shine" 30426 (Luke 1)
CG156, EL671, G192, GR217, S2173, SH102; V-3 (2), p. 48. Vocal Solo
+"Walking in the Light of God" No SS (Luke 1)
"Here I Am to Worship" 3266032 (Luke 1, Christ the King)
CG297, SH395, WS3177, ZS145
"Shine on Us" 1754646 (Luke 1)
"Hear our Praises" 2543402 (Luke 1)
"Everyday" 2798154 (Luke 1)
"Marvelous Light" 4491002 (Luke 1, Col)
+"Carry the Light" 126402 (Luke 1, Col)
+"You Keep Hope Alive" 7125876 (Luke 1, Col)
+"Freedom" 7078151 (Luke 1, Col)
+"Tremble" 7065049 (Luke 1, Col, Christ the King)
"You are the Light" 6238098 (Luke 1, Col, Luke 23)
+"Freedom Is Coming" 4194244 (Col, Christ the King)
G359, S2192, SH29, ZS110
+"O Freedom" OL-68414 (Col, Christ the King)
S2194 (PD-TO), Z102, ZS109
"Across the Lands" 3709898 (Col, Christ the King)
SH654, WS3032
"Came to My Rescue" 4705190 (Col, Luke 23)
"Here at the Cross" 7046292 (Luke 23)
"Awesome God" 41099 (Luke 23, Christ the King)
G616, S2040, ZS7
"The Power of the Cross" 4490766 (Luke 23, Christ the King)
CG190, GR237, WS3085
"Our God Reigns" 8458 (Luke 23, Christ the King)
"Blessing, Honour and Glory" 1001179 (Luke 23, Christ the King)
EL433
+"Majesty" 1527 (Christ the King)
CG346, GR63, SH212, UM176
"You Are Worthy" (*"Eres Digno"*) (Christ the King)
S2063
"All Hail King Jesus" 12877 (Christ the King)
S2069, ZS53
"King of Kings" 23952 (Christ the King)
S2075, VU167
"The King of Glory Comes" OL-81352 (Christ the King)
CG177, S2091, SH206
"Hosanna" 4785835 (Christ the King)
SH361, WS3188
"Crown Him King of Kings" 206009 (Luke 23, Christ the King)
"My Savior Lives" 4882965 (Luke 23, Christ the King)
"Forever Reign" 5639997 (Luke 23, Christ the King)
"The Highest and the Greatest" 4769758 (Christ the King)
"Prepare Ye the Way" 5286041 (Luke 1, Christ the King)
+"This Kingdom" 1650898 (Christ the King)
+"King of Kings" 7127647 (Christ the King)

Solo/Ensemble Suggestions

+"The People That Walked in Darkness" (aria) (Luke 1)
V-2
+"God Will Make a Way" (with "He Leadeth Me") (Luke 1, Col)
V-3 (2) p. 9
+"You Keep Hope Alive" (Luke 1, Col, Luke 23)
V-9 p. 132
+"Holy is the Lamb" (Luke 23)
V-5(1) p. 5
+"God Is the Lord of All" (Pss)
Handel/arr. Hopson; AEC-2 p. 55
2-part mixed, keyboard, opt. tpt (https://bit.ly/AEC-2-55)
"*Sizohamba Naye*" ("We Will Walk with God") (Luke 1)
arr. Terry Taylor; Choristers Guild CGA-1250
Unison (opt. SATB), piano (https://bit.ly/CGA-1250)

+Hymn Anthem

"Hail, Thou Once Despised Jesus" (Luke 23)
E495, GR271, UM325 (PD)
Introduction: Keyboard (organ) plays hymnal setting, measures 1-4. *Mezzo forte.*
Stanza 1: All voices, unison or in parts, *a cappella* or accompanied, sing measures 1-4. If *a cappella*, keyboard joins at measure 5 and plays to end of stanza. *Mezzo forte.*
Interlude: Keyboard plays S-1, #178 or another harmonization, measures 1-4, but without pedal line. *Mezzo piano.*
Stanza 2: S/A sing melody in measures 1-8. Keyboard may play S-1, #178 without pedal part. T/B sing measures 9-12. Keyboard continues without pedal part. All voices sing measures 13-16 and keyboard plays full setting of S-1, #178. This stanza is *mezzo piano.*
Stanza 3: Soloist sings this stanza. Keyboard plays S-1, #179 or another harmonization. *Mezzo forte.*
Stanza 4: All voices, unison. Keyboard plays full setting of S-1, #178. *Mezzo forte.*
Ending: While keyboard hold the last chord of S-1, #178, choir sings stanza 1, measures 1-4, in parts or unison. Keyboard joins choir on measures 3-4. *Ritard* and *fortissimo.*

Other Suggestions

For Thanksgiving Sunday, see Thanksgiving Day suggestions.
Visuals: Crown, Christus Rex
O Scattered/herding sheep, today's shepherds, branch
P Christus Rex, rescue, service, child, dawn, feet
E Glory, joy, light/dark, rescue, creation, Christ
G Skull, blood/lots/cross/clothes, INRI, wine, Luke 23:42
Introit: WS3047, st. 2. "God Almighty, We Are Waiting" (Jer)
Canticle: UM205 (Col) or UM208 (Luke 1)
Canticle: C137, UM208, VU900. "Zechariah" (Luke 1)
Greeting: N822 (Luke 1)
Prayer of Confession: N835 (Jer
Prayer: N853. Peace (Luke 1, Col)
Affirmation of Faith: WSL76. "We believe in one God" (Col)
Sung Confession: WS3084. "O Christ, You Hang upon a Cross" (Luke 23)
Prayer: UM466. An Invitation to Christ (Luke, Christ the King)
Prayer: UM721 (Christ the King)
Prayer: WSL34. "Enlighten our hearts" (Col)
Prayer of Thanksgiving: WSL63. "Our hearts are full" (Christ the King)
Prayers of the People: WSL26. "Jesus, remember us" (Luke 23)
+Sung Benediction: EL538, G747, S2184, SH718. *"Enviado Soy de Dios"* ("Sent Out in Jesus' Name") 6290823 (Jer, Col, Christ the King)
Alternate Lessons (see page 4): Jer. 23:1-6; Ps. 46
Theme Ideas: Cross, Jesus: Return and Reign, Justice, Peace

Notes

NRSVue

Deuteronomy 26:1-11

1“When you have come into the land that the LORD your God
is giving you as an inheritance to possess and you possess it and
settle in it, 2you shall take some of the first of all the fruit of the
ground, which you harvest from the land that the LORD your
God is giving you, and you shall put it in a basket and go to the
place that the LORD your God will choose as a dwelling for his
name. 3You shall go to the priest who is in office at that time
and say to him, ‘Today I declare to the LORD your God that I
have come into the land that the LORD swore to our ancestors to
give us.’ 4When the priest takes the basket from your hand and
sets it down before the altar of the LORD your God, 5you shall
make this response before the LORD your God: ‘A wandering
Aramean was my ancestor; he went down into Egypt and lived
there as an alien, few in number, and there he became a great
nation, mighty and populous. 6When the Egyptians treated us
harshly and afflicted us, by imposing hard labor on us, 7we cried
to the LORD, the God of our ancestors; the LORD heard our
voice and saw our affliction, our toil, and our oppression. 8The
LORD brought us out of Egypt with a mighty hand and an outstretched arm, with a terrifying display of power, and with signs
and wonders; 9and he brought us into this place and gave us this
land, a land flowing with milk and honey. 10So now I bring the
first of the fruit of the ground that you, O LORD, have given me.’
You shall set it down before the LORD your God and bow down
before the LORD your God. 11Then you, together with the Levites
and the aliens who reside among you, shall celebrate with all
the bounty that the LORD your God has given to you and to your
house.”

Psalm 100 (G385, N688, P220, UM821)

1Make a joyful noise to the LORD, all the earth.
 2Serve the LORD with gladness;
 come into his presence with singing.
3Know that the LORD is God.
 It is he who made us, and we are his;
 we are his people and the sheep of his pasture.
4Enter his gates with thanksgiving
 and his courts with praise.
 Give thanks to him; bless his name.
5For the LORD is good;
 his steadfast love endures forever
 and his faithfulness to all generations.

CEB

Deuteronomy 26:1-11

1Once you have entered the land the LORD your God is giving
you as an inheritance, and you take possession of it and are settled there, 2take some of the early produce of the fertile ground
that you have harvested from the land the LORD your God is giving you, and put it in a basket. Then go to the location the LORD
your God selects for his name to reside. 3Go to the priest who is
in office at that time and say to him: “I am declaring right now
before the LORD my God that I have indeed arrived in the land
the LORD swore to our ancestors to give us.”

4The priest will then take the basket from you and place it
before the LORD your God’s altar. 5Then you should solemnly
state before the LORD your God:

“My father was a starving Aramean. He went down to Egypt,
living as an immigrant there with few family members, but that
is where he became a great nation, mighty and numerous. 6The
Egyptians treated us terribly, oppressing us and forcing hard
labor on us. 7So we cried out for help to the LORD, our ancestor’s God. The LORD heard our call. God saw our misery, our
trouble, and our oppression. 8The LORD brought us out of Egypt
with a strong hand and an outstretched arm, with awesome
power, and with signs and wonders. 9He brought us to this place
and gave us this land—a land full of milk and honey. 10So now
I am bringing the early produce of the fertile ground that you,
LORD, have given me.”

Set the produce before the LORD your God, bowing down
before the LORD your God. 11Then celebrate all the good things
the LORD your God has done for you and your family—each
one of you along with the Levites and the immigrants who are
among you.

Psalm 100 (G385, N688, P220, UM821)

1Shout triumphantly to the LORD, all the earth!
2 Serve the LORD with celebration!
 Come before him with shouts of joy!
3Know that the LORD is God—
 he made us; we belong to him.
 We are his people,
 the sheep of his own pasture.
4Enter his gates with thanks;
 enter his courtyards with praise!
 Thank him! Bless his name!
5Because the LORD is good,
 his loyal love lasts forever;
 his faithfulness lasts generation after generation.

NRSVue

Philippians 4:4-9

[4]Rejoice in the Lord always; again I will say, Rejoice. [5]Let your gentleness be known to everyone. The Lord is near. [6]Do not be anxious about anything, but in everything by prayer and supplication with thanksgiving let your requests be made known to God. [7]And the peace of God, which surpasses all understanding, will guard your hearts and your minds in Christ Jesus.

[8]Finally, brothers and sisters, whatever is true, whatever is honorable, whatever is just, whatever is pure, whatever is pleasing, whatever is commendable, if there is any excellence and if there is anything worthy of praise, think about these things. [9]As for the things that you have learned and received and heard and noticed in me, do them, and the God of peace will be with you.

John 6:25-35

[25]When they found him on the other side of the sea, they said to him, "Rabbi, when did you come here?" [26]Jesus answered them, "Very truly, I tell you, you are looking for me not because you saw signs but because you ate your fill of the loaves. [27]Do not work for the food that perishes but for the food that endures for eternal life, which the Son of Man will give you. For it is on him that God the Father has set his seal." [28]Then they said to him, "What must we do to perform the works of God?" [29]Jesus answered them, "This is the work of God, that you believe in him whom he has sent." [30]So they said to him, "What sign are you going to give us, then, so that we may see it and believe you? What work are you performing? [31]Our ancestors ate the manna in the wilderness, as it is written, 'He gave them bread from heaven to eat.'" [32]Then Jesus said to them, "Very truly, I tell you, it was not Moses who gave you the bread from heaven, but it is my Father who gives you the true bread from heaven. [33]For the bread of God is that which comes down from heaven and gives life to the world." [34]They said to him, "Sir, give us this bread always."

[35]Jesus said to them, "I am the bread of life. Whoever comes to me will never be hungry, and whoever believes in me will never be thirsty."

CEB

Philippians 4:4-9

[4]Be glad in the Lord always! Again I say, be glad! [5]Let your gentleness show in your treatment of all people. The Lord is near. [6]Don't be anxious about anything; rather bring up all of your requests to God in your prayers and petitions, along with giving thanks. [7]Then the peace of God that exceeds all understanding will keep your hearts and minds safe in Christ Jesus.

[8]From now on, brothers and sisters, if anything is excellent and if anything is admirable, focus your thoughts on these things: all that is true, all that is holy, all that is just, all that is pure, all that is lovely, and all that is worthy of praise. [9]Practice these things: whatever you learned, received, heard, or saw in us. The God of peace will be with you.

John 6:25-35

[25]When they found him on the other side of the lake, they asked him, "Rabbi, when did you get here?"

[26]Jesus replied, "I assure you that you are looking for me not because you saw miraculous signs but because you ate all the food you wanted. [27]Don't work for the food that doesn't last but for the food that endures for eternal life, which the Human One will give you. God the Father has confirmed him as his agent to give life."

[28]They asked, "What must we do in order to accomplish what God requires?"

[29]Jesus replied, "This is what God requires, that you believe in him whom God sent."

[30]They asked, "What miraculous sign will you do, that we can see and believe you? What will you do? [31]Our ancestors ate manna in the wilderness, just as it is written, *He gave them bread from heaven to eat.*"

[32]Jesus told them, "I assure you, it wasn't Moses who gave the bread from heaven to you, but my Father gives you the true bread from heaven. [33]The bread of God is the one who comes down from heaven and gives life to the world."

[34]They said, "Sir, give us this bread all the time!"

[35]Jesus replied, "I am the bread of life. Whoever comes to me will never go hungry, and whoever believes in me will never be thirsty."

Primary Hymns and Songs for the Day

"Come, Ye Thankful People, Come" 50200 (Deut, Pss) (O)
C718, CG372, E290, EL693, G367, GR83, N422, P551, SH355, UM694 (PD), VU516
H-3 Hbl-54; Chr-58; Desc-94; Org-137
S-1 #302-303. Harms. with desc.

"All People That on Earth Do Dwell" (Pss)
C18, CG331, E377/378, EL883, G385, GR662, N7, P220, SH416, UM75 (PD), VU822 (Fr.)
H-3 Hbl-45; Chr-24; Desc-84, 85; Org-107
S-1 #257-259. Various treatments
S-2 #140. Desc.

"Now Thank We All Our God" 86638 (Pss)
C715, CG371, E396/397, EL839/840, G643, GR84, N419, P555, SH485, UM102 (PD), VU236 (Fr.)
H-3 Hbl-78; Chr-140; Desc-81; Org-98
S-1 #252-254. Various treatments

"Rejoice, Ye Pure in Heart" (Phil)
C15, CG312, E556/557, EL873/874, G804, GR62, N55/71, P145/146, UM160/161
H-3 Hbl-17, 90; Chr-166; Desc-73; Org-85
S-1 #228. Desc.

"Kum Ba Yah" 2749763 (Phil)
C561/590, G472 (PD), P338, UM494, Z139

"For the Beauty of the Earth" 43200 (John)
C56, CG341, E416, EL879, G14, GR82, P473, N28, SH21, UM92 (PD), VU226

"Guide Me, O Thou Great Jehovah" 1448 (Deut, John) (C)
C622, CG33, E690, EL618, G65, GR47, N18, P281, SH51, UM127 (PD), VU651 (Fr.)
H-3 Hbl-25, 51, 58; Chr-89; Desc-26; Org-23
S-1 #76-77. Desc. and harm.

Additional Hymn Suggestions

"What Gift Can We Bring" 216549 (Deut)
CG533, N370, UM87

+"We Gather Together" (Deut, Thanks.)
C276, CG61, G336, GR81, N421, P559, SH391, UM131

+"Great Is Thy Faithfulness" 18723 (Deut)
C86, CG48, EL733, G39, GR44, N423, P276, SH48, UM140, VU288

"God Be with You till We Meet Again" (Deut) (C)
C434, CG523, EL536, G541, GR688, N81, UM672 (PD), VU422, Z37

"God Be with You Till We Meet Again" (Deut (C)
G542, P540, UM673 (PD), VU423

"O God Beyond All Praising" (Deut)
CG366, EL880, S2009, VU256

"Praise God for This Holy Ground" (Deut, Thanks)
G405, WS3009

"Hope of the World" 643002 (Phil)
C538, E472, G734, N46, P360, UM178, VU215

"Take My Life, and Let It Be" 1390 (Phil) (C)
C609, CG490, E707, EL583/EL685, G697, GR586, P391, N448, SH627/628, UM399 (PD), VU506

"What a Friend We Have in Jesus" (Phil)
C585, CG409, EL742, G465, GR116, N506, P403, SH585/586, UM526 (PD), VU661

"Rejoice, the Lord Is King" 36592 (Phil)
C699, CG215, E481, EL430, G363, GR277, N303, P155, SH213, UM715/716, VU213

"Lord of All Hopefulness" 5579875 (Phil)
CG678, E482, EL765, G683, S2197, SH464

"My Life Flows On" (Phil, Thanks)
C619, CG592, EL763, G821, N476, S2212, VU716

"As Those of Old Their First Fruits Brought" 3468397 (John)
CG667, E705, G712, P414, VU518

"For the Fruits of This Creation" (John)
C714, CG376, E424, EL679, G36, GR85, N425, P553, UM97, VU227

"For the Healing of the Nations" 1510804 (John)
C668, CG698, G346, N576, UM428, VU678

"God the Sculptor of the Mountains" (John)
EL736, G5, S2060

"The Lily of the Valley" (John, Thanks)
CG624, GR142, S2062

"Gather Us In" OL-00031 (John, Thanks)
C284, EL532, G401, S2236, SH393

"Father, We Thank You" (John, Thanks)
E302/E303, EL478, GR394, SH686, UM563/565

"Eat This Bread" OL-00891 (John, Comm.)
C414, EL472, G527, N788, SH671, UM628, VU466

"You Satisfy the Hungry Heart" 84788 (John, Comm.)
C429, CG468, EL484, G523, P521, SH672, UM629, VU478

"Let All Things Now Living" 171701 (Thanks)
C717, CG379, EL881, G37, GR636, P554, S2008, SH23, VU242

"Praise Our God Above" (Thanks)
N424, P480, S2061

+"God of Great and God of Small" (Thanks)
G19, WS3033

Additional Contemporary and Modern Suggestions

"We Bring the Sacrifice of Praise" 9990 (Deut)
S2031, ZS213

"Blessed Be Your Name" 3798438 (Deut, Thanks)
SH449, WS3002

"Forever" 3148428 (Deut, Pss)
CG53, WS3023

+"Do It Again" 7067555 (Deut, Pss)

+"Promises" 6454250 (Deut, Pss)

+"Promises" 7149439 (Deut, Pss)

+"Great Things" 7111321 (Deut, Pss)

+"God, You're So Good" 7105729 (Pss)

+"Goodness of God" 7117726 (Pss)

"In the Lord I'll Be Ever Thankful" (Pss)
G654, S2195, SH316

"Grateful" 7023348 (Pss, Thanks.)

+"I Thank You for It All" No SS (Pss, Phil, Thanks)
https://bit.ly/ForItAll

+"Your Love, Oh Lord" 1894255 (Pss, John)

"Hallelujah" ("Your Love Is Amazing") 3091812 (Pss, John)
WS3027

"Jubilate Servite" ("Come, Rejoice in God") OL-31172 (Pss, Phil)
S2017

"Wait for the Lord" OL-00172 (Phil)
CG644, EL262, G90, SH580, VU22, WS3049

"In God Alone" OL-87508 (Phil)

"I Will Give Thanks" 6266091 (Phil, Thanks.)

"How Can I Keep from Singing" 4822372 (Phil)

"Halle, Halle, Halleluja" 2659190 (John, Thanks.)
C41, CG433, EL172, G591, N236, S2026, SH694, VU958, ZS76

"Fill My Cup, Lord" 15946 (John, Comm.)
C351, UM641 *(refrain only)*, WS3093

"There Will Be Bread" 4512352 (John, Comm.)

+"Reamo Leboga" ("To God Our Thanks We Give") (Thanks.)
EL682, https://bit.ly/ELW682

+"Thank You, Lord" 865000 (Thanks)
C531, SH496, UM84, Z228

+"Give Thanks" 20285 (Thanks.)
C528, CG373, G647, S2036, SH489, ZS127

+*"Tino tenda, Jesu"* ("Thank You, Jesus") OL-94999 (Thanks.)
S2081

"I Thank You, Jesus" OL-87176 (Thanks.)
C116, N41, WS3037, ZS124

Solo/Ensemble Suggestions

"Maybe the Rain" (Deut, John)
V-5 (2) p. 27
+"Make a Joyful Noise" (Pss, Thanks)
V-3 (5) p. 44
+"This Is the Time I Must Sing" (Pss, Thanks)
V-8 p. 45
"Life Indeed" (John, Comm.)
V-8 p. 271
"Now Thank We All Our God" (Thanks)
V-6 p. 8
"Thanks to God" (Thanks)
V-8 p. 296
"Jubilate Deo" (Pss, Thanks.)
Dale Wood; AEC-1 p. 36 (https://bit.ly/AEC-1)
2-part mixed, organ (SATB bit.ly/Augs-45779)
"Lord, Fill My Heart with Thankfulness" (Thanks.)
arr. Walter Krueger; AEC-3 p. 26
Unison, keyboard, opt. wind inst. (https://bit.ly/AEC-3)

+Hymn Anthem

"All People That on Earth Do Dwell" #75 (Pss)
C18, CG331, E377/378, EL883, G385, GR662, N7, P220, SH416, UM75 (PD), VU822 (Fr.)

Introduction: Keyboard plays Measures 1-2, through "earth do dwell." *Mezzo forte.*

Stanza 1: Choir sings in parts (or unison or S/A sing soprano part and T/B sing tenor part), *a cappella* or accompanied.

Stanza 2: S/A sing this stanza, unison, *mezzo piano.* Keyboard plays S-1, #257 or another alternate harmonization.

Stanza 3: Basses sing bass part, tenors sings melody, altos sing alto part, and sopranos sing the tenor part one octave higher (or perform as in stanza 1). *A cappella* or accompanied. *Mezzo forte.*

Stanza 4: All voices (and congregation), unison and *forte.* Keyboard plays S-1, #258 or another alternate harmonization. (Pianist may omit the middle line of #258 since it only doubles the melody being sung by the choir.) End *forte.*

Other Suggestions

Visuals: cornucopia, fruit, vegetables, etc.
O Produce, harvest, basket, altar, bricks, manacles
P Praise, singing, sheep, gates
E Rejoicing, Phil. 4:6, praying hands, Christ, Phil. 4:7
G Jesus teaching, loaves, John 6:27, manna, John 6:35

Call to Worship: WS3148, ZS103. "There's a Spirit of Love" (Phil)
Opening Prayer: WSL55. "Almight God, you sustained" (John)
Opening Prayer: C771 (John)
Prayer: N858. Providence of God (Deut, Thanks.)
Canticle: UM74. "Canticle of Thanksgiving (Pss)
Prayer: WSL203. "God of all nations" (Thanks.)
Communion Prayer: WSL81. "Creator God, how lovely" (John)
Offertory Prayer: WSL153. "Exalted one, we joyfully rejoice" (Pss)
Response: G635, WS3007. *"Laudate Dominum"* (Pss)
Prayer After Communion: WSL174. "We have gathered" (John)
Closing Prayer: WSL169. "As you have been fed" (John)
Sung Benediction: "Give Us Your Peace" 5767807 (Phil)
Theme Ideas: Bread of Life, God: Hunger / Thirst for God, Jesus: Mind of Christ, Peace, Praise, Stewardship, Thanksgiving / Gratitude

Notes

NRSVue

Isaiah 2:1-5

1The word that Isaiah son of Amoz saw concerning Judah and
Jerusalem.
2In days to come
the mountain of the Lord's house
shall be established as the highest of the mountains
and shall be raised above the hills;
all the nations shall stream to it.
3Many peoples shall come and say,
"Come, let us go up to the mountain of the LORD,
to the house of the God of Jacob,
that he may teach us his ways
and that we may walk in his paths."
For out of Zion shall go forth instruction
and the word of the LORD from Jerusalem.
4He shall judge between the nations
and shall arbitrate for many peoples;
they shall beat their swords into plowshares
and their spears into pruning hooks;
nation shall not lift up sword against nation;
neither shall they learn war any more.
5O house of Jacob,
come, let us walk
in the light of the LORD!

Psalm 122 (G400, N705, P235, UM845)

1I was glad when they said to me,
"Let us go to the house of the LORD!"
2Our feet are standing
within your gates, O Jerusalem.
3Jerusalem—built as a city
that is bound firmly together.
4To it the tribes go up,
the tribes of the LORD,
as was decreed for Israel,
to give thanks to the name of the LORD.
5For there the thrones for judgment were set up,
the thrones of the house of David.
6Pray for the peace of Jerusalem:
"May they prosper who love you.
7Peace be within your walls
and security within your towers."
8For the sake of my relatives and friends
I will say, "Peace be within you."
9For the sake of the house of the LORD our God,
I will seek your good.

CEB

Isaiah 2:1-5

1This is what Isaiah, Amoz's son, saw concerning Judah and
Jerusalem.
2In the days to come
the mountain of the LORD's house
will be the highest of the mountains.
It will be lifted above the hills;
peoples will stream to it.
3Many nations will go and say,
"Come, let's go up to the LORD's mountain,
to the house of Jacob's God
so that he may teach us his ways
and we may walk in God's paths."
Instruction will come from Zion;
the LORD's word from Jerusalem.
4God will judge between the nations,
and settle disputes of mighty nations.
Then they will beat their swords into iron plows
and their spears into pruning tools.
Nation will not take up sword against nation;
they will no longer learn how to make war.
5 Come, house of Jacob,
let's walk by the LORD's light.

Psalm 122 (G400, N705, P235, UM845)

1I rejoiced with those who said to me,
"Let's go to the LORD's house!"
2Now our feet are standing
in your gates, Jerusalem!
3Jerusalem is built like a city
joined together in unity.
4That is where the tribes go up—
the LORD's tribes!
It is the law for Israel
to give thanks there to the LORD's name
5because the thrones of justice are there—
the thrones of the house of David!
6Pray that Jerusalem has peace:
"Let those who love you have rest.
7 Let there be peace on your walls;
let there be rest on your fortifications."
8For the sake of my family and friends,
I say, "Peace be with you, Jerusalem."
9For the sake of the
LORD our God's house
I will pray for your good.

NRSVue

Romans 13:11-14

[11]Besides this, you know what time it is, how it is already the
moment for you to wake from sleep. For salvation is nearer to us
now than when we became believers; [12]the night is far gone; the
day is near. Let us then throw off the works of darkness and put
on the armor of light; [13]let us walk decently as in the day, not in
reveling and drunkenness, not in illicit sex and licentiousness,
not in quarreling and jealousy. [14]Instead, put on the Lord Jesus
Christ, and make no provision for the flesh, to gratify its desires.

Matthew 24:36-44

[36]"But about that day and hour no one knows, neither the
angels of heaven, nor the Son, but only the Father. [37]For as the
days of Noah were, so will be the coming of the Son of Man.
[38]For as in those days before the flood they were eating and
drinking, marrying and giving in marriage, until the day Noah
entered the ark, [39]and they knew nothing until the flood came
and swept them all away, so, too, will be the coming of the Son
of Man. [40]Then two will be in the field; one will be taken, and
one will be left. [41]Two women will be grinding meal together;
one will be taken, and one will be left. [42]Keep awake, therefore,
for you do not know on what day your Lord is coming. [43]But
understand this: if the owner of the house had known in what
part of the night the thief was coming, he would have stayed
awake and would not have let his house be broken into. [44]There-
fore you also must be ready, for the Son of Man is coming at an
hour you do not expect."

CEB

Romans 13:11-14

[11]As you do all this, you know what time it is. The hour has
already come for you to wake up from your sleep. Now our
salvation is nearer than when we first had faith. [12]The night is
almost over, and the day is near. So let's get rid of the actions
that belong to the darkness and put on the weapons of light.
[13]Let's behave appropriately as people who live in the day, not in
partying and getting drunk, not in sleeping around and obscene
behavior, not in fighting and obsession. [14]Instead, dress yourself
with the Lord Jesus Christ, and don't plan to indulge your selfish
desires.

Matthew 24:36-44

[36]"But nobody knows when that day or hour will come, not
the heavenly angels and not the Son. Only the Father knows.
[37]As it was in the time of Noah, so it will be at the coming of
the Human One. [38]In those days before the flood, people were
eating and drinking, marrying and giving in marriage, until the
day Noah entered the ark. [39]They didn't know what was happening until the flood came and swept them all away. The coming
of the Human One will be like that. [40]At that time there will
be two men in the field. One will be taken and the other left.
[41]Two women will be grinding at the mill. One will be taken and
the other left. [42]Therefore, stay alert! You don't know what day
the Lord is coming. [43]But you understand that if the head of
the house knew at what time the thief would come, he would
keep alert and wouldn't allow the thief to break into his house.
[44]Therefore you also should be prepared, because the Human
One will come at a time you don't know."

Primary Hymns and Songs for the Day
"Come, Thou Long-Expected Jesus" 31999 (Rom, Matt) (O)
E66, N122, G83, P1 (PD), SH64, VU2
H-3 Hbl-81; Chr-147; Desc-99; Org-158
S-1 #324. Descant
C125, CG83, G82, GR163, P2, UM196 (PD)
H-3 Hbl-46; Chr-26, 134; Desc-53; Org-56
S-1 #168-171. Various treatments
EL254
"O God of Every Nation" (Isa)
C680, CG46, E607, EL713, G756, P289, UM435, VU677
"You, Lord, Are Both Lamb and Shepherd" (Isa)
G274, SH210, VU210. WS3043
"Prepare the Way of the Lord" OL-00142 (Isa)
C121, G95, UM207, VU10
"Dona Nobis Pacem" 4340610 (Pss, Comm.)
C296/297, E712, EL753, G752, UM376 (PD)
"O-So-So" ("Come Now, O Prince of Peace") OL-AF20201411 (Isa, Matt)
EL247, G103, S2232, SH235
"Welcome" OL-232386 (Pss)
WS3152 (*See also* EL641, G301)
"Let Us Build a House Where Love Can Dwell" (Pss)
EL641, G301, SH228 (*See also* WS3152)
"Watchman, Tell Us of the Night" (Rom)
E640, G97, N103, P20
"Soon and Very Soon" 11249 (Matt) (C)
CG562, EL439, G384, GR629, SH357, UM706, Z198, ZS136,
S-2 #187. Piano arr.
"Wake, Awake, for Night Is Flying" (Rom, Matt)
E61, EL436, G349, P17, UM720 (PD), VU711
H-3 Chr-174, 203; Org-172
"We've a Story to Tell to the Nations" (Isa) (C)
C484, CG427, GR458, UM569 (PD)

Additional Hymn Suggestions
+"Blessed Be the God of Israel" 860627 (Isa, Advent)
C135, CG88, E444, EL250/552, G109, P602, UM209, VU901
"O God of Every Nation" (Isa)
C680, CG46, E607, EL713, G756, P289, UM435, VU677
+"Lead On, O King Eternal" (Isa)
C632, CG63, E555, EL805, G269, GR478, N573, P447/448, UM580
"O Day of Peace That Dimly Shines" (Isa)
C711, E597, EL711, G373, P450, UM729, VU682
"O Day of God, Draw Nigh" (PD) (Isa)
C700, E601, N611, P452, UM730 (PD), VU688/689 (Fr.)
"O Holy City, Seen of John" (PD-TO) (Isa, Pss)
E582/583, G374, N613, P453, UM726, VU709
"I Want to Walk as a Child of the Light" (Isa, Rom)
CG96, E490, EL815, G377, GR216, SH352, UM206
"Lead Me, Guide Me" (Isa, Rom, Advent)
C583, CG403, EL768, G740, S2214, SH582, ZS173
+"God of Grace and God of Glory" 43107 (Isa, Rom)
C464, CG285, E594/595, EL705, G307, GR45, N436, P420, SH250, UM577, VU686
"Awake, My Soul, and with the Sun" (Isa, Rom)
E11, EL557 (PD), G663, GR54, P456
"All Who Love and Serve Your City" 1277415 (Isa, Matt)
C670, CG674, E570/571, EL724, G351, P413, UM433
"Come, We That Love the Lord" 84159 (Isa, Matt)
CG549, E392, GR38, N379, UM732, VU715
"Marching to Zion" 144398 (Isa, Matt)
C707, CG550, EL625, GR626, N382, UM733, VU714, Z3
"When Morning Gilds the Skies" 69033 (Rom)
C100, CG345, E427, EL853 (PD), G667, GR110, N86, P487, SH466, UM185, VU339 (Fr.)
"Awake, O Sleeper" (Rom, Comm.)
E547, EL452, GR390, UM551, VU566
"People, Look East" (Rom, Matt)
C142, CG90, EL248, G105, P12, UM202, VU9
"My Lord, What a Morning" (PD-TO) (Rom, Matt)
C708, EL438, G352, P449, SH356, UM719, VU708, Z145
"O Come, O Come, Emmanuel" 3063194 (Matt)
C119, CG79, E56, EL257, G88, GR162, N116, P9, SH73, UM211, VU1 (Fr.)
"Savior of the Nations, Come" (Matt)
E54, EL263, G102, P14 (PD), SH67, UM214
"O Lord, How Shall I Meet You?" (Matt)
EL241, G104, N102, P11, VU31
"The King Shall Come When Morning Dawns" (Matt)
CG97, E73, EL260, GR286, SH346

Additional Contemporary and Modern Suggestions
"How Great Is Our God" 4348399 (Isa)
CG322, GR31, SH458, WS3003
"Step by Step" 696994 (Isa)
CG495, G743, GR671, WS3004
+"King of Kings" 23952 (Isa, Advent)
S2075, VU167
+"You Keep Hope Alive" 7125876 (Isa, Advent)
+"I Have a Hope" 5087587 (Isa, Advent)
"Everyday" 2798154 (Isa)
"Marvelous Light" 4491002 (Isa)
+"The Kingdom Is Yours" 7109354 (Isa, Pss, Advent)
+"Another World" No SS (Isa, Pss, Advent)
https://bit.ly/AW-KMeyer
"Give Us Your Peace" 5767807 (Isa, Pss)
"Come True Light" 5767773 (Isa, Rom, Advent)
"Siyahamba" ("We Are Marching") 1321512 (Isa, Rom)
C442, CG155, EL866, G853, N526, S2235-ab, SH717, VU646, ZS111
"Lord Jesus Christ, Your Light Shines" (Isa, Rom)
SH556, WS3137
+"Walking in the Light of God" No SS (Isa, Rom)
WS3163
"Here I Am to Worship" 3266032 (Isa, Rom, Advent)
CG297, SH395, WS3177, ZS145
"I Will Enter His Gates" 1493 (Pss)
S2270
"In the Lord I'll Be Ever Thankful" OL-00118 (Pss)
G654, S2195, SH316
"Awaken" 5491647 (Rom)
"Salvation Is Here" 4451327 (Rom)
"Waiting Here for You" 5925663 (Rom, Advent)
"There's Something About That Name" 14064 (Matt)
C115, GR124, UM171
"Wait for the Lord" OL-00172 (Matt, Advent)
CG644, EL262, G90, SH580, VU22, WS3049
+"Behold Him" 7133698 (Advent)
+"King of Kings" 7127647 (Advent)

Solo/Ensemble Suggestions
"Peace, Perfect Peace" (Isa, Pss)
V-5 (1) p. 69
+"Alleluia, Sing to Jesus" (Rom, Matt, Advent)
V-3 (3) p. 50
"Come, Thou Long Expected Jesus" (Rom, Matt, Advent)
V-10 p. 11
"Stir Up Your Power" (Rom, Matt, Advent)
Linda Cable Shute; AEC-1 p. 59
2-part mixed, keyboard, opt. cong. (https://bit.ly/AEC-1-59)
"An Advent Acclamation" (Advent, Thanksgiving)
Stacey Nordmeyer; Shawnee Press HL35032140
2-part mixed, keyboard, handbells (https://bit.ly/HL-32140)

+Hymn Anthem

"Wake, Awake, O Sleeper" (Rom.)
"Awake, O Sleeper" OL-24269 (Rom)
E547, UM551, VU566
"Wake, Awake, for Night Is Flying" ("Sleepers, Wake")
E61, EL436, G349, P17, UM720 (PD), VU711

In this anthem, the choir sings portions of "Wake, Awake" and two soloists, the "prophetic watchers," sing portions of "Awake, O Sleeper." If possible, the soloists should be separated from the choir.

The choir will only need to read "Wake, Awake." UM720 is in the public domain. Therefore, you may make copies of this hymn from that hymnal for use by your choir.

This hymn is found with different translations and tunes in the hymnals. However, this anthem can be used with any of these versions with little adaptation.

Introduction: Keyboard (organ) plays "Awake, O Sleeper" through one time. *Mezzo piano.*

"Wake, Awake"
Choir sings measures 1-8, stanza 1. SATB, SAB, or unison. Keyboard plays full accompaniment. *Mezzo forte.*

"Awake, O Sleeper"
T/B soloist sings stanza 1. Keyboards plays full accompaniment. *Mezzo forte.*

"Wake, Awake"
Choir continues stanza 1, measures 9-16. SATB, SAB, or unison. Keyboard plays full accompaniment. *Mezzo forte.*

"Awake, O Sleeper"
A S/A soloist sings stanza 2. Keyboard plays accompaniment one octave higher than written, but omitting all melody notes. Play all notes on last three words ("bond of peace").

"Wake, Awake"
Choir sings remainder of stanza 1. Begin in unison and move to four parts after "Alleluia." Keyboard plays full accompaniment. End *forte.*

Ending: Keyboard plays "Awake, O Sleeper" again, but *piano.*

Other Suggestions

Visuals:
O Mountain/hills/nations, paths, scales/justice, light
P Ps. 122:1, feet/gates, Jerusalem, worship, wall/tower
E Alarm clock, dawn, dark/light, armor, Rom 13:14
G Clock, angels, Christ, Noah/ark/flood, one in field

+Introit: E537, GR450, UM568 (PD), Stanza 1. "Christ for the World We Sing" (Isa)
Introit: WS3047, st. 2. "God Almighty, We Are Waiting" (Isa, Rom, Matt)
Introit: C583, CG403, EL768, G740, S2214, SH582, ZS173. "Lead Me, Guide Me" (Matt, Advent)
Opening Prayer: WSL2 (Isa, Rom)
Call to Worship: N823 (Advent)
Advent Candle Response: C128 or G85 (Advent)
+Response: S2090, stanza 1. "Light the Advent Candle" (Advent)
Call to Confession: N832 (Advent)
Response: C111, CG3, EL473, G595, N793, S2007, SH452, ZS48. "Holy, Holy, Holy" (*"Santo"*)
Response: C119, CG79, E56, EL257, G88, GR162, N116, P9, SH73, UM211, VU1, stanza 1. "O Come, O Come Emmanuel" (Rom, Matt, Advent)
Call to Prayer: WS3046. "Come, O Redeemer, Come" (Advent)
Offertory Prayer: WSL152. "Father, John the Baptist" (Advent)
Theme Ideas: Jesus: Return and Reign, Peace, Preparation, Waiting

Notes

NRSVue

Isaiah 11:1-10
1A shoot shall come out from the stump of Jesse,
and a branch shall grow out of his roots.
2The spirit of the LORD shall rest on him,
the spirit of wisdom and understanding,
the spirit of counsel and might,
the spirit of knowledge and the fear of the LORD.
3His delight shall be in the fear of the LORD.
He shall not judge by what his eyes see,
or decide by what his ears hear,
4but with righteousness he shall judge the poor
and decide with equity for the oppressed of the earth;
he shall strike the earth with the rod of his mouth,
and with the breath of his lips he shall kill the wicked.
5Righteousness shall be the belt around his waist
and faithfulness the belt around his loins.
6The wolf shall live with the lamb;
the leopard shall lie down with the kid;
the calf and the lion will feed together,
and a little child shall lead them.
7The cow and the bear shall graze;
their young shall lie down together;
and the lion shall eat straw like the ox.
8The nursing child shall play over the hole of the asp,
and the weaned child shall put its hand on the adder's den.
9They will not hurt or destroy
on all my holy mountain,
for the earth will be full of the knowledge of the LORD
as the waters cover the sea.
10On that day the root of Jesse shall stand as a signal to the
peoples; the nations shall inquire of him, and his dwelling shall
be glorious.

Psalm 72:1-7, 18-19 (G149, N667, P205, UM795)
1Give the king your justice, O God,
and your righteousness to a king's son.
2May he judge your people with righteousness
and your poor with justice.
3May the mountains yield prosperity for the people,
and the hills, in righteousness.
4May he defend the cause of the poor of the people,
give deliverance to the needy,
and crush the oppressor.
5May he live while the sun endures
and as long as the moon, throughout all generations.
6May he be like rain that falls on the mown grass,
like showers that water the earth.
7In his days may righteousness flourish
and peace abound, until the moon is no more.
. . . .
18Blessed be the LORD, the God of Israel,
who alone does wondrous things.
19Blessed be his glorious name forever;
may his glory fill the whole earth.
Amen and Amen.

CEB

Isaiah 11:1-10
1A shoot will grow up from the stump of Jesse;
a branch will sprout from his roots.
2The LORD's spirit will rest upon him,
a spirit of wisdom and understanding,
a spirit of planning and strength,
a spirit of knowledge and fear of the LORD.
3He will delight in fearing the LORD.
He won't judge by appearances,
nor decide by hearsay.
4He will judge the needy with righteousness,
and decide with equity for those who suffer in the land.
He will strike the violent with the rod of his mouth;
by the breath of his lips he will kill the wicked.
5Righteousness will be the belt around his hips,
and faithfulness the belt around his waist.
6The wolf will live with the lamb,
and the leopard will lie down with the young goat;
the calf and the young lion will feed together,
and a little child will lead them.
7The cow and the bear will graze.
Their young will lie down together,
and a lion will eat straw like an ox.
8A nursing child will play over the snake's hole;
toddlers will reach right over the serpent's den.
9They won't harm or destroy anywhere on my holy mountain.
The earth will surely be filled with the knowledge of the LORD,
just as the water covers the sea.
10On that day, the root of Jesse will stand as a signal to the
peoples. The nations will seek him out, and his dwelling will be
glorious.

Psalm 72:1-7, 18-19 (G149, N667, P205, UM795)
1God, give your judgments to the king.
Give your righteousness to the king's son.
2Let him judge your people with righteousness
and your poor ones with justice.
3Let the mountains bring peace to the people;
let the hills bring righteousness.
4Let the king bring justice to people who are poor;
let him save the children of those who are needy,
but let him crush oppressors!
5Let the king live as long as the sun,
as long as the moon,
generation to generation.
6Let him fall like rain upon fresh-cut grass,
like showers that water the earth.
7Let the righteous flourish throughout their lives,
and let peace prosper until the moon is no more.
. . . .
18Bless the LORD God, the God of Israel—
the only one who does wondrous things!
19Bless God's glorious name forever;
let his glory fill all the earth!
Amen and Amen!

NRSVue

Romans 15:4-13

4For whatever was written in former days was written for our
instruction, so that by steadfastness and by the encouragement
of the scriptures we might have hope. 5May the God of steadfastness and encouragement grant you to live in harmony with one
another, in accordance with Christ Jesus, 6so that together you
may with one voice glorify the God and Father of our Lord Jesus
Christ.

7Welcome one another, therefore, just as Christ has welcomed
you, for the glory of God. 8For I tell you that Christ has become
a servant of the circumcised on behalf of the truth of God in
order that he might confirm the promises given to the ancestors
9and that the gentiles might glorify God for his mercy. As it is
written,

"Therefore I will confess you among the gentiles
and sing praises to your name";

10and again he says,

"Rejoice, O gentiles, with his people";

11and again,

"Praise the Lord, all you gentiles,
and let all the peoples praise him";

12and again Isaiah says,

"The root of Jesse shall come,
the one who rises to rule the gentiles;
in him the gentiles shall hope."

13May the God of hope fill you with all joy and peace in believing, so that you may abound in hope by the power of the Holy
Spirit.

Matthew 3:1-12

1In those days John the Baptist appeared in the wilderness of
Judea, proclaiming, 2"Repent, for the kingdom of heaven has
come near." 3This is the one of whom the prophet Isaiah spoke
when he said,

"The voice of one crying out in the wilderness:
'Prepare the way of the Lord;
make his paths straight.' "

4Now John wore clothing of camel's hair with a leather belt
around his waist, and his food was locusts and wild honey. 5Then
Jerusalem and all Judea and all the region around the Jordan
were going out to him, 6and they were baptized by him in the
River Jordan, confessing their sins.

7But when he saw many of the Pharisees and Sadducees
coming for his baptism, he said to them, "You brood of vipers!
Who warned you to flee from the coming wrath? 8Therefore,
bear fruit worthy of repentance, 9and do not presume to say to
yourselves, 'We have Abraham as our ancestor,' for I tell you,
God is able from these stones to raise up children to Abraham.
10Even now the ax is lying at the root of the trees; therefore every
tree that does not bear good fruit will be cut down and thrown
into the fire.

11"I baptize you with water for repentance, but one who is
coming after me is more powerful than I, and I am not worthy
to carry his sandals. He will baptize you with the Holy Spirit and
fire. 12His winnowing fork is in his hand, and he will clear his
threshing floor and will gather his wheat into the granary, but
the chaff he will burn with unquenchable fire."

CEB

Romans 15:4-13

4Whatever was written in the past was written for our instruction so that we could have hope through endurance and
through the encouragement of the scriptures. 5May the God
of endurance and encouragement give you the same attitude
toward each other, similar to Christ Jesus' attitude. 6That way you
can glorify the God and Father of our Lord Jesus Christ together
with one voice.

7So welcome each other, in the same way that Christ also
welcomed you, for God's glory. 8I'm saying that Christ became a
servant of those who are circumcised for the sake of God's truth,
in order to confirm the promises given to the ancestors, 9and so
that the Gentiles could glorify God for his mercy. As it is written,

Because of this I will confess you among the Gentiles,
and I will sing praises to your name.

10And again, it says,

Rejoice, Gentiles, with his people.

11And again,

Praise the Lord, all you Gentiles,
and all the people should sing his praises.

12And again, Isaiah says,

There will be a root of Jesse,
who will also rise to rule the Gentiles.
The Gentiles will place their hope in him.

13May the God of hope fill you with all joy and peace in faith
so that you overflow with hope by the power of the Holy Spirit.

Matthew 3:1-12

1In those days John the Baptist appeared in the desert of
Judea announcing, 2"Change your hearts and lives! Here comes
the kingdom of heaven!" 3He was the one of whom Isaiah the
prophet spoke when he said:

The voice of one shouting in the wilderness,
"Prepare the way for the Lord;
make his paths straight."

4John wore clothes made of camel's hair, with a leather belt
around his waist. He ate locusts and wild honey.

5People from Jerusalem, throughout Judea, and all around
the Jordan River came to him. 6As they confessed their sins,
he baptized them in the Jordan River. 7Many Pharisees and
Sadducees came to be baptized by John. He said to them, "You
children of snakes! Who warned you to escape from the angry
judgment that is coming soon? 8Produce fruit that shows you
have changed your hearts and lives. 9And don't even think
about saying to yourselves, Abraham is our father. I tell you that
God is able to raise up Abraham's children from these stones.
10The ax is already at the root of the trees. Therefore, every
tree that doesn't produce good fruit will be chopped down and
tossed into the fire. 11I baptize with water those of you who have
changed your hearts and lives. The one who is coming after me
is stronger than I am. I'm not worthy to carry his sandals. He
will baptize you with the Holy Spirit and with fire. 12The shovel
he uses to sift the wheat from the husks is in his hands. He will
clean out his threshing area and bring the wheat into his barn.
But he will burn the husks with a fire that can't be put out."

Primary Hymns and Songs for the Day

"Hail to the Lord's Anointed" (PD) (Isa, Pss, Rom) (O)
C140, CG98, E616, EL311, G149, GR165, N104, P205, SH112, UM203, VU30
H-3 Hbl-16, 22, 68; Chr-101; Desc-37
S-1 #114. Desc.
#115. Harm.

"Lo, How a Rose E'er Blooming" (Isa)
C160, CG105, E81, EL272, G129, GR168, N127, P48 (PD), UM216, VU8
H-3 Chr-129; Org-38
S-2 #56-57. Various treatments

"Soon and Very Soon" 11249 (Isa)
CG562, EL439, G384, GR629, SH357, UM706, Z198, ZS136
S-2 #187. Piano arr.

"O Morning Star, How Fair and Bright" (Isa, Rom)
C105, E497, EL308, G827, N158, P69, UM247, VU98
H-3 Chr-147; Desc-104; Org-183

"Wild and Lone the Prophet's Voice" 3413029 (Matt)
G163, P409, S2089

"O Come, O Come, Emmanuel" 3063194 (Isa) (C)
C119, CG79, E56, EL257, G88, GR162, N116, P9, SH73, UM211, VU1(Fr.)
H-3 Hbl-14, 79; Chr-141; Org-168
S-1 #342. Handbell accompaniment

Additional Hymn Suggestions

"Isaiah the Prophet Has Written of Old" (Isa)
G77, N108, P337, VU680

"Who Would Think That What Was Needed" (Isa)
G138, N153

"I Come with Joy" (Isa, Comm.)
C420, CG456, E304, EL482, G515, N349, P507, SH682, UM617, VU477

+"O God of Every Nation" (Isa, Pss)
C680, CG46, E607, EL713, G756, P289, UM435, VU677

+"We've a Story to Tell to the Nations" (Isa, Pss)
C484, CG427, GR458, UM569 (PD)

"O Day of Peace That Dimly Shines" (Isa, Pss)
C711, E597, EL711, G373, P450, UM729, VU682

"O Day of God, Draw Nigh" (PD) (Isa, Pss)
C700, E601, N611, P452, UM730 (PD), VU688/689 (Fr.)

"Come, Thou Almighty King" 29073 (Isa, Pss)
C27, CG2, E365, EL408, G2, GR27, N275, P139, SH388, UM61 (PD), VU314

"Come, Thou Long-Expected Jesus" 31999 (Isa, Rom, Matt)
C125, CG83, E66, EL254, G82/83, GR163, N122, P1/2, SH64, UM196 (PD), VU2

"Savior of the Nations, Come" (Isa, Rom)
E54, EL263, G102, P14 (PD), SH67, UM214

"Blessed Be the God of Israel" 860627 (Isa, Matt)
C135, CG88, E444, EL250/552, G109, P602, UM209, VU901

"Toda la Tierra" ("All Earth Is Waiting") (Isa, Matt)
C139, EL266, N121, SH63, UM210, VU5

"Jesus Shall Reign" 1510 (Pss, Rom)
C95, CG158, E544, EL434, G265, GR282, N300, P423, SH209, UM157 (PD), VU330

"O For a World" (Rom)
C683, G372, N575, P386, VU697

"I Greet Thee, Who My Sure Redeemer Art" (Rom)
G624, GR41, N251, P457, VU393

"Jesus, the Very Thought of Thee" (Rom)
C102, CG386, E642, EL754, G629, GR127, N507, P310, UM175 (PD)

"Hope of the World" 643002 (Rom)
C538, E472, G734, N46, P360, UM178, VU215

"Help Us Accept Each Other" 133756 (Rom) (C)
C487, G754, N388, P358, UM560

"Jesus, United by Thy Grace" 4324227 (Rom, Comm.)
GR401, UM561 (PD), VU591

"Blessed Quietness" (Rom)
C267, CG244, N284 (PD), S2142, Z206

"Lord of All Hopefulness" 5579875 (Rom)
CG678, E482, EL765, G683, S2197, SH464

"On Jordan's Bank the Baptist's Cry" (Matt)
E76, EL249, G96, N115, P10, SH77, VU20

"Come, Holy Ghost, Our Souls Inspire" (Matt)
E503/504, N268, G278, P125, UM651, VU201

"God the Sculptor of the Mountains" (Matt)
EL736, G5, S2060

+"There's a Voice in the Wilderness" (Matt)
E75, EL255, N120, VU18

Additional Contemporary and Modern Suggestions

"Come, Emmanuel" 3999938 (Isa, Advent)
WS3130

+"Let Justice Roll" ("Like a River") 4974842 (Isa, Pss)

+"The Kingdom Is Yours" 7109354 (Isa, Pss, Rom)

+*"La Lucha"* ("The Struggle") OL-U01354 (Isa, Pss, Rom)
https://bit.ly/LaLucha-Miller

"Come True Light" 5767773 (Isa, Rom, Advent)

"I've Got Peace Like a River" (PD) (Isa, Rom)
C530, G623, N478, P368, S2145, SH276, VU577

"Give Us Your Peace" 5767807 (Isa, Rom)

+"Blessed Be the Name" 34525 (Pss)
CG350, GR67, UM63

"The King of Glory Comes" OL-81352 (Pss, Advent)
CG177, S2091, SH206

"Blessed Be Your Name" 3798438 (Pss)
SH449, WS3002

+"Holy Is the Lord" 4158039
WS3028

"Veni Sancte Spiritus" ("Holy Spirit, Come to Us") OL-TaizeVN57 (Pss, Matt)
EL406, G281, S2118

"Glorify Thy Name" 1383 (Rom)
CG8, S2016, SH427

"Canto de Esperanza" ("Song of Hope") 5193990 (Rom)
G765, P432, S2186, SH721, VU424

"Grace Alone" 2335524 (Rom)
CG43, S2162, ZS100

"Mighty to Save" 4591782 (Rom)
WS3038

+"You Keep Hope Alive" 7125876 (Rom)

"I Could Sing of Your Love Forever" 1043199 (Rom)

"Song of Hope" ("Heaven Come Down") 5111477 (Rom)

"Waiting Here for You" 5925663 (Rom, Matt, Advent)

"Spirit Song" 27824 (Rom, Matt)
C352, SH409, UM347

"Alleluia" 16811 (Matt)
C106, N765, SH699, UM186

"Jesus, Name above All Names" 21291 (Matt)
S2071, ZS27

"Breathe" 1874117 (Matt)
WS3112, ZS47

"I Will Never Be (the Same Again)" 1874911 (Matt)

"Refiner's Fire" 426298 (Matt)

"Prepare Ye the Way" 5286041 (Matt)

+"Prepare the Way" 7136724 (Matt)

+"Wesley Prayer" ("Fire") 7118633 (Matt)

Solo/Ensemble Suggestions

"In the First Light" (Isa, Rom, Advent)
V-5 (1) p. 28

"I Wonder as I Wander" (Pss, Advent)
V-8 p. 88

"Come Thou Long Expected Jesus" (Rom, Matt)
+ V-3(3) p. 50
V-10 p. 11
+"Prepare the Way of the Lord" (Matt)
V-3 (5) p. 30
"Come, My Light" (Isa)
Anne Krentz Organ; AEC-2 p. 30, Augsburg 9780800675813
2-part mixed, piano (https://bit.ly/AEC-2-30)
"Once He Came in Blessing" (Matt)
Arr. Mark Sedio; AEC-1 p. 40
2-part mixed, keyboard, flute (https://bit.ly/AEC-1)

+Hymn Anthem

"Hail to the Lord's Anointed" (PD) (Isa, Pss, Rom)
N104, GR165, UM203 (PD)

Introduction - Keyboard plays last system. Begin with melody only in both hands. Play last half ("and rule in equity.") as written.

Stanza 1: Systems 1&2 - All voices unison, *mezzo forte.* System 3 - "He comes to break oppression,": S/A only on their parts; "to set the captive free": tenors on melody, basses on their part. System 4 - All voices unison. Keyboard plays all parts.

Stanza 2 - T/B alone. Tenors sing melody, basses sing bass part. Accompaniment should be gentle, *mezzo forte.* May be accompanied by S-1, #115 or another harmonization.

Stanza 3 - S/A singing their parts. If possible, have several voices sing the tenor part in the soprano range. Keyboard plays the tenor and bass parts, but in both hands, doubling the parts an octave apart. On system 4, return to playing all four parts. Go immediately to stanza 4 with no *Ritard.*

Stanza 4 - For a full sound, have most of the choir sing their part. Add some S/A's voices singing the tenor line in their range (as in stanza 3) and some T/B singing the melody in their range, resulting in a six-part texture. Keyboard plays setting as written full, strong manner. Add r*itard* to the final phrase.

Other Suggestions

Visuals:

- **O** Stump/branch/roots, lamp, scales, belt, named animals, child, asp, adder's den, mountain/sea, nations
- **P** Crown, scales, mountains/hills, poor/needy, sun/moon, rain, lunar eclipse, Ps. 72:18, 19
- **E** Bible/OT, circle, welcome, nations/Christ, stump/root
- **G** Baptism, ax/root/fire, sandals, fork/wheat/chaff/fire

Introit: C121, G95, UM207, VU10. "Prepare the Way of the Lord" (Matt)
Introit: WS3044. "Make Way" (Matt, Advent)
Introit: WS3047, st. 1. "God Almighty, We Are Waiting" (Rom, Matt)
Opening Prayer: N816 (Advent)
Call or Response to Prayer: WS3046. "Come, O Redeemer, Come" (Advent)
Canticle: C126. "The Peaceful Realm" (Isa)
Call to Confession: N114. "Return, My People" (Isa)
Prayer: UM201. Advent (Isa, Matt)
Offertory Prayer: WSL152. "Father, John the Baptist" (Matt)
+Response: WS3088, stanza 1. "Easter Alleluia" OL-00580 (Pss)
Response: S2090, stanza 2. "Light the Advent Candle"
Advent Candle Response: C128 or G85(Advent)
+Sung Benediction: CG517, E347, UM670, VU418. "Go Forth for God" 5893898 (Isa, Pss)
Theme Ideas: Jesus: Return and Reign, Justice, Peace, Preparation, Waiting

Notes

NRSVue

Isaiah 35:1-10

1The wilderness and the dry land shall be glad;
the desert shall rejoice and blossom;
like the crocus 2it shall blossom abundantly
and rejoice with joy and shouting.
The glory of Lebanon shall be given to it,
the majesty of Carmel and Sharon.
They shall see the glory of the LORD,
the majesty of our God.
3Strengthen the weak hands
and make firm the feeble knees.
4Say to those who are of a fearful heart,
"Be strong, do not fear!
Here is your God.
He will come with vengeance,
with terrible recompense.
He will come and save you."
5Then the eyes of the blind shall be opened,
and the ears of the deaf shall be opened;
6then the lame shall leap like a deer,
and the tongue of the speechless sing for joy.
For waters shall break forth in the wilderness
and streams in the desert;
7the burning sand shall become a pool
and the thirsty ground springs of water;
the haunt of jackals shall become a swamp;
the grass shall become reeds and rushes.
8A highway shall be there,
and it shall be called the Holy Way;
the unclean shall not travel on it,
but it shall be for God's people;
no traveler, not even fools, shall go astray.
9No lion shall be there,
nor shall any ravenous beast come up on it;
they shall not be found there,
but the redeemed shall walk there.
10And the ransomed of the LORD shall return
and come to Zion with singing;
everlasting joy shall be upon their heads;
they shall obtain joy and gladness,
and sorrow and sighing shall flee away.

Luke 1:47-55

47"My soul magnifies the Lord,
and my spirit rejoices in God my Savior,
48for he has looked with favor on the lowly state of his servant.
Surely from now on all generations will call me blessed,
49for the Mighty One has done great things for me,
and holy is his name;
50indeed, his mercy is for those who fear him
from generation to generation.
51He has shown strength with his arm;
he has scattered the proud in the imagination of their hearts.
52He has brought down the powerful from their thrones
and lifted up the lowly;
53he has filled the hungry with good things
and sent the rich away empty.
54He has come to the aid of his child Israel,
in remembrance of his mercy,
55according to the promise he made to our ancestors,
to Abraham and to his descendants forever."

CEB

Isaiah 35:1-10

1The desert and the dry land will be glad;
the wilderness will rejoice and blossom like the crocus.
2They will burst into bloom,
and rejoice with joy and singing.
They will receive the glory of Lebanon,
the splendor of Carmel and Sharon.
They will see the LORD's glory,
the splendor of our God.
3Strengthen the weak hands,
and support the unsteady knees.
4Say to those who are panicking:
"Be strong! Don't fear!
Here's your God,
coming with vengeance;
with divine retribution
God will come to save you."
5Then the eyes of the blind will be opened,
and the ears of the deaf will be cleared.
6Then the lame will leap like the deer,
and the tongue of the speechless will sing.
Waters will spring up in the desert,
and streams in the wilderness.
7The burning sand will become a pool,
and the thirsty ground, fountains of water.
The jackals' habitat, a pasture;
grass will become reeds and rushes.
8A highway will be there.
It will be called The Holy Way.
The unclean won't travel on it,
but it will be for those walking on that way.
Even fools won't get lost on it;
9 no lion will be there,
and no predator will go up on it.
None of these will be there;
only the redeemed will walk on it.
10The LORD's ransomed ones will return and enter Zion with singing,
with everlasting joy upon their heads.
Happiness and joy will overwhelm them;
grief and groaning will flee away.

Luke 1:47-55

47"In the depths of who I am I rejoice in God my savior.
48He has looked with favor on the low status of his servant.
Look! From now on, everyone will consider me highly favored
49 because the mighty one has done great things for me.
Holy is his name.
50 He shows mercy to everyone,
from one generation to the next,
who honors him as God.
51He has shown strength with his arm.
He has scattered those with arrogant thoughts and proud inclinations.
52 He has pulled the powerful down from their thrones
and lifted up the lowly.
53He has filled the hungry with good things
and sent the rich away empty-handed.
54He has come to the aid of his servant Israel,
remembering his mercy,
55 just as he promised to our ancestors,
to Abraham and to Abraham's descendants forever."

NRSVue

James 5:7-10

7Be patient, therefore, brothers and sisters, until the coming
of the Lord. The farmer waits for the precious crop from the
earth, being patient with it until it receives the early and the
late rains. 8You also must be patient. Strengthen your hearts,
for the coming of the Lord is near. 9Brothers and sisters, do not
grumble against one another, so that you may not be judged.
See, the Judge is standing at the doors! 10As an example of suffering and patience, brothers and sisters, take the prophets who
spoke in the name of the Lord.

Matthew 11:2-11

2When John heard in prison what the Messiah was doing, he
sent word by his disciples 3and said to him, "Are you the one who
is to come, or are we to wait for another?" 4Jesus answered them,
"Go and tell John what you hear and see: 5the blind receive their
sight, the lame walk, those with a skin disease are cleansed, the
deaf hear, the dead are raised, and the poor have good news
brought to them. 6And blessed is anyone who takes no offense at
me."
7As they went away, Jesus began to speak to the crowds about
John: "What did you go out into the wilderness to look at? A
reed shaken by the wind? 8What, then, did you go out to see?
Someone dressed in soft robes? Look, those who wear soft
robes are in royal palaces. 9What, then, did you go out to see? A
prophet? Yes, I tell you, and more than a prophet. 10This is the
one about whom it is written,
'See, I am sending my messenger ahead of you,
who will prepare your way before you.'
11"Truly I tell you, among those born of women no one has
arisen greater than John the Baptist, yet the least in the kingdom
of heaven is greater than he."

CEB

James 5:7-10

7Therefore, brothers and sisters, you must be patient as you
wait for the coming of the Lord. Consider the farmer who waits
patiently for the coming of rain in the fall and spring, looking
forward to the precious fruit of the earth. 8You also must wait
patiently, strengthening your resolve, because the coming of the
Lord is near. 9Don't complain about each other, brothers and
sisters, so that you won't be judged. Look! The judge is standing
at the door!
10Brothers and sisters, take the prophets who spoke in
the name of the Lord as an example of patient resolve and
steadfastness.

Matthew 11:2-11

2Now when John heard in prison about the things Jesus was
doing, he sent word by his disciples to Jesus, asking, 3"Are you
the one who is to come, or should we look for another?"
4Jesus responded, "Go, report to John what you hear and see.
5*Those who were blind are able to see.* Those who were crippled are
walking. People with skin diseases are cleansed. Those *who were
deaf now hear. Those who were dead are raised up. The poor have good
news proclaimed to them.* 6Happy are those who don't stumble and
fall because of me."
7When John's disciples had gone, Jesus spoke to the crowds
about John: "What did you go out to the wilderness to see? A
stalk blowing in the wind? 8What did you go out to see? A man
dressed up in refined clothes? Look, those who wear refined
clothes are in royal palaces. 9What did you go out to see? A
prophet? Yes, I tell you, and more than a prophet. 10He is the
one of whom it is written: *Look, I'm sending my messenger before you,
who will prepare your way before you.*
11"I assure you that no one who has ever been born is greater
than John the Baptist. Yet whoever is least in the kingdom of
heaven is greater than he."

Primary Hymns and Songs for the Day

"Come, Thou Long-Expected Jesus" 31999 (Jas) (O)
E66, N122, G83, P1 (PD), SH64, VU2
H-3 Hbl-81; Chr-147; Desc-99; Org-158
S-1 #324. Descant
C125, CG83, G82, GR163, P2, UM196 (PD)
H-3 Hbl-46; Chr-26, 134; Desc-53; Org-56
S-1 #168-171. Various treatments
EL254
"While We Are Waiting, Come" 27525 (Jas)
G92
"My Soul Gives Glory to My God" OL-91855 (Luke)
C130, EL251, G99, N119, P600, UM198, VU899
H-3 Chr-139, 145; Desc-77
S-1 #241-242. Orff arr. and desc.
"Prepare the Way of the Lord" OL-00142 (Matt)
C121, G95, UM207, VU10
"O For a Thousand Tongues to Sing" 1369 (Isa, Matt) (C)
C5, CG332, E493, EL886, G610, GR1, N42, P466, SH439, UM57 (PD), VU326 (*See also* WS3001)
H-3 Hbl-79; Chr-142; Desc-17; Org-12
S-1 #33-38. Various Treatments
"I Want to Walk as a Child of the Light" (Isa, Jas) (C)
CG96, E490, EL815, G377, GR216, SH352, UM206

Additional Hymn Suggestions

"Awake! Awake, and Greet the New Morn" (Isa)
C138, EL242, G107, N107, SH66
"Lift Up Your Heads, Ye Mighty Gates" 1863214 (Isa)
C129, CG173, E436, G93, GR171, N117, P8, UM213 (PD)
"Lo, How a Rose E'er Blooming" (Isa)
C160, CG105, E81, EL272, G129, GR168, N127, P48 (PD), UM216, VU8
+"Dust and Ashes" (Isa)
N186, VU105, WS3098
"That Boy-Child of Mary" 78086 (Isa, Luke)
EL293, G139, P55, UM241
+"People, Look East" (Isa, Jas, Advent)
C142, CG90, EL248, G105, P12, UM202, VU9
"It Came Upon the Midnight Clear" 31078 (Isa, Jas, Matt)
C153, CG132, E89, EL282, G123, GR194, N131, P38, SH89, UM218 (PD), VU44
"Jesus Shall Reign" 1510 (Isa, Luke, Matt)
C95, CG158, E544, EL434, G265, GR282, N300, P423, SH209, UM157 (PD), VU330
"Hail to the Lord's Anointed" (PD) (Isa, Matt)
C140, CG98, E616, EL311, G149, GR165, N104, P205, SH112, UM203, VU30
"Good Christian Friends, Rejoice" 85158 (Isa, Matt)
C164, CG122, E107, EL288, G132, GR195, N129, P28, UM224, VU35
"Thou Didst Leave Thy Throne" (Isa, Matt, Advent)
CG165, GR202, S2100, SH86
"Canticle of the Turning" (Luke)
EL723, G100, SH68
"I'll Praise My Maker While I've Breath" (Luke)
C20, CG336, E429 (PD), G806, GR17, P253, UM60, VU867
"Tell Out, My Soul" 27051 (Luke)
CG94, E437/438, GR172, UM200
"To a Maid Engaged to Joseph" (Luke)
G98, P19, UM215, VU14
"The Snow lay on the Ground" (Luke)
E110, G116, S2093, P57
"I'm So Glad Jesus Lifted Me" (PD) (Luke)
C529, EL860 (PD), N474, S2151
"Blessed Be the God of Israel" 860627 (Luke, Matt)
C135, CG88, E444, EL250/552, G109, P602, UM209, VU901
"In the Cross of Christ I Glory" 36499 (Jas)
C207, CG183, E441/442, EL324, G213, GR239, N193, P84, UM295 (PD)
"If Thou But Suffer God to Guide Thee" 564215 (Jas)
C565, CG76, E635, EL769, G816, GR75, N410, P282, SH326, UM142 (PD), VU285 (Fr.) and VU286
"O Master, Let Me Walk with Thee" 158243 (Jas)
C602, CG660, E659/660, EL818, G738, GR596, N503, P357, SH612, UM430 (PD), VU560
"All Who Love and Serve Your City" 1277415 (Jas)
C670, CG674, E570/E571, EL724, G351, P413, UM433
"Be Still, My Soul" (Jas)
C566, CG57, G819, GR346, N488, SH330, UM534, VU652
"Watchman, Tell Us of the Night" (Jas)
E640, G97, N103, P20
"Prepare the Way, O Zion" (Jas)
CG95, EL264, G106, P13, VU882
"Because You Live, O Christ" (Matt)
G249, N231, P105
"Once in Royal David's City" 197156 (Matt)
C165, CG104, E102, EL269, G140, GR175, N145, P49, UM250 (PD), VU62
"Wake, Awake, for Night Is Flying" (Matt)
E61, EL436, G349, P17, UM720 (PD), VU711
"Wild and Lone the Prophet's Voice" 3413029 (Matt, Advent)
G163, P409, S2089

Additional Contemporary and Modern Suggestions

"Someone Asked the Question" 1640279 (Isa)
N523, S2144
"Come, O Redeemer, Come" 2069663 (Isa, Advent)
WS3046
+"Rise" 7036613 (Isa)
+"Springtime" 7146308 (Isa)
+"Freedom" 7078151 (Isa)
"All Who Are Thirsty" 2489542 (Isa, Advent)
"Awaken" 5491647 (Isa, Jas, Advent)
"Awesome in This Place" 847554 (Isa, Luke)
+"Chain Breaker" 7060031 (Isa, Luke)
+"Great Things" 7111321 (Isa, Luke)
+"The Kingdom Is Yours" 7109354 (Isa, Luke)
"Give Thanks" 20285 (Isa, Luke)
C528, CG373, G647, S2036, SH489, ZS127
"Please Enter My Heart, Hosanna" 2485371 (Jas, Advent)
S2154
"Forever" 3148428 (Jas, Luke)
CG53, WS3023
"Waiting Here for You" 5925663 (James, Luke, Advent)
"Shout to the North" 1562261 (Luke)
G319, WS3042
"Praise to the Lord" 89886 (Luke)
EL844, S2029, VU835
"Shout to the Lord" 1406918 (Luke)
CG348, EL821, GR124, S2074, SH426, ZS15
"How Great You Are" 6271677 (Luke)
WS3015
"Make Way" 121074 (Luke, Advent)
WS3044
"Your Grace Is Enough" 4477026 (Luke)
WS3106
"Great and Mighty Is He" 66665 (Luke)
"Good to Me" 313480 (Luke)
+"All the Poor and Powerless" 5881130 (Luke)
+"Daughters of Zion" 7133716 (Luke)
+"Let Justice Roll" ("Like a River") 4974842 (Luke)
"You Are My All in All" 825356 (Luke, Matt)
CG571, G519, SH335, WS3040, ZS184

"Welcome to Our World" 2317391 (Matt, Advent)
WS3067, V-5 (1), p. 34 Vocal Solo
"Here I Am to Worship" 3266032 (Matt)
CG297, SH395, WS3177, ZS145
"Emmanuel, Emmanuel" 12949 (Matt)
C134, CG120, UM204
"Prepare Ye the Way" 5286041 (Matt)
+"Prepare the Way" 7136724 (Matt)

Solo/Ensemble Suggestions
"He Shall Feed His Flock Like a Shepherd" (Isa)
V-2
"God Will Make a Way" (with "He Leadeth Me") (Isa)
V-3 (2) p. 9
"Lift Up Your Heads" (Isa, Advent)
V-10 p. 38
"Patiently Have I Waited for the Lord" (Jas)
V-4 p. 24
"Come, O Long-Expected Jesus" (Jas)
David Lasky; AEC-3 p. 10
2-part, keyboard (https://bit.ly/AEC-3)
+"Wild and Lone the Prophet's Voice" (Matt, Advent)
Machael Larkin; MorningStar MSM-50-0491
SATB, piano (https://bit.ly/MSM-50-0491)

+Hymn Anthem
"Blessed Be the God of Israel" 860627 (Luke, Matt)
C135, CG88, E444, EL250/552, G109, P602, UM209, VU901
Introduction: Keyboard plays first line melody, then line 4, treble parts only. Play both lines one octave higher than written.
Stanza 1: Female soloist sings stanza 1. Keyboard plays hymnal setting as written omitting all melody notes.
Stanza 2: All voices unison, *mezzo forte.* Keyboard plays hymnal setting as written.
Interlude: As choir reaches last note, keyboard plays last line again, *forte.* Choir holds final note for two measures.
Stanza 3: All voices, *forte.* Keyboard plays hymnal setting. For added brilliance, a flute or handbells may play the "alto" part of the accompaniment an octave higher than written. This stanza can be slower and more grand than the other two.

Other Suggestions
Visuals:
O Blooms, healing, singing, river/stream, oasis, spring
P Mary, joy, arm/scatter, toppled throne, feeding, chest
E Second Coming, farmer/cross, gavel, scales, doors
G John, prison, Jesus with men, Matt. 11:5 imagery
As an alternative to reading the Luke passage, have the choir lead the congregation in singing C130, G99, N119, P600, UM198, VU899, "My Soul Gives Glory to My God."
Additional Magnificat Settings: C131, CG91, E269, EL314, G100, SH68, N732, UM199, VU898 (Luke)
Introit: N142. *"Manglakat na Kita sa Belen"* ("Let Us Even Now Go to Bethlehem") (Luke, Advent)
Gathering Litany: WSL4. "We gather in preparation" (Isa, Matt)
Opening Prayer: WSL1. "O God, we are challenged" (Jas)
Call to Confession: N832 (Advent)
Canticle: UM199. "Canticle of Mary" ("Magnificat") (Luke)
Response: S2090, stanza 3. "Light the Advent Candle"
Advent Candle Response: C128 or G85(Advent)
Prayer: WSL148. "Loving God you have blessed us" (Luke)
Movement or dance can enhance the Luke songs and readings.
Theme Ideas: Hope, Jesus: Return and Reign, Justice, Patience, Preparation, Waiting

Notes

NRSVue

Isaiah 7:10-16

[10]Again the LORD spoke to Ahaz, saying, [11]"Ask a sign of the
LORD your God; let it be deep as Sheol or high as heaven."
[12]But Ahaz said, "I will not ask, and I will not put the LORD to
the test." [13]Then Isaiah said: "Hear then, O house of David! Is it
too little for you to weary mortals that you weary my God also?
[14]Therefore the Lord himself will give you a sign. Look, the
young woman is with child and shall bear a son and shall name
him Immanuel. [15]He shall eat curds and honey by the time he
knows how to refuse the evil and choose the good. [16]For before
the child knows how to refuse the evil and choose the good, the
land before whose two kings you are in dread will be deserted."

Psalm 80:1-7, 17-19 (G355, N672, P206, SH72, UM801)

[1]Give ear, O Shepherd of Israel,
you who lead Joseph like a flock!
You who are enthroned upon the cherubim, shine forth
[2] before Ephraim and Benjamin and Manasseh.
Stir up your might,
and come to save us!
[3]Restore us, O God;
let your face shine, that we may be saved.
[4]O LORD God of hosts,
how long will you be angry with your people's prayers?
[5]You have fed them with the bread of tears
and given them tears to drink in full measure.
[6]You make us the scorn of our neighbors;
our enemies laugh among themselves.
[7]Restore us, O God of hosts;
let your face shine, that we may be saved.
. . . .
[17]But let your hand be upon the one at your right hand,
the one whom you made strong for yourself.
[18]Then we will never turn back from you;
give us life, and we will call on your name.
[19]Restore us, O LORD God of hosts;
let your face shine, that we may be saved.

CEB

Isaiah 7:10-16

[10]Again the LORD spoke to Ahaz: [11]"Ask a sign from the LORD
your God. Make it as deep as the grave or as high as heaven."
[12]But Ahaz said, "I won't ask; I won't test the LORD."
[13]Then Isaiah said, "Listen, house of David! Isn't it enough for
you to be tiresome for people that you are also tiresome before
my God? [14]Therefore, the Lord will give you a sign. The young
woman is pregnant and is about to give birth to a son, and she
will name him Immanuel.[15]He will eat butter and honey, and
learn to reject evil and choose good. [16]Before the boy learns to
reject evil and choose good, the land of the two kings you dread
will be abandoned."

Psalm 80:1-7, 17-19 (G355, N672, P206, SH72, UM801)

[1]Shepherd of Israel, listen!
You, the one who leads Joseph as if he were a sheep.
You, who are enthroned upon the winged heavenly
creatures.
Show yourself [2]before Ephraim, Benjamin, and Manasseh!
Wake up your power!
Come to save us!
[3]Restore us, God!
Make your face shine so that we can be saved!
[4]LORD God of heavenly forces,
how long will you fume against your people's prayer?
[5]You've fed them bread made of tears;
you've given them tears to drink three times over!
[6]You've put us at odds with our neighbors;
our enemies make fun of us.
[7]Restore us, God of heavenly forces!
Make your face shine so that we can be saved!
. . . .
[17]Let your hand be with the one on your right side—
with the one whom you secured as your own—
[18] then we will not turn away from you!
Revive us so that we can call on your name.
[19] Restore us, LORD God of heavenly forces!
Make your face shine so that we can be saved!

NRSVue

Romans 1:1-7

1Paul, a servant of Christ Jesus, called to be an apostle, set
apart for the gospel of God, 2which he promised beforehand
through his prophets in the holy scriptures, 3the gospel concerning his Son, who was descended from David according to the
flesh 4and was declared to be Son of God with power according
to the spirit of holiness by resurrection from the dead, Jesus
Christ our Lord, 5through whom we have received grace and
apostleship to bring about the obedience of faith among all the
gentiles for the sake of his name, 6including you who are called
to belong to Jesus Christ,
7To all God's beloved in Rome, who are called to be saints:
Grace to you and peace from God our Father and the Lord
Jesus Christ.

Matthew 1:18-25

18Now the birth of Jesus the Messiah took place in this way.
When his mother Mary had been engaged to Joseph, but before
they lived together, she was found to be pregnant from the
Holy Spirit. 19Her husband Joseph, being a righteous man and
unwilling to expose her to public disgrace, planned to divorce
her quietly. 20But just when he had resolved to do this, an angel
of the Lord appeared to him in a dream and said, "Joseph, son
of David, do not be afraid to take Mary as your wife, for the child
conceived in her is from the Holy Spirit. 21She will bear a son,
and you are to name him Jesus, for he will save his people from
their sins." 22All this took place to fulfill what had been spoken
by the Lord through the prophet:
23 "Look, the virgin shall conceive and bear a son,
and they shall name him Emmanuel,"
which means, "God is with us." 24When Joseph awoke from
sleep, he did as the angel of the Lord commanded him; he took
her as his wife 25but had no marital relations with her until she
had given birth to a son, and he named him Jesus.

CEB

Romans 1:1-7

1From Paul, a slave of Christ Jesus, called to be an apostle and
set apart for God's good news. 2-3God promised this good news
about his Son ahead of time through his prophets in the holy
scriptures. His Son was descended from David. 4He was publicly
identified as God's Son with power through his resurrection
from the dead, which was based on the Spirit of holiness. This
Son is Jesus Christ our Lord. 5Through him we have received
God's grace and our appointment to be apostles. This was to
bring all Gentiles to faithful obedience for his name's sake. 6You
who are called by Jesus Christ are also included among these
Gentiles.
7To those in Rome who are dearly loved by God and called to
be God's people.
Grace to you and peace from God our Father and the Lord
Jesus Christ.

Matthew 1:18-25

18This is how the birth of Jesus Christ took place. When Mary
his mother was engaged to Joseph, before they were married,
she became pregnant by the Holy Spirit. 19Joseph her husband
was a righteous man. Because he didn't want to humiliate her,
he decided to call off their engagement quietly. 20As he was
thinking about this, an angel from the Lord appeared to him in
a dream and said, "Joseph son of David, don't be afraid to take
Mary as your wife, because the child she carries was conceived
by the Holy Spirit. 21She will give birth to a son, and you will call
him Jesus, because he will save his people from their sins." 22Now
all of this took place so that what the Lord had spoken through
the prophet would be fulfilled:
23 Look! A virgin will become pregnant and give birth to a son,
And they will call him, Emmanuel.
(Emmanuel means "God with us.")
24When Joseph woke up, he did just as an angel from God
commanded and took Mary as his wife. 25But he didn't have
sexual relations with her until she gave birth to a son. Joseph
called him Jesus.

Primary Hymns and Songs for the Day

"Emmanuel, Emmanuel" 12949 (Isa, Matt) (O)
C134, CG120, UM204
"O Come, O Come, Emmanuel" 3063194 (Isa, Matt) (O)
C119, CG79, E56, EL257, G88, GR162, N116, P9, SH73, UM211, VU1(Fr.)
H-3 Hbl-14, 79; Chr-141; Org-168
S-1 #342. Handbell accompaniment
"Once in Royal David's City" 197156 (Isa, Matt)
C165, CG104, E102, EL269, G140, GR175, N145, P49, UM250 (PD), VU62
H-3 Hbl-83; Chr-68, 156; Desc-57; Org-63
S-1 #182-184. Various treatments
"To a Maid Engaged to Joseph" (Isa, Matt)
G98, P19, UM215, VU14
"Joseph Dearest, Joseph Mine" (Matt)
N105, S2099
"The King of Glory Comes" OL-81352 (Matt)
CG177, S2091, SH206
"Hark! the Herald Angels Sing" (Matt) (C)
C150, CG127, E87, EL270, G119, GR180, N144, P31, SH94, UM240 (PD), VU48
H-3 Hbl-26, 67; Chr-91; Desc-75; Org-89
S-1 #234-6. Harms. and desc.

Additional Hymn Suggestions

"It Came Upon the Midnight Clear" 31078 (Isa)
C153, CG132, E89, EL282, G123, GR194, N131, P38, SH89, UM218 (PD), VU44
"I Want to Walk as a Child of the Light" (Isa, Pss, Advent)
CG96, E490, EL815, G377, GR216, SH352, UM206
"Toda la Tierra" ("All Earth Is Waiting") (Isa, Matt)
C139, EL266, N121, SH63, UM210, VU5
"Savior of the Nations, Come" (Isa, Matt)
E54, EL263, G102, P14 (PD), SH67, UM214
"Lo, How a Rose E'er Blooming" (Isa, Matt)
C160, CG105, E81, EL272, G129, GR168, N127, P48 (PD), UM216, VU8
"Come, Emmanuel" 3999938 (Isa, Matt, Advent)
WS3130
"Come, O Redeemer, Come" 2069663 (Pss, Advent)
WS3046
"Lead Me, Guide Me" (Pss, Advent)
C583, CG403, EL768, G740, S2214, SH582, ZS173
"People, Look East" (Pss, Advent)
C142, CG90, EL248, G105, P12, UM202, VU9
"Send Your Word" (Pss, Rom, Advent)
N317, UM195
"Alleluia, Alleluia" 32376 (Rom)
CG196, E178, G240, P106, SH189, UM162, VU179
"Rise, Shine, You People" (Rom, Advent)
EL665, UM187
"Jesus! the Name High over All" (Rom)
GR111, UM193 (PD)
"What Child Is This" 30983 (Rom)
C162, CG148, E115, EL296, G145, GR179, N148, P53, SH105, UM219 (PD), VU74
"While Shepherds Watched Their Flocks" (Rom)
C154, E94/95, CG123, G117/118, GR189, P58/59, UM236 (PD), VU75
"O Come, All Ye Faithful" 31054 (Rom, Matt)
C148, CG103, E83, EL283, G133, GR174, N135, P41, SH96, UM234 (PD), VU60 (Fr.)
"Come, Thou Long-Expected Jesus" 31999 (Matt)
C125, CG83, E66, EL254, G82/83, GR163, N122, P1/2, SH64, UM196 (PD), VU2
"Ye Who Claim the Faith of Jesus" (Matt)
E268/269, UM197
"My Soul Gives Glory to My God" OL-91855 (Matt)
C130, EL251, G99, N119, P600, UM198, VU899
"Tell Out, My Soul" 27051 (Matt)
CG94, E437/438, GR172, UM200
"Angels from the Realms of Glory" 31669 (Matt)
C149, CG126, E93, EL275, G143, GR190, N126, P22, SH99, UM220 (PD), VU36
"Il Est Né" ("He Is Born") (Matt)
CG106, UM228, VU50
"O Little Town of Bethlehem" 27879 (Matt) (C)
C144, CG107, E78/79, EL279, G121, GR192, N133, P43/44, SH80, UM230, VU64
"Go, Tell It on the Mountain" 3063235 (Matt)
C167, CG143, E99, EL290, G136, GR203, N154, P29, SH90, UM251, VU43, Z75 (PD), ZS59
"The First One Ever" (Matt)
E673, UM276
"Like a Child" (Matt)
C133, S2092, VU366
"Rise Up, Shepherd, and Follow" (Matt)
G135, P50, S2096, VU70
"O Holy Spirit, Root of Life" (Matt, Advent)
C251, EL399, N57, S2121, VU379
"A Star Shone Bright" (Matt, Advent)
WS3051

Additional Contemporary and Modern Suggestions

"All Hail King Jesus" 12877 (Isa, Matt)
S2069, ZS53
"Jesus, Name above All Names" 21291 (Isa, Matt)
S2071, ZS27
+"Love Has Come" (Isa, Matt)
EL292, G110, WS3059
+"Behold Him" 7133698 (Isa, Matt, Advent)
"Glory in the Highest" 4822451 (Isa, Matt)
"Shine, Jesus, Shine" 30426 (Pss)
CG156, EL671, G192, GR217, S2173, SH102; V-3 (2), p. 48. Vocal Solo
+"In Christ Alone" 3350395 (Pss)
CG569, GR106, SH656, WS3105
"The Power of Your Love" 917491 (Pss)
"Refresh My Heart" 917518 (Rom, Advent)
"Let the Peace of God Reign" 1839987 (Rom)
"There's Something About That Name" 14064 (Matt)
C115, GR124, UM171
"Jesus, the Light of the World" 6363190 (Matt, Advent)
WS3056 (*See also* CG129, G127, GR214, N160, SH103, ZS62)
"Lord, I Lift Your Name on High" 117947 (Matt, Christmas)
CG606, EL857, S2088, SH205
"Jesus, We Crown You with Praise" 1453284 (Matt)

Solo/Ensemble Suggestions

"Behold! A Virgin Shall Conceive" and
"O Thou That Tellest Good Tidings to Zion" (Isa, Matt)
V-2
"Lost in the Night" (Pss, Matt)
V-5 (1) p. 18
"Who Is This Boy?" (Matt)
V-8 p. 223
+"O Come, O Come, Emmanuel" (Isa, Matt)
Taylor Scott Davis; MorningStarr MSM-50-7716
SATB, piano (https://bit.ly/50-7716)
"While Shepherds Watched Their Flocks" (Rom)
John Carter; AEC-2 p. 90
3-part mixed, piano (https://bit.ly/AEC-2)

+Hymn Anthem
"To a Maid Engaged to Joseph" 220700, OL-08935, OL-08937 (Isa, Matt)
G98, P19, UM215, VU14
Sing the story of the annunciation. Choose three soloists to sing the text which is attributed their character: Narrator (treble or bass voice), Angel (treble or bass voice), and Mary (treble voice, perhaps a teenager).
Introduction - Keyboard plays 1st system, melody only. *Piano.*
Stanza 1 - Narrator and Angel. Soft accompaniment. *Mezzo piano.*
Stanza 2 - Angel. Same accompaniment. *Mezzo piano.*
Stanza 3 - Full choir, unison. Voices and accompaniment. *Mezzo forte.*
Stanza 4 - Angel and accompaniment. *Mezzo forte.*
Stanza 5 - Mary and Angel, stronger accompaniment. *Forte*
Stanza 6 - Full choir, *forte.* Keyboard full. Left hand may double the bass notes in octaves, leaving out the bass clef notes above them, or catching with the right hand when possible. Choir may sing four parts on last system, with some sopranos singing the alto part up an octave. Strong ending, *forte.*

Other Suggestions
Visuals:
O Test, pregnant woman, baby, Immanuel, curds/honey
P Shepherd, seat, anger/tears/laughter, returning
E Letter, Bible, resurrection, Rom. 1:7b
G Pregnant Mary, Joseph, Spirit symbol, birth, angel Emmanuel (God with us), "Jesus"
Use UM211 with the printed spoken antiphons. For processional, stop each time an antiphon is read, moving during the singing of each stanza.
Introit: N137, P52, VU52. *"Hitsuji wa nemureri"* ("Sheep Fast Asleep") (Isa)
Greeting: WSL4 (Matt)
Prayer: WSL6. "Gracious God, your servant Mary" (Matt)
Response: C158. "Her Baby, Newly Breathing" (Matt)
Response: S2090, stanza 4. "Light the Advent Candle" (Advent)
Advent Candle Response: C128 or G85(Advent)
Prayer: WSL11. "Radiant Morning Star" (Matt)
Offertory Prayer: WSL125. "Precious Lord, amid the twinkling lights" (Matt, Advent)
Blessing: WSL7. "The light that enlivens" (Pss)
Theme Ideas: Grace, Jesus: Incarnation, Redemption / Salvation

Notes

NRSVue

Isaiah 9:2-7
2The people who walked in darkness
have seen a great light;
those who lived in a land of deep darkness—
on them light has shined.
3You have multiplied exultation;
you have increased its joy;
they rejoice before you
as with joy at the harvest,
as people exult when dividing plunder.
4For the yoke of their burden
and the bar across their shoulders,
the rod of their oppressor,
you have broken as on the day of Midian.
5For all the boots of the tramping warriors
and all the garments rolled in blood
shall be burned as fuel for the fire.
6For a child has been born for us,
a son given to us;
authority rests upon his shoulders,
and he is named
Wonderful Counselor, Mighty God,
Everlasting Father, Prince of Peace.
7Great will be his authority,
and there shall be endless peace
for the throne of David and his kingdom.
He will establish and uphold it
with justice and with righteousness
from this time onward and forevermore.
The zeal of the LORD of hosts will do this.

Psalm 96 (G304, N684, P216/217, SH648, UM815)
1O sing to the LORD a new song;
sing to the LORD, all the earth.
2Sing to the LORD, bless his name;
tell of his salvation from day to day.
3Declare his glory among the nations,
his marvelous works among all the peoples.
4For great is the LORD and greatly to be praised;
he is to be revered above all gods.
5For all the gods of the peoples are idols,
but the LORD made the heavens.
6Honor and majesty are before him;
strength and beauty are in his sanctuary.
7Ascribe to the LORD, O families of the peoples,
ascribe to the LORD glory and strength.
8Ascribe to the LORD the glory due his name;
bring an offering, and come into his courts.
9Worship the LORD in holy splendor;
tremble before him, all the earth.
10Say among the nations, "The LORD is king!
The world is firmly established; it shall never be moved.
He will judge the peoples with equity."
11Let the heavens be glad, and let the earth rejoice;
let the sea roar and all that fills it;
12let the field exult, and everything in it.
Then shall all the trees of the forest sing for joy
13before the LORD, for he is coming,
for he is coming to judge the earth.
He will judge the world with righteousness
and the peoples with his truth.

CEB

Isaiah 9:2-7
2The people walking in darkness have seen a great light.
On those living in a pitch-dark land, light has dawned.
3You have made the nation great;
you have increased its joy.
They rejoiced before you as with joy at the harvest,
as those who divide plunder rejoice.
4As on the day of Midian, you've shattered the yoke that burdened them,
the staff on their shoulders,
and the rod of their oppressor.
5Because every boot of the thundering warriors,
and every garment rolled in blood
will be burned, fuel for the fire.
6A child is born to us, a son is given to us,
and authority will be on his shoulders.
He will be named
Wonderful Counselor, Mighty God,
Eternal Father, Prince of Peace.
7There will be vast authority and endless peace
for David's throne and for his kingdom,
establishing and sustaining it
with justice and righteousness
now and forever.
The zeal of the LORD of heavenly forces will do this.

Psalm 96 (G304, N684, P216/217, SH648, UM815)
1Sing to the LORD a new song!
Sing to the LORD, all the earth!
2Sing to the LORD! Bless his name!
Share the news of his saving work every single day!
3Declare God's glory among the nations;
declare his wondrous works among all people
4because the LORD is great and so worthy of praise.
He is awesome beyond all other gods
5because all the gods of the nations are just idols,
but it is the LORD who created heaven!
6Greatness and grandeur are in front of him;
strength and beauty are in his sanctuary.
7Give to the LORD, all families of the nations—
give to the LORD glory and power!
8Give to the LORD the glory due his name!
Bring gifts!
Enter his courtyards!
9Bow down to the LORD in his holy splendor!
Tremble before him, all the earth!
10Tell the nations, "The LORD rules!
Yes, he set the world firmly in place;
it won't be shaken.
He will judge all people fairly."
11Let heaven celebrate! Let the earth rejoice!
Let the sea and everything in it roar!
12 Let the countryside and everything in it celebrate!
Then all the trees of the forest too
will shout out joyfully
13 before the LORD because he is coming!
He is coming to establish justice on the earth!
He will establish justice in the world rightly.
He will establish justice among all people fairly.

NRSVue

Titus 2:11-14

11For the grace of God has appeared, bringing salvation to all,
12training us to renounce impiety and worldly passions and in
the present age to live lives that are self-controlled, upright, and
godly, 13while we wait for the blessed hope and the manifestation
of the glory of our great God and Savior, Jesus Christ. 14He it is
who gave himself for us that he might redeem us from all iniquity and purify for himself a people of his own who are zealous
for good deeds.

Luke 2:1-14, (15-20)

1In those days a decree went out from Caesar Augustus that
all the world should be registered. 2This was the first registration
and was taken while Quirinius was governor of Syria. 3All went
to their own towns to be registered. 4Joseph also went from the
town of Nazareth in Galilee to Judea, to the city of David called
Bethlehem, because he was descended from the house and
family of David. 5He went to be registered with Mary, to whom
he was engaged and who was expecting a child. 6While they were
there, the time came for her to deliver her child. 7And she gave
birth to her firstborn son and wrapped him in bands of cloth
and laid him in a manger, because there was no place for them
in the guest room.

8Now in that same region there were shepherds living in the
fields, keeping watch over their flock by night. 9Then an angel
of the Lord stood before them, and the glory of the Lord shone
around them, and they were terrified. 10But the angel said to
them, "Do not be afraid, for see, I am bringing you good news of
great joy for all the people: 11to you is born this day in the city of
David a Savior, who is the Messiah, the Lord. 12This will be a sign
for you: you will find a child wrapped in bands of cloth and lying
in a manger." 13And suddenly there was with the angel a multitude of the heavenly host, praising God and saying,

14 "Glory to God in the highest heaven,
and on earth peace among those whom he favors!"

15When the angels had left them and gone into heaven, the
shepherds said to one another, "Let us go now to Bethlehem
and see this thing that has taken place, which the Lord has made
known to us." 16So they went with haste and found Mary and
Joseph and the child lying in the manger. 17When they saw this,
they made known what had been told them about this child,
18and all who heard it were amazed at what the shepherds told
them, 19and Mary treasured all these words and pondered them
in her heart. 20The shepherds returned, glorifying and praising
God for all they had heard and seen, as it had been told them.

CEB

Titus 2:11-14

11The grace of God has appeared, bringing salvation to all
people. 12It educates us so that we can live sensible, ethical, and
godly lives right now by rejecting ungodly lives and the desires
of this world. 13At the same time we wait for the blessed hope
and the glorious appearance of our great God and savior Jesus
Christ. 14He gave himself for us in order to rescue us from every
kind of lawless behavior, and cleanse a special people for himself
who are eager to do good actions.

Luke 2:1-14 (15-20)

1In those days Caesar Augustus declared that everyone
throughout the empire should be enrolled in the tax lists.
2This first enrollment occurred when Quirinius governed Syria.
3Everyone went to their own cities to be enrolled. 4Since Joseph
belonged to David's house and family line, he went up from
the city of Nazareth in Galilee to David's city, called Bethlehem,
in Judea. 5He went to be enrolled together with Mary, who was
promised to him in marriage and who was pregnant. 6While they
were there, the time came for Mary to have her baby. 7She gave
birth to her firstborn child, a son, wrapped him snugly, and laid
him in a manger, because there was no place for them in the
guestroom.

8Nearby shepherds were living in the fields, guarding their
sheep at night. 9The Lord's angel stood before them, the Lord's
glory shone around them, and they were terrified.

10The angel said, "Don't be afraid! Look! I bring good news
to you—wonderful, joyous news for all people. 11Your savior is
born today in David's city. He is Christ the Lord. 12This is a sign
for you: you will find a newborn baby wrapped snugly and lying
in a manger." 13Suddenly a great assembly of the heavenly forces
was with the angel praising God. They said, 14"Glory to God in
heaven, and on earth peace among those whom he favors."

15When the angels returned to heaven, the shepherds said to
each other, "Let's go right now to Bethlehem and see what's happened. Let's confirm what the Lord has revealed to us." 16They
went quickly and found Mary and Joseph, and the baby lying in
the manger. 17When they saw this, they reported what they had
been told about this child. 18Everyone who heard it was amazed
at what the shepherds told them. 19Mary committed these things
to memory and considered them carefully. 20The shepherds
returned home, glorifying and praising God for all they had
heard and seen. Everything happened just as they had been told.

Primary Hymns and Songs for the Day

"Angels We Have Heard on High" 27721 (Luke) (O)
C155, CG125, E96, EL289, G113, GR191, P23, N125, SH93, UM238, VU38 (Fr.)
H-3 Hbl-47; Chr-31; Desc-43; Org-45

"On Christmas Night" (Isa, Titus, Luke)
CG133, EL274, G112, N143, WS3064

"Silent Night, Holy Night" 27862 (Luke)
C145, CG134, E111, EL281, G122, GR199, N134, P60, SH83, UM239 (PD), VU67 (Fr.)
H-3 Hbl-92; Chr-171; Desc-99; Org-159
S-1 #322. Desc.
#323. Guitar/Autoharp chords
S-2 #167. Handbell arrangement

"Joy to the World" 24016 (Titus, Luke) (C)
C143, CG102, E100, EL267, G134, GR201, N132, P40, SH95, UM246 (PD), VU59
S-1 #19-20. Trumpet desc.

"Go, Tell It on the Mountain" 3063235 (Luke) (C)
C167, CG143, E99, EL290, G136, GR203, N154, P29, SH90, UM251, VU43, Z75 (PD), ZS59
H-3 Hbl-17; Chr-73; Desc-45; Org-46

Additional Hymn Suggestions

"Born in the Night, Mary's Child" 2574505 (Isa)
G158, N152, P30, VU95

"Break Forth, O Beauteous Heavenly Light" (Isa)
E91, G130, GR206, N140, P26, UM223, VU83

"O Morning Star, How Fair and Bright" (Isa)
C105, E497, EL308, G827, N158, P69, UM247, VU98

"O-So-So" ("Come Now, O Prince of Peace") OL-AF20201411 (Isa)
EL247, G103, S2232, SH235

"It Came Upon the Midnight Clear" 31078 (Isa, Luke) (O)
C153, CG132, E89, EL282, G123, GR194, N131, P38, SH89, UM218 (PD), VU44

"Angels from the Realms of Glory" 31669 (Isa, Luke)
C149, CG126, E93, EL275, G143, GR190, N126, P22, SH99, UM220 (PD), VU36

+"Hark! the Herald Angels Sing" ("Jesus, the Light of the World") (Isa, Luke)
CG129, G127, GR214, N160, SH103, ZS62 (*See also* WS3056)

"Hark! the Herald Angels Sing" (Isa, Luke) (O)
C150, CG127, E87, EL270, G119, GR180, N144, P31, SH94, UM240 (PD), VU48

"Love Has Come" (Isa, Titus, Luke, Christmas)
EL292, G110, WS3059

+"Jesus, Jesus, Oh, What a Wonderful Child" 4206259 (Isa, Luke, Christmas)
EL297, G126, N136, WS3060

+"On Christmas Night" (Isa, Luke, Christmas)
CG133, EL274, G112, N143, WS3064

"I Come with Joy" (Pss, Comm.)
C420, CG456, E304, EL482, G515, N349, P507, SH682, UM617, VU477

"In the Bleak Midwinter" (Pss, Titus, Luke)
CG131, E112, EL294, G144, GR186, N128, P36, UM221 (PD), VU55

+"Fairest Lord Jesus" (Titus)
C97, CG159, E383/384, EL838, G630, GR113, N44, P306, SH7, UM189 (PD), VU341

"Love Came Down at Christmas" (Titus, Luke)
CG147, E84, GR181, N165, UM242

"Here, O My Lord, I See Thee" 136265(Titus, Comm.)
C416, CG460, E318, G517, GR411, N336, P520, UM623, VU459

"Away in a Manger" 38583 (Luke)
C147, CG110/111, E101, EL277, G114/115, GR197, N124, P24/P25, SH79, UM217, VU69

"What Child Is This" 30983 (Luke)
C162, CG148, E115, EL296, G145, GR179, N148, P53, SH105, UM219 (PD), VU74

"Good Christian Friends, Rejoice" (Luke)
C164, CG122, E107, EL288, G132, GR195, N129, P28, UM224, VU35

"The Friendly Beasts" ("Jesus, Our Brother") (Luke)
N138, UM227, VU56

"Infant Holy, Infant Lowly" 162538 (Luke)
C163, CG139, EL276, G128, P37, UM229, VU58

"O Come, All Ye Faithful" 31054 (Luke)
C148, CG103, E83, EL283, G133, GR174, N135, P41, SH96, UM234 (PD), VU60 (Fr.)

+"While Shepherds Watched Their Flocks" (Luke)
C154, E94/95, CG123, G117/118, GR189, P58/59, UM236 (PD), VU75

"'Twas in the Moon of Wintertime" (Luke)
C166, E114, EL284, G142, N151, P61, UM244, VU71

+"The First Noel" (Luke)
C151, CG124, E109, EL300, G147, GR188, N139, P56, UM245 (PD), VU90 (Fr.) and VU91

"Once in Royal David's City" 197156 (Luke)
C165, CG104, E102, EL269, G140, GR175, N145, P49, UM250 (PD), VU62

"Rise Up, Shepherd, and Follow" (Luke)
G135, P50, S2096, VU70

"Still, Still, Still" (Luke)
CG117, G124, P47, VU47, WS3066

"From Heaven Above" (Luke)
C146, CG128, E80, EL268, G111, N130, P54, VU72

Additional Contemporary and Modern Suggestions

"His Name Is Wonderful" 1122230 (Isa)
CG343, SH454, UM174, ZS31

"How Majestic Is Your Name" 26007 (Isa)
C63, CG326, G613, S2023, ZS26

"Jesus, Jesus, Oh, What a Wonderful Child" 4206259 (Isa, Luke)
EL297, G126, N136, WS3060

"Marvelous Light" 4491002 (Isa)

"You are the Light" 6238098 (Isa)

"How Great Is Our God" 4348399 (Isa, Pss)
CG322, GR31, SH458, WS3003

"Sing Alleluia to the Lord" 26272 (Titus)
C32, S2258, SH685

"Lord, I Lift Your Name on High" 117947 (Luke)
CG606, EL857, S2088, SH205

"Bethlehem" (Luke)
WS3053, ZS58

"Gloria en las Alturas" ("Glory in the Highest") OL-71336 (Luke)
WS3057

"Welcome to Our World" 2317391 (Luke)
WS3067, V-5 (1), p. 34 Vocal Solo

"Peace in the Manger" 7104263 (Luke, Christmas)

"What Love Has Done" 5836965 (Luke, Christmas)

+"Behold Him" 7133698 (Luke, Christmas)

+"King of Kings" 7127647 (Christmas)

Solo/Ensemble Suggestions

"Hark! The Herald Angels Sing" (Luke, Christmas)
V-1 p. 13

+"Silent Night" (Luke, Christmas)
V-3 (4) p. 58

"O Holy Night" (Luke, Christmas)
V-8 p. 93

"Sleep, Little Baby" (Luke, Christmas)
V-10 p. 27
+"In the First Light" (Christmas)
V-5(1) p. 28
+"Some Children See Him" OL-31741 (Luke, Christmas)
WS3065
"Before the Marvel of This Night" (Luke)
Carl Schalk; AEC-1 p. 14
2-part mixed, keyboard (https://bit.ly/AEC-1-14)
"The Friendly Beasts" (Luke)
Arr. David M. Kellermeyer; AEC-3 p. 14
Unison, keyboard, opt. C-Instrument (https://bit.ly/AEC-3)

+Hymn Anthem

"Carol Medley"

This medley works well if all the hymnal arrangements are in F Major. Spice it up with alternate harmonizations. Use the first stanza for all hymns. This can be performed from memory by singers of all ages.

Introduction: Keyboard plays first four and last four measures of "Away in a Manger"

"Away in a Manger" – All voices, unison, with keyboard.

Interlude: As singers reach last word ("hay"), keyboard plays refrain of "Hark! the Herald Angels Sing."

"Hark! the Herald Angels Sing" – All, in parts or unison.

"Good Christian Friends, Rejoice" – Keyboard moves immediately from the previous hymn to this one. The pulse remains the same.
Keyboard: mm. 1-2, holding the last note.
Choir: Sing mm. 1-2, holding the last note.
Keyboard: mm. 3-4, holding the last note.
Choir: Sing mm. 3-4, holding the last note.
Keyboard and choir continue as written.

Interlude: As choir singes last word of previous hymn ("today"), keyboard plays the last seven measures of the next hymn. Pulse remains the same

"Angel We Have Heard on High" – All sing in unison, with keyboard. Sing in parts on the final refrain.

Other Suggestions

Visuals:
O Darkness/light, joy, yoke, boots, fire, child, names
P New song, nations, glory, Ps. 96:10a, gavel, nature images
E Jesus, Second Coming, crucifix
G Tax register, manger scene, shepherds, angels, Luke 2:14

Introit or Sung Benediction: G158, N152, P30, VU95, stanzas 1-2. "Born in the Night, Mary's Child" (Luke, Christmas)
Introit: EL819, G388, S2274, SH405. "Come, All You People" (Pss)
Introit: C146. "From Heaven Above" (Luke)
Greeting: WSL4. "We gather in preparation" (Luke, Christmas)
Prayer Confession: WSL5. "Merciful God" (Luke)
Prayer of Preparation: WSL8. "God of glory" (Isa, Luke)
Prayer: UM231. Christmas (Luke)
Reading: C152, CG108 (Luke)
Response: G584, CG321, N756/758, SH100, VU895. "Gloria" (Luke)
Response: S3190, stanza 1. "Mary Had a Little Lamb" (Luke)
Offertory Prayer: WSL127. "Joy to the world" (Luke)
Communion Hymn: EL487, WS3170. "What Feast of Love" (Same tune as "What Child Is This")
Blessing: WSL7. "The light that enlivens" (Isa)
Additional Scriptures for Christmas Day: Isa 52:7-10; Ps 98; Heb 1:1-4, (5-12); John 1:1-14
Theme Ideas: Grace, Jesus: Incarnation, Light, Praise

Notes

NRSVue

Isaiah 63:7-9
7I will recount the gracious deeds of the LORD,
the praiseworthy acts of the LORD,
because of all that the LORD has done for us
and the great favor to the house of Israel
that he has shown them according to his mercy,
according to the abundance of his steadfast love.
8For he said, "Surely they are my people,
children who will not act deceitfully,"
and he became their savior
9 in all their distress.
It was no messenger or angel
but his presence that saved them;
in his love and pity it was he who redeemed them;
he lifted them up and carried them all the days of old.

Psalm 148 (G16/17, N721, P256, UM861)
1Praise the LORD!
Praise the LORD from the heavens;
praise him in the heights!
2Praise him, all his angels;
praise him, all his host!
3Praise him, sun and moon;
praise him, all you shining stars!
4Praise him, you highest heavens
and you waters above the heavens!
5Let them praise the name of the LORD,
for he commanded and they were created.
6He established them forever and ever;
he fixed their bounds, which cannot be passed.
7Praise the LORD from the earth,
you sea monsters and all deeps,
8fire and hail, snow and frost,
stormy wind fulfilling his command!
9Mountains and all hills,
fruit trees and all cedars!
10Wild animals and all cattle,
creeping things and flying birds!
11Kings of the earth and all peoples,
princes and all rulers of the earth!
12Young men and women alike,
old and young together!
13Let them praise the name of the LORD,
for his name alone is exalted;
his glory is above earth and heaven.
14He has raised up a horn for his people,
praise for all his faithful,
for the people of Israel who are close to him.
Praise the LORD!

CEB

Isaiah 63:7-9
7I will recount the LORD's faithful acts;
I will sing the LORD's praises,
because of all the LORD did for us,
for God's great favor toward the house of Israel.
God treated them compassionately
and with deep affection.
8God said, "Truly, they are my people,
children who won't do what is wrong."
God became their savior.
9During all their distress, God also was distressed,
so a messenger who served him saved them.
In love and mercy God redeemed them,
lifting and carrying them throughout earlier times.

Psalm 148 (G16/17, N721, P256, UM861)
1Praise the LORD!
Praise the LORD from heaven!
Praise God on the heights!
2Praise God, all of you who are his messengers!
Praise God, all of you who comprise his heavenly forces!
3Sun and moon, praise God!
All of you bright stars, praise God!
4You highest heaven, praise God!
Do the same, you waters that are above the sky!
5Let all of these praise the LORD's name
because God gave the command and they were created!
6God set them in place always and forever.
God made a law that will not be broken.
7Praise the LORD from the earth,
you sea monsters and all you ocean depths!
8Do the same, fire and hail, snow and smoke,
stormy wind that does what God says!
9Do the same, you mountains, every single hill,
fruit trees, and every single cedar!
10Do the same, you animals—wild or tame—
you creatures that creep along and you birds that fly!
11Do the same, you kings of the earth and every single person,
you princes and every single ruler on earth!
12Do the same, you young men—young women too!—
you who are old together with you who are young!
13Let all of these praise the LORD's name
because only God's name is high over all.
Only God's majesty is over earth and heaven.
14God raised the strength of his people,
the praise of all his faithful ones—
that's the Israelites,
the people who are close to him.
Praise the LORD!

NRSVue

Hebrews 2:10-18

[10]It was fitting that God, for whom and through whom all
things exist, in bringing many children to glory, should make
the pioneer of their salvation perfect through sufferings. [11]For
the one who sanctifies and those who are sanctified all have one
Father. For this reason Jesus is not ashamed to call them brothers and sisters, [12]saying,

"I will proclaim your name to my brothers and sisters;
in the midst of the congregation I will praise you."

[13]And again,

"I will put my trust in him."

And again,

"Here am I and the children whom God has given me."

[14]Since, therefore, the children share flesh and blood, he
himself likewise shared the same things, so that through death
he might destroy the one who has the power of death, that is,
the devil, [15]and free those who all their lives were held in slavery
by the fear of death. [16]For it is clear that he did not come to help
angels but the descendants of Abraham. [17]Therefore he had to
become like his brothers and sisters in every respect, so that he
might become a merciful and faithful high priest in the service
of God, to make a sacrifice of atonement for the sins of the
people. [18]Because he himself was tested by what he suffered, he
is able to help those who are being tested.

Matthew 2:13-23

[13]Now after they had left, an angel of the Lord appeared to
Joseph in a dream and said, "Get up, take the child and his
mother, and flee to Egypt, and remain there until I tell you, for
Herod is about to search for the child, to destroy him." [14]Then
Joseph got up, took the child and his mother by night, and went
to Egypt [15]and remained there until the death of Herod. This
was to fulfill what had been spoken by the Lord through the
prophet, "Out of Egypt I have called my son."

[16]When Herod saw that he had been tricked by the magi, he
was infuriated, and he sent and killed all the children in and
around Bethlehem who were two years old or under, according
to the time that he had learned from the magi. [17]Then what had
been spoken through the prophet Jeremiah was fulfilled:

18 "A voice was heard in Ramah,
wailing and loud lamentation,
Rachel weeping for her children;
she refused to be consoled, because they are no more."

[19]When Herod died, an angel of the Lord suddenly appeared
in a dream to Joseph in Egypt and said, [20]"Get up, take the child
and his mother, and go to the land of Israel, for those who were
seeking the child's life are dead." [21]Then Joseph got up, took the
child and his mother, and went to the land of Israel. [22]But when
he heard that Archelaus was ruling Judea in place of his father
Herod, he was afraid to go there. And after being warned in a
dream, he went away to the district of Galilee. [23]There he made
his home in a town called Nazareth, so that what had been spoken through the prophets might be fulfilled, "He will be called a
Nazarene."

CEB

Hebrews 2:10-18

[10]It was appropriate for God, for whom and through whom
everything exists, to use experiences of suffering to make perfect
the pioneer of salvation. This salvation belongs to many sons
and daughters whom he's leading to glory. [11]This is because the
one who makes people holy and the people who are being made
holy all come from one source. That is why Jesus isn't ashamed
to call them brothers and sisters when he says,

[12]I will publicly announce your name to my brothers and
sisters.

I will praise you in the middle of the assembly.

[13]He also says,

I will rely on him.

And also,

Here I am with the children whom God has given to me.

[14]Therefore, since the children share in flesh and blood,
he also shared the same things in the same way. He did this to
destroy the one who holds the power over death—the devil—by
dying. [15]He set free those who were held in slavery their entire
lives by their fear of death. [16]Of course, he isn't trying to help
angels, but rather he's helping Abraham's descendants. [17]There-
fore, he had to be made like his brothers and sisters in every way.
This was so that he could become a merciful and faithful high
priest in things relating to God, in order to wipe away the sins
of the people. [18]He's able to help those who are being tempted,
since he himself experienced suffering when he was tempted.

Matthew 2:13-23

[13]When the magi had departed, an angel from the Lord
appeared to Joseph in a dream and said, "Get up. Take the
child and his mother and escape to Egypt. Stay there until I tell
you, for Herod will soon search for the child in order to kill
him." [14]Joseph got up and, during the night, took the child and
his mother to Egypt. [15]He stayed there until Herod died. This
fulfilled what the Lord had spoken through the prophet: *I have
called my son out of Egypt.*

[16]When Herod knew the magi had fooled him, he grew very
angry. He sent soldiers to kill all the male children in Bethlehem
and in all the surrounding territory who were two years old and
younger, according to the time that he had learned from the
magi. [17]This fulfilled the word spoken through Jeremiah the
prophet:

18 *A voice was heard in Ramah,
weeping and much grieving.
Rachel weeping for her children,
and she did not want to be comforted,
because they were no more.*

[19]After King Herod died, an angel from the Lord appeared in
a dream to Joseph in Egypt. [20]"Get up," the angel said, "and take
the child and his mother and go to the land of Israel. Those who
were trying to kill the child are dead." [21]Joseph got up, took the
child and his mother, and went to the land of Israel. [22]But when
he heard that Archelaus ruled over Judea in place of his father
Herod, Joseph was afraid to go there. Having been warned in a
dream, he went to the area of Galilee. [23]He settled in a city called
Nazareth so that what was spoken through the prophets might
be fulfilled: He will be called a Nazarene.

Primary Hymns and Songs for the Day

"Hark! the Herald Angels Sing" (Isa, Matt) (O)
C150, CG127, E87, EL270, G119, GR180, N144, P31, SH94, UM240 (PD), VU48
H-3 Hbl-26, 67; Chr-91; Desc-75; Org-89
S-1 #234-6. Harms. and desc.
"O Sing a Song of Bethlehem" 2798408 (Isa, Heb, Matt)
CG164, G159, N51, P308, UM179 (PD)
H-3 Hbl-15, 20, 34, 84; Chr-150; Org-67
S-2 #100-103. Various treatments
"Jesus, the Light of the World" 6363190 (Isa, Matt, Epiphany)
WS3056 (*See also* CG129, G127, GR214, N160, SH103, ZS62)
"All Creatures of Our God and King" 2420288 (Pss) (O)
C22, CG307, E400, EL835, G15, GR34, N17, P455, SH16, UM62, VU217 (Fr.)
H-3 Hbl-44; Chr-21; Desc-66; Org-73
S-1 #198-204. Various treatments
"What Child Is This" 30983 (Matt, Christmas, Epiphany) (C)
C162, CG148, E115, EL296, G145, GR179, N148, P53, SH105, UM219 (PD), VU74
H-3 Hbl-102; Chr-210; Desc-46; Org-47
S-1 #150. Guitar chords
"Joy to the World" 24016 (Matt, Christmas, Epiphany) (C)
C143, CG102, E100, EL267, G134, GR201, N132, P40, SH95, UM246 (PD), VU59

Additional Hymn Suggestions

"Great Is Thy Faithfulness" 18723 (Isa)
C86, CG48, EL733, G39, GR44, N423, P276, SH48, UM140, VU288
"Children of the Heavenly Father" (Isa)
CG69, EL781, GR56, N487, SH42, UM141
"We Sing of Your Glory" (Isa, Christmas)
EL849, S2011, SH622
"On Christmas Night" (Isa, Pss, Christmas)
CG133, EL274, G112, N143, WS3064
"Love Came Down at Christmas" (Isa, Matt) (C)
CG147, E84, GR181, N165, UM242
"Good Christian Friends, Rejoice" 85158 (Pss, Heb, Matt)
C164, CG122, E107, EL288, G132, GR195, N129, P28, UM224, VU35
"O God, We Bear the Imprint of Your Face" (Heb)
C681, G759, N585, P385
"Jesus Entered Egypt" (Heb)
G154
"Holy God, We Praise Thy Name" 114555 (Heb) (O)
CG9, E366, EL414 (PD), G4, GR2, N276, P460, SH431, UM79, VU894 (Fr.)
"To God Be the Glory" (Heb)
C72, CG349, G634, GR531, P485, SH545, UM98 (PD)
"Thou Hidden Source of Calm Repose" (Heb)
GR123, UM153 (PD)
"At the Name of Jesus" (Heb)
CG424, E435, EL416, G264, GR105, P148, SH657, UM168, VU335
"The Friendly Beasts" (Heb)
N138, UM227, VU56
"In Bethlehem a Newborn Boy" OL-59261 (Matt)
E246, G153, P35 (PD), VU77
"Niño Lindo" ("Child So Lovely") (Matt)
UM222
"Break Forth, O Beauteous Heavenly Light" (Heb, Matt)
E91, G130, GR206, N140, P26, UM223, VU83
"Infant Holy, Infant Lowly" 162538 (Heb, Matt)
C163, CG139, EL276, G128, P37, UM229, VU58
"Rock-a-Bye, My Dear Little Boy" (Matt)
UM235
"Once in Royal David's City" 197156 (Heb, Matt) (O)
C165, CG104, E102, EL269, G140, GR175, N145, P49, UM250 (PD), VU62
"Our Parent, by Whose Name" (Matt)
E587, EL640, UM447, VU555
"O Food to Pilgrims Given" (Matt, Comm.)
E308/E309, UM631
"Star-Child" (Matt)
CG145, S2095, ZS63
"Joseph Dearest, Joseph Mine" (Matt)
N105, S2099
"Bethlehem" (Matt, Christmas)
WS3053, ZS58
"Welcome to Our World" 2317391 (Matt, Christmas)
WS3067, V-5 (1), p. 34 Vocal Solo
"Bread of the World" (Comm.)
C387, E301, G499, GR412, N346, P502, UM624, VU461

Additional Contemporary and Modern Suggestions

"Great Is the Lord" 1149 (Isa)
CG325, G614, S2022, SH459
+"Mighty to Save" 4591782 (Isa)
WS3038
+"Glory in the highest" (*"Gloria en las Alturas"*) OL-71336 (Isa, Christmas)
WS3057
"The Steadfast Love of the Lord" 21590 (Isa)
"Because of Your Love" 4662501 (Isa)
+"I Could Sing of Your Love Forever" 1043199 (Isa)
+"What Love Has Done" 5836965 (Isa, Christmas)
"Gloria a Dios" ("Glory to God") (PD) (Pss, Christmas)
CG320, EL164, G585, S2033, SH381
"We Will Glorify the King of Kings" 19038 (Pss)
CG360, S2087
"God of Wonders" 3118757 (Pss)
SH9, WS3034
"Doxology" 5465879 (Pss)
"Let Everything That Has Breath" 2430979 (Pss)
+"Alpha and Omega" 4654148 (Pss)
+"Every Praise" 6623483 (Pss)
"Glory in the Highest" 4822451 (Pss, Christmas)
"Sing the Praise of God Our Maker" OL-80079 (Heb)
WS3013
"You Are My All in All" 825356 (Heb)
CG571, G519, SH335, WS3040, ZS184
"You Are My King" ("Amazing Love") 2456623 (Heb)
SH539, WS3102
"He Is Able" 115420 (Heb)
"Before the Throne of God Above" 2306412 (Heb)
"Once Again" 1564362 (Heb)
"Amazing Love" 192553 (Heb)
"That's Why We Praise Him" 2668576 (Heb)
+"Is He Worthy?" 7108951 (Heb)
+"Behold Him" 7133698 (Heb, Christmas)
+"King of Kings" 7127647 (Heb, Christmas)
+"New Wine" 7102397 (Heb, New Year)
+"Mary Had a Little Lamb" OL-88810 (Heb, Matt)
WS3190
"The Virgin Mary Had a Baby Boy" 2957081 (Matt, Christmas)
S2098, VU73, ZS60
+"The Family Prayer Song" 1680466 (Matt)
S2188
"Peace in the Manger" 7104263 (Matt, Christmas)

Solo/Ensemble Suggestions

"Sing a Song of Joy" (Pss)
V-4 p. 2
"Little Baby Jesus" (Matt, Christmas)
V-8 p. 96
"Jesus, What a Wonderful Child" (Matt, Christmas)
V-5 (1) p. 48
"To Touch His Tiny Hand" (Matt, Christmas)
V-10 p. 22
+ Gentle Jesus, Meek and Mild (Matt, Christmas)
V-1 p. 11
+"I Wonder as I Wander" (Matt, Christmas)
V-8 p. 88
+"The Coventry Carol" (Matt)
V-3 (4) p. 44
+"A Cradle Song" (Matt)
David Hurd: Augsburg 9781506495200
SATB, organ, opt. C instrument (https://bit.ly/Aug-95200)
"Angel Song" (Christmas)
Patricia Mock & Jon Paige; Hal Leonard 00274491
SAB, piano (https://bit.ly/H-4491)

+Hymn Anthem

"Go, Tell It on the Mountain" 3063235 (Matt) (C)
C167, CG143, E99, EL290, G136, GR203, N154, P29, SH90, UM251, VU43, Z75 (PD), ZS59

This spiritual setting should not be performed faster than MM = 88. Place a strong emphasis on the first and third beats of each measure. Have the choir step from side to side in rehearsal, if not in performance, to feel this slow swinging beat.

Refrain: Male soloist sings refrain once in a declamatory manner, adding improvised notes to the melody. *A cappella.*

Stanza 1: Soloist continues, but without improvisation. Keyboard plays only the chords on the first beat of each measure. Sustain the chord throughout the measure. Play last measure as written.

Refrain: All voices, unison. Keyboard plays only notes on the four beats of each measure, omitting dotted rhythms, syncopations, etc. *Mezzo piano.*

Stanza 2: All voices in parts (SATB, SA, SAB), *a cappella* (or accompanied). Gradual crescendo throughout the stanza to *forte.*

Refrain: SATB (or unison), *forte.* Keyboard plays hymnal setting, with strength.

Stanza 3: Female soloist sings this stanza. Choir may accompany the soloist by singing parts on an "ooh" vowel. *Mezzo piano.*

Refrain: SATB (or unison), piano. Female soloist lightly sings alto part one octave higher on an "ah" vowel. *A cappella* or lightly accompanied.

Other Suggestions

You may also choose to use Watch Night (Dec. 31) scriptures for this service.

Visuals:
O Salvation history, people, children, Christ
P Ps. 148;1a, angels, sun/moon/stars, nature imagery
E Pioneer, crucifix, brothers/sisters, Jesus, manacles
G Angel/Joseph, escape, Herod/Wise Men, suffering children, return, Nazareth

Prayer: WSL11. "Radiant Morning Star" (Matt)

For children: N138, UM227, VU56. "The Friendly Beasts." Accompany a soloist with guitar or piano. This tune is also recommended for 12/31, using another text.

Theme Ideas: Children / Family of God, Jesus: Childhood, Lament, Praise, Redemption / Salvation

Notes

NRSVue

Ecclesiastes 3:1-13

For everything there is a season and a time for every matter
under heaven:
2 a time to be born, and a time to die;
a time to plant and a time to pluck up what is planted;
3 a time to kill and a time to heal;
a time to break down and a time to build up;
4 a time to weep and a time to laugh;
a time to mourn and a time to dance;
5 a time to throw away stones and a time to gather stones
together;
a time to embrace and a time to refrain from embracing;
6 a time to seek and a time to lose;
a time to keep and a time to throw away;
7 a time to tear and a time to sew;
a time to keep silent and a time to speak;
8 a time to love and a time to hate;
a time for war and a time for peace.
9 What gain have the workers from their toil? 10 I have seen the
business that God has given to everyone to be busy with. 11 He
has made everything suitable for its time; moreover, he has put
a sense of past and future into their minds, yet they cannot find
out what God has done from the beginning to the end. 12 I know
that there is nothing better for them than to be happy and enjoy
themselves as long as they live; 13 moreover, it is God's gift that all
should eat and drink and take pleasure in all their toil.

Psalm 8 (G25, N624, P162/163, SH6, UM743)

1 O LORD, our Sovereign,
how majestic is your name in all the earth!
You have set your glory above the heavens.
2 Out of the mouths of babes and infants
you have founded a bulwark because of your foes,
to silence the enemy and the avenger.
3 When I look at your heavens, the work of your fingers,
the moon and the stars that you have established;
4 what are human beings that you are mindful of them,
mortals that you care for them?
5 Yet you have made them a little lower than God
and crowned them with glory and honor.
6 You have given them dominion over the works of your hands;
you have put all things under their feet,
7 all sheep and oxen,
and also the beasts of the field,
8 the birds of the air, and the fish of the sea,
whatever passes along the paths of the seas.
9 O LORD, our Sovereign,
how majestic is your name in all the earth!

CEB

Ecclesiastes 3:1-13

1 There's a season for everything and a time for every matter
under the heavens:
2 a time for giving birth and a time for dying,
a time for planting and a time for uprooting what was
planted,
3 a time for killing and a time for healing,
a time for tearing down and a time for building up,
4 a time for crying and a time for laughing,
a time for mourning and a time for dancing,
5 a time for throwing stones and a time for gathering stones,
a time for embracing and a time for avoiding embraces,
6 a time for searching and a time for losing,
a time for keeping and a time for throwing away,
7 a time for tearing and a time for repairing,
a time for keeping silent and a time for speaking,
8 a time for loving and a time for hating,
a time for war and a time for peace.
9 What do workers gain from all their hard work? 10 I have
observed the task that God has given human beings. 11 God has
made everything fitting in its time, but has also placed eternity
in their hearts, without enabling them to discover what God has
done from beginning to end.
12 I know that there's nothing better for them but to enjoy
themselves and do what's good while they live. 13 Moreover, this is
the gift of God: that all people should eat, drink, and enjoy the
results of their hard work.

Psalm 8 (G25, N624, P162/163, SH6, UM743)

1 LORD, our Lord, how majestic
is your name throughout the earth!
You made your glory higher than heaven!
2 From the mouths of nursing babies
you have laid a strong foundation
because of your foes,
in order to stop vengeful enemies.
3 When I look up at your skies,
at what your fingers made—
the moon and the stars
that you set firmly in place—
4 what are human beings
that you think about them;
what are human beings
that you pay attention to them?
5 You've made them only slightly less than divine,
crowning them with glory and grandeur.
6 You've let them rule over your handiwork,
putting everything under their feet—
7 all sheep and all cattle,
the wild animals too,
8 the birds in the sky,
the fish of the ocean,
everything that travels the pathways of the sea.
9 LORD, our Lord, how majestic is your name throughout the
earth!

NRSVue

Revelation 21:1-6a

1Then I saw a new heaven and a new earth, for the first
heaven and the first earth had passed away, and the sea was no
more. 2And I saw the holy city, the new Jerusalem, coming down
out of heaven from God, prepared as a bride adorned for her
husband. 3And I heard a loud voice from the throne saying,

"See, the home of God is among mortals.
He will dwell with them;
they will be his peoples,
and God himself will be with them and be their God;
4 he will wipe every tear from their eyes.
Death will be no more;
mourning and crying and pain will be no more,
for the first things have passed away."

5And the one who was seated on the throne said, "See, I am
making all things new." Also he said, "Write this, for these words
are trustworthy and true." 6aThen he said to me, "It is done! I am
the Alpha and the Omega, the Beginning and the End."

Matthew 25:31-46

31"When the Son of Man comes in his glory and all the angels
with him, then he will sit on the throne of his glory. 32All the
nations will be gathered before him, and he will separate people
one from another as a shepherd separates the sheep from the
goats, 33and he will put the sheep at his right hand and the goats
at the left. 34Then the king will say to those at his right hand,
'Come, you that are blessed by my Father, inherit the kingdom
prepared for you from the foundation of the world, 35for I was
hungry and you gave me food, I was thirsty and you gave me
something to drink, I was a stranger and you welcomed me, 36I
was naked and you gave me clothing, I was sick and you took
care of me, I was in prison and you visited me.' 37Then the righteous will answer him, 'Lord, when was it that we saw you hungry
and gave you food or thirsty and gave you something to drink?
38And when was it that we saw you a stranger and welcomed you
or naked and gave you clothing? 39And when was it that we saw
you sick or in prison and visited you?' 40And the king will answer
them, 'Truly I tell you, just as you did it to one of the least of
these brothers and sisters of mine, you did it to me.' 41Then he
will say to those at his left hand, 'You who are accursed, depart
from me into the eternal fire prepared for the devil and his
angels, 42for I was hungry and you gave me no food, I was thirsty
and you gave me nothing to drink, 43I was a stranger and you
did not welcome me, naked and you did not give me clothing,
sick and in prison and you did not visit me.' 44Then they also will
answer, 'Lord, when was it that we saw you hungry or thirsty or
a stranger or naked or sick or in prison and did not take care
of you?' 45Then he will answer them, 'Truly I tell you, just as you
did not do it to one of the least of these, you did not do it to
me.' 46And these will go away into eternal punishment but the
righteous into eternal life."

CEB

Revelation 21:1-6a

1Then I saw a new heaven and a new earth, for the former
heaven and the former earth had passed away, and the sea was
no more. 2I saw the holy city, New Jerusalem, coming down out
of heaven from God, made ready as a bride beautifully dressed
for her husband. 3I heard a loud voice from the throne say,
"Look! God's dwelling is here with humankind. He will dwell
with them, and they will be his peoples. God himself will be with
them as their God. 4He will wipe away every tear from their eyes.
Death will be no more. There will be no mourning, crying, or
pain anymore, for the former things have passed away." 5Then
the one seated on the throne said, "Look! I'm making all things
new." He also said, "Write this down, for these words are trustworthy and true." 6aThen he said to me, "All is done. I am the
Alpha and the Omega, the beginning and the end."

Matthew 25:31-46

31"Now when the Human One comes in his majesty and all his
angels are with him, he will sit on his majestic throne. 32All the
nations will be gathered in front of him. He will separate them
from each other, just as a shepherd separates the sheep from the
goats. 33He will put the sheep on his right side. But the goats he
will put on his left.

34"Then the king will say to those on his right, 'Come, you
who will receive good things from my Father. Inherit the kingdom that was prepared for you before the world began. 35I was
hungry and you gave me food to eat. I was thirsty and you gave
me a drink. I was a stranger and you welcomed me. 36I was naked
and you gave me clothes to wear. I was sick and you took care of
me. I was in prison and you visited me.'

37"Then those who are righteous will reply to him, 'Lord,
when did we see you hungry and feed you, or thirsty and give
you a drink? 38When did we see you as a stranger and welcome
you, or naked and give you clothes to wear? 39When did we see
you sick or in prison and visit you?'

40"Then the king will reply to them, 'I assure you that when
you have done it for one of the least of these brothers and sisters
of mine, you have done it for me.'

41"Then he will say to those on his left, 'Get away from me, you
who will receive terrible things. Go into the unending fire that
has been prepared for the devil and his angels. 42I was hungry
and you didn't give me food to eat. I was thirsty and you didn't
give me anything to drink. 43I was a stranger and you didn't
welcome me. I was naked and you didn't give me clothes to wear.
I was sick and in prison, and you didn't visit me.'

44"Then they will reply, 'Lord, when did we see you hungry
or thirsty or a stranger or naked or sick or in prison and didn't
do anything to help you?' 45Then he will answer, 'I assure you
that when you haven't done it for one of the least of these, you
haven't done it for me.' 46And they will go away into eternal punishment. But the righteous ones will go into eternal life."

Primary Hymns and Songs for the Day
"O God, Our Help in Ages Past" 43152 (Eccl) (O)
C67, CG566, E680, EL632, G687, GR15, N25, P210, SH41, UM117 (PD), VU806
H-3 Hbl-33, 80; Chr-60, 143; Desc-93; Org-132
S-1 #293-296. Various treatments
"Hymn of Promise" 126529 (Eccl)
C638, CG545, G250, N433, UM707, VU703
"How Great Thou Art" 14181 (Pss)
C33, CG323, EL856, G625, GR32, N35, P467, SH14, UM77, VU238 (Fr.)
"O Holy City, Seen of John" (PD-TO) (Rev)
E582/583, G374, N613, P453, UM726, VU709
H-3 Chr-139, 145; Desc-77
S-1 #241-242. Orff arr. and desc.
"Cuando el Pobre" ("When the Poor Ones") OL-97385 (Matt)
C662, EL725, G762, P407, SH240, UM434, VU702
"Here Am I" (Matt) (C)
C654, S2178

Additional Hymn Suggestions
"O God, in a Mysterious Way" (PD) (Eccl)
CG39, E677, G30, GR51N412, P270, SH47
"For the Beauty of the Earth" 43200 (Eccl)
C56, CG341, E416, EL879, G14, GR82, P473, N28, SH21, UM92 (PD), VU226
"Sing Praise to God Who Reigns Above" 7061649 (Eccl)
C6, CG315, E408, EL871, G645, GR5, N6, P483, UM126 (PD), VU216
"Great Is Thy Faithfulness" 18723 (Eccl) (O)
C86, CG48, EL733, G39, GR44, N423, P276, SH48, UM140, VU288
"Many and Great, O God" (Eccl)
C58, CG28, E385, EL837, G21, N3, N341, P271 (PD), SH5, UM148, VU308
"By Gracious Powers" (Eccl)
E695/696, EL626, G818, N413, P342, UM517
"Rejoice! Rejoice, Believers" (Rev)
E68, EL244, G362, P15
"This Is a Day of New Beginnings" 231043 (Rev)
C518, N417, UM383
"For the Healing of the Nations" 1510804 (Rev)
C668, CG698, G346, N576, UM428, VU678
"This Is the Feast of Victory" (Rev, Comm.)
E417/418, EL165/EL166/EL167, G513, P594, UM638, VU904
"I Want to Be Ready" (Rev)
N616, UM722 (PD-TO), Z151
"O What Their Joy and Their Glory Must Be" (PD) (Rev)
E623, N385, UM727 (PD)
"Blessed Quietness" (Rev)
C267, CG244, N284 (PD), S2142, Z206
"Come, Ye Disconsolate" (Rev, Matt)
C502, EL607, GR347, SH342, UM510 (PD)
"All Who Hunger" (Rev, Matt)
C419, CG303, EL461, G509, S2126, VU460
"Like a Mother Who Has Borne Us" (Matt)
G44, N583
"We Praise You, O God, Our Redeemer" (Matt)
CG356, EL870, G612, GR42, N420, VU218
"There's a Spirit in the Air" (Matt) (C)
C257, N294, P433, UM192, VU582
"Where Cross the Crowded Ways of Life" 2961345 (Matt)
C665, CG657, E609, EL719, G343, N543, P408, UM427 (PD), VU681
"Jesu, Jesu" 3049039 (Matt)
C600, CG656, E602, EL708, G203, N498, P367, SH155, UM432, VU593, S-1 #63. Vocal part
"All Who Love and Serve Your City" 1277415 (Matt)
C670, CG674, E570/571, EL724, G351, P413, UM433
+"The Voice of God is Calling" (PD) (Matt)
C666, UM436 (PD)
"Christ for the World We Sing" (Matt)
E537, GR450, UM568 (PD)
"Lord, Whose Love Through Humble Service" (Matt)
C461, CG650, E610, EL712, GR454, P427, SH239, UM581
"Rescue the Perishing" 34549 (Matt)
CG480, GR457, UM591 (PD)
"I Come with Joy" (Matt, New Year, Comm.)
C420, CG456, E304, EL482, G515, N349, P507, SH682, UM617, VU477
"Together We Serve" (Matt)
G767, S2175
"In Remembrance of Me" 25156 (Matt, Comm.)
C403, CG462, G521, S2254, SH667, ZS203
+"As We Gather at Your Table" (Matt, Comm.)
EL522, N332, S2268, SH411, VU457
+"Come, Share the Lord" (Matt, Comm.)
C408, CG459, G510, S2269, VU469

Additional Contemporary and Modern Suggestions
"I Could Sing of Your Love Forever" 1043199 (Eccl)
"Be Glorified" 2732646 (Eccl)
+"Jesus at the Center" 6115180 (Eccl, Rev)
+"Beautiful Things" 5665521 (Eccl, Rev)
"How Majestic Is Your Name" 26007 (Pss)
C63, CG326, G613, S2023, ZS26
"How Great Is Our God" 4348399 (Pss)
CG322, GR31, SH458, WS3003
"Across the Lands" 3709898 (Pss, Christmas)
SH654, WS3032
"God of Wonders" 3118757 (Pss)
SH9, WS3034
"Majestic" 4573308 (Pss)
"You Have Saved Us" 5548514 (Pss)
+"Friend of God" 3991651 (Pss)
"There's Something About That Name" 14064 (Rev)
C115, GR124, UM171
"Spirit Song" 27824 (Rev)
C352, SH409, UM347
"Soon and Very Soon" 11249 (Rev)
CG562, EL439, G384, GR629, SH357, UM706, Z198, ZS136, S-2 #187. Piano arr.
"We Will Glorify the King of Kings" 19038 (Rev)
CG360, S2087
"You Who Are Thirsty" 814453 (Rev)
S2132
"O Freedom" OL-68414 (Rev)
S2194 (PD-TO), Z102, ZS109
"There Is a Higher Throne" 3994672 (Rev)
WS3189
+"You Are" 4387343 (Rev)
+"Alpha and Omega" 4654148 (Rev)
+"Behold Him" 7133698 (Rev, Christmas)
+"Called Me Higher" 5887880 (Rev, Matt)
+"Head to the Heart" 7047283 (Rev, Matt)
"Holy and Anointed One" 164361 (Rev, Matt)
"To Him Who Sits on the Throne" 20429 (Rev, Matt)
+"New Wine" 7102397 (Rev, Matt, New Year)
+"No Outsiders" 7101035 (Matt)
+"We Resist" ("Prayer Chant") (Matt)
ConvergenceMP.com
+"Let Justice Roll" ("Like a River") 4974842 (Matt)
"All of Me" 6290160 (Matt, Covenant, New Year)
"Peace in the Manger" 7104263 (Matt, Christmas)

Solo/Ensemble Suggestions

+"A Time for Everything" (Eccl)
V-3 (5) p. 23
"I Will Sing of Thy Great Mercies" (Eccl, Pss)
V-4 p. 43
"My Lord, What a Morning" (Rev)
V-3 (1) p. 39
V-3 (4) p. 32
"Maybe the Rain" (Rev)
V-5 (2) p. 27
"Sing for Christ Is Born" (Rev, Christmas)
V-10 p. 16
"Come to the Water" (Rev, Matt)
WS3114
"Reach Out to Your Neighbor" (Matt)
V-8 p. 372
"In All These You Welcomed Me" (Matt)
William Bradley Roberts; AEC-2 p. 63
Mixed unison, organ (https://bit.ly/AEC-2-63)
"God has Work for Us to Do" (Matt)
Mark Miller; Choristers Guild CGA-1288
SATB, piano (https://bit.ly/CG-1288)

+Hymn Anthem

"This Is the Feast of Victory" (Rev, Comm.)
E417, G513, P594, UM638, VU904
Introduction: Keyboard (organ) plays antiphon. *Forte.*
Antiphon: All sing in unison each time the antiphon is sung. Congregation may be invited to sing from the beginning, or after the antiphon has been sung 2-3 times. *Forte.*
Stanza 1: All voices, unison. *Mezzo forte.*
Stanza 2: S/A only, unison. *Mezzo forte.*
Stanza 3: Soloist. *Mezzo forte.*
Stanza 4: T/B only, unison. *Mezzo forte.*
Stanza 5: All voices, unison. *Molto ritard* the last two measures, and *crescendo* to *forte.*
Final antiphon: All voices unison. Tempo should be slower that before. *Forte.*
Ending: Instead of playing the final chord in the final antiphon, the keyboard returns to the beginning of the antiphon. The choir holds the final "A" for two measures and then rests two measures. Choir joins the keyboard for the final "alleluias." Choir may sing SATB on the last "alleluia."

Other Suggestions

These scriptures may also be used on January 1.
Visuals:
O Clock, birth/death, mourn/dance, weep/laugh, etc.
P Glory, newborns, fingers, moon/stars, humanity, earth
E Earth/space, heaven, bride, throne, wipe tears, Rev. 21:5a
G Second Coming, nations, goats/sheep, feeding, etc.
Opening Prayer: WSL64. "God of all creation" (Pss, Covenant)
Prayer: WSL217. "Lord of the morning" (Matt, New Year)
Prayer: WSL199. "O God of the crucified Christ" (Matt)
Canticle: UM734. "Canticle of Hope" (Rev)
Offertory Prayer: WSL98 (Matt) or WSL105 (Rev)
Litany: WSL158. "Here in this sanctuary" (Matt)
Litany: C157. "For All Who Give You a Face" (Matt)
Response: C638, CG545, G250, N433, UM707, VU703, stanza 3. "Hymn of Promise" (Eccl)
Blessing: WSL27 or WSL159 or WSL169 (Matt)
Theme Ideas: Compassion, God: Glory of God, Justice, New Creation, Patience

Notes

NRSVue

Jeremiah 31:7-14
7For thus says the LORD:
Sing aloud with gladness for Jacob,
and raise shouts for the chief of the nations;
proclaim, give praise, and say,
"Save, O LORD, your people,
the remnant of Israel."
8See, I am going to bring them from the land of the north
and gather them from the farthest parts of the earth,
among them the blind and the lame,
those with child and those in labor together;
a great company, they shall return here.
9With weeping they shall come,
and with consolations I will lead them back;
I will let them walk by brooks of water,
in a straight path where they shall not stumble,
for I have become a father to Israel,
and Ephraim is my firstborn.
10Hear the word of the LORD, O nations,
and declare it in the coastlands far away;
say, "He who scattered Israel will gather him
and will keep him as a shepherd does a flock."
11For the LORD has ransomed Jacob
and has redeemed him from hands too strong for him.
12They shall come and sing aloud on the height of Zion,
and they shall be radiant over the goodness of the LORD,
over the grain, the wine, and the oil,
and over the young of the flock and the herd;
their life shall become like a watered garden,
and they shall never languish again.
13Then shall the young women rejoice in the dance,
and the young men and the old shall be merry.
I will turn their mourning into joy;
I will comfort them and give them gladness for sorrow.
14I will give the priests their fill of fatness,
and my people shall be satisfied with my bounty,
says the LORD.

Psalm 147:12-20 (G657, N720, P255, UM859)
12Extol the LORD, O Jerusalem!
Praise your God, O Zion!
13For he strengthens the bars of your gates;
he blesses your children within you.
14He grants peace within your borders;
he fills you with the finest of wheat.
15He sends out his command to the earth;
his word runs swiftly.
16He gives snow like wool;
he scatters frost like ashes.
17He hurls down hail like crumbs—
who can stand before his cold?
18He sends out his word and melts them;
he makes his wind blow, and the waters flow.
19He declares his word to Jacob,
his statutes and ordinances to Israel.
20He has not dealt thus with any other nation;
they do not know his ordinances.
Praise the LORD!

CEB

Jeremiah 31:7-14
7The LORD proclaims:
Sing joyfully for the people of Jacob;
shout for the leading nation.
Raise your voices with praise and call out:
"The LORD has saved his people,
the remaining few in Israel!"
8I'm going to bring them back from the north;
I will gather them from the ends of the earth.
Among them will be the blind and the disabled,
expectant mothers and those in labor;
a great throng will return here.
9With tears of joy they will come;
while they pray, I will bring them back.
I will lead them by quiet streams
and on smooth paths so they don't stumble.
I will be Israel's father,
Ephraim will be my oldest child.
10Listen to the LORD's word, you nations,
and announce it to the distant islands:
The one who scattered Israel will gather them
and keep them safe, as a shepherd his flock.
11The LORD will rescue the people of Jacob
and deliver them from the power of those stronger than they
are.
12They will come shouting for joy on the hills of Zion,
jubilant over the LORD's gifts:
grain, wine, oil, flocks, and herds.
Their lives will be like a lush garden;
they will grieve no more.
13Then the young women will dance for joy;
the young and old men will join in.
I will turn their mourning into laughter
and their sadness into joy;
I will comfort them.
14I will lavish the priests with abundance
and shower my people with my gifts,
declares the LORD.

Psalm 147:12-20 (G657, N720, P255, UM859)
12Worship the LORD, Jerusalem!
Praise your God, Zion!
13Because God secures the bars on your gates,
God blesses the children you have there.
14God establishes your borders peacefully.
God fills you full with the very best wheat.
15God issues his command to the earth—
God's word speeds off fast!
16God spreads snow like it was wool;
God scatters frost like it was ashes;
17God throws his hail down like crumbs—
who can endure God's freezing cold?
18Then God issues his word and melts it all away!
God makes his winds blow;
the water flows again.
19God proclaims his word to Jacob;
his statutes and rules to Israel.
20God hasn't done that with any other nation;
those nations have no knowledge of God's rules.
Praise the LORD!

NRSVue

Ephesians 1:3-14

[3]Blessed be the God and Father of our Lord Jesus Christ, who has blessed us in Christ with every spiritual blessing in the heavenly places, [4]just as he chose us in Christ before the foundation of the world to be holy and blameless before him in love. [5]He destined us for adoption as his children through Jesus Christ, according to the good pleasure of his will, [6]to the praise of his glorious grace that he freely bestowed on us in the Beloved. [7]In him we have redemption through his blood, the forgiveness of our trespasses, according to the riches of his grace [8]that he lavished on us. With all wisdom and insight [9]he has made known to us the mystery of his will, according to his good pleasure that he set forth in Christ, [10]as a plan for the fullness of time, to gather up all things in him, things in heaven and things on earth. [11]In Christ we have also obtained an inheritance, having been destined according to the purpose of him who accomplishes all things according to his counsel and will, [12]so that we, who were the first to set our hope on Christ, might live for the praise of his glory. [13]In him you also, when you had heard the word of truth, the gospel of your salvation, and had believed in him, were marked with the seal of the promised Holy Spirit; [14]this is the pledge of our inheritance toward redemption as God's own people, to the praise of his glory.

John 1: (1-9), 10-18

In the beginning was the Word, and the Word was with God, and the Word was God. [2]He was in the beginning with God. [3]All things came into being through him, and without him not one thing came into being. What has come into being [4]in him was life, and the life was the light of all people. [5]The light shines in the darkness, and the darkness did not overtake it.

[6]There was a man sent from God whose name was John. [7]He came as a witness to testify to the light, so that all might believe through him. [8]He himself was not the light, but he came to testify to the light. [9]The true light, which enlightens everyone, was coming into the world.

[10]He was in the world, and the world came into being through him, yet the world did not know him. [11]He came to what was his own, and his own people did not accept him. [12]But to all who received him, who believed in his name, he gave power to become children of God, [13]who were born, not of blood or of the will of the flesh or of the will of man, but of God.

[14]And the Word became flesh and lived among us, and we have seen his glory, the glory as of a father's only son, full of grace and truth. [15](John testified to him and cried out, "This was he of whom I said, 'He who comes after me ranks ahead of me because he was before me.' ") [16]From his fullness we have all received, grace upon grace. [17]The law indeed was given through Moses; grace and truth came through Jesus Christ. [18]No one has ever seen God. It is the only Son, himself God, who is close to the Father's heart, who has made him known.

CEB

Ephesians 1:3-14

[3]Bless the God and Father of our Lord Jesus Christ! He has blessed us in Christ with every spiritual blessing that comes from heaven. [4]God chose us in Christ to be holy and blameless in God's presence before the creation of the world. [5]God destined us to be his adopted children through Jesus Christ because of his love. This was according to his goodwill and plan [6]and to honor his glorious grace that he has given to us freely through the Son whom he loves. [7]We have been ransomed through his Son's blood, and we have forgiveness for our failures based on his overflowing grace, [8]which he poured over us with wisdom and understanding. [9]God revealed his hidden design to us, which is according to his goodwill and the plan that he intended to accomplish through his Son. [10]This is what God planned for the climax of all times: to bring all things together in Christ, the things in heaven along with the things on earth. [11]We have also received an inheritance in Christ. We were destined by the plan of God, who accomplishes everything according to his design. [12]We are called to be an honor to God's glory because we were the first to hope in Christ. [13]You too heard the word of truth in Christ, which is the good news of your salvation. You were sealed with the promised Holy Spirit because you believed in Christ. [14]The Holy Spirit is the down payment on our inheritance, which is applied toward our redemption as God's own people, resulting in the honor of God's glory.

John 1: (1-9), 10-18

In the beginning was the Word
and the Word was with God
and the Word was God.
[2]The Word was with God in the beginning.
[3]Everything came into being through the Word,
and without the Word
nothing came into being.
What came into being
4 through the Word was life,
and the life was the light for all people.
[5]The light shines in the darkness,
and the darkness doesn't extinguish the light.

[6]A man named John was sent from God. [7]He came as a witness to testify concerning the light, so that through him everyone would believe in the light. [8]He himself wasn't the light, but his mission was to testify concerning the light.

[9]The true light that shines on all people
was coming into the world.
[10]The light was in the world,
and the world came into being through the light,
but the world didn't recognize the light.
[11]The light came to his own people,
and his own people didn't welcome him.
[12]But those who did welcome him,
those who believed in his name,
he authorized to become God's children,
13 born not from blood
nor from human desire or passion,
but born from God.
[14]The Word became flesh
and made his home among us.
We have seen his glory,
glory like that of a father's only son,
full of grace and truth.

[15]John testified about him, crying out, "This is the one of whom I said, 'He who comes after me is greater than me because he existed before me.'"

[16]From his fullness we have all received grace upon grace;
17 as the Law was given through Moses,
so grace and truth came into being through Jesus Christ.
[18]No one has ever seen God.
God the only Son,
who is at the Father's side,
has made God known.

Primary Hymns and Songs for the Day

"Hark! The Herald Angels Sing" (John) (O)
C150, CG127, E87, EL270, G119, GR180, N144, P31, SH94, UM240 (PD), VU48
H-3 Hbl-26, 67; Chr-91; Desc-75; Org-89
S-1 #234-6. Harmonizations and descant
"Go, Tell It on the Mountain" 3063235 (John) (O)
C167, CG143, E99, EL290, G136, GR203, N154, P29, SH90, UM251, VU43, Z75 (PD), ZS59
H-3 Hbl-17; Chr-73; Desc-45; Org-46
"Break Forth, O Beauteous Heavenly Light" (Jer)
E91, G130, GR206, N140, P26, UM223, VU83
"Alleluia" 16811 (Jer)
C106, N765, SH699, UM186
"Shout to the North" 1562261 (Jer)
G319, WS3042
"Lord of the Dance" 78529 (John)
G157, P302, UM261, VU352
H-3 Chr-106; Org-81
"Joy to the World" 24016 (Eph, John, Christmas) (C)
C143, CG102, E100, EL267, G134, GR201, N132, P40, SH95, UM246 (PD), VU59
S-1 #19-20. Trumpet descants

Additional Hymn Suggestions

"All Things Bright and Beautiful" (Jer)
C61, CG23, E405, G20, GR20, N31, P267, SH1, UM147 (PD), VU291
"Shall We Gather at the River" 93731 (Jer)
C701, CG561, EL423, G375, GR632, N597, SH366, UM723, VU710
"Live Into Hope" (Jer)
G772, P332, VU699
"Child of Blessing, Child of Promise" (Jer, Eph)
G486, P498, N325, UM611, VU444
"Gather Us In" OL-00031 (Jer, John, Epiphany)
C284, EL532, G401, S2236, SH393
"There's a Wideness in God's Mercy" 3063417 (Eph)
C73, CG41, E469/470, EL587/588, G435, GR64, N23, P298, SH526, UM121, VU271
"The First Noel" (Eph)
C151, CG124, E109, EL300, G147, GR188, N139, P56, UM245 (PD), VU90 (Fr.) and VU91
"It Is Well with My Soul" 25376 (Eph)
C561, CG573, EL785, G840, GR344, N438, SH305, UM377 (PD), Z20
+"Amazing Grace" 22025 (Eph)
C546, CG587, E671, EL779, G649, GR572, N547/548, P280, SH523, UM378 (PD), VU266 (Fr.), Z211
"The Church's One Foundation" 55377 (Eph)
C272, CG246, E525, EL654, G321, GR388/646, N386, P442, SH233, UM545/546, VU332 (Fr.)
"Christ Is Made the Sure Foundation" 7036287 (Eph)
C275, CG248, E518, EL645, G394, GR101, N400, P416/417, SH225, UM559 (PD), VU325
"God of Grace and God of Glory" 43107 (Eph)
C464, CG285, E594/595, EL705, G307, GR45, N436, P420, SH250, UM577, VU686
"I'm Gonna Live So God Can Use Me" (Eph)
C614, G700, GR615, P369, S2153, SH632, VU575
"Wonder of Wonders" (Eph)
C378, G489, N328, P499, S2247
+"Depth of Mercy" 1320726 (Eph)
GR234, UM355
+"Take, O Take Me as I Am" 4562041 (Eph, New Year)
EL814, G698, SH620, WS3119
"On Jordan's Bank the Baptist's Cry" (John)
E76, EL249, G96, N115, P10, SH77, VU20
"Of the Father's Love Begotten" (John)
C104, CG113, E82, EL295, G108, GR166, N118, P309, SH81, UM184, VU61
"Savior of the Nations, Come" (John)
E54, EL263, G102, P14 (PD), SH67, UM214
"Love Came Down at Christmas" (John)
CG147, E84, GR181, N165, UM242
+"O Morning Star, How Fair and Bright" (John, Epiph.)
C105, E497, EL308, G827, N158, P69, UM247, VU98
"On This Day Earth Shall Ring" (John)
E92, G141, P46, UM248 (PD)
"Jesus, Lover of My Soul" (John)
C542, CG406, E699, G440, GR120, N546, P303, SH542/543, UM479, VU669
"O Splendor of God's Glory Bright" (John)
E5, G666, N87, P474, UM679, VU413
"Thou Didst Leave Thy Throne" (John)
CG165, GR202, S2100, SH86
"Just a Closer Walk with Thee" (John)
C557, EL697, G835, S2158, SH584, Z46 (PD)
+*"Siyahamba"* ("We Are Marching") 1321512 (John, Epiphany)
C442, CG155, EL866, G853, N526, S2235-ab, SH717, VU646, ZS111
"Jesus, the Light of the World" 6363190 (John)
WS3056 (*See also* CG129, G127, GR214, N160, SH103, ZS62)

Additional Contemporary and Modern Suggestions

"Trading My Sorrows" 2574653 (Jer)
3108
"I Will Rise" 5183450 (Jer)
+"Beautiful Things" 5665521 (Jer)
+"You Keep Hope Alive" 7125876 (Jer, John)
"Someone Asked the Question" 1640279 (Jer, Pss)
N523, S2144
"My Tribute" 11218 (Eph)
C39, CG574, GR580, N14, SH434, UM99; V-8, p. 5. Vocal Solo
+"Holy, Holy" 18792 (Eph)
P140, S2039
+"Hallelujah" ("Your Love Is Amazing") 3091812 (Eph)
WS3027
+"You Are My King" ("Amazing Love") 2456623 (Eph)
SH539, WS3102
+"Amazing Grace" ("My Chains Are Gone") 4768151 (Eph)
GR574, WS3104
+"We Fall Down" 2437367 (Eph)
G368, WS3187
"Foundation" 706151 (Eph)
+"Grace Like Rain" 3689877 (Eph)
+"His Mercy Is More" 7065053 (Eph)
+ "Love Came Down" 5148938 (Eph)
+"No Outsiders" 7101035 (Eph)
+"Love Moves You" ("Love Alone") 5775514 (Eph)
+"Shine on Us" 1754646 (John)
+"You are the Light" 6238098 (John)
+"Tremble" 7065049 (John)
+"Trinity Song" 7068847 (John)
+"Behold Him" 7133698 (John, Christmas)
"Behold, What Manner of Love" 1596 (John)
"Shine, Jesus, Shine" 30426 (John, Epiphany)
CG156, EL671, G192, GR217, S2173, SH102; V-3 (2), p. 48. Vocal Solo
+"Light of the World" 73342 (John, Epiphany)
S2204
"Goodness Is Stronger than Evil" OL-02636 (John)
EL721, G750, S2219

+"How Great Is Our God" 4348399 (John)
CG322, GR31, SH458, WS3003
+"Here I Am to Worship" 3266032 (John, Epiphany)
CG297, SH395, WS3177, ZS145

Solo/Ensemble Suggestions

"A Song of Trust" (Jer)
V-4 p. 20
+"Come, Thou Fount of Every Blessing" (Jer, Eph)
V-3 (3) p. 22
V-3 (4) p. 3
V-6 p. 4
+"And Can It Be That I Should Gain" (Eph)
V-1 p. 29
+"Grace Greater Than Our Sin" (Eph)
V-8 p. 180
+"Love Moved First" (Eph)
V-9 p. 56
+"In the Image of God" (Eph, John)
V-8 p. 362
+"In the First Light" (John, Epiphany)
V-5(1) p. 28
+"O Splendor of God's Glory Bright" (John)
Arr. Brenda Portman; Augsburg 9781506495347
Unison or 2-part, organ (https://bit.ly/Aug-95347)
+"Christmas Hymn" (John)
Arr. Keith Christopher; Daybreak 00125044
SATB, piano, opt. instruments (https://bit.ly/HL-25044)

+Hymn Anthem

"Jesus, Joy of Our Desiring" (John, Comm.)
GR129, UM644 (PD), VU328

A simple anthem can be fashioned from the choir singing this hymn while the keyboard plays the well-known J.S. Bach chorale prelude on this tune. The choir can sing in unison or parts. Bach used this arrangement in one of his many cantatas. Most keyboard editions of this work are in G Major, so the choir will be singing one whole step higher than printed in the hymnal.

Bach Prelude Measures	Hymn Measures
9-12	1-4
14-17	5-8
24-27	9-12
29-32	13-16
40-43	17-20
46-49	21-24
52-55	25-28
57-60	29-32

Other Suggestions

This Sunday may also be celebrated as Epiphany of the Lord Sunday using the scriptures and ideas for January 6.

Visuals:
- **O** Praise, singing, old and young dancing, blind, lame, children, pregnant woman
- **P** Gates, children, wheat, runner, winter
- **E** Christ, children, adoption certificate, wrapped gift, crucifix
- **G** Creation, light/darkness, Christ (Word), John the Baptist

Introit: WS3152. "Welcome" OL-232386 (*See also* EL641, G301) (Jer)

Benediction: WSL167. "Go! Never stop going out" (John)

Theme Ideas: Joy, Redemption/Salvation, Peace, Grace, Light

Notes

NRSVue

Isaiah 60:1-6

Arise, shine, for your light has come,
and the glory of the LORD has risen upon you.
2For darkness shall cover the earth
and thick darkness the peoples,
but the LORD will arise upon you,
and his glory will appear over you.
3Nations shall come to your light
and kings to the brightness of your dawn.
4Lift up your eyes and look around;
they all gather together; they come to you;
your sons shall come from far away,
and your daughters shall be carried in their nurses' arms.
5Then you shall see and be radiant;
your heart shall thrill and rejoice,
because the abundance of the sea shall be brought to you;
the wealth of the nations shall come to you.
6A multitude of camels shall cover you,
the young camels of Midian and Ephah;
all those from Sheba shall come.
They shall bring gold and frankincense
and shall proclaim the praise of the LORD.

Psalm 72:1-7, 10-14 (G149, N667, P205, UM795)

Give the king your justice, O God,
and your righteousness to a king's son.
2May he judge your people with righteousness
and your poor with justice.
3May the mountains yield prosperity for the people,
and the hills, in righteousness.
4May he defend the cause of the poor of the people,
give deliverance to the needy,
and crush the oppressor.
5May he live while the sun endures
and as long as the moon, throughout all generations.
6May he be like rain that falls on the mown grass,
like showers that water the earth.
7In his days may righteousness flourish
and peace abound, until the moon is no more.
. . . .
10May the kings of Tarshish and of the isles
render him tribute;
may the kings of Sheba and Seba
bring gifts.
11May all kings fall down before him,
all nations give him service.
12For he delivers the needy when they call,
the poor and those who have no helper.
13He has pity on the weak and the needy
and saves the lives of the needy.
14From oppression and violence he redeems their life,
and precious is their blood in his sight.

CEB

Isaiah 60:1-6

Arise! Shine! Your light has come;
the LORD's glory has shone upon you.
2Though darkness covers the earth
and gloom the nations,
the LORD will shine upon you;
God's glory will appear over you.
3Nations will come to your light
and kings to your dawning radiance.
4Lift up your eyes and look all around:
they are all gathered; they have come to you.
Your sons will come from far away,
and your daughters on caregivers' hips.
5Then you will see and be radiant;
your heart will tremble and open wide,
because the sea's abundance will be turned over to you;
the nations' wealth will come to you.
6Countless camels will cover your land,
young camels from Midian and Ephah.
They will all come from Sheba,
carrying gold and incense,
proclaiming the LORD's praises.

Psalm 72:1-7, 10-14 (G149, N667, P205, UM795)

God, give your judgments to the king.
Give your righteousness to the king's son.
2Let him judge your people with righteousness
and your poor ones with justice.
3Let the mountains bring peace to the people;
let the hills bring righteousness.
4Let the king bring justice to people who are poor;
let him save the children of those who are needy,
but let him crush oppressors!
5Let the king live as long as the sun,
as long as the moon,
generation to generation.
6Let him fall like rain upon fresh-cut grass,
like showers that water the earth.
7Let the righteous flourish throughout their lives,
and let peace prosper until the moon is no more.
. . . .
10Let the kings of Tarshish and the islands bring tribute;
let the kings of Sheba and Seba present gifts.
11Let all the kings bow down before him;
let all the nations serve him.
12Let it be so, because he delivers the needy who cry out,
the poor, and those who have no helper.
13He has compassion on the weak and the needy;
he saves the lives of those who are in need.
14He redeems their lives from oppression and violence;
their blood is precious in his eyes.

NRSVue

Ephesians 3:1-12

This is the reason that I, Paul, am a prisoner for Christ Jesus for the sake of you gentiles, 2for surely you have already heard of the commission of God's grace that was given me for you 3and how the mystery was made known to me by revelation, as I wrote above in a few words, 4a reading of which will enable you to perceive my understanding of the mystery of Christ. 5In former generations this mystery was not made known to humankind, as it has now been revealed to his holy apostles and prophets by the Spirit: 6that is, the gentiles have become fellow heirs, members of the same body, and sharers in the promise in Christ Jesus through the gospel.

7Of this gospel I have become a servant according to the gift of God's grace that was given me by the working of his power. 8Although I am the very least of all the saints, this grace was given to me to bring to the gentiles the news of the boundless riches of Christ 9and to make everyone see what is the plan of the mystery hidden for ages in God, who created all things, 10so that through the church the wisdom of God in its rich variety might now be made known to the rulers and authorities in the heavenly places. 11This was in accordance with the eternal purpose that he has carried out in Christ Jesus our Lord, 12in whom we have access in boldness and confidence through faith in him.

Matthew 2:1-12

In the time of King Herod, after Jesus was born in Bethlehem of Judea, magi from the east came to Jerusalem, 2asking, "Where is the child who has been born king of the Jews? For we observed his star in the east and have come to pay him homage." 3When King Herod heard this, he was frightened, and all Jerusalem with him, 4and calling together all the chief priests and scribes of the people, he inquired of them where the Messiah was to be born. 5They told him, "In Bethlehem of Judea, for so it has been written by the prophet:

6 'And you, Bethlehem, in the land of Judah,
are by no means least among the rulers of Judah,
for from you shall come a ruler
who is to shepherd my people Israel.' "

7Then Herod secretly called for the magi and learned from them the exact time when the star had appeared. 8Then he sent them to Bethlehem, saying, "Go and search diligently for the child, and when you have found him, bring me word so that I may also go and pay him homage." 9When they had heard the king, they set out, and there, ahead of them, went the star that they had seen in the east, until it stopped over the place where the child was. 10When they saw that the star had stopped, they were overwhelmed with joy. 11On entering the house, they saw the child with Mary his mother, and they knelt down and paid him homage. Then, opening their treasure chests, they offered him gifts of gold, frankincense, and myrrh. 12And having been warned in a dream not to return to Herod, they left for their own country by another road.

CEB

Ephesians 3:1-12

This is why I, Paul, am a prisoner of Christ for you Gentiles. 2You've heard, of course, about the responsibility to distribute God's grace, which God gave to me for you, right? 3God showed me his secret plan in a revelation, as I mentioned briefly before (4when you read this, you'll understand my insight into the secret plan about Christ). 5Earlier generations didn't know this hidden plan that God has now revealed to his holy apostles and prophets through the Spirit. 6This plan is that the Gentiles would be coheirs and parts of the same body, and that they would share with the Jews in the promises of God in Christ Jesus through the gospel. 7I became a servant of the gospel because of the grace that God showed me through the exercise of his power.

8God gave his grace to me, the least of all God's people, to preach the good news about the immeasurable riches of Christ to the Gentiles. 9God sent me to reveal the secret plan that had been hidden since the beginning of time by God, who created everything. 10God's purpose is now to show the rulers and powers in the heavens the many different varieties of his wisdom through the church. 11This was consistent with the plan he had from the beginning of time that he accomplished through Christ Jesus our Lord. 12In Christ we have bold and confident access to God through faith in him.

Matthew 2:1-12

After Jesus was born in Bethlehem in the territory of Judea during the rule of King Herod, magi came from the east to Jerusalem. 2They asked, "Where is the newborn king of the Jews? We've seen his star in the east, and we've come to honor him."

3When King Herod heard this, he was troubled, and everyone in Jerusalem was troubled with him. 4He gathered all the chief priests and the legal experts and asked them where the Christ was to be born. 5They said, "In Bethlehem of Judea, for this is what the prophet wrote:

6 *You, Bethlehem, land of Judah,*
by no means are you least among the rulers of Judah,
because from you will come one who governs,
who will shepherd my people Israel."

7Then Herod secretly called for the magi and found out from them the time when the star had first appeared. 8He sent them to Bethlehem, saying, "Go and search carefully for the child. When you've found him, report to me so that I too may go and honor him." 9When they heard the king, they went; and look, the star they had seen in the east went ahead of them until it stood over the place where the child was. 10When they saw the star, they were filled with joy. 11They entered the house and saw the child with Mary his mother. Falling to their knees, they honored him. Then they opened their treasure chests and presented him with gifts of gold, frankincense, and myrrh. 12Because they were warned in a dream not to return to Herod, they went back to their own country by another route.

Primary Hymns and Songs for the Day

"Hail to the Lord's Anointed" (PD) (Pss) (O)
C140, CG98, E616, EL311, G149, GR165, N104, P205, SH112, UM203, VU30
"Arise, Shine" (Isa)
S2005
"We Three Kings" 30983 " (Matt, Pss)
C172, CG151, E128, G151, GR208, P66, SH107, UM254 (PD)
H-3 Chr-208; Org-65
S-2 #97-98. Various treatments
"O Morning Star, How Fair and Bright" (Isa, Pss, Eph, Matt)
C105, E497, EL308, G827, N158, P69, UM247, VU98
"Star-Child" (Matt)
CG145, S2095, ZS63
"A Star Shone Bright" (Matt)
WS3051
"Siyahamba" ("We Are Marching") 1321512 (Matt, Epiphany)
C442, CG155, EL866, G853, N526, S2235-ab, SH717, VU646, ZS111
"Jesus Shall Reign" 1510 (Isa, Pss, Eph) (C)
C95, CG158, E544, EL434, G265, GR282, N300, P423, SH209, UM157 (PD), VU330
"Go, Tell It on the Mountain" 3063235 (Eph, Christmas) (C)
C167, CG143, E99, EL290, G136, GR203, N154, P29, SH90, UM251, VU43, Z75 (PD), ZS59
H-3 Hbl-17, 28, 61; Chr-73; Desc-45; Org-46

Additional Hymn Suggestions

"Awake! Awake, and Greet the New Morn" (Isa)
C138, EL242, G107, N107, SH66
"Arise, Your Light Is Come" OL-07293 (Isa)
CG87, EL314, G744, N164, P411, VU79
"Blessed Be the God of Israel" 860627 (Isa)
C135, CG88, E444, EL250/552, G109, P602, UM209, VU901
"Break Forth, O Beauteous Heavenly Light" (Isa)
E91, G130, GR206, N140, P26, UM223, VU83
"This Little Light of Mine" 5305434, OL-22794 (Isa)
N525, UM585, Z132 (*See also* EL677, N524, SH257)
"Deck Thyself, My Soul, with Gladness" (Isa, Comm.)
E339, EL488/EL489, G514, P506, UM612 (PD), VU463
+"Gather Us In" OL-00031 (Isa, Epiphany)
C284, EL532, G401, S2236, SH393
"There's a Song in the Air" (Isa, Pss, Matt)
C159, GR193, UM249 (PD)
"Christ, Whose Glory Fills the Skies" 808926 (Eph)
E7, EL553, G662, GR211, P462, UM173 (PD), VU336
"Ye Servants of God" 90765 (Eph)
C110, CG420, E535, EL825 (PD), G299, GR40, N305, P477, UM181 (PD), VU342
"Christ Is the World's Light" (Eph)
CG154, UM188
"Make Me a Captive, Lord" 1228206 (Eph)
GR587, P378, SH639, UM421
"Christ for the World We Sing" (Eph)
E537, GR450, UM568 (PD)
"Blessed Jesus, At Thy Word" (Eph)
E440, EL520, G395, N74, P454, UM596 (PD), VU500
"I'm Gonna Live So God Can Use Me" (Eph)
C614, G700, GR615, P369, S2153, SH632, VU575
"What Star Is This, with Beams So Bright" (Matt)
E124, G152, P68
"What Child Is This" 30983 (Matt)
C162, CG148, E115, EL296, G145, GR179, N148, P53, SH105, UM219 (PD), VU74
"In the Bleak Midwinter" (Matt)
CG131, E112, EL294, G144, GR186, N128, P36, UM221 (PD), VU55
"Love Came Down at Christmas" (Matt)
CG147, E84, GR181, N165, UM242
"De Tierra Lejana Venimos" ("From a Distant Home") (Matt)
P64, SH110, UM243, VU89
"The First Noel" 31047 (Matt)
C151, CG124, E109, EL300, G147, GR188, N139, P56, UM245 (PD), VU90 (Fr.) and VU91
"On This Day Earth Shall Ring" (Matt)
E92, G141, P46, UM248 (PD)
"O the Depth of Love Divine" (Matt, Comm.)
GR422, UM627
"Carol of the Epiphany" OL-32151 (Matt)
S2094
"Rise Up, Shepherd, and Follow" (Matt)
G135, P50, S2096, VU70
"The Virgin Mary Had a Baby Boy" 2957081 (Matt)
S2098, VU73, ZS60
+"Come, Little Children" OL-88797 (Matt)
WS3055
+"Some Children See Him" OL-31741 (Matt, Christmas)
WS3065
"Love Has Come" (Matt, Epiphany)
EL292, G110, WS3059
"Spirit-Child Jesus" 2477279 (Matt, Epiphany)
WS3062
"If I Could Visit Bethlehem" 442894 (Matt, Epiphany)
WS3063

Additional Contemporary and Modern Suggestions

"Shine, Jesus, Shine" 30426 (Isa, Epiphany)
CG156, EL671, G192, GR217, S2173, SH102; V-3 (2), p. 48. Vocal Solo
"Mighty to Save" 4591782 (Isa)
WS3038
"Arise, Shine" 13797 (Isa)
"Let It Rise" 2240585 (Isa)
"Shine on Us" 1754646 (Isa, Epiphany)
"You are the Light" 6238098 (Isa, Pss, Epiphany)
+"The Kingdom Is Yours" 7109354 (Pss)
+"Let Justice Roll" ("Like a River") 4974842 (Pss)
"Veni Sancte Spiritus" ("Holy Spirit, Come to Us") OL-TaizeVN57 (Pss)
EL406, G281, S2118
"Grace Alone" 2335524 (Eph)
CG43, S2162, ZS100
"Alleluia" 16811 (Matt)
C106, N765, SH699, UM186
+"Honor and Praise" 1867485 (Matt, Epiphany)
S2018
"All Hail King Jesus" 12877 (Matt, Epiphany)
S2069, ZS53
"A Place at the Table" (Matt, Comm.)
G769, WS3149
"Here I Am to Worship" 3266032 (Matt, Epiphany)
CG297, SH395, WS3177, ZS145
+"We Worship and Adore You" 551194 (Matt, Epiphany)
+"Come and Behold Him" 2653581 (Matt, Epiphany)

Solo/Ensemble Suggestions

"For Behold, Darkness Shall Cover the Earth" and
"The People That Walked in Darkness" (Isa)
V-2
"Jesus, What a Wonderful Child" (Eph, Matt, Christmas)
V-5 (1) p. 48
"Love Came Down at Christmas" (Matt)
V-8 p. 90
+"Behold that Star!" (Matt, Epiphany)
V-3 (1) p. 34

"A Scottish Christmas Song" (Matt, Epiphany)
V-4 p. 4
"Fit for a King" (Matt, Epiphany)
V-10 p. 32
+"Go, Tell It on the Mountain" (Epiphany)
V-3 (1) p. 10
+"We Three Kings" (Matt)
Teresa Yoder; Paraclete Press 1847M
SAB, piano (https://bit.ly/PP-1847)
"The Silent Stars Shine Down on Us" (Epiphany)
arr. Thomas Keesecker; AEC-1 p. 76
2-part mixed, piano (https://bit.ly/AEC-1)

+Hymn Anthem

"That Boy-Child of Mary" (Epiphany)
EL293, G139, P55, UM241

Write 5 simple, one measure rhythm patterns and assign them to five un-pitched rhythm instruments (blocks, hand drum, claves, shakers, hand claps, etc). The accompaniment will be led by guitar (see S-1, #45 for guitar chords) or piano and these recurring rhythm patterns. Guitar (or piano) may continue during the entire anthem. Experiment!

Introduction: Start with rhythm pattern #1 for 2 measures, then add pattern #2 for 2 measures. Keep adding a pattern at 2 measure intervals until all are playing. Add guitar on F Major chord strums for the final two measures.
Refrain: All sing melody with all instruments accompanying.
Stanza 1: Soloist, guitar, and pattern #1.
Refrain: All sing melody with all instruments accompanying.
Stanza 2: Another soloist, guitar, and pattern #2.
Refrain: All sing melody with all instruments accompanying.
Stanza 3: Another soloist or small group, guitar, and pattern #3.
Continue in this manner until . . .
Stanza 6: All sing with guitar and all rhythm instruments.
Refrain: All sing melody with all instruments accompanying.
Ending: Do the reverse of the introduction, subtracting an instrument every 2 measures.

Invite the congregation to sing the refrain with you after they have heard it several times and are comfortable with it. You might ask children or youth to play the rhythm instrument parts.

Other Suggestions

These scriptures and ideas can be used on January 4 as Epiphany of the Lord Sunday.

Visuals:
O Light, glory, darkness, daughters/nurses, sea, camels
P Scales of justice, Christ, mountains/hills, poor/needy
E Manacles, letter, Christ, all nations
G Herod, Wise Men, star, Bethlehem, Mary/baby, gifts

Introit: C160, CG105, E81, EL272, G129, GR168, N127, P48 (PD), UM216, VU8. "Lo, How a Rose E'er Blooming" (Matt)
Canticle: N808. "Song of Simeon" (Pss, Matt)
Canticle: UM225. "Canticle of Simeon" (Pss, Matt)
Prayer: UM255 (Isa, Epiphany)
Response: C175. "Lovely Star in the Sky" (Matt)
Offertory Prayer: WSL150. "God of new beginnings" (New Year)
Sung Benediction: WS3062. "Spirit-Child Jesus" 2477279 (Matt)
Theme Ideas: Light, Justice, God: Wisdom, Grace, Jesus: Childhood

Notes

NRSVue

Isaiah 42:1-9

[1]Here is my servant, whom I uphold,
my chosen, in whom my soul delights;
I have put my spirit upon him;
he will bring forth justice to the nations.
[2]He will not cry out or lift up his voice,
or make it heard in the street;
[3]a bruised reed he will not break,
and a dimly burning wick he will not quench;
he will faithfully bring forth justice.
[4]He will not grow faint or be crushed
until he has established justice in the earth,
and the coastlands wait for his teaching.
[5]Thus says God, the LORD,
who created the heavens and stretched them out,
who spread out the earth and what comes from it,
who gives breath to the people upon it
and spirit to those who walk in it:
[6]I am the LORD, I have called you in righteousness;
I have taken you by the hand and kept you;
I have given you as a covenant to the people,
a light to the nations,
[7]to open the eyes that are blind,
to bring out the prisoners from the dungeon,
from the prison those who sit in darkness.
[8]I am the LORD; that is my name;
my glory I give to no other,
nor my praise to idols.
[9]See, the former things have come to pass,
and new things I now declare;
before they spring forth,
I tell you of them.

Psalm 29 (G10, N638, P180, UM761)

Ascribe to the LORD, O heavenly beings,
ascribe to the LORD glory and strength.
[2]Ascribe to the LORD the glory of his name;
worship the LORD in holy splendor.
[3]The voice of the LORD is over the waters;
the God of glory thunders,
the LORD, over mighty waters.
[4]The voice of the LORD is powerful;
the voice of the LORD is full of majesty.
[5]The voice of the LORD breaks the cedars;
the LORD breaks the cedars of Lebanon.
[6]He makes Lebanon skip like a calf
and Sirion like a young wild ox.
[7]The voice of the LORD flashes forth flames of fire.
[8]The voice of the LORD shakes the wilderness;
the LORD shakes the wilderness of Kadesh.
[9]The voice of the LORD causes the oaks to whirl
and strips the forest bare,
and in his temple all say, "Glory!"
[10]The LORD sits enthroned over the flood;
the LORD sits enthroned as king forever.
[11]May the LORD give strength to his people!
May the LORD bless his people with peace!

CEB

Isaiah 42:1-9

[1]But here is my servant, the one I uphold;
my chosen, who brings me delight.
I've put my spirit upon him;
he will bring justice to the nations.
[2]He won't cry out or shout aloud
or make his voice heard in public.
[3]He won't break a bruised reed;
he won't extinguish a faint wick,
but he will surely bring justice.
[4]He won't be extinguished or broken
until he has established justice in the land.
The coastlands await his teaching.
[5]God the LORD says—
the one who created the heavens,
the one who stretched them out,
the one who spread out the earth and its offspring,
the one who gave breath to its people
and life to those who walk on it—
[6]I, the LORD, have called you for a good reason.
I will grasp your hand and guard you,
and give you as a covenant to the people,
as a light to the nations,
[7] to open blind eyes, to lead the prisoners from prison,
and those who sit in darkness from the dungeon.
[8]I am the LORD;
that is my name;
I don't hand out my glory to others
or my praise to idols.
[9]The things announced in the past—look—they've already happened,
but I'm declaring new things.
Before they even appear,
I tell you about them.

Psalm 29 (G10, N638, P180, UM761)

You, divine beings! Give to the LORD—
give to the LORD glory and power!
[2]Give to the LORD the glory due his name!
Bow down to the LORD in holy splendor!
[3]The LORD's voice is over the waters;
the glorious God thunders;
the LORD is over the mighty waters.
[4]The LORD's voice is strong;
the LORD's voice is majestic.
[5]The LORD's voice breaks cedar trees—
yes, the LORD shatters the cedars of Lebanon.
[6]He makes Lebanon jump around like a young bull,
makes Sirion jump around like a young wild ox.
[7]The LORD's voice unleashes fiery flames;
[8] the LORD's voice shakes the wilderness—
yes, the LORD shakes the wilderness of Kadesh.
[9]The LORD's voice convulses the oaks,
strips the forests bare,
but in his temple everyone shouts, "Glory!"
[10]The LORD sits enthroned over the floodwaters;
the LORD sits enthroned—king forever!
[11]Let the LORD give strength to his people!
Let the LORD bless his people with peace!

NRSVue

Acts 10:34-43

[34]Then Peter began to speak to them: "I truly understand
that God shows no partiality, [35]but in every people anyone who
fears him and practices righteousness is acceptable to him. [36]You
know the message he sent to the people of Israel, preaching
peace by Jesus Christ—he is Lord of all. [37]That message spread
throughout Judea, beginning in Galilee after the baptism that
John announced: [38]how God anointed Jesus of Nazareth with
the Holy Spirit and with power; how he went about doing good
and healing all who were oppressed by the devil, for God was
with him. [39]We are witnesses to all that he did both in Judea
and in Jerusalem. They put him to death by hanging him on a
tree, [40]but God raised him on the third day and allowed him to
appear, [41]not to all the people but to us who were chosen by God
as witnesses and who ate and drank with him after he rose from
the dead. [42]He commanded us to preach to the people and to
testify that he is the one ordained by God as judge of the living
and the dead. [43]All the prophets testify about him that everyone
who believes in him receives forgiveness of sins through his
name."

Matthew 3:13-17

[13]Then Jesus came from Galilee to John at the Jordan, to be
baptized by him. [14]John would have prevented him, saying, "I
need to be baptized by you, and do you come to me?" [15]But Jesus
answered him, "Let it be so now, for it is proper for us in this
way to fulfill all righteousness." Then he consented. [16]And when
Jesus had been baptized, just as he came up from the water, suddenly the heavens were opened to him and he saw God's Spirit
descending like a dove and alighting on him. [17]And a voice from
the heavens said, "This is my Son, the Beloved, with whom I am
well pleased."

CEB

Acts 10:34-43

[34] Peter said, "I really am learning that God doesn't show
partiality to one group of people over another. [35]Rather, in
every nation, whoever worships him and does what is right is
acceptable to him. [36]This is the message of peace he sent to the
Israelites by proclaiming the good news through Jesus Christ:
He is Lord of all! [37]You know what happened throughout Judea,
beginning in Galilee after the baptism John preached. [38]You
know about Jesus of Nazareth, whom God anointed with the
Holy Spirit and endowed with power. Jesus traveled around
doing good and healing everyone oppressed by the devil
because God was with him. [39]We are witnesses of everything he
did, both in Judea and in Jerusalem. They killed him by hanging him on a tree, [40]but God raised him up on the third day
and allowed him to be seen, [41]not by everyone but by us. We are
witnesses whom God chose beforehand, who ate and drank with
him after God raised him from the dead. [42]He commanded us to
preach to the people and to testify that he is the one whom God
appointed as judge of the living and the dead. [43]All the prophets
testify about him that everyone who believes in him receives
forgiveness of sins through his name."

Matthew 3:13-17

[13]At that time Jesus came from Galilee to the Jordan River so
that John would baptize him. [14]John tried to stop him and said,
"I need to be baptized by you, yet you come to me?"

[15]Jesus answered, "Allow me to be baptized now. This is necessary to fulfill all righteousness."

So John agreed to baptize Jesus. [16]When Jesus was baptized,
he immediately came up out of the water. Heaven was opened
to him, and he saw the Spirit of God coming down like a dove
and resting on him. [17]A voice from heaven said, "This is my Son
whom I dearly love; I find happiness in him."

Primary Hymns and Songs for the Day

"Fairest Lord Jesus" 27800 (Isa, Matt) (O)
C97, CG159, E383/384, EL838, G630, GR113, N44, P306, SH7, UM189 (PD), VU341
H-3 Hbl-57; Chr-63; Desc-25, 94; Org-22, 135
S-1 #301. Descant
S-2 #158. Choral harmonization

"When Jesus Came to Jordan" 2678157 (Isa, Matt)
CG152, EL305, P72, SH113, UM252
H-3 Chr-211

"Spirit Song" 27824 (Matt)
C352, SH409, UM347

"Spirit of God, Descend upon My Heart" 2083 (Matt)
C265, CG243, EL800, G688, GR294, N290, P326, SH277, UM500 (PD), VU378

"Take Me to the Water" (PD) (Matt, Baptism)
C367, G480, N322, SH665, WS3165, ZS190

"Canto de Esperanza" ("Song of Hope") 5193990 (Isa) (C)
G765, P432, S2186, SH721, VU424

Additional Hymn Suggestions

"Today We All Are Called to Be Disciples" (Isa)
G757, P434, VU507

"Jesus Shall Reign" 1510 (Isa)
C95, CG158, E544, EL434, G265, GR282, N300, P423, SH209, UM157 (PD), VU330

"Jesus, the Very Thought of Thee" (Isa)
C102, CG386, E642, EL754, G629, GR127, N507, P310, UM175 (PD)

"Breathe on Me, Breath of God" 99481 (Isa)
C254, CG235, E508, G286, GR304, N292, P316, SH224/273, UM420 (PD), VU382 (Fr.)

"The Church of Christ, in Every Age" (Isa) (C)
C475, EL729, G320, N306, P421, UM589, VU601

"Gather Us In" OL-00031 (Isa)
C284, EL532, G401, S2236, SH393

"For the Healing of the Nations" 1510804 (Isa, Acts)
C668, CG698, G346, N576, UM428, VU678

"O For a Thousand Tongues to Sing" 1369 (Isa, Pss) (O)
C5, CG332, E493, EL886, G610, GR1, N42, P466, SH439, UM57 (PD), VU326 (*See also* WS3001)

+"He Is Lord" 1515225 (Acts)
C117, CG208, GR268, SH657, UM177, Z233

"The Strife is O'er, the Battle Done" (Acts)
C221, E208, EL366, G236, GR256, N242, P119, SH193, UM306, VU159

"Come, Ye Faithful, Raise the Strain" 355929 (Acts)
C215, CG218, E199/200, EL363, G234, GR253, N230, P115/114, UM315 (PD), VU165

"This Is My Song" (Acts)
C722, CG697, EL887, G340, N591, UM437

"Filled with the Spirit's Power" (Acts)
N266, UM537, VU194

"In Christ There Is No East or West" 2608952 (UMH ONLY St. 3 OL-13651) (Acts, Matt)
C687, CG273, E529, EL650 (PD), G317/318, GR392, N394/395, P439/440, UM548, VU606, Z65 (PD)

"On Jordan's Bank the Baptist's Cry" (Acts, Matt)
E76, EL249, G96, N115, P10, SH77, VU20

"I Come with Joy" (Acts, Comm.)
C420, CG456, E304, EL482, G515, N349, P507, SH682, UM617, VU477

"Wild and Lone the Prophet's Voice" 3413029 (Acts, Matt)
G163, P409, S2089

"At the Font We Start Our Journey" (Acts, Baptism)
N308, S2114

"Down to the River to Pray" 4369457 (Acts, Baptism)
WS3164

"We Know That Christ Is Raised" OL-40344 (Acts, Baptism)
E296, EL449, G485, P495, UM610, VU448

"Spirit of Faith, Come Down" (Acts, Matt)
GR289, UM332 (PD)

"See How Great a Flame Aspires" (Acts, Matt)
GR465, UM541

+"O Breath of Life" OL-90731 (Acts, Matt)
WS3146

"Sweet, Sweet Spirit" (Matt)
C261, CG241, G408, GR361, N293, P398, SH410, UM334

"Come, Holy Ghost, Our Hearts Inspire" (Matt)
GR291, UM603 (PD)

+"Down Galilee's Slow Roadways" (Matt)
G164

"I Was There to Hear Your Borning Cry" (Matt, Baptism)
C75, EL732, G488, N351, S2051, VU644

"Wash, O God, Our Sons and Daughters" (Matt, Baptism)
C365, EL445, G490, SH669, UM605, VU442, ZS191

"Loving Spirit" 3379424 (Matt, Baptism)
C244, EL397, G293, P323, S2123, VU387

"Wonder of Wonders" (Matt, Baptism)
C378, G489, N328, P499, S2247

"Baptized in Water" 5853694 (Matt, Baptism)
CG449, E294, EL456, P492, S2248, SH666

"Water, River, Spirit, Grace" OL-126179 (Matt, Baptism)
C366, N169, S2253

"Soplo de Dios" ("Breath of the Living God") (Matt)
EL407, N56, SH8

Additional Contemporary and Modern Suggestions

"From Ashes to Beauty" 5288953 (Isa)
+"The Kingdom Is Yours" 7109354 (Isa)
+"Daughters of Zion" 7133716 (Isa)
+"Let Justice Roll" ("Like a River") 4974842 (Isa)
"I'm Goin'a Sing When the Spirit Says Sing" (Isa, Matt)
GR330, UM333, Z81 (PD)
"Santo" ("Holy") (Isa)
EL762, G594, SH39, S2019
"Siyahamba" ("We Are Marching") 1321512 (Isa)
C442, CG155, EL866, G853, N526, S2235-ab, SH717, VU646, ZS111
"O For a Thousand Tongues to Sing" 4048754 (Isa, Pss)
WS3001
"Awesome God" 41099 (Pss)
G616, S2040, ZS7
"God Is the Strength of My Heart" 80919 (Pss)
"Ah, Lord God" 17896 (Pss)
+"You Are My Strength" 4869940 (Pss)
+"See His Glory" 229921 (Pss, Matt)
"Great and Mighty Is He" 66665 (Pss, Matt)
"Holy and Anointed One" 164361 (Acts)
+"The Highest and the Greatest" 4769758 (Acts)
"Surely the Presence of the Lord" 7909 (Matt)
C263, GR306, UM328; S-2 #200. Stanzas for soloist
"Wade in the Water" OL-246943 (Matt, Baptism)
C371, EL459 (PD), S2107, Z129 (PD), ZS189
"Oh, I Know the Lord's Laid His Hands on Me" (PD) (Matt)
S2139 (PD), Z166
+"Prepare the Way" 7136724 (Matt)
+"Wesley Prayer" ("Fire") 7118633 (Matt, Baptism)

Solo/Ensemble Suggestions

+"The Heavens Declare His Glory" (Pss)
V-8 p. 248
+"Above All" (Eph)
V-3 (2) p. 17
"Wash, O God, Our Sons and Daughters" (Matt, Baptism)
V-5 (1) p. 64

+"Wash Me in Your Water" (Matt, Baptism)
V-5(2) p. 18
+"Waterlife" (Matt, Baptism)
V-5(3) p. 17
+"I've Just Come from the Fountain" (Matt, Baptism)
V-7 p. 54/59
"Washed Anew" (Matt, Baptism)
Thomas Keesecker; AEC-2 p. 83
SATB, piano, opt. handbells (https://bit.ly/AEC-2-83)
"I'm Going on a Journey" (1 Cor, Baptism)
Arr. Mark Hayes; AEC-1 p. 27
Unison/2-part, piano, opt. flute (https://bit.ly/AEC-1-27)

+Hymn Anthem
"Fairest Lord Jesus" 27800 (Isa, Matt) (O)
C97, CG159, E383/384, EL838, G630, GR113, N44, P306, SH7, UM189 (PD), VU341
Introduction: Keyboard (organ) plays the last seven measures. *Mezzo piano*
Stanza 1: Child soloist or adult with a very light voice. Keyboard accompanies playing lower three parts only. *Mezzo piano.*
Stanza 2: *Mezzo forte.*
Option 1: S/A sing unison or parts. Keyboard plays full accompaniment.
Option 2: SATB, *a cappella* (or accompanied). S/A sing text, T/B sing "ooh."
Stanza 3:
Option 1: T/B sing melody. Keyboard plays bass clef as written, and alto part 8va higher. Omit upper part.
Option 2: Four-part men's quartet or ensemble, *a cappella* (or accompanied). Be sure that the melody predominates. In an ensemble, some singers may need to be added to that part. *Mezzo forte.*
Tenor 1 – Alto part as written
Tenor 2 – Tenor part as written
Bass 1 – Melody
Bass 2 – Bass part
Interlude: As singers sing the last word of stanza 3, keyboard repeats last seven measures, increasing volume.
Stanza 4: Unison or SATB, accompanied, *forte.* Some sopranos and tenors may sing a descant such as S-1, #301. *Ritard* at ending.

Other Suggestions
Visuals:
O Christ, dove, scales, bent reed, lighted wick, earth
P Ps. 29:1-2, worship, sea, storm, cedars, calf, ox, flames
E Jesus/baptism/dove, healing, risen Christ, witness
G John baptizing Jesus, dove, Matt 3:17
Baptism reaffirmation resources: UM608, CG451, S2252, S2249, WS3164, SH665, WS3165
+Introit or Call to Prayer: EL406, G281, S2118. *"Veni Sancte Spiritus"* ("Holy Spirit, Come to Us") OL-TaizeVN57 (Pss)
Call to Worship: WS3044. "Make Way" (Isa)
Opening Prayer: N829 (Matt)
Sung Confession: WS3111. "Redemption" (Isa)
Prayer: WSL12. "Great God of waves" (Isa, Matt, Baptism)
Prayer: UM253. Baptism of the Lord.
+Call to Baptism: CG451, S2252, ZS188. "Come, Be Baptized" 239485 (Acts, Matt, Baptism)
Baptism Readings: C370, C372, C377
+Sung Benediction: EL538, G747, S2184, SH718. *"Enviado Soy de Dios"* ("Sent Out in Jesus' Name") 6290823 (Isa, Acts)
Theme Ideas: Baptism, Covenant, God: Glory of God, Holy Spirit, Inclusion, Light, New Creation

Notes

NRSVue

Isaiah 49:1-7

1Listen to me, O coastlands;
pay attention, you peoples from far away!
The LORD called me before I was born;
while I was in my mother's womb he named me.
2He made my mouth like a sharp sword;
in the shadow of his hand he hid me;
he made me a polished arrow;
in his quiver he hid me away.
3And he said to me, "You are my servant,
Israel, in whom I will be glorified."
4But I said, "I have labored in vain;
I have spent my strength for nothing and vanity;
yet surely my cause is with the LORD,
and my reward with my God."
5And now the LORD says,
who formed me in the womb to be his servant,
to bring Jacob back to him,
and that Israel might be gathered to him,
for I am honored in the sight of the LORD,
and my God has become my strength—
6he says,
"It is too light a thing that you should be my servant
to raise up the tribes of Jacob
and to restore the survivors of Israel;
I will give you as a light to the nations,
that my salvation may reach to the end of the earth."
7Thus says the LORD,
the Redeemer of Israel and his Holy One,
to one deeply despised, abhorred by the nations,
the slave of rulers,
"Kings shall see and stand up,
princes, and they shall prostrate themselves,
because of the LORD, who is faithful,
the Holy One of Israel, who has chosen you."

Psalm 40:1-11 (G651, N647, SH607, UM774)

1I waited patiently for the LORD;
he inclined to me and heard my cry.
2He drew me up from the desolate pit,
out of the miry bog,
and set my feet upon a rock,
making my steps secure.
3He put a new song in my mouth,
a song of praise to our God.
Many will see and fear
and put their trust in the LORD.
4Happy are those who make
the LORD their trust,
who do not turn to the proud,
to those who go astray after false gods.
5You have multiplied, O LORD my God,
your wondrous deeds and your thoughts toward us;
none can compare with you.
Were I to proclaim and tell of them,
they would be more than can be counted.
6Sacrifice and offering you do not desire,
but you have given me an open ear.
Burnt offering and sin offering
you have not required.
7Then I said, "Here I am;
in the scroll of the book it is written of me.
8I delight to do your will, O my God;
your law is within my heart."
9I have told the glad news of deliverance
in the great congregation;
see, I have not restrained my lips,
as you know, O LORD.

CEB

Isaiah 49:1-7

1Listen to me, coastlands;
pay attention, peoples far away.
The LORD called me before my birth,
called my name when I was in my mother's womb.
2He made my mouth like a sharp sword,
and hid me in the shadow of God's own hand.
He made me a sharpened arrow,
and concealed me in God's quiver,
3 saying to me, "You are my servant,
Israel, in whom I show my glory."
4But I said, "I have wearied myself in vain.
I have used up my strength for nothing."
Nevertheless, the LORD will grant me justice;
my reward is with my God.
5And now the LORD has decided—
the one who formed me from the womb as his servant—
to restore Jacob to God,
so that Israel might return to him.
Moreover, I'm honored in the LORD's eyes;
my God has become my strength.
6He said: It is not enough, since you are my servant,
to raise up the tribes of Jacob
and to bring back the survivors of Israel.
Hence, I will also appoint you as light to the nations
so that my salvation may reach to the end of the earth.
7The LORD, redeemer of Israel and its holy one,
says to one despised,
rejected by nations,
to the slave of rulers:
Kings will see and stand up;
commanders will bow down
on account of the LORD, who is faithful,
the holy one of Israel,
who has chosen you.

Psalm 40:1-11 (G651, N647, SH607, UM774)

1I put all my hope in the LORD.
He leaned down to me;
he listened to my cry for help.
2He lifted me out of the pit of death,
out of the mud and filth,
and set my feet on solid rock.
He steadied my legs.
3He put a new song in my mouth,
a song of praise for our God.
Many people will learn of this and be amazed;
they will trust the LORD.
4Those who put their trust in the LORD,
who pay no attention to the proud
or to those who follow lies,
are truly happy!
5You, LORD my God!
You've done so many things—
your wonderful deeds and your plans for us—
no one can compare with you!
If I were to proclaim and talk about all of them,
they would be too numerous to count!
6You don't relish sacrifices or offerings;
you don't require entirely burned offerings or compensation offerings—
but you have given me ears!
7So I said, "Here I come!
I'm inscribed in the written scroll.
8 I want to do your will, my God.
Your Instruction is deep within me."
9I've told the good news of your righteousness
in the great assembly.

NRSVue

Psalm 40:1-11 (continued)

[10]I have not hidden your saving help within my heart;
  I have spoken of your faithfulness and your salvation;
I have not concealed your steadfast love and your faithfulness
  from the great congregation.
[11]Do not, O LORD, withhold
  your mercy from me;
let your steadfast love and your faithfulness
  keep me safe forever.

---

1 Corinthians 1:1-9

[1]Paul, called to be an apostle of Christ Jesus by the will of
God, and our brother Sosthenes,
[2]To the church of God that is in Corinth, to those who are
sanctified in Christ Jesus, called to be saints, together with all
those who in every place call on the name of our Lord Jesus
Christ, both their Lord and ours:
[3]Grace to you and peace from God our Father and the Lord
Jesus Christ.
[4]I give thanks to my God always for you because of the grace
of God that has been given you in Christ Jesus, [5]for in every way
you have been enriched in him, in speech and knowledge of
every kind—[6]just as the testimony of Christ has been strengthened among you—[7]so that you are not lacking in any gift as
you wait for the revealing of our Lord Jesus Christ. [8]He will also
strengthen you to the end, so that you may be blameless on the
day of our Lord Jesus Christ. [9]God is faithful, by whom you were
called into the partnership of his Son, Jesus Christ our Lord.

John 1:29-42

[29]The next day he saw Jesus coming toward him and declared,
"Here is the Lamb of God who takes away the sin of the world!
[30]This is he of whom I said, 'After me comes a man who ranks
ahead of me because he was before me.' [31]I myself did not know
him, but I came baptizing with water for this reason, that he
might be revealed to Israel." [32]And John testified, "I saw the
Spirit descending from heaven like a dove, and it remained on
him. [33]I myself did not know him, but the one who sent me to
baptize with water said to me, 'He on whom you see the Spirit
descend and remain is the one who baptizes with the Holy
Spirit.' [34]And I myself have seen and have testified that this is the
Chosen One."
[35]The next day John again was standing with two of his disciples, [36]and as he watched Jesus walk by he exclaimed, "Look,
here is the Lamb of God!" [37]The two disciples heard him say this,
and they followed Jesus. [38]When Jesus turned and saw them following, he said to them, "What are you looking for?" They said
to him, "Rabbi" (which translated means Teacher), "where are
you staying?" [39]He said to them, "Come and see." They came and
saw where he was staying, and they remained with him that day.
It was about four o'clock in the afternoon. [40]One of the two who
heard John speak and followed him was Andrew, Simon Peter's
brother. [41]He first found his brother Simon and said to him,
"We have found the Messiah" (which is translated Anointed).
[42]He brought Simon to Jesus, who looked at him and said, "You
are Simon son of John. You are to be called Cephas" (which is
translated Peter).

CEB

Psalm 40:1-11 (continued)

  I didn't hold anything back—
    as you well know, LORD!
[10]I didn't keep your righteousness only to myself.
  I declared your faithfulness and your salvation.
I didn't hide your loyal love and trustworthiness
  from the great assembly.
[11]So now you, LORD—
  don't hold back any of your compassion from me.
Let your loyal love and faithfulness always protect me.

---

1 Corinthians 1:1-9

[1]From Paul, called by God's will to be an apostle of Jesus
Christ, and from Sosthenes our brother.
[2]To God's church that is in Corinth:
To those who have been made holy to God in Christ Jesus,
who are called to be God's people.
Together with all those who call upon the name of our Lord
Jesus Christ in every place—he's their Lord and ours!
[3]Grace to you and peace from God our Father and the Lord
Jesus Christ.
[4]I thank my God always for you, because of God's grace that
was given to you in Christ Jesus. [5]That is, you were made rich
through him in everything: in all your communication and every
kind of knowledge, [6]in the same way that the testimony about
Christ was confirmed with you. [7]The result is that you aren't
missing any spiritual gift while you wait for our Lord Jesus Christ
to be revealed. [8]He will also confirm your testimony about Christ
until the end so that you will be blameless on the day of our
Lord Jesus Christ. [9]God is faithful, and you were called by him to
partnership with his Son, Jesus Christ our Lord.

John 1:29-42

[29]The next day John saw Jesus coming toward him and said,
"Look! The Lamb of God who takes away the sin of the world!
[30]This is the one about whom I said, 'He who comes after me is
really greater than me because he existed before me.' [31]Even I
didn't recognize him, but I came baptizing with water so that
he might be made known to Israel." [32]John testified, "I saw the
Spirit coming down from heaven like a dove, and it rested on
him. [33]Even I didn't recognize him, but the one who sent me to
baptize with water said to me, 'The one on whom you see the
Spirit coming down and resting is the one who baptizes with
the Holy Spirit.' [34]I have seen and testified that this one is God's
Son."
[35]The next day John was standing again with two of his disciples. [36]When he saw Jesus walking along he said, "Look! The
Lamb of God!" [37]The two disciples heard what he said, and they
followed Jesus.
[38]When Jesus turned and saw them following, he asked, "What
are you looking for?"
They said, "Rabbi (which is translated *Teacher*), where are you
staying?"
[39]He replied, "Come and see." So they went and saw where he
was staying, and they remained with him that day. It was about
four o'clock in the afternoon.
[40]One of the two disciples who heard what John said and followed Jesus was Andrew, the brother of Simon Peter. [41]He first
found his own brother Simon and said to him, "We have found
the Messiah" (which is translated *Christ*). [42]He led him to Jesus.
Jesus looked at him and said, "You are Simon, son of John.
You will be called Cephas" (which is translated *Peter*).

Primary Hymns and Songs for the Day

"Great Is Thy Faithfulness" 18723 (Isa, 1 Cor) (O)
C86, CG48, EL733, G39, GR44, N423, P276, SH48, UM140, VU288
H-3 Chr-87; Desc-39; Org-39
S-2 #59. Piano arrangement
"O Jesus, I Have Promised" 40454 (1 Cor)
C612, E655, EL810, G724/725, GR592, N493, P388/389, SH623, UM396 (PD), VU120
"The Summons" ("Will You Come and Follow Me") 4668756 (John)
CG473, EL798, G726, S2130, SH598, VU567
"Siyahamba" ("We Are Marching") 1321512 (Isa, Human Relations) (C)
C442, CG155, EL866, G853, N526, S2235-ab, SH717, VU646, ZS111

Additional Hymn Suggestions

"Holy God, We Praise Thy Name" 114555 (Isa) (O)
CG9, E366, EL414 (PD), G4, GR2, N276, P460, SH431, UM79, VU894 (Fr.)
"Immortal, Invisible, God Only Wise" 124466 (Isa) (C)
C66, CG58, E423, EL834, G12, GR7, N1, P263, UM103 (PD), VU264 (*See also* ZS4)
"Ye Servants of God" 90765 (Rom)
C110, CG420, E535, EL825 (PD), G299, GR40, N305, P477, UM181 (PD), VU342
"Womb of Life" (Isa)
C14, G3, N274, S2046
"I Was There to Hear Your Borning Cry" (Isa)
C75, EL732, G488, N351, S2051, VU644
"O Zion, Haste" (Isa, Human Relations)
C482, CG479, E539, EL668, GR451, UM573 (PD)
"This Little Light of Mine" 5305434, OL-22794 (Isa, Epiphany)
N525, UM585, Z132 (*See also* EL677, N524, SH257)
"Mothering God, You Gave Me Birth" (Isa, Comm.)
C83, EL735, G7, N467, S2050, VU320
"Jesus, Thou Joy of Loving Hearts" (1 Cor)
C101, CG394, E649, G494, GR128, N329, P510, SH688, VU472
"How Great Thou Art" 14181 (1 Cor)
C33, CG323, EL856, G625, GR32, N35, P467, SH14, UM77, VU238 (Fr.)
"Leaning on the Everlasting Arms" (1 Cor)
C560, CG640, EL774, G837, GR61, N471, UM133, Z53
"Blessed Be the God of Israel" 860627 (1 Cor)
C135, CG88, E444, EL250/552, G109, P602, UM209, VU901
"Holy Spirit, Come, Confirm Us" (1 Cor)
N264, UM331
"Amazing Grace" 22025 (1 Cor)
C546, CG587, E671, EL779, G649, GR572, N547/548, P280, SH523, UM378 (PD), VU266 (Fr.), Z211
"Christ for the World We Sing" (1 Cor, John, Human Relations)
E537, GR450, UM568 (PD)
"I Sing a Song of the Saints of God" (1 Cor, John, Human Relations)
E293, G730, GR482, N295, P364, UM712 (PD)
"I Know Whom I Have Believed" (1 Cor, John)
CG588, GR571, SH529, UM714 (PD)
"Come, Holy Spirit, Heavenly Dove" (John)
C248, E510, G279, GR290, N281, P126
"I Love to Tell the Story" (John)
C480, CG581, EL661, G462, GR160, N522, SH569, UM156 (PD), VU343
"Jesus! the Name High over All" (John)
GR111, UM193 (PD)
"Sweet, Sweet Spirit" (John)
C261, CG241, G408, GR361, N293, P398, SH410, UM334
"Just as I Am" (John)
C339, CG500, E693, EL592, G442, GR509, N207, P370, SH500, UM357 (PD), VU508, Z208
"Spirit of God, Descend upon My Heart" 2083 (John)
C265, CG243, EL800, G688, GR294, N290, P326, SH277, UM500 (PD), VU378
"Jesus, Priceless Treasure" (John)
E701, EL775, G830, GR114, N480 P365, UM532 (PD), VU667 / VU668 (Fr.)
"Lead On, O King Eternal" (John)
C632, CG63, E555, EL805, G269, GR478, N573, P447/448, UM580
"Rescue the Perishing" 34549 (John)
CG480, GR457, UM591 (PD)
"Wild and Lone the Prophet's Voice" 3413029 (John)
G163, P409, S2089
"Lamb of God" 16787 (John)
EL336, G518, S2113, ZS74
"Songs of Thankfulness and Praise" (John)
E135 (PD), EL310, GR212, SH104, VU101

Additional Contemporary and Modern Suggestions

"Lord, Be Glorified" 26368 (Isa)
EL744, G468, S2150, SH420
"Shout to the North" 1562261 (Isa)
G319, WS3042
"Be Glorified" 429226 (Isa)
"Be Glorified" 2732646 (Isa)
"Good to Me" 313480 (Isa)
"You Are My All in All" 825356 (Isa, John)
CG571, G519, SH335, WS3040, ZS184
+"Say So" 4944016 (Isa, Pss, John)
+"Goodness of God" 7117726 (Isa, Pss)
+"All Things Are Possible" 2245140 (Isa, Pss)
"Shout to the Lord" 1406918 (Pss)
CG348, EL821, GR124, S2074, SH426, ZS15
"You Are Good" 3383788 (Pss)
SH455, WS3014
"Forever" 3148428 (Pss)
CG53, WS3023
"Hallelujah" ("Your Love Is Amazing") 3091812 (Pss)
WS3027
"Your Love, Oh Lord" 1894255 (Pss)
"You Are My Hiding Place" 21442 (Pss)
C554, S2055, SH46
"Waiting Here for You" 5925663 (Pss)
+"God Is Good All the Time" 1729073 (Pss)
+"God, You're So Good" 7105729 (Pss)
+"Never Runs Out" 7193998 (Pss)
+"No Outsiders" 7101035 (Pss)
"Oh, I Know the Lord's Laid His Hands on Me" (PD) (1 Cor)
S2139 (PD), Z166
"Amazing Grace" ("My Chains Are Gone") 4768151 (1 Cor)
GR574, WS3104
"Let the Peace of God Reign" 1839987 (1 Cor)
"Grace Like Rain" 3689877 (1 Cor)
+"His Mercy Is More" 7065053 (1 Cor)
"Spirit Song" 27824 (John)
C352, SH409, UM347
"Jesus, Name above All Names" 21291 (John)
S2071, ZS27
"Cry of My Heart" 844980 (John)
S2165
"Step by Step" 696994 (John)
CG495, G743, GR671, WS3004
"Now Behold the Lamb" (John)
EL341, WS3081

"Somlandela" ("We Will Follow") (PD-TO) (John)
WS3160
"Agnus Dei" 626713 (John)
CG351
"Come Just As You Are" 1189479 (John)
+"Behold Him" 7133698 (John)
+"Lead Me, Lord" 1609045 (John)

Solo/Ensemble Suggestions

"Patiently Have I Waited for the Lord" (Pss)
V-4 p. 24
"Holy is the Lamb" (John)
V-5 (1) p. 5
"Lamb of God" (John)
V-5 (2) p. 5
+"Grace Greater Than Our Sin" (John)
V-8 p. 180
"I Waited for the Lord" (Pss)
F. Mendelssohn; Theodore Presser 312-10269
SATB, keyboard (https://bit.ly/TP-10269)
"Just as I Am, I Come" (John)
Victor Johnson; Lorenz Music 10/4078L
SATB, piano, opt. clarinet (https://bit.ly/10-4078L)

+Hymn Anthem

"Spirit Song" 27824 (John)
C352, SH409, UM347
This simple melody is best sung without much fuss, letting the text sing itself. Accompany with piano and/or guitar, allowing for improvisation.
Introduction: Piano and/or guitar play the refrain, using the first ending.
Stanza 1: Full choir, *mezzo forte.* Unison singing throughout stanza and refrain.
Interlude: As the choir sings the last word of the refrain, "lambs," play the last 8 measures of the refrain.
Stanza 2: Full choir, unison, *mezzo forte.* On refrain, allow for singers to add harmony notes (add congregation?). Keyboard supports throughout. Instead of the second ending, play the last measure just before the refrain, leading back into a repeat of the refrain.
Ending: Final refrain with full choir (and congregation?), unison, soft. End prayerfully.

Other Suggestions

This day may include observances of Martin Luther King Jr. Day.
Visuals:
O Coast, pregnancy, hand, arrow, light, earth, Christ
P Clasped hands, pit, bog, feet/rock, sing, preach
E People, speak, learning, Bible, gifts, Second Coming
G Jesus, Lamb, baptism, Spirit, John, witnessing
Opening Prayer: WSL22. "From Bethlehem to Nazareth" (John)
Prayer: N863. Justice (Martin Luther King Day)
Litany: C664. Litany for the World (Martin Luther King Day)
Canticle: UM82 or UM83. "Canticle of God's Glory" (John)
Response: UM300. "O The Lamb" (John)
Medley: "Take This Moment, Sign, and Space" (WS3118) and "Take, O Take Me As I Am" (EL814, G698, SH620, WS3119) (John)
Prayer: WSL67 (Isa)
+Response: EL152, S2275. *"Kyrie"* (Pss)
Theme Ideas: Call of God, Discipleship / Following God, Light, Spiritual Gifts, Waiting

Notes

NRSVue

Isaiah 9:1-4

1 But there will be no gloom for those who were in anguish. In
the former time he brought into contempt the land of Zebulun
and the land of Naphtali, but in the latter time he will make
glorious the way of the sea, the land beyond the Jordan, Galilee
of the nations.

2 The people who walked in darkness
have seen a great light;
those who lived in a land of deep darkness—
on them light has shined.
3 You have multiplied exultation;
you have increased its joy;
they rejoice before you
as with joy at the harvest,
as people exult when dividing plunder.
4 For the yoke of their burden,
and the bar across their shoulders,
the rod of their oppressor,
you have broken as on the day of Midian.

Psalm 27:1, 4-9 (G90/841/842, N637, P179, UM758)

1 The LORD is my light and my salvation;
whom shall I fear?
The LORD is the stronghold of my life;
of whom shall I be afraid?

. . . .

4 One thing I asked of the LORD;
this I seek:
to live in the house of the LORD
all the days of my life,
to behold the beauty of the LORD,
and to inquire in his temple.
5 For he will hide me in his shelter
in the day of trouble;
he will conceal me under the cover of his tent;
he will set me high on a rock.
6 Now my head is lifted up
above my enemies all around me,
and I will offer in his tent
sacrifices with shouts of joy;
I will sing and make melody to the LORD.
7 Hear, O LORD, when I cry aloud;
be gracious to me and answer me!
8 "Come," my heart says, "seek his face!"
Your face, LORD, do I seek.
9 Do not hide your face from me.
Do not turn your servant away in anger,
you who have been my help.
Do not cast me off, do not forsake me,
O God of my salvation!

CEB

Isaiah 9:1-4

1 Nonetheless, those who were in distress won't be exhausted.
At an earlier time, God cursed the land of Zebulun and the land
of Naphtali, but later he glorified the way of the sea, the far side
of the Jordan, and the Galilee of the nations.

2 The people walking in darkness
have seen a great light.
On those living in a pitch-dark land,
light has dawned.
3 You have made the nation great;
you have increased its joy.
They rejoiced before you
as with joy at the harvest,
as those who divide plunder rejoice.
4 As on the day of Midian,
you've shattered the yoke
that burdened them,
the staff on their shoulders,
and the rod of their oppressor.

Psalm 27:1, 4-9 (G90/841/842, N637, P179, UM758)

1 The LORD is my light and my salvation.
Should I fear anyone?
The LORD is a fortress protecting my life.
Should I be frightened of anything?

. . . .

4 I have asked one thing from the LORD—
it's all I seek—
to live in the LORD's house all the days of my life,
seeing the LORD's beauty
and constantly adoring his temple.
5 Because he will shelter me in his own dwelling
during troubling times;
he will hide me in a secret place in his own tent;
he will set me up high, safe on a rock.
6 Now my head is higher than the enemies surrounding me,
and I will offer sacrifices in God's tent—
sacrifices with shouts of joy!
I will sing and praise the LORD.
7 LORD, listen to my voice when I cry out—
have mercy on me and answer me!
8 Come, my heart says, seek God's face.
LORD, I do seek your face!
9 Please don't hide it from me!
Don't push your servant aside angrily—
you have been my help!
God who saves me,
don't neglect me!
Don't leave me all alone!

NRSVue

1 Corinthians 1:10-18

[10]Now I appeal to you, brothers and sisters, by the name of
our Lord Jesus Christ, that all of you be in agreement and that
there be no divisions among you but that you be knit together
in the same mind and the same purpose. [11]For it has been made
clear to me by Chloe's people that there are quarrels among
you, my brothers and sisters. [12]What I mean is that each of you
says, "I belong to Paul," or "I belong to Apollos," or "I belong
to Cephas," or "I belong to Christ." [13]Has Christ been divided?
Was Paul crucified for you? Or were you baptized in the name of
Paul? [14]I thank God that I baptized none of you except Crispus
and Gaius, [15]so that no one can say that you were baptized in my
name. [16]I did baptize also the household of Stephanas; beyond
that, I do not know whether I baptized anyone else. [17]For Christ
did not send me to baptize but to proclaim the gospel—and not
with eloquent wisdom, so that the cross of Christ might not be
emptied of its power.

[18]For the message about the cross is foolishness to those who
are perishing, but to us who are being saved it is the power of
God.

Matthew 4:12-23

[12]Now when Jesus heard that John had been arrested, he
withdrew to Galilee. [13]He left Nazareth and made his home in
Capernaum by the sea, in the territory of Zebulun and Naphtali, [14]so that what had been spoken through the prophet Isaiah
might be fulfilled:

15 "Land of Zebulun, land of Naphtali,
on the road by the sea, across the Jordan, Galilee of the
gentiles—
16 the people who sat in darkness
have seen a great light,
and for those who sat in the region and shadow of death
light has dawned."

[17]From that time Jesus began to proclaim, "Repent, for the
kingdom of heaven has come near."

[18]As he walked by the Sea of Galilee, he saw two brothers,
Simon, who is called Peter, and Andrew his brother, casting a net
into the sea—for they were fishermen. [19]And he said to them,
"Follow me, and I will make you fishers of people." [20]Immedi-
ately they left their nets and followed him. [21]As he went from
there, he saw two other brothers, James son of Zebedee and his
brother John, in the boat with their father Zebedee, mending
their nets, and he called them. [22]Immediately they left the boat
and their father and followed him.

[23]Jesus went throughout Galilee, teaching in their synagogues
and proclaiming the good news of the kingdom and curing
every disease and every sickness among the people.

CEB

1 Corinthians 1:10-18

[10]Now I encourage you, brothers and sisters, in the name
of our Lord Jesus Christ: Agree with each other and don't be
divided into rival groups. Instead, be restored with the same
mind and the same purpose. [11]My brothers and sisters, Chloe's
people gave me some information about you, that you're fighting with each other. [12]What I mean is this: that each one of
you says, "I belong to Paul," "I belong to Apollos," "I belong to
Cephas," "I belong to Christ." [13]Has Christ been divided? Was
Paul crucified for you, or were you baptized in Paul's name?
[14]Thank God that I didn't baptize any of you, except Crispus
and Gaius, [15]so that nobody can say that you were baptized in my
name! [16]Oh, I baptized the house of Stephanas too. Otherwise, I
don't know if I baptized anyone else. [17]Christ didn't send me to
baptize but to preach the good news. And Christ didn't send me
to preach the good news with clever words so that Christ's cross
won't be emptied of its meaning.

[18]The message of the cross is foolishness to those who are
being destroyed. But it is the power of God for those of us who
are being saved.

Matthew 4:12-23

[12]Now when Jesus heard that John was arrested, he went to
Galilee. [13]He left Nazareth and settled in Capernaum, which lies
alongside the sea in the area of Zebulun and Naphtali. [14]This
fulfilled what Isaiah the prophet said:

15 *Land of Zebulun and land of Naphtali,*
alongside the sea, across the Jordan, Galilee of the Gentiles,
16 *the people who lived in the dark have seen a great light,*
and a light has come upon those who lived in the region and in
shadow of death.

[17]From that time Jesus began to announce, "Change your
hearts and lives! Here comes the kingdom of heaven!"

[18]As Jesus walked alongside the Galilee Sea, he saw two brothers, Simon, who is called Peter, and Andrew, throwing fishing
nets into the sea, because they were fishermen. [19]"Come, follow
me," he said, "and I'll show you how to fish for people." [20]Right
away, they left their nets and followed him. [21]Continuing on, he
saw another set of brothers, James the son of Zebedee and his
brother John. They were in a boat with Zebedee their father
repairing their nets. Jesus called them and [22]immediately they
left the boat and their father and followed him.

[23]Jesus traveled throughout Galilee, teaching in their synagogues. He announced the good news of the kingdom and
healed every disease and sickness among the people.

Primary Hymns and Songs for the Day

"The Church's One Foundation" 55377 (1 Cor) (O)
C272, CG246, E525, EL654, G321, GR388/646, N386, P442, SH233, UM545/546, VU332 (Fr.)
H-3 Hbl-94; Chr-180; Desc-16; Org-9
S-1 #25-26. Desc. and harm.
"Somos Uno en Cristo" ("We Are One in Christ Jesus") 6368975 (1 Cor)
C493, EL643, G322, S2229, SH227
"Fight the Good Fight" (1 Cor)
E552, G846, GR473, P307 (PD), VU674
"Jesus Calls Us" 68900 (Matt)
C337, EL696, G720, GR520, N172, SH604, UM398, VU562
H-3 Chr-115
S-2 #65. Harmonization
CG486, E549/550, N171
"I Have Decided to Follow Jesus" (Matt) (C)
C344, CG497, GR603, S2129, SH610

Additional Hymn Suggestions

"Christ, Whose Glory Fills the Skies" 808926 (Isa, Matt)
E7, EL553, G662, GR211, P462, UM173 (PD), VU336
"I Want to Walk as a Child of the Light" (Isa, Matt)
CG96, E490, EL815, G377, GR216, SH352, UM206
"Break Forth, O Beauteous Heavenly Light" (Isa)
E91, G130, GR206, N140, P26, UM223, VU83
"How Firm a Foundation" 107816 (Isa)
C618, CG425, E636, EL796, G463, GR46, N407, P361, SH291, UM529 (PD), VU660
"Christ, Be Our Light" (*"Cristo, la Luz"*) (Isa, Pss, Matt)
EL715, G314, SH242
"O Morning Star, How Fair and Bright" (Isa, Matt)
C105, E497, EL308, G827, N158, P69, UM247, VU98
"Goodness Is Stronger than Evil" OL-02636 (Isa, Matt)
EL721, G750, S2219
"Gather Us In" OL-00031 (Isa, Matt)
C284, EL532, G401, S2236, SH393
"Where Charity and Love Prevail" 40313 (1 Cor)
CG264, E581, EL359, G316, N396, SH271, UM549
"All My Hope Is Firmly Grounded" 3594474 (1 Cor)
C88, E665, EL757, GR68, N408, UM132, VU654/655
"In the Cross of Christ I Glory" 36499 (1 Cor)
C207, CG183, E441/442, EL324, G213, GR239, N193, P84, UM295 (PD)
"When I Survey the Wondrous Cross" 721333 (1 Cor)
C195, CG186, E474, EL803, G223/ 224, GR221, N224, P100/101, SH163/164, UM298/299, VU149 (Fr.)
+"In Christ There Is No East or West" 2608952 (1 Cor)
C687, CG273, E529, EL650 (PD), G317/318, GR392, N394/395, P439/440, UM548, VU606, Z65 (PD)
"Blest Be the Tie that Binds" 7106572 (1 Cor) (C)
C433, CG267, EL656, G306, GR405, N393, P438, SH701, UM557 (PD), VU602
"Help Us Accept Each Other" 133756 (1 Cor)
C487, G754, N388, P358, UM560
"Lord of the Dance" 78529 (Matt)
G157, P302, UM261, VU352
"Tell Me the Stories of Jesus" 2627445 (Matt)
C190, GR159, UM277 (PD), VU357
"Softly and Tenderly Jesus Is Calling" (Matt)
C340, CG474, EL608 (PD), G418, GR504, N449, SH601, UM348
"Dear Lord and Father of Mankind" 106185 (Matt)
(Alternate Text: "Dear God, Embracing Humankind")
C594, CG413, E652/563, G169, GR499, N502, P345, UM358 (PD), VU608
"O Jesus, I Have Promised" 40454 (Matt)
C612, E655, EL810, G724/725, GR592, N493, P388/389, SH623, UM396 (PD), VU120
+"Take My Life, and Let It Be" 1390 (Matt)
C609, CG490, E707, EL583/L685, G697, GR586, P391, N448, SH627/628, UM399 (PD), VU506
"Where Cross the Crowded Ways of Life" 2961345 (Matt)
C665, CG657, E609, EL719, G343, N543, P408, UM427 (PD), VU681
"O Master, Let Me Walk with Thee" 158243 (Matt)
C602, CG660, E659/660, EL818, G738, GR596, N503, P357, SH612, UM430 (PD), VU560
"The Summons" ("Will You Come and Follow Me") 4668756 (Matt)
CG473, EL798, G726, S2130, SH598, VU567
"Somebody's Knockin' at Your Door" (PD-TO) (Matt)
G728, P382, SH597, WS3095 (PD-TO), Z154

Additional Contemporary and Modern Suggestions

"Foundation" 706151 (Isa, 1 Cor)
+"Tremble" 7065049 (Isa, Pss, Matt)
+"Way Maker" 7115744 (Isa, Pss, Matt)
+"Carry the Light" 126402 (Isa, Matt)
"How Great Is Our God" 4348399 (Isa, Pss, Matt)
CG322, GR31, SH458, WS3003
"Here I Am to Worship" 3266032 (Isa, Pss, Matt)
CG297, SH395, WS3177, ZS145
"Shine, Jesus, Shine" 30426 (Isa, Pss, Matt)
CG156, EL671, G192, GR217, S2173, SH102; V-3 (2), p. 48. Vocal Solo
"Shine on Us" 1754646 (Isa, Pss, Matt)
"You are the Light" 6238098 (Isa, Pss, Matt)
"I Will Call upon the Lord" 11263 (Pss)
G621, S2002
"Shout to the Lord" 1406918 (Pss)
CG348, EL821, GR124, S2074, SH426, ZS15
+"Nothing to Fear" 7133723 (Pss)
+"Our God Saves" 4972837 (Pss)
+"You Never Let Go" 4674166 (Pss)
"Today" 5775617 (Pss)
"The Lord Is My Light" 41240 (Pss)
"All Heaven Declares" 120556 (Pss)
"Better Is One Day" 1097451 (Pss)
"Marvelous Light" 4491002 (Pss, Matt)
"Siyahamba" ("We Are Marching") 1321512 (Pss, Matt)
C442, CG155, EL866, G853, N526, S2235-ab, SH717, VU646, ZS111
"Step by Step" 696994 (Pss, Matt)
CG495, G743, GR671, WS3004
"I Stand Amazed" 769450 (Pss, Matt)
"Let It Be Said of Us" 1855882 (1 Cor)
"The Wonderful Cross" 3148435 (1 Cor)
"I Will Boast" 4662350 (1 Cor)
+"Won't Stop Now" 7111932 (1 Cor, Matt)
+"You're Worthy of My Praise" 487976 (Matt)
+"Called Me Higher" 5887880 (Matt)
+"Lead Me, Lord" 1609045 (Matt)
"Everyday" 2798154 (Matt)
+"As We Go" 5043277 (Matt) (C)
WS3183

Solo/Ensemble Suggestions

"The People That Walked in Darkness" (Isa)
V-2
+"On Eagle's Wings" (Pss)
V-3 (3) p. 4
V-3 (2) p. 2
"The Lord Is My Light" (Pss)
V-8 p. 57
"Softly and Tenderly" (Matt)
V-5 (3) p. 52

"Arise! Sing Forth!" (Isa)
Purcell/arr. Hopson; Augsburg AEC-2 p. 5
SAB, piano (https://bit.ly/AEC-2)
"Who At My Door Is Standing?" (Matt)
arr. K. Lee Scott; Hinshaw HMC728
2-part mixed, keyboard (https://bit.ly/KLS-728)

+Hymn Anthem
"I Want to Walk as a Child of the Light" (Isa, Matt)
CG96, E490, EL815, G377, GR216, SH352, UM206
Introduction: Keyboard plays last system, very simply, perhaps only melody and 1st and 3rd beats of bass part.
Stanza 1: Solo by a light, young treble voice. Continue simple accompaniment. Refrain: Add some S/A with light voices to the melody. Keyboard plays setting as written.
Stanza 2: Systems 1&2 – S/A sing their parts, *mezzo-forte.* Systems 3&4 – Tenors sing melody in their range, basses sing their part, *mezzo-forte.* Keyboard plays setting as written, *mezzo-forte.*
Refrain: All voices sing four-parts (or unison). Keyboard plays full setting.
Interlude: On last measure of refrain, keyboard begins playing refrain again. Voices hold last note for two beats only. Keyboard grows in power while playing interlude.
Stanza 3: All voices in unison, *forte,* with great strength and certainty. Somewhat slower. *Decrescendo* and *ritard* on 4th system on "joy of Jesus."
Refrain: Return to four parts (or unison), slower, softer, and more emotional. *Crescendo* slightly on third system of refrain, returning to *piano* after "God." Sing last system softly and prayerfully.
Ending: Keyboard begins refrain again, with simple accompaniment as at beginning. Selected light voices, S/A and/or T/B, sing melody on very focused "oo" vowel. Beginning soloist sings last system alone, ending very quietly and simply.

Other Suggestions
Visuals:
O Light/darkness, sea/land, joy, harvest, yoke, rod
P Light, church, seekers, tent/rock, joy, singing
E Walls torn down, baptism, crucifix, stone
G John, sea, light/darkness, dawn, fishnet, net with people, mending nets, boat, Jesus teaching
Introit: S2127. "Come and See" (*"Kyrie"*) (Matt)
Confession: WSL43. "We often act" (1 Cor)
Confession: WSL97. "Your light has filled our lives" (Isa)
Prayer of Confession: N835 (Matt)
Response: SH556, WS3137. "Lord Jesus Christ, Your Light Shines" (Isa, Pss)
Canticle: UM205. "Canticle of Light and Darkness" (Isa)
Litany: N880 (Isa, Matt)
Litany: C664. A Litany for the World (Isa, Matt)
+Call to Prayer: CG399, EL751, G471, S2200, SH311/517. "O Lord, Hear My Prayer" (Pss)
+Sung Benediction: G80, S2279, VU884. "The Trees of the Field" 20546 (Pss)
+Vespers Sung Benediction: WS3185, stanza 1. "Send Us Your Spirit" (Isa, Matt)
Blessing: WSL7. "The light that enlivens" (Isa)
Response: N161, P299, S2072 (PD-TO), Z147. "Amen, Amen" (Matt, Closing)
Theme Ideas: Call of God, Cross, Discipleship / Following God, Inclusion, Light, Unity

Notes

NRSVue

Micah 6:1-8

1Hear what the LORD says:
Rise, plead your case before the mountains,
and let the hills hear your voice.
2Hear, you mountains, the controversy of the LORD,
and you enduring foundations of the earth,
for the LORD has a case against his people,
and he will contend with Israel.
3"O my people, what have I done to you?
In what have I wearied you? Answer me!
4For I brought you up from the land of Egypt
and redeemed you from the house of slavery,
and I sent before you Moses,
Aaron, and Miriam.
5O my people, remember now what King Balak of Moab devised,
what Balaam son of Beor answered him,
and what happened from Shittim to Gilgal,
that you may know the saving acts of the LORD."
6"With what shall I come before the LORD
and bow myself before God on high?
Shall I come before him with burnt offerings,
with calves a year old?
7Will the LORD be pleased with thousands of rams,
with ten thousands of rivers of oil?
Shall I give my firstborn for my transgression,
the fruit of my body for the sin of my soul?"
8He has told you, O mortal, what is good;
and what does the LORD require of you
but to do justice, and to love kindness
and to walk humbly with your God?

Psalm 15 (G419, N627, P164, UM747)

1O LORD, who may abide in your tent?
Who may dwell on your holy hill?
2Those who walk blamelessly, and do what is right
and speak the truth from their heart;
3who do not slander with their tongue
and do no evil to their friends
nor heap shame upon their neighbors;
4in whose eyes the wicked are despised
but who honor those who fear the LORD;
who stand by their oath even to their hurt;
5who do not lend money at interest
and do not take a bribe against the innocent.
Those who do these things shall never be moved.

CEB

Micah 6:1-8

1Hear what the LORD is saying:
Arise, lay out the lawsuit before the mountains;
let the hills hear your voice!
2Hear, mountains, the lawsuit of the LORD!
Hear, eternal foundations of the earth!
The LORD has a lawsuit against his people;
with Israel he will argue.
3"My people, what did I ever do to you?
How have I wearied you? Answer me!
4I brought you up out of the land of Egypt;
I redeemed you from the house of slavery.
I sent Moses, Aaron, and Miriam before you.
5My people, remember what Moab's King Balak had planned,
and how Balaam, Beor's son, answered him!
Remember everything from Shittim to Gilgal,
that you might learn to recognize the righteous acts of the LORD!"
6With what should I approach the LORD
and bow down before God on high?
Should I come before him with entirely burned offerings,
with year-old calves?
7Will the LORD be pleased with thousands of rams,
with many torrents of oil?
Should I give my oldest child for my crime;
the fruit of my body for the sin of my spirit?
8He has told you, human one, what is good and
what the LORD requires from you:
to do justice, embrace faithful love, and walk humbly with your God.

Psalm 15 (G419, N627, P164, UM747)

1Who can live in your tent, LORD?
Who can dwell on your holy mountain?
2The person who
lives free of blame,
does what is right,
and speaks the truth sincerely;
3 who does no damage with their talk,
does no harm to a friend,
doesn't insult a neighbor;
4 someone who despises
those who act wickedly,
but who honors those
who honor the LORD;
someone who keeps their promise even when it hurts;
5 someone who doesn't lend money with interest,
who won't accept a bribe against any innocent person.
Whoever does these things will never stumble.

NRSVue

1 Corinthians 1:18-31

[18]For the message about the cross is foolishness to those who
are perishing, but to us who are being saved it is the power of
God. [19]For it is written,
"I will destroy the wisdom of the wise,
and the discernment of the discerning I will thwart."
[20]Where is the one who is wise? Where is the scribe? Where is
the debater of this age? Has not God made foolish the wisdom
of the world? [21]For since, in the wisdom of God, the world did
not know God through wisdom, God decided, through the
foolishness of the proclamation, to save those who believe. [22]For
Jews ask for signs and Greeks desire wisdom, [23]but we proclaim
Christ crucified, a stumbling block to Jews and foolishness to
gentiles, [24]but to those who are the called, both Jews and Greeks,
Christ the power of God and the wisdom of God. [25]For God's
foolishness is wiser than human wisdom, and God's weakness is
stronger than human strength.
[26]Consider your own call, brothers and sisters: not many of
you were wise by human standards, not many were powerful, not
many were of noble birth. [27]But God chose what is foolish in the
world to shame the wise; God chose what is weak in the world to
shame the strong; [28]God chose what is low and despised in the
world, things that are not, to abolish things that are, [29]so that
no one might boast in the presence of God. [30]In contrast, God
is why you are in Christ Jesus, who became for us wisdom from
God, and righteousness and sanctification and redemption, [31]in
order that, as it is written, "Let the one who boasts, boast in the
Lord."

Matthew 5:1-12

[1]When Jesus saw the crowds, he went up the mountain, and
after he sat down, his disciples came to him. [2]And he began to
speak and taught them, saying:
[3]"Blessed are the poor in spirit, for theirs is the kingdom of
heaven.
[4]"Blessed are those who mourn, for they will be comforted.
[5]"Blessed are the meek, for they will inherit the earth.
[6]"Blessed are those who hunger and thirst for righteousness,
for they will be filled.
[7]"Blessed are the merciful, for they will receive mercy.
[8]"Blessed are the pure in heart, for they will see God.
[9]"Blessed are the peacemakers, for they will be called children
of God.
[10]"Blessed are those who are persecuted for the sake of righteousness, for theirs is the kingdom of heaven.
[11]"Blessed are you when people revile you and persecute you
and utter all kinds of evil against you falsely on my account.
[12]Rejoice and be glad, for your reward is great in heaven, for
in the same way they persecuted the prophets who were before
you."

CEB

1 Corinthians 1:18-31

[18]The message of the cross is foolishness to those who are
being destroyed. But it is the power of God for those of us who
are being saved. [19]It is written in scripture: *I will destroy the wisdom
of the wise, and I will reject the intelligence of the intelligent.* [20]Where
are the wise? Where are the legal experts? Where are today's
debaters? Hasn't God made the wisdom of the world foolish?
[21]In God's wisdom, he determined that the world wouldn't come
to know him through its wisdom. Instead, God was pleased to
save those who believe through the foolishness of preaching.
[22]Jews ask for signs, and Greeks look for wisdom, [23]but we preach
Christ crucified, which is a scandal to Jews and foolishness to
Gentiles. [24]But to those who are called—both Jews and Greeks—
Christ is God's power and God's wisdom. [25]This is because the
foolishness of God is wiser than human wisdom, and the weakness of God is stronger than human strength.
[26]Look at your situation when you were called, brothers and
sisters! By ordinary human standards not many were wise, not
many were powerful, not many were from the upper class.
[27]But God chose what the world considers foolish to shame the
wise. God chose what the world considers weak to shame the
strong. [28]And God chose what the world considers low-class and
low-life—what is considered to be nothing—to reduce what is
considered to be something to nothing. [29]So no human being
can brag in God's presence. [30]It is because of God that you are
in Christ Jesus. He became wisdom from God for us. This means
that he made us righteous and holy, and he delivered us. [31]This
is consistent with what was written: *The one who brags should brag
in the Lord!*

Matthew 5:1-12

[1]Now when Jesus saw the crowds, he went up a mountain. He
sat down and his disciples came to him. [2]He taught them, saying:
[3]"Happy are people who are hopeless, because the kingdom
of heaven is theirs.
[4]"Happy are people who grieve, because they will be made
glad.
[5]"Happy are people who are humble, because they will inherit
the earth.
[6]"Happy are people who are hungry and thirsty for righteousness, because they will be fed until they are full.
[7]"Happy are people who show mercy, because they will receive
mercy.
[8]"Happy are people who have pure hearts, because they will
see God.
[9]"Happy are people who make peace, because they will be
called God's children.
[10]"Happy are people whose lives are harassed because they are
righteous, because the kingdom of heaven is theirs.
[11]"Happy are you when people insult you and harass you and
speak all kinds of bad and false things about you, all because of
me. [12]Be full of joy and be glad, because you have a great reward
in heaven. In the same way, people harassed the prophets who
came before you."

Primary Hymns and Songs for the Day

"Rejoice in God's Saints" (Matt) (O)
C476, EL418, G732, UM708
H-3 Hbl-90, 105; Chr-221; Desc-49; Org-51
S-2 #71-74. Intro. and harms.
"What Does the Lord Require of You" 456859 (Mic)
C661, CG690, G70, S2174, VU701
"Be Thou My Vision" UM 5021907 (1 Cor, Matt)
C595, CG71, E488, EL793, G450, GR49, N451, P339, SH640, UM451, VU642
H-3 Hbl-15, 48; Chr-36; Org-153
S-1 #319. Arr. for organ and voices in canon
"Lord, You Give the Great Commission" 230673 (Mic, Pss) (C)
C459, CG651/CG653, E528, EL579, G298, GR463, P429, S2176, UM584, VU512
H-3 Hbl-61; Chr-132; Org-2
S-1 #4-5. Instrumental and vocal desc.
"*Enviado Soy de Dios*" ("Sent Out in Jesus' Name") 6290823 (Mic) (C)
EL538, G747, S2184, SH718

Additional Hymn Suggestions

"O for a Closer Walk with God" (Mic)
CG679, E684, G739, GR327, N450, P396
"Softly and Tenderly Jesus Is Calling" (Mic)
C340, CG474, EL608 (PD), G418, GR504, N449, SH601, UM348
+"Lord, Whose Love Through Humble Service" (Mic)
C461, CG650, E610, EL712, GR454, P427, SH239, UM581
"When Jesus Wept" (Mic)
C199, E715, G194, N192, P312, S2106, VU146
"I'm Gonna Live So God Can Use Me" (Mic)
C614, G700, GR615, P369, S2153, SH632, VU575
"Healer of Our Every Ill" OL-00115 (Mic)
C506, EL612, G795, S2213, SH339, VU619
"Lead On, O Cloud of Presence" (Mic)
C633, S2234, VU421
"What Gift Can We Bring" 216549 (Mic, Matt)
CG533, N370, UM87
"All Who Love and Serve Your City" 1277415 (Mic, Matt)
C670, CG674, E570/571, EL724, G351, P413, UM433
"*Cuando el Pobre*" ("When the Poor Ones") OL-97385 (Mic, Matt)
C662, EL725, G762, P407, SH240, UM434, VU702
"Lift Up Your Heads, Ye Mighty Gates" 1863214 (Pss, Matt)
C129, CG173, E436, G93, GR171, N117, P8, UM213 (PD)
"All My Hope Is Firmly Grounded" 3594474 (1 Cor)
C88, E665, EL757, GR68, N408, UM132, VU654/655
"Ask Ye What Great Thing I Know" (1 Cor)
CG443, GR107, N49, UM163 (PD), VU338
"Fairest Lord Jesus" 27800 (1 Cor)
C97, CG159, E383/384, EL838, G630, GR113, N44, P306, SH7, UM189 (PD), VU341
"In the Cross of Christ I Glory" 36499 (1 Cor)
C207, CG183, E441/442, EL324, G213, GR239, N193, P84, UM295 (PD)
"When I Survey the Wondrous Cross" 721333 (1 Cor)
C195, CG186, E474, EL803, G223/ 224, GR221, N224, P100/101, SH163/164, UM298/299, VU149 (Fr.)
"Thine Be the Glory" (1 Cor)
C218, CG222, EL376, G238, GR255, N253, P122, SH192, UM308, VU173 (Fr.)
"The Old Rugged Cross" (1 Cor)
C548, CG185, GR236, N195, SH165, UM504 (PD)
"Help Us Accept Each Other" 133756 (1 Cor)
C487, G754, N388, P358, UM560
"O For a World" (1 Cor)
C683, G372, N575, P386, VU697
"My Faith Looks Up to Thee" 43334 (1 Cor, Matt)
C576, CG407, E691, EL759, G829, GR351, P383, UM452 (PD), VU663, Z215
"Holy Spirit, Truth Divine" 300431 (1 Cor, Matt)
C241, EL398, GR320, N63, P321, UM465, VU368
"O Love That Wilt Not Let Me Go" (1 Cor, Matt)
C540, CG631, G833, GR92, N485, P384, SH314, UM480 (PD), VU658
"Lord, I Want to be a Christian" 3184437 (Matt)
C589, CG507, G729, GR611, N454, P372 (PD), SH621, UM402, Z76 (PD-TO)
"Near to the Heart of God" (Matt)
C581, CG383, G824, GR357, P527, UM472 (PD)
"For All the Saints" 90590 (Matt)
C637, CG567, E287, EL422, G326, GR480, N299, P526, SH231, UM711 (PD), VU705
"I Sing a Song of the Saints of God" (Matt)
E293, G730, GR482, N295, P364, UM712 (PD)
"*Santo*" ("Holy") (Matt)
EL762, G594, SH39, S2019
"All Who Hunger" (Matt)
C419, CG303, EL461, G509, S2126, VU460
"Since Jesus Came into My Heart" (Matt)
CG614, GR552, S2140

Additional Contemporary and Modern Suggestions

+"The Kingdom Is Yours" 7109354 (Mic)
+"Called Me Higher" 5887880 (Mic)
+"Come to the Table" 7130008 (Mic)
+"Daughters of Zion" 7133716 (Mic)
+"Let Justice Roll" ("Like a River") 4974842 (Mic)
+"The Heart of Worship" 2296522 (Mic)
+"From the Inside Out" 4705176 (Mic)
"*Ubi Caritas*" ("Live in Charity") OL-00798 (Mic)
C523, EL642, G205, S2179
"Rule of Life" (PD-TO) (Mic, Matt)
WS3117, ZS95
"Here I Am to Worship" 3266032 (Mic, 1 Cor)
CG297, SH395, WS3177, ZS145
"You Are My All in All" 825356 (1 Cor)
CG571, G519, SH335, WS3040, ZS184
"Let It Be Said of Us" 1855882 (1 Cor)
"The Wonderful Cross" 3148435 (1 Cor)
"I Will Boast" 4662350 (1 Cor)
+"Won't Stop Now" 7111932 (1 Cor)
+"Yet Not I but Through Christ in Me" 7121852 (1 Cor)
+"My Worth Is Not in What I Own" 7024758 (1 Cor)
+"Let Justice Roll" ("Like a River") 4974842 (1 Cor, Matt)
+"The Kingdom Is Yours" 7109354 (1 Cor, Matt)
"Give Thanks" 20285 (1 Cor, Matt)
C528, CG373, G647, S2036, SH489, ZS127
"Open Our Eyes, Lord" 1572 (Matt)
CG392, S2086, SH562
"Blessed Be Your Name" 3798438 (Matt)
SH449, WS3002
"Open the Eyes of My Heart" 2298355 (Matt)
G452, SH378, WS3008
"Restless" 5775569 (Matt)
+"Pure and Holy" 7181776 (Matt)
+"You Keep Hope Alive" 7125876 (Matt)
+"Come to the Table" 7130008 (Matt, Comm.)

Solo/Ensemble Suggestions

"Fit for a King" (Mic)
V-10 p. 32
+"Who You Are to Me" (Pss, Matt)
V-9 p. 124

"Maybe the Rain" (Matt)
V-5 (2) p. 27
"This Is My Commandment" (Matt)
V-8 p. 284
"As This Broken Bread" (Heb)
Wayne Wold; AEC-1 p.5
2-part mixed, organ (https://bit.ly/AEC-1-5)
"Walking on Our Way with God" (Mic)
Jayne Southwick Cool; AEC-3 p. 78
2-part mixed, piano (https://bit.ly/AEC-3)

+Hymn Anthem

"Cuando el Pobre" ("When the Poor Ones") (Mic, Matt)
C662, EL725, G762, P407, SH240, UM434, VU702

Guitar accompaniment is highly desired, though piano may be used in addition to or instead of a guitar. Simple use of maracas and claves will also be effective. The outline below may be adapted in many ways. Experiment with text language and accompaniment.

Introduction: Piano plays first measure two times, bass clef only.

Stanza 1: (Spanish) Male soloist sings stanza and refrain. Piano plays only bass clef accompaniment.

Stanza 1: (English) Another soloist sings and choir joins on refrain. Add guitar to the piano playing the full accompaniment.

Stanza 2: (English) S/A only, singing parts when there are two notes in the treble clef. Guitar only. Continue in this manner through the refrain.

Stanza 3: (English) T/B only on melody. S/A (and congregation) join on refrain. Piano plays full accompaniment. Claves (or rhythm sticks) play rhythm of bass clef, measure 1, throughout.

Stanza 4: (English) All voices (with congregation), unison. Accompany with piano, guitar, claves (as in stanza 3) and maracas playing two eighth notes at the beginning of every measure.

Ending: (Spanish) Refrain only, stanza 1 soloist, accompanied by guitar.

Other Suggestions

February is Black History Month, which can be reflected in your choice of music and liturgy.

Visuals:

O Briefcase, Exodus, prayer, scales of justice, ministry
P Tent, hill, walking, speaking, destructive behavior, ministry, justice, money
E Empty cross, clown, debate, crucifix, block, Christ, world upside down
G Jesus teaching, examples of ministry described

Opening Prayer: WSL60. "As the sun rises" (Mic)
Affirmation of Faith: WSL83. "We believe" (Matt)
Litany: WSL49. "For rebirth and resilience" (Matt)
Prayer: N860. "Those in Need" (Mic)
Prayer: WSL199. "O God of the crucified Christ" (Matt)
Prayer: WSL200. "Show us, good Lord" (Matt)
Prayer: UM392 (Matt)
Prayer: UM456 (Mic, 1 Cor)
Response: WS3103. "Purify My Heart" (Matt)
Canticle: C185. "The Beatitudes" (Matt)
Dance Solo: N180. "Blessed Are the Poor in Spirit" (Matt)
Offertory Prayer: WSL129. "Blessed One" (Matt)
Blessing: WSL160. "What does the Lord require" (Mic)

Theme Ideas: Beatitudes/Blessings, Cross, Faithfulness, God: Hunger / Thirst for God, God: Wisdom, Humility, Justice, Saints

Notes

NRSVue

Isaiah 58:1-9a (9b-12)
1Shout out; do not hold back!
Lift up your voice like a trumpet!
Announce to my people their rebellion,
to the house of Jacob their sins.
2Yet day after day they seek me
and delight to know my ways,
as if they were a nation that practiced righteousness
and did not forsake the ordinance of their God;
they ask of me righteous judgments;
they want God on their side.
3"Why do we fast, but you do not see?
Why humble ourselves, but you do not notice?"
Look, you serve your own interest on your fast day
and oppress all your workers.
4You fast only to quarrel and to fight
and to strike with a wicked fist.
Such fasting as you do today
will not make your voice heard on high.
5Is such the fast that I choose,
a day to humble oneself?
Is it to bow down the head like a bulrush
and to lie in sackcloth and ashes?
Will you call this a fast,
a day acceptable to the LORD?
6Is not this the fast that I choose:
to loose the bonds of injustice,
to undo the straps of the yoke,
to let the oppressed go free,
and to break every yoke?
7Is it not to share your bread with the hungry
and bring the homeless poor into your house;
when you see the naked, to cover them
and not to hide yourself from your own kin?
8Then your light shall break forth like the dawn,
and your healing shall spring up quickly;
your vindicator shall go before you;
the glory of the LORD shall be your rear guard.
9Then you shall call, and the LORD will answer;
you shall cry for help, and he will say, "Here I am."
If you remove the yoke from among you,
the pointing of the finger, the speaking of evil,
10if you offer your food to the hungry
and satisfy the needs of the afflicted,
then your light shall rise in the darkness
and your gloom be like the noonday.
11The LORD will guide you continually
and satisfy your needs in parched places
and make your bones strong,
and you shall be like a watered garden,
like a spring of water
whose waters never fail.
12Your ancient ruins shall be rebuilt;
you shall raise up the foundations of many generations;
you shall be called the repairer of the breach,
the restorer of streets to live in.

Psalm 112:1-9 (10) (G755, N697, UM833)
1Praise the LORD!
Happy are those who fear the LORD,
who greatly delight in his commandments.
2Their descendants will be mighty in the land;
the generation of the upright will be blessed.
3Wealth and riches are in their houses,
and their righteousness endures forever.
4They rise in the darkness as a light for the upright;
they are gracious, merciful, and righteous.
5It is well with those who deal generously and lend,
who conduct their affairs with justice.

CEB

Isaiah 58:1-9a (9b-12)
1Shout loudly; don't hold back;
raise your voice like a trumpet!
Announce to my people their crime,
to the house of Jacob their sins.
2They seek me day after day,
desiring knowledge of my ways
like a nation that acted righteously,
that didn't abandon their God.
They ask me for righteous judgments,
wanting to be close to God.
3"Why do we fast and you don't see;
why afflict ourselves and you don't notice?"
Yet on your fast day you do whatever you want,
and oppress all your workers.
4You quarrel and brawl, and then you fast;
you hit each other violently with your fists.
You shouldn't fast as you are doing today
if you want to make your voice heard on high.
5Is this the kind of fast I choose,
a day of self-affliction,
of bending one's head like a reed
and of lying down in mourning clothing and ashes?
Is this what you call a fast,
a day acceptable to the LORD?
6Isn't this the fast I choose:
releasing wicked restraints, untying the ropes of a yoke,
setting free the mistreated,
and breaking every yoke?
7Isn't it sharing your bread with the hungry
and bringing the homeless poor into your house,
covering the naked when you see them,
and not hiding from your own family?
8Then your light will break out like the dawn,
and you will be healed quickly.
Your own righteousness will walk before you,
and the LORD's glory will be your rear guard.
9Then you will call, and the LORD will answer;
you will cry for help, and God will say, "I'm here."
If you remove the yoke from among you,
the finger-pointing, the wicked speech;
10 if you open your heart to the hungry,
and provide abundantly for those who are afflicted,
your light will shine in the darkness,
and your gloom will be like the noon.
11The LORD will guide you continually
and provide for you, even in parched places.
He will rescue your bones.
You will be like a watered garden,
like a spring of water that won't run dry.
12They will rebuild ancient ruins on your account;
the foundations of generations past you will restore.
You will be called Mender of Broken Walls,
Restorer of Livable Streets.

Psalm 112:1-9 (10) (G755, N697, UM833)
1Praise the LORD!
Those who honor the LORD,
who adore God's commandments, are truly happy!
2Their descendants will be strong throughout the land.
The offspring of those who do right will be blessed;
3 wealth and riches will be in their houses.
Their righteousness stands forever.
4They shine in the dark for others who do right.
They are merciful, compassionate, and righteous.
5Those who lend generously are good people—
as are those who conduct their affairs with justice.
6Yes, these sorts of people will never be shaken;
the righteous will be remembered forever!

NRSVue

Psalm 112:1-9 (10) (continued)

6For the righteous will never be moved;
  they will be remembered forever.
7They are not afraid of evil tidings;
  their hearts are firm, secure in the LORD.
8Their hearts are steady; they will not be afraid;
  in the end they will look in triumph on their foes.
9They have distributed freely; they have given to the poor;
  their righteousness endures forever;
  their horn is exalted in honor.
10The wicked see it and are angry;
  they gnash their teeth and melt away;
  the desire of the wicked comes to nothing.

---

1 Corinthians 2:1-12 (13-16)

1When I came to you, brothers and sisters, I did not come proclaiming the testimony of God to you with superior speech or wisdom. 2For I decided to know nothing among you except Jesus Christ and him crucified. 3And I came to you in weakness and in fear and in much trembling. 4My speech and my proclamation were made not with persuasive words of wisdom but with a demonstration of the Spirit and of power, 5so that your faith might rest not on human wisdom but on the power of God.

6Yet among the mature we do speak wisdom, though it is not a wisdom of this age or of the rulers of this age, who are being destroyed. 7But we speak God's wisdom, a hidden mystery, which God decreed before the ages for our glory 8and which none of the rulers of this age understood, for if they had, they would not have crucified the Lord of glory. 9But, as it is written,

"What no eye has seen, nor ear heard,
    nor the human heart conceived,
  what God has prepared for those who love him"—

10God has revealed to us through the Spirit, for the Spirit searches everything, even the depths of God. 11For what human knows what is truly human except the human spirit that is within? So also no one comprehends what is truly God's except the Spirit of God. 12Now we have received not the spirit of the world but the Spirit that is from God, so that we may understand the gifts bestowed on us by God. 13And we speak of these things in words not taught by human wisdom but taught by the Spirit, interpreting spiritual things to those who are spiritual.

14Those who are unspiritual do not receive the gifts of God's Spirit, for they are foolishness to them, and they are unable to understand them because they are spiritually discerned. 15Those who are spiritual discern all things, and they are themselves subject to no one else's scrutiny. But we have the mind of Christ.

16 "For who has known the mind of the Lord
    so as to instruct him?"
  But we have the mind of Christ.

Matthew 5:13-20

13"You are the salt of the earth, but if salt has lost its taste, how can its saltiness be restored? It is no longer good for anything but is thrown out and trampled under foot.

14"You are the light of the world. A city built on a hill cannot be hid. 15People do not light a lamp and put it under the bushel basket; rather, they put it on the lampstand, and it gives light to all in the house. 16In the same way, let your light shine before others, so that they may see your good works and give glory to your Father in heaven.

17"Do not think that I have come to abolish the Law or the Prophets; I have come not to abolish but to fulfill. 18For truly I tell you, until heaven and earth pass away, not one letter, not one stroke of a letter, will pass from the law until all is accomplished. 19Therefore, whoever breaks one of the least of these commandments and teaches others to do the same will be called least in the kingdom of heaven, but whoever does them and teaches them will be called great in the kingdom of heaven. 20For I tell you, unless your righteousness exceeds that of the scribes and Pharisees, you will never enter the kingdom of heaven."

CEB

Psalm 112:1-9 (10) (continued)

7They won't be frightened at bad news.
  Their hearts are steady, trusting in the LORD.
8Their hearts are firm; they aren't afraid.
  In the end, they will witness their enemies' defeat.
9They give freely to those in need.
  Their righteousness stands forever.
  Their strength increases gloriously.
10The wicked see all this and fume;
    they grind their teeth, but disappear to nothing.
  What the wicked want to see happen comes to nothing!

---

1 Corinthians 2:1-12 (13-16)

1When I came to you, brothers and sisters, I didn't come preaching God's secrets to you like I was an expert in speech or wisdom. 2I had made up my mind not to think about anything while I was with you except Jesus Christ, and to preach him as crucified. 3I stood in front of you with weakness, fear, and a lot of shaking. 4My message and my preaching weren't presented with convincing wise words but with a demonstration of the Spirit and of power. 5I did this so that your faith might not depend on the wisdom of people but on the power of God.

6What we say is wisdom to people who are mature. It isn't a wisdom that comes from the present day or from today's leaders who are being reduced to nothing. 7We talk about God's wisdom, which has been hidden as a secret. God determined this wisdom in advance, before time began, for our glory. 8It is a wisdom that none of the present-day rulers have understood, because if they did understand it, they would never have crucified the Lord of glory! 9But this is precisely what is written: *God has prepared things for those who love him that no eye has seen, or ear has heard, or that haven't crossed the mind of any human being.* 10God has revealed these things to us through the Spirit. The Spirit searches everything, including the depths of God. 11Who knows a person's depths except their own spirit that lives in them? In the same way, no one has known the depths of God except God's Spirit. 12We haven't received the world's spirit but God's Spirit so that we can know the things given to us by God. 13These are the things we are talking about—not with words taught by human wisdom but with words taught by the Spirit—we are interpreting spiritual things to spiritual people. 14But people who are unspiritual don't accept the things from God's Spirit. They are foolishness to them and can't be understood, because they can only be comprehended in a spiritual way. 15Spiritual people comprehend everything, but they themselves aren't understood by anyone. 16*Who has known the mind of the Lord, who will advise him?* But we have the mind of Christ.

Matthew 5:13-20

13"You are the salt of the earth. But if salt loses its saltiness, how will it become salty again? It's good for nothing except to be thrown away and trampled under people's feet. 14You are the light of the world. A city on top of a hill can't be hidden. 15Neither do people light a lamp and put it under a basket. Instead, they put it on top of a lampstand, and it shines on all who are in the house. 16In the same way, let your light shine before people, so they can see the good things you do and praise your Father who is in heaven.

17"Don't even begin to think that I have come to do away with the Law and the Prophets. I haven't come to do away with them but to fulfill them. 18I say to you very seriously that as long as heaven and earth exist, neither the smallest letter nor even the smallest stroke of a pen will be erased from the Law until everything there becomes a reality. 19Therefore, whoever ignores one of the least of these commands and teaches others to do the same will be called the lowest in the kingdom of heaven. But whoever keeps these commands and teaches people to keep them will be called great in the kingdom of heaven. 20I say to you that unless your righteousness is greater than the righteousness of the legal experts and the Pharisees, you will never enter the kingdom of heaven."

Primary Hymns and Songs for the Day
"Gather Us In" OL-00031 (Isa, Matt, Comm.) (O)
C284, EL532, G401, S2236, SH393
"For the Healing of the Nations" 1510804 (Isa) (O)
C668, CG698, G346, N576, UM428, VU678
"Awake, My Soul, and with the Sun" (Isa)
E11, EL557 (PD), G663, GR54, P456
"All Who Love and Serve Your City" 1277415 (Isa)
C670, CG674, E570/571, EL724, G351, P413, UM433
H-3 Chr-26, 65; Org-19
S-1 #62. Desc.
"I Want to Walk as a Child of the Light" (Matt)
CG96, E490, EL815, G377, GR216, SH352, UM206
S-2 #91. Desc.
"This Little Light of Mine" 5305434, OL-22794 (Matt, Black History) (C)
N525, UM585, Z132 (*See also* EL677, N524, SH257)

Additional Hymn Suggestions
"O For a Thousand Tongues to Sing" 1369 (Isa)
C5, CG332, E493, EL886, G610, GR1, N42, P466, SH439, UM57 (PD), VU326 (*See also* WS3001)
+"I'll Praise My Maker While I've Breath" (Isa)
C20, CG336, E429 (PD), G806, GR17, P253, UM60, VU867
"Guide Me, O Thou Great Jehovah" 1448 (Isa)
C622, CG33, E690, EL618, G65, GR47, N18, P281, SH51, UM127 (PD), VU651 (Fr.)
"Cuando el Pobre" ("When the Poor Ones") OL-97385 (Isa)
C662, EL725, G762, P407, SH240, UM434, VU702
"Mine Eyes Have Seen the Glory" (Isa)
C705, CG439, EL890, G354, GR283, N610, UM717 (PD), Z24/213
"God Is So Good" 4956994 (Isa)
G658, GR52, S2056, SH461, Z231
"What Does the Lord Require of You" 456859 (Isa)
C661, CG690, G70, S2174, VU701
"Guide My Feet" OL-LMGM2537 (Isa, Black History)
CG637, G741, GR326, N497, P354, S2208, SH54, ZS141
+"Lead On, O Cloud of Presence" (Isa)
C633, S2234, VU421
"Here I Am, Lord" OL-80670 (Isa, Matt)
C452, CG482, EL574, G69, GR589, P525, SH608, UM593, VU509
"Christ, Be Our Light" (*"Cristo, la Luz"*) (Isa, Matt)
EL715, G314, SH242
"Lord, Whose Love Through Humble Service" (Isa, 1 Cor, Matt)
C461, CG650, E610, EL712, GR454, P427, SH239, UM581
"We've a Story to Tell to the Nations" (Isa, Matt)
C484, CG427, GR458, UM569 (PD)
"Bring Forth the Kingdom" (Isa, Matt)
N181, S2190, SH130
"Lead Me, Guide Me" (Isa, Matt)
C583, CG403, EL768, G740, S2214, SH582, ZS173
"I Will Trust in the Lord" (Pss, Black History)
N416, UM464, Z14 (PD-TO)
"All Praise to Thee, for Thou, O King Divine" (Pss, 1 Cor)
CG352, E477, GR281, UM166, VU327
"Lord, Speak to Me" 2769286 (Pss, 1 Cor)
CG503, EL676, G722, GR439, N531, P426, SH557, UM463 (PD), VU589
"Ask Ye What Great Thing I Know" (1 Cor)
CG443, GR107, N49, UM163 (PD), VU338
"Jesus, the Very Thought of Thee" (1 Cor)
C102, CG386, E642, EL754, G629, GR127, N507, P310, UM175 (PD)
"Forth in Thy Name, O Lord" (1 Cor)
GR685, UM438 (PD), VU416
"Blest Be the Dear Uniting Love" (1 Cor)
GR389, UM566 (PD)
"Come, Holy Ghost, Our Hearts Inspire" (1 Cor)
GR291, UM603 (PD)
"Spirit of Faith, Come Down" (1 Cor)
GR289, UM332 (PD)
"Be Thou My Vision" UM 5021907 (1 Cor)
C595, CG71, E488, EL793, G450, GR49, N451, P339, SH640, UM451, VU642
"Woke Up This Morning" (1 Cor)
C623, N85, S2082, Z146, ZS105
"Christ Beside Me" (1 Cor)
G702, S2166
"Blessed Jesus, At Thy Word" (Matt)
E440, EL520, G395, N74, P454, UM596 (PD), VU500
"I'm Gonna Live So God Can Use Me" (Matt)
C614, G700, GR615, P369, S2153, SH632, VU575
"Together We Serve" (Matt)
G767, S2175
"We All Are One in Mission" 3176809 (Matt)
CG269, EL576, G733, P435, S2243, ZS99
"Today We All Are Called to Be Disciples" (Matt)
G757, P434, VU507

Additional Contemporary and Modern Suggestions
"Shout to the Lord" 1406918 (Isa)
CG348, EL821, GR124, S2074, SH426, ZS15
+"All the Poor and Powerless" 5881130 (Isa)
+"Called Me Higher" 5887880 (Isa, Matt)
+"Won't Stop Now" 7111932 (Isa, 1 Cor)
+"The Jesus in Me" (PD) (1 Cor)
WS3151, ZS132
"Knowing You" 1045238 (1 Cor)
"In the Secret" 1810119 (1 Cor)
"Let It Be Said of Us" 1855882 (1 Cor)
"Take My Life" 1617154 1 Cor)
"I Will Boast" 4662350 (1 Cor)
"I Have a Hope" 5087587 (1 Cor)
+"Presence" 7116947 (1 Cor)
+"The Kingdom Is Yours" 7109354 (1 Cor, Matt)
"Shine, Jesus, Shine" 30426 (Matt)
CG156, EL671, G192, GR217, S2173, SH102, V-3 (2), p. 48 Vocal Solo
"Light of the World" 73342 (Matt)
S2204
"Siyahamba" ("We Are Marching") 1321512 (Matt)
C442, CG155, EL866, G853, N526, S2235-ab, SH717, VU646, ZS111
"Mighty to Save" 4591782 (Matt)
WS3038
+"Whatever You Do" (Matt)
WS3128
"Lord Jesus Christ, Your Light Shines" (Matt)
SH556, WS3137
+"Walking in the Light of God" (Matt)
"Here I Am to Worship" 3266032 (Matt)
CG297, SH395, WS3177, ZS145
+"As We Go" 5043277 (Matt) (C)
WS3183
"Carry the Light" 126402 (Matt)
"Song for the Nations" 20340 (Matt)
"Shine on Us" 1754646 (Matt)
"Everyday" 2798154 (Matt)
"Freedom in the Spirit" 7127886 (Matt)
+"Start a Fire" 7017142 (Matt)
+"Say So" 4944016 (Matt)

Solo/Ensemble Suggestions

"God Will Make a Way" (with "He Leadeth Me") (Isa)
V-3 (2) p. 9
+"Shout to the Lord" (with "All Creatures of Our God and King") (Isa)
V-3 (2) p. 32
+"May the Mind of Christ" (1 Cor)
V-8 p. 114
+"The Blessing" (1 Cor)
V-9 p. 10
"We All Are One in Mission" (1 Cor, MLK Day)
Arr. Joel Martinson; AEC-2 p. 23
SATB, organ (https://bit.ly/AEC-2)
"Teach Me, O Lord" (Pss)
Thomas Atwood; MorningStar MSM-50-3425
SATB *a cappella* (https://bit.ly/MSM-50-3425)

+Hymn Anthem

"This Little Light of Mine" 5305434, OL-22794 (Matt, Black History)
N525, UM585, Z132

This setting is different from the faster, syncopated version that is familiar to many singers. It can be reproduced with CCLI or OneLicense licenses.

Sing slowly and with emotion. Vary the tempos between verses. Accompany with soft organ or piano if necessary, but *a cappella* singing is preferable. Sing it in either D or E flat major if possible.

Introduction: All voices sing entire setting in four-parts on "oo" vowel or hum.

Stanza 1: All voices continue "oo" or hum in four-parts, treble soloist sings melody and text. Systems 3 & 4, all sing text in four parts.

Stanza 2: T/B only (quartet). Tenor I: alto part, in the alto range. Tenor II: tenor part. Baritone: melody. Bass: bass part. If this is not possible, all sing in four parts. This stanza should move a little more and be a little louder.

Stanza 3: Full and strong, but slower, with rubato as the conductor wishes. Four parts continue, but assign other parts to two sopranos. One singer may sing the bass part up 2 octaves. The other may sing the alto part up one octave. These parts should remain on C and G during the last two measures. This will give an improvisatory feel to this stanza. Increase intensity throughout this stanza. End strong and intense.

Other Suggestions

This day may include an observance of Scout Sunday.

Visuals:

O Trumpet, fist, open shackles, yoke, bread, light, water
P Bible, light/dark, justice, heart, ministry to poor, anger
E Bible, heart, emotion, praise, walking
G Salt/light, globe, city, lamp/basket/lampstand, Bible, teaching

Opening Prayer: WSL218. "Lord, set your blessing" (Isa)
Confession: WSL97. "Your light has filled our lives" (Matt)
Confession: WSL87. "Almighty God" (Isa)
Canticle: UM125. Canticle of Covenant Faithfulness (Isa)
Prayer: WSL57. "Days pass and the years vanish" (1 Cor)
Prayer: UM456. For Courage to Do Justice (Isa)
Blessing: WSL59. "You are the salt" (Matt)
Theme Ideas: Discipleship / Following God, Faithfulness, God: Wisdom, Jesus: Mind of Christ, Justice, Light, Redemption / Salvation

Notes

NRSVue

Exodus 24:12-18

12The LORD said to Moses, "Come up to me on the mountain
and wait there; I will give you the tablets of stone, with the law
and the commandment, which I have written for their instruction." 13So Moses set out with his assistant Joshua, and Moses
went up into the mountain of God. 14To the elders he had said,
"Wait here for us, until we come back to you. Look, Aaron and
Hur are with you; whoever has a dispute may go to them."
15Then Moses went up on the mountain, and the cloud covered the mountain. 16The glory of the LORD settled on Mount
Sinai, and the cloud covered it for six days; on the seventh day
he called to Moses out of the cloud. 17Now the appearance of
the glory of the LORD was like a devouring fire on the top of
the mountain in the sight of the Israelites. 18Moses entered the
cloud and went up on the mountain. Moses was on the mountain for forty days and forty nights.

Psalm 99 (G57, N687, UM819)

1The LORD is king; let the peoples tremble!
  He sits enthroned upon the cherubim; let the earth quake!
2The LORD is great in Zion;
  he is exalted over all the peoples.
3Let them praise your great and awesome name.
  Holy is he!
4Mighty King, lover of justice,
  you have established equity;
you have executed justice
  and righteousness in Jacob.
5Extol the LORD our God;
  worship at his footstool.
  Holy is he!
6Moses and Aaron were among his priests,
  Samuel also was among those who called on his name.
  They cried to the LORD, and he answered them.
7He spoke to them in the pillar of cloud;
  they kept his decrees
  and the statutes that he gave them.
8O LORD our God, you answered them;
  you were a forgiving God to them
  but an avenger of their wrongdoings.
9Extol the LORD our God,
  and worship at his holy mountain,
  for the LORD our God is holy.

CEB

Exodus 24:12-18

12The LORD said to Moses, "Come up to me on the mountain
and wait there. I'll give you the stone tablets with the instructions and the commandments that I've written in order to teach
them."
13So Moses and his assistant Joshua got up, and Moses went up
God's mountain. 14Moses had said to the elders, "Wait for us here
until we come back to you. Aaron and Hur will be here with you.
Whoever has a legal dispute may go to them."
15Then Moses went up the mountain, and the cloud covered
the mountain. 16The LORD's glorious presence settled on Mount
Sinai, and the cloud covered it for six days. On the seventh day
the LORD called to Moses from the cloud. 17To the Israelites,
the LORD's glorious presence looked like a blazing fire on top
of the mountain. 18Moses entered the cloud and went up the
mountain. Moses stayed on the mountain for forty days and forty
nights.

Psalm 99 (G57, N687, UM819)

1The LORD rules—
  the nations shake!
  He sits enthroned on the winged heavenly creatures—
  the earth quakes!
2The LORD is great in Zion;
  he is exalted over all the nations.
3Let them thank your great and awesome name.
  He is holy!
4Strong king who loves justice,
  you are the one who established what is fair.
  You worked justice and righteousness in Jacob.
5Magnify the LORD, our God!
  Bow low at his footstool!
  He is holy!
6Moses and Aaron were among his priests,
  Samuel too among those who called on his name.
They cried out to the LORD, and he himself answered them—
7 he spoke to them from a pillar of cloud.
They kept the laws and the rules God gave to them.
8LORD our God, you answered them.
  To them you were a God who forgives
  but also the one who avenged their wrong deeds.
9Magnify the LORD our God!
  Bow low at his holy mountain
  because the LORD our God is holy!

NRSVue

2 Peter 1:16-21

16For we did not follow cleverly devised myths when we made known to you the power and coming of our Lord Jesus Christ, but we had been eyewitnesses of his majesty. 17For he received honor and glory from God the Father when that voice was conveyed to him by the Majestic Glory, saying, "This is my Son, my Beloved, with whom I am well pleased." 18We ourselves heard this voice come from heaven, while we were with him on the holy mountain.

19So we have the prophetic message more fully confirmed. You will do well to be attentive to this as to a lamp shining in a dark place, until the day dawns and the morning star rises in your hearts. 20First of all you must understand this, that no prophecy of scripture is a matter of one's own interpretation, 21because no prophecy ever came by human will, but men and women moved by the Holy Spirit spoke from God.

Matthew 17:1-9

1Six days later, Jesus took with him Peter and James and his brother John and led them up a high mountain, by themselves. 2And he was transfigured before them, and his face shone like the sun, and his clothes became bright as light. 3Suddenly there appeared to them Moses and Elijah, talking with him. 4Then Peter said to Jesus, "Lord, it is good for us to be here; if you wish, I will set up three tents here, one for you, one for Moses, and one for Elijah." 5While he was still speaking, suddenly a bright cloud overshadowed them, and a voice from the cloud said, "This is my Son, the Beloved; with him I am well pleased; listen to him!" 6When the disciples heard this, they fell to the ground and were overcome by fear. 7But Jesus came and touched them, saying, "Get up and do not be afraid." 8And when they raised their eyes, they saw no one except Jesus himself alone.

9As they were coming down the mountain, Jesus ordered them, "Tell no one about the vision until after the Son of Man has been raised from the dead."

CEB

2 Peter 1:16-21

16We didn't repeat crafty myths when we told you about the powerful coming of our Lord Jesus Christ. Quite the contrary, we witnessed his majesty with our own eyes. 17He received honor and glory from God the Father when a voice came to him from the magnificent glory, saying, "This is my dearly loved Son, with whom I am well-pleased." 18We ourselves heard this voice from heaven while we were with him on the holy mountain. 19In addition, we have a most reliable prophetic word, and you would do well to pay attention to it, just as you would to a lamp shining in a dark place, until the day dawns and the morning star rises in your hearts. 20Most important, you must know that no prophecy of scripture represents the prophet's own understanding of things, 21because no prophecy ever came by human will. Instead, men and women led by the Holy Spirit spoke from God.

Matthew 17:1-9

1Six days later Jesus took Peter, James, and John his brother, and brought them to the top of a very high mountain. 2He was transformed in front of them. His face shone like the sun, and his clothes became as white as light.

3Moses and Elijah appeared to them, talking with Jesus. 4Peter reacted to all of this by saying to Jesus, "Lord, it's good that we're here. If you want, I'll make three shrines: one for you, one for Moses, and one for Elijah."

5While he was still speaking, look, a bright cloud overshadowed them. A voice from the cloud said, "This is my Son whom I dearly love. I am very pleased with him. Listen to him!" 6Hearing this, the disciples fell on their faces, filled with awe.

7But Jesus came and touched them. "Get up," he said. "Don't be afraid." 8When they looked up, they saw no one except Jesus.

9As they were coming down the mountain, Jesus commanded them, "Don't tell anybody about the vision until the Human One is raised from the dead."

Primary Hymns and Songs for the Day
"Christ, Whose Glory Fills the Skies" 808926 (2 Pet, Matt) (O)
E7, EL553, G662, GR211, P462, UM173 (PD), VU336
H-3 Hbl-51; Chr-206; Desc-89; Org-120
S-1 #278-279. Harms.
"Open the Eyes of My Heart" 2298355 (2 Pet)
G452, SH378, WS3008
"O Wondrous Sight! O Vision Fair" (PD) h(2 Pet, Matt)
E137, UM258 (PD)
H-3 Hbl-93; Chr-84; Desc-102; Org-175
S-2 #191. Harm.
E136, EL316 (PD), G189, N184, P75
"Swiftly Pass the Clouds of Glory" (Matt)
G190, P73, S2102
H-3 Chr-98; Org-43
"Holy Ground" 21198 (Matt)
C112, G406, S2272
"You, Lord, Are Both Lamb and Shepherd" (Matt)
G274, SH210, VU210. WS3043
"Immortal, Invisible, God Only Wise" 124466 (Exod) (C)
C66, CG58, E423, EL834, G12, GR7, N1, P263, UM103 (PD), VU264 (*See also* ZS4)
H-3 Hbl-15, 71; Chr-65; Desc-93; Org-135
S-1 #300. Harm.

Additional Hymn Suggestions
"O Worship the King" (Exod)
C17, CG52, E388, EL842, G41, GR11, N26, P476, SH255, UM73 (PD), VU235
"Source and Sovereign, Rock and Cloud" (Exod)
C12, G11, UM113
"Guide Me, O Thou Great Jehovah" 1448 (Exod)
C622, CG33, E690, EL618, G65, GR47, N18, P281, SH51, UM127 (PD), VU651 (Fr.)
"Glorious Things of Thee Are Spoken" 99371 (Exod)
C709, CG282, E522/523, EL647, G81, GR395, N307, P446, UM731 (PD)
"You Alone Are Holy" (Exod, Transfig.)
S2077, SH457
"Spirit, Spirit of Gentleness" (Exod)
C249, EL396, G291, N286, P319, S2120, VU375 (Fr.)
"Praise God for This Holy Ground" (Exod, Matt)
G405, WS3009
"The God of Abraham Praise" 484742 (Exod, Matt)
C24, CG45, E401, EL831, G49, GR16, N24, P488, SH50, UM116 (PD), VU255
"Every Time I Feel the Spirit" (PD-TO) (Exod, Matt)
C592, G66, GR446, N282, P315, UM404, Z121 (PD)
"Be Thou My Vision" UM 5021907 (Exod, Matt, Transfig.)
C595, CG71, E488, EL793, G450, GR49, N451, P339, SH640, UM451, VU642
"La Palabra Del Señor Es Recta" ("Righteous and Just Is the Word of the Lord") (Pss)
G40, UM107, SH4
"Praise to the Lord, the Almighty" 785135 (Pss)
C25, CG319, E390, EL858 (PD)/859, G35, GR3, N22, P482, SH453, UM139, VU220 (Fr.) and VU221
"A Hymn of Glory Let Us Sing" (2 Pet)
E218, G258, N259, P141
"Lord of All Hopefulness" 5579875 (2 Pet)
CG678, E482, EL765, G683, S2197, SH464
"Deep in the Shadows of the Past" (2 Pet)
G50, N320, P330, S2246
"Jesus, the Light of the World" 6363190 (2 Pet)
WS3056 (*See also* CG129, G127, GR214, N160, SH103, ZS62)
"O Morning Star, How Fair and Bright" (2 Pet, Matt)
C105, E497, EL308, G827, N158, P69, UM247, VU98

"Christ, Upon the Mountain Peak" (2 Pet, Matt)
E129/E130, EL317, P74, UM260, VU102
"Jesus, Take Us to the Mountain" OL-11329 (Matt)
G193, N183
+"Joyful, Joyful, We Adore Thee" (Matt)
C2, CG310, E376, EL836, G611, GR8, N4, P464, SH390, UM89 (PD), VU232
"I Stand Amazed in the Presence" (Matt)
CG576, GR122, SH537, UM371 (PD)
"Jesus, Joy of Our Desiring" (Matt, Comm.)
GR129, UM644 (PD), VU328
"Here, O My Lord, I See Thee" 136265(Matt, Comm.)
C416, CG460, E318, G517, GR411, N336, P520, UM623, VU459
"Let Us with a Joyful Mind" (Matt)
E389, G31, N16, P244, S2012, VU234
"We Have Come at Christ's Own Bidding" (Matt)
CG162, G191, N182, S2103, VU104
"How Good, Lord, to Be Here!" (*"Es bueno estar aquí"*) (Matt)
EL315, SH133, VU103
"Come Away with Me" 2496559 (Matt, Transfig.)
S2202
"O Living God" 3308921 (Transfig.)
WS3089

Additional Contemporary and Modern Suggestions
"Awesome God" 41099 (Exod, Pss)
G616, S2040, ZS7
"Doxology" 5465879 (Exod, Pss)
"Majesty" 1527 (Pss, Transfig.)
CG346, GR63, SH212, UM176
+"From the Inside Out" 4705176 (Pss)
+"Daughters of Zion" 7133716 (Pss)
+"Let Justice Roll" ("Like a River") 4974842 (Pss)
"Awesome Is the Lord Most High" 4674159 (Pss)
"Famous One" 3599431 (Pss, 2 Pet)
"Ancient Words" 2986399 (2 Pet)
+"Beautiful Savior" 2492216 (2 Pet, Matt, Transfig.)
+"Beautiful Savior" 4600051 (2 Pet, Matt, Transfig.)
+"You Are" 4387343 (2 Pet, Matt, Transfig.)
"Turn Your Eyes upon Jesus" 15960 (Matt)
CG472, GR670, UM349
"All Hail King Jesus" 12877 (Matt, Transfig.)
S2069, ZS53
"He Is Exalted" 17827 (Matt, Transfig.)
CG342, S2070, SH423
"Shine, Jesus, Shine" 30426 (Matt, Transfig.)
CG156, EL671, G192, GR217, S2173, SH102; V-3 (2), p. 48. Vocal Solo
"We Fall Down" 2437367 (Matt, Transfig)
G368, WS3187
"Awesome in This Place" 847554 (Matt, Transfig.)
"We Declare Your Majesty" 121483 (Matt, Transfig.)
"Great and Mighty Is He" 66665 (Transfig.)
+"Oh, the Glory of Your Presence" 16529 (Transfig.)
+"See His Glory" 229921 (Transfig.)
"Honor and Praise" 1867485 (Transfig.)
S2018
"Hosanna" 4785835 (Transfig.)
SH361, WS3188

Solo/Ensemble Suggestions

"Be Thou My Vision" (Exod, Matt, Transfig.)
V-6 p. 13
"I Saw the Lord, and All Beside Was Darkness" (Exod, Matt)
V-8 p. 268
+"O Lord of Darkness and of Light" (2 Pet, Matt)
Justin Wedgewood; Oregon Catholic Press 30149538
SAB, piano, opt. instruments (https://bit.ly/OCP-9538)
+"Vision Prayer" (2 Pet, Matt)
Molly Ijmaes; Lorenz 10/4336L
SATB, piano, opt. cello (https://bit.ly/L-4336L)

+Hymn Anthem

"Christ, Whose Glory Fills the Skies" 808926 (2 Pet, Matt) (O)
E7, EL553, G662, GR211, P462, UM173 (PD), VU336

Introduction: S-1, #330. Though in 3/4 time, it will serve well as an introduction. Play the "Ossia" passage at the end Hold the last chord six beats. Or create an introduction from the hymnal setting.

Stanza 1: All sing, *forte*, either in parts or unison. O plays hymnal setting.

Stanza 2: This stanza should be slower and softer. Organ plays S-1, #278 or another suitable harmonzation. T/B alone, unison, for first four measures; S/A alone, unison, next four measures; all voices, unison, complete the stanza with a gradual *crescendo* to the words "warms my heart."

Interlude: Organs plays S-1, #330 again. (Or omit interlude.)

Stanza 3: Full and strong. Voices in unison. Organ plays S-1, #279, or another harmonization. In the last two measures, a few sopranos may sing the alto part up 1 octave. *Ritard* these last two measures, ending *forte.*

Other Suggestions

Visuals:
O Exod. 24:12b, mountain, tablets, cloud, glory, volcano
P Throne, quake, Ps. 99:3, scales, footstool, cloud, tablet
E Majesty, 2 Pet. 1:17b, mountain, lamp, dawn, star
G Mountain, three figures/booths, cloud, Matt 17:5b

Introit: EL819, G388, S2274, SH405. "Come, All You People" (Pss)
Introit: N742. "Gathered Here in the Mystery" (Transfiguration)
Sung Confession: UM82 "Canticle of God's Glory" (Exod, Matt)
Call to Prayer: EL529, G392, S2273, SH611, ZS148. "Jesus, We Are Here" (Matt)
Prayer: UM259, WSL13 (Matt, Transfig.)
Prayer: WSL11 (2 Pet)
Prayer: N831 (Matt, Transfiguration)
Blessing: N872 (Exod., Matt, Transfiguration)
Alternate Lesson (see page 4): Psalm 2
Theme Ideas: God: Glory of God, God: Wisdom, Praise

Notes

NRSVue

Joel 2:1-2, 12-17
[1] Blow the trumpet in Zion;
sound the alarm on my holy mountain!
Let all the inhabitants of the land tremble,
for the day of the LORD is coming, it is near—
[2]a day of darkness and gloom,
a day of clouds and thick darkness!
Like blackness spread upon the mountains,
a great and powerful army comes;
their like has never been from of old,
nor will be again after them
in ages to come.
. . . .
[12]Yet even now, says the LORD,
return to me with all your heart,
with fasting, with weeping, and with mourning;
[13]rend your hearts and not your clothing.
Return to the LORD, your God,
for he is gracious and merciful,
slow to anger, and abounding in steadfast love,
and relents from punishment.
[14]Who knows whether he will not turn and relent
and leave a blessing behind him,
a grain offering and a drink offering
for the LORD your God?
[15]Blow the trumpet in Zion;
consecrate a fast;
call a solemn assembly;
[16]gather the people.
Consecrate the congregation;
assemble the aged;
gather the children,
even infants at the breast.
Let the bridegroom leave his room
and the bride her canopy.
[17]Between the vestibule and the altar,
let the priests, the ministers of the LORD, weep.
Let them say, "Spare your people, O LORD,
and do not make your heritage a mockery,
a byword among the nations.
Why should it be said among the peoples,
'Where is their God?'"

Psalm 51:1-17 (G421/422/423, N657, P195/196, UM785)
[1]Have mercy on me, O God,
according to your steadfast love;
according to your abundant mercy,
blot out my transgressions.
[2]Wash me thoroughly from my iniquity,
and cleanse me from my sin.
[3]For I know my transgressions,
and my sin is ever before me.
[4]Against you, you alone, have I sinned
and done what is evil in your sight,
so that you are justified in your sentence
and blameless when you pass judgment.
[5]Indeed, I was born guilty,
a sinner when my mother conceived me.
[6]You desire truth in the inward being;
therefore teach me wisdom in my secret heart.
[7]Purge me with hyssop, and I shall be clean;
wash me, and I shall be whiter than snow.
[8]Let me hear joy and gladness;
let the bones that you have crushed rejoice.
[9]Hide your face from my sins,
and blot out all my iniquities.

CEB

Joel 2:1-2, 12-17
[1]Blow the horn in Zion;
give a shout on my holy mountain!
Let all the people of the land tremble,
for the day of the LORD is coming.
It is near—
[2] a day of darkness and no light,
a day of clouds and thick darkness!
Like blackness spread out upon the mountains,
a great and powerful army comes,
unlike any that has ever come before them,
or will come after them in centuries ahead.
. . . .
[12]Yet even now, says the LORD,
return to me with all your hearts,
with fasting, with weeping, and with sorrow;
[13]tear your hearts
and not your clothing.
Return to the LORD your God,
for he is merciful and compassionate,
very patient, full of faithful love,
and ready to forgive.
[14]Who knows whether he will have a change of heart
and leave a blessing behind him,
a grain offering and a drink offering
for the LORD your God?
[15]Blow the horn in Zion;
demand a fast;
request a special assembly.
[16]Gather the people;
prepare a holy meeting;
assemble the elders;
gather the children,
even nursing infants.
Let the groom leave his room
and the bride her chamber.
[17]Between the porch and the altar
let the priests, the LORD's ministers, weep.
Let them say, "Have mercy, LORD, on your people,
and don't make your inheritance a disgrace,
an example of failure among the nations.
Why should they say among the peoples,
'Where is their God?'"

Psalm 51:1-17 (G421/422/423, N657, P195/196, UM785)
[1]Have mercy on me, God, according to your faithful love!
Wipe away my wrongdoings according to your great
compassion!
[2]Wash me completely clean of my guilt;
purify me from my sin!
[3]Because I know my wrongdoings,
my sin is always right in front of me.
[4]I've sinned against you—you alone.
I've committed evil in your sight.
That's why you are justified when you render your verdict,
completely correct when you issue your judgment.
[5]Yes, I was born in guilt, in sin,
from the moment my mother conceived me.
[6]And yes, you want truth in the most hidden places;
you teach me wisdom in the most secret space.
[7]Purify me with hyssop and I will be clean;
wash me and I will be whiter than snow.
[8]Let me hear joy and celebration again;
let the bones you crushed
rejoice once more.
[9]Hide your face from my sins;
wipe away all my guilty deeds!
[10]Create a clean heart for me, God;
put a new, faithful spirit deep inside me!

NRSVue

Psalm 51:1-17 (continued)
[10]Create in me a clean heart, O God,
and put a new and right spirit within me.
[11]Do not cast me away from your presence,
and do not take your holy spirit from me.
[12]Restore to me the joy of your salvation,
and sustain in me a willing spirit.
[13]Then I will teach transgressors your ways,
and sinners will return to you.
[14]Deliver me from bloodshed, O God,
O God of my salvation,
and my tongue will sing aloud of your deliverance.
[15]O Lord, open my lips,
and my mouth will declare your praise.
[16]For you have no delight in sacrifice;
if I were to give a burnt offering, you would not be pleased.
[17]The sacrifice acceptable to God is a broken spirit;
a broken and contrite heart, O God, you will not despise.

---

2 Corinthians 5:20b–6:10
[20b]we entreat you on behalf of Christ: be reconciled to God. [21]For
our sake God made the one who knew no sin to be sin, so that in
him we might become the righteousness of God.
6 As we work together with him, we entreat you also not to accept
the grace of God in vain. [2]For he says,
"At an acceptable time I have listened to you,
and on a day of salvation I have helped you."
Look, now is the acceptable time; look, now is the day of salvation! [3]We are putting no obstacle in anyone's way, so that no fault
may be found with our ministry, [4]but as servants of God we have
commended ourselves in every way: in great endurance, afflictions,
hardships, calamities, [5]beatings, imprisonments, riots, labors, sleepless nights, hunger; [6]in purity, knowledge, patience, kindness, holiness of spirit, genuine love, [7]truthful speech, and the power of God;
with the weapons of righteousness for the right hand and for the
left; [8]in honor and dishonor, in ill repute and good repute. We are
treated as impostors and yet are true, [9]as unknown and yet are well
known, as dying and look—we are alive, as punished and yet not
killed, [10]as sorrowful yet always rejoicing, as poor yet making many
rich, as having nothing and yet possessing everything.

Matthew 6:1-6, 16-21
[1]"Beware of practicing your righteousness before others in order
to be seen by them, for then you have no reward from your Father
in heaven.
[2]"So whenever you give alms, do not sound a trumpet before you,
as the hypocrites do in the synagogues and in the streets, so that
they may be praised by others. Truly I tell you, they have received
their reward. [3]But when you give alms, do not let your left hand
know what your right hand is doing, [4]so that your alms may be done
in secret, and your Father who sees in secret will reward you.
[5]"And whenever you pray, do not be like the hypocrites, for they
love to stand and pray in the synagogues and at the street corners, so
that they may be seen by others. Truly I tell you, they have received
their reward. [6]But whenever you pray, go into your room and shut
the door and pray to your Father who is in secret, and your Father
who sees in secret will reward you. . . .
[16]"And whenever you fast, do not look somber, like the hypocrites,
for they mark their faces to show others that they are fasting. Truly I
tell you, they have received their reward. [17]But when you fast, put oil
on your head and wash your face, [18]so that your fasting may be seen
not by others but by your Father who is in secret, and your Father
who sees in secret will reward you.
[19]"Do not store up for yourselves treasures on earth, where moth
and rust consume and where thieves break in and steal, [20]but store
up for yourselves treasures in heaven, where neither moth nor rust
consumes and where thieves do not break in and steal. [21]For where
your treasure is, there your heart will be also."

CEB

Psalm 51:1-17 (continued)
[11]Please don't throw me out of your presence;
please don't take your holy spirit away from me.
[12]Return the joy of your salvation to me
and sustain me with a willing spirit.
[13]Then I will teach wrongdoers your ways,
and sinners will come back to you.
[14]Deliver me from violence, God, God of my salvation,
so that my tongue can sing of your righteousness.
[15]Lord, open my lips,
and my mouth will proclaim your praise.
[16]You don't want sacrifices.
If I gave an entirely burned offering,
you wouldn't be pleased.
[17]A broken spirit is my sacrifice, God.
You won't despise a heart, God, that is broken and crushed.

---

2 Corinthians 5:20b–6:10
[20b]We beg you as Christ's representatives, "Be reconciled to
God!" [21]God caused the one who didn't know sin to be sin for our
sake so that through him we could become the righteousness of
God.
6 Since we work together with him, we are also begging you not
to receive the grace of God in vain. [2]He says, *I listened to you at the
right time, and I helped you on the day of salvation.* Look, now is the
right time! Look, now is the day of salvation!
[3]We don't give anyone any reason to be offended about
anything so that our ministry won't be criticized. [4]Instead, we com-
mend ourselves as ministers of God in every way. We did this with
our great endurance through problems, disasters, and stressful
situations. [5]We went through beatings, imprisonments, and riots.
We experienced hard work, sleepless nights, and hunger. [6]We
displayed purity, knowledge, patience, and generosity. We served
with the Holy Spirit, genuine love, [7]telling the truth, and God's
power. We carried the weapons of righteousness in our right hand
and our left hand. [8]We were treated with honor and dishonor and
with verbal abuse and good evaluation. We were seen as both fake
and real, [9]as unknown and well known, as dying—and look, we are
alive! We were seen as punished but not killed, [10]as going through
pain but always happy, as poor but making many rich, and as having nothing but owning everything.

Matthew 6:1-6, 16-21
[1]"Be careful that you don't practice your religion in front of
people to draw their attention. If you do, you will have no reward
from your Father who is in heaven.
[2]"Whenever you give to the poor, don't blow your trumpet as the
hypocrites do in the synagogues and in the streets so that they may
get praise from people. I assure you, that's the only reward they'll
get. [3]But when you give to the poor, don't let your left hand know
what your right hand is doing [4]so that you may give to the poor in
secret. Your Father who sees what you do in secret will reward you.
[5]"When you pray, don't be like hypocrites. They love to pray
standing in the synagogues and on the street corners so that people
will see them. I assure you, that's the only reward they'll get. [6]But
when you pray, go to your room, shut the door, and pray to your
Father who is present in that secret place. Your Father who sees what
you do in secret will reward you. . . .
[16]"And when you fast, don't put on a sad face like the hypocrites.
They distort their faces so people will know they are fasting. I
assure you that they have their reward. [17]When you fast, brush your
hair and wash your face. [18]Then you won't look like you are fasting
to people, but only to your Father who is present in that secret
place. Your Father who sees in secret will reward you.
[19]"Stop collecting treasures for your own benefit on earth, where
moth and rust eat them and where thieves break in and steal them.
[20]Instead, collect treasures for yourselves in heaven, where moth and
rust don't eat them and where thieves don't break in and steal them.
[21]Where your treasure is, there your heart will be also."

Primary Hymns and Songs for the Day

"What Wondrous Love Is This" 197297 (2 Cor) (O)
C200, CG171, E439, EL666, G215, GR233, N223, P85, SH177, UM292, VU147 (Fr.)
H-3 Hbl-102; Chr-212; Org-185
S-1 #347. Harm.
"Take Time to Be Holy" (Matt) (O)
C572, GR316, UM395 (PD), VU672
H-3 Chr-178
S-1 #159. Harm.
"Give Me a Clean Heart" 314764 (Pss, Ash Wed.)
C515, N188, S2133, Z182, ZS116
"Lord, I Want to Be a Christian" 3184437 (Joel, Matt) (C)
C589, CG507, G729, GR611, N454, P372 (PD), SH621, UM402, Z76 (PD-TO)
H-3 Chr-130
"O Master, Let Me Walk with Thee" 158243 (Joel) (C)
C602, CG660, E659/660, EL818, G738, GR596, N503, P357, SH612, UM430 (PD), VU560
H-3 Hbl-81; Chr-147; Desc-74; Org-87
S-2 #118. Descant

Additional Hymn Suggestions

"There's a Wideness in God's Mercy" 3063417 (Joel)
C73, CG41, E469/470, EL587/588, G435, GR64, N23, P298, SH526, UM121, VU271
"Come Back Quickly to the Lord" (Joel)
G416, P381, UM343
"Today We All Are Called to Be Disciples" (Joel)
G757, P434, VU507
+"Dust and Ashes" (Pss, Matt, Ash Wednesday)
N186, VU105, WS3098
"Give Me Jesus" (PD-TO) (Pss, Matt)
CG546, EL770, N409, SH306, WS3140, Z165, ZS84
"Jesus, the Very Thought of Thee" (2 Cor)
C102, CG386, E642, EL754, G629, GR127, N507, P310, UM175 (PD)
"Alas! and Did My Savior Bleed" 106123 (2 Cor, Lent)
CG182, EL337, G212, GR231, N200, P78, UM294 (PD)
"Alas! and Did My Savior Bleed" 29499 (2 Cor, Lent)
C204, CG595, GR564, N199, SH172, UM359 (PD), Z8, ZS67
"Lord, Speak to Me" 2769286 (2 Cor)
CG503, EL676, G722, GR439, N531, P426, SH557, UM463 (PD), VU589
"We Walk by Faith" 2591911 (2 Cor, Matt)
CG634, E209, EL635, G817, N256, P399, S2196, SH660
"Lord, Who Throughout These Forty Days" 2312509 (Matt, Lent) (C)
C180, CG169, E142, EL319, G166, GR223, N211, P81, UM269
"Amazing Grace" 22025 (Matt, Comm.)
C546, CG587, E671, EL779, G649, GR572, N547/548, P280, SH523, UM378 (PD), VU266 (Fr.), Z211
"Be Thou My Vision" 5021907 (Matt)
C595, CG71, E488, EL793, G450, GR49, N451, P339, SH640, UM451, VU642
"More Love to Thee, O Christ" 36750 (Matt)
C527, CG365, G828, GR588, N456, P359, UM453 (PD)
"Prayer Is the Soul's Sincere Desire" (Matt)
CG391, GR438, N508, UM492
"Sweet Hour of Prayer" (Matt)
C570, CG412, GR440, N505, SH578, UM496 (PD)
"Near to the Heart of God" (Matt)
C581, CG383, G824, GR357, P527, UM472 (PD)
"Here, O My Lord, I See Thee" 136265(Matt, Comm.)
C416, CG460, E318, G517, GR411, N336, P520, UM623, VU459
"Lord of All Hopefulness" 5579875 (Matt)
CG678, E482, EL765, G683, S2197, SH464
"The Glory of These Forty Days" 954904 (Matt)
E143, EL320, G165, P87
"Forty Days and Forty Nights" 4775326 (Matt)
C179, E150, G167, N205, P77, SH116, VU114
"The Lord's Prayer" (Matt, Lent)
C307-C310, G464, GR441, P589, S2278, SH595, UM271, WS3068/3069/3071

Additional Contemporary and Modern Suggestions

+"Hosanna" 4785835 (Joel, Pss)
SH361, WS3188
+"Because of Your Love" 4662501 (Joel, Pss)
+"You Have Saved Us" 5548514 (Joel, Pss)
+"Restored" 5894615 (Joel, Pss, Ash Wed)
"You Are My Hiding Place" 21442 (Pss)
C554, S2055, SH46
"Open Our Eyes, Lord" 1572 (Pss)
CG392, S2086, SH562
"Change My Heart, O God" 1565 (Pss)
EL801, G695, S2152, SH507, ZS178
"Open the Eyes of My Heart" 2298355 (Pss)
G452, SH378, WS3008
"Purify My Heart" OL-73195 / OL-86873 (Pss)
"Refresh My Heart" 917518 (Pss)
"Refiner's Fire" 426298 (Pss)
"Purified" 3409710 (Pss)
"I Give You My Heart" 1866132 (Pss)
"Give Us Clean Hands" 2060208 (Pss)
+"Beautiful Things" 5665521 (Pss)
+"Head to the Heart" 7047283 (Pss)
+"Pure and Holy" 7181776 (Pss)
+"Create In Me" 7104652 (Pss)
+"Prepare the Way" 7136724 (Pss)
+"The Heart of Worship" 2296522 (Pss, Matt)
+"Take My Life" 1617154 (Pss, Matt)
+"Grace Like Rain" 3689877 (Pss, Matt)
"Come, Emmanuel" 3999938 (Pss, 2 Cor, Ash Wed.)
WS3130
"This is My Story" 7046375 (2 Cor)
"We Want to See Jesus Lifted High" 1033408 (2 Cor)
"That's Why We Praise Him" 2668576 (2 Cor)
+"Do It Again" 7067555 (2 Cor)
"Amazing Grace" ("My Chains Are Gone") 4768151 (Matt)
GR574, WS3104
+"His Mercy Is More" 7065053 (Matt)
+"Graves into Gardens" 7138219 (Matt)
+"My Worth Is Not in What I Own" 7024758 (Matt)
"In the Silence" 6182357 (Matt)
"In the Secret" 1810119 (Matt)
"When It's All Been Said and Done" 2788353 (Matt)
"You Are My All in All" 825356 (Matt, Lent)
CG571, G519, SH335, WS3040, ZS184

Solo/Ensemble Suggestions

"If With All Your Hearts" (Joel)
V-8 p. 277
"A Contrite Heart" (Pss)
V-4 p. 10
"Turn My Heart to You" (Pss, Ash Wednesday)
V-5 (2) p. 14
"Give Me Jesus" (Pss, Lent)
V-3 (1) p. 53
V-3 (4) p. 9
V-7 p. 24/28
V-8 p. 256

+"Clean Before My Lord" (Pss)
V-8 p. 233
"How Quiet Is the Night" (Matt, Ash Wednesday)
V-8 p. 158
+"Graves Into Gardens" 7138219 (Matt)
V-9 p. 15
"A Right Spirit" (Pss)
Stephan Casurella; AEC-3 p. 5
Treble voices, organ, opt. descant (https://bit.ly/AEC-3)
"That Priceless Grace" (John)
arr. John Helgen; AEC-1 p. 64, Augsburg 0800658590
Unison, piano, opt. descant (https://bit.ly/AEC-1-64)

+Hymn Anthem

"O The Lamb" 1510220 (John)
UM300

Cello is recommended as the accompanying instrument, but its part could be played by organ, synthesizer, or even omitted.

Introduction: Cello plays melody once. Perform freely and without rhythmic restraint. Hold some notes longer, speed up others.

Setting 1: Solo, *a cappella*. Preferably a S/A with a rich vocal quality.

Setting 2: T/B sing melody. Accompany with continuous drone on cello on a low B.

Setting 3: This setting is sung as a round. The S/A sing the first phrase, "O the Lamb, the loving Lamb." As they continue the T/B begin. S/A hold last note until T/B finish.

Setting 4: Divide choir into four equal parts. Sing the melody as a four-part round. Cello plays drone. Each group sings the melody twice. They start *piano*, crescendo to *forte* by the time they begin the melody a second time, and then *decrescendo* to *piano* by the end of their part. Each group holds its last note until all are finished.

Setting 5: Soloist begins the melody once again, beginning when the last group of Setting 4 reaches the final word, "me." Choir and cello continue to hold "B" very softly while soloist sings.

Other Suggestions

Visuals: Ashes, rough fabrics
O Black cloth, grain, trumpet, empty plate, weeping
P Water, snow, rejoicing, Ps. 51:10, 15, 17, heart
E Clock, calendar with today's date, black/gold
G Praying hands, oil/water, closed door, empty plate, rusty items, Matt 6:21, ashes of last year's palms, oil

Isaiah 58:1-12 gives another interpretation of fasting.

Responsive Reading: CG166. (Lent)
Call to Confession: N833 or WSL93 (Pss, Healing)
Confession: WSL14 (Joel, Pss, Ash Wed)
+Response: C299, EL152, G576, S2275, S2277, WS3133. "Lord, Have Mercy" (Pss)
Call to Prayer or Introit: EL538, G466, S2157. "Come and Fill Our Hearts" (Pss)
Prayer: N846 or UM353 (Pss, Ash Wednesday)
Prayer: WSL15. "O God, you delight not in pomp" (Matt, Pss)
+Sung Prayer: S2201. "Prayers of the People" (Matt)
Response: WS3122. "Christ Has Broken Down the Wall" (2 Cor)
+Sung Communion Offering: S2262, SH644. *"Te Ofrecemos Padre Nuestro"* ("Let Us Offer to the Father") (Pss, Matt)
Offertory Prayer: WSL109. "O great and holy God" (2 Cor)
Offertory Prayer: WSL123. "Gracious God" (Matt)
Meditative Songs in Taizé Style: S2057, S2058, S2118, S2133, S2156, S2157, S2159, S2200, S2275
Theme Ideas: Patience, Prayer, Redemption / Salvation, Repentance, Sin and Forgiveness

Notes

NRSVue

Genesis 2:15-17; 3:1-7

15The LORD God took the man and put him in the garden of
Eden to till it and keep it. 16And the LORD God commanded the
man, "You may freely eat of every tree of the garden, 17but of the
tree of the knowledge of good and evil you shall not eat, for in
the day that you eat of it you shall die." . . .

3 Now the serpent was more crafty than any other wild animal
that the LORD God had made. He said to the woman, "Did
God say, 'You shall not eat from any tree in the garden'?" 2The
woman said to the serpent, "We may eat of the fruit of the trees
in the garden, 3but God said, 'You shall not eat of the fruit of the
tree that is in the middle of the garden, nor shall you touch it,
or you shall die.'" 4But the serpent said to the woman, "You will
not die, 5for God knows that when you eat of it your eyes will be
opened, and you will be like God, knowing good and evil." 6So
when the woman saw that the tree was good for food and that it
was a delight to the eyes and that the tree was to be desired to
make one wise, she took of its fruit and ate, and she also gave
some to her husband, who was with her, and he ate. 7Then the
eyes of both were opened, and they knew that they were naked,
and they sewed fig leaves together and made loincloths for
themselves.

Psalm 32 (G446, N642, P184, SH527, UM766)

1Happy are those whose transgression is forgiven,
    whose sin is covered.
2Happy are those to whom the LORD imputes no iniquity
    and in whose spirit there is no deceit.
3While I kept silent, my body wasted away
    through my groaning all day long.
4For day and night your hand was heavy upon me;
    my strength was dried up as by the heat of summer. *[Selah]*
5Then I acknowledged my sin to you,
    and I did not hide my iniquity;
I said, "I will confess my transgressions to the LORD,"
    and you forgave the guilt of my sin. *[Selah]*
6Therefore let all who are faithful
    offer prayer to you;
at a time of distress, the rush of mighty waters
    shall not reach them.
7You are a hiding place for me;
    you preserve me from trouble;
    you surround me with glad cries of deliverance. *[Selah]*
8I will instruct you and teach you the way you should go;
    I will counsel you with my eye upon you.
9Do not be like a horse or a mule, without understanding,
    whose temper must be curbed with bit and bridle,
    else it will not stay near you.
10Many are the torments of the wicked,
    but steadfast love surrounds those who trust in the LORD.
11Be glad in the LORD and rejoice, O righteous,
    and shout for joy, all you upright in heart.

CEB

Genesis 2:15-17; 3:1-7

15The LORD God took the human and settled him in the
garden of Eden to farm it and to take care of it. 16The LORD God
commanded the human, "Eat your fill from all of the garden's
trees; 17but don't eat from the tree of the knowledge of good and
evil, because on the day you eat from it, you will die!" . . .

3 The snake was the most intelligent of all the wild animals
that the LORD God had made. He said to the woman, "Did God
really say that you shouldn't eat from any tree in the garden?"

2The woman said to the snake, "We may eat the fruit of the
garden's trees 3but not the fruit of the tree in the middle of the
garden. God said, 'Don't eat from it, and don't touch it, or you
will die.'"

4The snake said to the woman, "You won't die! 5God knows
that on the day you eat from it, you will see clearly and you will
be like God, knowing good and evil." 6The woman saw that
the tree was beautiful with delicious food and that the tree
would provide wisdom, so she took some of its fruit and ate
it, and also gave some to her husband, who was with her, and
he ate it. 7Then they both saw clearly and knew that they were
naked. So they sewed fig leaves together and made garments for
themselves.

Psalm 32 (G446, N642, P184, SH527, UM766)

1 The one whose wrongdoing is forgiven,
    whose sin is covered over is truly happy!
2 The one the LORD doesn't consider guilty—
    in whose spirit there is no dishonesty—
    that one is truly happy!
3 When I kept quiet, my bones wore out;
    I was groaning all day long—
    every day, every night!—
4 because your hand was heavy upon me.
    My energy was sapped as if in a summer drought. *[Selah]*
5 So I admitted my sin to you;
    I didn't conceal my guilt.
    "I'll confess my sins to the LORD," is what I said.
    Then you removed the guilt of my sin. *[Selah]*
6 That's why all the faithful should pray to you during troubled
        times,
    so that a great flood of water won't reach them.
7 You are my secret hideout!
    You protect me from trouble.
    You surround me with songs of rescue! *[Selah]*
8 I will instruct you and teach you
    about the direction you should go.
    I'll advise you and keep my eye on you.
9 Don't be like some senseless horse or mule,
    whose movement must be controlled
    with a bit and a bridle.
        Don't be anything like that!
10 The pain of the wicked is severe,
    but faithful love surrounds the one who trusts the LORD.
11 You who are righteous, rejoice in the LORD and be glad!
    All you whose hearts are right, sing out in joy!

NRSVue

Romans 5:12-19

12Therefore, just as sin came into the world through one man, and death came through sin, and so death spread to all because all have sinned—13for sin was indeed in the world before the law, but sin is not reckoned when there is no law. 14Yet death reigned from Adam to Moses, even over those who did not sin in the likeness of Adam, who is a pattern of the one who was to come.

15But the free gift is not like the trespass. For if the many died through the one man's trespass, much more surely have the grace of God and the gift in the grace of the one man, Jesus Christ, abounded for the many. 16And the gift is not like the effect of the one man's sin. For the judgment following one trespass brought condemnation, but the gift following many trespasses brings justification. 17If, because of the one man's trespass, death reigned through that one, much more surely will those who receive the abundance of grace and the gift of righteousness reign in life through the one man, Jesus Christ.

18Therefore just as one man's trespass led to condemnation for all, so one man's act of righteousness leads to justification and life for all. 19For just as through the one man's disobedience the many were made sinners, so through the one man's obedience the many will be made righteous.

Matthew 4:1-11

1Then Jesus was led up by the Spirit into the wilderness to be tested by the devil. 2He fasted forty days and forty nights, and afterward he was famished. 3The tempter came and said to him, "If you are the Son of God, command these stones to become loaves of bread." 4But he answered, "It is written,

'One does not live by bread alone,
but by every word that comes from the mouth of God.'"

5Then the devil took him to the holy city and placed him on the pinnacle of the temple, 6saying to him, "If you are the Son of God, throw yourself down, for it is written,

'He will command his angels concerning you,'
and 'On their hands they will bear you up,
so that you will not dash your foot against a stone.'"

7Jesus said to him, "Again it is written, 'Do not put the Lord your God to the test.'"

8Again, the devil took him to a very high mountain and showed him all the kingdoms of the world and their glory, 9and he said to him, "All these I will give you, if you will fall down and worship me." 10Jesus said to him, "Away with you, Satan! for it is written,

'Worship the Lord your God,
and serve only him.'"

11Then the devil left him, and suddenly angels came and waited on him.

CEB

Romans 5:12-19

12So, in the same way that sin entered the world through one person, and death came through sin, so death spread to all human beings with the result that all sinned. 13Although sin was in the world, since there was no Law, it wasn't taken into account until the Law came. 14But death ruled from Adam until Moses, even over those who didn't sin in the same way Adam did—Adam was a type of the one who was coming.

15But the free gift of Christ isn't like Adam's failure. If many people died through what one person did wrong, God's grace is multiplied even more for many people with the gift—of the one person Jesus Christ—that comes through grace. 16The gift isn't like the consequences of one person's sin. The judgment that came from one person's sin led to punishment, but the free gift that came out of many failures led to the verdict of acquittal. 17If death ruled because of one person's failure, those who receive the multiplied grace and the gift of righteousness will even more certainly rule in life through the one person Jesus Christ.

18So now the righteous requirements necessary for life are met for everyone through the righteous act of one person, just as judgment fell on everyone through the failure of one person. 19Many people were made righteous through the obedience of one person, just as many people were made sinners through the disobedience of one person.

Matthew 4:1-11

1Then the Spirit led Jesus up into the wilderness so that the devil might tempt him.2After Jesus had fasted for forty days and forty nights, he was starving. 3The tempter came to him and said, "Since you are God's Son, command these stones to become bread."

4Jesus replied, "It's written, *People won't live only by bread, but by every word spoken by God.*"

5After that the devil brought him into the holy city and stood him at the highest point of the temple. He said to him, 6"Since you are God's Son, throw yourself down; for it is written, *I will command my angels concerning you, and they will take you up in their hands so that you won't hit your foot on a stone.*"

7Jesus replied, "Again it's written, *Don't test the Lord your God.*"

8Then the devil brought him to a very high mountain and showed him all the kingdoms of the world and their glory. 9He said, "I'll give you all these if you bow down and worship me."

10Jesus responded, "Go away, Satan, because it's written, *You will worship the Lord your God and serve only him.*" 11The devil left him, and angels came and took care of him.

Primary Hymns and Songs for the Day

"Lord, Who Throughout These Forty Days" 2312509 (Matt) (O)
C180, CG169, E142, G166, N211, P81
H-3 Chr-132; Desc-94; Org-137
UM269
H-3 Chr-106; Desc-65; Org-72
S-2 #105. Flute/violin desc.
#106. Harm.
EL319, GR223
H-3 Chr-139, 145; Desc-77
S-1 #241-242. Orff arr. And descant
"Jesus, Tempted in the Desert" OL-09669 (Matt)
S2105, VU115
H-3 Chr-53; Org-33
S-1 #109-10. Desc. and harm.
"Jesus Walked This Lonesome Valley" 4715434 (Matt)
C211, P80, S2112
"Amazing Grace" 22025 (Pss, Rom, Comm.) (C)
C546, CG587, E671, EL779, G649, GR572, N547/548, P280, SH523, UM378 (PD), VU266 (Fr.), Z211
H-3 Hbl-14, 46; Chr-27; Desc-14; Org-4
S-2 #5-7. Various treatments

Additional Hymn Suggestions

+"O God, Our Help in Ages Past" 43152 (Gen)
C67, CG566, E680, EL632, G687, GR15, N25, P210, SH41, UM117 (PD), VU806
"All My Hope Is Firmly Grounded" 3594474 (Gen)
C88, E665, EL757, GR68, N408, UM132, VU654/655
"God Who Stretched the Spangled Heavens" (Gen)
C651, CG21, E580, EL771, G24, N556, P268, UM150
+"It's Me, It's Me, O Lord" (Gen)
C579, GR444, N519, UM352, Z110 (PD), ZS149
"O Love That Wilt Not Let Me Go" (Gen)
C540, CG631, G833, GR92, N485, P384, SH314, UM480 (PD), VU658
"Creator of the Stars of Night" (Gen)
C127, E60, EL245, G84, N111, P4, SH74, UM692 (PD)
+*"Perdón, Señor"* ("Forgive Us, Lord") 3409466 (Gen)
G431, S2134, SH505
"God Made from One Blood" (Gen)
C500, CG686, N427, S2170, VU554
+"Deep in the Shadows of the Past" (Gen)
G50, N320, P330, S2246
"There in God's Garden" (Gen)
EL342, G226, VU346
"Today We All Are Called to Be Disciples" (Gen)
G757, P434, VU507
"O Worship the King" (Gen, Rom)
C17, CG52, E388, EL842, G41, GR11, N26, P476, SH255, UM73 (PD), VU235
"Grace Greater than Our Sin" (Pss, Rom)
CG586, GR558, UM365
"O Love Divine, What Hast Thou Done" (PD) (Rom)
GR244, UM287 (PD)
"Alas! and Did My Savior Bleed" 106123 (Rom)
CG182, EL337, G212, GR231, N200, P78, UM294 (PD)
"Alas! and Did My Savior Bleed" 29499 (Rom)
C204, CG595, GR564, N199, SH172, UM359 (PD), Z8, ZS67
"When I Survey the Wondrous Cross" 27893 (Rom) (C)
C195, CG186, EL803, G223, GR221, N224, P101, SH163/164, UM298 (PD)
"When I Survey the Wondrous Cross" 721333 (Rom) (C)
E474, G224, P100, UM299 (PD), VU149 (Fr.)
"Cristo Vive" ("Christ Is Risen") (Rom)
N235, P109, SH184, UM313
"And Can It Be that I Should Gain" 25280 (Rom)
CG605, GR569, SH540, UM363 (PD)
"Because He Lives" (Rom,)
C562, CG620, GR265, SH200, UM364
"Lord, Dismiss Us With Thy Blessing" 4529091 (Rom) (C)
C439, E344, EL545, G546, GR686, N77, P538, UM671 (PD), VU425
"In the Singing" (Rom, Comm.)
EL466, G533, S2255
"Bread of the World" (Rom, Matt, Comm.)
C387, E301, G499, GR412, N346, P502, UM624, VU461
"O Love, How Deep" (Matt)
E448/449, EL322, G618, GR95, N209, P83, SH115, UM267, VU348
"It Is Well with My Soul" 25376 (Matt)
C561, CG573, EL785, G840, GR344, N438, SH305, UM377 (PD), Z20
+"Have Thine Own Way, Lord" (Matt)
C588, CG493, GR343, SH626, UM382 (PD)
"Be Still, My Soul" (Matt)
C566, CG57, G819, GR346, N488, SH330, UM534, VU652
"I Was There to Hear Your Borning Cry" (Matt)
C75, EL732, G488, N351, S2051, VU644
"My Song Is Love Unknown" 2399704 (Matt, Lent)
E458, EL343, G209, N222, P76, S2083, VU143
"Praise God for This Holy Ground" (Matt, Lent)
G405, WS3009
"The Glory of These Forty Days" 954904 (Matt)
E143, EL320, G165, P87
"Forty Days and Forty Nights" 4775326 (Matt)
C179, E150, G167, N205, P77, SH116, VU114
"Wild and Lone the Prophet's Voice" 3413029 (Lent)
G163, P409, S2089

Additional Contemporary and Modern Suggestions

"Daughter of God" 4509781 (Gen)
+"Who You Say You Are" 7130503 (Gen, Pss)
+"Do It Again" 7067555 (Gen, Pss)
+"Promises" 7149439 (Gen, Pss)
"Able" 1256560 (Gen, Pss, Lent)
"My Redeemer Lives" 2397964 (Gen, Pss, Lent)
"You Are My Hiding Place" 21442 (Pss)
C554, S2055, SH46
"All Things Are Possible" 2245140 (Pss)
"Hallelujah" ("Your Love Is Amazing") 3091812 (Pss, Lent)
WS3027
"Amazing Grace" ("My Chains Are Gone") 4768151 (Pss, Rom)
GR574, WS3104
"Grace Like Rain" 3689877 (Pss, Rom)
+"His Mercy Is More" 7065053 (Pss, Rom)
+"No Outsiders" 7101035 (Pss, Rom)
+"The Way" 7089024 (Pss, Rom)
+"Won't Stop Now" 7111932 (Rom)
+"Love Moves You" ("Love Alone") 5775514 (Rom)
"We Fall Down" 2437367 (Rom)
G368, WS3187
"Oh Lord, You're Beautiful" 14514 (Rom)
S2064
"Sing Alleluia to the Lord" 26272 (Rom)
C32, S2258, SH685
"Restored" 5894615 (Rom, Lent)
"Lamb of God" 16787 (Matt, Lent)
EL336, G518, S2113, ZS74
"Lord, I Lift Your Name on High" 117947 (Matt, Lent)
CG606, EL857, S2088, SH205
"We Walk His Way" OL-72482 (Matt, Lent)
WS3073

Solo/Ensemble Suggestions

"In the Image of God" (Gen, Rom, Lent)
V-8 p. 362
+"City Called Heaven" (Gen, Matt)
V-7 p. 4/9
+"And Can It Be That I Should Gain" (Rom)
V-1 p. 29
"Amazing Grace" (Rom)
V-8 p. 56
"Grace Greater Than Our Sin" (Rom)
V-8 p. 180
+"Love Moved First" (Rom, Matt)
V-9 p. 56
"Holy is the Lamb" (Matt)
V-5 (1) p. 5
+"Celtic Amazing Grace" (Rom)
arr. Michael Ware; Shawnee Press 35031911
SATB, piano, opt. instruments (https://bit.ly/SP-2179)
+"A Lenten Prayer" (Matt)
arr. Hal Hopson: MorningStar MSM-50-3225)
SATB, piano, opt. handbells (https://bit.ly/M-3225)

+Hymn Anthem

"O Love, How Deep" (Matt)
E448/449, EL322, G618, GR95, N209, P83, SH115, UM267, VU348

Introduction: Keyboard plays S-1, #82 or another harmonization. *Forte*, with force. Handbells may play the treble clef notes with the keyboard.

Stanza 1: All voices, unison. Keyboard plays S-1, #83 or a second harmonization. *Forte.*

Stanza 2: S/A sing melody. Keyboard plays hymnal setting one octave higher than written, omitting the melody notes. *Mezzo piano.*

Stanza 3: T sing melody, B sing bass part (or melody). Keyboard plays hymnal setting as written. *Mezzo forte.*

Interlude: Handbells or keyboard plays S-1, #84 (or omit).

Stanza 6: All voices, unison. Keyboard and handbells play S-1, #82 as in introduction. *Forte.* This stanza may be a bit slower than the previous stanzas.

Other Suggestions

Visuals:
O Garden, fruit tree, serpent, fig leaves/loin cloth
P Hand, dry/heat, praying hands, waterfall, hiding place, teaching, bit/bridle, joy, Ps. 32:11
E Target/arrows (sin), gift, Christ, crucifix
G Dove/flames, 40/40, stones/bread, Bible, pinnacle, angels ministering, Matt 4:7, mountain, vista

Introit: G274, SH210, VU210. WS3043, stanza 3. "You, Lord, are Both Lamb and Shepherd" (Matt, Lent)

Call to Prayer: UM330. "Daw-Kee, Aim Daw-Tis-Taw" ("Great Spirit, Now I Pray") (Matt)

+Sung Confession: C594, CG413, E652/563, G169, GR499, N502, P345, UM358 (PD), VU608, stanza 1. "Dear Lord and Father of Mankind" 106185 *(Alternate Text: "Dear God, Embracing Humankind")* (Gen)

Prayer: UM366. For Guidance (Gen, Rom)

Prayer: WSL16 or WSL19 (Matt, Lent)

Canticle: UM167. "Canticle of Christ's Obedience" (Rom, Matt)

Blessing: WSL18. "May the blessing of God" (Matt, Lent)

+Sung Benediction: G80, S2279, VU884. "The Trees of the Field" 20546 (Pss)

Theme Ideas: Covenant, Grace, Jesus: Temptation, Sin and Forgiveness

Notes

NRSVue

Genesis 12:1-4a

1 Now the LORD said to Abram, "Go from your country and
your kindred and your father's house to the land that I will show
you. 2 I will make of you a great nation, and I will bless you and
make your name great, so that you will be a blessing. 3 I will bless
those who bless you, and the one who curses you I will curse,
and in you all the families of the earth shall be blessed."
4a So Abram went, as the LORD had told him, and Lot went
with him.

Psalm 121 (P45/845, N704, P234, UM844)

1 I lift up my eyes to the hills—
from where will my help come?
2 My help comes from the LORD,
who made heaven and earth.
3 He will not let your foot be moved;
he who keeps you will not slumber.
4 He who keeps Israel
will neither slumber nor sleep.
5 The LORD is your keeper;
the LORD is your shade at your right hand.
6 The sun shall not strike you by day,
nor the moon by night.
7 The LORD will keep you from all evil;
he will keep your life.
8 The LORD will keep
your going out and your coming in
from this time on and forevermore.

CEB

Genesis 12:1-4a

1 The LORD said to Abram, "Leave your land, your family, and
your father's household for the land that I will show you. 2 I will
make of you a great nation and will bless you. I will make your
name respected, and you will be a blessing.
3 I will bless those who bless you,
those who curse you I will curse;
all the families of earth
will be blessed because of you."
4a Abram left just as the LORD told him, and Lot went with him.

Psalm 121 (P45/845, N704, P234, UM844)

1 I raise my eyes toward the mountains.
Where will my help come from?
2 My help comes from the LORD,
the maker of heaven and earth.
3 God won't let your foot slip.
Your protector won't fall asleep on the job.
4 No! Israel's protector
never sleeps or rests!
5 The LORD is your protector;
the LORD is your shade right beside you.
6 The sun won't strike you during the day;
neither will the moon at night.
7 The LORD will protect you from all evil;
God will protect your very life.
8 The LORD will protect you on your journeys—
whether going or coming—
from now until forever from now.

NRSVue

Romans 4:1-5, 13-17

1What then are we to say was gained by Abraham, our ancestor according to the flesh? 2For if Abraham was justified by works, he has something to boast about, but not before God. 3For what does the scripture say? "Abraham believed God, and it was reckoned to him as righteousness." 4Now to one who works, wages are not reckoned as a gift but as something due. 5But to one who does not work but trusts him who justifies the ungodly, such faith is reckoned as righteousness. . . .

13For the promise that he would inherit the world did not come to Abraham or to his descendants through the law but through the righteousness of faith. 14For if it is the adherents of the law who are to be the heirs, faith is null and the promise is void. 15For the law brings wrath, but where there is no law, neither is there transgression.

16For this reason the promise depends on faith, in order that it may rest on grace, so that it may be guaranteed to all his descendants, not only to the adherents of the law but also to those who share the faith of Abraham (who is the father of all of us, 17as it is written, "I have made you the father of many nations"), in the presence of the God in whom he believed, who gives life to the dead and calls into existence the things that do not exist.

John 3:1-17

1Now there was a Pharisee named Nicodemus, a leader of the Jews. 2He came to Jesus by night and said to him, "Rabbi, we know that you are a teacher who has come from God, for no one can do these signs that you do unless God is with that person." 3Jesus answered him, "Very truly, I tell you, no one can see the kingdom of God without being born from above." 4Nicodemus said to him, "How can anyone be born after having grown old? Can one enter a second time into the mother's womb and be born?" 5Jesus answered, "Very truly, I tell you, no one can enter the kingdom of God without being born of water and Spirit. 6What is born of the flesh is flesh, and what is born of the Spirit is spirit. 7Do not be astonished that I said to you, 'You must be born from above.' 8The wind blows where it chooses, and you hear the sound of it, but you do not know where it comes from or where it goes. So it is with everyone who is born of the Spirit." 9Nicodemus said to him, "How can these things be?" 10Jesus answered him, "Are you the teacher of Israel, and yet you do not understand these things?

11"Very truly, I tell you, we speak of what we know and testify to what we have seen, yet you do not receive our testimony. 12If I have told you about earthly things and you do not believe, how can you believe if I tell you about heavenly things? 13No one has ascended into heaven except the one who descended from heaven, the Son of Man. 14And just as Moses lifted up the serpent in the wilderness, so must the Son of Man be lifted up, 15that whoever believes in him may have eternal life.

16"For God so loved the world that he gave his only Son, so that everyone who believes in him may not perish but may have eternal life.

17"Indeed, God did not send the Son into the world to condemn the world but in order that the world might be saved through him."

CEB

Romans 4:1-5, 13-17

1So what are we going to say? Are we going to find that Abraham is our ancestor on the basis of genealogy? 2Because if Abraham was made righteous because of his actions, he would have had a reason to brag, but not in front of God. 3What does the scripture say? *Abraham had faith in God, and it was credited to him as righteousness.* 4Workers' salaries aren't credited to them on the basis of an employer's grace but rather on the basis of what they deserve. 5But faith is credited as righteousness to those who don't work, because they have faith in God who makes the ungodly righteous. . . .

13The promise to Abraham and to his descendants, that he would inherit the world, didn't come through the Law but through the righteousness that comes from faith. 14If they inherit because of the Law, then faith has no effect and the promise has been canceled. 15The Law brings about wrath. But when there isn't any law, there isn't any violation of the law. 16That's why the inheritance comes through faith, so that it will be on the basis of God's grace. In that way, the promise is secure for all of Abraham's descendants, not just for those who are related by Law but also for those who are related by the faith of Abraham, who is the father of all of us. 17As it is written: *I have appointed you to be the father of many nations.* So Abraham is our father in the eyes of God in whom he had faith, the God who gives life to the dead and calls things that don't exist into existence.

John 3:1-17

1There was a Pharisee named Nicodemus, a Jewish leader. 2He came to Jesus at night and said to him, "Rabbi, we know that you are a teacher who has come from God, for no one could do these miraculous signs that you do unless God is with him."

3Jesus answered, "I assure you, unless someone is born anew, it's not possible to see God's kingdom."

4Nicodemus asked, "How is it possible for an adult to be born? It's impossible to enter the mother's womb for a second time and be born, isn't it?"

5Jesus answered, "I assure you, unless someone is born of water and the Spirit, it's not possible to enter God's kingdom. 6Whatever is born of the flesh is flesh, and whatever is born of the Spirit is spirit. 7Don't be surprised that I said to you, 'You must be born anew.' 8God's Spirit blows wherever it wishes. You hear its sound, but you don't know where it comes from or where it is going. It's the same with everyone who is born of the Spirit."

9Nicodemus said, "How are these things possible?"

10Jesus answered, "You are a teacher of Israel and you don't know these things? 11I assure you that we speak about what we know and testify about what we have seen, but you don't receive our testimony. 12If I have told you about earthly things and you don't believe, how will you believe if I tell you about heavenly things? 13No one has gone up to heaven except the one who came down from heaven, the Human One. 14Just as Moses lifted up the snake in the wilderness, so must the Human One be lifted up 15so that everyone who believes in him will have eternal life. 16God so loved the world that he gave his only Son, so that everyone who believes in him won't perish but will have eternal life. 17God didn't send his Son into the world to judge the world, but that the world might be saved through him."

Primary Hymns and Songs for the Day

"The God of Abraham Praise" 484742 (Gen) (O)
C24, CG45, E401, EL831, G49, GR16, N24, P488, SH50, UM116 (PD), VU255
H-3 Hbl-62, 95; Chr-59; Org-77
S-1 #211. Harm.
"To God Be the Glory" (John)
C72, CG349, G634, GR531, P485, SH545, UM98 (PD)
H-3 Chr-201
S-2 #176. Piano arrangement
"Lift High the Cross" 5169 (John)
C108, CG415, E473, EL660, G826, GR226, N198, P371, SH162, UM159, VU151
H-3 Hbl-75; Chr-128; Desc-25; Org-21
S-1 #71-75. Various treatments
"He Came Down" 4679219 (John)
EL253, G137, S2085, SH88, ZS54
+"It Is Well with My Soul" 25376 (Rom, John) (C)
C561, CG573, EL785, G840, GR344, N438, SH305, UM377 (PD), Z20
H-3 Chr-113

Additional Hymn Suggestions

+"Lead On, O King Eternal" (Gen)
C632, CG63, E555, EL805, G269, GR478, N573, P447/448, UM580
+"Here I Am, Lord" OL-80670 (Gen)
C452, CG482, EL574, G69, GR589, P525, SH608, UM593, VU509
"Let All Things Now Living" 171701 (Gen)
C717, CG379, EL881, G37, GR636, P554, S2008, SH23, VU242
"Deep in the Shadows of the Past" (Gen)
G50, N320, P330, S2246
"O God, Our Help in Ages Past" 43152 (Gen, Pss)
C67, CG566, E680, EL632, G687, GR15, N25, P210, SH41, UM117 (PD), VU806
"If Thou But Suffer God to Guide Thee" 564215 (Gen, Pss)
C565, CG76, E635, EL769, G816, GR75, N410, P282, SH326, UM142 (PD), VU285 (Fr.) and VU286
"Faith of Our Fathers" 7029079 (Gen, Rom)
C635, CG645, EL812/813, N381, UM710 (PD), VU580
+"We've a Story to Tell to the Nations" (Gen, John)
C484, CG427, GR458, UM569 (PD)
+"O Zion, Haste" (Gen, John)
C482, CG479, E539, EL668, GR451, UM573 (PD)
"Immortal, Invisible, God Only Wise" 124466 (Pss, Rom)
C66, CG58, E423, EL834, G12, GR7, N1, P263, UM103 (PD), VU264 (*See also* ZS4)
"Jesus, Lover of My Soul" (Pss, Rom)
C542, CG406, E699, G440, GR120, N546, P303, SH542/543, UM479, VU669
"Let Us Plead for Faith Alone" (Rom)
GR541, UM385 (PD)
"My Faith Looks Up to Thee" 43334 (Rom)
C576, CG407, E691, EL759, G829, GR351, P383, UM452 (PD), VU663, Z215
"See How Great a Flame Aspires" (Rom)
GR465, UM541
"We Walk by Faith" 2591911 (Rom)
CG634, E209, EL635, G817, N256, P399, S2196, SH660
"In the Singing" (Rom, Comm.)
EL466, G533, S2255
+"Healer of Our Every Ill" OL-00115 (Rom, John)
C506, EL612, G795, S2213, SH339, VU619
"Of the Father's Love Begotten" (John)
C104, CG113, E82, EL295, G108, GR166, N118, P309, SH81, UM184, VU61
"Because He Lives" (John)
C562, CG620, GR265, SH200, UM364
"Blessed Assurance" (John)
C543, CG619, EL638, G839, GR570, N473, P341, SH320, UM369 (PD), VU337
+"I Stand Amazed in the Presence" (John)
CG576, GR122, SH537, UM371 (PD)
"Wash, O God, Our Sons and Daughters" (John, Baptism)
C365, EL445, G490, SH669, UM605, VU442, ZS191
"We Know That Christ Is Raised" OL-40344 (John, Baptism)
E296, EL449, G485, P495, UM610, VU448
"You Satisfy the Hungry Heart" 84788 (John, Comm.)
C429, CG468, EL484, G523, P521, SH672, UM629, VU478
"How Blest Are They Who Trust in Christ" (John)
C646, N365, UM654
"Womb of Life" (John, Comm.)
C14, G3, N274, S2046
"Mothering God, You Gave Me Birth" (John, Comm.)
C83, EL735, G7, N467, S2050, VU320
"O Holy Spirit, Root of Life" (John)
C251, EL399, N57, S2121, VU379
"Living for Jesus" (John)
C610, GR595, S2149
"Gather Us In" OL-00031 (John)
C284, EL532, G401, S2236, SH393
"Dearest Jesus, We Are Here" (John)
EL443, G483, P493

Additional Contemporary and Modern Suggestions

+"Promises" 7149439 (Gen, Pss)
+"Won't Stop Now" 7111932 (Gen, Rom)
"Love Moves You" ("Love Alone") 5775514 (Gen, John)
+"Good Grace" 7122177 (Pss)
+"All Things Are Possible" 2245140 (Pss)
+"You Are My Strength" 4869940 (Pss, Rom)
+"No Outsiders" 7101035 (Pss, Rom)
+"Grace Like Rain" 3689877 (Rom)
"Sing Alleluia to the Lord" 26272 (Rom)
C32, S2258, SH685
"Here Is Bread, Here Is Wine" 983717 (Rom, Comm.)
EL483, S2266
+"Presence" 7116947 (Rom, John)
+"Say So" 4944016 (Rom, John)
+"Who You Say I Am" 7102401 (Rom, John)
+"Good Grace" 7122177 (Rom, John)
+"His Mercy Is More" 7065053 (Rom, John)
+"Living Hope" 7106807 (Rom, John)
+"Love Came Down" 5148938 (Rom, John)
+"In Christ Alone" 3350395 (Rom, John)
"O How He Loves You and Me" 15850 (John)
CG600, S2108, SH535, ZS208
"Lord, I Lift Your Name on High" 117947 (John, Lent)
CG606, EL857, S2088, SH205
"There Is a Redeemer" 11483 (John)
CG377, G443, GR30, SH495
"You Are My All in All" 825356 (John)
CG571, G519, SH335, WS3040, ZS184
"I Believe in Jesus" 61282 (John)
"No Greater Love" 930887 (John, Lent)
"God Is Good All the Time" 1729073 (John)
"I Could Sing of Your Love Forever" 1043199 (John)
"You Are My King" ("Amazing Love") 2456623 (John)
SH539, WS3102
"That's Why We Praise Him" 2668576 (John)
"I Come to the Cross" 1965249 (John, Lent)
+"Behold Him" 7133698 (John)
+"God, You're So Good" 7105729 (John)
+"New Wine" 7102397 (John)
+"God Is Love" 7136019 (John)

Solo/Ensemble Suggestions

+"The Blessing" (Pss)
V-9 p. 10
"Redeeming Grace" (Rom)
V-4 p. 47
"Oh, What Love!" (Rom, John)
V-8 p. 144
"The Gospel of Grace" (Rom, John)
V-3 (1) p.44
"Wash Me in Your Water" (John, Baptism)
V-5 (2) p. 18
"Waterlife" (John, Baptism)
V-5 (3) p. 17
+"Gentle Like Jesus" (John)
V-8 p. 42
+"God So Loved" (John)
V-9 p. 28
+"He Watching Over Israel" (Pss)
Arr. Hal Hopson; Jubilate 00-46850
SA(T)B, keyboard (https://bit.ly/J-46850)
+"God So Loved the World" (John)
Tom Kendzia; Oregon Catholic Press 30146879
SATB, keyboard, opt. violin/guitar (https://bit.ly/O-6879)

+Hymn Anthem

"You Satisfy the Hungry Heart" 84788 (John, Comm.)
C429, CG468, EL484, G523, P521, SH672, UM629, VU478
The congregation may be invited to sing the refrain and the stanzas later beginning with stanza 3.
Introduction: Keyboard plays refrain.
Refrain: All voices, unison.
Stanza 1: Male soloist.
Refrain: All voices, unison.
Stanza 2: All voices, unison.
Refrain: All voices unison. *A cappella* or accompanied.
Stanza 3: S/A, unison.
Refrain: All voices unison.
Stanza 4: TB, unison.
Refrain: All voices, unison.
Stanza 5: All voices, unison.
Refrain: All voices, unison.

Other Suggestions

Visuals:
O Luggage, multitude, farewell, walking
P Hills, foot, sleep, sun/moon, evils, open door
E Abraham, paycheck, will, trust
G Cloak/night, newborn, water/Spirit, wind, serpent lifted, crucifix, John 3:16, Ascension, world

The scripture from John makes today an excellent day to schedule baptisms.

+Introit: CG255, S2220, stanza 1. "We Are God's People" (John)
Greeting: N819 (Pss)
Call to Prayer: G782, WS3131, stanza 1. "Hear My Prayer, O God" (Pss)
Confession: WSL88. "Lord, we have come to see" (Rom, Matt)
+Prayer: UM570. Prayer of Ignatius of Loyola (Gen)
Prayer for Illumination: WSL75. "Holy God" (John)
Offering Prayer: WSL110. "Jesus gave himself for us" (John)
Theme Ideas: Covenant, Faith, God: Providence / God our Help, Holy Spirit, Resurrection

Notes

NRSVue

Exodus 17:1-7

1From the wilderness of Sin the whole congregation of the
Israelites journeyed by stages, as the LORD commanded. They
camped at Rephidim, but there was no water for the people
to drink. 2The people quarreled with Moses and said, "Give us
water to drink." Moses said to them, "Why do you quarrel with
me? Why do you test the LORD?" 3But the people thirsted there
for water, and the people complained against Moses and said,
"Why did you bring us out of Egypt, to kill us and our children
and livestock with thirst?" 4So Moses cried out to the LORD,
"What shall I do for this people? They are almost ready to stone
me." 5The LORD said to Moses, "Go on ahead of the people and
take some of the elders of Israel with you; take in your hand the
staff with which you struck the Nile and go. 6I will be standing
there in front of you on the rock at Horeb. Strike the rock, and
water will come out of it, so that the people may drink." Moses
did so, in the sight of the elders of Israel. 7He called the place
Massah and Meribah, because the Israelites quarreled and tested
the LORD, saying, "Is the LORD among us or not?"

Psalm 95 (G386/638, N683, P214/215, SH401, UM814)

1O come, let us sing to the LORD; / let us make a joyful noise
to the rock of our salvation! / 2Let us come into his presence
with thanksgiving; / let us make a joyful noise to him with songs
of praise! / 3For the LORD is a great God / and a great King
above all gods. / 4In his hand are the depths of the earth; / the
heights of the mountains are his also. / 5The sea is his, for he
made it, / and the dry land, which his hands have formed.

6O come, let us worship and bow down; / let us kneel before
the LORD, our Maker! / 7For he is our God, / and we are the
people of his pasture / and the sheep of his hand. / O that
today you would listen to his voice! / 8Do not harden your
hearts, as at Meribah, / as on the day at Massah in the wilderness, / 9when your ancestors tested me / and put me to the
proof, though they had seen my work. / 10For forty years I
loathed that generation / and said, "They are a people whose
hearts go astray, / and they do not regard my ways." / 11There-
fore in my anger I swore, / "They shall not enter my rest."

Romans 5:1-11

1Therefore, since we are justified by faith, we have peace with
God through our Lord Jesus Christ, 2through whom we have
obtained access to this grace in which we stand, and we boast in
our hope of sharing the glory of God. 3And not only that, but
we also boast in our afflictions, knowing that affliction produces
endurance, 4and endurance produces character, and character
produces hope, 5and hope does not put us to shame, because
God's love has been poured into our hearts through the Holy
Spirit that has been given to us.

6For while we were still weak, at the right time Christ died
for the ungodly. 7Indeed, rarely will anyone die for a righteous
person—though perhaps for a good person someone might actually dare to die. 8But God proves his love for us in that while we
still were sinners Christ died for us. 9Much more surely, therefore, since we have now been justified by his blood, will we be
saved through him from the wrath of God. 10For if while we were
enemies we were reconciled to God through the death of his Son,
much more surely, having been reconciled, will we be saved by his
life. 11But more than that, we even boast in God through our Lord
Jesus Christ, through whom we have now received reconciliation.

John 4:5-42

5So he came to a Samaritan city called Sychar, near the plot of
ground that Jacob had given to his son Joseph. 6Jacob's well was
there, and Jesus, tired out by his journey, was sitting by the well.
It was about noon.

CEB

Exodus 17:1-7

1The whole Israelite community broke camp and set out from
the Sin desert to continue their journey, as the LORD commanded. They set up their camp at Rephidim, but there was no
water for the people to drink. 2The people argued with Moses
and said, "Give us water to drink."

Moses said to them, "Why are you arguing with me? Why are
you testing the LORD?"

3But the people were very thirsty for water there, and they
complained to Moses, "Why did you bring us out of Egypt to kill
us, our children, and our livestock with thirst?"

4So Moses cried out to the LORD, "What should I do with this
people? They are getting ready to stone me."

5The LORD said to Moses, "Go on ahead of the people, and
take some of Israel's elders with you. Take in your hand the
shepherd's rod that you used to strike the Nile River, and go. 6I'll
be standing there in front of you on the rock at Horeb. Hit the
rock. Water will come out of it, and the people will be able to
drink." Moses did so while Israel's elders watched. 7He called the
place Massah and Meribah, because the Israelites argued with
and tested the LORD, asking, "Is the LORD really with us or not?"

Psalm 95 (G386/638, N683, P214/215, SH401, UM814)

1Come, let's sing out loud to the LORD! / Let's raise a joyful
shout to the rock of our salvation! / 2Let's come before him with
thanks! / Let's shout songs of joy to him! / 3The Lord is a great
God, / the great king over all other gods. / 4The earth's depths
are in his hands; / the mountain heights belong to him; / 5the
sea, which he made, is his / along with the dry ground, / which
his own hands formed.

6Come, let's worship and bow down! / Let's kneel before the
LORD, our maker! / 7He is our God, / and we are the people of
his pasture, / the sheep in his hands. / If only you would listen
to his voice right now! / 8"Don't harden your hearts / like you
did at Meribah, / like you did when you were at Massah, / in the
wilderness, / 9when your ancestors tested me / and scrutinized
me, / even though they had already seen my acts. / 10For forty
years I despised that generation; / I said, 'These people have
twisted hearts. / They don't know my ways.' / 11So in anger I
swore: / 'They will never enter my place of rest!' "

Romans 5:1-11

1Therefore, since we have been made righteous through his
faithfulness combined with our faith, we have peace with God
through our Lord Jesus Christ. 2We have access by faith into this
grace in which we stand through him, and we boast in the hope
of God's glory. 3But not only that! We even take pride in our
problems, because we know that trouble produces endurance,
4endurance produces character, and character produces hope.
5This hope doesn't put us to shame, because the love of God has
been poured out in our hearts through the Holy Spirit, who has
been given to us.

6While we were still weak, at the right moment, Christ died
for ungodly people. 7It isn't often that someone will die for a
righteous person, though maybe someone might dare to die for
a good person. 8But God shows his love for us, because while we
were still sinners Christ died for us. 9So, now that we have been
made righteous by his blood, we can be even more certain that
we will be saved from God's wrath through him. 10If we were
reconciled to God through the death of his Son while we were
still enemies, now that we have been reconciled, how much more
certain is it that we will be saved by his life? 11And not only that:
we even take pride in God through our Lord Jesus Christ, the one
through whom we now have a restored relationship with God.

John 4:5-42

5He came to a Samaritan city called Sychar, which was near the
land Jacob had given to his son Joseph. 6Jacob's well was there. Jesus
was tired from his journey, so he sat down at the well. It was about
noon.

NRSVue

John 4:5-42 (continued)

[7]A Samaritan woman came to draw water, and Jesus said to her, "Give me a drink." [8](His disciples had gone to the city to buy food.) [9]The Samaritan woman said to him, "How is it that you, a Jew, ask a drink of me, a woman of Samaria?" (Jews do not share things in common with Samaritans.) [10]Jesus answered her, "If you knew the gift of God and who it is that is saying to you, 'Give me a drink,' you would have asked him, and he would have given you living water." [11]The woman said to him, "Sir, you have no bucket, and the well is deep. Where do you get that living water? [12]Are you greater than our ancestor Jacob, who gave us the well and with his sons and his flocks drank from it?" [13]Jesus said to her, "Everyone who drinks of this water will be thirsty again, [14]but those who drink of the water that I will give them will never be thirsty. The water that I will give will become in them a spring of water gushing up to eternal life." [15]The woman said to him, "Sir, give me this water, so that I may never be thirsty or have to keep coming here to draw water."

[16]Jesus said to her, "Go, call your husband, and come back." [17]The woman answered him, "I have no husband." Jesus said to her, "You are right in saying, 'I have no husband,' [18]for you have had five husbands, and the one you have now is not your husband. What you have said is true!" [19]The woman said to him, "Sir, I see that you are a prophet. [20]Our ancestors worshiped on this mountain, but you say that the place where people must worship is in Jerusalem." [21]Jesus said to her, "Woman, believe me, the hour is coming when you will worship the Father neither on this mountain nor in Jerusalem. [22]You worship what you do not know; we worship what we know, for salvation is from the Jews. [23]But the hour is coming and is now here when the true worshipers will worship the Father in spirit and truth, for the Father seeks such as these to worship him. [24]God is spirit, and those who worship him must worship in spirit and truth." [25]The woman said to him, "I know that Messiah is coming" (who is called Christ). "When he comes, he will proclaim all things to us." [26]Jesus said to her, "I am he, the one who is speaking to you."

[27]Just then his disciples came. They were astonished that he was speaking with a woman, but no one said, "What do you want?" or, "Why are you speaking with her?" [28]Then the woman left her water jar and went back to the city. She said to the people, [29]"Come and see a man who told me everything I have ever done! He cannot be the Messiah, can he?" [30]They left the city and were on their way to him.

[31]Meanwhile the disciples were urging him, "Rabbi, eat something." [32]But he said to them, "I have food to eat that you do not know about." [33]So the disciples said to one another, "Surely no one has brought him something to eat?" [34]Jesus said to them, "My food is to do the will of him who sent me and to complete his work. [35]Do you not say, 'Four months more, then comes the harvest'? But I tell you, look around you, and see how the fields are ripe for harvesting. [36]The reaper is already receiving wages and is gathering fruit for eternal life, so that sower and reaper may rejoice together. [37]For here the saying holds true, 'One sows and another reaps.' [38]I sent you to reap that for which you did not labor. Others have labored, and you have entered into their labor."

[39]Many Samaritans from that city believed in him because of the woman's testimony, "He told me everything I have ever done." [40]So when the Samaritans came to him, they asked him to stay with them, and he stayed there two days. [41]And many more believed because of his word. [42]They said to the woman, "It is no longer because of what you said that we believe, for we have heard for ourselves, and we know that this is truly the Savior of the world."

CEB

John 4:5-42 (continued)

[7]A Samaritan woman came to the well to draw water. Jesus said to her, "Give me some water to drink." [8]His disciples had gone into the city to buy him some food.

[9]The Samaritan woman asked, "Why do you, a Jewish man, ask for something to drink from me, a Samaritan woman?" (Jews and Samaritans didn't associate with each other.)

[10]Jesus responded, "If you recognized God's gift and who is saying to you, 'Give me some water to drink,' you would be asking him and he would give you living water."

[11]The woman said to him, "Sir, you don't have a bucket and the well is deep. Where would you get this living water? [12]You aren't greater than our father Jacob, are you? He gave this well to us, and he drank from it himself, as did his sons and his livestock."

[13]Jesus answered, "Everyone who drinks this water will be thirsty again, [14]but whoever drinks from the water that I will give will never be thirsty again. The water that I give will become in those who drink it a spring of water that bubbles up into eternal life."

[15]The woman said to him, "Sir, give me this water, so that I will never be thirsty and will never need to come here to draw water!"

[16]Jesus said to her, "Go, get your husband, and come back here."

[17]The woman replied, "I don't have a husband."

"You are right to say, 'I don't have a husband,'" Jesus answered. [18]"You've had five husbands, and the man you are with now isn't your husband. You've spoken the truth."

[19]The woman said, "Sir, I see that you are a prophet. [20]Our ancestors worshipped on this mountain, but you and your people say that it is necessary to worship in Jerusalem."

[21]Jesus said to her, "Believe me, woman, the time is coming when you and your people will worship the Father neither on this mountain nor in Jerusalem. [22]You and your people worship what you don't know; we worship what we know because salvation is from the Jews. [23]But the time is coming—and is here!—when true worshippers will worship in spirit and truth. The Father looks for those who worship him this way. [24]God is spirit, and it is necessary to worship God in spirit and truth."

[25]The woman said, "I know that the Messiah is coming, the one who is called the Christ. When he comes, he will teach everything to us."

[26]Jesus said to her, "I Am—the one who speaks with you."

[27]Just then, Jesus' disciples arrived and were shocked that he was talking with a woman. But no one asked, "What do you want?" or "Why are you talking with her?" [28]The woman put down her water jar and went into the city. She said to the people, [29]"Come and see a man who has told me everything I've done! Could this man be the Christ?" [30]They left the city and were on their way to see Jesus.

[31]In the meantime the disciples spoke to Jesus, saying, "Rabbi, eat."

[32]Jesus said to them, "I have food to eat that you don't know about."

[33]The disciples asked each other, "Has someone brought him food?"

[34]Jesus said to them, "I am fed by doing the will of the one who sent me and by completing his work. [35]Don't you have a saying, 'Four more months and then it's time for harvest'? Look, I tell you: open your eyes and notice that the fields are already ripe for the harvest. [36]Those who harvest are receiving their pay and gathering fruit for eternal life so that those who sow and those who harvest can celebrate together. [37]This is a true saying, that one sows and another harvests. [38]I have sent you to harvest what you didn't work hard for; others worked hard, and you will share in their hard work."

[39]Many Samaritans in that city believed in Jesus because of the woman's word when she testified, "He told me everything I've ever done." [40]So when the Samaritans came to Jesus, they asked him to stay with them, and he stayed there two days. [41]Many more believed because of his word, [42]and they said to the woman, "We no longer believe because of what you said, for we have heard for ourselves and know that this one is truly the savior of the world."

Primary Hymns and Songs for the Day

"Guide Me, O Thou Great Jehovah" 1448 (Exod, John) (O)
C622, CG33, E690, EL618, G65, GR47, N18, P281, SH51, UM127 (PD), VU651 (Fr.)
H-3 Hbl-25, 51, 58; Chr-89; Desc-26; Org-23
S-1 #76-77. Desc. and harm.
"O How He Loves You and Me" 15850 (Rom)
CG600, S2108, SH535, ZS208
"When I Survey the Wondrous Cross" 27893 (Rom) (C)
C195, CG186, EL803, G223, GR221, N224, P101, SH163/164, UM298 (PD)
H-3 Hbl-6, 102; Chr-213; Desc-49; Org-49
S-1 #155. Descant
"When I Survey the Wondrous Cross" 721333 (Rom) (C)
E474, G224, P100, UM299 (PD), VU149 (Fr.)
H-3 Hbl-47; Chr-214; Desc-90; Org-127
S-1 #288. Transposition to E-flat major

Additional Hymn Suggestions

"All My Hope Is Firmly Grounded" 3594474 (Exod)
C88, E665, EL757, GR68, N408, UM132, VU654/655
"Rock of Ages, Cleft for Me" (Exod)
C214, E685, EL623, G438, GR242, N596, SH301, UM361 (PD)
+"Dust and Ashes" (Exod)
N186, VU105, WS3098
"Jesus, Thou Joy of Loving Hearts" (Exod, John)
C101, CG394, E649, G494, GR128, N329, P510, SH6688, VU472
"Glorious Things of Thee Are Spoken" 99371 (Exod, John)
C709, CG282, E522/523, EL647, G81, GR395, N307, P446, UM731 (PD)
"We Walk by Faith" 2591911 (Pss, Rom)
CG634, E209, EL635, G817, N256, P399, S2196, SH660
"O Love That Wilt Not Let Me Go" (Rom)
C540, CG631, G833, GR92, N485, P384, SH314, UM480 (PD), VU658
"Spirit of God, Descend upon My Heart" 2083 (Rom)
C265, CG243, EL800, G688, GR294, N290, P326, SH277, UM500 (PD), VU378
"In the Singing" (Rom, Comm.)
EL466, G533, S2255
"You, Lord, are Both Lamb and Shepherd" (Rom, Lent)
G274, SH210, VU210, WS3043
"Hope of the World" 643002 (Rom, John)
C538, E472, G734, N46, P360, UM178, VU215
"Healer of Our Every Ill" OL-00115 (Rom, John)
C506, EL612, G795, S2213, SH339, VU619
"The King of Love, My Shepherd Is" (John)
CG64, E645/646, EL502, G802, GR90, N248, P171, SH359, UM138 (PD), VU273
+"I Love to Tell the Story" (John)
C480, CG581, EL661, G462, GR160, N522, SH569, UM156 (PD), VU343
+"Jesus Is All the World to Me" (John)
CG612, SH323, UM469, Z216
"Jesus, Lover of My Soul" (John)
C542, CG406, E699, G440, GR120, N546, P303, SH542/543, UM479, VU669
"You Satisfy the Hungry Heart" 84788 (John, Comm.)
C429, CG468, EL484, G523, P521, SH672, UM629, VU478
"Jesus, Joy of Our Desiring" (John)
GR129, UM644 (PD), VU328
"O Splendor of God's Glory Bright" (John)
E5, G666, N87, P474, UM679, VU413
"Come, Labor On" (John)
E541, G719, N532, P415
"Gather Us In" OL-00031 (John)
C284, EL532, G401, S2236, SH393
"De Tu Cántaro Dame" ("The Samaritan Woman") (John)
SH119
"All Who Hunger" (John, Comm.)
C419, CG303, EL461, G509, S2126, VU460

Additional Contemporary and Modern Suggestions

"Forever" 3148428 (Exod, Pss)
CG53, WS3023
"God of Wonders" 3118757 (Exod, Pss)
SH9, WS3034
+"Here Again" 7111925 (Exod, Pss)
"Restless" 5775569 (Exod, Pss, John)
"I Will Call upon the Lord" 11263 (Pss)
G621, S2002
"Great Is the Lord" 1149 (Pss)
CG325, G614, S2022, SH459
+"He Is Exalted" 17827 (Pss)
CG342, S2070, SH423
"Uyai Mose" ("Come, All You People") OL-00027 (Pss)
EL819, G388, S2274, SH405
"Rock of Ages" 2240547 (Pss)
+"We Worship and Adore You" 551194 (Pss)
+"Yes I Will" 7105442 (Pss)
+"You Are My Strength" 4869940 (Pss)
"I Could Sing of Your Love Forever" 1043199 (Pss, Rom)
"You Are My King" ("Amazing Love") 2456623 (Rom)
SH539, WS3102
"That's Why We Praise Him" 2668576 (Rom)
+"Yet Not I but Through Christ in Me" 7121852 (Rom)
+"My Worth Is Not in What I Own" 7024758 (Rom)
+"Never Runs Out" 7193998 (Rom, John)
+"No Outsiders" 7101035 (Rom, John)
+"Presence" 7116947 (Rom, John)
+"Say So" 4944016 (Rom, John)
+"Who You Say I Am" 7102401 (Rom, John)
+"All the Poor and Powerless" 5881130 (Rom, John)
"Love Moves You" ("Love Alone") 5775514 (Rom, John)
"Song of Hope" ("Heaven Come Down") 5111477 (Rom, John)
"Here Is Bread, Here Is Wine" 983717 (Rom, John, Comm.)
EL483, S2266
"Jesus, Name above All Names" 21291 (John)
S2071, ZS27
"Fill My Cup, Lord" 15946 (John, Comm.)
C351, UM641 *(refrain only)*, WS3093
"Hungry" ("Falling on My Knees") 2650364 (John)
WS3099
"Stand in Awe" (John)
WS3162
"Here at the Cross" 7046292 (John, Lent)
"The River Is Here" 1475231 (John)
"Who Can Satisfy My Soul Like You?" 208492 (John)
"More Love, More Power" 60661 (John)
"Come Just As You Are" 1189479 (John)
"All Who Are Thirsty" 2489542 (John)
"Just to Be with You" 5585120 (John)
+"Enough" 3599479 (John)
+"Reckless Love" 7089641 (John)
+"Rise" 7036613 (John)
+"Springtime" 7146308 (John)
+"Beautiful Things" 5665521 (John)
+"The Goodness of Jesus" 7121854 (John)
+"Come to the Table" 7130008 (John, Comm.)

Solo/Ensemble Suggestions

+"Ho! Everyone Who Is Thirsty" (Exod, John)
V-8 p. 244
"Redeeming Grace" (Rom)
V-4 p. 47
"Maybe the Rain" (John)
V-5 (2) p. 27
"Life Indeed" (John)
V-8 p. 271
+"God So Loved" (John)
V-9 p. 28
"Oh, Come Let Us Sing!" (Pss)
William M. Schoenfeld; AEC-3 p. 33
2-part, keyboard (https://bit.ly/AEC-3)
"Uyai Mose" (Pss)
Arr. Kevin Holland; Choristers Guild CGA-1373
SATB, opt. percussion (https://bit.ly/CGA-1373)

+Hymn Anthem

"Woman in the Night" (John)
C188, G161, UM274
There are various tunes in these hymnals, but these instructions work for all.
Use a children's choir or teenagers to tell the story and teach this hymn. Involve the congregation in singing the refrain. You might choose to use the refrain as a response to a litany earlier or later in this service.
Introduction: Keyboard plays refrain one time.
Stanza 1: All children or a child soloist sings the stanza, followed by all children (or S/A) singing refrain.
Stanza 2: All children sing stanza, followed by children and S/A singing refrain.
Interlude: On last measure of previous refrain, begin playing refrain again.
Stanza 3: S/A soloist sing this stanza a bit slower than the previous one. Refrain is sung by children and choir.
Interlude: On last measure of previous refrain, begin playing refrain again.
Stanza 4: T/B soloist on stanza. All, including congregation on refrain.
Stanza 5: S/A soloist on stanza. All on refrain.
Stanza 6: All children and choir on stanza. Congregation joins on refrain. Hold last note throughout ending.
Ending: On last measure or previous refrain, begin playing the last system again while choir holds last note.

Other Suggestions

Daylight Savings Time begins today.
This day may include an observance of Girl Scout Sunday.
Visuals:
O Wilderness, quarrel, stones, staff, rock, water, Exod. 17:7c
P Singing, rock, instruments, mountain, sea, dry land
E Christ, glory/suffering, hearts/Spirit, crucifix
G Well, noon, water jar, living water, clock
Introit: WS3113, st. 1. "A Wilderness Wandering People" (Exod, Lent)
Opening Prayer: WSL19. "God of the wilderness" (Exod)
Canticle: UM91. "Canticle of Praise to God" (Pss)
Greeting: N820 (John) or N821 (Pss)
Call to Confession: N833 (Lent)
Words of Assurance: Romans 5:8
Prayer: WSL57. "Days pass and the years vanish" (Exod)
Prayer: WSL52. "O God, you pour out" (John)
Litany: WSL53. "We also boast in our sufferings" (Rom)
Benediction: WSL167. "Go! Never stop going out" (John)
Theme Ideas: Faith, God: Hunger / Thirst for God, God: Love of God, God: Shepherd, Hope, Praise, Sin and Forgiveness

Notes

NRSVue

1 Samuel 16:1-13

[1]The LORD said to Samuel, "How long will you grieve over Saul? I have rejected him from being king over Israel. Fill your horn with oil and set out; I will send you to Jesse the Bethlehemite, for I have provided for myself a king among his sons." [2]Samuel said, "How can I go? If Saul hears of it, he will kill me." And the LORD said, "Take a heifer with you and say, 'I have come to sacrifice to the LORD.' [3]Invite Jesse to the sacrifice, and I will show you what you shall do, and you shall anoint for me the one whom I name to you." [4]Samuel did what the LORD commanded and came to Bethlehem. The elders of the city came to meet him trembling and said, "Do you come peaceably?" [5]He said, "Peaceably. I have come to sacrifice to the LORD; sanctify yourselves and come with me to the sacrifice." And he sanctified Jesse and his sons and invited them to the sacrifice.

[6]When they came, he looked on Eliab and thought, "Surely his anointed is now before the LORD." [7]But the LORD said to Samuel, "Do not look on his appearance or on the height of his stature, because I have rejected him, for the LORD does not see as mortals see; they look on the outward appearance, but the LORD looks on the heart." [8]Then Jesse called Abinadab and made him pass before Samuel. He said, "Neither has the LORD chosen this one." [9]Then Jesse made Shammah pass by. And he said, "Neither has the LORD chosen this one." [10]Jesse made seven of his sons pass before Samuel, and Samuel said to Jesse, "The LORD has not chosen any of these." [11]Samuel said to Jesse, "Are all your sons here?" And he said, "There remains yet the youngest, but he is keeping the sheep." And Samuel said to Jesse, "Send and bring him, for we will not sit down until he comes here." [12]He sent and brought him in. Now he was ruddy and had beautiful eyes and was handsome. The LORD said, "Rise and anoint him, for this is the one." [13]Then Samuel took the horn of oil and anointed him in the presence of his brothers, and the spirit of the LORD came mightily upon David from that day forward. Samuel then set out and went to Ramah.

Psalm 23 (G473/801-803, N633, P170-175, SH295/307, UM134/754)

[1]The LORD is my shepherd; I shall not want. / [2]He makes me lie down in green pastures; / he leads me beside still waters; / [3]he restores my soul. / He leads me in right paths / for his name's sake. / [4]Even though I walk through the darkest valley, / I fear no evil, / for you are with me; / your rod and your staff, / they comfort me. / [5]You prepare a table before me / in the presence of my enemies; / you anoint my head with oil; / my cup overflows. / [6]Surely goodness and mercy shall follow me / all the days of my life, / and I shall dwell in the house of the LORD / my whole life long.

Ephesians 5:8-14

[8]For once you were darkness, but now in the Lord you are light. Walk as children of light, [9]for the fruit of the light is found in all that is good and right and true. [10]Try to find out what is pleasing to the Lord. [11]Take no part in the unfruitful works of darkness; rather, expose them. [12]For it is shameful even to mention what such people do secretly, [13]but everything exposed by the light becomes visible, [14]for everything that becomes visible is light. Therefore it says,

"Sleeper, awake!
Rise from the dead,
and Christ will shine on you."

John 9:1-41

[1]As he walked along, he saw a man blind from birth. [2]His disciples asked him, "Rabbi, who sinned, this man or his parents, that he was born blind?" [3]Jesus answered, "Neither this man nor his parents sinned; he was born blind so that God's works might be revealed in him. [4]We must work the works of him who sent me

CEB

1 Samuel 16:1-13

[1]The LORD said to Samuel, "How long are you going to grieve over Saul? I have rejected him as king over Israel. Fill your horn with oil and get going. I'm sending you to Jesse of Bethlehem because I have found my next king among his sons."

[2]"How can I do that?" Samuel asked. "When Saul hears of it he'll kill me!"

"Take a heifer with you," the LORD replied, "and say, 'I have come to make a sacrifice to the LORD.' [3]Invite Jesse to the sacrifice, and I will make clear to you what you should do. You will anoint for me the person I point out to you."

[4]Samuel did what the LORD instructed. When he came to Bethlehem, the city elders came to meet him. They were shaking with fear. "Do you come in peace?" they asked.

[5]"Yes," Samuel answered. "I've come to make a sacrifice to the LORD. Now make yourselves holy, then come with me to the sacrifice." Samuel made Jesse and his sons holy and invited them to the sacrifice as well.

[6]When they arrived, Samuel looked at Eliab and thought, That must be the LORD's anointed right in front.

[7]But the LORD said to Samuel, "Have no regard for his appearance or stature, because I haven't selected him. God doesn't look at things like humans do. Humans see only what is visible to the eyes, but the LORD sees into the heart."

[8]Next Jesse called for Abinadab, who presented himself to Samuel, but he said, "The LORD hasn't chosen this one either." [9]So Jesse presented Shammah, but Samuel said, "No, the LORD hasn't chosen this one." [10]Jesse presented seven of his sons to Samuel, but Samuel said to Jesse, "The LORD hasn't picked any of these." [11]Then Samuel asked Jesse, "Is that all of your boys?"

"There is still the youngest one," Jesse answered, "but he's out keeping the sheep."

"Send for him," Samuel told Jesse, "because we can't proceed until he gets here."

[12]So Jesse sent and brought him in. He was reddish brown, had beautiful eyes, and was good-looking. The LORD said, "That's the one. Go anoint him." [13]So Samuel took the horn of oil and anointed him right there in front of his brothers. The LORD's spirit came over David from that point forward.

Then Samuel left and went to Ramah.

Psalm 23 (G473/801-803, N633, P170-175, SH295/307, UM134/754)

[1]The LORD is my shepherd. / I lack nothing. / [2]He lets me rest in grassy meadows; / he leads me to restful waters; / [3]he keeps me alive. / He guides me in proper paths / for the sake of his good name. / [4]Even when I walk / through the darkest valley, / I fear no danger because you are with me. / Your rod and your staff— / they protect me. / [5]You set a table for me / right in front of my enemies. / You bathe my head in oil; / my cup is so full it spills over! / [6]Yes, goodness and faithful love / will pursue me all the days of my life, / and I will live in the LORD's house / as long as I live.

Ephesians 5:8-14

[8]You were once darkness, but now you are light in the Lord, so live your life as children of light. [9]Light produces fruit that consists of every sort of goodness, justice, and truth.[10]Therefore, test everything to see what's pleasing to the Lord,[11]and don't participate in the unfruitful actions of darkness. Instead, you should reveal the truth about them. [12]It's embarrassing to even talk about what certain persons do in secret. [13]But everything exposed to the light is revealed by the light. [14]Everything that is revealed by the light is light. Therefore, it says, *Wake up, sleeper! Get up from the dead, and Christ will shine on you.*

John 9:1-41

[1]As Jesus walked along, he saw a man who was blind from birth. [2]Jesus' disciples asked, "Rabbi, who sinned so that he was born blind, this man or his parents?"

[3]Jesus answered, "Neither he nor his parents. This happened so that God's mighty works might be displayed in him. [4]While it's

NRSVue

John 9:1-41 (continued)

while it is day; night is coming, when no one can work. 5As long as I am in the world, I am the light of the world." 6When he had said this, he spat on the ground and made mud with the saliva and spread the mud on the man's eyes, 7saying to him, "Go, wash in the pool of Siloam" (which means Sent). Then he went and washed and came back able to see. 8The neighbors and those who had seen him before as a beggar began to ask, "Is this not the man who used to sit and beg?" 9Some were saying, "It is he." Others were saying, "No, but it is someone like him." He kept saying, "I am he." 10But they kept asking him, "Then how were your eyes opened?" 11He answered, "The man called Jesus made mud, spread it on my eyes, and said to me, 'Go to Siloam and wash.' Then I went and washed and received my sight." 12They said to him, "Where is he?" He said, "I do not know."

13They brought to the Pharisees the man who had formerly been blind. 14Now it was a sabbath day when Jesus made the mud and opened his eyes. 15Then the Pharisees also began to ask him how he had received his sight. He said to them, "He put mud on my eyes. Then I washed, and now I see." 16Some of the Pharisees said, "This man is not from God, for he does not observe the sabbath." Others said, "How can a man who is a sinner perform such signs?" And they were divided. 17So they said again to the blind man, "What do you say about him? It was your eyes he opened." He said, "He is a prophet."

18The Jews did not believe that he had been blind and had received his sight until they called the parents of the man who had received his sight 19and asked them, "Is this your son, who you say was born blind? How then does he now see?" 20His parents answered, "We know that this is our son and that he was born blind; 21but we do not know how it is that now he sees, nor do we know who opened his eyes. Ask him; he is of age. He will speak for himself." 22His parents said this because they were afraid of the Jews, for the Jews had already agreed that anyone who confessed Jesus to be the Messiah would be put out of the synagogue. 23Therefore his parents said, "He is of age; ask him."

24So for the second time they called the man who had been blind, and they said to him, "Give glory to God! We know that this man is a sinner." 25He answered, "I do not know whether he is a sinner. One thing I do know, that though I was blind, now I see." 26They said to him, "What did he do to you? How did he open your eyes?" 27He answered them, "I have told you already, and you would not listen. Why do you want to hear it again? Do you also want to become his disciples?" 28Then they reviled him, saying, "You are his disciple, but we are disciples of Moses. 29We know that God has spoken to Moses, but as for this man, we do not know where he comes from." 30The man answered, "Here is an astonishing thing! You do not know where he comes from, yet he opened my eyes. 31We know that God does not listen to sinners, but he does listen to one who worships him and obeys his will. 32Never since the world began has it been heard that anyone opened the eyes of a person born blind. 33If this man were not from God, he could do nothing." 34They answered him, "You were born entirely in sins, and are you trying to teach us?" And they drove him out.

35Jesus heard that they had driven him out, and when he found him he said, "Do you believe in the Son of Man?" 36He answered, "And who is he, sir? Tell me, so that I may believe in him." 37Jesus said to him, "You have seen him, and the one speaking with you is he." 38He said, "Lord, I believe." And he worshiped him. 39Jesus said, "I came into this world for judgment, so that those who do not see may see and those who do see may become blind." 40Some of the Pharisees who were with him heard this and said to him, "Surely we are not blind, are we?" 41Jesus said to them, "If you were blind, you would not have sin. But now that you say, 'We see,' your sin remains."

CEB

John 9:1-41 (continued)

daytime, we must do the works of him who sent me. Night is coming when no one can work. 5While I am in the world, I am the light of the world." 6After he said this, he spit on the ground, made mud with the saliva, and smeared the mud on the man's eyes. 7Jesus said to him, "Go, wash in the pool of Siloam" (this word means *sent*). So the man went away and washed. When he returned, he could see.

8The man's neighbors and those who used to see him when he was a beggar said, "Isn't this the man who used to sit and beg?"

9Some said, "It is," and others said, "No, it's someone who looks like him."

But the man said, "Yes, it's me!"

10So they asked him, "How are you now able to see?"

11He answered, "The man they call Jesus made mud, smeared it on my eyes, and said, 'Go to the Pool of Siloam and wash.' So I went and washed, and then I could see."

12They asked, "Where is this man?"

He replied, "I don't know."

13Then they led the man who had been born blind to the Pharisees. 14Now Jesus made the mud and smeared it on the man's eyes on a Sabbath day. 15So Pharisees also asked him how he was able to see.

The man told them, "He put mud on my eyes, I washed, and now I see."

16Some Pharisees said, "This man isn't from God, because he breaks the Sabbath law." Others said, "How can a sinner do miraculous signs like these?" So they were divided. 17Some of the Pharisees questioned the man who had been born blind again: "What do you have to say about him, since he healed your eyes?"

He replied, "He's a prophet."

18The Jewish leaders didn't believe the man had been blind and received his sight until they called for his parents. 19The Jewish leaders asked them, "Is this your son? Are you saying he was born blind? How can he now see?"

20His parents answered, "We know he is our son. We know he was born blind. 21But we don't know how he now sees, and we don't know who healed his eyes. Ask him. He's old enough to speak for himself." 22His parents said this because they feared the Jewish authorities. This is because the Jewish authorities had already decided that whoever confessed Jesus to be the Christ would be expelled from the synagogue. 23That's why his parents said, "He's old enough. Ask him."

24Therefore, they called a second time for the man who had been born blind and said to him, "Give glory to God. We know this man is a sinner."

25The man answered, "I don't know whether he's a sinner. Here's what I do know: I was blind and now I see."

26They questioned him: "What did he do to you? How did he heal your eyes?"

27He replied, "I already told you, and you didn't listen. Why do you want to hear it again? Do you want to become his disciples too?"

28They insulted him: "You are his disciple, but we are Moses' disciples. 29We know that God spoke to Moses, but we don't know where this man is from."

30The man answered, "This is incredible! You don't know where he is from, yet he healed my eyes! 31We know that God doesn't listen to sinners. God listens to anyone who is devout and does God's will. 32No one has ever heard of a healing of the eyes of someone born blind. 33If this man wasn't from God, he couldn't do this."

34They responded, "You were born completely in sin! How is it that you dare to teach us?" Then they expelled him.

35Jesus heard they had expelled the man born blind. Finding him, Jesus said, "Do you believe in the Human One?"

36He answered, "Who is he, sir? I want to believe in him."

37Jesus said, "You have seen him. In fact, he is the one speaking with you."

38The man said, "Lord, I believe." And he worshipped Jesus.

39Jesus said, "I have come into the world to exercise judgment so that those who don't see can see and those who see will become blind."

40Some Pharisees who were with him heard what he said and asked, "Surely we aren't blind, are we?"

41Jesus said to them, "If you were blind, you wouldn't have any sin, but now that you say, 'We see,' your sin remains."

Primary Hymns and Songs for the Day
"Savior, Like a Shepherd Lead Us" 24078 (1 Sam, Pss) (O)
C558, CG405, EL789, G187, GR130, N252, P387, SH538, UM381 (PD)
H-3 Chr-167; Org-15
S-2 #29. Harmonization
"Open My Eyes, That I May See" 68003 (John) (O)
C586, CG395, G451, GR311, P324, SH583, UM454, VU371
H-3 Chr-157; Org-108
"Shepherd Me, O God" OL-00751 (1 Sam, Pss)
EL780, G473, S2058, SH365
"Siyahamba" ("We Are Marching") 1321512 (Eph)
C442, CG155, EL866, G853, N526, S2235-ab, SH717, VU646, ZS111
"Open Our Eyes, Lord" 1572 (John)
CG392, S2086, SH562
"I Want to Walk as a Child of the Light" (Eph, John) (C)
CG96, E490, EL815, G377, GR216, SH352, UM206
S-2 #91. Desc.
"He Leadeth Me: O Blessed Thought" (1 Sam, Pss) (C)
C545, CG68, GR73, SH304, UM128 (PD), VU657

Additional Hymn Suggestions
"O God, in a Mysterious Way" (PD) (1 Sam)
CG39, E677, G30, GR51N412, P270, SH47
"Awake, My Soul, and with the Sun" (1 Sam)
E11, EL557 (PD), G663, GR54, P456
"Great Is Thy Faithfulness" 18723 (1 Sam)
C86, CG48, EL733, G39, GR44, N423, P276, SH48, UM140, VU288
"I Sing the Almighty Power of God" 738058 (1 Sam)
C64, CG19, E398, G32, GR4, N12, P288, SH15, UM152, VU231
"Spirit of the Living God" 23488 (1 Sam)
C259, CG233, G288, GR299, N283, P322, SH555, UM393, VU376, Z226, S-1 #212 Vocal desc. idea
"Precious Lord, Take My Hand" 7205306 (1 Sam, Pss)
C628, CG400, EL773, G834, N472, P404, SH336, UM474, VU670, Z179
"The Lord's My Shepherd" (Pss)
C78/79, CG65, EL778, G801, N479, GR377/657, P170, SH375, UM136, VU747/748
"My Shepherd Will Supply My Need" (Pss)
C80, CG66, E664, EL782 (PD), G803, GR50, N247, P172, SH44
"Jesus Walked This Lonesome Valley" 4715434 (Pss, Lent)
C211, P80, S2112
+"Lead On, O Cloud of Presence" (Pss)
C633, S2234, VU421
+"Feed Us, Lord" 4636207 (Pss, Comm.)
G501, WS3167
"Lead Me, Guide Me" (Pss, Eph)
C583, CG403, EL768, G740, S2214, SH582, ZS173
"O for a Closer Walk with God" (Eph)
CG679, E684, G739, GR327, N450, P396
"Gather Us In" OL-00031 (Eph, Comm.)
C284, EL532, G401, S2236, SH393
"Christ, Be Our Light" (*"Cristo, la Luz"*) (Eph, John)
EL715, G314, SH242
"O Christ, the Healer" 1730268 (John)
C503. EL610, G793, N175, P380, UM265
"All Who Love and Serve Your City" 1277415 (John)
C670, CG674, E570/571, EL724, G351, P413, UM433
"Lord, Whose Love Through Humble Service" (John)
C461, CG650, E610, EL712, GR454, P427, SH239, UM581
"Wash, O God, Our Sons and Daughters" (John)
C365, EL445, G490, SH669, UM605, VU442, ZS191
"Come, Labor On" (John)
E541, G719, N532, P415
"In Remembrance of Me" 25156 (John, Comm.)
C403, CG462, G521, S2254, SH667, ZS203

Additional Contemporary and Modern Suggestions
"Oh, I Know the Lord's Laid His Hands on Me" (PD) (1 Sam)
S2139 (PD), Z166
"Nada Te Turbe" ("Nothing Can Trouble") OL-00128 (Pss)
CG73, G820, N772, S2054, SH292, VU290
"God Is Good All the Time" OL-88288 (Pss)
WS3026, ZS18
"Gentle Shepherd" 15609 (Pss, Lent)
WS3096
"Your Grace Is Enough" 4477026 (Pss, Lent)
"God Is Good All the Time" 1729073 (Pss)
+"Lead Me, Lord" 1609045 (Pss)
+"Nothing to Fear" 7133723 (Pss)
+"Psalm 23" ("I Am Not Alone") 7111981 (Pss)
+"Tremble" 7065049 (Pss)
+"Surrounded" (Fight My Battles) 7098758 (Pss)
+"Be Still" 7116946 (Pss)
"God Will Make a Way" 458620 (Pss)
SH57
"The King of Love My Shepherd Is" 7023979 (Pss)
WS3106
"I Stand Amazed" 769450 (Pss, Lent)
"You Never Let Go" 4674166 (Pss, Eph, John)
"I Have a Hope" 5087587 (Pss, Eph, John)
+"Here Again" 7111925 (Pss, John)
+"Called Me Higher" 5887880 (Pss, Eph, John)
+"Freedom"7078151 (Pss, John)
+"Good Grace" 7122177 (Pss, John)
+"You Are My Strength" 4869940 (Pss, John)
"For Us" 7119349 (Pss, John, Lent)
"Awaken" 5491647 (Eph)
"Shine on Us" 1754646 (Eph)
"Everyday" 2798154 (Eph)
+"Walking in the Light of God" No SS (Eph)
+"You are the Light" 6238098 (Eph, John)
"Shine, Jesus, Shine" 30426 (Eph, John)
CG156, EL671, G192, GR217, S2173, SH102, V-3 (2), p. 48. Vocal Solo
"Turn Your Eyes upon Jesus" 15960 (John)
CG472, GR670, UM349
"Water, River, Spirit, Grace" OL-126179 (John, Baptism)
C366, N169, S2253
"Open the Eyes of My Heart" 2298355 (John)
G452, SH378, WS3008
+"Word of God, Speak" 3912788 (John)
+"You Keep Hope Alive" 7125876 (John)
+"You Hear" 6005063 (John, Lent)
"Restored" 5894615 (John, Lent)
"The Power of Your Love" 917491 (John)
+"I Am the Light of the World" (*"Del mundo yo soy la luz"*) 954502 (John)
"Good to Me" 313480 (John)
"There Is a Redeemer" 11483 (John, Comm.)
CG377, G443, GR30, SH495
"You Hear" 6005063 (John, Lent)

Solo/Ensemble Suggestions
"God, Our Ever Faithful Shepherd" (Pss)
V-4 p. 15
"Holy is the Lamb" (Pss, Lent)
V-5 (1) p. 5

"The Lord is My Shepherd" (Pss)
V-5 (3) p. 30
"Shepherd of Love" (Pss)
V-8 p. 142
"My Shepherd Will Supply My Need" (Pss)
V-10 p. 4
+"I Want Jesus to Walk with Me" (Pss, John)
V-7 p. 50/54
V-8 p. 187
+"I Will Fear No More" (Pss, John)
V-9 p. 42
"Psalms, Hymns and Spiritual Songs" (Eph)
V-3 (5) p. 3
+"Redeeming Grace" (John)
V-4 p. 47
+"Still Rolling Stones" (John)
V-9 p. 104
"Savior, Like a Shepherd Lead Us" (Pss)
William Bradley Roberts; AEC-1 p. 54
Unison, keyboard, opt. C-inst. (https://bit.ly/AEC-1-54)
+*"Nada me falta"* (Pss)
Mark Sedio; Augsburg 9781506495309
SATB, organ, opt. perc. (https://bit.ly/Aug-95309)

+Hymn Anthem

"The King of Love My Shepherd Is" (Pss)
CG64, E645/646, EL502, G802, GR90, N248, P171, SH359, UM138 (PD), VU273
Suggested Harmonizations:
Alternate Harmonization #1: S-1, #299 or another harmonization.
Alternate Harmonization #2: S-1, #298 or another harmonization that includes a descant that can be played on trumpet.
Introduction: Keyboard (organ) plays last four measures of harmonization #1. *Mezzo forte.*
Stanza 1: All voices, unison. Keyboard plays hymnal setting. *Mezzo forte.*
Stanza 2: Soloist, accompanied by keyboard playing hymnal setting.
Stanza 3: All voices in unison, accompanied by harmonization #2.
Interlude: Last four measures of harmonization #1, *forte.*
Stanza 6: All voices, unison. Keyboard plays harmonization #1. *Forte,* with breadth and conviction.

Other Suggestions

Visuals:
O Oil/horn, crown, heifer, washing hands, seven sons
P Shepherd/sheep, pasture, water, path, dark valley, rod/ staff, banquet, oil, overflowing cup, house of God
E Dark/light, children, ministry, waking, Christ
G Mud, dark glasses, day/night, light/dark, water
Introit: C593, GR332, N774, UM473 (PD), VU662. "Lead Me, Lord" (Pss)
Invocation: WSL22. "From Bethlehem to Nazareth" (John, Lent)
Bilingual Sung Response: SH294/613. *"El Señor es mi pastor"* ("The Lord is My Shepherd") (Pss)
Canticle: UM137 (Pss)
Prayer: WSL17. "A wilderness beckons" (Pss, Lent)
Prayer: UM489. For God's Gifts (Eph)
Prayer: C81. Knee-bowed and Body-Bent (Pss, John)
Litany: N880. A Litany of Darkness and Light (Eph)
Benediction: WSL18. "May the blessing of God" (John)
Theme Ideas: Call of God, God: Shepherd, Healing, Light, Vision

Notes

NRSVue

Ezekiel 37:1-14

1The hand of the Lord came upon me, and he brought me out by the spirit of the Lord and set me down in the middle of a valley; it was full of bones. 2He led me all around them; there were very many lying in the valley, and they were very dry. 3He said to me, "Mortal, can these bones live?" I answered, "O Lord God, you know." 4Then he said to me, "Prophesy to these bones and say to them: O dry bones, hear the word of the Lord. 5Thus says the Lord God to these bones: I will cause breath to enter you, and you shall live. 6I will lay sinews on you and will cause flesh to come upon you and cover you with skin and put breath in you, and you shall live, and you shall know that I am the Lord."

7So I prophesied as I had been commanded, and as I prophesied, suddenly there was a noise, a rattling, and the bones came together, bone to its bone. 8I looked, and there were sinews on them, and flesh had come upon them, and skin had covered them, but there was no breath in them. 9Then he said to me, "Prophesy to the breath, prophesy, mortal, and say to the breath: Thus says the Lord God: Come from the four winds, O breath, and breathe upon these slain, that they may live." 10I prophesied as he commanded me, and the breath came into them, and they lived, and stood on their feet, a vast multitude.

11Then he said to me, "Mortal, these bones are the whole house of Israel. They say, 'Our bones are dried up, and our hope is lost; we are cut off completely.' 12Therefore prophesy and say to them: Thus says the Lord God: I am going to open your graves and bring you up from your graves, O my people, and I will bring you back to the land of Israel. 13And you shall know that I am the Lord when I open your graves and bring you up from your graves, O my people. 14I will put my spirit within you, and you shall live, and I will place you on your own soil; then you shall know that I, the Lord, have spoken and will act, says the Lord."

Psalm 130 (G424/791, N709, P240, SH573, UM848)

1Out of the depths I cry to you, O Lord. / 2Lord, hear my voice! / Let your ears be attentive / to the voice of my supplications! / 3If you, O Lord, should mark iniquities, / Lord, who could stand? / 4But there is forgiveness with you, / so that you may be revered. / 5I wait for the Lord; my soul waits, / and in his word I hope; / 6my soul waits for the Lord / more than those who watch for the morning, / more than those who watch for the morning. / 7O Israel, hope in the Lord! / For with the Lord there is steadfast love, / and with him is great power to redeem. / 8It is he who will redeem Israel / from all its iniquities.

Romans 8:6-11

6To set the mind on the flesh is death, but to set the mind on the Spirit is life and peace. 7For this reason the mind that is set on the flesh is hostile to God; it does not submit to God's law—indeed, it cannot, 8and those who are in the flesh cannot please God.

9But you are not in the flesh; you are in the Spirit, since the Spirit of God dwells in you. Anyone who does not have the Spirit of Christ does not belong to him. 10But if Christ is in you, then the body is dead because of sin, but the Spirit is life because of righteousness. 11If the Spirit of him who raised Jesus from the dead dwells in you, he who raised Christ Jesus from the dead will give life to your mortal bodies also through his Spirit that dwells in you.

John 11:1-45

1Now a certain man was ill, Lazarus of Bethany, the village of Mary and her sister Martha. 2Mary was the one who anointed the Lord with perfume and wiped his feet with her hair; her brother Lazarus was ill. 3So the sisters sent a message to Jesus, "Lord, he whom you love is ill." 4But when Jesus heard it, he said, "This illness does not lead to death; rather, it is for God's glory, so that

CEB

Ezekiel 37:1-14

1The Lord's power overcame me, and while I was in the Lord's spirit, he led me out and set me down in the middle of a certain valley. It was full of bones. 2He led me through them all around, and I saw that there were a great many of them on the valley floor, and they were very dry.

3He asked me, "Human one, can these bones live again?"

I said, "Lord God, only you know."

4He said to me, "Prophesy over these bones, and say to them, Dry bones, hear the Lord's word! 5The Lord God proclaims to these bones: I am about to put breath in you, and you will live again. 6I will put sinews on you, place flesh on you, and cover you with skin. When I put breath in you, and you come to life, you will know that I am the Lord."

7I prophesied just as I was commanded. There was a great noise as I was prophesying, then a great quaking, and the bones came together, bone by bone. 8When I looked, suddenly there were sinews on them. The flesh appeared, and then they were covered over with skin. But there was still no breath in them.

9He said to me, "Prophesy to the breath; prophesy, human one! Say to the breath, The Lord God proclaims: Come from the four winds, breath! Breathe into these dead bodies and let them live."

10I prophesied just as he commanded me. When the breath entered them, they came to life and stood on their feet, an extraordinarily large company.

11He said to me, "Human one, these bones are the entire house of Israel. They say, 'Our bones are dried up, and our hope has perished. We are completely finished.' 12So now, prophesy and say to them, The Lord God proclaims: I'm opening your graves! I will raise you up from your graves, my people, and I will bring you to Israel's fertile land. 13You will know that I am the Lord, when I open your graves and raise you up from your graves, my people. 14I will put my breath in you, and you will live. I will plant you on your fertile land, and you will know that I am the Lord. I've spoken, and I will do it. This is what the Lord says."

Psalm 130 (G424/791, N709, P240, SH573, UM848)

1I cry out to you from the depths, Lord— / 2my Lord, listen to my voice! / Let your ears pay close attention to my request for mercy! / 3If you kept track of sins, Lord— / my Lord, who would stand a chance? / 4But forgiveness is with you— / that's why you are honored. / 5I hope, Lord. / My whole being hopes, / and I wait for God's promise. / 6My whole being waits for my Lord— / more than the night watch waits for morning; / yes, more than the night watch waits for morning! / 7Israel, wait for the Lord! / Because faithful love is with the Lord; / because great redemption is with our God! / 8He is the one who will redeem Israel / from all its sin.

Romans 8:6-11

6The attitude that comes from selfishness leads to death, but the attitude that comes from the Spirit leads to life and peace. 7So the attitude that comes from selfishness is hostile to God. It doesn't submit to God's Law, because it can't. 8People who are self-centered aren't able to please God.

9But you aren't self-centered. Instead you are in the Spirit, if in fact God's Spirit lives in you. If anyone doesn't have the Spirit of Christ, they don't belong to him. 10If Christ is in you, the Spirit is your life because of God's righteousness, but the body is dead because of sin. 11If the Spirit of the one who raised Jesus from the dead lives in you, the one who raised Christ from the dead will give life to your human bodies also, through his Spirit that lives in you.

John 11:1-45

1A certain man, Lazarus, was ill. He was from Bethany, the village of Mary and her sister Martha. (2This was the Mary who anointed the Lord with fragrant oil and wiped his feet with her hair. Her brother Lazarus was ill.) 3So the sisters sent word to Jesus, saying, "Lord, the one whom you love is ill."

NRSVue

John 11:1-45 (continued)

the Son of God may be glorified through it." 5Accordingly, though Jesus loved Martha and her sister and Lazarus, 6after having heard that Lazarus was ill, he stayed two days longer in the place where he was.

7Then after this he said to the disciples, "Let us go to Judea again." 8The disciples said to him, "Rabbi, the Jews were just now trying to stone you, and are you going there again?" 9Jesus answered, "Are there not twelve hours of daylight? Those who walk during the day do not stumble because they see the light of this world. 10But those who walk at night stumble because the light is not in them." 11After saying this, he told them, "Our friend Lazarus has fallen asleep, but I am going there to awaken him." 12The disciples said to him, "Lord, if he has fallen asleep, he will be all right." 13Jesus, however, had been speaking about his death, but they thought that he was referring merely to sleep. 14Then Jesus told them plainly, "Lazarus is dead. 15For your sake I am glad I was not there, so that you may believe. But let us go to him." 16Thomas, who was called the Twin, said to his fellow disciples, "Let us also go, that we may die with him."

17When Jesus arrived, he found that Lazarus had already been in the tomb four days. 18Now Bethany was near Jerusalem, some two miles away, 19and many of the Jews had come to Martha and Mary to console them about their brother. 20When Martha heard that Jesus was coming, she went and met him, while Mary stayed at home. 21Martha said to Jesus, "Lord, if you had been here, my brother would not have died. 22But even now I know that God will give you whatever you ask of him." 23Jesus said to her, "Your brother will rise again." 24Martha said to him, "I know that he will rise again in the resurrection on the last day." 25Jesus said to her, "I am the resurrection and the life. Those who believe in me, even though they die, will live, 26and everyone who lives and believes in me will never die. Do you believe this?" 27She said to him, "Yes, Lord, I believe that you are the Messiah, the Son of God, the one coming into the world."

28When she had said this, she went back and called her sister Mary and told her privately, "The Teacher is here and is calling for you." 29And when she heard it, she got up quickly and went to him. 30Now Jesus had not yet come to the village but was still at the place where Martha had met him. 31The Jews who were with her in the house consoling her saw Mary get up quickly and go out. They followed her because they thought that she was going to the tomb to weep there. 32When Mary came where Jesus was and saw him, she knelt at his feet and said to him, "Lord, if you had been here, my brother would not have died." 33When Jesus saw her weeping and the Jews who came with her also weeping, he was greatly disturbed in spirit and deeply moved. 34He said, "Where have you laid him?" They said to him, "Lord, come and see." 35Jesus began to weep. 36So the Jews said, "See how he loved him!" 37But some of them said, "Could not he who opened the eyes of the blind man have kept this man from dying?"

38Then Jesus, again greatly disturbed, came to the tomb. It was a cave, and a stone was lying against it. 39Jesus said, "Take away the stone." Martha, the sister of the dead man, said to him, "Lord, already there is a stench because he has been dead four days." 40Jesus said to her, "Did I not tell you that if you believed you would see the glory of God?" 41So they took away the stone. And Jesus looked upward and said, "Father, I thank you for having heard me. 42I knew that you always hear me, but I have said this for the sake of the crowd standing here, so that they may believe that you sent me." 43When he had said this, he cried with a loud voice, "Lazarus, come out!" 44The dead man came out, his hands and feet bound with strips of cloth and his face wrapped in a cloth. Jesus said to them, "Unbind him, and let him go."

45Many of the Jews therefore, who had come with Mary and had seen what Jesus did believed in him.

CEB

John 11:1-45 (continued)

4When he heard this, Jesus said, "This illness isn't fatal. It's for the glory of God so that God's Son can be glorified through it." 5Jesus loved Martha, her sister, and Lazarus. 6When he heard that Lazarus was ill, he stayed where he was. After two days, 7he said to his disciples, "Let's return to Judea again."

8The disciples replied, "Rabbi, the Jewish opposition wants to stone you, but you want to go back?"

9Jesus answered, "Aren't there twelve hours in the day? Whoever walks in the day doesn't stumble because they see the light of the world. 10But whoever walks in the night does stumble because the light isn't in them."

11He continued, "Our friend Lazarus is sleeping, but I am going in order to wake him up."

12The disciples said, "Lord, if he's sleeping, he will get well." 13They thought Jesus meant that Lazarus was in a deep sleep, but Jesus had spoken about Lazarus' death.

14Jesus told them plainly, "Lazarus has died. 15For your sakes, I'm glad I wasn't there so that you can believe. Let's go to him."

16Then Thomas (the one called Didymus) said to the other disciples, "Let us go too so that we may die with Jesus."

17When Jesus arrived, he found that Lazarus had already been in the tomb for four days. 18Bethany was a little less than two miles from Jerusalem. 19Many Jews had come to comfort Martha and Mary after their brother's death. 20When Martha heard that Jesus was coming, she went to meet him, while Mary remained in the house. 21Martha said to Jesus, "Lord, if you had been here, my brother wouldn't have died. 22Even now I know that whatever you ask God, God will give you."

23Jesus told her, "Your brother will rise again."

24Martha replied, "I know that he will rise in the resurrection on the last day."

25Jesus said to her, "I am the resurrection and the life. Whoever believes in me will live, even though they die. 26Everyone who lives and believes in me will never die. Do you believe this?"

27She replied, "Yes, Lord, I believe that you are the Christ, God's Son, the one who is coming into the world."

28After she said this, she went and spoke privately to her sister Mary, "The teacher is here and he's calling for you." 29When Mary heard this, she got up quickly and went to Jesus. 30He hadn't entered the village but was still in the place where Martha had met him. 31When the Jews who were comforting Mary in the house saw her get up quickly and leave, they followed her. They assumed she was going to mourn at the tomb.

32When Mary arrived where Jesus was and saw him, she fell at his feet and said, "Lord, if you had been here, my brother wouldn't have died."

33When Jesus saw her crying and the Jews who had come with her crying also, he was deeply disturbed and troubled. 34He asked, "Where have you laid him?"

They replied, "Lord, come and see."

35Jesus began to cry. 36The Jews said, "See how much he loved him!" 37But some of them said, "He healed the eyes of the man born blind. Couldn't he have kept Lazarus from dying?"

38Jesus was deeply disturbed again when he came to the tomb. It was a cave, and a stone covered the entrance. 39Jesus said, "Remove the stone."

Martha, the sister of the dead man, said, "Lord, the smell will be awful! He's been dead four days."

40Jesus replied, "Didn't I tell you that if you believe, you will see God's glory?" 41So they removed the stone. Jesus looked up and said, "Father, thank you for hearing me. 42I know you always hear me. I say this for the benefit of the crowd standing here so that they will believe that you sent me." 43Having said this, Jesus shouted with a loud voice, "Lazarus, come out!" 44The dead man came out, his feet bound and his hands tied, and his face covered with a cloth. Jesus said to them, "Untie him and let him go."

45Therefore, many of the Jews who came with Mary and saw what Jesus did believed in him.

Primary Hymns and Songs for the Day

"Lord of the Dance" 78529 (John, Lent) (O)
G157, P302, UM261, VU352
"Now the Green Blade Riseth" 1476522 (Ezek, John)
C230, E204, EL379, G247, N238, SH187, UM311, VU186
"This Is a Day of New Beginnings" 231043 (Ezek, John, Comm.)
C518, N417, UM383
H-3 Chr-196
"Spirit of the Living God" (Rom, Comm.)
C259, CG233, G288, GR299, N283, P322, SH555, UM393, VU376, Z226, S-1 #212 Vocal desc. idea
H-3 Chr-176
S-1 #212. Vocal descant idea
"Why Has God Forsaken Me?" (Pss, John)
G809, P406, S2110, VU154
H-3 Chr-220
"Every Time I Feel the Spirit" (PD-TO) (Rom)
C592, G66, GR446, N282, P315, UM404, Z121 (PD)
"Welcome" OL-232386 (John)
WS3152 (*See also* EL641, G301)
"Let Us Build a House Where Love Can Dwell" OL-00004 (John)
EL641, G301, SH228 (*See also* WS3152)
"Somebody's Knockin' at Your Door" (PD-TO) (John)
G728, P382, SH597, WS3095 (PD-TO), Z154
"Breathe on Me, Breath of God" 99481 (Ezek) (C)
C254, CG235, E508, G286, GR304, N292, P316, SH224/273, UM420 (PD), VU382 (Fr.)

Additional Hymn Suggestions

"Let It Breathe on Me" (Ezek)
C260, N288, UM503, Z224 (PD)
"Hope of the World" 643002 (Ezek, John)
C538, E472, G734, N46, P360, UM178, VU215
"The Day of Resurrection" 197417 (Ezek, John)
C228, CG214, E210, EL361, G233, GR254, N245, P118, SH186, UM303 (PD), VU164
"Come, Ye Faithful, Raise the Strain" 355929 (Ezek, John)
C215, CG218, E199/200, EL363, G234, GR253, N230, P115/114, UM315 (PD), VU165
+"Give Me Jesus" (PD-TO) (Pss, John)
CG546, EL770, N409, SH306, WS3140, Z165, ZS84
"To God Be the Glory" (Rom)
C72, CG349, G634, GR531, P485, SH545, UM98 (PD)
"Spirit Divine, Attend Our Prayers" (Rom)
E509, G407, P325, SH571, VU385
"Holy Spirit, Truth Divine" 300431 (Rom)
C241, EL398, GR320, N63, P321, UM465, VU368
"Christ Beside Me" (Rom)
G702, S2166
"Trust and Obey" (Rom, John)
C556, CG509, GR334, SH636, UM467 (PD)
"Spirit of God, Descend upon My Heart" 2083 (Rom, John)
C265, CG243, EL800, G688, GR294, N290, P326, SH277, UM500 (PD), VU378
"Jesús Es Mi Rey Soberano" ("O Jesus, My King and My Sovereign") (John)
C109, P157, SH211, UM180
"Heal Me, Hands of Jesus" (John)
C504, CG541, UM262, VU621
"O Christ, the Healer"1730268 (John)
C503. EL610, G793, N175, P380, UM265
"Woman in the Night" (John)
C188, G161, UM274
"He Lives" (John)
C226, CG622, GR257, SH198, UM310, Z30
"Cristo Vive" ("Christ Is Risen") (John)
N235, P109, SH184, UM313
"In the Garden" (John)
C227, CG200, GR342. N237, UM314, Z44 (PD)
"Christ Jesus Lay in Death's Strong Bonds" (John)
E186, EL370, G237, P110, UM319 (PD)
"Hymn of Promise" 126529 (John)
C638, CG545, G250, N433, UM707, VU703
"When Jesus Wept" (John)
C199, E715, G194, N192, P312, S2106, VU146
"Just a Closer Walk with Thee" (John, Lent)
C557, EL697, G835, S2158, SH584, Z46 (PD)
"Lead Me, Guide Me" (John, Lent)
C583, CG403, EL768, G740, S2214, SH582, ZS173
"Come, Join the Dance of Trinity" OL-06029 (John, Lent)
EL412, WS3017
"Jesus is a Rock in a Weary Land" (PD) (John, Lent)
EL333, WS3074 (PD)

Additional Contemporary and Modern Suggestions

"Veni Sancte Spiritus" ("Holy Spirit, Come to Us") OL-TaizeVN57 (Ezek)
EL406, G281, S2118
"Oh, I Know the Lord's Laid His Hands on Me" (PD) (Ezek, John)
S2139 (PD), Z166
"Lord, I Lift Your Name on High" 117947 (Ezek, Rom, John, Lent)
CG606, EL857, S2088, SH205
"Restored" 5894615 (Ezekiel, Pss, Rom, John, Lent)
"Let Your Spirit Rise Within Me" 15355 (Ezek, Rom, John)
+"Tremble" 7065049 (Ezek, John)
+"Nothing to Fear" 7133723 (Ezek, John)
+"Made a Way" 7071768 (Ezek, John)
+"Here Again" 7111925 (Ezek, John)
+"Do It Again" 7067555 (Ezek, John)
+"Freedom" 7078151 (Ezek, John)
+"Another in the Fire" 7124907 (Ezek, John)
+"Graves Into Gardens" 7138219 (Ezek, John)
"Hungry" ("Falling on My Knees") 2650364 (Pss)
WS3099
"Come to Me" OL-01983 (Pss, John)
WS3094
"Lord, Be Glorified" 26368 (Rom, John)
EL744, G468, S2150, SH420
"Cares Chorus" 25974 (John)
S2215
"Halle, Halle, Halleluja" 2659190 (John)
C41, CG433, EL172, G591, N236, S2026, SH694, VU958, ZS76
"Light of the World" 73342 (John)
S2204
"Siyahamba" ("We Are Marching") 1321512 (John)
C442, CG155, EL866, G853, N526, S2235-ab, SH717, VU646, ZS111
"I Believe in Jesus" 61282 (John)
"Everyday" 2798154 (John)
"Awaken" 5491647 (John)
"The Dark Is Not Your Home" 7132934 (John)
+"Chain Breaker" 7060031 (John)
+"Stand in Your Love" 7107821 (John)
+"Rise Up" ("Lazarus") 7146618 (John)
V-9, p. 97. Vocal Solo

Solo/Ensemble Suggestions

+"Famous For" ("I Believe") 7096220 (Ezek)
V-9 p. 22
"Like a Child" (Pss)
V-8 p. 356

+"Give Me Jesus" (Pss, John)
V-3 (1) p. 53
V-3 (4) p. 9
V-7 p. 24/28
V-8 p. 256
"Just a Closer Walk with Thee" (John, Lent)
V-5 (2) p. 31
V-8 p. 323
"Out of the Depths I Cry to Thee" (Pss)
arr. K. Lee Scott; AEC-1 p. 47
2-part mixed, keyboard (https://bit.ly/AEC-1)
"*Lacrymosa*: Do not stand at my grave and weep" (John)
Howard Goodall; MorningStar MSM-56-0053
Baritone solo, SATB, piano (https://bit.ly/56-0053)

+Hymn Anthem

"Jesus' Healing Hands" (John)
UM273, VU570 and UM263, VU358

This anthem uses two hymns that are both covered by CCLI and OneLicense for reproduction for your choir.

"Jesus' Hands Were Kind Hands" 2325651, OL-13235 and OL-34023

"When Jesus the Healer Passed Through Galilee" 458888, OL-44225

Introduction: Keyboard plays "Jesus' Hands . . . ," last 4 measures.

"Jesus' Hands . . . ," Stanza 1: Child or adult soloist or all voices sing melody. Keyboard plays hymnal setting.

"When Jesus the Healer . . . ," Stanza 1: Adult T/B soloist sings "Leader" parts. All other voices sing sections marked "All." Keyboard plays only when full choir sings. Lively, *mezzo forte*.

"When Jesus the Healer . . . ," Interlude: Keyboard plays full setting. Full choir sings "All" sections only.

"When Jesus the Healer . . . ," Stanzas 6-7: Soloists sing "Leader" parts, with full choir responding. Keyboard plays full setting. *Ritard* last choir response. Choir holds last note while keyboard plays measures 3-4 of "Jesus' Hands . . . ."

"Jesus' Hands . . . ," Stanza 2: Soloist (or sopranos) sing melody while choir sing other notes on "oo." *Mezzo piano. A cappella.* (Or: All sing melody, piano, accompanied by keyboard.) *Ritard* ending.

Other Suggestions

Visuals:
O Valley/bones, wilderness, multitude, open graves
P Listening, praying hands/waiting, rescue
E Coffin, Spirit symbols, Christ, open tomb
G Jar/woman, hair/feet, message, night/stumbling block, woman/Jesus/kneeling, tears, tomb, strips of cloth

Plan this service so that it moves from the quietness of the tomb and the Psalm to the joy of Lazarus' resurrection.

Introit: G249, N231, P105, stanza 1. "Because You Live" (Ezek, John)
Opening Prayer: N831 (John) or WSL52 (Ezek, Rom)
Opening Prayer: WSL52. "O God, you pour out" (Ezek, Rom)
+ Call to Prayer: G782, WS3131, stanza 1. "Hear My Prayer, O God" (Pss)
Sung Confession: WS3111. "Redemption" (Rom, Lent)
Canticle: UM516. "Canticle of Redemption" (Pss)
Prayer: UM461. For Those Who Mourn (John)
Prayer: WSL28. "Eternal God, rock and refuge" (Ezek, John)
Prayer after Communion: WSL32. "God of Life" (Lent)
Blessing: WSL178. "May the God who made heaven" (John)
Theme Ideas: Healing, Jesus: Mind of Christ, Lament, New Creation, Repentance, Resurrection

Notes

Palm Readings

NRSVue

Matthew 21:1-11

1When they had come near Jerusalem and had reached Bethphage, at the Mount of Olives, Jesus sent two disciples, 2saying to them, "Go into the village ahead of you, and immediately you will find a donkey tied and a colt with her; untie them and bring them to me. 3If anyone says anything to you, just say this, 'The Lord needs them.' And he will send them immediately." 4This took place to fulfill what had been spoken through the prophet:

5"Tell the daughter of Zion,
Look, your king is coming to you,
humble and mounted on a donkey,
and on a colt, the foal of a donkey."

6The disciples went and did as Jesus had directed them; 7they brought the donkey and the colt and put their cloaks on them, and he sat on them. 8A very large crowd spread their cloaks on the road, and others cut branches from the trees and spread them on the road. 9The crowds that went ahead of him and that followed were shouting,

"Hosanna to the Son of David!
Blessed is the one who comes in the name of the Lord!
Hosanna in the highest heaven!"

10When he entered Jerusalem, the whole city was in turmoil, asking, "Who is this?" 11The crowds were saying, "This is the prophet Jesus from Nazareth in Galilee."

Psalm 118:1-2, 19-29 (G391/681, N700, P232, UM839)

O give thanks to the LORD, for he is good;
his steadfast love endures forever!
2Let Israel say,
"His steadfast love endures forever."

. . . .

19Open to me the gates of righteousness,
that I may enter through them
and give thanks to the LORD.
20This is the gate of the LORD;
the righteous shall enter through it.
21I thank you that you have answered me
and have become my salvation.
22The stone that the builders rejected
has become the chief cornerstone.
23This is the LORD's doing;
it is marvelous in our eyes.
24This is the day that the LORD has made;
let us rejoice and be glad in it.
25Save us, we beseech you, O LORD!
O LORD, we beseech you, give us success!
26Blessed is the one who comes in the name of the LORD.
We bless you from the house of the LORD.
27The LORD is God,
and he has given us light.
Bind the festal procession with branches,
up to the horns of the altar.
28You are my God, and I will give thanks to you;
you are my God; I will extol you.
29O give thanks to the LORD, for he is good,
for his steadfast love endures forever.

Palm Readings

CEB

Matthew 21:1-11

1When they approached Jerusalem and came to Bethphage on the Mount of Olives, Jesus gave two disciples a task. 2He said to them, "Go into the village over there. As soon as you enter, you will find a donkey tied up and a colt with it. Untie them and bring them to me. 3If anybody says anything to you, say that the Lord needs it." He sent them off right away. 4Now this happened to fulfill what the prophet said, 5*Say to Daughter Zion, "Look, your king is coming to you, humble and riding on a donkey, and on a colt the donkey's offspring.*" 6The disciples went and did just as Jesus had ordered them. 7They brought the donkey and the colt and laid their clothes on them. Then he sat on them.

8Now a large crowd spread their clothes on the road. Others cut palm branches off the trees and spread them on the road. 9The crowds in front of him and behind him shouted, "*Hosanna* to the Son of David! *Blessings on the one who comes in the name of the Lord! Hosanna* in the highest!" 10And when Jesus entered Jerusalem, the whole city was stirred up. "Who is this?" they asked. 11The crowds answered, "It's the prophet Jesus from Nazareth in Galilee."

Psalm 118:1-2, 19-29 (G391/681, N700, P232, UM839)

1Give thanks to the LORD because he is good,
because his faithful love lasts forever.
2Let Israel say it:
"God's faithful love lasts forever!"

. . . .

19Open the gates of righteousness for me
so I can come in and give thanks to the LORD!
20This is the LORD's gate;
those who are righteous enter through it.
21I thank you because you answered me,
because you were my saving help.
22The stone rejected by the builders
is now the main foundation stone!
23This has happened because of the LORD;
it is astounding in our sight!
24This is the day the LORD acted;
we will rejoice and celebrate in it!
25LORD, please save us!
LORD, please let us succeed!
26The one who enters in the LORD's name is blessed;
we bless all of you
from the LORD's house.
27The LORD is God!
He has shined a light on us!
So lead the festival offering with ropes
all the way to the horns of the altar.
28You are my God—I will give thanks to you!
You are my God—I will lift you up high!
29Give thanks to the LORD because he is good,
because his faithful love lasts forever.

Passion Readings

NRSVue

Isaiah 50:4-9a

[4]The Lord God has given me
a trained tongue,
that I may know how to sustain
the weary with a word.
Morning by morning he wakens,
wakens my ear
to listen as those who are taught.
[5]The Lord God has opened my ear,
and I was not rebellious;
I did not turn backward.
[6]I gave my back to those who struck me
and my cheeks to those who pulled out the beard;
I did not hide my face
from insult and spitting.
[7]The Lord God helps me;
therefore I have not been disgraced;
therefore I have set my face like flint,
and I know that I shall not be put to shame;
[8] he who vindicates me is near.
Who will contend with me?
Let us stand in court together.
Who are my adversaries?
Let them confront me.
[9a]It is the Lord God who helps me;
who will declare me guilty?

Psalm 31:9-16 (G214/814, N641, P182, UM764)

[9]Be gracious to me, O Lord, for I am in distress;
my eye wastes away from grief,
my soul and body also.
[10]For my life is spent with sorrow
and my years with sighing;
my strength fails because of my misery,
and my bones waste away.
[11]I am the scorn of all my adversaries,
a horror to my neighbors,
an object of dread to my acquaintances;
those who see me in the street flee from me.
[12]I have passed out of mind like one who is dead;
I have become like a broken vessel.
[13]For I hear the whispering of many—
terror all around!—
as they scheme together against me,
as they plot to take my life.
[14]But I trust in you, O Lord;
I say, "You are my God."
[15]My times are in your hand;
deliver me from the hand of my enemies and persecutors.
[16]Let your face shine upon your servant;
save me in your steadfast love.

Passion Readings

CEB

Isaiah 50:4-9a

[4]The Lord God gave me an educated tongue
to know how to respond to the weary
with a word that will awaken them in the morning.
God awakens my ear in the morning to listen,
as educated people do.
[5]The Lord God opened my ear;
I didn't rebel; I didn't turn my back.
[6]Instead, I gave my body to attackers,
and my cheeks to beard pluckers.
I didn't hide my face
from insults and spitting.
[7]The Lord God will help me;
therefore, I haven't been insulted.
Therefore, I set my face like flint,
and knew I wouldn't be ashamed.
[8]The one who will declare me innocent is near.
Who will argue with me?
Let's stand up together.
Who will bring judgment against me?
Let him approach me.
[9a]Look! The Lord God will help me.
Who will condemn me?

Psalm 31:9-16 (G214/814, N641, P182, UM764)

[9]Have mercy on me, Lord, because I'm depressed.
My vision fails because of my grief,
as do my spirit and my body.
[10]My life is consumed with sadness;
my years are consumed with groaning.
Strength fails me because of my suffering;
my bones dry up.
[11]I'm a joke to all my enemies,
still worse to my neighbors.
I scare my friends,
and whoever sees me in the street runs away!
[12]I am forgotten, like I'm dead,
completely out of mind;
I am like a piece of pottery, destroyed.
[13]Yes, I've heard all the gossiping,
terror all around;
so many gang up together against me,
they plan to take my life!
[14]But me? I trust you, Lord!
I affirm, "You are my God."
[15]My future is in your hands.
Don't hand me over to my enemies,
to all who are out to get me!
[16]Shine your face on your servant;
save me by your faithful love!

NRSVue

Philippians 2:5-11

5Let the same mind be in you that was in Christ Jesus,
6 who, though he existed in the form of God,
did not regard equality with God
as something to be grasped,
7 but emptied himself,
taking the form of a slave,
assuming human likeness.
And being found in appearance as a human,
8 he humbled himself
and became obedient to the point of death—
even death on a cross.
9 Therefore God exalted him even more highly
and gave him the name
that is above every other name,
10 so that at the name given to Jesus
every knee should bend,
in heaven and on earth and under the earth,
11 and every tongue should confess
that Jesus Christ is Lord,
to the glory of God the Father.

Matthew 26:14–27:66 (or 27:11-54)

14Then one of the twelve, who was called Judas Iscariot, went
to the chief priests 15and said, "What will you give me if I betray
him to you?" They paid him thirty pieces of silver. 16And from
that moment he began to look for an opportunity to betray him.
17On the first day of Unleavened Bread the disciples came to
Jesus, saying, "Where do you want us to make the preparations
for you to eat the Passover?" 18He said, "Go into the city to a
certain man and say to him, 'The Teacher says, My time is near; I
will keep the Passover at your house with my disciples.'" 19So the
disciples did as Jesus had directed them, and they prepared the
Passover meal.
20When it was evening, he took his place with the twelve
disciples, 21and while they were eating he said, "Truly I tell you,
one of you will betray me." 22And they became greatly distressed
and began to say to him one after another, "Surely not I, Lord?"
23He answered, "The one who has dipped his hand into the bowl
with me will betray me. 24The Son of Man goes as it is written of
him, but woe to that one by whom the Son of Man is betrayed!
It would have been better for that one not to have been born."
25Judas, who betrayed him, said, "Surely not I, Rabbi?" He
replied, "You have said so."
26While they were eating, Jesus took a loaf of bread, and after
blessing it he broke it, gave it to the disciples, and said, "Take,
eat; this is my body." 27Then he took a cup, and after giving
thanks he gave it to them, saying, "Drink from it, all of you, 28for
this is my blood of the covenant, which is poured out for many
for the forgiveness of sins. 29I tell you, I will never again drink of
this fruit of the vine until that day when I drink it new with you
in my Father's kingdom."
30When they had sung the hymn, they went out to the Mount
of Olives.
31Then Jesus said to them, "You will all fall away because of me
this night, for it is written,
'I will strike the shepherd,
and the sheep of the flock will be scattered.'
32But after I am raised up, I will go ahead of you to Galilee."
33Peter said to him, "Even if all fall away because of you, I will
never fall away." 34Jesus said to him, "Truly I tell you, this very
night, before the cock crows, you will deny me three times."
35Peter said to him, "Even though I must die with you, I will not
deny you." And so said all the disciples.
36Then Jesus went with them to a place called Gethsemane,
and he said to his disciples, "Sit here while I go over there and
pray." 37He took with him Peter and the two sons of Zebedee

CEB

Philippians 2:5-11

5Adopt the attitude that was in Christ Jesus:
6 Though he was in the form of God,
he did not consider being equal with God something to
exploit.
7 But he emptied himself
by taking the form of a slave
and by becoming like human beings.
When he found himself in the form of a human,
8 he humbled himself by becoming obedient to the point of
death,
even death on a cross.
9 Therefore, God highly honored him
and gave him a name above all names,
10 so that at the name of Jesus everyone
in heaven, on earth, and under the earth might bow
11 and every tongue confess that
Jesus Christ is Lord, to the glory of God the Father.

Matthew 26:14–27:66 (or 27:11-54)

14Then one of the Twelve, who was called Judas Iscariot, went
to the chief priests 15and said, "What will you give me if I turn
Jesus over to you?" They paid him thirty pieces of silver. 16From
that time on he was looking for an opportunity to turn him in.
17On the first day of the Festival of Unleavened Bread, the disciples came to Jesus and said, "Where do you want us to prepare
for you to eat the Passover meal?"
18He replied, "Go into the city, to a certain man, and say, 'The
teacher says, "My time is near. I'm going to celebrate the Passover with my disciples at your house." ' " 19The disciples did just
as Jesus instructed them. They prepared the Passover.
20That evening he took his place at the table with the twelve
disciples. 21As they were eating he said, "I assure you that one of
you will betray me."
22Deeply saddened, each one said to him, "I'm not the one,
am I, Lord?"
23He replied, "The one who will betray me is the one who dips
his hand with me into this bowl. 24The Human One goes to his
death just as it is written about him. But how terrible it is for that
person who betrays the Human One! It would have been better
for him if he had never been born."
25Now Judas, who would betray him, replied, "It's not me, is it,
Rabbi?"
Jesus answered, "You said it."
26While they were eating, Jesus took bread, blessed it, broke
it, and gave it to the disciples and said, "Take and eat. This is my
body." 27He took a cup, gave thanks, and gave it to them, saying,
"Drink from this, all of you. 28This is my blood of the covenant,
which is poured out for many so that their sins may be forgiven.
29I tell you, I won't drink wine again until that day when I drink
it in a new way with you in my Father's kingdom." 30Then, after
singing songs of praise, they went to the Mount of Olives.
31Then Jesus said to his disciples, "Tonight you will all fall away
because of me. This is because it is written, *I will hit the shepherd,
and the sheep of the flock will go off in all directions.* 32But after I'm
raised up, I'll go before you to Galilee."
33Peter replied, "If everyone else stumbles because of you, I'll
never stumble."
34Jesus said to him, "I assure you that, before the rooster crows
tonight, you will deny me three times."
35Peter said, "Even if I must die alongside you, I won't deny
you." All the disciples said the same thing.
36Then Jesus went with his disciples to a place called Gethsemane. He said to the disciples, "Stay here while I go and pray
over there." 37When he took Peter and Zebedee's two sons, he
began to feel sad and anxious. 38Then he said to them, "I'm very
sad. It's as if I'm dying. Stay here and keep alert with me."

NRSVue

Matthew 26:14–27:66 (27:11-54) (continued)

and began to be grieved and agitated. 38Then he said to them, "My soul is deeply grieved, even to death; remain here, and stay awake with me." 39And going a little farther, he threw himself on the ground and prayed, "My Father, if it is possible, let this cup pass from me, yet not what I want but what you want." 40Then he came to the disciples and found them sleeping, and he said to Peter, "So, could you not stay awake with me one hour? 41Stay awake and pray that you may not come into the time of trial; the spirit indeed is willing, but the flesh is weak." 42Again he went away for the second time and prayed, "My Father, if this cannot pass unless I drink it, your will be done." 43Again he came and found them sleeping, for their eyes were heavy. 44So leaving them again, he went away and prayed for the third time, saying the same words. 45Then he came to the disciples and said to them, "Are you still sleeping and taking your rest? Now the hour is at hand, and the Son of Man is betrayed into the hands of sinners. 46Get up, let us be going. Look, my betrayer is at hand."

47While he was still speaking, Judas, one of the twelve, arrived; with him was a large crowd with swords and clubs, from the chief priests and the elders of the people. 48Now the betrayer had given them a sign, saying, "The one I will kiss is the man; arrest him." 49At once he came up to Jesus and said, "Greetings, Rabbi!" and kissed him. 50Jesus said to him, "Friend, do what you are here to do." Then they came and laid hands on Jesus and arrested him. 51Suddenly one of those with Jesus put his hand on his sword, drew it, and struck the slave of the high priest, cutting off his ear. 52Then Jesus said to him, "Put your sword back into its place, for all who take the sword will die by the sword. 53Do you think that I cannot appeal to my Father, and he will at once send me more than twelve legions of angels? 54But how then would the scriptures be fulfilled, which say it must happen in this way?" 55At that hour Jesus said to the crowds, "Have you come out with swords and clubs to arrest me as though I were a rebel? Day after day I sat in the temple teaching, and you did not arrest me. 56But all this has taken place, so that the scriptures of the prophets may be fulfilled." Then all the disciples deserted him and fled.

57Those who had arrested Jesus took him to Caiaphas the high priest, where the scribes and the elders had gathered. 58But Peter was following him at a distance, as far as the courtyard of the high priest, and going inside he sat with the guards in order to see how this would end. 59Now the chief priests and the whole council were looking for false testimony against Jesus so that they might put him to death, 60but they found none, though many false witnesses came forward. At last two came forward 61and said, "This fellow said, 'I am able to destroy the temple of God and to build it in three days.'" 62The high priest stood up and said, "Have you no answer? What is it that they testify against you?" 63But Jesus was silent. Then the high priest said to him, "I put you under oath before the living God, tell us if you are the Messiah, the Son of God." 64Jesus said to him, "You have said so. But I tell you,

From now on you will see the Son of Man
seated at the right hand of Power
and coming on the clouds of heaven."

65Then the high priest tore his clothes and said, "He has blasphemed! Why do we still need witnesses? You have now heard his blasphemy. 66What do you think?" They answered, "He deserves death." 67Then they spat in his face and struck him, and some slapped him, 68saying, "Prophesy to us, you Messiah! Who is it that struck you?"

CEB

Matthew 26:14–27:66 (27:11-54) (continued)

39Then he went a short distance farther and fell on his face and prayed, "My Father, if it's possible, take this cup of suffering away from me. However—not what I want but what you want."

40He came back to the disciples and found them sleeping. He said to Peter, "Couldn't you stay alert one hour with me? 41Stay alert and pray so that you won't give in to temptation. The spirit is eager, but the flesh is weak." 42A second time he went away and prayed, "My Father, if it's not possible that this cup be taken away unless I drink it, then let it be what you want."

43Again he came and found them sleeping. Their eyes were heavy with sleep. 44But he left them and again went and prayed the same words for the third time. 45Then he came to his disciples and said to them, "Will you sleep and rest all night? Look, the time has come for the Human One to be betrayed into the hands of sinners. 46Get up. Let's go. Look, here comes my betrayer."

47While Jesus was still speaking, Judas, one of the Twelve, came. With him was a large crowd carrying swords and clubs. They had been sent by the chief priests and elders of the people. 48His betrayer had given them a sign: "Arrest the man I kiss." 49Just then he came to Jesus and said, "Hello, Rabbi." Then he kissed him.

50But Jesus said to him, "Friend, do what you came to do." Then they came and grabbed Jesus and arrested him.

51One of those with Jesus reached for his sword. Striking the high priest's slave, he cut off his ear. 52Then Jesus said to him, "Put the sword back into its place. All those who use the sword will die by the sword. 53Or do you think that I'm not able to ask my Father and he will send to me more than twelve battle groups of angels right away? 54But if I did that, how would the scriptures be fulfilled that say this must happen?" 55Then Jesus said to the crowds, "Have you come with swords and clubs to arrest me, like a thief? Day after day, I sat in the temple teaching, but you didn't arrest me. 56But all this has happened so that what the prophets said in the scriptures might be fulfilled." Then all the disciples left Jesus and ran away.

57Those who arrested Jesus led him to Caiaphas the high priest. The legal experts and the elders had gathered there. 58Peter followed him from a distance until he came to the high priest's courtyard. He entered that area and sat outside with the officers to see how it would turn out.

59The chief priests and the whole council were looking for false testimony against Jesus so that they could put him to death. 60They didn't find anything they could use from the many false witnesses who were willing to come forward. But finally they found two 61who said, "This man said, 'I can destroy God's temple and rebuild it in three days.'"

62Then the high priest stood and said to Jesus, "Aren't you going to respond to the testimony these people have brought against you?"

63But Jesus was silent.

The high priest said, "By the living God, I demand that you tell us whether you are the Christ, God's Son."

64"You said it," Jesus replied. "But I say to you that from now on you'll see *the Human One sitting on the right side of the Almighty and coming on the heavenly clouds.*"

65Then the high priest tore his clothes and said, "He's insulting God! Why do we need any more witnesses? Look, you've heard his insult against God. 66What do you think?"

And they answered, "He deserves to die!" 67Then they spit in his face and beat him. They hit him 68and said, "Prophesy for us, Christ! Who hit you?"

69Meanwhile, Peter was sitting outside in the courtyard. A servant woman came and said to him, "You were also with Jesus the Galilean."

70But he denied it in front of all of them, saying, "I don't know what you are talking about."

NRSVue

Matthew 26:14–27:66 (27:11-54) (continued)

69Now Peter was sitting outside in the courtyard. A female servant came to him and said, "You also were with Jesus the Galilean." 70But he denied it before all of them, saying, "I do not know what you are talking about." 71When he went out to the porch, another female servant saw him, and she said to the bystanders, "This man was with Jesus the Nazarene." 72Again he denied it with an oath, "I do not know the man." 73After a little while the bystanders came up and said to Peter, "Certainly you are also one of them, for your accent betrays you." 74Then he began to curse, and he swore an oath, "I do not know the man!" At that moment the cock crowed. 75Then Peter remembered what Jesus had said: "Before the cock crows, you will deny me three times." And he went out and wept bitterly.

27 When morning came, all the chief priests and the elders of the people conferred together against Jesus in order to bring about his death. 2They bound him, led him away, and handed him over to Pilate the governor.

3When Judas, his betrayer, saw that Jesus was condemned, he repented and brought back the thirty pieces of silver to the chief priests and the elders. 4He said, "I have sinned by betraying innocent blood." But they said, "What is that to us? See to it yourself." 5Throwing down the pieces of silver in the temple, he departed, and he went and hanged himself. 6But the chief priests, taking the pieces of silver, said, "It is not lawful to put them into the treasury, since they are blood money." 7After conferring together, they used them to buy the potter's field as a place to bury foreigners. 8For this reason that field has been called the Field of Blood to this day. 9Then was fulfilled what had been spoken through the prophet Jeremiah, "And they took the thirty pieces of silver, the price of the one on whom a price had been set, on whom some of the people of Israel had set a price, 10and they gave them for the potter's field, as the Lord commanded me."

11Now Jesus stood before the governor, and the governor asked him, "Are you the King of the Jews?" Jesus said, "You say so." 12But when he was accused by the chief priests and elders, he did not answer. 13Then Pilate said to him, "Do you not hear how many accusations they make against you?" 14But he gave him no answer, not even to a single charge, so that the governor was greatly amazed.

15Now at the festival the governor was accustomed to release a prisoner for the crowd, anyone whom they wanted. 16At that time they had a notorious prisoner, called Jesus Barabbas. 17So after they had gathered, Pilate said to them, "Whom do you want me to release for you, Jesus Barabbas or Jesus who is called the Messiah?" 18For he realized that it was out of jealousy that they had handed him over. 19While he was sitting on the judgment seat, his wife sent word to him, "Have nothing to do with that innocent man, for today I have suffered a great deal because of a dream about him." 20Now the chief priests and the elders persuaded the crowds to ask for Barabbas and to have Jesus killed. 21The governor again said to them, "Which of the two do you want me to release for you?" And they said, "Barabbas." 22Pilate said to them, "Then what should I do with Jesus who is called the Messiah?" All of them said, "Let him be crucified!" 23Then he asked, "Why, what evil has he done?" But they shouted all the more, "Let him be crucified!"

24So when Pilate saw that he could do nothing but rather that a riot was beginning, he took some water and washed his hands before the crowd, saying, "I am innocent of this man's blood; see to it yourselves." 25Then the people as a whole answered, "His blood be on us and on our children!" 26So he released Barabbas for them, and after flogging Jesus he handed him over to be crucified.

CEB

Matthew 26:14–27:66 (27:11-54) (continued)

71When he went over to the gate, another woman saw him and said to those who were there, "This man was with Jesus, the man from Nazareth."

72With a solemn pledge, he denied it again, saying, "I don't know the man."

73A short time later those standing there came and said to Peter, "You must be one of them. The way you talk gives you away."

74Then he cursed and swore, "I don't know the man!" At that very moment the rooster crowed. 75Peter remembered Jesus' words, "Before the rooster crows you will deny me three times." And Peter went out and cried uncontrollably.

27 Early in the morning all the chief priests and the elders of the people reached the decision to have Jesus put to death. They bound him, led him away, and turned him over to Pilate the governor.

3When Judas, who betrayed Jesus, saw that Jesus was condemned to die, he felt deep regret. He returned the thirty pieces of silver to the chief priests and elders, and 4said, "I did wrong because I betrayed an innocent man."

But they said, "What is that to us? That's your problem." 5Judas threw the silver pieces into the temple and left. Then he went and hanged himself.

6The chief priests picked up the silver pieces and said, "According to the Law it's not right to put this money in the treasury. Since it was used to pay for someone's life, it's unclean." 7So they decided to use it to buy the potter's field where strangers could be buried. 8That's why that field is called "Field of Blood" to this very day. 9This fulfilled the words of Jeremiah the prophet: *And I took the thirty pieces of silver, the price for the one whose price had been set by some of the Israelites,* 10*and I gave them for the potter's field, as the Lord commanded me.*

11Jesus was brought before the governor. The governor said, "Are you the king of the Jews?"

Jesus replied, "That's what you say." 12But he didn't answer when the chief priests and elders accused him.

13Then Pilate said, "Don't you hear the testimony they bring against you?" 14But he didn't answer, not even a single word. So the governor was greatly amazed.

15It was customary during the festival for the governor to release to the crowd one prisoner, whomever they might choose. 16At that time there was a well-known prisoner named Jesus Barabbas. 17When the crowd had come together, Pilate asked them, "Whom would you like me to release to you, Jesus Barabbas or Jesus who is called Christ?" 18He knew that the leaders of the people had handed him over because of jealousy.

19While he was serving as judge, his wife sent this message to him, "Leave that righteous man alone. I've suffered much today in a dream because of him."

20But the chief priests and the elders persuaded the crowds to ask for Barabbas and kill Jesus. 21The governor said, "Which of the two do you want me to release to you?"

"Barabbas," they replied.

22Pilate said, "Then what should I do with Jesus who is called Christ?"

They all said, "Crucify him!"

23But he said, "Why? What wrong has he done?"

They shouted even louder, "Crucify him!"

24Pilate saw that he was getting nowhere and that a riot was starting. So he took water and washed his hands in front of the crowd. "I'm innocent of this man's blood," he said. "It's your problem."

25All the people replied, "Let his blood be on us and on our children." 26Then he released Barabbas to them. He had Jesus whipped, then handed him over to be crucified.

27The governor's soldiers took Jesus into the governor's house, and they gathered the whole company of soldiers around him.

NRSVue

Matthew 26:14–27:66 (27:11-54) (continued)

27 Then the soldiers of the governor took Jesus into the governor's headquarters, and they gathered the whole cohort around him. 28 They stripped him and put a scarlet robe on him, 29 and after twisting some thorns into a crown they put it on his head. They put a reed in his right hand and knelt before him and mocked him, saying, "Hail, King of the Jews!" 30 They spat on him and took the reed and struck him on the head. 31 After mocking him, they stripped him of the robe and put his own clothes on him. Then they led him away to crucify him.

32 As they went out, they came upon a man from Cyrene named Simon; they compelled this man to carry his cross. 33 And when they came to a place called Golgotha (which means Place of a Skull), 34 they offered him wine to drink, mixed with gall, but when he tasted it, he would not drink it. 35 And when they had crucified him, they divided his clothes among themselves by casting lots; 36 then they sat down there and kept watch over him. 37 Over his head they put the charge against him, which read, "This is Jesus, the King of the Jews."

38 Then two rebels were crucified with him, one on his right and one on his left. 39 Those who passed by derided him, shaking their heads 40 and saying, "You who would destroy the temple and build it in three days, save yourself! If you are the Son of God, come down from the cross." 41 In the same way the chief priests also, along with the scribes and elders, were mocking him, saying, 42 "He saved others; he cannot save himself. He is the King of Israel; let him come down from the cross now, and we will believe in him. 43 He trusts in God; let God deliver him now, if he wants to, for he said, 'I am God's Son.'" 44 The rebels who were crucified with him also taunted him in the same way.

45 From noon on, darkness came over the whole land until three in the afternoon. 46 And about three o'clock Jesus cried with a loud voice, "Eli, Eli, lema sabachthani?" that is, "My God, my God, why have you forsaken me?" 47 When some of the bystanders heard it, they said, "This man is calling for Elijah." 48 At once one of them ran and got a sponge, filled it with sour wine, put it on a stick, and gave it to him to drink. 49 But the others said, "Wait, let us see whether Elijah will come to save him." 50 Then Jesus cried again with a loud voice and breathed his last. 51 At that moment the curtain of the temple was torn in two, from top to bottom. The earth shook, and the rocks were split. 52 The tombs also were opened, and many bodies of the saints who had fallen asleep were raised. 53 After his resurrection they came out of the tombs and entered the holy city and appeared to many. 54 Now when the centurion and those with him, who were keeping watch over Jesus, saw the earthquake and what took place, they were terrified and said, "Truly this man was God's Son!"

55 Many women were also there, looking on from a distance; they had followed Jesus from Galilee, ministering to him. 56 Among them were Mary Magdalene, and Mary the mother of James and Joseph, and the mother of the sons of Zebedee.

57 When it was evening, there came a rich man from Arimathea named Joseph, who also was himself a disciple of Jesus. 58 He went to Pilate and asked for the body of Jesus; then Pilate ordered it to be given to him. 59 So Joseph took the body and wrapped it in a clean linen cloth 60 and laid it in his new tomb, which he had hewn in the rock. He then rolled a great stone to the door of the tomb and went away. 61 Mary Magdalene and the other Mary were there, sitting opposite the tomb.

62 The next day, that is, after the day of Preparation, the chief priests and the Pharisees gathered before Pilate 63 and said, "Sir, we remember what that impostor said while he was still alive, 'After three days I will rise again.' 64 Therefore command the tomb to be made secure until the third day; otherwise, his disciples may go and steal him away and tell the people, 'He has been raised from the dead,' and the last deception would be worse than the first." 65 Pilate said to them, "You have a guard of soldiers; go, make it as secure as you can." 66 So they went with the guard and made the tomb secure by sealing the stone.

CEB

Matthew 26:14–27:66 (27:11-54) (continued)

28 They stripped him and put a red military coat on him. 29 They twisted together a crown of thorns and put it on his head. They put a stick in his right hand. Then they bowed down in front of him and mocked him, saying, "Hey! King of the Jews!" 30 After they spit on him, they took the stick and struck his head again and again. 31 When they finished mocking him, they stripped him of the military coat and put his own clothes back on him. They led him away to crucify him.

32 As they were going out, they found Simon, a man from Cyrene. They forced him to carry his cross. 33 When they came to a place called Golgotha, which means Skull Place, 34 they gave Jesus wine mixed with vinegar to drink. But after tasting it, he didn't want to drink it. 35 After they crucified him, they divided up his clothes among them by drawing lots. 36 They sat there, guarding him. 37 They placed above his head the charge against him. It read, "This is Jesus, the king of the Jews." 38 They crucified with him two outlaws, one on his right side and one on his left.

39 Those who were walking by insulted Jesus, shaking their heads 40 and saying, "So you were going to destroy the temple and rebuild it in three days, were you? Save yourself! If you are God's Son, come down from the cross."

41 In the same way, the chief priests, along with the legal experts and the elders, were making fun of him, saying, 42 "He saved others, but he can't save himself. He's the king of Israel, so let him come down from the cross now. Then we'll believe in him. 43 He trusts in God, so let God deliver him now if he wants to. He said, 'I'm God's Son.'" 44 The outlaws who were crucified with him insulted him in the same way.

45 From noon until three in the afternoon the whole earth was dark. 46 At about three Jesus cried out with a loud shout, *"Eli, Eli, lama sabachthani,"* which means, "My God, my God, why have you left me?"

47 After hearing him, some standing there said, "He's calling Elijah." 48 One of them ran over, took a sponge full of vinegar, and put it on a pole. He offered it to Jesus to drink.

49 But the rest of them said, "Let's see if Elijah will come and save him."

50 Again Jesus cried out with a loud shout. Then he died.

51 Look, the curtain of the sanctuary was torn in two from top to bottom. The earth shook, the rocks split, 52 and the bodies of many holy people who had died were raised. 53 After Jesus' resurrection they came out of their graves and went into the holy city where they appeared to many people. 54 When the centurion and those with him who were guarding Jesus saw the earthquake and what had just happened, they were filled with awe and said, "This was certainly God's Son."

55 Many women were watching from a distance. They had followed Jesus from Galilee to serve him. 56 Among them were Mary Magdalene, Mary the mother of James and Joseph, and the mother of Zebedee's sons.

57 That evening a man named Joseph came. He was a rich man from Arimathea who had become a disciple of Jesus. 58 He came to Pilate and asked for Jesus' body. Pilate gave him permission to take it. 59 Joseph took the body, wrapped it in a clean linen cloth, 60 and laid it in his own new tomb, which he had carved out of the rock. After he rolled a large stone at the door of the tomb, he went away. 61 Mary Magdalene and the other Mary were there, sitting in front of the tomb.

62 The next day, which was the day after Preparation Day, the chief priests and the Pharisees gathered before Pilate. 63 They said, "Sir, we remember that while that deceiver was still alive he said, 'After three days I will arise.' 64 Therefore, order the grave to be sealed until the third day. Otherwise, his disciples may come and steal the body and tell the people, 'He's been raised from the dead.' This last deception will be worse than the first."

65 Pilate replied, "You have soldiers for guard duty. Go and make it as secure as you know how." 66 Then they went and secured the tomb by sealing the stone and posting the guard.

Primary Hymns and Songs for the Day

"Hosanna, Loud Hosanna" 7101236 (Palms Gospel) (O)
C G172, G197, GR227, N213, P89, SH146, UM278 (PD), VU123
H-3 Hbl-16, 22, 68; Chr-101; Desc-37
S-1 #114. Descant
#115. Harmonization
"Tell Me the Stories of Jesus" 2627445 (Palms Gospel)
C190, GR159, UM277 (PD), VU357
"Mantos y Palmas" ("Filled with Excitement") (Palms Gospel)
G199, N214, SH144, UM279
S-2 #90. Performance note
#89. Harm.
"Lamb of God" 16787 (Passion Gospel)
EL336, G518, S2113, ZS74
"Nohu pū" ("Stay with Me") OL-03065 (Passion Gospel)
EL348, G204, S2198, SH157
"O Sacred Head, Now Wounded" 4224059 (Passion)
C202, CG191, E168/169, EL351/352, G221/117, GR245, N226, P98, SH168, UM286, VU145 (Fr.)
H-3 Hbl-82; Chr-148; Desc-86; Org-111
"Lord Whose Love Through Humble Service" (C) (Passion)
C461, CG650, E610, EL712, GR454, P427, SH239, UM581

Additional Hymn Suggestions

"All Glory, Laud, and Honor" 29509 (Palms Gospel) (O)
C192, CG175, E154/ E155, EL344, G196, GR228, N216/ N217, P88, SH143, UM280 (PD), VU122
"Ride On! Ride On in Majesty!" 7005466 (Palms Gospel)
C191, EL346, G198, GR229, N215, P90/91, VU127
"Santo" ("Holy") (Palms Gospel)
EL762, G594, SH39, S2019
+"Thank You, Lord" 865000 (Ps 118)
C531, SH496, UM84, Z228
+"This Is the Day" 32754 (Ps 118)
C286, N84, SH379, UM657, VU412
"Rejoice, Ye Pure in Heart" (Phil, Palms)
C15, CG312, E556/557, EL873/874, G804, GR62, N55/71, P145/146, UM160/161
"All Praise to Thee, for Thou, O King Divine" (Phil)
CG352, E477, GR281, UM166, VU327
"Thou Didst Leave Thy Throne" (Phil, Passion)
CG165, GR202, S2100, SH86
"Ah, Holy Jesus" 749188 (Passion Gospel)
C210, E158, EL349, G218, GR235, N218, P93, UM289 (PD), VU138
+"Beneath the Cross of Jesus" (Passion, Holy Week)
C197, CG184, E498, EL338, G216, GR248, N190, P92, SH166, UM297 (PD), VU135
+"Jesus, Keep Me Near the Cross" (Passion, Holy Week)
C587, CG642, EL335, GR241, N197, UM301 (PD), VU142, Z19
"My Song Is Love Unknown" 2399704 (Palms/Passion)
E458, EL343, G209, N222, P76, S2083, VU143
"An Upper Room Did Our Lord Prepare" (Passion Gospel)
C385, G202, P94, VU130
+"In Remembrance of Me" (Passion Gospel, Comm.)
C403, CG462, G521, S2254, SH667, ZS203
+"Broken for Me" (Passion Gospel, Comm.)
S2263, ZS199
+"Jesus is a Rock in a Weary Land" (PD) (Passion)
EL333, WS3074 (PD)
+"Jesus, You Are the New Day" OL-13732 (Passion)
WS3143

Additional Contemporary and Modern Suggestions

"All Hail King Jesus" 12877 (Palms Gospel)
S2069, ZS53
"Make Way" 121074 (Palms Gospel)
WS3044
"Hosanna" 4785835 (Palms Gospel, Ps 118)
SH361, WS3188
+"Hosanna" (Palms Gospel, Ps 118) 66050
"Hosanna" (Palms Gospel, Ps 118)
WS3079
"Alleluia" OL-81263 (Ps 118)
EL174, G587, S2043
"I Will Enter His Gates" 1493 (Ps 118)
S2270
+"You Are Good" 3383788 (Ps 118)
SH455, WS3014
"Forever" 3148428 (Ps 118)
CG53, WS3023
"Hallelujah" ("Your Love Is Amazing") 3091812 (Pss)
WS3027
+"Goodness of God" 7117726 (Ps 118)
+"Today Is the Day" 5200924 (Ps 118)
+"Never Runs Out" 7193998 (Ps 118)
+"Rise" 7036613 (Ps 118)
+"God, You're So Good" 7105729 (Ps 118, Lent)
+"Not in a Hurry" 7047889 (Isa)
+"Open Our Eyes, Lord" 1572 (Isa)
CG392, S2086, SH562
+"Open the Eyes of My Heart" 2298355 (Isa)
G452, SH378, WS3008
+"I Stand Amazed" 4026484 (Ps 31, Lent)
+"Beautiful Savior" 2492216 (Ps 31, Holy Week)
"He Is Lord" 1515225 (Phil)
C117, CG208, GR268, SH657, UM177, Z233
"How Majestic Is Your Name" 26007 (Phil)
C63, CG326, G613, S2023, ZS26
"Shout to the North" 1562261 (Phil)
G319, WS3042
"I Exalt You" 17803 (Phil)
"Ancient of Days" 798108 (Phil)
"Majestic" 4573308 (Phil)
+"Promises" 7149439 (Phil)
+"Won't Stop Now" 7111932 (Phil)
+"Take My Life" 1617154 (Phil)
+"Wesley Prayer" ("Fire") 7118633 (Phil)
+"At the Cross" 4591816 (Phil, Holy Week)
"Adoremus te Christe" ("We Adore You, Jesus Christ") OL-12694 (Phil, Passion Gospel, Holy Week)
WS3083
+"The Power of the Cross" 4490766 (Passion Gospel)
CG190, GR237, WS3085
"Jesus, We Crown You with Praise" 1453284 (Passion)
"Once Again" 1564362 (Passion Gospel)
"You Hear" 6005063 (Passion Gospel, Holy Week)

Solo/Ensemble Suggestions

"Ride On, Ride On in Majesty!" (Palm Sunday)
V-5 (2) p. 57
"The Shepherd Became a Lamb" (Palm/Passion)
V-10 p. 48
+"He Was Despised" from Messiah (Isa, Passion)
V-2
+"Refuge and Strength" (Ps 31)
V-3 (5) p. 14
+"In Jesus' Name" (Phil)
V-8 p. 188
+"Holy is the Lamb" (Passion Gospel)
V-5(1) p. 5

"Lamb of God" (Passion Gospel)
V-5 (2) p. 5
+"Blessed Is He" (Palms Gospel)
Dennis & Nan Allen; Celebrating Grace 622032304
Unison/2-part, piano, (https://bit.ly/CG-2304)
+"Glorious the Mystery of Christ" (Phil, Passion Gospel)
Marty Parks; Celebrating Grace 810090
SATB, piano, opt. cello (https://bit.ly/CG-090)

+Hymn Anthem

"Mantos y Palmas" ("Filled with Excitement") (Palms Gospel)
G199, N214, SH144, UM279

This exciting hymn is divided into three parts. The stanza is the first part, telling or commenting upon Jesus' entry into Jerusalem. The *estribillo* (refrain) is divided into the second and third parts. The second part ("From every corner . . .") leads into the triumphant third part ("Hosanna, hosanna to the King! . . ."). This hymn is arranged as an introit anthem, but it can be adapted and sung as an anthem later in the service. Accompany throughout with piano, guitar, maracas, and claves, allowing the instrumentalists to improvise and create their own accompaniment. Add organ in the "Hosanna!" section if desired.

Stanza 1: Children sing this stanza from the front of the worship space.

Refrain: The eight measures may be sung by a small group of S/A from the back of the worship space. They may sing in unison or in two parts, adapted from the hymnal. *Ritard* a bit before going into the final section. On "Hosanna," all sing, children in the front waving palm branches, adults in the back singing in unison or in improvised parts from the hymnal. Add organ on this section for added fullness.

Interlude: Accompaniment plays entire hymn while adults process from back and children wave palm branches. Accompaniment should be rhythmic and exciting.

Stanza 2: An adult soloist (the pastor, maybe) sings this stanza.

Refrain: Any combination of voices sing the first section of the refrain, with a slight *ritard* before the final section. Add the congregation on the "Hosanna's," especially if they have been given palm branches to wave. Repeat the "Hosanna" section at least one more time, adding a *molto ritard* on the final measure.

Other Suggestions

Visuals:

Palms Gospel	Donkey, colt/cloaks/crowd/branches
Ps	Gate, cornerstone, branches, joy
O	Jesus teaching, morning, Christ, passion, flint
Ps 31	Tears, praying/comforting hands, broken pottery
E	Manacles, wood cross, crucifix, resurrection
Passion Gospel	Thirty coins, Praying hands, sword, robe, crucifix, crown of thorns, INRI, dice/robe, tombstone

For additional Passion ideas, consult Good Friday suggestions.
Introit: WS3078. "Hosanna" OL-93800 (Palms Gospel, Ps 118)
Greeting: WSL21. "Hosanna!" (Palms Gospel, Ps 118)
Canticle: UM167. "Canticle of Christ's Obedience" (Phil)
Affirmation of Faith: WSL76 or WSL 80. "We believe" (Phil)
Prayer: UM281. Passion/Palm Sunday
Offertory Prayer: WSL141. "Holy One" (Holy Week)
+Response: G654, S2195, SH316. "In the Lord I'll Be Ever Thankful" OL-00118 (Pss)
Theme Ideas: God: Glory of God, Jesus: Crucifixion, Jesus: Mind of Christ, Lament, Praise, Thanksgiving / Gratitude

Notes

NRSVue

Exodus 12:1-4 (5-10) 11-14

The LORD said to Moses and Aaron in the land of Egypt,
2“This month shall mark for you the beginning of months; it
shall be the first month of the year for you. 3Tell the whole
congregation of Israel that on the tenth of this month they are
to take a lamb for each family, a lamb for each household. 4If a
household is too small for a whole lamb, it shall join its closest
neighbor in obtaining one; the lamb shall be divided in proportion to the number of people who eat of it. 5Your lamb shall be
without blemish, a year-old male; you may take it from the sheep
or from the goats. 6You shall keep it until the fourteenth day of
this month; then the whole assembled congregation of Israel
shall slaughter it at twilight. 7They shall take some of the blood
and put it on the two doorposts and the lintel of the houses in
which they eat it. 8They shall eat the lamb that same night; they
shall eat it roasted over the fire with unleavened bread and bitter herbs. 9Do not eat any of it raw or boiled in water but roasted
over the fire, with its head, legs, and inner organs. 10You shall let
none of it remain until the morning; anything that remains until
the morning you shall burn with fire. 11This is how you shall eat
it: your loins girded, your sandals on your feet, and your staff
in your hand, and you shall eat it hurriedly. It is the Passover
of the LORD. 12I will pass through the land of Egypt that night,
and I will strike down every firstborn in the land of Egypt, from
human to animal, and on all the gods of Egypt I will execute
judgments: I am the LORD. 13The blood shall be a sign for you
on the houses where you live: when I see the blood, I will pass
over you, and no plague shall destroy you when I strike the land
of Egypt.

14“This day shall be a day of remembrance for you. You shall
celebrate it as a festival to the LORD; throughout your generations you shall observe it as a perpetual ordinance.

Psalm 116:1-4, 12-19 (G655, N699, P228, SH344, UM837)

I love the LORD because he has heard
  my voice and my supplications.
2Because he inclined his ear to me,
  therefore I will call on him as long as I live.
3The snares of death encompassed me;
  the pangs of Sheol laid hold on me;
  I suffered distress and anguish.
4Then I called on the name of the LORD,
  “O LORD, I pray, save my life!”
. . . .
12What shall I return to the LORD
  for all his bounty to me?
13I will lift up the cup of salvation
  and call on the name of the LORD;
14I will pay my vows to the LORD
  in the presence of all his people.
15Precious in the sight of the LORD
  is the death of his faithful ones.
16O LORD, I am your servant;
  I am your servant, the child of your serving girl.
  You have loosed my bonds.
17I will offer to you a thanksgiving sacrifice
  and call on the name of the LORD.
18I will pay my vows to the LORD
  in the presence of all his people,
19in the courts of the house of the LORD,
  in your midst, O Jerusalem.
Praise the LORD!

CEB

Exodus 12:1-4 (5-10) 11-14

The LORD said to Moses and Aaron in the land of Egypt,
2“This month will be the first month; it will be the first month
of the year for you. 3Tell the whole Israelite community: On the
tenth day of this month they must take a lamb for each household, a lamb per house. 4If a household is too small for a lamb, it
should share one with a neighbor nearby. You should divide the
lamb in proportion to the number of people who will be eating
it. 5Your lamb should be a flawless year-old male. You may take it
from the sheep or from the goats. 6You should keep close watch
over it until the fourteenth day of this month. At twilight on that
day, the whole assembled Israelite community should slaughter
their lambs. 7They should take some of the blood and smear
it on the two doorposts and on the beam over the door of the
houses in which they are eating. 8That same night they should
eat the meat roasted over the fire. They should eat it along with
unleavened bread and bitter herbs. 9Don’t eat any of it raw or
boiled in water, but roasted over fire with its head, legs, and
internal organs. 10Don’t let any of it remain until morning, and
burn any of it left over in the morning. 11This is how you should
eat it. You should be dressed, with your sandals on your feet and
your walking stick in your hand. You should eat the meal in a
hurry. It is the Passover of the LORD. 12I’ll pass through the land
of Egypt that night, and I’ll strike down every oldest child in the
land of Egypt, both humans and animals. I’ll impose judgments
on all the gods of Egypt. I am the LORD. 13The blood will be your
sign on the houses where you live. Whenever I see the blood, I’ll
pass over you. No plague will destroy you when I strike the land
of Egypt.

14“This day will be a day of remembering for you. You will
observe it as a festival to the LORD. You will observe it in every
generation as a regulation for all time.

Psalm 116:1-4, 12-19 (G655, N699, P228, SH344, UM837)

I love the LORD because he hears
  my requests for mercy.
2I’ll call out to him as long as I live,
  because he listens closely to me.
3Death’s ropes bound me;
  the distress of the grave found me—
  I came face-to-face with trouble and grief.
4So I called on the LORD’s name:
  “LORD, please save me!”
. . . .
12What can I give back to the LORD
  for all the good things he has done for me?
13I’ll lift up the cup of salvation.
  I’ll call on the LORD’s name.
14I’ll keep the promises I made to the LORD
  in the presence of all God’s people.
15The death of the LORD’s faithful
  is a costly loss in his eyes.
16Oh yes, LORD, I am definitely your servant!
  I am your servant and the son of your female servant—
  you’ve freed me from my chains.
17So I’ll offer a sacrifice of thanksgiving to you,
  and I’ll call on the LORD’s name.
18I’ll keep the promises I made to the LORD
  in the presence of all God’s people,
19 in the courtyards of the LORD’s house,
    which is in the center of Jerusalem.
Praise the LORD!

NRSVue

1 Corinthians 11:23-26

23For I received from the Lord what I also handed on to you, that the Lord Jesus on the night when he was betrayed took a loaf of bread, 24and when he had given thanks, he broke it and said, "This is my body that is for you. Do this in remembrance of me." 25In the same way he took the cup also, after supper, saying, "This cup is the new covenant in my blood. Do this, as often as you drink it, in remembrance of me." 26For as often as you eat this bread and drink the cup, you proclaim the Lord's death until he comes.

John 13:1-17, 31b-35

Now before the festival of the Passover, Jesus knew that his hour had come to depart from this world and go to the Father. Having loved his own who were in the world, he loved them to the end. 2The devil had already decided that Judas son of Simon Iscariot would betray Jesus. And during supper 3Jesus, knowing that the Father had given all things into his hands and that he had come from God and was going to God, 4got up from supper, took off his outer robe, and tied a towel around himself. 5Then he poured water into a basin and began to wash the disciples' feet and to wipe them with the towel that was tied around him. 6He came to Simon Peter, who said to him, "Lord, are you going to wash my feet?" 7Jesus answered, "You do not know now what I am doing, but later you will understand." 8Peter said to him, "You will never wash my feet." Jesus answered, "Unless I wash you, you have no share with me." 9Simon Peter said to him, "Lord, not my feet only but also my hands and my head!" 10Jesus said to him, "One who has bathed does not need to wash, except for the feet, but is entirely clean. And you are clean, though not all of you." 11For he knew who was to betray him; for this reason he said, "Not all of you are clean."

12After he had washed their feet, had put on his robe, and had reclined again, he said to them, "Do you know what I have done to you? 13You call me Teacher and Lord, and you are right, for that is what I am. 14So if I, your Lord and Teacher, have washed your feet, you also ought to wash one another's feet. 15For I have set you an example, that you also should do as I have done to you. 16Very truly, I tell you, slaves are not greater than their master, nor are messengers greater than the one who sent them. 17If you know these things, you are blessed if you do them.

. . .

31b"Now the Son of Man has been glorified, and God has been glorified in him. 32If God has been glorified in him, God will also glorify him in himself and will glorify him at once. 33Little children, I am with you only a little longer. You will look for me, and as I said to the Jews so now I say to you, 'Where I am going, you cannot come.' 34I give you a new commandment, that you love one another. Just as I have loved you, you also should love one another. 35By this everyone will know that you are my disciples, if you have love for one another."

CEB

1 Corinthians 11:23-26

23I received a tradition from the Lord, which I also handed on to you: on the night on which he was betrayed, the Lord Jesus took bread. 24After giving thanks, he broke it and said, "This is my body, which is for you; do this to remember me." 25He did the same thing with the cup, after they had eaten, saying, "This cup is the new covenant in my blood. Every time you drink it, do this to remember me." 26Every time you eat this bread and drink this cup, you broadcast the death of the Lord until he comes.

John 13:1-17, 31b-35

Before the Festival of Passover, Jesus knew that his time had come to leave this world and go to the Father. Having loved his own who were in the world, he loved them fully.

2Jesus and his disciples were sharing the evening meal. The devil had already provoked Judas, Simon Iscariot's son, to betray Jesus. 3Jesus knew the Father had given everything into his hands and that he had come from God and was returning to God. 4So he got up from the table and took off his robes. Picking up a linen towel, he tied it around his waist. 5Then he poured water into a washbasin and began to wash the disciples' feet, drying them with the towel he was wearing. 6When Jesus came to Simon Peter, Peter said to him, "Lord, are you going to wash my feet?"

7Jesus replied, "You don't understand what I'm doing now, but you will understand later."

8"No!" Peter said. "You will never wash my feet!"

Jesus replied, "Unless I wash you, you won't have a place with me."

9Simon Peter said, "Lord, not only my feet but also my hands and my head!"

10Jesus responded, "Those who have bathed need only to have their feet washed, because they are completely clean. You disciples are clean, but not every one of you." 11He knew who would betray him. That's why he said, "Not every one of you is clean."

12After he washed the disciples' feet, he put on his robes and returned to his place at the table. He said to them, "Do you know what I've done for you? 13You call me 'Teacher' and 'Lord,' and you speak correctly, because I am. 14If I, your Lord and teacher, have washed your feet, you too must wash each other's feet. 15I have given you an example: Just as I have done, you also must do. 16I assure you, servants aren't greater than their master, nor are those who are sent greater than the one who sent them. 17Since you know these things, you will be happy if you do them.

. . .

31b"Now the Human One has been glorified, and God has been glorified in him. 32If God has been glorified in him, God will also glorify the Human One in himself and will glorify him immediately. 33Little children, I'm with you for a little while longer. You will look for me—but, just as I told the Jewish leaders, I also tell you now—'Where I'm going, you can't come.'

34"I give you a new commandment: Love each other. Just as I have loved you, so you also must love each other. 35This is how everyone will know that you are my disciples, when you love each other."

Primary Hymns and Songs for the Day

"What Wondrous Love Is This" 197297 (Pss, John) (O)
C200, CG171, E439, EL666, G215, GR233, N223, P85, SH177, UM292, VU147 (Fr.)
H-3 Hbl-102; Chr-212; Org-185
S-1 #347. Harm.
"In Remembrance of Me" 25156 (Pss, 1 Cor, Comm.)
C403, CG462, G521, S2254, SH667, ZS203
"Jesu, Jesu" 3049039 (John, Footwashing) (C)
S-1 #63. Vocal part
C600, CG656, E602, EL708, G203, N498, P367, SH155, UM432, VU593, S-1 #63. Vocal part

Additional Hymn Suggestions

+"Wellspring of Wisdom" (Exod)
C596, UM506, VU287
+"Here, O My Lord, I See Thee" 136265 (Exod, Comm.)
C416, CG460, E318, G517, GR411, N336, P520, UM623, VU459
"Deep in the Shadows of the Past" (Exod)
G50, N320, P330, S2246
"Saranam, Saranam" ("Refuge") (Exod, Pss)
G789, UM523
"Fill My Cup, Lord" 15946 (Pss, Comm.)
C351, UM641 *(refrain only)*, WS3093
"The Church of Christ, in Every Age" (1 Cor)
C475, EL729, G320, N306, P421, UM589, VU601
"For the Bread Which You Have Broken" (1 Cor, Comm.)
C411, E340/341, EL494, G516, P508/509, UM614/615, VU470
"For the Bread Which You Have Broken" (1 Cor, Comm.)
+"Bread of the World" (1 Cor, Comm.)
C387, E301, G499, GR412, N346, P502, UM624, VU461
+"The Bread of Life for All is Broken" (1 Cor, Comm.)
E342, N333, UM633
"Broken for Me" (1 Cor, Lent, Comm.)
S2263, ZS199
"Come, Share the Lord" (1 Cor, Comm.)
C408, CG459, G510, S2269, VU469
+"As We Gather at Your Table" (1 Cor, John, Comm.)
"Ah, Holy Jesus" 749188 (John)
C210, E158, EL349, G218, GR235, N218, P93, UM289 (PD), VU138
"Make Me a Captive, Lord" 1228206 (John)
GR587, P378, SH639, UM421
"O Master, Let Me Walk with Thee" 158243 (John)
C602, CG660, E659/660, EL818, G738, GR596, N503, P357, SH612, UM430 (PD), VU560
+"By Gracious Powers" (John)
E695/696, EL626, G818, N413, P342, UM517
"Lord God, Your Love Has Called Us Here" 1517065 (John)
EL358. P353, UM579
"Lavapés" ("The Washing of Feet") (John, Foot Washing)
SH154
"Draw Us in the Spirit's Tether" (John, Comm.)
C392, EL470, G529, N337, P504, UM632, VU479
"We Sang Our Glad Hosannas" (John, Holy Week)
S2111
"Together We Serve" (John)
G767, S2175
"Healer of Our Every Ill" OL-00115 (John)
C506, EL612, G795, S2213, SH339, VU619
"As We Gather at Your Table" (John, Comm.)
EL522, N332, S2268, SH411, VU457
"Jesus is a Rock in a Weary Land" (PD) (John, Holy Week)
EL333, WS3074 (PD)
+"Glory in the Cross" (John, Holy Week)
WS3075
+"Father, We Have Heard You Calling" (John)
WS3150

Additional Contemporary and Modern Suggestions

+"Nothing to Fear" 7133723 (Exod)
+"Freedom" 7078151 (Exod, Pss)
"I Will Call upon the Lord" 11263 (Pss)
G621, S2002
"We Bring the Sacrifice of Praise" 9990 (Pss)
S2031, ZS213
"I Love You, Lord" 25266 (Pss)
CG362, G627, S2068, SH417, ZS40
+"Fill My Cup, Lord" 15946 (Pss, Comm.)
+"Chain Breaker" 7060031 (Pss)
"I Stand Amazed" 769450 (Pss, Lent)
"I Will Not Forget You" 2694306 (Pss)
"Beautiful Savior" 2492216 (Pss, Holy Week)
"This is My Story" 7046375 (Pss, John)
"Eat This Bread" OL-00891 (1 Cor, Comm.)
C414, EL472, G527, N788, SH671, UM628, VU466
"Here Is Bread, Here Is Wine" 983717 (1 Cor, Comm.)
EL483, S2266
"Take Our Bread" (1 Cor, John, Comm.)
C413, UM640
"We Remember We Believe" 5767711 (1 Cor, John, Comm.)
"Father, I Adore You" 26557 (John)
CG4, S2038, SH587
"Make Me a Servant" 33131 (John)
CG651, S2176
"Ubi Caritas" ("Live in Charity") OL-00798 (John)
C523, EL642, G205, S2179
"The Servant Song" 72673 (John)
C490, CG289, EL659, G727, N539, S2222, SH264, VU595
"They'll Know We Are Christians" 26997 (John)
C494, CG272, G300, S2223, SH232
"Make Us One" 695737 (John)
S2224, ZS93
"Bind Us Together" 1228 (John)
S2226
"There's a Spirit of Love in This Place" OL-38821 (John)
WS3148, ZS103
"The Jesus in Me" (PD) (John)
WS3151, ZS132
+"Draw the Circle Wide" OL-117657 / OL-101422 (John)
WS3154
+"Let Justice Roll" ("Like a River") 4974842 (John)
+"Come to the Table" 7130008 (John, Comm.)
"There Will Be Bread" 4512352 (John, Comm.)
"For Us" 7119349 (John, Holy Week)

Solo/Ensemble Suggestions

+"Great Things" 7111321 (Exod, Pss)
V-9 p. 36
"In Remembrance" (John, Comm.)
V-5 (2) p. 7
"He Breaks the Bread, He Pours the Wine" (John)
V-10 p. 43
+"This Is My Commandment" (John)
V-8 p. 284
"Now The Silence" (Comm.)
C415, E333, EL460, G534, UM619, VU475

"When Twilight Comes" (John)
arr. Robert Buckley Farlee; AEC-1 p. 82
2-part mixed, piano (https://bit.ly/AEC-Twilight)
"How Beautiful" (John)
arr. Lloyd Larson; Hope C5258
SAB, keyboard (https://bit.ly/C5258)

+Hymn Anthem

"What Wondrous Love Is This" 197297 (Pss, John) (O)
C200, CG171, E439, EL666, G215, GR233, N223, P85, SH177, UM292, VU147 (Fr.)
Stanza 1: Have a soloist sing this stanza *a cappella* from the back of the worship space.
Stanza 2: All voices, unison. Add a triangle, or finger cymbals, or handbells playing the open fifth D-A in any octave, sounding on the downbeats of measures 1, 5, 8, 10, 12, 16, and after 18.
Stanza 3: All voices unison, accompanied by S-1, #347, or another harmonization.
Stanza 4: Sing in parts or unison, accompanied by hymnal setting.

Other Suggestions

Visuals:
O Goat/lamb, blood/doorposts, unleavened bread, sandals, staff, Exod. 12:11b, 14a
P Praying hands, lifted cup, death, open manacles
E Broken loaf, cup, Last Supper
G Robe/towel/water/basin, John 13:12b or 13:34ab, Last Supper, Jesus speaking, acts of love
For additional Passion ideas, consult Good Friday suggestions.
+Introit: WS3150, stanza 1. "Father, We Have Heard Your Calling" (Pss, John)
+Opening Prayer: N827 (John)
+Readings: C189 (2 Cor, John, Lent)
+Call to Prayer: EL348, G204, S2198, SH157. "Stay with Me" (Holy Thursday)
+Sung Confession: "Let Justice Roll" ("Like a River") 4974842 (John, Lent)
Prayer: UM283. Holy Thursday
+Prayer: C332. God of Wondrous Darkness (Exod)
Reading: C388. Remember Me (1 Cor)
+Response: EL152, S2275, WS3133. *"Kyrie"* (Lent, Comm.)
Offertory Prayer: WSL154. "Heavenly Father" (John)
+Call to Communion: S2265. "Time Now to Gather" (1 Cor)
Invitation to Communion: WS3152. "Welcome" (John)
Sung Communion: WS3171. "Communion Setting" (1 Cor)
Closing Prayer: WSL17. "A wilderness beckons" (Holy Week)
Blessing: WSL27. "May the Christ who walks" (John, Holy Week)
Theme Ideas: Communion, God: Providence / God Our Help, Jesus: Crucifixion, Jesus: Jesus Our Savior, Love, Servanthood / Service

Notes

NRSVue

Isaiah 52:13–53:12

13 See, my servant shall prosper;
he shall be exalted and lifted up
and shall be very high.
14 Just as there were many who were astonished at him
—so marred was his appearance, beyond human semblance,
and his form beyond that of mortals—
15 so he shall startle many nations;
kings shall shut their mouths because of him,
for that which had not been told them they shall see,
and that which they had not heard they shall contemplate.
53 Who has believed what we have heard?
And to whom has the arm of the LORD been revealed?
2 For he grew up before him like a young plant
and like a root out of dry ground;
he had no form or majesty that we should look at him,
nothing in his appearance that we should desire him.
3 He was despised and rejected by others;
a man of suffering and acquainted with infirmity,
and as one from whom others hide their faces
he was despised, and we held him of no account.
4 Surely he has borne our infirmities
and carried our diseases,
yet we accounted him stricken,
struck down by God, and afflicted.
5 But he was wounded for our transgressions,
crushed for our iniquities;
upon him was the punishment that made us whole,
and by his bruises we are healed.
6 All we like sheep have gone astray;
we have all turned to our own way,
and the LORD has laid on him
the iniquity of us all.
7 He was oppressed, and he was afflicted,
yet he did not open his mouth;
like a lamb that is led to the slaughter
and like a sheep that before its shearers is silent,
so he did not open his mouth.
8 By a perversion of justice he was taken away.
Who could have imagined his future?
For he was cut off from the land of the living,
stricken for the transgression of my people.
9 They made his grave with the wicked
and his tomb with the rich,
although he had done no violence,
and there was no deceit in his mouth.
10 Yet it was the will of the LORD to crush him with affliction.
When you make his life an offering for sin,
he shall see his offspring and shall prolong his days;
through him the will of the LORD shall prosper.
11 Out of his anguish he shall see;
he shall find satisfaction through his knowledge.
The righteous one, my servant, shall make many righteous,
and he shall bear their iniquities.
12 Therefore I will allot him a portion with the great,
and he shall divide the spoil with the strong,
because he poured out himself to death
and was numbered with the transgressors,
yet he bore the sin of many
and made intercession for the transgressors.

CEB

Isaiah 52:13–53:12

13 Look, my servant will succeed.
He will be exalted and lifted very high.
14 Just as many were appalled by you,
he too appeared disfigured, inhuman,
his appearance unlike that of mortals.
15 But he will astonish many nations.
Kings will be silenced because of him,
because they will see what they haven't seen before;
what they haven't heard before, they will ponder.
53 Who can believe what we have heard,
and for whose sake has the LORD's arm been revealed?
2 He grew up like a young plant before us,
like a root from dry ground.
He possessed no splendid form for us to see,
no desirable appearance.
3 He was despised and avoided by others;
a man who suffered, who knew sickness well.
Like someone from whom people hid their faces,
he was despised, and we didn't think about him.
4 It was certainly our sickness that he carried,
and our sufferings that he bore,
but we thought him afflicted,
struck down by God and tormented.
5 He was pierced because of our rebellions
and crushed because of our crimes.
He bore the punishment that made us whole;
by his wounds we are healed.
6 Like sheep we had all wandered away,
each going its own way,
but the LORD let fall on him all our crimes.
7 He was oppressed and tormented,
but didn't open his mouth.
Like a lamb being brought to slaughter,
like a ewe silent before her shearers,
he didn't open his mouth.
8 Due to an unjust ruling he was taken away,
and his fate—who will think about it?
He was eliminated from the land of the living,
struck dead because of my people's rebellion.
9 His grave was among the wicked,
his tomb with evildoers,
though he had done no violence,
and had spoken nothing false.
10 But the LORD wanted to crush him
and to make him suffer.
If his life is offered as restitution,
he will see his offspring; he will enjoy long life.
The LORD's plans will come to fruition through him.
11 After his deep anguish he will see light, and he will be satisfied.
Through his knowledge, the righteous one, my servant,
will make many righteous,
and will bear their guilt.
12 Therefore, I will give him a share with the great,
and he will divide the spoil with the strong,
in return for exposing his life to death
and being numbered with rebels,
though he carried the sin of many
and pleaded on behalf of those who rebelled.

NRSVue

Psalm 22 (G210/631, N632, P168, SH178, UM752)

My God, my God, why have you forsaken me?
Why are you so far from helping me, from the words of my groaning?
2 O my God, I cry by day, but you do not answer;
and by night but find no rest.
3 Yet you are holy,
enthroned on the praises of Israel.
4 In you our ancestors trusted;
they trusted, and you delivered them.
5 To you they cried and were saved;
in you they trusted and were not put to shame.
6 But I am a worm and not human,
scorned by others and despised by the people.
7 All who see me mock me;
they sneer at me; they shake their heads;
8 "Commit your cause to the LORD; let him deliver—
let him rescue the one in whom he delights!"
9 Yet it was you who took me from the womb;
you kept me safe on my mother's breast.
10 On you I was cast from my birth,
and since my mother bore me you have been my God.
11 Do not be far from me,
for trouble is near,
and there is no one to help.
12 Many bulls encircle me;
strong bulls of Bashan surround me;
13 they open wide their mouths at me,
like a ravening and roaring lion.
14 I am poured out like water,
and all my bones are out of joint;
my heart is like wax;
it is melted within my breast;
15 my mouth is dried up like a potsherd,
and my tongue sticks to my jaws;
you lay me in the dust of death.
16 For dogs are all around me;
a company of evildoers encircles me;
they bound my hands and feet.
17 I can count all my bones.
They stare and gloat over me;
18 they divide my clothes among themselves,
and for my clothing they cast lots.
19 But you, O LORD, do not be far away!
O my help, come quickly to my aid!
20 Deliver my soul from the sword,
my life from the power of the dog!
21 Save me from the mouth of the lion!
From the horns of the wild oxen you have rescued me.
22 I will tell of your name to my brothers and sisters;
in the midst of the congregation I will praise you:
23 You who fear the LORD, praise him!
All you offspring of Jacob, glorify him;
stand in awe of him, all you offspring of Israel!
24 For he did not despise or abhor
the affliction of the afflicted;
he did not hide his face from me
but heard when I cried to him.
25 From you comes my praise in the great congregation;
my vows I will pay before those who fear him.
26 The poor shall eat and be satisfied;
those who seek him shall praise the LORD.
May your hearts live forever!

CEB

Psalm 22 (G210/631, N632, P168, SH178, UM752)

My God! My God,
why have you left me all alone?
Why are you so far from saving me—
so far from my anguished groans?
2 My God, I cry out during the day,
but you don't answer;
even at nighttime I don't stop.
3 You are the holy one, enthroned.
You are Israel's praise.
4 Our ancestors trusted you—
they trusted you and you rescued them;
5 they cried out to you and they were saved;
they trusted you and they weren't ashamed.
6 But I'm just a worm, less than human;
insulted by one person, despised by another.
7 All who see me make fun of me—
they gape, shaking their heads:
8 "He committed himself to the LORD,
so let God rescue him;
let God deliver him
because God likes him so much."
9 But you are the one who pulled me from the womb,
placing me safely at my mother's breasts.
10 I was thrown on you from birth;
you've been my God
since I was in my mother's womb.
11 Please don't be far from me,
because trouble is near
and there's no one to help.
12 Many bulls surround me;
mighty bulls from Bashan encircle me.
13 They open their mouths at me
like a lion ripping and roaring!
14 I'm poured out like water.
All my bones have fallen apart.
My heart is like wax;
it melts inside me.
15 My strength is dried up
like a piece of broken pottery.
My tongue sticks to the roof of my mouth;
you've set me down in the dirt of death.
16 Dogs surround me;
a pack of evil people circle me like a lion—
oh, my poor hands and feet!
17 I can count all my bones!
Meanwhile, they just stare at me, watching me.
18 They divvy up my garments among themselves;
they cast lots for my clothes.
19 But you, LORD! Don't be far away!
You are my strength!
Come quick and help me!
20 Deliver me from the sword.
Deliver my life from the power of the dog.
21 Save me from the mouth of the lion.
From the horns of the wild oxen
you have answered me!
22 I will declare your name to my brothers and sisters;
I will praise you in the very center of the congregation!
23 All of you who revere the LORD—praise him!
All of you who are Jacob's descendants—honor him!
All of you who are all Israel's offspring—
stand in awe of him!
24 Because he didn't despise or detest
the suffering of the one who suffered—
he didn't hide his face from me.
No, he listened when I cried out to him for help.
25 I offer praise in the great congregation
because of you;
I will fulfill my promises
in the presence of those who honor God.
26 Let all those who are suffering eat and be full!
Let all who seek the LORD praise him!
I pray your hearts live forever!

NRSVue

Psalm 22 (continued)

27All the ends of the earth shall remember
and turn to the LORD,
and all the families of the nations
shall worship before him.
28For dominion belongs to the LORD,
and he rules over the nations.
29To him, indeed, shall all who sleep in the earth bow down;
before him shall bow all who go down to the dust,
and I shall live for him.
30Posterity will serve him;
future generations will be told about the Lord
31and proclaim his deliverance to a people yet unborn,
saying that he has done it.

Hebrews 10:16-25

16"This is the covenant that I will make with them
after those days, says the Lord:
I will put my laws in their hearts,
and I will write them on their minds,"
17and he adds,
"I will remember their sins and their lawless deeds no more."
18Where there is forgiveness of these, there is no longer any
offering for sin.
19Therefore, my brothers and sisters, since we have confidence to enter the sanctuary by the blood of Jesus, 20by the new
and living way that he opened for us through the curtain (that
is, through his flesh), 21and since we have a great priest over
the house of God, 22let us approach with a true heart in full
assurance of faith, with our hearts sprinkled clean from an evil
conscience and our bodies washed with pure water. 23Let us hold
fast to the confession of our hope without wavering, for he who
has promised is faithful. 24And let us consider how to provoke
one another to love and good deeds, 25not neglecting to meet
together, as is the habit of some, but encouraging one another,
and all the more as you see the Day approaching.

John 18:1–19:42

After Jesus had spoken these words, he went out with his
disciples across the Kidron Valley to a place where there was a
garden, which he and his disciples entered. 2Now Judas, who
betrayed him, also knew the place because Jesus often met there
with his disciples. 3So Judas brought a detachment of soldiers
together with police from the chief priests and the Pharisees,
and they came there with lanterns and torches and weapons.
4Then Jesus, knowing all that was to happen to him, came
forward and asked them, "Whom are you looking for?" 5They
answered, "Jesus of Nazareth." Jesus replied, "I am he." Judas,
who betrayed him, was standing with them. 6When Jesus said
to them, "I am he," they stepped back and fell to the ground.
7Again he asked them, "Whom are you looking for?" And they
said, "Jesus of Nazareth." 8Jesus answered, "I told you that I am
he. So if you are looking for me, let these people go." 9This was
to fulfill the word that he had spoken, "I did not lose a single
one of those whom you gave me." 10Then Simon Peter, who had
a sword, drew it, struck the high priest's slave, and cut off his
right ear. The slave's name was Malchus. 11Jesus said to Peter,
"Put your sword back into its sheath. Am I not to drink the cup
that the Father has given me?"
12So the soldiers, their officer, and the Jewish police arrested
Jesus and bound him. 13First they took him to Annas, who was
the father-in-law of Caiaphas, the high priest that year. 14Caia-
phas was the one who had advised the Jews that it was better to
have one person die for the people.

CEB

Psalm 22 (continued)

27Every part of the earth
will remember and come back to the LORD;
every family among all the nations will worship you.
28Because the right to rule belongs to the LORD,
he rules all nations.
29Indeed, all the earth's powerful
will worship him;
all who are descending to the dust
will kneel before him;
my being also lives for him.
30Future descendants will serve him;
generations to come will be told about my LORD.
31They will proclaim God's righteousness
to those not yet born,
telling them what God has done.

Hebrews 10:16-25

16This is the covenant that I will make with them.
After these days, says the LORD,
I will place my laws in their hearts
and write them on their minds.
17And I won't remember their sins
and their lawless behavior anymore.
18When there is forgiveness for these things, there is no longer an
offering for sin.
19Brothers and sisters, we have confidence that we can enter the
holy of holies by means of Jesus' blood, 20through a new and living
way that he opened up for us through the curtain, which is his body,
21and we have a great high priest over God's house.
22Therefore, let's draw near with a genuine heart with the certainty that our faith gives us, since our hearts are sprinkled clean
from an evil conscience and our bodies are washed with pure water.
23Let's hold on to the confession of our hope without wavering,
because the one who made the promises is reliable.
24And let us consider each other carefully for the purpose of
sparking love and good deeds. 25Don't stop meeting together with
other believers, which some people have gotten into the habit of
doing. Instead, encourage each other, especially as you see the day
drawing near.

John 18:1–19:42

After he said these things, Jesus went out with his disciples and
crossed over to the other side of the Kidron Valley. He and his
disciples entered a garden there. 2Judas, his betrayer, also knew the
place because Jesus often gathered there with his disciples. 3Judas
brought a company of soldiers and some guards from the chief
priests and Pharisees. They came there carrying lanterns, torches,
and weapons. 4Jesus knew everything that was to happen to him, so
he went out and asked, "Who are you looking for?"
5They answered, "Jesus the Nazarene."
He said to them, "I Am." (Judas, his betrayer, was standing with
them.) 6When he said, "I Am," they shrank back and fell to the
ground. 7He asked them again, "Who are you looking for?"
They said, "Jesus the Nazarene."
8Jesus answered, "I told you, 'I Am.' If you are looking for me,
then let these people go." 9This was so that the word he had spoken
might be fulfilled: "I didn't lose anyone of those whom you gave
me."
10Then Simon Peter, who had a sword, drew it and struck the high
priest's servant, cutting off his right ear. (The servant's name was
Malchus.) 11Jesus told Peter, "Put your sword away! Am I not to drink
the cup the Father has given me?" 12Then the company of soldiers,
the commander, and the guards from the Jewish leaders took Jesus
into custody. They bound him 13and led him first to Annas. He was
the father-in-law of Caiaphas, the high priest that year. (14Caiaphas
was the one who had advised the Jewish leaders that it was better for
one person to die for the people.)

NRSVue

John 18:1–19:42 (continued)

15Simon Peter and another disciple followed Jesus. Since that
disciple was known to the high priest, he went with Jesus into
the courtyard of the high priest, 16but Peter was standing outside
at the gate. So the other disciple, who was known to the high
priest, went out, spoke to the woman who guarded the gate, and
brought Peter in. 17The woman said to Peter, "You are not also
one of this man's disciples, are you?" He said, "I am not." 18Now
the slaves and the police had made a charcoal fire because it was
cold, and they were standing around it and warming themselves.
Peter also was standing with them and warming himself.

19Then the high priest questioned Jesus about his disciples
and about his teaching. 20Jesus answered, "I have spoken openly
to the world; I have always taught in synagogues and in the
temple, where all the Jews come together. I have said nothing
in secret. 21Why do you ask me? Ask those who heard what I said
to them; they know what I said." 22When he had said this, one
of the police standing nearby struck Jesus on the face, saying,
"Is that how you answer the high priest?" 23Jesus answered, "If I
have spoken wrongly, testify to the wrong. But if I have spoken
rightly, why do you strike me?" 24Then Annas sent him bound to
Caiaphas the high priest.

25Now Simon Peter was standing and warming himself. They
asked him, "You are not also one of his disciples, are you?" He
denied it and said, "I am not." 26One of the slaves of the high
priest, a relative of the man whose ear Peter had cut off, asked,
"Did I not see you in the garden with him?" 27Again Peter denied
it, and at that moment the cock crowed.

28Then they took Jesus from Caiaphas to Pilate's headquarters.
It was early in the morning. They themselves did not enter the
headquarters, so as to avoid ritual defilement and to be able to
eat the Passover. 29So Pilate went out to them and said, "What
accusation do you bring against this man?" 30They answered, "If
this man were not a criminal, we would not have handed him
over to you." 31Pilate said to them, "Take him yourselves and
judge him according to your law." The Jews replied, "We are not
permitted to put anyone to death." 32(This was to fulfill what
Jesus had said when he indicated the kind of death he was to
die.)

33Then Pilate entered the headquarters again, summoned
Jesus, and asked him, "Are you the King of the Jews?" 34Jesus
answered, "Do you ask this on your own, or did others tell you
about me?" 35Pilate replied, "I am not a Jew, am I? Your own
nation and the chief priests have handed you over to me. What
have you done?" 36Jesus answered, "My kingdom does not belong
to this world. If my kingdom belonged to this world, my followers would be fighting to keep me from being handed over to the
Jews. But as it is, my kingdom is not from here." 37Pilate asked
him, "So you are a king?" Jesus answered, "You say that I am a
king. For this I was born, and for this I came into the world, to
testify to the truth. Everyone who belongs to the truth listens to
my voice." 38Pilate asked him, "What is truth?"

After he had said this, he went out to the Jews again and told
them, "I find no case against him. 39But you have a custom that
I release someone for you at the Passover. Do you want me to
release for you the King of the Jews?" 40They shouted in reply,
"Not this man but Barabbas!" Now Barabbas was a rebel.

CEB

John 18:1–19:42 (continued)

15Simon Peter and another disciple followed Jesus. Because
this other disciple was known to the high priest, he went with
Jesus into the high priest's courtyard. 16However, Peter stood
outside near the gate. Then the other disciple (the one known
to the high priest) came out and spoke to the woman stationed
at the gate, and she brought Peter in. 17The servant woman
stationed at the gate asked Peter, "Aren't you one of this man's
disciples?"

"I'm not," he replied. 18The servants and the guards had made
a fire because it was cold. They were standing around it, warming themselves. Peter joined them there, standing by the fire
and warming himself.

19Meanwhile, the chief priest questioned Jesus about his
disciples and his teaching. 20Jesus answered, "I've spoken openly
to the world. I've always taught in synagogues and in the temple,
where all the Jews gather. I've said nothing in private. 21Why ask
me? Ask those who heard what I told them. They know what I
said."

22After Jesus spoke, one of the guards standing there slapped
Jesus in the face. "Is that how you would answer the high priest?"
he asked.

23Jesus replied, "If I speak wrongly, testify about what was
wrong. But if I speak correctly, why do you strike me?" 24Then
Annas sent him, bound, to Caiaphas the high priest.

25Meanwhile, Simon Peter was still standing with the guards,
warming himself. They asked, "Aren't you one of his disciples?"

Peter denied it, saying, "I'm not."

26A servant of the high priest, a relative of the one whose ear
Peter had cut off, said to him, "Didn't I see you in the garden
with him?" 27Peter denied it again, and immediately a rooster
crowed.

28The Jewish leaders led Jesus from Caiaphas to the Roman
governor's palace. It was early in the morning. So that they could
eat the Passover, the Jewish leaders wouldn't enter the palace;
entering the palace would have made them ritually impure.

29So Pilate went out to them and asked, "What charge do you
bring against this man?"

30They answered, "If he had done nothing wrong, we wouldn't
have handed him over to you."

31Pilate responded, "Take him yourselves and judge him
according to your Law."

The Jewish leaders replied, "The Law doesn't allow us to kill
anyone." (32This was so that Jesus' word might be fulfilled when
he indicated how he was going to die.)

33Pilate went back into the palace. He summoned Jesus and
asked, "Are you the king of the Jews?"

34Jesus answered, "Do you say this on your own or have others
spoken to you about me?"

35Pilate responded, "I'm not a Jew, am I? Your nation and its
chief priests handed you over to me. What have you done?"

36Jesus replied, "My kingdom doesn't originate from this
world. If it did, my guards would fight so that I wouldn't have
been arrested by the Jewish leaders. My kingdom isn't from
here."

37"So you are a king?" Pilate said.

Jesus answered, "You say that I am a king. I was born and
came into the world for this reason: to testify to the truth. Whoever accepts the truth listens to my voice."

38"What is truth?" Pilate asked.

After Pilate said this, he returned to the Jewish leaders and
said, "I find no grounds for any charge against him. 39You have
a custom that I release one prisoner for you at Passover. Do you
want me to release for you the king of the Jews?"

40They shouted, "Not this man! Give us Barabbas!" (Barabbas
was an outlaw.)

NRSVue

John 18:1–19:42 (continued)

19 Then Pilate took Jesus and had him flogged. 2And the
soldiers wove a crown of thorns and put it on his head, and they
dressed him in a purple robe. 3They kept coming up to him,
saying, "Hail, King of the Jews!" and striking him on the face.
4Pilate went out again and said to them, "Look, I am bringing
him out to you to let you know that I find no case against him."
5So Jesus came out wearing the crown of thorns and the purple
robe. Pilate said to them, "Behold the man!" 6When the chief
priests and the police saw him, they shouted, "Crucify him! Crucify him!" Pilate said to them, "Take him yourselves and crucify
him; I find no case against him." 7The Jews answered him, "We
have a law, and according to that law he ought to die because he
has claimed to be the Son of God."

8Now when Pilate heard this, he was more afraid than ever.
9He entered his headquarters again and asked Jesus, "Where are
you from?" But Jesus gave him no answer. 10Pilate therefore said
to him, "Do you refuse to speak to me? Do you not know that
I have power to release you and power to crucify you?" 11Jesus
answered him, "You would have no power over me unless it had
been given you from above; therefore the one who handed me
over to you is guilty of a greater sin." 12From then on Pilate tried
to release him, but the Jews cried out, "If you release this man,
you are no friend of Caesar. Everyone who claims to be a king
sets himself against Caesar."

13When Pilate heard these words, he brought Jesus outside
and sat on the judge's bench at a place called The Stone Pavement, or in Hebrew Gabbatha. 14Now it was the day of Preparation for the Passover, and it was about noon. He said to the Jews,
"Here is your King!" 15They cried out, "Away with him! Away
with him! Crucify him!" Pilate asked them, "Shall I crucify your
King?" The chief priests answered, "We have no king but Caesar." 16Then he handed him over to them to be crucified.

So they took Jesus, 17and carrying the cross by himself he went
out to what is called the Place of the Skull, which in Hebrew is
called Golgotha. 18There they crucified him and with him two
others, one on either side, with Jesus between them. 19Pilate also
had an inscription written and put on the cross. It read, "Jesus
of Nazareth, the King of the Jews." 20Many of the Jews read this
inscription because the place where Jesus was crucified was near
the city, and it was written in Hebrew, in Latin, and in Greek.
21Then the chief priests of the Jews said to Pilate, "Do not write,
'The King of the Jews,' but, 'This man said, I am King of the
Jews.' " 22Pilate answered, "What I have written I have written."
23When the soldiers had crucified Jesus, they took his clothes
and divided them into four parts, one for each soldier. They also
took his tunic; now the tunic was seamless, woven in one piece
from the top. 24So they said to one another, "Let us not tear it
but cast lots for it to see who will get it." This was to fulfill what
the scripture says,

"They divided my clothes among themselves,
and for my clothing they cast lots."

25And that is what the soldiers did.

Meanwhile, standing near the cross of Jesus were his mother,
and his mother's sister, Mary the wife of Clopas, and Mary
Magdalene. 26When Jesus saw his mother and the disciple whom
he loved standing beside her, he said to his mother, "Woman,
here is your son." 27Then he said to the disciple, "Here is your
mother." And from that hour the disciple took her into his own
home.

28After this, when Jesus knew that all was now finished, he
said (in order to fulfill the scripture), "I am thirsty." 29A jar full
of sour wine was standing there. So they put a sponge full of the
wine on a branch of hyssop and held it to his mouth. 30When
Jesus had received the wine, he said, "It is finished." Then he
bowed his head and gave up his spirit.

CEB

John 18:1–19:42 (continued)

19 Then Pilate had Jesus taken and whipped. 2The soldiers
twisted together a crown of thorns and put it on his head, and
dressed him in a purple robe. 3Over and over they went up to him
and said, "Greetings, king of the Jews!" And they slapped him in the
face.

4Pilate came out of the palace again and said to the Jewish leaders, "Look! I'm bringing him out to you to let you know that I find
no grounds for a charge against him." 5When Jesus came out, wearing the crown of thorns and the purple robe, Pilate said to them,
"Here's the man."

6When the chief priests and their deputies saw him, they shouted
out, "Crucify, crucify!"

Pilate told them, "You take him and crucify him. I don't find any
grounds for a charge against him."

7The Jewish leaders replied, "We have a Law, and according to
this Law he ought to die because he made himself out to be God's
Son."

8When Pilate heard this word, he was even more afraid. 9He went
back into the residence and spoke to Jesus, "Where are you from?"
Jesus didn't answer. 10So Pilate said, "You won't speak to me? Don't
you know that I have authority to release you and also to crucify
you?"

11Jesus replied, "You would have no authority over me if it had
not been given to you from above. That's why the one who handed
me over to you has the greater sin." 12From that moment on, Pilate
wanted to release Jesus.

However, the Jewish leaders cried out, saying, "If you release this
man, you aren't a friend of the emperor! Anyone who makes himself
out to be a king opposes the emperor!"

13When Pilate heard these words, he led Jesus out and seated
him on the judge's bench at the place called Stone Pavement (in
Aramaic, *Gabbatha*). 14It was about noon on the Preparation Day for
the Passover. Pilate said to the Jewish leaders, "Here's your king."

15The Jewish leaders cried out, "Take him away! Take him away!
Crucify him!"

Pilate responded, "What? Do you want me to crucify your king?"

"We have no king except the emperor," the chief priests
answered. 16Then Pilate handed Jesus over to be crucified.

The soldiers took Jesus prisoner. 17Carrying his cross by himself,
he went out to a place called Skull Place (in Aramaic, *Golgotha*).
18That's where they crucified him—and two others with him, one on
each side and Jesus in the middle. 19Pilate had a public notice written and posted on the cross. It read "Jesus the Nazarene, the king
of the Jews." 20Many of the Jews read this sign, for the place where
Jesus was crucified was near the city and it was written in Aramaic,
Latin, and Greek. 21Therefore, the Jewish chief priests complained
to Pilate, "Don't write, 'The king of the Jews' but 'This man said, "I
am the king of the Jews." ' "

22Pilate answered, "What I've written, I've written."

23When the soldiers crucified Jesus, they took his clothes and his
sandals, and divided them into four shares, one for each soldier. His
shirt was seamless, woven as one piece from the top to the bottom.
24They said to each other, "Let's not tear it. Let's cast lots to see who
will get it." This was to fulfill the scripture,

They divided my clothes among themselves,
and they cast lots for my clothing.

That's what the soldiers did.

25Jesus' mother and his mother's sister, Mary the wife of Clopas,
and Mary Magdalene stood near the cross. 26When Jesus saw his
mother and the disciple whom he loved standing nearby, he said
to his mother, "Woman, here is your son." 27Then he said to the
disciple, "Here is your mother." And from that time on, this disciple
took her into his home.

28After this, knowing that everything was already completed, in
order to fulfill the scripture, Jesus said, "I am thirsty." 29A jar full of
sour wine was nearby, so the soldiers soaked a sponge in it, placed
it on a hyssop branch, and held it up to his lips. 30When he had
received the sour wine, Jesus said, "It is completed." Bowing his
head, he gave up his life.

NRSVue

John 18:1–19:42 (continued)

31 Since it was the day of Preparation, the Jews did not want the bodies left on the cross during the Sabbath, especially because that Sabbath was a day of great solemnity. So they asked Pilate to have the legs of the crucified men broken and the bodies removed. 32 Then the soldiers came and broke the legs of the first and of the other who had been crucified with him. 33 But when they came to Jesus and saw that he was already dead, they did not break his legs. 34 Instead, one of the soldiers pierced his side with a spear, and at once blood and water came out. 35 (He who saw this has testified so that you also may believe. His testimony is true, and he knows that he tells the truth, so that you also may continue to believe.) 36 These things occurred so that the scripture might be fulfilled, "None of his bones shall be broken." 37 And again another passage of scripture says, "They will look on the one whom they have pierced."

38 After these things, Joseph of Arimathea, who was a disciple of Jesus, though a secret one because of his fear of the Jews, asked Pilate to let him take away the body of Jesus. Pilate gave him permission, so he came and removed his body. 39 Nicodemus, who had at first come to Jesus by night, also came, bringing a mixture of myrrh and aloes, weighing about a hundred pounds. 40 They took the body of Jesus and wrapped it with the spices in linen cloths, according to the burial custom of the Jews. 41 Now there was a garden in the place where he was crucified, and in the garden there was a new tomb in which no one had ever been laid. 42 And so, because it was the Jewish day of Preparation and the tomb was nearby, they laid Jesus there.

CEB

John 18:1–19:42 (continued)

31 It was the Preparation Day and the Jewish leaders didn't want the bodies to remain on the cross on the Sabbath, especially since that Sabbath was an important day. So they asked Pilate to have the legs of those crucified broken and the bodies taken down. 32 Therefore, the soldiers came and broke the legs of the two men who were crucified with Jesus. 33 When they came to Jesus, they saw that he was already dead so they didn't break his legs. 34 However, one of the soldiers pierced his side with a spear, and immediately blood and water came out. 35 The one who saw this has testified, and his testimony is true. He knows that he speaks the truth, and he has testified so that you also can believe. 36 These things happened to fulfill the scripture, *They won't break any of his bones.* 37 And another scripture says, *They will look at him whom they have pierced.*

38 After this Joseph of Arimathea asked Pilate if he could take away the body of Jesus. Joseph was a disciple of Jesus, but a secret one because he feared the Jewish authorities. Pilate gave him permission, so he came and took the body away. 39 Nicodemus, the one who at first had come to Jesus at night, was there too. He brought a mixture of myrrh and aloe, nearly seventy-five pounds in all. 40 Following Jewish burial customs, they took Jesus' body and wrapped it, with the spices, in linen cloths. 41 There was a garden in the place where Jesus was crucified, and in the garden was a new tomb in which no one had ever been laid. 42 Because it was the Jewish Preparation Day and the tomb was nearby, they laid Jesus in it.

Primary Hymns and Songs for the Day

"Hallelujah! What a Savior" 29530 (Isa) (O)
CG188, GR503, UM165 (PD)
H-3 Chr-134
"O Sacred Head, Now Wounded" 4224059 (John)
C202, CG191, E168/169, EL351/352, G221/117, GR245, N226, P98, SH168, UM286, VU145 (Fr.)
H-3 Hbl-82; Chr-148; Desc-86; Org-111
"Were You There" 3177994 (John)
C198, CG192, E172, EL353, G228, GR249, N229, P102, SH176, UM288 (PD-TO), VU144, Z126
H-3 Hbl-101; Chr-209
S-2 #195-196. Desc. and harm.
"When I Survey the Wondrous Cross" 27893 (John) (C)
C195, CG186, EL803, G223, GR221, N224, P101, SH163/164, UM298 (PD)
H-3 Hbl-6, 102; Chr-213; Desc-49; Org-49
S-1 #155. Descant
"When I Survey the Wondrous Cross" 721333 (John) (C)
E474, G224, P100, UM299 (PD), VU149 (Fr.)
H-3 Hbl-47; Chr-214; Desc-90; Org-127
S-1 #288. Transposition to E-flat major

Additional Hymn Suggestions

"He Never Said a Mumbalin' Word" (PD-TO) (Isa, John)
C208, EL350, G219, P95, UM291, VU141, Z101 (PD)
+"What Wondrous Love Is This" 197297 (Isa, John)
C200, CG171, E439, EL666, G215, GR233, N223, P85, SH177, UM292, VU147 (Fr.)
"Alas! and Did My Savior Bleed" 106123 (Isa, John)
CG182, EL337, G212, GR231, N200, P78, UM294 (PD)
+"Alas! and Did My Savior Bleed" 29499 (Isa, John)
C204, CG595, GR564, N199, SH172, UM359 (PD), Z8, ZS67
"Out of the Depths I Cry to You" OL-03328 (Pss)
EL600, G424, N483, P240, SH513, UM515
"Nobody Knows the Trouble I See" (Pss)
UM520, Z170 (PD)
"Why Stand So Far Away, My God?" OL-30234 (Pss, John)
C671, G786, S2180
+"And Can It Be that I Should Gain" 25280 (Heb, John)
CG605, GR569, SH540, UM363 (PD)
+"O Love, How Deep" (John)
E448/449, EL322, G618, GR95, N209, P83, SH115, UM267, VU348
"'Tis Finished! The Messiah Dies" (John)
GR246, UM282 (PD)
+"O Love Divine, What Hast Thou Done" (PD) (John)
GR244, UM287 (PD)
"Ah, Holy Jesus" 749188 (John)
C210, E158, EL349, G218, GR235, N218, P93, UM289 (PD), VU138
+"Beneath the Cross of Jesus" (John, Good Friday)
C197, CG184, E498, EL338, G216, GR248, N190, P92, SH166, UM297 (PD), VU135
+"Jesus, Keep Me Near the Cross" (John, Good Friday)
C587, CG642, EL335, GR241, N197, UM301 (PD), VU142, Z19
"Depth of Mercy" 1320726 (John)
GR234, UM355
"Depth of Mercy" 5412781 (John)
WS3097
"Must Jesus Bear the Cross Alone" (John)
CG505, GR598, UM424 (PD)
"Why Has God Forsaken Me?" (John)
G809, P406, S2110, VU154
+"Mary Had a Little Lamb" OL-88810 (Good Friday)
WS3190

Additional Contemporary and Modern Suggestions

"Our God Reigns" 8458 (Isa)
+"You Are More Than Enough " 6005063 (Isa, Good Friday)
+"Now Behold the Lamb" (Isa, Good Friday)
EL341, WS3081
"O How He Loves You and Me" 15850 (Isa, John)
CG600, S2108, SH535, ZS208
"There Is a Redeemer" 11483 (Isa, John)
+"Is He Worthy?" 7108951 (Isa, John)
+"Living Hope" 7106807 (Isa, John)
+"Better Than A Hallelujah" 5622564 (Pss, Good Friday)
CG377, G443, GR30, SH495
"Here at the Cross" 7046292 (Pss, Heb, Lent)
"You Are My King" ("Amazing Love") 2456623 (Heb)
SH539, WS3102
"Take Our Bread" (Heb, Comm.)
C413, UM640
"Before the Throne of God Above" 2306412 (Heb)
"Amazing Love" 192553 (Heb, Good Friday)
"Because of Your Love" 4662501 (Heb, Good Friday)
"I Come to the Cross" 1965249 (Heb, Good Friday)
"This is My Story" 7046375 (John, Good Friday)
"Jesus, Remember Me" OL-00122 (John, Good Friday)
C569, CG393, EL616, G227, P599, SH175, UM488, VU148
"Nohu pū" ("Stay with Me") OL-03065 (Good Friday)
EL348, G204, S2198, SH157
"Lamb of God" 16787 (Good Friday)
EL336, G518, S2113, ZS74
"The Power of the Cross" 4490766 (John, Good Friday)
CG190, GR237, WS3085
"In Christ Alone" 3350395 (John, Good Friday)
CG569, GR106, SH656, WS3105
"The Wonderful Cross" 3148435 (Good Friday)
"Above All" 2672885 (John, Good Friday)
V-3 (2), p. 17. Vocal Solo
+"At the Cross" 4591816 (John, Good Friday)
+"The Wonderful Cross" 3148435 (John, Good Friday)
+"Love Moves You" ("Love Alone") 5775514 (Good Friday)
+"You Are More Than Enough" 5951998 (Good Friday)
"Revelation Song" 4447960 (Good Friday)

Solo/Ensemble Suggestions

"He was Cut Off Out of the Land of the Living" (recitative) (Isa)
"But Thou Didst Not Leave His Soul in Hell" (aria) (John)
V-2
+"Steal Away to Heaven" (Pss, Good Friday)
V-3 (1) p. 17
+"Into the Sea" ("It's Gonna Be OK") (Pss, John)
V-9 p. 48
+"'Tis Finished! The Messiah Dies" (John, Good Friday)
V-1 p. 63
"Sing of Mary, Pure and Lowly" (John, Good Friday)
V-5 (1) p. 21
"Lamb of God" (John, Good Friday)
V-5 (2) p. 5
"Ah, Holy Jesus" (John, Good Friday)
V-6 p. 24
"He Carried My Cross" (John, Good Friday)
V-8 p. 213
+"Ten Thousand Angels" (John, Good Friday)
V-8 p. 218
"They Led Him Away" (John)
V-8 p. 245
+"Love Moved First" (Good Friday)
V-9 p. 56
"Cross of Jesus" (John)
Robert Benson; AEC-2 p. 46
Unison, keyboard (https://bit.ly/AEC-2)

"*Recordare*: Drop, drop slow tears" (John, Good Friday)
Howard Goodall; MorningStar MSM-56-0055
Soprano solo, SATB, piano (https://bit.ly/56-0055)

+Hymn Anthem
"O The Lamb" 1510220 (John)
UM300
Cello is recommended as the accompanying instrument, but its part could be played by organ, synthesizer, or even omitted.
Introduction: Cello plays melody once. Perform freely and without rhythmic restraint. Hold some notes longer, speed up others.
Setting 1: Solo, *a cappella*. Preferably a S/A with a rich vocal quality.
Setting 2: T/B sing melody. Accompany with continuous drone on cello on a low B.
Setting 3: This setting is sung as a round. The S/A sing the first phrase, "O the Lamb, the loving Lamb." As they continue the T/B begin. S/A hold last note until T/B finish.
Setting 4: Divide choir into four equal parts. Sing the melody as a four-part round. Cello plays drone. Each group sings the melody twice. They start *piano*, crescendo to *forte* by the time they begin the melody a second time, and then *decrescendo* to *piano* by the end of their part. Each group holds its last note until all are finished.
Setting 5: Soloist begins the melody once again, beginning when the last group of Setting 4 reaches the final word, "me." Choir and cello continue to hold "B" very softly while soloist sings.

Other Suggestions
Visuals: Black-draped cross, altar stripped
O Plant, root, suffering, crucifix, lamb/shears
P Crucifix, Exodus, nursing, water, bones, sword, dog/lion/ox, feeding the poor
E Heb. 10:16b, eraser, crucifix, curtain, worship
G Sword, fire, cock, whip, robe, rugged cross, crucifix nails, crown (thorns), ladder, sponge, spear, shroud
For additional ideas, consult Palm/Passion Sunday suggestions.
+Introit: WS3081. "Now Behold the Lamb" (Isa, Lent)
Call to Worship: WSL22 (Isa, John)
Opening Prayer: WSL25. "Today the carpenter's hands" (John)
Confession: WSL24. "Holy Savior" (John)
+Response: C299, G576, S2277. "Lord, Have Mercy" (Good Friday)
+Words of Assurance: N841 (Good Friday)
Psalm: SH178. Psalm 22 with stanzas of "What Wondrous Love Is This" (Pss)
Prayer: UM284. Good Friday (John)
Offertory Prayer: WSL155. "God of the Crucified Jesus" (John)
Prayers: N833, N880, and UM284 (John)
Litany: C201 or C209 (John)
Reading: UM293. Behold the Savior of Mankind (Good Friday)
Reading: C205, UM293 (John, Good Friday)
Reading: C196, CG180, E171, EL347, G220, GR576, N219, P97, SH171, UM290 (PD), VU133. "Go to Dark Gethsemane." Use this hymn to supplement the reading of the John passage. Stanza 1 before beginning 18:1. Sing stanza 2 after 19:3. Sing stanza 3 after 19:30. Sing UM288, stanza 5 at the conclusion of the reading.
Closing Prayer: WSL28. "Eternal God" (Good Friday)
Blessing: N872 (Holy Week)
+Blessing: WSL27 (Good Friday)
Theme Ideas: Covenant, Cross, Jesus: Crucifixion, Jesus: Jesus Our Savior, Lament

Notes

NRSVue

Acts 10:34-43

[34]Then Peter began to speak to them: “I truly understand that
God shows no partiality, [35]but in every people anyone who fears
him and practices righteousness is acceptable to him. [36]You know
the message he sent to the people of Israel, preaching peace by
Jesus Christ—he is Lord of all. [37]That message spread throughout Judea, beginning in Galilee after the baptism that John
announced: [38]how God anointed Jesus of Nazareth with the Holy
Spirit and with power; how he went about doing good and healing
all who were oppressed by the devil, for God was with him. [39]We
are witnesses to all that he did both in Judea and in Jerusalem.
They put him to death by hanging him on a tree, [40]but God raised
him on the third day and allowed him to appear, [41]not to all the
people but to us who were chosen by God as witnesses and who
ate and drank with him after he rose from the dead. [42]He commanded us to preach to the people and to testify that he is the
one ordained by God as judge of the living and the dead. [43]All
the prophets testify about him that everyone who believes in him
receives forgiveness of sins through his name.”

Psalm 118:1-2, 14-24 (G391/681, N700, P230/232, UM839)

O give thanks to the LORD, for he is good;
  his steadfast love endures forever!
[2]Let Israel say,
  “His steadfast love endures forever.”
. . . .
[14]The LORD is my strength and my might;
  he has become my salvation.
[15]There are glad songs of victory in the tents of the righteous:
  “The right hand of the LORD does valiantly;
[16]the right hand of the LORD is exalted;
  the right hand of the LORD does valiantly.”
[17]I shall not die, but I shall live
  and recount the deeds of the LORD.
[18]The LORD has punished me severely,
  but he did not give me over to death.
[19]Open to me the gates of righteousness,
  that I may enter through them
  and give thanks to the LORD.
[20]This is the gate of the LORD;
  the righteous shall enter through it.
[21]I thank you that you have answered me
  and have become my salvation.
[22]The stone that the builders rejected
  has become the chief cornerstone.
[23]This is the LORD’s doing;
  it is marvelous in our eyes.
[24]This is the day that the LORD has made;
  let us rejoice and be glad in it.

Colossians 3:1-4

[1]So if you have been raised with Christ, seek the things that
are above, where Christ is, seated at the right hand of God. [2]Set
your minds on the things that are above, not on the things that
are on earth, [3]for you have died, and your life is hidden with
Christ in God. [4]When Christ who is your life is revealed, then
you also will be revealed with him in glory.

CEB

Acts 10:34-43

[34]Peter said, “I really am learning that God doesn’t show partiality to one group of people over another. [35]Rather, in every nation,
whoever worships him and does what is right is acceptable to him.
[36]This is the message of peace he sent to the Israelites by proclaiming the good news through Jesus Christ: He is LORD of all! [37]You
know what happened throughout Judea, beginning in Galilee
after the baptism John preached. [38]You know about Jesus of Nazareth, whom God anointed with the Holy Spirit and endowed with
power. Jesus traveled around doing good and healing everyone
oppressed by the devil because God was with him. [39]We are witnesses of everything he did, both in Judea and in Jerusalem. They
killed him by hanging him on a tree, [40]but God raised him up on
the third day and allowed him to be seen, [41]not by everyone but by
us. We are witnesses whom God chose beforehand, who ate and
drank with him after God raised him from the dead. [42]He commanded us to preach to the people and to testify that he is the one
whom God appointed as judge of the living and the dead. [43]All
the prophets testify about him that everyone who believes in him
receives forgiveness of sins through his name.”

Psalm 118:1-2, 14-24 (G391/681, N700, P230/232, UM839)

Give thanks to the LORD because he is good,
  because his faithful love lasts forever.
[2]Let Israel say it:
  “God’s faithful love lasts forever!”
. . . .
[14]The LORD was my strength and protection;
  he was my saving help!
[15]The sounds of joyful songs and deliverance
  are heard in the tents of the righteous:
  “The LORD’s strong hand is victorious!
16 The LORD’s strong hand is ready to strike!
    The LORD’s strong hand is victorious!”
[17]I won’t die—no, I will live
  and declare what the LORD has done.
[18]Yes, the LORD definitely disciplined me,
  but he didn’t hand me over to death.
[19]Open the gates of righteousness for me
  so I can come in and give thanks to the LORD!
[20]This is the LORD’s gate;
  those who are righteous enter through it.
[21]I thank you because you answered me,
  because you were my saving help.
[22]The stone rejected by the builders
  is now the main foundation stone!
[23]This has happened because of the LORD;
  it is astounding in our sight!
[24]This is the day the LORD acted;
  we will rejoice and celebrate in it!

Colossians 3:1-4

[1]Therefore if you were raised with Christ, look for the things
that are above where Christ is sitting at God’s right side. [2]Think
about the things above and not things on earth. [3]You died, and
your life is hidden with Christ in God. [4]When Christ, who is your
life, is revealed, then you also will be revealed with him in glory.

NRSVue

John 20:1-18 (or Matthew 28:1-10)

Early on the first day of the week, while it was still dark, Mary Magdalene came to the tomb and saw that the stone had been removed from the tomb. 2So she ran and went to Simon Peter and the other disciple, the one whom Jesus loved, and said to them, "They have taken the Lord out of the tomb, and we do not know where they have laid him." 3Then Peter and the other disciple set out and went toward the tomb. 4The two were running together, but the other disciple outran Peter and reached the tomb first. 5He bent down to look in and saw the linen wrappings lying there, but he did not go in. 6Then Simon Peter came, following him, and went into the tomb. He saw the linen wrappings lying there, 7and the cloth that had been on Jesus's head, not lying with the linen wrappings but rolled up in a place by itself. 8Then the other disciple, who reached the tomb first, also went in, and he saw and believed, 9for as yet they did not understand the scripture, that he must rise from the dead. 10Then the disciples returned to their homes.

11But Mary stood weeping outside the tomb. As she wept, she bent over to look into the tomb, 12and she saw two angels in white sitting where the body of Jesus had been lying, one at the head and the other at the feet. 13They said to her, "Woman, why are you weeping?" She said to them, "They have taken away my Lord, and I do not know where they have laid him." 14When she had said this, she turned around and saw Jesus standing there, but she did not know that it was Jesus. 15Jesus said to her, "Woman, why are you weeping? Whom are you looking for?" Supposing him to be the gardener, she said to him, "Sir, if you have carried him away, tell me where you have laid him, and I will take him away." 16Jesus said to her, "Mary!" She turned and said to him in Hebrew, "Rabbouni!" (which means Teacher). 17Jesus said to her, "Do not touch me, because I have not yet ascended to the Father. But go to my brothers and say to them, 'I am ascending to my Father and your Father, to my God and your God.'" 18Mary Magdalene went and announced to the disciples, "I have seen the Lord," and she told them that he had said these things to her.

[Matthew 28:1-10] 1After the sabbath, as the first day of the week was dawning, Mary Magdalene and the other Mary went to see the tomb. 2And suddenly there was a great earthquake, for an angel of the Lord, descending from heaven, came and rolled back the stone and sat on it. 3His appearance was like lightning and his clothing white as snow. 4For fear of him the guards shook and became like dead men. 5But the angel said to the women, "Do not be afraid, for I know that you are looking for Jesus who was crucified. 6He is not here, for he has been raised, as he said. Come, see the place where he lay. 7Then go quickly and tell his disciples, 'He has been raised from the dead, and indeed he is going ahead of you to Galilee; there you will see him.' This is my message for you." 8So they left the tomb quickly with fear and great joy and ran to tell his disciples. 9Suddenly Jesus met them and said, "Greetings!" And they came to him, took hold of his feet, and worshiped him. 10Then Jesus said to them, "Do not be afraid; go and tell my brothers and sisters to go to Galilee; there they will see me."

CEB

John 20:1-18 (or Matthew 28:1-10)

Early in the morning of the first day of the week, while it was still dark, Mary Magdalene came to the tomb and saw that the stone had been taken away from the tomb. 2She ran to Simon Peter and the other disciple, the one whom Jesus loved, and said, "They have taken the Lord from the tomb, and we don't know where they've put him." 3Peter and the other disciple left to go to the tomb. 4They were running together, but the other disciple ran faster than Peter and was the first to arrive at the tomb. 5Bending down to take a look, he saw the linen cloths lying there, but he didn't go in. 6Following him, Simon Peter entered the tomb and saw the linen cloths lying there. 7He also saw the face cloth that had been on Jesus' head. It wasn't with the other clothes but was folded up in its own place. 8Then the other disciple, the one who arrived at the tomb first, also went inside. He saw and believed. 9They didn't yet understand the scripture that Jesus must rise from the dead. 10Then the disciples returned to the place where they were staying.

11Mary stood outside near the tomb, crying. As she cried, she bent down to look into the tomb. 12She saw two angels dressed in white, seated where the body of Jesus had been, one at the head and one at the foot. 13The angels asked her, "Woman, why are you crying?"

She replied, "They have taken away my Lord, and I don't know where they've put him." 14As soon as she had said this, she turned around and saw Jesus standing there, but she didn't know it was Jesus.

15Jesus said to her, "Woman, why are you crying? Who are you looking for?"

Thinking he was the gardener, she replied, "Sir, if you have carried him away, tell me where you have put him and I will get him."

16Jesus said to her, "Mary."

She turned and said to him in Aramaic, "Rabbouni" (which means *Teacher*).

17Jesus said to her, "Don't hold on to me, for I haven't yet gone up to my Father. Go to my brothers and sisters and tell them, 'I'm going up to my Father and your Father, to my God and your God.'"

18Mary Magdalene left and announced to the disciples, "I've seen the Lord." Then she told them what he said to her.

[Matthew 28:1-10] 1After the Sabbath, at dawn on the first day of the week, Mary Magdalene and the other Mary came to look at the tomb. 2Look, there was a great earthquake, for an angel from the Lord came down from heaven. Coming to the stone, he rolled it away and sat on it. 3Now his face was like lightning and his clothes as white as snow. 4The guards were so terrified of him that they shook with fear and became like dead men. 5But the angel said to the women, "Don't be afraid. I know that you are looking for Jesus who was crucified. 6He isn't here, because he's been raised from the dead, just as he said. Come, see the place where they laid him. 7Now hurry, go and tell his disciples, 'He's been raised from the dead. He's going on ahead of you to Galilee. You will see him there.' I've given the message to you."

8With great fear and excitement, they hurried away from the tomb and ran to tell his disciples. 9But Jesus met them and greeted them. They came and grabbed his feet and worshipped him. 10Then Jesus said to them, "Don't be afraid. Go and tell my brothers that I am going into Galilee. They will see me there."

Primary Hymns and Songs for the Day

"Christ the Lord Is Risen Today" 27965 (John, Matt) (O)
C216, CG194, GR251, N233, SH181, UM302 (PD), VU155/157
H-3 Hbl-8, 51; Chr-49; Desc-31; Org-32
S-1 #104-108. Various treatments
G245, P113
H-3 Hbl-72; Chr-50; Desc-69; Org-78
S-1 #213. Desc.
EL373
"The Day of Resurrection" 197417 (John, Matt)
C228, CG214, E210, EL361, G233, GR254, N245, P118, SH186, UM303 (PD), VU164
H-3 Hbl-74; Chr-123; Desc-64; Org-71
S-1 #195-197. Various treatments
"Crown Him with Many Crowns" (John) (C)
C234, CG223. E494, EL855, G268, GR278, N301, P151, SH208, UM327 (PD), VU211
H-3 Hbl-55; Chr-60; Desc-30; Org-27
S-1 #86-88. Various treatments

Additional Hymn Suggestions

"At the Font We Start Our Journey" (Acts, Baptism)
N308, S2114
+"Ask Ye What Great Thing I Know" (Acts, Easter)
CG443, GR107, N49, UM163 (PD), VU338
"Lord of the Dance" 78529 (Acts)
G157, P302, UM261, VU352
"The Strife Is O'er, the Battle Done" (Acts)
C221, E208, EL366, G236, GR256, N242, P119, SH193, UM306, VU159
"This Is the Day the Lord Hath Made" (Pss)
E50, G681, GR448, P230, UM658 (PD), Z243
"Taste and See" OL-00155 (Pss, Comm.)
EL493, G520, S2267, SH691, ZS205
"O Sons and Daughters, Let Us Sing" (Pss, John)
C220, CG212, E203, EL386/E387, G235/255, N244, P116 (PD), SH190, UM317, VU170
+"All Praise to Thee, for Thou, O King Divine" (Col)
CG352, E477, GR281, UM166, VU327
"Woke Up This Morning" (Col)
C623, N85, S2082, Z146, ZS105
"Woman in the Night" (John)
C188, G161, UM274
"Thine Be the Glory" (John, Matt)
C218, CG222, EL376, G238, GR255, N253, P122, SH192, UM308, VU173 (Fr.)
"He Lives" (John, Matt)
C226, CG622, GR257, SH198, UM310, Z30
"*Cristo Vive*" ("Christ Is Risen") (John, Matt)
N235, P109, SH184, UM313
"In the Garden" (John)
C227, CG200, GR342. N237, UM314, Z44 (PD)
"Come, Ye Faithful, Raise the Strain" 355929 (John, Matt)
C215, CG218, E199/200, EL363, G234, GR253, N230, P115/114, UM315 (PD), VU165
"He Rose" (John, Matt)
GR267, N239, UM316, Z168 (PD)
"Christ Is Alive" (John, Matt)
CG205, E182, EL389, G246, P108, UM318, VU158
"Up from the Grave He Arose" (John, Matt)
C224, CG207, GR252, SH185, UM322 (PD)
"You Alone Are Holy" (John, Easter)
S2077, SH457
"You, Lord, Are Both Lamb and Shepherd" (John)
G274, SH210, VU210. WS3043
"Deck Thyself, My Soul, with Gladness" (Easter, Comm.)
E339, EL488/EL489, G514, P506, UM612 (PD), VU463

Additional Contemporary and Modern Suggestions

"Halle, Halle, Halleluja" 2659190 (Easter, Opening)
C41, CG433, EL172, G591, N236, S2026, SH694, VU958, ZS76
"Holy and Anointed One" 164361 (Acts)
+"The Highest and the Greatest" 4769758 (Acts)
+"Here at the Cross" 7046292 (Acts, Easter)
+"You Are More Than Enough " 5951998 (Acts, Easter)
+"Rise" 7036613 (Acts, Pss)
+"God, You're So Good" 7105729 (Pss)
+"Goodness of God" 7117726 (Pss)
+"Never Runs Out" 7193998 (Pss)
"In the Lord I'll Be Ever Thankful" OL-00118 (Pss)
G654, S2195, SH316
"You Are Good" 3383788 (Pss)
SH455, WS3014
"You Are My All in All" 825356 (Pss)
CG571, G519, SH335, WS3040, ZS184
"Forever" 3148428 (Pss)
CG53, WS3023
"Christ Beside Me" (Col)
G702, S2166
"Lord, I Lift Your Name on High" 117947 (Col, Easter)
CG606, EL857, S2088, SH205
+"Purify My Heart" 1314323 (Col)
+ "Take My Life" 1617154 (Col)
+"All the Poor and Powerless" 5881130 (Col)
+"Stand in Your Love" 7107821 (John, Matt)
"Alleluia" 16811 (John, Matt, Easter)
C106, N765, SH699, UM186
"Christ the Lord Is Risen" 230240 (John, Matt, Easter)
S2116
+"Living Hope" 7106807 (John, Matt, Easter)
+"Springtime" 7146308 (John, Matt, Easter)
+"You Keep Hope Alive" 7125876 (John, Matt, Easter)
V-9, p. 132. Vocal Solo
+"Resurrection Hymn" ("See What a Morning") 4108797 (John, Matt, Easter)
+"Happy Day" 4847027 (John, Matt, Easter)
"Our God Reigns" 8458 (John, Matt, Easter)
"Celebrate Jesus" 16859 (John, Matt, Easter)
"Jesus Is Alive" 550652 (John, Matt, Easter)
"See What a Morning" ("Resurrection Hymn") 4108797 (John, Matt, Easter)
"Blessing, Honour and Glory" 1001179 (Easter)
EL433
"My Redeemer Lives" 2397964 (Easter)
"Holy, Holy" 18792 (Easter)
P140, S2039
"Alleluia" OL-81263 (Easter)
EL174, G587, S2043
"Sing Alleluia to the Lord" 26272 (Easter, Comm.)
C32, S2258, SH685
"Amen, Amen" OL-50011 (Easter, Closing)
N161, P299, S2072 (PD-TO), Z147
"Alive Forever, Amen" 4190176 (Easter, Closing)

Solo/Ensemble Suggestions

+"Waterlife" (Col, Baptism)
V-5(3) p. 17
+"Jesus Christ is Risen Today" (Matt, John, Easter)
V-1 p. 50
"I Know That My Redeemer Liveth" (Easter)
V-2
V-8 p. 202
"I Know That My Redeemer Lives" (Easter)
V-5 (2) p. 22

+"Rise Again" (Easter)
V-8 p. 31
+"Great Things" 7111321 (Easter)
V-9 p. 36
"Taste and See the Goodness of the Lord" (Pss, Comm.)
Thomas Keesecker; AEC-3 p. 71
Unison or 2-part, keyboard (https://bit.ly/AEC-3-71)
+"Christ Is Risen! Christ Is Alive!" (John)
Larson/Wren; Hope C6136
SATB, piano, trumpet (https://bit.ly/C6136)

+Hymn Anthem

"Cristo Vive" ("Christ Is Risen") (John, Matt)
N235, P109, SH184, UM313

Organ is the preferred accompanying instrument. Measures 1-8 may be accompanied by playing the setting as written on one of the manuals while the pedal plays a repeated pedal point measure. Each measure of this pedal point consists of an eighth rest followed by the low "E" played on the "and" of beat 1. The manuals should be played in a detached style. Pianists may adapt the suggestions given to the piano. Tempo should be about MM = 100.

Introduction: Organ plays melody in octaves, through the first phrase (to "be unafraid").

Stanza 1: Voices in unison, *forte*, with strength and a full tone. Keyboard plays measures 1-8 with pedal point. Play measures 9-16 as written.

Stanza 2: S/A sing their parts and all T/B sing the tenor part. *Mezzo forte*. Keyboard plays only these upper three parts, *legato*.

Interlude: Keyboard plays measures 9 (with pickup notes) - 16, manuals only, but *forte*.

Stanza 3: Slower, with certainty. All voices sing melody. Keyboard plays measures 1-8 with pedal point. Measures 9-16 play as written with a strong pedal stop. Some sopranos may sing the alto part an octave higher beginning in measure 12, but return to the melody note on the final measure. All voices hold last note while keyboard plays ending.

Ending: Keyboard plays measures 1-4 with pedal point, *fortissimo*. Hold chord on beat 1 of measure 4.

Other Suggestions

Visuals:
O Crucifix, resurrection, Acts 10:39a
P Ps. 118:29, singing, tents, gates, cornerstone
E Butterfly, empty cross, open tomb, Christ returning
G Basket/spices, open tomb, grave clothes, napkin, runners, tears, risen Christ, "I have seen . . ."

+Introit: E175, EL394, G277, N262, P120, UM324, VU163. "Hail Thee, Festival Day" (Mark)
Introit: WS3044. "Make Way" (Pss, Easter)
Greeting: WSL29. "Christ is Risen" (John, Easter)
Call to Worship: WSL22. "From Bethlehem" (Acts, Easter)
Opening Prayer: WSL28. "Eternal God, Rock" (John, Easter)
+Affirmation of Faith: WSL29, WSL33, or UM888 (1 Cor)
Litany: C217. Easter Affirmations
+Response: S2039, stanza 5. "Holy, Holy" (Easter)
Litany: WSL36. "When the World Divides Us" (Acts)
Response: S2167. "More Like You" 2145051 (Col)
Response: C531, SH496, UM84, Z228. "Thank You, Lord" (Pss)
Benediction: N872 (John)
Blessing: WSL27. "May the Christ who Walks" (John, Easter)
Theme Ideas: God: Glory of God, Inclusion, Jesus: Mind of Christ, Resurrection, Thanksgiving / Gratitude

Notes

NRSVue

Acts 2:14a, 22-32

14aBut Peter, standing with the eleven, raised his voice and
addressed them, . . .
22"Fellow Israelites, listen to what I have to say: Jesus of
Nazareth, a man attested to you by God with deeds of power,
wonders, and signs that God did through him among you, as you
yourselves know—23this man, handed over to you according to
the definite plan and foreknowledge of God, you crucified and
killed by the hands of those outside the law. 24But God raised
him up, having released him from the agony of death, because
it was impossible for him to be held in its power. 25For David says
concerning him,
'I saw the Lord always before me,
for he is at my right hand so that I will not be shaken;
26therefore my heart was glad, and my tongue rejoiced;
moreover, my flesh will live in hope.
27For you will not abandon my soul to Hades
or let your Holy One experience corruption.
28You have made known to me the ways of life;
you will make me full of gladness with your presence.'
29"Fellow Israelites, I may say to you confidently of our ancestor David that he both died and was buried, and his tomb is
with us to this day. 30Since he was a prophet, he knew that God
had sworn with an oath to him that he would put one of his
descendants on his throne. 31Foreseeing this, David spoke of the
resurrection of the Messiah, saying,
'He was not abandoned to Hades,
nor did his flesh experience corruption.'
32This Jesus God raised up, and of that all of us are witnesses.

Psalm 16 (G810, N628, P165, UM748)

1Protect me, O God, for in you I take refuge.
2I say to the LORD, "You are my Lord;
I have no good apart from you."
3As for the holy ones in the land, they are the noble ones
in whom is all my delight.
4Those who choose another god multiply their sorrows;
their drink offerings of blood I will not pour out
or take their names upon my lips.
5The LORD is my chosen portion and my cup;
you hold my lot.
6The boundary lines have fallen for me in pleasant places;
I have a goodly heritage.
7I bless the LORD, who gives me counsel;
in the night also my heart instructs me.
8I keep the LORD always before me;
because he is at my right hand, I shall not be moved.
9Therefore my heart is glad, and my soul rejoices;
my body also rests secure.
10For you do not give me up to Sheol
or let your faithful one see the Pit.
11You show me the path of life.
In your presence there is fullness of joy;
in your right hand are pleasures forevermore.

CEB

Acts 2:14a, 22-32

14aPeter stood with the other eleven apostles. He raised his
voice and declared, . . .
22"Fellow Israelites, listen to these words! Jesus the Nazarene was a man whose credentials God proved to you through
miracles, wonders, and signs, which God performed through
him among you. You yourselves know this. 23In accordance with
God's established plan and foreknowledge, he was betrayed.
You, with the help of wicked men, had Jesus killed by nailing
him to a cross. 24God raised him up! God freed him from death's
dreadful grip, since it was impossible for death to hang on to
him. 25David says about him,
I foresaw that the Lord was always with me;
because he is at my right hand I won't be shaken.
26 *Therefore, my heart was glad*
and my tongue rejoiced.
Moreover, my body will live in hope,
27 *because you won't abandon me to the grave,*
nor permit your holy one to experience decay.
28 *You have shown me the paths of life;*
your presence will fill me with happiness.
29"Brothers and sisters, I can speak confidently about the
patriarch David. He died and was buried, and his tomb is with us
to this very day. 30Because he was a prophet, he knew that God
promised him with a solemn pledge to seat one of his descendants on his throne. 31Having seen this beforehand, David spoke
about the resurrection of Christ, that *he wasn't abandoned to the*
grave, nor did his body experience decay. 32This Jesus, God raised up.
We are all witnesses to that fact.

Psalm 16 (G810, N628, P165, UM748)

2I say to the LORD, "You are my Lord.
Apart from you, I have nothing good."
3Now as for the "holy ones" in the land,
the "magnificent ones" that I was so happy about;
4 let their suffering increase because
they hurried after a different god.
I won't participate in their blood offerings;
I won't let their names cross my lips.
5You, LORD, are my portion, my cup;
you control my destiny.
6The property lines have fallen beautifully for me;
yes, I have a lovely home.
7I will bless the LORD who advises me;
even at night I am instructed
in the depths of my mind.
8I always put the LORD in front of me;
I will not stumble because he is on my right side.
9That's why my heart celebrates and my mood is joyous;
yes, my whole body will rest in safety
10 because you won't abandon my life to the grave;
you won't let your faithful follower see the pit.
11You teach me the way of life.
In your presence is total celebration.
Beautiful things are always in your right hand.

NRSVue

1 Peter 1:3-9

3 Blessed be the God and Father of our Lord Jesus Christ! By
his great mercy he has given us a new birth into a living hope
through the resurrection of Jesus Christ from the dead 4 and into
an inheritance that is imperishable, undefiled, and unfading,
kept in heaven for you, 5 who are being protected by the power
of God through faith for a salvation ready to be revealed in the
last time. 6 In this you rejoice, even if now for a little while you
have had to suffer various trials, 7 so that the genuineness of your
faith—being more precious than gold that, though perishable,
is tested by fire—may be found to result in praise and glory and
honor when Jesus Christ is revealed. 8 Although you have not
seen him, you love him, and even though you do not see him
now, you believe in him and rejoice with an indescribable and
glorious joy, 9 for you are receiving the outcome of your faith, the
salvation of your souls.

John 20:19-31

19 When it was evening on that day, the first day of the week,
and the doors were locked where the disciples were, for fear of
the Jews, Jesus came and stood among them and said, "Peace be
with you." 20 After he said this, he showed them his hands and
his side. Then the disciples rejoiced when they saw the Lord.
21 Jesus said to them again, "Peace be with you. As the Father has
sent me, so I send you." 22 When he had said this, he breathed on
them and said to them, "Receive the Holy Spirit. 23 If you forgive
the sins of any, they are forgiven them; if you retain the sins of
any, they are retained."

24 But Thomas (who was called the Twin), one of the twelve,
was not with them when Jesus came. 25 So the other disciples told
him, "We have seen the Lord." But he said to them, "Unless I see
the mark of the nails in his hands and put my finger in the mark
of the nails and my hand in his side, I will not believe."

26 A week later his disciples were again in the house, and
Thomas was with them. Although the doors were shut, Jesus
came and stood among them and said, "Peace be with you."
27 Then he said to Thomas, "Put your finger here and see my
hands. Reach out your hand and put it in my side. Do not doubt
but believe." 28 Thomas answered him, "My Lord and my God!"
29 Jesus said to him, "Have you believed because you have seen
me? Blessed are those who have not seen and yet have come to
believe."

30 Now Jesus did many other signs in the presence of his
disciples that are not written in this book. 31 But these are written
so that you may continue to believe that Jesus is the Messiah, the
Son of God, and that through believing you may have life in his
name.

CEB

1 Peter 1:3-9

3 May the God and Father of our Lord Jesus Christ be blessed!
On account of his vast mercy, he has given us new birth. You
have been born anew into a living hope through the resurrection of Jesus Christ from the dead. 4 You have a pure and
enduring inheritance that cannot perish—an inheritance that
is presently kept safe in heaven for you. 5 Through his faithfulness, you are guarded by God's power so that you can receive the
salvation he is ready to reveal in the last time.

6 You now rejoice in this hope, even if it's necessary for you to
be distressed for a short time by various trials. 7 This is necessary so that your faith may be found genuine. (Your faith is
more valuable than gold, which will be destroyed even though
it is itself tested by fire.) Your genuine faith will result in
praise, glory, and honor for you when Jesus Christ is revealed.
8 Although you've never seen him, you love him. Even though
you don't see him now, you trust him and so rejoice with a glorious joy that is too much for words. 9 You are receiving the goal of
your faith: your salvation.

John 20:19-31

19 It was still the first day of the week. That evening, while the
disciples were behind closed doors because they were afraid of
the Jewish authorities, Jesus came and stood among them. He
said, "Peace be with you." 20 After he said this, he showed them
his hands and his side. When the disciples saw the Lord, they
were filled with joy. 21 Jesus said to them again, "Peace be with
you. As the Father sent me, so I am sending you." 22 Then he
breathed on them and said, "Receive the Holy Spirit. 23 If you forgive anyone's sins, they are forgiven; if you don't forgive them,
they aren't forgiven."

24 Thomas, the one called Didymus, one of the Twelve, wasn't
with the disciples when Jesus came. 25 The other disciples told
him, "We've seen the Lord!"

But he replied, "Unless I see the nail marks in his hands, put
my finger in the wounds left by the nails, and put my hand into
his side, I won't believe."

26 After eight days his disciples were again in a house and
Thomas was with them. Even though the doors were locked,
Jesus entered and stood among them. He said, "Peace be with
you." 27 Then he said to Thomas, "Put your finger here. Look
at my hands. Put your hand into my side. No more disbelief.
Believe!"

28 Thomas responded to Jesus, "My Lord and my God!"

29 Jesus replied, "Do you believe because you see me? Happy
are those who don't see and yet believe."

30 Then Jesus did many other miraculous signs in his disciples'
presence, signs that aren't recorded in this scroll. 31 But these
things are written so that you will believe that Jesus is the Christ,
God's Son, and that believing, you will have life in his name.

Primary Hymns and Songs for the Day

"Hail the Day That Sees Him Rise" 95997 (Acts) (O)
CG219, E214, GR269, N260, SH203, UM312, VU189
H-3 Hbl-72; Chr-50; Desc-69; Org-78
S-1 #213. Descant
"Alleluia, Alleluia" 32376 (Acts)
CG196, E178, G240, P106, SH189, UM162, VU179
H-3 Hbl-46; Chr-26
S-1 #14. Desc.
"We Walk by Faith" 2591911 (1 Pet, John)
CG634, E209, EL635, G817, N256, P399, S2196, SH660
"That Easter Day with Joy Was Bright" (John, Easter)
C229, CG204, E193, EL384 (PD), G254, P121
H-3 Chr-19
"Dona Nobis Pacem" 4340610 (John)
C296/297, E712, EL753, G752, UM376 (PD)
"Thine Be the Glory" (Acts, John) (C)
C218, CG222, EL376, G238, GR255, N253, P122, SH192, UM308, VU173 (Fr.)
H-3 Hbl-98; Chr-195; Desc-59
S-1 #190. Arrangement
S-2 #95. Various treatments

Additional Hymn Suggestions

"This Joyful Eastertide" (Acts)
E192, EL391, G244, N232, VU177
"Hail Thee, Festival Day" (Acts)
E175, EL394, G277, N262, P120, UM324, VU163
"How Firm a Foundation" 107816 (Acts, 1 Pet)
C618, CG425, E636, EL796, G463, GR46, N407, P361, SH291, UM529 (PD), VU660
"Praise God for This Holy Ground" (Acts, John)
G405, WS3009
"Alleluia" (Pss, Easter)
EL174, G587, S2043
"To God Be the Glory" (1 Pet)
C72, CG349, G634, GR531, P485, SH545, UM98 (PD)
"Jesus, the Very Thought of Thee" (1 Pet)
C102, CG386, E642, EL754, G629, GR127, N507, P310, UM175 (PD)
"Hope of the World" 643002 (1 Pet)
C538, E472, G734, N46, P360, UM178, VU215
"He Lives" (1 Pet)
C226, CG622, GR257, SH198, UM310, Z30
"Mothering God, You Gave Me Birth" (1 Pet, Comm.)
C83, EL735, G7, N467, S2050, VU320
"There Are Some Things I May Not Know" (1 Pet)
N405, S2147, Z201 (PD), ZS172
"The Day of Resurrection" 197417 (1 Pet, John, Easter)
C228, CG214, E210, EL361, G233, GR254, N245, P118, SH186, UM303 (PD), VU164
"Depth of Mercy" 1320726 (1 Pet, John)
GR234, UM355
"Depth of Mercy" 5412781 (1 Pet, John)
WS3097
"O Sons and Daughters, Let Us Sing" (John)
C220, CG212, E203, EL386/E387, G235/255, N244, P116 (PD), SH190, UM317, VU170
"Christ Jesus Lay in Death's Strong Band" (John)
E186, EL370, G237, P110, UM319 (PD)
"Holy Spirit, Come, Confirm Us" (John)
N264, UM331
"Spirit of Faith, Come Down" (John)
GR289, UM332 (PD)
"Love Divine, All Loves Excelling" 40306 (John, Comm.)
C517, CG281, E657, EL631, G366, GR88, N43, P376, SH353/354, UM384 (PD), VU333
"Breathe on Me, Breath of God" 99481 (John)
C254, CG235, E508, G286, GR304, N292, P316, SH224/273, UM420 (PD), VU382 (Fr.)
"Holy Spirit, Truth Divine" 300431 (John)
C241, EL398, GR320, N63, P321, UM465, VU368
"Let it Breathe on Me" (John)
C260, N288, UM503, Z224 (PD)
"In the Singing" (John, Comm.)
EL466, G533, S2255
"Come, Share the Lord" (John, Comm.)
C408, CG459, G510, S2269, VU469
+"Peace of Our Praying" (John, Comm.)
WS3022
"I Know that My Redeemer Lives!" (John)
CG210, EL619 (PD), GR261, SH199

Additional Contemporary and Modern Suggestions

"I Will Enter His Gates" 1493 (Acts)
S2270
+"Made a Way" 7071768 (Acts, Pss)
"Foundation" 706151 (Acts, 1 Pet)
+"Won't Stop Now" 7111932 (Acts, John)
"Surely the Presence of the Lord" 7909 (Acts, John)
C263, GR306, UM328; S-2 #200. Stanzas for soloist
"Holy Ground" 21198 (Acts, John)
C112, G406, S2272
+"There's a Spirit of Love in This Place" OL-38821 (Acts, John)
WS3148, ZS103
"Awesome in This Place" 847554 (Acts, John)
"I Believe In Jesus" 61282 (Acts, John)
"All Things Are Possible" 2245140 (Pss)
"Alleluia" OL-81263 (Pss, Easter)
EL174, G587, S2043
"More Precious than Silver" 11335 (Pss, 1 Pet)
S2065
+"You Are My Strength" 4869940 (Pss, 1 Pet)
+"No Outsiders" 7101035 (Pss, John)
+"Stand in Your Love" 7107821 (Pss, John, Easter)
"Knowing You" 1045238 (Pss, 1 Pet, John)
"Song of Hope" ("Heaven Come Down") 5111477 (1 Pet)
"My Tribute" 11218 (1 Pet)
C39, CG574, GR580, N14, SH434, UM99; V-8 p. 5. Vocal Solo
"Please Enter My Heart, Hosanna" 2485371 (1 Pet, John)
S2154
"I'm So Glad Jesus Lifted Me" (PD) (1 Pet, John)
C529, EL860 (PD), N474, S2151
"God Is Good All the Time" OL-88288 (1 Pet, John)
WS3026, ZS18
"God Is Good All the Time" 1729073 (1 Pet, John)
"Blessing, Honour and Glory" 1001179 (1 Pet, John, Easter)
EL433
"There Is a Redeemer" 11483 (1 Pet, John)
CG377, G443, GR30, SH495
+"You Keep Hope Alive" 7125876 (1 Pet, John, Easter)
+"Living Hope" 7106807 (1 Pet, John, Easter)
"My Life Is in You, Lord" 17315 (John)
S2032
"Open Our Eyes, Lord" 1572 (John)
CG392, S2086, SH562
"Where the Spirit of the Lord Is" 27484 (John, Comm.)
C264, S2119
"Here Is Bread, Here Is Wine" 983717 (John, Comm.)
EL483, S2266
"Open the Eyes of My Heart" 2298355 (John)
G452, SH378, WS3008
"The Power of Your Love" 917491 (John)
"In the Secret" 1810119 (John)
"Our God Reigns" 8458 (John)

+"Your Spirit" 7091513 (John)
+"Here Again" 7111925 (John)
+"Presence" 7116947 (John)
+"Love Moves You" ("Love Alone") 5775514 (John)

Solo/Ensemble Suggestions

"Crown Him, the Risen King" (Acts, 1 Pet, Easter)
V-10 p. 55
+"Refuge and Strength" (Pss)
V-3 (5) p. 14
+"Because He Lives" (John, Easter)
V-8 p. 24
+"Love Moved First" (John, Easter)
V-9 p. 56
"The Journey of Faith" (1 Pet, John)
Joseph M. Martin; Daybreak HL 00125169
SATB, piano, opt. instruments (https://bit.ly/HL-5169)
+*"Cristo Resucito"* ("Christ Is Risen") (John)
Luis Bojos; Oregon Catholic Press 30149210
SAB, piano, guitar, C-Instrument (https://bit.ly/O-9210)
+"We Walk by Faith" (John)
Karen Marrolli; MorningStar 50-6213
SAB, piano (https://bit.ly/M-6213)

+Hymn Anthem

"Alleluia, Alleluia" 32376 (Acts)
CG196, E178, G240, P106, SH189, UM162, VU179
Piano plays full hymnal setting throughout, varying dynamics depending on the vocal dynamics.
Introduction: Piano plays refrain, playing the first ending.
Refrain: All voices unison.
Stanza 1: S/A only, singing two parts.
Refrain: All voices unison.
Stanza 2: T/B sing melody, altos (or S/A) sing the alto part.
Refrain: All voices unison.
Stanza 3: Sopranos (or S/A) sing soprano part. Tenors (or T/B) sing tenor part.
Refrain: All voices unison.
Stanza 4: This stanza is the loudest. Basses sing bass part. Tenors sing melody. Altos sing alto part. Sopranos sing melody, some sopranos sing tenor part up one octave.
Refrain: All voices unison. Some sopranos on descant, S-1, #14 (or another descant). Strong, *forte.*

Other Suggestions

Visuals:
O Eleven men, preaching, crucifix, open tomb, heart, joy
P Cup, boundary line, prayer, joy, rest, path, hand
E Newborn, butterfly/chrysalis, gold/fire, joy
G Locked door, Jesus, "Peace. . .," wind, wounds, John 20:29b
Litany: WSL33. "This is the Good News" (1 Pet, Easter)
Opening Prayer: WSL37. "Holy Spirit, Rain Down" (John)
+Call to Prayer: CG203, G252, EL374, WS3086, stanza 2. "Day of Arising" (John)
Prayers: N827 and N847 (John)
+Confession Response: EL152, S2275, WS3133. *"Kyrie"* (1 Pet)
Offertory: WSL131. "Blessed One, the Resurrection" (1 Pet)
Blessing: WSL27. "May the Christ who Walks" (John, Easter)
Response: UM376. *"Dona Nobis Pacem"* (John)
Benediction: WSL161. "Sisters and Brothers" (John)
+Sung Benediction: C436, UM666 . "Shalom to You" 114122
Theme Ideas: Doubt, Faith, Holy Spirit, Hope, New Creation, Resurrection

Notes

NRSVue

Acts 2:14a, 36-41

14aBut Peter, standing with the eleven, raised his voice and
addressed them, . . .
36"Therefore let the entire house of Israel know with certainty
that God has made him both Lord and Messiah, this Jesus whom
you crucified."
37Now when they heard this, they were cut to the heart and
said to Peter and to the other apostles, "Brothers, what should
we do?" 38Peter said to them, "Repent and be baptized every
one of you in the name of Jesus Christ so that your sins may be
forgiven, and you will receive the gift of the Holy Spirit. 39For
the promise is for you, for your children, and for all who are far
away, everyone whom the Lord our God calls to him." 40And he
testified with many other arguments and exhorted them, saying,
"Save yourselves from this corrupt generation." 41So those who
welcomed his message were baptized, and that day about three
thousand persons were added.

Psalm 116:1-4, 12-19 (G655, N699, P228, SH344, UM837)

1I love the LORD, because he has heard
  my voice and my supplications.
2Because he inclined his ear to me,
  therefore I will call on him as long as I live.
3The snares of death encompassed me;
  the pangs of Sheol laid hold on me;
  I suffered distress and anguish.
4Then I called on the name of the LORD,
  "O LORD, I pray, save my life!"
. . . .
12What shall I return to the LORD
  for all his bounty to me?
13I will lift up the cup of salvation
  and call on the name of the LORD;
14I will pay my vows to the LORD
  in the presence of all his people.
15Precious in the sight of the LORD
  is the death of his faithful ones.
16O LORD, I am your servant;
  I am your servant, the child of your serving girl.
  You have loosed my bonds.
17I will offer to you a thanksgiving sacrifice
  and call on the name of the LORD.
18I will pay my vows to the LORD
  in the presence of all his people,
19in the courts of the house of the LORD,
  in your midst, O Jerusalem.
Praise the LORD!

CEB

Acts 2:14a, 36-41

14aPeter stood with the other eleven apostles. He raised his
voice and declared, . . .
36"Therefore, let all Israel know beyond question that God has
made this Jesus, whom you crucified, both Lord and Christ."
37When the crowd heard this, they were deeply troubled. They
said to Peter and the other apostles, "Brothers, what should we
do?"
38Peter replied, "Change your hearts and lives. Each of you
must be baptized in the name of Jesus Christ for the forgiveness
of your sins. Then you will receive the gift of the Holy Spirit.
39This promise is for you, your children, and for all who are far
away—as many as the Lord our God invites." 40With many other
words he testified to them and encouraged them, saying, "Be
saved from this perverse generation." 41Those who accepted
Peter's message were baptized. God brought about three thousand people into the community on that day.

Psalm 116:1-4, 12-19 (G655, N699, P228, SH344, UM837)

1I love the LORD because he hears
  my requests for mercy.
2I'll call out to him as long as I live
  because he listens closely to me.
3Death's ropes bound me;
  the distress of the grave found me—
  I came face-to-face
    with trouble and grief.
4So I called on the LORD's name:
  "LORD, please save me!"
. . . .
12What can I give back to the LORD
  for all the good things he has done for me?
13I'll lift up the cup of salvation.
  I'll call on the LORD's name.
14I'll keep the promises I made to the LORD
  in the presence of all God's people.
15The death of the LORD's faithful
  is a costly loss in his eyes.
16Oh yes, LORD, I am definitely your servant!
  I am your servant and the son of your female servant—
  you've freed me from my chains.
17 So I'll offer a sacrifice of thanksgiving to you,
  and I'll call on the LORD's name.
18 I'll keep the promises I made to the LORD
  in the presence of all God's people,
19 in the courtyards of the LORD's house,
    which is in the center of Jerusalem.
Praise the LORD!

NRSVue

1 Peter 1:17-23

17If you invoke as Father the one who judges impartially according to each person's work, live in fear during the time of your exile. 18You know that you were ransomed from the futile conduct inherited from your ancestors, not with perishable things like silver or gold 19but with the precious blood of Christ, like that of a lamb without defect or blemish. 20He was destined before the foundation of the world but was revealed at the end of the ages for your sake. 21Through him you have come to trust in God, who raised him from the dead and gave him glory, so that your trust and hope are in God.

22Now that you have purified your souls by your obedience to the truth so that you have genuine mutual affection, love one another deeply from the heart. 23You have been born anew, not of perishable but of imperishable seed, through the living and enduring word of God.

Luke 24:13-35

13Now on that same day two of them were going to a village called Emmaus, about seven miles from Jerusalem, 14and talking with each other about all these things that had happened. 15While they were talking and discussing, Jesus himself came near and went with them, 16but their eyes were kept from recognizing him. 17And he said to them, "What are you discussing with each other while you walk along?" They stood still, looking sad. 18Then one of them, whose name was Cleopas, answered him, "Are you the only stranger in Jerusalem who does not know the things that have taken place there in these days?" 19He asked them, "What things?" They replied, "The things about Jesus of Nazareth, who was a prophet mighty in deed and word before God and all the people, 20and how our chief priests and leaders handed him over to be condemned to death and crucified him. 21But we had hoped that he was the one to redeem Israel. Yes, and besides all this, it is now the third day since these things took place. 22Moreover, some women of our group astounded us. They were at the tomb early this morning, 23and when they did not find his body there they came back and told us that they had indeed seen a vision of angels who said that he was alive. 24Some of those who were with us went to the tomb and found it just as the women had said, but they did not see him." 25Then he said to them, "Oh, how foolish you are and how slow of heart to believe all that the prophets have declared! 26Was it not necessary that the Messiah should suffer these things and then enter into his glory?" 27Then beginning with Moses and all the prophets, he interpreted to them the things about himself in all the scriptures.

28As they came near the village to which they were going, he walked ahead as if he were going on. 29But they urged him strongly, saying, "Stay with us, because it is almost evening and the day is now nearly over." So he went in to stay with them. 30When he was at the table with them, he took bread, blessed and broke it, and gave it to them. 31Then their eyes were opened, and they recognized him, and he vanished from their sight. 32They said to each other, "Were not our hearts burning within us while he was talking to us on the road, while he was opening the scriptures to us?" 33That same hour they got up and returned to Jerusalem, and they found the eleven and their companions gathered together. 34They were saying, "The Lord has risen indeed, and he has appeared to Simon!" 35Then they told what had happened on the road and how he had been made known to them in the breaking of the bread.

CEB

1 Peter 1:17-23

17Since you call upon a Father who judges all people according to their actions without favoritism, you should conduct yourselves with reverence during the time of your dwelling in a strange land. 18Live in this way, knowing that you were not liberated by perishable things like silver or gold from the empty lifestyle you inherited from your ancestors. 19Instead, you were liberated by the precious blood of Christ, like that of a flawless, spotless lamb. 20Christ was chosen before the creation of the world, but was only revealed at the end of time. This was done for you, 21who through Christ are faithful to the God who raised him from the dead and gave him glory. So now, your faith and hope should rest in God.

22As you set yourselves apart by your obedience to the truth so that you might have genuine affection for your fellow believers, love each other deeply and earnestly. 23Do this because you have been given new birth—not from the type of seed that decays but from seed that doesn't. This seed is God's life-giving and enduring word.

Luke 24:13-35

13On that same day, two disciples were traveling to a village called Emmaus, about seven miles from Jerusalem. 14They were talking to each other about everything that had happened. 15While they were discussing these things, Jesus himself arrived and joined them on their journey. 16They were prevented from recognizing him.

17He said to them, "What are you talking about as you walk along?" They stopped, their faces downcast.

18The one named Cleopas replied, "Are you the only visitor to Jerusalem who is unaware of the things that have taken place there over the last few days?"

19He said to them, "What things?"

They said to him, "The things about Jesus of Nazareth. Because of his powerful deeds and words, he was recognized by God and all the people as a prophet. 20But our chief priests and our leaders handed him over to be sentenced to death, and they crucified him. 21We had hoped he was the one who would redeem Israel. All these things happened three days ago. 22But there's more: Some women from our group have left us stunned. They went to the tomb early this morning 23and didn't find his body. They came to us saying that they had even seen a vision of angels who told them he is alive. 24Some of those who were with us went to the tomb and found things just as the women said. They didn't see him."

25Then Jesus said to them, "You foolish people! Your dull minds keep you from believing all that the prophets talked about. 26 Wasn't it necessary for the Christ to suffer these things and then enter into his glory?" 27Then he interpreted for them the things written about himself in all the scriptures, starting with Moses and going through all the Prophets.

28When they came to Emmaus, he acted as if he was going on ahead. 29But they urged him, saying, "Stay with us. It's nearly evening, and the day is almost over." So he went in to stay with them. 30After he took his seat at the table with them, he took the bread, blessed and broke it, and gave it to them. 31Their eyes were opened and they recognized him, but he disappeared from their sight. 32They said to each other, "Weren't our hearts on fire when he spoke to us along the road and when he explained the scriptures for us?"

33They got up right then and returned to Jerusalem. They found the eleven and their companions gathered together. 34They were saying to each other, "The Lord really has risen! He appeared to Simon!" 35Then the two disciples described what had happened along the road and how Jesus was made known to them as he broke the bread.

Primary Hymns and Songs for the Day

"We Know That Christ Is Raised" OL-40344 (Acts) (O)
E296, EL449, G485, P495, UM610, VU448
H-3 Hbl-100; Chr-214; Desc- ; Org-37
S-1 #118-127. Various treatments
"I Love the Lord" 1168957 (Pss)
CG613, G799, P362, N511, SH343, VU617, WS3142, ZS176
"Jesus, the Very Thought of Thee" (1 Pet)
C102, CG386, E642, EL754, G629, GR127, N507, P310, UM175 (PD)
"Christ Is Alive" (Luke)
CG205, E182, EL389, G246, P108, UM318, VU158
H-3 Hbl-91; Chr-129; Desc-101; Org-167
S-1 #334-5. Descant and harmonization
"Day of Arising" (Luke, Comm.)
CG203, G252, EL374, WS3086
H-3 Hbl-77; Chr-136; Desc-21; Org-16
S-1 #50-51. Flute and vocal desc.
"Open My Eyes, That I May See" 68003 (Luke)
C586, CG395, G451, GR311, P324, SH583, UM454, VU371
H-3 Chr-157; Org-108
"Lord, I Want to Be a Christian" 3184437 (1 Pet) (C)
C589, CG507, G729, GR611, N454, P372 (PD), SH621, UM402, Z76 (PD-TO)
H-3 Chr-130

Additional Hymn Suggestions

"What Is this Place" (Acts)
C289, EL524, G404
"Let Us Talents and Tongues Employ" (Acts)
C422, CG458, EL674, G526, N347, P514, VU468, ZS206
"Wash, O God, Our Sons and Daughters" (Acts)
C365, EL445, G490, SH669, UM605, VU442, ZS191
"Let Us Break Bread Together" (Acts, Comm.)
C425, CG461, EL471 (PD), G525, GR418, N330, P513, SH674, UM618, VU480, Z88 (PD)
"Wonder of Wonders" (Acts, Baptism)
C378, G489, N328, P499, S2247
+"O God Beyond All Praising" (Pss)
CG366, EL880, S2009, VU256
"Just As I Am, Without One Plea" 1039000 (1 Pet)
C339, CG500, E693, EL592, G442, GR509, N207, P370, SH500, UM357 (PD), VU508, Z208
"Blessed Assurance" (1 Pet)
C543, CG619, EL638, G839, GR570, N473, P341, SH320, UM369 (PD), VU337
"It Is Well with My Soul" 25376 (1 Pet)
C561, CG573, EL785, G840, GR344, N438, SH305, UM377 (PD), Z20
"Amazing Grace" 22025 (1 Pet)
C546, CG587, E671, EL779, G649, GR572, N547/548, P280, SH523, UM378 (PD), VU266 (Fr.), Z211
"My Faith Looks Up to Thee" 43334 (1 Pet)
C576, CG407, E691, EL759, G829, GR351, P383, UM452 (PD), VU663, Z215
"Jesus, Priceless Treasure" (1 Pet)
E701, EL775, G830, GR114, N480 P365, UM532 (PD), VU667 / VU668 (Fr.)
"The Church's One Foundation" 55377 (1 Pet)
C272, CG246, E525, EL654, G321, GR388/646, N386, P442, SH233, UM545/546, VU332 (Fr.)
"Blessed Quietness" (1 Pet)
C267, CG244, N284 (PD), S2142, Z206
"Healer of Our Every Ill" OL-00115 (1 Pet)
C506, EL612, G795, S2213, SH339, VU619
"The King Shall Come When Morning Dawns" (1 Pet)
CG97, E73, EL260, GR286, SH346
"Baptized in Water" 5853694 (1 Pet, Baptism)
CG449, E294, EL456, G482, P492, S2248, SH666
"Leaning on the Everlasting Arms" (Luke)
C560, CG640, EL774, G837, GR61, N471, UM133, Z53
"Cuando el Pobre" ("When the Poor Ones") OL-97385 (Luke)
C662, EL725, G762, P407, SH240, UM434, VU702
"By Gracious Powers" (Luke)
E695/696, EL626, G818, N413, P342, UM517
"God the Sculptor of the Mountains" (Luke)
EL736, G5, S2060
"Just a Closer Walk with Thee" (Luke)
C557, EL697, G835, S2158, SH584, Z46 (PD)
"We Walk by Faith" 2591911 (Luke)
CG634, E209, EL635, G817, N256, P399, S2196, SH660
"Come, Share the Lord" (Luke, Comm.)
C408, CG459, G510, S2269, VU469
"Feed Us, Lord" 4636207 (Luke, Comm.)
G501, WS3167
"Be Known to Us in Breaking Bread" (Luke)
C398, G500, N342, P505
"Sing of One Who Walks Beside Us" (Luke)
C231

Additional Contemporary and Modern Suggestions

"Able" 1256560 (Acts, 1 Pet)
"Come, Be Baptized" 239485 (Acts, Baptism)
CG451, S2252, ZS188
"I Love You, Lord" 25266 (Pss)
CG362, G627, S2068, SH417, ZS40
"Beautiful Savior" 2492216 (Pss)
+"Because of Your Love" 4662501 (Pss)
+"Chain Breaker" 7060031 (Pss)
+"Freedom" 7078151 (Pss)
+"Great Things" 7111321 (Pss)
+"Living Hope" 7106807 (Pss)
+"Made a Way" 7071768 (Pss)
"Amazing Grace" ("My Chains Are Gone") 4768151 (1 Pet)
GR574, WS3104
"Take, O Take Me as I Am" 4562041 (1 Pet)
EL814, G698, SH620, WS3119
"Live in Charity" (*"Ubi Caritas"*) OL-00798 (1 Pet)
C523, EL642, G205, S2179
"They'll Know We Are Christians" 26997 (1 Pet)
C494, CG272, G300, S2223, SH232
+"His Mercy Is More" 7065053 (1 Pet)
+"Knowing You" 1045238 (1 Pet)
+"Come to the Table" 7130008 (1 Pet, Comm.)
"Let Us Be Bread" OL-00124 (1 Pet, Luke, Comm.)
S2260
"Agnus Dei" 626713 (1 Pet, Easter)
CG351
"Hallelujah to the Lamb" 2316323 (1 Pet, Easter)
"We Will Worship the Lamb" 208409 (1 Pet, Easter)
"Grace Like Rain" 3689877 (1 Pet)
"Turn Your Eyes upon Jesus" 15960 (Luke)
CG472, GR670, UM349
"Jesus, We Want to Meet" (Luke)
UM661
"Open Our Eyes, Lord" 1572 (Luke)
CG392, S2086, SH562
"The Servant Song" 72673 (Luke)
C490, CG289, EL659, G727, N539, S2222, SH264, VU595
"Open the Eyes of My Heart" 2298355 (Luke)
G452, SH378, WS3008
"We Walk His Way" OL-72482 (Luke, Easter)
WS3073
+"The Kingdom Is Yours" 7109354 (Luke)
+"Wesley Prayer" ("Fire") 7118633 (Luke)

Solo/Ensemble Suggestions

"Wash, O God, Our Sons and Daughters" (Acts, Baptism)
V-5 (1) p. 64
+"Great Things" 7111321 (Pss)
V-9 p. 36
"Worthy Is the Lamb" (1 Pet, Easter)
V-8 p. 228
"Just a Closer Walk with Thee" (Luke)
V-5 (2) p. 31
V-8 p. 323
+"I Walked Today Where Jesus Walked" (Luke)
V-8 p. 14
"Day of Arising" (Luke, Comm.)
Carl Schalk; AEC-2 p. 50 (https://bit.ly/AEC-2)
2-part mixed, organ (https://bit.ly/AEC-2)
"Assurance" (1 Pet)
arr. John Ness Beck; Beckenhorst BP1097
SATB, keyboard (https://bit.ly/BP1097)

+Hymn Anthem

"En el Frío Invernal" ("Cold December Flies Away") OL-09572 (Acts, 1 Pet)

For accompaniment, use a flute on the melody, a cello or bassoon on the bass part, and tambourine on a repeated pattern (i.e., one quarter note followed by two eighths). Flute and bass instrument should play in a detached manner throughout. Keyboard may play the instrumental parts as described if they are not available. Keep the tempo up, perhaps MM = 80. Perform without *ritard,* with a driving excitement.

Introduction, Interludes between each verse, and Ending – measures 1-2 only. Flute on melody, cello or bassoon on bass, tambourine on rhythm pattern.

Stanza 1 – Three soloists, each taking a sentence of the text. Accompany with bass instrument only. Follow with interlude.

Stanza 2 – All voices on melody. Begin very soft, but excited. Begin getting louder on the third system, going to a full *forte* by the end of the stanza. Begin accompaniment with bass instrument only, adding flute on the third system. Follow with interlude.

Stanza 3 – T/B sing first phrase to "bloom" and hold it while S/A sing "and the world awakens." T/B sing second phrase to "flower" and hold it while S/A sing "dwells a wondrous fragrance." All voices unison, *forte* to the end. Accompany with all three instruments. Follow with ending.

Other Suggestions

Visuals:
O Christus Rex, repent, baptism, gift, Spirit, 3000
P Ear, snare, anguish, prayer, cup, shackles, gifts
E Silver/gold, blood, lamb, Jesus, baptism, Bible
G Jesus, three men walking, Bible, broken bread, burning heart, blindness/vision

Introit: EL529, G392, S2273, SH611, ZS148. "Jesus, We Are Here" (Luke)
Call to Worship: WSL31. "The Risen Savior" (1 Pet)
Opening Prayer: WSL66. "Lord of all nations" (Luke)
Opening Prayer: N831 (Luke)
Prayer: WSL72. "Loving God" (Luke)
Response: UM300. "O the Lamb" (1 Pet, Easter)
Call to Communion: C418. Behold These Emblems (Luke)
Theme Ideas: Assurance, Baptism, Bread of Life, Communion, Grace, Holy Spirit, Resurrection

Notes

NRSVue

Acts 2:42-47

42They devoted themselves to the apostles' teaching and fellowship, to the breaking of bread and the prayers.
43Awe came upon everyone, because many wonders and signs
were being done through the apostles. 44All who believed were
together and had all things in common; 45they would sell their
possessions and goods and distribute the proceeds to all, as any
had need. 46Day by day, as they spent much time together in the
temple, they broke bread at home and ate their food with glad
and generous hearts, 47praising God and having the goodwill of
all the people. And day by day the Lord added to their number
those who were being saved.

Psalm 23 (G473/801-803, N633, P170-175, SH295/307, UM134/754)

1The LORD is my shepherd, I shall not want.
2 He makes me lie down in green pastures;
he leads me beside still waters;
3 he restores my soul.
He leads me in right paths
for his name's sake.
4Even though I walk through the darkest valley,
I fear no evil,
for you are with me;
your rod and your staff,
they comfort me.
5You prepare a table before me
in the presence of my enemies;
you anoint my head with oil;
my cup overflows.
6Surely goodness and mercy shall follow me
all the days of my life,
and I shall dwell in the house of the LORD
my whole life long.

CEB

Acts 2:42-47

42The believers devoted themselves to the apostles' teaching,
to the community, to their shared meals, and to their prayers.
43A sense of awe came over everyone. God performed many
wonders and signs through the apostles. 44All the believers were
united and shared everything. 45They would sell pieces of property and possessions and distribute the proceeds to everyone
who needed them. 46Every day, they met together in the temple
and ate in their homes. They shared food with gladness and
simplicity. 47They praised God and demonstrated God's goodness to everyone. The Lord added daily to the community those
who were being saved.

Psalm 23 (G473/801-803, N633, P170-175, SH295/307, UM134/754)

1 The LORD is my shepherd.
I lack nothing.
2 He lets me rest in grassy meadows;
he leads me to restful waters;
3 he keeps me alive.
He guides me in proper paths
for the sake of his good name.
4 Even when I walk
through the darkest valley,
I fear no danger because you are with me.
Your rod and your staff—
they protect me.
5 You set a table for me
right in front of my enemies.
You bathe my head in oil;
my cup is so full it spills over!
6 Yes, goodness and faithful love
will pursue me all the days of my life,
and I will live in the LORD's house
as long as I live.

NRSVue

1 Peter 2:19-25

19For it is a commendable thing if, being aware of God, a person endures pain while suffering unjustly. 20If you endure when you are beaten for doing wrong, what credit is that? But if you endure when you do good and suffer for it, this is a commendable thing before God. 21For to this you have been called, because Christ also suffered for you, leaving you an example, so that you should follow in his steps.

22"He committed no sin,
and no deceit was found in his mouth."

23When he was abused, he did not return abuse; when he suffered, he did not threaten, but he entrusted himself to the one who judges justly. 24He himself bore our sins in his body on the cross, so that, having died to sins, we might live for righteousness; by his wounds you have been healed. 25For you were going astray like sheep, but now you have returned to the shepherd and guardian of your souls.

John 10:1-10

1"Very truly, I tell you, anyone who does not enter the sheepfold by the gate but climbs in by another way is a thief and a bandit. 2The one who enters by the gate is the shepherd of the sheep. 3The gatekeeper opens the gate for him, and the sheep hear his voice. He calls his own sheep by name and leads them out. 4When he has brought out all his own, he goes ahead of them, and the sheep follow him because they know his voice. 5They will not follow a stranger, but they will run from him because they do not know the voice of strangers." 6Jesus used this figure of speech with them, but they did not understand what he was saying to them.

7So again Jesus said to them, "Very truly, I tell you, I am the gate for the sheep. 8All who came before me are thieves and bandits, but the sheep did not listen to them. 9I am the gate. Whoever enters by me will be saved and will come in and go out and find pasture. 10The thief comes only to steal and kill and destroy. I came that they may have life and have it abundantly."

CEB

1 Peter 2:19-25

19Now, it is commendable if, because of one's understanding of God, someone should endure pain through suffering unjustly. 20But what praise comes from enduring patiently when you have sinned and are beaten for it? But if you endure steadfastly when you've done good and suffer for it, this is commendable before God.

21You were called to this kind of endurance, because Christ suffered on your behalf. He left you an example so that you might follow in his footsteps. 22He committed no sin, nor did he ever speak in ways meant to deceive. 23When he was insulted, he did not reply with insults. When he suffered, he did not threaten revenge. Instead, he entrusted himself to the one who judges justly. 24He carried in his own body on the cross the sins we committed. He did this so that we might live in righteousness, having nothing to do with sin. By his wounds you were healed. 25Though you were like straying sheep, you have now returned to the shepherd and guardian of your lives.

John 10:1-10

1"I assure you that whoever doesn't enter into the sheep pen through the gate but climbs over the wall is a thief and an outlaw. 2The one who enters through the gate is the shepherd of the sheep. 3The guard at the gate opens the gate for him, and the sheep listen to his voice. He calls his own sheep by name and leads them out. 4Whenever he has gathered all of his sheep, he goes before them and they follow him, because they know his voice. 5They won't follow a stranger but will run away because they don't know the stranger's voice." 6Those who heard Jesus use this analogy didn't understand what he was saying.

7So Jesus spoke again, "I assure you that I am the gate of the sheep. 8All who came before me were thieves and outlaws, but the sheep didn't listen to them. 9I am the gate. Whoever enters through me will be saved. They will come in and go out and find pasture. 10The thief enters only to steal, kill, and destroy. I came so that they could have life—indeed, so that they could live life to the fullest."

Primary Hymns and Songs for the Day

"The Lord's My Shepherd, I'll Not Want" 1671200 (Pss, John) (O)
C78/79, CG65, EL778, G801, N479, GR377/657, P170, SH375, UM136, VU747/748
"Where Charity and Love Prevail" 40313 (Acts)
SH271, UM549
H-3 Hbl-71, 104; Chr-219; Desc-95; Org-143
S-2 #162. Harmonization
E581, CG264, EL359, G316, N396
"The King of Love My Shepherd Is" (Pss, 1 Pet)
CG64, E645/646, EL502, G802, GR90, N248, P171, SH359, UM138 (PD), VU273
S-1 #298-299. Harms.
"Shepherd Me, O God" OL-00751 (Pss, John)
EL780, G473, S2058, SH365
"They'll Know We Are Christians" 26997 (Acts) (C)
C494, CG272, G300, S2223, SH232

Additional Hymn Suggestions

"Let Us Talents and Tongues Employ" (Acts)
C422, CG458, EL674, G526, N347, P514, VU468, ZS206
+"O For a World" (Acts)
C683, G372, N575, P386, VU697
"Great Is Thy Faithfulness" 18723 (Acts)
C86, CG48, EL733, G39, GR44, N423, P276, SH48, UM140, VU288
"Sweet, Sweet Spirit" (Acts, 1 Pet)
C261, CG241, G408, GR361, N293, P398, SH410, UM334
+*"Cuando el Pobre"* ("When the Poor Ones") OL-97385 (Acts)
C662, EL725, G762, P407, SH240, UM434, VU702
"Blest Be the Tie That Binds" 7106572 (Acts)
C433, CG267, EL656, G306, GR405, N393, P438, SH701, UM557 (PD), VU602
+"Blest Be the Dear Uniting Love" (Acts)
GR389, UM566 (PD)
"I Come with Joy" (Acts, Comm.)
C420, CG456, E304, EL482, G515, N349, P507, SH682, UM617, VU477
"Let Us Break Bread Together" (Acts, Comm.)
C425, CG461, EL471 (PD), G525, GR418, N330, P513, SH674, UM618, VU480, Z88 (PD)
"In the Midst of New Dimensions" (Acts)
C458, G315, N391, S2238
"We All Are One in Mission" 3176809 (Acts)
CG269, EL576, G733, P435, S2243, ZS99
"Come, Share the Lord" (Acts, Comm.)
C408, CG459, G510, S2269, VU469
+"Father, We Have Heard You Calling" OL-86142 (Acts)
WS3150
"My Shepherd Will Supply My Need" (Pss)
C80, CG66, E664, EL782 (PD), G803, GR50, N247, P172, SH44
"He Leadeth Me: O Blessed Thought" (Pss)
C545, CG68, GR73, SH304, UM128 (PD), VU657
"Close to Thee" (Pss)
GR335, UM407 (PD), Z7
"Since Jesus Came into My Heart" (Pss, 1 Pet)
CG614, GR552, S2140
+"Lead On, O Cloud of Presence" (Pss, 1 Pet)
C633, S2234, VU421
+"God of Great and God of Small" (Pss, John)
G19, WS3033
+"You, Lord, Are Both Lamb and Shepherd" (Pss, John)
G274, SH210, VU210. WS3043
"Savior, Like a Shepherd Lead Us" 24078 (Pss, John)
C558, CG405, EL789, G187, GR130, N252, P387, SH538, UM381 (PD)
"Lead Me, Guide Me" (Pss, John)
C583, CG403, EL768, G740, S2214, SH582, ZS173
"In the Cross of Christ I Glory" 36499 (1 Pet)
C207, CG183, E441/442, EL324, G213, GR239, N193, P84, UM295 (PD)
"Christ Is Alive" (1 Pet)
CG205, E182, EL389, G246, P108, UM318, VU158
"O Jesus, I Have Promised" 40454 (1 Pet)
C612, E655, EL810, G724/725, GR592, N493, P388/389, SH623, UM396 (PD), VU120
"Take Up Thy Cross" 2154808 (1 Pet)
E675, EL667, G718, GR220,N204, P393, SH605, UM415, VU561
"Lord of the Dance" 78529 (John, Easter)
G157, P302, UM261, VU352
"You Satisfy the Hungry Heart" 84788 (John, Comm.)
C429, CG468, EL484, G523, P521, SH672, UM629, VU478
"God Be with You till We Meet Again" (John) (C)
C434, CG523, EL536, G541, GR688, N81, UM672 (PD), VU422, Z37
"God Be with You Till We Meet Again" (John) (C)
G542, P540, UM673 (PD), VU423
+"God Be with You" (John) (C)
C435, N809, Z203, ZS215

Additional Contemporary and Modern Suggestions

+"Let Justice Roll" ("Like a River") 4974842 (Acts)
"If You Believe and I Believe" 3273104 (Acts)
WS3121
"One Bread, One Body" OL-80673 (Acts, Comm.)
C393, EL496, G530, SH678, UM620, VU467
"Make Us One" 695737 (Acts)
S2224, ZS93
"One God and Father of Us All" 3417678 (Acts)
S2240
"Your Grace Is Enough" 4477026 (Acts, Pss)
WS3106
"Nada Te Turbe" ("Nothing Can Trouble") OL-00128 (Pss)
CG73, G820, N772, S2054, SH292, VU290
"Gentle Shepherd" 15609 (Pss)
WS3096
"God Will Make a Way" 458620 (Pss)
SH57
"For Us" 7119349 (Pss)
"The King of Love My Shepherd Is" 7023979 (Pss)
"Lead Me, Lord" 1609045 (Pss, 1 Pet)
+"Called Me Higher" 5887880 (Pss, 1 Pet)
"His Name Is Wonderful" 1122230 (Pss, John)
CG343, SH454, UM174, ZS31
"The Power of the Cross" 4490766 (1 Pet, Easter)
CG190, GR237, WS3085
+"At the Cross" 4591816 (1 Pet, Easter)
+"Living Hope" 7106807 (1 Pet, Easter)
+"Love Came Down" 5148938 (1 Pet, John)
+"Yet Not I but Through Christ in Me" 7121852 (1 Pet, John)
+"Good Grace" 7122177 (1 Pet, John)
+"His Mercy Is More" 7065053 (1 Pet, John)
+"Won't Stop Now" 7111932 (1 Pet, John)
"Who Can Satisfy My Soul Like You?" 208492 (John)
"People Need the Lord" 18084 (John)
S2244

Solo/Ensemble Suggestions

+"God Will Make a Way" (with "He Leadeth Me") (Pss, 1 Pet)
V-3 (2) p. 9
"The Lord is My Shepherd" (Pss, John)
V-5 (3) p. 30

"God, Our Ever Faithful Shepherd" (Pss, John)
V-4 p. 15
"My Shepherd Will Supply My Need" (Pss, John)
V-10 p. 4
"Maybe the Rain" (Pss, John)
V-5 (2) p. 27
"Come, Praise the Lord!" (Pss, Easter)
V-8 p. 304
+"The New 23rd" (Pss)
V-8 p. 340
"In the Image of God" (1 Pet)
V-8 p. 362
+"Graves Into Gardens" 7138219 (John, Easter)
V-9 p. 15
"Shepherd Me, Lord" (Pss)
William M. Schoenfeld; AEC-3 p. 46
2-part, piano, flute or recorder (https://bit.ly/AEC-3)
"Show Me, Teach Me, Lead Me" (Pss)
Nancy M. Raabe; AEC-3 p. 66
Unison, piano (https://bit.ly/AEC-3)

+Hymn Anthem

"One Bread, One Body" OL-80673 (Acts, Comm.)
C393, EL496, G530, SH678, UM620, VU467

This anthem will be enhanced with the use of improvised piano playing, guitars, and movement. The choir and congregation sing the refrain together. Vary the singing of the stanzas: lower voices, upper voices, soloists, etc. The movement described here may be done by all, even the seated congregation. Further movement may be devised for the stanzas and performed by a small group. If available, use a flute to double the refrain melody.

Suggested movement for refrain:
"One bread," - Right arm, palm up, moves left to right, in front of body.
"one body," - Left arm, palm up, moves right to left, in front of body.
"one Lord of all," - Create "praying hands" in front of chest.
"one cup of blessing . . ." - Keeping wrist together, but fingers apart, raise hands above head, creating a "cup."
"And we . . . the earth" - Slowly lower arms, palms up, arms extended.
"We are one body . . . one Lord." - Grasp hands of neighbors and lower arms to side.

Other Suggestions

Visuals:
O Teaching, fellowship, broken bread, prayer, meal
P Shepherd/sheep, pasture, lake, path, valley, rod, staff, banquet table, cup, sanctuary
E Whip/club, Passion, crucifix, healing, sheep
G Sheepfold, gate, robber's mask, sheep/shepherd

+Introit: C273, CG247, EL652, WS3147, stanza 3. "Built on a Rock" (Acts)
Canticle: UM137. Psalm 23 (Pss, John)
Confession: WSL43. "We often act" (Acts, 1 Pet, John)
Prayer: WSL17. "A wilderness beckons" (Acts, Pss, John)
+Call to Commitment: S2101, stanza 4. "Two Fishermen" (1 Pet)
Litany: UM556. Litany for Christian Unity (Acts)
+Sung Benediction: C273, CG247, EL652, WS3147, stanza 6. "Built on a Rock" (John)
Theme Ideas: Discipleship / Following God, Endurance, God: Shepherd, Holy Spirit, Unity

Notes

NRSVue

Acts 7:55-60

55But filled with the Holy Spirit, he gazed into heaven and saw
the glory of God and Jesus standing at the right hand of God.
56"Look," he said, "I see the heavens opened and the Son of Man
standing at the right hand of God!" 57But they covered their ears,
and with a loud shout all rushed together against him. 58Then
they dragged him out of the city and began to stone him, and
the witnesses laid their coats at the feet of a young man named
Saul. 59While they were stoning Stephen, he prayed, "Lord Jesus,
receive my spirit." 60Then he knelt down and cried out in a loud
voice, "Lord, do not hold this sin against them." When he had
said this, he died.

Psalm 31:1-5, 15-16 (G214/811, N640/641, P182/183, UM764)

1In you, O LORD, I seek refuge;
  do not let me ever be put to shame;
  in your righteousness deliver me.
2Incline your ear to me;
  rescue me speedily.
Be a rock of refuge for me,
  a strong fortress to save me.
3You are indeed my rock and my fortress;
  for your name's sake lead me and guide me;
4take me out of the net that is hidden for me,
  for you are my refuge.
5Into your hand I commit my spirit;
  you have redeemed me, O LORD, faithful God.

. . . .

15My times are in your hand;
  deliver me from the hand of my enemies and persecutors.
16Let your face shine upon your servant;
  save me in your steadfast love.

CEB

Acts 7:55-60

55But Stephen, enabled by the Holy Spirit, stared into heaven
and saw God's majesty and Jesus standing at God's right side.
56He exclaimed, "Look! I can see heaven on display and the
Human One standing at God's right side!" 57At this, they
shrieked and covered their ears. Together, they charged at
him, 58threw him out of the city, and began to stone him. The
witnesses placed their coats in the care of a young man named
Saul. 59As they battered him with stones, Stephen prayed, "Lord
Jesus, accept my life!" 60Falling to his knees, he shouted, "Lord,
don't hold this sin against them!" Then he died.

Psalm 31:1-5, 15-16 (G214/811, N640/641, P182/183, UM764)

1I take refuge in you, LORD.
  Please never let me be put to shame.
    Rescue me by your righteousness!
2Listen closely to me!
  Deliver me quickly;
    be a rock that protects me;
    be a strong fortress that saves me!
3You are definitely my rock and my fortress.
  Guide me and lead me for the sake of your good name!
4Get me out of this net that's been set for me
  because you are my protective fortress.
5I entrust my spirit into your hands;
  you, LORD, God of faithfulness—
  you have saved me.

. . . .

15My future is in your hands.
  Don't hand me over to my enemies,
  to all who are out to get me!
16Shine your face on your servant;
  save me by your faithful love!

NRSVue

1 Peter 2:2-10

[2]Like newborn infants, long for the pure, spiritual milk, so that by it you may grow into salvation—[3]if indeed you have tasted that the Lord is good.

[4]Come to him, a living stone, though rejected by mortals yet chosen and precious in God's sight, and [5]like living stones let yourselves be built into a spiritual house, to be a holy priesthood, to offer spiritual sacrifices acceptable to God through Jesus Christ. [6]For it stands in scripture:

"See, I am laying in Zion a stone,
a cornerstone chosen and precious,
and whoever believes in him will not be put to shame."

[7]This honor, then, is for you who believe, but for those who do not believe,

"The stone that the builders rejected
has become the very head of the corner,"

[8]and

"A stone that makes them stumble,
and a rock that makes them fall."

They stumble because they disobey the word, as they were destined to do.

[9]But you are a chosen people, a royal priesthood, a holy nation, God's own people, in order that you may proclaim the excellence of him who called you out of darkness into his marvelous light.

[10]Once you were not a people,
but now you are God's people;
once you had not received mercy,
but now you have received mercy.

John 14:1-14

[1]"Do not let your hearts be troubled. Believe in God; believe also in me. [2]In my Father's house there are many dwelling places. If it were not so, would I have told you that I go to prepare a place for you? [3]And if I go and prepare a place for you, I will come again and will take you to myself, so that where I am, there you may be also. [4]And you know the way to the place where I am going." [5]Thomas said to him, "Lord, we do not know where you are going. How can we know the way?" [6]Jesus said to him, "I am the way and the truth and the life. No one comes to the Father except through me. [7]If you know me, you will know my Father also. From now on you do know him and have seen him."

[8]Philip said to him, "Lord, show us the Father, and we will be satisfied." [9]Jesus said to him, "Have I been with you all this time, Philip, and you still do not know me? Whoever has seen me has seen the Father. How can you say, 'Show us the Father'? [10]Do you not believe that I am in the Father and the Father is in me? The words that I say to you I do not speak on my own, but the Father who dwells in me does his works. [11]Believe me that I am in the Father and the Father is in me, but if you do not, then believe because of the works themselves. [12]Very truly, I tell you, the one who believes in me will also do the works that I do and, in fact, will do greater works than these, because I am going to the Father. [13]I will do whatever you ask in my name, so that the Father may be glorified in the Son. [14]If in my name you ask me for anything, I will do it."

CEB

1 Peter 2:2-10

[2]Instead, like a newborn baby, desire the pure milk of the word. Nourished by it, you will grow into salvation, [3]since you have tasted that the Lord is good.

[4]Now you are coming to him as to a living stone. Even though this stone was rejected by humans, from God's perspective it is chosen, valuable. [5]You yourselves are being built like living stones into a spiritual temple. You are being made into a holy priesthood to offer up spiritual sacrifices that are acceptable to God through Jesus Christ. [6]Thus it is written in scripture, *Look! I am laying a cornerstone in Zion, chosen, valuable. The person who believes in him will never be shamed.* [7]So God honors you who believe. For those who refuse to believe, though, the stone the builders tossed aside has become the capstone. [8]This is a stone that makes people stumble and a rock that makes them fall. Because they refuse to believe in the word, they stumble. Indeed, this is the end to which they were appointed. [9]But you are a chosen race, a royal priesthood, a holy nation, a people who are God's own possession. You have become this people so that you may speak of the wonderful acts of the one who called you out of darkness into his amazing light. [10]Once you weren't a people, but now you are God's people. Once you hadn't received mercy, but now you have received mercy.

John 14:1-14

[1]"Don't be troubled. Trust in God. Trust also in me. [2]My Father's house has room to spare. If that weren't the case, would I have told you that I'm going to prepare a place for you? [3]When I go to prepare a place for you, I will return and take you to be with me so that where I am you will be too. [4]You know the way to the place I'm going."

[5]Thomas asked, "Lord, we don't know where you are going. How can we know the way?"

[6]Jesus answered, "I am the way, the truth, and the life. No one comes to the Father except through me. [7]If you have really known me, you will also know the Father. From now on you know him and have seen him."

[8]Philip said, "Lord, show us the Father; that will be enough for us."

[9]Jesus replied, "Don't you know me, Philip, even after I have been with you all this time? Whoever has seen me has seen the Father. How can you say, 'Show us the Father'? [10]Don't you believe that I am in the Father and the Father is in me? The words I have spoken to you I don't speak on my own. The Father who dwells in me does his works. [11]Trust me when I say that I am in the Father and the Father is in me, or at least believe on account of the works themselves. [12]I assure you that whoever believes in me will do the works that I do. They will do even greater works than these because I am going to the Father. [13]I will do whatever you ask for in my name, so that the Father can be glorified in the Son. [14]When you ask me for anything in my name, I will do it."

Primary Hymns and Songs for the Day

"The Church's One Foundation" 55377 (1 Pet, John) (O)
C272, CG246, E525, EL654, G321, GR388/646, N386, P442, SH233, UM545/546, VU332 (Fr.)
H-3 Hbl-94; Chr-180; Desc-16; Org-9
S-1 #25-26. Desc. and harm.
"Be Still, My Soul" (Acts, Pss)
C566, CG57, G819, GR346, N488, SH330, UM534, VU652
H-3 Chr-36
"Nada Te Turbe" ("Nothing Can Trouble") OL-00128 (John)
CG73, G820, N772, S2054, SH292, VU290
"His Eye Is on the Sparrow" 77692 (Pss, John)
C82, G661, GR380, N475, S2146, SH322, Z33 (PD)
"Christ Is Made the Sure Foundation" 7036287 (1 Pet, Comm.) (C)
C275, CG248, E518, EL645, G394, GR101, N400, P416/417, SH225, UM559 (PD), VU325
H-3 Chr-49; Desc-103; Org-180
S-1 #346. Desc.

Additional Hymn Suggestions

"God of Grace and God of Glory" 43107 (Acts)
C464, CG285, E594/595, EL705, G307, GR45, N436, P420, SH250, UM577, VU686
"Dear Lord and Father of Mankind" 106185 (Acts)
(Alternate Text: "Dear God, Embracing Humankind")
C594, CG413, E652/563, G169, GR499, N502, P345, UM358 (PD), VU608
"God of Our Life" (Acts)
C713, G686, N366, P275
"Deep in the Shadows of the Past" (Acts)
G50, N320, P330, S2246
"Guide My Feet" OL-LMGM2537 (Acts, Pss)
CG637, G741, GR326, N497, P354, S2208, SH54, ZS141
"Lead Me, Guide Me" (Acts, Pss)
C583, CG403, EL768, G740, S2214, SH582, ZS173
"Saranam, Saranam" ("Refuge") (Acts, Pss)
G789, UM523
"How Firm a Foundation" 107816 (Acts, 1 Pet)
C618, CG425, E636, EL796, G463, GR46, N407, P361, SH291, UM529 (PD), VU660
+"Feed Us, Lord" 4636207 (Pss, Comm.)
G501, WS3167
"From All That Dwell Below the Skies" (1 Pet)
C49, CG330, E380, G327, GR76, N27, P229, UM101 (PD)
"Sing Praise to God Who Reigns Above" 7061649 (1 Pet)
C6, CG315, E408, EL871, G645, GR5, N6, P483, UM126 (PD), VU216
"God Is Here" 223549 (1 Pet)
C280, CG298, EL526, G409, GR393, N70, P461, UM660, VU389
"Christ, the Great Foundation" (1 Pet)
G361, P443
"Come, O Spirit, Dwell Among Us" (1 Pet)
G280, N267, P129, VU198
"Spirit Divine, Attend Our Prayers" (John)
E509, G407, P325, SH571, VU385
"Come, My Way, My Truth, My Life" (John)
E487, EL816, N331, UM164 (PD), VU628
"My Jesus, I Love Thee" (John)
C349, CG361, GR117, SH303, UM172 (PD)
"Victory in Jesus" (John)
CG627, GR119, UM370
"Prayer Is the Soul's Sincere Desire" (John)
CG391, GR438, N508, UM492
"Here, O Lord, Your Servants Gather" (John)
C278, EL530, G311, N72, P465, UM552, VU362
"When We All Get to Heaven" (John)
CG548, GR616, UM701 (PD), Z15, ZS131
"Healer of Our Every Ill" OL-00115 (John)
C506, EL612, G795, S2213, SH339, VU619
"In Remembrance of Me" 25156 (John, Comm.)
C403, CG462, G521, S2254, SH667, ZS203
"I'll Fly Away" (John)
N595, S2282, Z183
"In God Alone" OL-87508 (John)
G814, WS3135
"Solamente en Cristo" ("Only in Christ Jesus") (John)
SH131
"Let Us Break Bread Together" (Comm.)
C425, CG461, EL471 (PD), G525, GR418, N330, P513, SH674, UM618, VU480, Z88 (PD)

Additional Contemporary and Modern Suggestions

"Holy Ground" 21198 (Acts)
C112, G406, S2272
+"Presence" 7116947 (Acts)
+"Awesome in This Place" 847554 (Acts)
"Foundation" 706151 (Acts, 1 Pet)
"You are the Light" 6238098 (Acts, 1 Pet)
"Guide My Feet" OL-LMGM2537 (Acts, Pss)
CG637, G741, GR326, N497, P354, S2208, SH54, ZS141
"I Will Call upon the Lord" 11263 (Pss)
G621, S2002
"Rock of Ages" 2240547 (Pss)
"Lead Me, Lord" 1609045 (Pss)
"God Will Make a Way" 458620 (Pss, John)
SH57
+"Made a Way" 7071768 (Pss, John)
+"Do It Again" 7067555 (Pss, John)
+"Nothing to Fear" 7133723 (Pss, John)
"Grace Alone" 2335524 (1 Pet)
CG43, S2162, ZS100
"Cornerstone" 6158927 (1 Pet)
"Knowing You" 1045238 (1 Pet)
"Marvelous Light" 4491002 (1 Pet)
+"Promises" 7149439 (1 Pet)
+"All of Me" 6290160 (1 Pet)
"Here I Am to Worship" 3266032 (1 Pet)
CG297, SH395, WS3177, ZS145
"Someone Asked the Question" 1640279 (John)
N523, S2144
"People Need the Lord" 18084 (John)
S2244
"Be Glorified" 429226 (John)
"Be Glorified" 2732646 (John)
"Behold, What Manner of Love" 1596 (John)
"Give Us Your Peace" 5767807 (John)
"Jesus I Trust in You" 4510828 (John)
+"One Way" 4222082 (John)
+"You Are" 4387343 (John)
+"Good Grace" 7122177 (John)
+"The Way" 7089024 (John)
+"Who You Say You Are" 7130503 (John)
"My Savior Lives" 4882965 (John, Easter)
"That's Why We Praise Him" 2668576 (John, Easter)
"For All You've Done" 4254689 (John, Easter)
"Halle, Halle, Halleluja" 2659190 (John, Easter)
C41, CG433, EL172, G591, N236, S2026, SH694, VU958, ZS76

Solo/Ensemble Suggestions

+"Refuge and Strength" (Pss)
V-3 (5) p. 14
+"Famous For" ("I Believe") 7096220 (Pss)
V-9 p. 22

"How Firm a Foundation" (1 Pet)
V-6 p. 31
"Because He Lives" (1 Pet, Easter)
V-8 p. 24
"The Call" (John)
V-4 p. 31
"In Bright Mansions Above" (John)
V-4 p. 39
"They Led Him Away" (John, Easter)
V-8 p. 245
"The Chief Cornerstone" (1 Pet)
Bradley Ellingboe; AEC-1 p. 69
2-part mixed, keyboard, opt. trumpet (bit.ly/AEC-1-69)
+"Come, My Way, My Truth, My Life" (John)
Gerald Near; MorningStar AE175
SATB, organ (https://bit.ly/M-175)

+Hymn Anthem

"Here, O Lord, Your Servants Gather" (John)
C278, EL530, G311, N72, P465, UM552, VU362

This melody is pentatonic, however, the accompaniment in the hymnal is not pentatonic. You may invent your own accompaniments using handbells, resonator bells, Orff instruments, and percussions instruments or see S-1, #333.

Introduction: Flute, recorder, or keyboard plays phrase 1 melody.

Stanza 1: *A cappella.* One voice sings phrase 1 (mm 1-4), three voices sing phrase 2 (mm 5-8), five to six voices sing phrase 3 (mm 9-12), and all voices sing phrase 4 (mm 13-16). This obviously gives a "gathering" effect.

Stanza 2: Phrases 1-2, T/B sing English text, S/A lightly sing Japanese phonetic transcription. Phrases 3-4, reverse: S/A on English, T/B on Japanese. (Or sing the stanza as a round with the second group starting one measure after the first.) Keyboard plays hymnal accompaniment.

Stanza 3: All voices sing stanza in English. Flute or recorder may double melody. Keyboard plays hymnal accompaniment. Strongest stanza, though reducing volume in phrase 4.

Stanza 4: All voices sing, *mezzo piano*, prayerfully. Keyboard left hand plays bass clef, lower part as written; right hand plays bass clef, upper part two octaves higher than written. Flute or recorder may play treble clef, lower part one or two octaves higher. End quietly and slowly.

Other Suggestions

Visuals:

O Spirit/flames/dove, Christ, heavens opened, stones, coats, Acts 7:59b, 60b, life/death
P Rock, Ps. 31:3a, fortress, net, hands, Ps. 31:16ab
E Newborn, milk, stone(s), cornerstone, stumbling blocks, 1 Pet. 2:9a, crowd, nations, dark/light
G Hearts, mourning, dwellings, Christ, works, John 14:13, 14

Affirmation of Faith: WSL33. "This is the good news" (1 Pet, Easter)
Litany of Preparation: WSL73. "We come broken" (John)
Prayer: UM466. An Invitation to Christ (John)
Prayer: N856. Eternal Life (John)
Prayer: UM535. A Refuge amid Distraction (Acts, Pss)
+Sung Benediction: C436, UM666. "Shalom to You" 114122 (John)
+Sung Benediction: C273, CG247, EL652, WS3147, stanza 6. "Built on a Rock" (John)
Theme Ideas: Comfort, God: Providence / God our Help, Holy Spirit, Jesus: Cornerstone, Lament

Notes

NRSVue

Acts 17:22-31

22Then Paul stood in front of the Areopagus and said, "Athe-
nians, I see how extremely spiritual you are in every way. 23For
as I went through the city and looked carefully at the objects of
your worship, I found among them an altar with the inscription,
'To an unknown god.' What therefore you worship as unknown,
this I proclaim to you. 24The God who made the world and everything in it, he who is Lord of heaven and earth, does not live
in shrines made by human hands, 25nor is he served by human
hands, as though he needed anything, since he himself gives to
all mortals life and breath and all things. 26From one ancestor he
made all peoples to inhabit the whole earth, and he allotted the
times of their existence and the boundaries of the places where
they would live, 27so that they would search for God and perhaps
fumble about for him and find him—though indeed he is not
far from each one of us. 28For 'In him we live and move and have
our being'; as even some of your own poets have said,
'For we, too, are his offspring.'

29Since we are God's offspring, we ought not to think that the
deity is like gold or silver or stone, an image formed by the art
and imagination of mortals. 30While God has overlooked the
times of human ignorance, now he commands all people everywhere to repent, 31because he has fixed a day on which he will
have the world judged in righteousness by a man whom he has
appointed, and of this he has given assurance to all by raising
him from the dead."

Psalm 66:8-20 (G54, N662, UM790)

8Bless our God, O peoples;
  let the sound of his praise be heard,
9who has kept us among the living
  and has not let our feet slip.
10For you, O God, have tested us;
  you have tried us as silver is tried.
11You brought us into the net;
  you laid burdens on our backs;
12you let people ride over our heads;
  we went through fire and through water;
yet you have brought us out to a spacious place.
13I will come into your house with burnt offerings;
  I will pay you my vows,
14those that my lips uttered
  and my mouth promised when I was in trouble.
15I will offer to you burnt offerings of fatted calves,
  with the smoke of the sacrifice of rams;
I will make an offering of bulls and goats. *[Selah]*
16Come and hear, all you who fear God,
  and I will tell what he has done for me.
17I cried aloud to him,
  and he was extolled with my tongue.
18If I had cherished iniquity in my heart,
  the Lord would not have listened.
19But truly God has listened;
  he has heard the words of my prayer.
20Blessed be God,
  who has not rejected my prayer
  or removed his steadfast love from me.

CEB

Acts 17:22-31

22Paul stood up in the middle of the council on Mars Hill and
said, "People of Athens, I see that you are very religious in every
way. 23As I was walking through town and carefully observing
your objects of worship, I even found an altar with this inscription: 'To an unknown God.' What you worship as unknown, I
now proclaim to you. 24God, who made the world and everything
in it, is Lord of heaven and earth. He doesn't live in temples
made with human hands. 25Nor is God served by human hands,
as though he needed something, since he is the one who gives
life, breath, and everything else. 26From one person God created
every human nation to live on the whole earth, having determined their appointed times and the boundaries of their lands.
27God made the nations so they would seek him, perhaps even
reach out to him and find him. In fact, God isn't far away from
any of us. 28In God we live, move, and exist. As some of your own
poets said, 'We are his offspring.'

29"Therefore, as God's offspring, we have no need to imagine
that the divine being is like a gold, silver, or stone image made
by human skill and thought. 30God overlooks ignorance of these
things in times past, but now directs everyone everywhere to
change their hearts and lives. 31This is because God has set a
day when he intends to judge the world justly by a man he has
appointed. God has given proof of this to everyone by raising
him from the dead."

Psalm 66:8-20 (G54, N662, UM790)

8All you nations, bless our God!
  Let the sound of his praise be heard!
9God preserved us among the living;
  he didn't let our feet slip a bit.
10But you, God, have tested us—
  you've refined us like silver,
11 trapped us in a net,
  laid burdens on our backs,
12 let other people run right over our heads—
  we've been through fire and water.
But you brought us out to freedom!
13 So I'll enter your house
    with entirely burned offerings.
  I'll keep the promises I made to you,
14   the ones my lips uttered,
    the ones my mouth spoke when I was in deep trouble.
15I will offer the best burned offerings to you
  along with the smoke of sacrificed rams.
  I will offer both bulls and goats. *[Selah]*
16Come close and listen,
  all you who honor God;
  I will tell you what God has done for me:
17My mouth cried out to him
  with praise on my tongue.
18If I had cherished evil in my heart,
  my Lord would not have listened.
19But God definitely listened.
  He heard the sound of my prayer.
20Bless God! He didn't reject my prayer;
  he didn't withhold his faithful love from me.

NRSVue

1 Peter 3:13-22

13Now who will harm you if you are eager to do what is good?
14But even if you do suffer for doing what is right, you are
blessed. Do not fear what they fear, and do not be intimidated,
15but in your hearts sanctify Christ as Lord. Always be ready
to make your defense to anyone who demands from you an
accounting for the hope that is in you, 16yet do it with gentleness
and respect. Maintain a good conscience so that, when you are
maligned, those who abuse you for your good conduct in Christ
may be put to shame. 17For it is better to suffer for doing good,
if suffering should be God's will, than to suffer for doing evil.
18For Christ also suffered for sins once for all, the righteous for
the unrighteous, in order to bring you to God. He was put to
death in the flesh but made alive in the spirit, 19in which also
he went and made a proclamation to the spirits in prison, 20who
in former times did not obey, when God waited patiently in the
days of Noah, during the building of the ark, in which a few, that
is, eight lives, were saved through water. 21And baptism, which
this prefigured, now saves you—not as a removal of dirt from the
body but as an appeal to God for a good conscience, through
the resurrection of Jesus Christ, 22who has gone into heaven and
is at the right hand of God, with angels, authorities, and powers
made subject to him.

John 14:15-21

15"If you love me, you will keep my commandments. 16And I
will ask the Father, and he will give you another Advocate, to be
with you forever. 17This is the Spirit of truth, whom the world
cannot receive because it neither sees him nor knows him. You
know him because he abides with you, and he will be in you.
18"I will not leave you orphaned; I am coming to you. 19In a
little while the world will no longer see me, but you will see me;
because I live, you also will live. 20On that day you will know that
I am in my Father, and you in me, and I in you. 21They who have
my commandments and keep them are those who love me, and
those who love me will be loved by my Father, and I will love
them and reveal myself to them."

CEB

1 Peter 3:13-22

13Who will harm you if you are zealous for good? 14But happy
are you, even if you suffer because of righteousness! Don't be
terrified or upset by them. 15Instead, regard Christ as holy in
your hearts. Whenever anyone asks you to speak of your hope,
be ready to defend it. 16Yet do this with respectful humility,
maintaining a good conscience. Act in this way so that those who
malign your good lifestyle in Christ may be ashamed when they
slander you. 17It is better to suffer for doing good (if this could
possibly be God's will) than for doing evil.
18Christ himself suffered on account of sins, once for all, the
righteous one on behalf of the unrighteous. He did this in order
to bring you into the presence of God. Christ was put to death as
a human, but made alive by the Spirit. 19And it was by the Spirit
that he went to preach to the spirits in prison. 20In the past,
these spirits were disobedient—when God patiently waited during the time of Noah. Noah built an ark in which a few (that is,
eight) lives were rescued through water. 21Baptism is like that. It
saves you now—not because it removes dirt from your body but
because it is the mark of a good conscience toward God. Your
salvation comes through the resurrection of Jesus Christ, 22who
is at God's right side. Now that he has gone into heaven, he rules
over all angels, authorities, and powers.

John 14:15-21

15"If you love me, you will keep my commandments. 16I will ask
the Father, and he will send another Companion, who will be
with you forever. 17This Companion is the Spirit of Truth, whom
the world can't receive because it neither sees him nor recog-
nizes him. You know him, because he lives with you and will be
with you.
18"I won't leave you as orphans. I will come to you. 19Soon the
world will no longer see me, but you will see me. Because I live,
you will live too. 20On that day you will know that I am in my
Father, you are in me, and I am in you. 21Whoever has my commandments and keeps them loves me. Whoever loves me will
be loved by my Father, and I will love them and reveal myself to
them."

Primary Hymns and Songs for the Day
"I Sing the Almighty Power of God" 738058 (Acts, John) (O)
C64, G32, N12, P288 (PD), SH15
H-3 Hbl-16, 22, 68; Chr-101; Desc-37
S-1 #115. Harmonization
CG19, E398, GR4, UM152 (PD)
H-3 Hbl-44; Chr-21; Desc-40; Org-40
S-1 #131-132. Introduction and descant
VU231 (PD)
H-3 Hbl-44; Chr-21; Desc-40; Org-40
S-1 #131-132. Intro. and desc.
"Spirit of the Living God" 23488 (Acts, John)
C259, CG233, G288, GR299, N283, P322, SH555, UM393, VU376, Z226, S-1 #212 Vocal desc. idea
H-3 Chr-176
S-1 #212. Vocal descant idea
"Love Divine, All Loves Excelling" 40306 (John) (C)
C517, CG281, E657, EL631, G366, GR88, N43, P376, SH353/354, UM384 (PD), VU333
H-3 Chr-134; Desc-18; Org-13
S-1 #41-42. Desc. and harm.

Additional Hymn Suggestions
"From All That Dwell Below the Skies" (Acts)
C49, CG330, E380, G327, GR76, N27, P229, UM101 (PD)
+"I Need Thee Every Hour" (Acts)
C578, CG404, G735, GR340, N517, UM397, VU671
+"Near to the Heart of God" (Acts)
C581, CG383, G824, GR357, P527, UM472 (PD)
+"O for a Closer Walk with God" (Acts)
CG679, E684, G739, GR327, N450, P396
"God Is Here" 223549 (Acts)
C280, CG298, EL526, G409, GR393, N70, P461, UM660, VU389
"I Greet Thee, Who My Sure Redeemer Art" (Acts, 1 Pet)
G624, GR41, N251, P457, VU393
"Rejoice, the Lord Is King" 36592 (Acts, 1 Pet)
C699, CG215, E481, EL430, G363, GR277, N303, P155, SH213, UM715/716, VU213
"O For a World" (1 Pet)
C683, G372, N575, P386, VU697
"To God Be the Glory" (1 Pet)
C72, CG349, G634, GR531, P485, SH545, UM98 (PD)
"Rejoice, Ye Pure in Heart" (1 Pet)
C15, CG312, E556/557, EL873/874, G804, GR62, N55/71, P145/146, UM160/161
"Wash, O God, Our Sons and Daughters" (1 Pet, Baptism)
C365, EL445, G490, SH669, UM605, VU442, ZS191
"Spirit Divine, Attend Our Prayers" (John)
E509, G407, P325, SH571, VU385
+"Take Me to the Water" (PD) (1 Pet, Baptism)
C367, G480, N322, SH665, WS3165, ZS190
"Cristo Vive" ("Christ is Risen") (John)
N235, P109, SH184, UM313
"Pues Si Vivimos" ("When We Are Living") 4968810 (John)
C536, CG265, EL639, G822, N499, P400, SH299, UM356, VU581
"Because He Lives" (John, Easter)
C562, CG620, GR265, SH200, UM364
"There's Within My Heart a Melody" (John)
C550, CG597, GR144, UM380 (PD)
"Lord, I Want to Be a Christian" 3184437 (John)
C589, CG507, G729, GR611, N454, P372 (PD), SH621, UM402, Z76 (PD-TO)
"The Gift of Love" 67327 (John)
C526, CG440, G693, P335, UM408, VU372
"Holy Spirit, Truth Divine" 300431 (John)
C241, EL398, GR320, N63, P321, UM465, VU368
"Come Down, O Love Divine" 761678 (John)
C582, E516, EL804, G282, GR293, N289, P313, UM475 (PD), VU367
"O Spirit of the Living God" (PD) (John)
N263, SH222, UM539
"Blessed Jesus, At Thy Word" (John)
E440, EL520, G395, N74, P454, UM596 (PD), VU500
"Abide with Me" (John)
C636, CG543, E662, EL629, G836, GR678, N99, P543, SH475, UM700 (PD), VU436
"Blessed Quietness" (John, Comm.)
C267, CG244, N284 (PD), S2142, Z206
"Love the Lord Your God" 1400093 (John)
G62, S2168
+"In Remembrance of Me" 25156 (John, Comm.)
C403, CG462, G521, S2254, SH667, ZS203
"Joyful, Joyful, We Adore Thee" (John, Easter, Mother's Day)
C2, CG310, E376, EL836, G611, GR8, N4, P464, SH390, UM89 (PD), VU232
+"O Lord, May Church and Home Combine" (Mother's Day)
CG684, UM695
"Loving Spirit" 3379424 (Mother's Day)
C244, EL397, G293, P323, S2123, VU387

Additional Contemporary and Modern Suggestions
"Awesome in This Place" 847554 (Acts)
"Doxology" 5465879 (Acts)
"More Precious than Silver" 11335 (Acts)
S2065
"Someone Asked the Question" 1640279 (Pss)
N523, S2144
"Blessed Be Your Name" 3798438 (Pss)
SH449, WS3002
+"Shout to the North" 1562261 (Pss)
G319, WS3042
"Refiner's Fire" 426298 (Pss)
+"Purified" 3409710 (Pss)
"All Heaven Declares" 120556 (Pss, Easter)
+"Say So" 4944016 (Pss, John)
+"Purify My Heart" 1314323 (Pss, John)
+"Purify My Heart" OL-73195 / OL-86873 (Pss, John)
WS3103
"Veni Sancte Spiritus" ("Holy Spirit, Come to Us") OL-TaizeVN57 (John)
EL406, G281, S2118
"Where the Spirit of the Lord Is" 27484 (John)
C264, S2119
+"He Who Began a Good Work in You" 15238 (John)
S2163, ZS98
"Live in Charity" (*"Ubi Caritas"*) OL-00798 (John)
C523, EL642, G205, S2179
"Fill Us with Your Love, O Lord" OL-87676 (John)
WS3005
+"Come, Holy Spirit" 3383953 (John)
WS3092 (*See also* SH223, WS3091)
"Love the Lord" 4572938 (John)
WS3116
"There's a Spirit of Love in This Place" OL-38821 (John)
WS3148, ZS103
+"The Jesus in Me" (PD) (John)
WS3151, ZS132
+"Your Spirit" 7091513 (John)
+"Here Again" 7111925 (John)
+"Presence" 7116947 (John)
+"Wesley Prayer" ("Fire") 7118633 (John)
+"The Kingdom Is Yours" 7109354 (John)

+"God Is Love" 7136019 (John)
"Behold, What Manner of Love" 1596 (John)
"Let Your Spirit Rise Within Me" 15355 (John)
"The Power of Your Love" 917491 (John)
"Holy Spirit, Rain Down" 2405227 (John)
"Dwell" 4085652 (John)
"Holy and Anointed One" 164361 (John, Easter)

Solo/Ensemble Suggestions
"Wash, O God, Our Sons and Daughters" (1 Pet, Baptism)
V-5 (1) p. 64
"Gentle Like Jesus" (John, Easter)
V-8 p. 42
"This Is My Commandment" (John)
V-8 p. 284
+"All Creatures of Our God and King" (Acts)
Tim Sarsany; MorningStar MSM- 60-2283
SATB, organ, opt. cong. (https://bit.ly/MSM-60-2283)
"If You Love Me, Keep My Commandments" (John)
Tallis/arr. Hopson; MorningStar MSM-50-5550
2-part mixed, keyboard (https://bit.ly/MSM-50-5550)

+Hymn Anthem
"Easter People, Raise Your Voices" 424764 (Acts, 1 Pet)
UM304, Z6
Introduction: Keyboard (organ) play hymn setting, first two measures, then last two measures. Full, with power.
Stanza 1: All voices begin in unison, with keyboard playing hymnal setting. Strong, *forte.* If desired, sing parts from the first "Alleluia!" to the end of the stanza.
Stanza 2: All voices singing parts, *a cappella* or softly accompanied. May be performed by women only singing parts or unison, accompanied.
Interlude: Same as introduction.
Stanza 3: All voices unison, keyboard plays S-1, #281, with some sopranos singing S-1, #280 (or use another harmonization with descant). Full, *forte* and a bit slower. Descant may be played by trumpet if desired.
Ending: Similar to introduction. All voices sing first two measures unison, *a cappella,* using text of Stanza 1, "Easter people. . . ." Then sing last two measures ("Easter people let us sing.") in parts with some sopranos singing alto part up one octave. Accompany with full organ or piano.

Other Suggestions
Visuals:
O Preaching, globe, Acts 17:28a, risen Christ
P Feet, refine silver, fire/water, offering, prayer
E Hearts, readiness, briefcase, accounting, Christ, crucifix, prisoners, resurrection
G Advocate (briefcase), Spirit, open Bible, child
Introit: C263, GR306, UM328. "Surely the Presence of the Lord" 7909 (Acts, John)
Opening Prayer: WSL37. "Holy Spirit, Rain Down" (John)
+Response: "Holy Spirit, Rain Down" 2405227 (John)
Prayer of Confession: N836 (Mother's Day)
Prayer: WSL42. "God, whose fingers sculpt" (Acts)
Prayer: WSL201. "God our Creator" (Mother's Day)
Litany: C189. Love One Another (John)
Sung Benediction: N249. "Peace I Leave with You" (John)
+Sung Benediction: C436, UM666. "Shalom to You" 114122 (John)
Blessing: WSL40. "May the Spirit of God" (John)
Theme Ideas: Baptism, God: Faithfulness, Holy Spirit, Love

Notes

NRSVue

Acts 1:1-11

[1]In the first book, Theophilus, I wrote about all that Jesus
began to do and teach [2]until the day when he was taken up to
heaven, after giving instructions through the Holy Spirit to the
apostles whom he had chosen. [3]After his suffering he presented
himself alive to them by many convincing proofs, appearing to
them during forty days and speaking about the kingdom of God.
[4]While staying with them, he ordered them not to leave Jerusalem but to wait there for the promise of the Father. “This,” he
said, “is what you have heard from me; [5]for John baptized with
water, but you will be baptized with the Holy Spirit not many
days from now.”

[6]So when they had come together, they asked him, “Lord, is
this the time when you will restore the kingdom to Israel?” [7]He
replied, “It is not for you to know the times or periods that the
Father has set by his own authority. [8]But you will receive power
when the Holy Spirit has come upon you, and you will be my
witnesses in Jerusalem, in all Judea and Samaria, and to the ends
of the earth.” [9]When he had said this, as they were watching, he
was lifted up, and a cloud took him out of their sight. [10]While he
was going and they were gazing up toward heaven, suddenly two
men in white robes stood by them. [11]They said, “Men of Galilee,
why do you stand looking up toward heaven? This Jesus, who has
been taken up from you into heaven, will come in the same way
as you saw him go into heaven.”

Psalm 47 (G261, N653, P194, UM781)

[1]Clap your hands, all you peoples;
shout to God with loud songs of joy.
[2]For the LORD, the Most High, is awesome,
a great king over all the earth.
[3]He subdued peoples under us
and nations under our feet.
[4]He chose our heritage for us,
the pride of Jacob whom he loves. *[Selah]*
[5]God has gone up with a shout,
the LORD with the sound of a trumpet.
[6]Sing praises to God, sing praises;
sing praises to our King, sing praises.
[7]For God is the king of all the earth;
sing praises with a psalm.
[8]God is king over the nations;
God sits on his holy throne.
[9]The princes of the peoples gather
as the people of the God of Abraham.
For the shields of the earth belong to God;
he is highly exalted.

CEB

Acts 1:1-11

[1]Theophilus, the first scroll I wrote concerned everything
Jesus did and taught from the beginning, [2]right up to the day
when he was taken up into heaven. Before he was taken up,
working in the power of the Holy Spirit, Jesus instructed the
apostles he had chosen. [3]After his suffering, he showed them
that he was alive with many convincing proofs. He appeared to
them over a period of forty days, speaking to them about God’s
kingdom. [4]While they were eating together, he ordered them
not to leave Jerusalem but to wait for what the Father had promised. He said, “This is what you heard from me: [5]John baptized
with water, but in only a few days you will be baptized with the
Holy Spirit.”

[6]As a result, those who had gathered together asked Jesus,
“Lord, are you going to restore the kingdom to Israel now?”

[7]Jesus replied, “It isn’t for you to know the times or seasons
that the Father has set by his own authority. [8]Rather, you will
receive power when the Holy Spirit has come upon you, and you
will be my witnesses in Jerusalem, in all Judea and Samaria, and
to the end of the earth.”

[9]After Jesus said these things, as they were watching, he was
lifted up and a cloud took him out of their sight. [10]While he was
going away and as they were staring toward heaven, suddenly
two men in white robes stood next to them. [11]They said, “Galileans, why are you standing here, looking toward heaven? This
Jesus, who was taken up from you into heaven, will come in the
same way that you saw him go into heaven.”

Psalm 47 (G261, N653, P194, UM781)

[1]Clap your hands, all you people!
Shout joyfully to God with a joyous shout!
[2]Because the LORD Most High is awesome,
he is the great king of the whole world.
[3]He subdues the nations under us,
subdues all people beneath our feet.
[4]He chooses our inheritance for us:
the heights of Jacob, which he loves. *[Selah]*
[5]God has gone up with a joyous shout—
the LORD with the blast of the ram’s horn.
[6]Sing praises to God! Sing praises!
Sing praises to our king! Sing praises
7 because God is king of the whole world!
Sing praises with a song of instruction!
[8]God is king over the nations.
God sits on his holy throne.
[9]The leaders of all people are gathered
with the people of Abraham’s God
because the earth’s guardians belong to God;
God is exalted beyond all.

NRSVue

Ephesians 1:15-23

[15]I have heard of your faith in the Lord Jesus and your love toward all the saints, and for this reason [16]I do not cease to give thanks for you as I remember you in my prayers, [17]that the God of our Lord Jesus Christ, the Father of glory, may give you a spirit of wisdom and revelation as you come to know him, [18]so that, with the eyes of your heart enlightened, you may perceive what is the hope to which he has called you, what are the riches of his glorious inheritance among the saints, [19]and what is the immeasurable greatness of his power for us who believe, according to the working of his great power. [20]God put this power to work in Christ when he raised him from the dead and seated him at his right hand in the heavenly places, [21]far above all rule and authority and power and dominion and above every name that is named, not only in this age but also in the age to come. [22]And he has put all things under his feet and has made him the head over all things for the church, [23]which is his body, the fullness of him who fills all in all.

Luke 24:44-53

[44]Then he said to them, "These are my words that I spoke to you while I was still with you—that everything written about me in the law of Moses, the prophets, and the psalms must be fulfilled." [45]Then he opened their minds to understand the scriptures, [46]and he said to them, "Thus it is written, that the Messiah is to suffer and to rise from the dead on the third day, [47]and that repentance and forgiveness of sins is to be proclaimed in his name to all nations, beginning from Jerusalem. [48]You are witnesses of these things. [49]And see, I am sending upon you what my Father promised, so stay here in the city until you have been clothed with power from on high."

[50]Then he led them out as far as Bethany, and, lifting up his hands, he blessed them. [51]While he was blessing them, he withdrew from them and was carried up into heaven. [52]And they worshiped him and returned to Jerusalem with great joy, [53]and they were continually in the temple blessing God.

CEB

Ephesians 1:15-23

[15]Since I heard about your faith in the Lord Jesus and your love for all God's people, this is the reason that [16]I don't stop giving thanks to God for you when I remember you in my prayers. [17]I pray that the God of our Lord Jesus Christ, the Father of glory, will give you a spirit of wisdom and revelation that makes God known to you. [18]I pray that the eyes of your heart will have enough light to see what is the hope of God's call, what is the richness of God's glorious inheritance among believers, [19]and what is the overwhelming greatness of God's power that is working among us believers. This power is conferred by the energy of God's powerful strength. [20]God's power was at work in Christ when God raised him from the dead and sat him at God's right side in the heavens, [21]far above every ruler and authority and power and angelic power, any power that might be named not only now but in the future. [22]God put everything under Christ's feet and made him head of everything in the church, [23]which is his body. His body, the church, is the fullness of Christ, who fills everything in every way.

Luke 24:44-53

[44]Jesus said to them, "These are my words that I spoke to you while I was still with you—that everything written about me in the Law of Moses, the Prophets, and the Psalms must be fulfilled." [45]Then he opened their minds to understand the scriptures. [46]He said to them, "This is what is written: the Christ will suffer and rise from the dead on the third day, [47]and a change of heart and life for the forgiveness of sins must be preached in his name to all nations, beginning from Jerusalem. [48]You are witnesses of these things. [49]Look, I'm sending to you what my Father promised, but you are to stay in the city until you have been furnished with heavenly power."

[50]He led them out as far as Bethany, where he lifted his hands and blessed them. [51]As he blessed them, he left them and was taken up to heaven. [52]They worshipped him and returned to Jerusalem overwhelmed with joy. [53]And they were continuously in the temple praising God.

Primary Hymns and Songs for the Day

"Hail the Day That Sees Him Rise" 95997 (Acts, Luke) (O)
CG219, E214, GR269, N260, SH203, UM312, VU189
H-3 Hbl-72; Chr-50; Desc-69; Org-78
S-1 #213-214. Transposition with desc.
S-1 #213. Desc.
"Crown Him with Many Crowns" (Acts, Luke)
C234, CG223. E494, EL855, G268, GR278, N301, P151, SH208, UM327 (PD), VU211
H-3 Hbl-55; Chr-60; Desc-30; Org-27
S-1 #86-88. Various treatments
"He Is Exalted" 17827 (Acts, Pss, Luke, Ascension) (C)
CG342, S2070, SH423
"Thine Be the Glory" (Acts, Pss, Luke) (C)
C218, CG222, EL376, G238, GR255, N253, P122, SH192, UM308, VU173 (Fr.)

Additional Hymn Suggestions

"A Hymn of Glory Let Us Sing" (Acts)
E218, G258, N259, P141
"Jesus Shall Reign" 1510 (Acts)
C95, CG158, E544, EL434, G265, GR282, N300, P423, SH209, UM157 (PD), VU330
"I Love to Tell the Story" (Acts)
C480, CG581, EL661, G462, GR160, N522, SH569, UM156 (PD), VU343
"Loving Spirit" 3379424 (Acts)
C244, EL397, G293, P323, S2123, VU387
"Wonder of Wonders" (Acts, Baptism)
C378, G489, N328, P499, S2247
"I'll Fly Away" (Acts, Ascension)
N595, S2282, Z183
+"Christ, Whose Glory Fills the Skies" 808926 (Acts, Luke)
E7, EL553, G662, GR211, P462, UM173 (PD), VU336
"Christ the Lord Is Risen Today" 27965 (Acts, Luke)
C216, CG194, EL373, G245, GR251, N233, P113, SH181, UM302 (PD), VU155/157
"Come, Ye Faithful, Raise the Strain" 355929 (Acts, Luke)
C215, CG218, E199/200, EL363, G234, GR253, N230, P115/114, UM315 (PD), VU165
"Christ Jesus Lay in Death's Strong Bands" (Acts, Luke)
E186, EL370, G237, P110, UM319 (PD)
"Hail Thee, Festival Day" (Acts, Luke, Ascension)
E175, EL394, G277, N262, UM324, VU163
"Blessed Jesus, At Thy Word" (Acts, Luke)
E440, EL520, G395, N74, P454, UM596 (PD), VU500
"At the Font We Start Our Journey" (Acts, Luke, Baptism)
N308, S2114
"Because You Live, O Christ" (Eph)
G249, N231, P105
"Holy God, We Praise Thy Name" 114555 (Eph)
CG9, E366, EL414 (PD), G4, GR2, N276, P460, SH431, UM79, VU894 (Fr.)
"Praise to the Lord, the Almighty" 785135 (Eph)
C25, CG319, E390, EL858 (PD)/859, G35, GR3, N22, P482, SH453, UM139, VU220 (Fr.) and VU221
"All Hail the Power of Jesus' Name" 196858 (Eph)
C91/C92, CG339/340, E450/451, EL634, G263, GR279/280, N304, P142/143, SH207, UM154/155, VU334
"At the Name of Jesus" (Eph)
CG424, E435, EL416, G264, GR105, P148, SH657, UM168, VU335
"Hope of the World" 643002 (Eph)
C538, E472, G734, N46, P360, UM178, VU215
"My Hope Is Built" (PD) (Eph)
C537, CG590, EL596/597, G353, GR102, N403, P379, SH324, UM368 (PD), ZS182
"For All the Saints" 90590 (Eph)
C637, CG567, E287, EL422, G326, GR480, N299, P526, SH231, UM711 (PD), VU705
"There Are Some Things I May Not Know" (Eph)
N405, S2147, Z201 (PD), ZS172
"Come, Share the Lord" (Eph, Comm.)
C408, CG459, G510, S2269, VU469
"Give Me Jesus" (PD-TO) (Eph)
CG546, EL770, N409, SH306, WS3140, Z165, ZS84
+"One Is the Body" 1099301 (Eph, Ascension)
WS3156
"Alleluia! Sing to Jesus!" (Luke)
C233, CG217, E460/E461, EL392, G260, GR146, N257, P144 (PD), SH204
"Christ the Lord Is Risen Today" 27965 (Luke Ascension)
C216, CG194, EL373, G245, GR251, N233, P113, SH181, UM302 (PD), VU155/157
"You Alone Are Holy" (Luke, Ascension)
S2077, SH457
"Enviado Soy de Dios" ("Sent Out in Jesus' Name") 6290823 (Luke)
EL538, G747, S2184, SH718
+"Go to the World" (Luke)
CG481, G295, SH720, VU420, WS3158

Additional Contemporary and Modern Suggestions

"Veni Sancte Spiritus" ("Holy Spirit, Come to Us") OL-TaizeVN57 (Acts)
EL406, G281, S2118
"Come, Holy Spirit" 26351 (Acts)
S2125 (*See also* S2124)
"Come, Holy Spirit" 3383953 (Acts)
WS3092 (*See also* SH223, WS3091)
"Jesu, Tawa Pano" ("Jesus, We Are Here") OL-17487 (Acts, Luke)
EL529, G392, S2273, SH611, ZS148
"Holy Spirit, Rain Down" 2405227 (Acts, Eph)
"Clap Your Hands" 806674 (Pss)
S2028, ZS10
"Shout to the Lord" 1406918 (Pss)
CG348, EL821, GR124, S2074, SH426, ZS15
"Lord, I Lift Your Name on High" 117947 (Pss, Ascension)
CG606, EL857, S2088, SH205
"Forever" 3148428 (Pss)
CG53, WS3023
"Awesome Is the Lord Most High" 4674159 (Pss, Ascension)
+"All the Poor and Powerless" 5881130 (Pss)
"Open the Eyes of My Heart" 2298355 (Eph)
G452, SH378, WS3008
+"Not in a Hurry" 7047889 (Eph, Luke)
+"Behold Him" 7133698 (Eph, Luke, Ascension)
"Above All" 2672885 (Eph, Ascension)
V-3 (2), p. 17. Vocal Solo
+"Your Spirit" 7091513 (Luke)
+"Presence" 7116947 (Luke, Ascension)
+"Rise" 7036613 (Luke, Ascension)
"Lord God Almighty" (Luke, Ascension)
S2006
"Alleluia" OL-81263 (Ascension, Easter)
G589, S2078
"Once Again" 1564362 (Ascension)
+"Great Things" 7111321 (Ascension)
V-9, p. 36. Vocal Solo

Solo/Ensemble Suggestions

+"Crown Him, the Risen King" (Acts 1, Ascension)
V-10 p. 55
+"Shout to the Lord" (with "All Creatures of Our God and King") (Pss)
V-3 (2) p. 32

"Give Me Jesus" (Eph)
V-3 (1) p. 53
V-3 (4) p. 9
V-7 p. 24/28
V-8 p. 256
+"Jesus Christ is Risen Today" (Luke, Ascension)
V-1 p. 50
+"Thou Art Gone Up On High" (Ascension)
V-2
"Rise Again" (Ascension, Easter)
V-8 p. 31
+"Hail the Day That Sees Him Rise" (Acts, Luke)
Arr. Victor C. Johnson; Lorenz 10/4348L
SAB, organ, opt. Trumpet/Brass (https://bit.ly/L-4348)
SATB (10/4335L)
"Psalm 150" (Pss, Luke)
Nathan Jensen; AEC-3 p. 41
Unison, keyboard, opt. congregation (https://bit.ly/AEC-3)

+Hymn Anthem

"Hail the Day That Sees Him Rise" 95997 (Acts, Luke)
CG219, E214, GR269, SH203, UM312
Write a trumpet part by transposing the melocy line up one whole step. Or locate harmonizations of this hymn in F Major for the keyboard (S-1, #214 or some hymnals) and G Major for the trumpet (UM312 and some hymnals).
Introduction: Trumpet plays first four measures. Keyboard joins trumpet on measures 3-4.
Stanza 1: All voices, unison. Trumpet plays melody, keyboard plays full hymn setting.
Stanza 2: All voices sing unison, except on "Alleluia's" and System 3, where they may sing parts. May be *a cappella* or accompanied by keyboard.
Stanza 3: System 1, tenors sing melody, basses sing their part, or unison melody. System 2, S/A sing their parts, or unison melody. May be *a cappella* or accompanied by keyboard.
Interlude: Keyboard plays last 8 measures.
Stanza 4: All voices unison. Keyboard plays full hymnal setting. Trumpet may play a descant part, such as S-1, #213 (transposition found in back of S-1, p. 362). Grand, majestic, *forte* ending.

Other Suggestions

These ideas may be used on May 17 as Ascension Sunday.
Visuals:
O Risen Christ, baptism, seven flames, ascension, angels
P Clapping, singing, shouting, crown/throne, shields
E Open Bible, Christ, right hand, feet, Church
G Open Bible, crucifix, Christ, lifted hands
Introit: N742. "Gathered Here" (Acts, Luke)
+Introit: C220, CG212, E203, EL386/E387, G235/255, N244, P116 (PD), SH190, UM317, VU170, stanza 1. "O Sons and Daughters, Let Us Sing" (Luke)
Greeting: Acts 1:8. Receive power from the Holy Spirit.
Call to Worship: WSL35. "Let us gather" (Acts)
Affirmation of Faith: WSL76. "We believe" (Eph)
Prayer: UM323. (Ascension, Acts, Luke, Eph)
Song of Preparation: WS3047, stanza 3. "God Almighty, We Are Waiting" (Luke)
Offering Prayer: WSL119. "Alleluia! Christ is risen!" (Eph, Easter)
Blessing: WSL163. "From where we are" (Luke)
+Sung Benediction: S2101, stanza 4. "Two Fishermen" (Luke)
Theme Ideas: Call of God, Discipleship / Following God, Faith, Holy Spirit, Praise, Resurrection

Notes

NRSVue

Acts 1:6-14

[6]So when they had come together, they asked him, "Lord, is
this the time when you will restore the kingdom to Israel?" [7]He
replied, "It is not for you to know the times or periods that the
Father has set by his own authority. [8]But you will receive power
when the Holy Spirit has come upon you, and you will be my
witnesses in Jerusalem, in all Judea and Samaria, and to the ends
of the earth." [9]When he had said this, as they were watching, he
was lifted up, and a cloud took him out of their sight. [10]While he
was going and they were gazing up toward heaven, suddenly two
men in white robes stood by them. [11]They said, "Men of Galilee,
why do you stand looking up toward heaven? This Jesus, who has
been taken up from you into heaven, will come in the same way
as you saw him go into heaven."
[12]Then they returned to Jerusalem from the mount called
Olivet, which is near Jerusalem, a Sabbath day's journey away.
[13]When they had entered the city, they went to the room
upstairs where they were staying: Peter, and John, and James,
and Andrew, Philip and Thomas, Bartholomew and Matthew,
James son of Alphaeus, and Simon the Zealot, and Judas son of
James. [14]All these were constantly devoting themselves to prayer,
together with certain women, including Mary the mother of
Jesus, as well as his brothers.

Psalm 68:1-10, 32-35 (G55, N664, UM792)

[1]Let God rise up; let his enemies be scattered;
let those who hate him flee before him.
[2]As smoke is driven away, so drive them away;
as wax melts before the fire,
let the wicked perish before God.
[3]But let the righteous be joyful;
let them exult before God;
let them be jubilant with joy.
[4]Sing to God; sing praises to his name;
lift up a song to him who rides upon the clouds—
his name is the LORD—
be exultant before him.
[5]Father of orphans and protector of widows
is God in his holy habitation.
[6]God gives the desolate a home to live in;
he leads out the prisoners to prosperity,
but the rebellious live in a parched land.
[7]O God, when you went out before your people,
when you marched through the wilderness, *[Selah]*
[8]the earth quaked, the heavens poured down rain
at the presence of God, the God of Sinai,
at the presence of God, the God of Israel.
[9]Rain in abundance, O God, you showered abroad;
you restored your heritage when it languished;
[10]your flock found a dwelling in it;
in your goodness, O God, you provided for the needy.

. . . .

[32]Sing to God, O kingdoms of the earth;
sing praises to the Lord, *[Selah]*
[33]O rider in the heavens, the ancient heavens;
listen, he sends out his voice, his mighty voice.
[34]Ascribe power to God,
whose majesty is over Israel
and whose power is in the skies.
[35]Awesome is God in his sanctuary,
the God of Israel;
he gives power and strength to his people.
Blessed be God!

CEB

Acts 1:6-14

[6]As a result, those who had gathered together asked Jesus,
"Lord, are you going to restore the kingdom to Israel now?"
[7]Jesus replied, "It isn't for you to know the times or seasons
that the Father has set by his own authority. [8]Rather, you will
receive power when the Holy Spirit has come upon you, and you
will be my witnesses in Jerusalem, in all Judea and Samaria, and
to the end of the earth."
[9]After Jesus said these things, as they were watching, he was
lifted up and a cloud took him out of their sight. [10]While he was
going away and as they were staring toward heaven, suddenly
two men in white robes stood next to them. [11]They said, "Galileans, why are you standing here, looking toward heaven? This
Jesus, who was taken up from you into heaven, will come in the
same way that you saw him go into heaven."
[12]Then they returned to Jerusalem from the Mount of Olives,
which is near Jerusalem—a sabbath day's journey away. [13]When
they entered the city, they went to the upstairs room where
they were staying. Peter, John, James, and Andrew; Philip and
Thomas; Bartholomew and Matthew; James, Alphaeus' son;
Simon the zealot; and Judas, James' son—[14]all were united in
their devotion to prayer, along with some women, including
Mary the mother of Jesus, and his brothers.

Psalm 68:1-10, 32-35 (G55, N664, UM792)

[1]Let God rise up;
let his enemies scatter;
let those who hate him
run scared before him!
[2]Like smoke is driven away,
drive them away!
Like wax melting before fire,
let the wicked perish before God!
[3]But let the righteous be glad
and celebrate before God.
Let them rejoice with gladness!
[4]Sing to God! Sing praises to his name!
Exalt the one who rides the clouds!
The LORD is his name.
Celebrate before him!
[5]Father of orphans and defender of widows
is God in his holy habitation.
[6]God settles the lonely in their homes;
he sets prisoners free with happiness,
but the rebellious dwell in a parched land.
[7]When you went forth before your people, God,
when you marched through the wasteland, *[Selah]*
[8] the earth shook!
Yes, heaven poured down
before God, the one from Sinai—
before God, the God of Israel!
[9]You showered down abundant rain, God;
when your inheritance grew weary,
you restored it yourself,
[10] and your creatures settled in it.
In your goodness, God,
you provided for the poor.

. . . .

NRSVue

1 Peter 4:12-14; 5:6-11

[12]Beloved, do not be surprised at the fiery ordeal that is taking place among you to test you, as though something strange were happening to you. [13]But rejoice insofar as you are sharing Christ's sufferings, so that you may also be glad and shout for joy when his glory is revealed. [14]If you are reviled for the name of Christ, you are blessed, because the spirit of glory, which is the Spirit of God, is resting on you. . . .

5 . . . [6]Humble yourselves, therefore, under the mighty hand of God, so that he may exalt you in due time. [7]Cast all your anxiety on him, because he cares for you. [8]Discipline yourselves; keep alert. Like a roaring lion your adversary the devil prowls around, looking for someone to devour. [9]Resist him, steadfast in your faith, for you know that your brothers and sisters in all the world are undergoing the same kinds of suffering. [10]And after you have suffered for a little while, the God of all grace, who has called you to his eternal glory in Christ, will himself restore, support, strengthen, and establish you. [11]To him be the power forever and ever. Amen.

John 17:1-11

[1]After Jesus had spoken these words, he looked up to heaven and said, "Father, the hour has come; glorify your Son so that the Son may glorify you, [2]since you have given him authority over all people, to give eternal life to all whom you have given him. [3]And this is eternal life, that they may know you, the only true God, and Jesus Christ whom you have sent. [4]I glorified you on earth by finishing the work that you gave me to do. [5]So now, Father, glorify me in your own presence with the glory that I had in your presence before the world existed.

[6]"I have made your name known to those whom you gave me from the world. They were yours, and you gave them to me, and they have kept your word. [7]Now they know that everything you have given me is from you, [8]for the words that you gave to me I have given to them, and they have received them and know in truth that I came from you, and they have believed that you sent me. [9]I am asking on their behalf; I am not asking on behalf of the world but on behalf of those whom you gave me, because they are yours. [10]All mine are yours, and yours are mine, and I have been glorified in them. [11]And now I am no longer in the world, but they are in the world, and I am coming to you. Holy Father, protect them in your name that you have given me, so that they may be one, as we are one."

CEB

Psalm 68:1-10, 32-35 (continued)

[32]Sing to God, all kingdoms of the earth!
  Sing praises to my Lord. *[Selah]*
[33]Sing to the one who rides through heaven,
  the most ancient heaven.
  Look! God sends forth his voice,
    his mighty voice.
[34]Recognize how strong God is!
  His majesty extends over Israel;
  his strength is in the clouds.
[35]You are awesome, God, in your sanctuaries—
  the God of Israel who gives strength and power to his people!
Bless God!

---

1 Peter 4:12-14; 5:6-11

[12]Dear friends, don't be surprised about the fiery trials that have come among you to test you. These are not strange happenings. [13]Instead, rejoice as you share Christ's suffering. You share his suffering now so that you may also have overwhelming joy when his glory is revealed. [14]If you are mocked because of Christ's name, you are blessed, for the Spirit of glory—indeed, the Spirit of God—rests on you.

5 . . . [6]Therefore, humble yourselves under God's power so that he may raise you up in the last day. [7]Throw all your anxiety onto him, because he cares about you. [8]Be clearheaded. Keep alert. Your accuser, the devil, is on the prowl like a roaring lion, seeking someone to devour. [9]Resist him, standing firm in the faith. Do so in the knowledge that your fellow believers are enduring the same suffering throughout the world. [10]After you have suffered for a little while, the God of all grace, the one who called you into his eternal glory in Christ Jesus, will himself restore, empower, strengthen, and establish you. [11]To him be power forever and always. Amen.

John 17:1-11

[1]When Jesus finished saying these things, he looked up to heaven and said, "Father, the time has come. Glorify your Son, so that the Son can glorify you. [2]You gave him authority over everyone so that he could give eternal life to everyone you gave him. [3]This is eternal life: to know you, the only true God, and Jesus Christ whom you sent. [4]I have glorified you on earth by finishing the work you gave me to do. [5]Now, Father, glorify me in your presence with the glory I shared with you before the world was created.

[6]"I have revealed your name to the people you gave me from this world. They were yours and you gave them to me, and they have kept your word. [7]Now they know that everything you have given me comes from you. [8]This is because I gave them the words that you gave me, and they received them. They truly understood that I came from you, and they believed that you sent me.

[9]"I'm praying for them. I'm not praying for the world but for those you gave me, because they are yours. [10]Everything that is mine is yours and everything that is yours is mine; I have been glorified in them. [11]I'm no longer in the world, but they are in the world, even as I'm coming to you. Holy Father, watch over them in your name, the name you gave me, that they will be one just as we are one."

Primary Hymns and Songs for the Day

"Hail the Day That Sees Him Rise" 95997 (Acts) (O)
CG219, E214, GR269, N260, SH203, UM312, VU189
H-3 Hbl-72; Chr-50; Desc-69; Org-78
S-1 #213-214. Transposition with desc.
S-1 #213. Desc.
"Alleluia! Sing to Jesus!" (Heb) (O)
C233, CG217, E460/E461, EL392, G260, GR146, N257, P144 (PD), SH204
H-3 Hbl-46; Chr-26, 134; Desc-53; Org-56
S-1 #168-171. Various treatments
"Come, Ye Faithful, Raise the Strain" 355929 (Acts)
C215, CG218, E199/200, EL363, G234, GR253, N230, P115/114, UM315 (PD), VU165
"He Is Exalted" 17827 (Acts)
CG342, S2070, SH423
"How Firm a Foundation" 107816 (Acts, Pss, 1 Pet) (C)
C618, CG425, E636, EL796, G463, GR46, N407, P361, SH291, UM529 (PD), VU660
H-3 Hbl-27, 69; Chr-102; Desc-41; Org-41
S-1 #133. Harm.
#134. Performance note

Additional Hymn Suggestions

"Lo, He Comes with Clouds Descending" 4923769 (Acts)
CG100, E57/58, EL435, G348, GR285, P6, UM718, VU25
"Loving Spirit" 3379424 (Acts)
C244, EL397, G293, P323, S2123, VU387
"Wonder of Wonders" (Acts, Baptism)
C378, G489, N328, P499, S2247
"I'll Fly Away" (Acts)
N595, S2282, Z183
"Hail Thee, Festival Day" (Acts)
E175, EL394, G277, N262, P120, UM324, VU163
+*"Kum Ba Yah"* 2749763 (Acts)
C561/590, G472 (PD), P338, UM494, Z139
"Immortal, Invisible, God Only Wise" 124466 (Acts, John)
C66, CG58, E423, EL834, G12, GR7, N1, P263, UM103 (PD), VU264 (*See also* ZS4)
"Christ, Whose Glory Fills the Skies" 808926 (Acts, John)
E7, EL553, G662, GR211, P462, UM173 (PD), VU336
"A Hymn of Glory Let Us Sing" (Acts)
E218, G258, N259, P141
"Spirit Divine, Attend Our Prayers" (Acts)
E509, G407, P325, SH571, VU385
"Joyful, Joyful, We Adore Thee" (Pss, John)
C2, CG310, E376, EL836, G611, GR8, N4, P464, SH390, UM89 (PD), VU232
"Lift Every Voice and Sing" 7071034 (Pss, 1 Pet)
C631, CG638, E599, EL841, G339, GR408, N593, P563, SH36, UM519, Z32 (PD), Z210, ZS113
"Christ Is Alive" (1 Pet)
CG205, E182, EL389, G246, P108, UM318, VU158
"I Surrender All" (1 Pet)
CG499, SH619, GR607, UM354, Z67 (PD)
"Blessed Assurance" (1 Pet)
C543, CG619, EL638, G839, GR570, N473, P341, SH320, UM369 (PD), VU337
"Stand By Me" (1 Pet)
C629, GR352, UM512, Z41 (PD-TO), ZS164
"The Trees of the Field" 20546 (1 Pet)
G80, S2279, VU884
"We Cannot Measure How You Heal" 4751065 (1 Pet)
CG540, G797, SH341, VU613, WS3139
"Lead Me, Guide Me" (1 Pet)
C583, CG403, EL768, G740, S2214, SH582, ZS173
"Fight the Good Fight" (1 Pet)
E552, G846, GR473, P307 (PD), VU674
"By Gracious Powers" (1 Pet, John)
E695/696, EL626, G818, N413, P342, UM517
"O Jesus, I Have Promised" 40454 (John)
C612, E655, EL810, G724/725, GR592, N493, P388/389, SH623, UM396 (PD), VU120
"A Charge to Keep I Have" 118850 (John)
CG623, GR456, SH634, UM413 (PD)
"We All Are One in Mission" 3176809 (John)
CG269, EL576, G733, P435, S2243, ZS99

Additional Contemporary and Modern Suggestions

"Veni Sancte Spiritus" ("Holy Spirit, Come to Us") OL-TaizeVN57 (Acts)
EL406, G281, S2118
"Come, Holy Spirit" 26351 (Acts)
S2125 (*See also* S2124)
"Come, Holy Spirit" 3383953 (Acts)
WS3092 (*See also* SH223, WS3091)
"Waiting Here for You" 5925663 (Acts)
"Holy Spirit, Rain Down" 2405227 (Acts, Pss)
+"Won't Stop Now" 7111932 (Acts, Pss, John)
"Foundation" 706151 (Acts, Pss, 1 Pet)
+"Our God Saves" 4972837 (Pss, 1 Pet)
+"Nothing to Fear" 7133723 (Pss, 1 Pet)
+"The Blessing" 7147007 (Pss, John)
"Lord, I Lift Your Name on High" 117947 (Pss)
CG606, EL857, S2088, SH205
"Shout to the Lord" 1406918 (Pss)
CG348, EL821, GR124, S2074, SH426, ZS15
"God Is So Good" 4956994 (1 Pet)
G658, GR52, S2056, SH461, Z231
"Humble Thyself in the Sight of the Lord" 26564 (1 Pet)
G80, S2279, VU884
"God Is Good All the Time" OL-88288 (1 Pet)
WS3026, ZS18
"God Is Good All the Time" 1729073 (1 Pet)
+"Freedom" 7078151 (1 Pet)
+"Surrounded" ("Fight My Battles") 7098758 (1 Pet)
+"Jesus I Trust in You" 4510828 (1 Pet)
"Cares Chorus" 25974 (1 Pet, John)
S2215
"Time Now to Gather" 2890911 (1 Pet, Comm.)
S2265
"Today Is the Day" 5200924 (1 Pet)
"I Will Boast" 4662350 (1 Pet)
"Freedom in the Spirit" 7127886 (1 Pet, John)
"Praise You" 863806 (John)
S2003, ZS170
"Lord, Be Glorified" 26368 (John)
EL744, G468, S2150, SH420
"Be Glorified" 429226 (John)
"Be Glorified" 2732646 (John)
+"Be Lifted" 7060780 (John)

Solo/Ensemble Suggestions

+"Crown Him, the Risen King" (Acts 1, Pss)
V-10 p. 55
+"Make a Joyful Noise" (Pss)
V-3 (5) p. 44
+"Man of Your Word" (1 Pet)
V-9 p. 71
"My Heart Is Steadfast" (1 Pet, John)
V-5 (2) p. 40
+"Hail the Day That Sees Him Rise" (Acts, John)
Arr. Victor C. Johnson; Lorenz 10/4348L
SAB, organ, opt. Trumpet/Brass (https://bit.ly/L-4348)
SATB (10/4335L)

+"Lift Every Voice and Sing" (Pss, 1 Pet)
Arr. Rollo Dilworth; Hal Leonard HL 00456058
SAB, piano (https://bit.ly/HL-6058)
SATB (HL 00456057)

+Hymn Anthem

"How Firm a Foundation" 107816 (Acts, Pss, 1 Pet) (C)
C618, CG425, E636, EL796, G463, GR46, N407, P361, SH291, UM529 (PD), VU660

Introduction: Handbells ring four whole notes. Use all A flats and E flats that are available, but be sure the lowest note sounding is an A flat. Or piano can play these notes with sustain pedal held throughout.

Stanza 1: All voices unison, *forte*, with strength. Handbells continue ringing whole notes.

Stanza 2: S/A sing their parts. E flat bells continue whole notes.

Stanza 3: Four part round. Each group enters after the previous group sing "When through." Group 1-sopranos; group 2-tenors; group 3-altos; group 4-basses. Groups 1, 2, and 3 sing *piano*, creating the effect of flowing water. Basses sing *forte*, but restrained. Accompany if necessary with A flat bells ringing whole notes.

Stanza 4: All voices sing parts. (Or omit temor and/or bass parts.) Accompany if necessary with keyboard.

Interlude: Same as introduction, but *mezzo piano.*

Stanza 5: All voices, unison. Begin *mezzo piano* and *decrescendo* to piano by the end. Hold last note as bells ring two more chords. Let sound of bells and choir fade away.

Other Suggestions

Today may also be celebrated as Ascension Sunday using the ideas for May 14.

Visuals:

Acts Cloud, ascension, Jesus ascending, angels, prayer
P Melting candle, music notes, clouds, broken chains, abundant rain
E Fire, trials, testing, suffering, relief from suffering
G Jesus ascending, sun, lifted hands

Introit: EL529, G392, S2273, SH611, ZS148. *"Jesu, Tawa Pano"* ("Jesus, We Are Here") (Acts)

Call to Worship: WSL35. "Let us gather" (Acts)

Opening Prayer: N827 or N831 (Acts, Pentecost)

Confession and Assurance: N837 and N841 (Acts)

Prayer: WSL34, WSL42, or WSL67 (Acts)

Offertory: S2262, SH644. *"Te Ofrecemos Padre Nuestro"* ("Let Us Offer to the Father") (1 Pet)

Song of Preparation: WS3047, stanza 3. "God Almighty, We Are Waiting" (Acts)

Introit and Sung Benediction: EL412, WS3017, verses 1 and 3. "Come, Join the Dance of Trinity" OL-06029 (Luke)

Theme Ideas: Assurance, Discipleship / Following God, God: Providence / God our Help, Holy Spirit, Waiting

Notes

NRSVue

Acts 2:1-21

[1]When the day of Pentecost had come, they were all together
in one place. [2]And suddenly from heaven there came a sound
like the rush of a violent wind, and it filled the entire house
where they were sitting. [3]Divided tongues, as of fire, appeared
among them, and a tongue rested on each of them. [4]All of them
were filled with the Holy Spirit and began to speak in other
languages, as the Spirit gave them ability.
[5]Now there were devout Jews from every people under heaven
living in Jerusalem. [6]And at this sound the crowd gathered and
was bewildered, because each one heard them speaking in the
native language of each. [7]Amazed and astonished, they asked,
"Are not all these who are speaking Galileans? [8]And how is it
that we hear, each of us, in our own native language? [9]Parthians,
Medes, Elamites, and residents of Mesopotamia, Judea and Cappadocia, Pontus and Asia, [10]Phrygia and Pamphylia, Egypt and
the parts of Libya belonging to Cyrene, and visitors from Rome,
both Jews and proselytes, [11]Cretans and Arabs—in our own
languages we hear them speaking about God's deeds of power."
[12]All were amazed and perplexed, saying to one another, "What
does this mean?" [13]But others sneered and said, "They are filled
with new wine."
[14]But Peter, standing with the eleven, raised his voice and
addressed them, "Fellow Jews and all who live in Jerusalem, let
this be known to you, and listen to what I say. [15]Indeed, these
are not drunk, as you suppose, for it is only nine o'clock in the
morning. [16]No, this is what was spoken through the prophet Joel:

17 'In the last days it will be, God declares,
that I will pour out my Spirit upon all flesh,
and your sons and your daughters shall prophesy,
and your young men shall see visions,
and your old men shall dream dreams.
18 Even upon my slaves, both men and women,
in those days I will pour out my Spirit;
and they shall prophesy.
19 And I will show portents in the heaven above
and signs on the earth below,
blood, and fire, and smoky mist.
20 The sun shall be turned to darkness
and the moon to blood,
before the coming of the Lord's great and glorious
day.
21 Then everyone who calls on the name of the Lord shall be
saved.'"

CEB

Acts 2:1-21

[1]When Pentecost Day arrived, they were all together in one
place. [2]Suddenly a sound from heaven like the howling of a
fierce wind filled the entire house where they were sitting. [3]They
saw what seemed to be individual flames of fire alighting on
each one of them. [4]They were all filled with the Holy Spirit and
began to speak in other languages as the Spirit enabled them to
speak.
[5]There were pious Jews from every nation under heaven living
in Jerusalem. [6]When they heard this sound, a crowd gathered.
They were mystified because everyone heard them speaking in
their native languages. [7]They were surprised and amazed, saying,
"Look, aren't all the people who are speaking Galileans, every
one of them? [8]How then can each of us hear them speaking in
our native language? [9]Parthians, Medes, and Elamites; as well as
residents of Mesopotamia, Judea, and Cappadocia, Pontus and
Asia, [10]Phrygia and Pamphylia, Egypt and the regions of Libya
bordering Cyrene; and visitors from Rome (both Jews and con-
verts to Judaism), [11]Cretans and Arabs—we hear them declaring
the mighty works of God in our own languages!" [12]They were all
surprised and bewildered. Some asked each other, "What does
this mean?" [13]Others jeered at them, saying, "They're full of new
wine!"
[14]Peter stood with the other eleven apostles. He raised his
voice and declared, "Judeans and everyone living in Jerusalem!
Know this! Listen carefully to my words! [15]These people aren't
drunk, as you suspect; after all, it's only nine o'clock in the
morning! [16]Rather, this is what was spoken through the prophet
Joel:

17 *In the last days, God says,*
I will pour out my Spirit on all people.
Your sons and daughters will prophesy.
Your young will see visions.
Your elders will dream dreams.
18 *Even upon my servants, men and women,*
I will pour out my Spirit in those days,
and they will prophesy.
19 *I will cause wonders to occur in the heavens above*
and signs on the earth below,
blood and fire and a cloud of smoke.
20 *The sun will be changed into darkness,*
and the moon will be changed into blood,
before the great and spectacular day of the Lord comes.
21 *And everyone who calls on the name of the Lord will be saved.*

NRSVue

Psalm 104:24-34, 35b (G34, N889/890, P224, SH219, UM826)

24 O LORD, how manifold are your works!
In wisdom you have made them all;
the earth is full of your creatures.
25 There is the sea, great and wide;
creeping things innumerable are there,
living things both small and great.
26 There go the ships
and Leviathan that you formed to sport in it.
27 These all look to you
to give them their food in due season;
28 when you give to them, they gather it up;
when you open your hand, they are filled with good things.
29 When you hide your face, they are dismayed;
when you take away their breath, they die
and return to their dust.
30 When you send forth your spirit, they are created,
and you renew the face of the ground.
31 May the glory of the LORD endure forever;
may the LORD rejoice in his works—
32 who looks on the earth and it trembles,
who touches the mountains and they smoke.
33 I will sing to the LORD as long as I live;
I will sing praise to my God while I have being.
34 May my meditation be pleasing to him,
for I rejoice in the LORD.
35 . . .
b Bless the LORD, O my soul.
Praise the LORD!

---

1 Corinthians 12:3b-13

3b [N]o one can say "Jesus is Lord" except by the Holy Spirit.
4 Now there are varieties of gifts but the same Spirit, 5 and there
are varieties of services but the same Lord, 6 and there are varieties of activities, but it is the same God who activates all of them
in everyone. 7 To each is given the manifestation of the Spirit
for the common good. 8 To one is given through the Spirit the
utterance of wisdom and to another the utterance of knowledge
according to the same Spirit, 9 to another faith by the same
Spirit, to another gifts of healing by the one Spirit, 10 to another
the working of powerful deeds, to another prophecy, to another
the discernment of spirits, to another various kinds of tongues,
to another the interpretation of tongues. 11 All these are activated
by one and the same Spirit, who allots to each one individually
just as the Spirit chooses.
12 For just as the body is one and has many members, and all
the members of the body, though many, are one body, so it is
with Christ. 13 For in the one Spirit we were all baptized into one
body—Jews or Greeks, slaves or free—and we were all made to
drink of one Spirit.

John 7:37-39

37 On the last day of the festival, the great day, while Jesus was
standing there, he cried out, "Let anyone who is thirsty come to
me, 38 and let the one who believes in me drink. As the scripture
has said, 'Out of the believer's heart shall flow rivers of living
water.'" 39 Now he said this about the Spirit, which believers in
him were to receive; for as yet there was no Spirit because Jesus
was not yet glorified.

CEB

Psalm 104:24-34, 35b (G34, N889/890, P224, SH219, UM826)

24 LORD, you have done so many things!
You made them all so wisely!
The earth is full of your creations!
25 And then there's the sea, wide and deep,
with its countless creatures—
living things both small and large.
26 There go the ships on it,
and Leviathan, which you made, plays in it!
27 All your creations wait for you
to give them their food on time.
28 When you give it to them, they gather it up;
when you open your hand, they are filled completely full!
29 But when you hide your face, they are terrified;
when you take away their breath,
they die and return to dust.
30 When you let loose your breath, they are created,
and you make the surface of the ground brand-new again.
31 Let the LORD's glory last forever!
Let the LORD rejoice in all he has made!
32 He has only to look at the earth, and it shakes.
God just touches the mountains, and they erupt in smoke.
33 I will sing to the LORD as long as I live;
I will sing praises to my God while I'm still alive.
34 Let my praise be pleasing to him;
I'm rejoicing in the LORD!
. . . .
35 b But let my whole being bless the Lord!
Praise the Lord!

---

1 Corinthians 12:3b-13

3b [N]o one can say, "Jesus is Lord," except by the Holy Spirit.
4 There are different spiritual gifts but the same Spirit; 5 and there
are different ministries and the same Lord; 6 and there are different activities but the same God who produces all of them in
everyone. 7 A demonstration of the Spirit is given to each person
for the common good. 8 A word of wisdom is given by the Spirit
to one person, a word of knowledge to another according to
the same Spirit, 9 faith to still another by the same Spirit, gifts of
healing to another in the one Spirit, 10 performance of miracles
to another, prophecy to another, the ability to tell spirits apart to
another, different kinds of tongues to another, and the interpretation of the tongues to another. 11 All these things are produced
by the one and same Spirit who gives what he wants to each
person.
12 Christ is just like the human body—a body is a unit and has
many parts; and all the parts of the body are one body, even
though there are many. 13 We were all baptized by one Spirit into
one body, whether Jew or Greek, or slave or free, and we all were
given one Spirit to drink.

John 7:37-39

37 On the last and most important day of the festival, Jesus
stood up and shouted,
"All who are thirsty should come to me!
38 All who believe in me should drink!
As the scriptures said concerning me,
Rivers of living water will flow out from within him."
39 Jesus said this concerning the Spirit. Those who believed in
him would soon receive the Spirit, but they hadn't experienced
the Spirit yet since Jesus hadn't yet been glorified.

Primary Hymns and Songs for the Day

"On Pentecost They Gathered" 40207 (Acts) (O)
C237, CG225, G289, N272, P128, VU195
H-3 Hbl-86; Chr-153; Org-95
S-1 #243. Harmonization

"Every Time I Feel the Spirit" (PD-TO) (Acts)
C592, G66, GR446, N282, P315, UM404, Z121 (PD)

"O Spirit of the Living God" (PD) (Acts) (O)
N263, SH222, UM539
H-3 Hbl-44; Chr-21; Desc-40; Org-40
S-1 #131-132. Intro. and desc.

"Holy Ground" 21198 (Acts)
C112, G406, S2272

"Spirit of the Living God" 23488 (Acts, Pentecost)
C259, CG233, G288, GR299, N283, P322, SH555, UM393, VU376, Z226, S-1 #212 Vocal desc. idea
H-3 Chr-176
S-1 #212. Vocal descant idea

"Somos Uno en Cristo" ("We Are One in Christ Jesus") 6368975 (1 Cor)
C493, EL643, G322, S2229, SH227

"Forward through the Ages" (PD) (1 Cor) (C)
N377, UM555 (PD)
H-3 Hbl-59; Chr-156; Org-140

"Breathe on Me, Breath of God" 99481 (Acts) (C)
C254, CG235, E508, G286, GR304, N292, P316, SH224/273, UM420 (PD), VU382 (Fr.)
H-3 Hbl-49; Chr-45; Desc-101; Org-166

Additional Hymn Suggestions

"What Is this Place" (Acts)
C289, EL524, G404

"Hail Thee, Festival Day" (Acts)
E225, EL394, G277, N262, UM324, VU163

"Come, O Spirit, Dwell Among Us" (Acts, 1 Cor)
G280, N267, P129, VU198

+"O Breath of Life" OL-90731 (Acts, Comm.)
WS3146

+"Come, Holy Ghost, Our Hearts Inspire" (Acts)
GR291, UM603 (PD)

"Spirit, Spirit of Gentleness" (Acts, Pentecost)
C249, EL396, G291, N286, P319, S2120, VU375 (Fr.)

"Loving Spirit" 3379424 (Acts, Pentecost)
C244, EL397, G293, P323, S2123, VU387

+"Healer of Our Every Ill" OL-00115 (Acts)
C506, EL612, G795, S2213, SH339, VU619

"In the Midst of New Dimensions" (Acts, Pentecost)
C458, G315, N391, S2238

"Deep in the Shadows of the Past" (Acts, Pentecost)
G50, N320, P330, S2246

"Come, Share the Lord" (Acts, Comm.)
C408, CG459, G510, S2269, VU469

+"Praise God for This Holy Ground" (Acts, Pentecost)
G405, WS3009

"Like the Murmur of the Dove's Song" (Acts, 1 Cor)
C245, CG233, E513, EL403, G285, N270, P314, SH407, UM544, VU205

"Here, O Lord, Your Servants Gather" (Acts, 1 Cor)
C278, EL530, G311, N72, P465, UM552, VU362

"I'm Goin'a Sing When the Spirit Says Sing" (1 Cor, Pentecost)
GR330, UM333, Z81 (PD)

+"In Christ There Is No East or West" 2608952 (UMH ONLY St. 3 OL-13651) (1 Cor)
C687, CG273, E529, EL650 (PD), G317/318, GR392, N394/395, P439/440, UM548, VU606, Z65 (PD)

+"Where Charity and Love Prevail" 40313 (1 Cor)
CG264, E581, EL359, G316, N396, SH271, UM549

+"In Unity We Lift Our Song" (1 Cor)
CG563, S2221

+"They'll Know We Are Christians" 26997 (1 Cor)
C494, CG272, G300, S2223, SH232

"We All Are One in Mission" 3176809 (1 Cor)
CG269, EL576, G733, P435, S2243, ZS99

+"Let Us Be Bread" OL-00124 (1 Cor, Comm.)
S2260

+"Christ Has Broken Down the Wall" (1 Cor)
WS3122

+"A Place at the Table" (1 Cor, Comm.)
G769, WS3149

+"Spirit of God, Descend upon My Heart" 2083 (John, Pentecost)
C265, CG243, EL800, G688, GR294, N290, P326, SH277, UM500 (PD), VU378

+"Shalom to You" 114122 (John)
C436, UM666

+"Feed Us, Lord" 4636207 (John, Comm.)
G501, WS3167

Additional Contemporary and Modern Suggestions

"Surely the Presence of the Lord" 7909 (Acts, Pentecost)
C263, GR306, UM328; S-2 #200. Stanzas for soloist

"Sweet, Sweet Spirit" 18204 (Acts, Pentecost)
C261, CG241, G408, GR361, N293, P398, SH410, UM334

"Spirit Song" 27824 (Acts, Pentecost)
C352, SH409, UM347

"Holy, Holy" 18792 (Acts, Pentecost)
P140, S2039

"Dios Está Aquí" ("God Is Here Today") 3170575 (Acts)
G411, S2049, SH382

"Open Our Eyes, Lord" 1572 (Acts)
CG392, S2086, SH562

"Where the Spirit of the Lord Is" 27484 (Acts, Pentecost)
C264, S2119

"Open the Eyes of My Heart" 2298355 (Acts)
G452, SH378, WS3008

"Come, Holy Spirit" 3383953 (Acts)
WS3092 (*See also* SH223, WS3091)

"There's a Spirit of Love in This Place" OL-38821 (Acts)
WS3148, ZS103

"Holy Spirit, Rain Down" 2405227 (Acts)

"Let It Rise" 2240585 (Acts)

+"Prepare the Way" 7136724 (Acts)

+"As We Gather" 35469 (Acts)

+"Here Again" 7111925 (Acts)

+"From the Inside Out" 4705176 (Acts)

+"Here As In Heaven" 7051506 (Acts)

+"Presence" 7116947 (Acts)

+"No Outsiders" 7101035 (Acts, 1 Cor)

+"Let Justice Roll" ("Like a River") 4974842 (Acts, 1 Cor)

+"The Kingdom Is Yours" 7109354 (Acts, 1 Cor)

+"Good Grace" 7122177 (Acts, Pss, 1 Cor)

+"So Will I" ("100 Billion X") 7084123 (Pss)

+"O Bless the Lord My Soul" ("Psalm 104") 7017883 (Pss)

"God of Wonders" 3118757 (Pss)
SH9, WS3034

"We Are the Body of Christ" 2220206 (1 Cor)
S2227

+"Trinity Song" 7068847 (1 Cor)

"You Who Are Thirsty" 814453 (John)
S2132

"The River Is Here" 1475231 (John, Pentecost)

"Who Can Satisfy My Soul Like You?" 208492 (John)

"Holy and Anointed One" 164361 (John)

"All Who Are Thirsty" 2489542 (John)

+"Springtime" 7146308 (John)

+"King of Kings" 7127647 (Pentecost)

"Dwell" 4085652 (Pentecost)

Solo/Ensemble Suggestions

+"Spirit of Faith Come Down" (Acts, Pentecost)
V-1 p. 43
"Spirit of God" (Acts, Pentecost)
V-8 p. 170
"I Feel the Spirit Moving" (Acts, 1 Cor)
V-3 (1) p.22
"One Bread, One Body" (1 Cor)
V-3 (2) p. 40
"Ho! Everyone Who Is Thirsty" (John)
V-8 p. 244
+"Pentecost" (Acts)
Tom Shelton; MorningStar MSM-50-8881
SAB, piano (https://bit.ly/MS-8881)
"Gracious Spirit, Dwell with Me" (Matt, Baptism)
arr. K. Lee Scott; AEC-1 p. 21, Augsburg 0800646134
2-part mixed, organ (https://bit.ly/AEC-1-21)

+Hymn Anthem

"Wind Who Makes All Winds That Blow" (Acts)
C236, CG226, N271, P131, UM538, VU196
Keyboard (piano, harpsichord, or organ) and flute (or recorder) play through entire anthem.
Introduction: Flute plays melody, and keyboard plays all other notes. Maintain a simple, floating feel, with both instruments playing as smoothly as possible.
Stanza 1: S/A sing melody mm 1-4. T/B sing melody mm 5-8. All voices, unison, mm 9-19. Keyboard plays full setting. *Mezzo forte.*
Stanza 2: Keyboard plays full setting. T/B sing mm. 1-8. *Mezzo forte.* S/A sing remainder of stanza with keyboard, but *mezzo piano.*
Stanza 3: All voices, unison throughout. *Forte.* Keyboard plays full setting. Flute plays "alto" part up one or two octaves. *Ritard* the last measures.

Other Suggestions

Visuals:
O Wind, tongues of fire, praise, all races
P Sea/ships, whales, dove, volcano, quake, Ps. 104:35b
E Pile of gifts, seven flames, clasped hands, circle, baptism, drinking glasses
G Water/pitcher/glasses, river fountain
Introit: G283, S2124/2125, VU383, SH223, WS3091/3092. "Come, Holy Spirit" (Acts)
Call to Worship: WSL39. "Spirit of the living God" (Acts, Pentecost)
+Call to Prayer: UM330. "Daw-Kee, Aim Daw-Tis-Taw" ("Great Spirit, Now I Pray") (Matt)
Prayers: WSL37/38, N826/857, UM329/335, UM542/574, C52/243 (Pentecost)
Response: S2118. "Holy Spirit, Come to Us" (Acts, 1 Cor) EL406, G281, S2118
Song of Preparation: WS3047, stanza 3. "God Almighty, We Are Waiting" (Acts)
+Litany for Christian Unity: UM556 (Acts, 1 Cor)
Offertory Prayer: WSL132. "Loving Father" (Acts, John)
Sung Communion: WS3172. "Communion Setting"
Blessing: WSL41. "Wisdom, knowledge, faith" (1 Cor, Acts)
Sung Benediction: WS3183. "As We Go" (Pentecost)
Theme Ideas: God: Glory of God, God: Hunger / Thirst for God, Holy Spirit, Spiritual Gifts, Unity

Notes

NRSVue

Genesis 1:1–2:4a

1When God began to create the heavens and the earth, 2the earth was complete chaos, and darkness covered the face of the deep, while a wind from God swept over the face of the waters. 3Then God said, "Let there be light," and there was light. 4And God saw that the light was good; and God separated the light from the darkness. 5God called the light Day, and the darkness he called Night. And there was evening and there was morning, the first day.

6And God said, "Let there be a dome in the midst of the waters, and let it separate the waters from the waters." 7So God made the dome and separated the waters that were under the dome from the waters that were above the dome. And it was so. 8God called the dome Sky. And there was evening and there was morning, the second day.

9And God said, "Let the waters under the sky be gathered together into one place, and let the dry land appear." And it was so. 10God called the dry land Earth, and the waters that were gathered together he called Seas. And God saw that it was good. 11Then God said, "Let the earth put forth vegetation: plants yielding seed and fruit trees of every kind on earth that bear fruit with the seed in it." And it was so. 12The earth brought forth vegetation: plants yielding seed of every kind and trees of every kind bearing fruit with the seed in it. And God saw that it was good. 13And there was evening and there was morning, the third day.

14And God said, "Let there be lights in the dome of the sky to separate the day from the night, and let them be for signs and for seasons and for days and years, 15and let them be lights in the dome of the sky to give light upon the earth." And it was so. 16God made the two great lights—the greater light to rule the day and the lesser light to rule the night—and the stars. 17God set them in the dome of the sky to give light upon the earth, 18to rule over the day and over the night, and to separate the light from the darkness. And God saw that it was good. 19And there was evening and there was morning, the fourth day.

20And God said, "Let the waters bring forth swarms of living creatures, and let birds fly above the earth across the dome of the sky." 21So God created the great sea monsters and every living creature that moves, of every kind, with which the waters swarm and every winged bird of every kind. And God saw that it was good. 22God blessed them, saying, "Be fruitful and multiply and fill the waters in the seas, and let birds multiply on the earth." 23And there was evening and there was morning, the fifth day.

24And God said, "Let the earth bring forth living creatures of every kind: cattle and creeping things and wild animals of the earth of every kind." And it was so. 25God made the wild animals of the earth of every kind and the cattle of every kind and everything that creeps upon the ground of every kind. And God saw that it was good.

26Then God said, "Let us make humans in our image, according to our likeness, and let them have dominion over the fish of the sea and over the birds of the air and over the cattle and over all the wild animals of the earth and over every creeping thing that creeps upon the earth."

27So God created humankind in his image,
in the image of God he created them;
male and female he created them.

28God blessed them, and God said to them, "Be fruitful and multiply and fill the earth and subdue it and have dominion over the fish of the sea and over the birds of the air and over every living thing that moves upon the earth." 29God said, "See, I have given you every plant yielding seed that is upon the face of all the earth and every tree with seed in its fruit; you shall have them for food. 30And to every beast of the earth and to every bird of the air and to everything that creeps on the earth, everything that has the breath of life, I have given every green plant for food." And it was so. 31God saw everything that he had made, and indeed, it was very good. And there was evening and there was morning, the sixth day.

2 Thus the heavens and the earth were finished and all their multitude. 2On the sixth day God finished the work that he had done, and he rested on the seventh day from all the work that he had done. 3So God blessed the seventh day and hallowed it, because on it God rested from all the work that he had done in creation.

4aThese are the generations of the heavens and the earth when they were created.

CEB

Genesis 1:1–2:4a

1When God began to create the heavens and the earth—2the earth was without shape or form, it was dark over the deep sea, and God's wind swept over the waters—3God said, "Let there be light." And so light appeared. 4God saw how good the light was. God separated the light from the darkness. 5God named the light Day and the darkness Night.

There was evening and there was morning: the first day.

6God said, "Let there be a dome in the middle of the waters to separate the waters from each other." 7God made the dome and separated the waters under the dome from the waters above the dome. And it happened in that way. 8God named the dome Sky.

There was evening and there was morning: the second day.

9God said, "Let the waters under the sky come together into one place so that the dry land can appear." And that's what happened. 10God named the dry land Earth, and he named the gathered waters Seas. God saw how good it was. 11God said, "Let the earth grow plant life: plants yielding seeds and fruit trees bearing fruit with seeds inside it, each according to its kind throughout the earth." And that's what happened. 12The earth produced plant life: plants yielding seeds, each according to its kind, and trees bearing fruit with seeds inside it, each according to its kind. God saw how good it was.

13There was evening and there was morning: the third day.

14God said, "Let there be lights in the dome of the sky to separate the day from the night. They will mark events, sacred seasons, days, and years. 15They will be lights in the dome of the sky to shine on the earth." And that's what happened. 16God made the stars and two great lights: the larger light to rule over the day and the smaller light to rule over the night. 17God put them in the dome of the sky to shine on the earth, 18to rule over the day and over the night, and to separate the light from the darkness. God saw how good it was.

19There was evening and there was morning: the fourth day.

20God said, "Let the waters swarm with living things, and let birds fly above the earth up in the dome of the sky." 21God created the great sea animals and all the tiny living things that swarm in the waters, each according to its kind, and all the winged birds, each according to its kind. God saw how good it was. 22Then God blessed them: "Be fertile and multiply and fill the waters in the seas, and let the birds multiply on the earth."

23There was evening and there was morning: the fifth day.

24God said, "Let the earth produce every kind of living thing: livestock, crawling things, and wildlife." And that's what happened. 25God made every kind of wildlife, every kind of livestock, and every kind of creature that crawls on the ground. God saw how good it was. 26Then God said, "Let us make humanity in our image to resemble us so that they may take charge of the fish of the sea, the birds of the sky, the livestock, all the earth, and all the crawling things on earth."

27God created humanity in God's own image,
in the divine image God created them,
male and female God created them.

28God blessed them and said to them, "Be fertile and multiply; fill the earth and master it. Take charge of the fish of the sea, the birds of the sky, and everything crawling on the ground." 29Then God said, "I now give to you all the plants on the earth that yield seeds and all the trees whose fruit produces its seeds within it. These will be your food. 30To all wildlife, to all the birds of the sky, and to everything crawling on the ground—to everything that breathes—I give all the green grasses for food." And that's what happened. 31God saw everything he had made: it was supremely good.

There was evening and there was morning: the sixth day.

2 The heavens and the earth and all who live in them were completed. 2On the sixth day God completed all the work that he had done, and on the seventh day God rested from all the work that he had done. 3God blessed the seventh day and made it holy, because on it God rested from all the work of creation. 4aThis is the account of the heavens and the earth when they were created.

NRSVue

Psalm 8 (G25, N624, P162/163, SH6, UM743)

[1]O LORD, our Sovereign,
how majestic is your name in all the earth!
You have set your glory above the heavens.
[2]Out of the mouths of babes and infants
you have founded a bulwark because of your foes,
to silence the enemy and the avenger.
[3]When I look at your heavens, the work of your fingers,
the moon and the stars that you have established;
[4]what are human beings that you are mindful of them,
mortals that you care for them?
[5]Yet you have made them a little lower than God
and crowned them with glory and honor.
[6]You have given them dominion over the works of your hands;
you have put all things under their feet,
[7]all sheep and oxen,
and also the beasts of the field,
[8]the birds of the air, and the fish of the sea,
whatever passes along the paths of the seas.
[9]O LORD, our Sovereign,
how majestic is your name in all the earth!

---

2 Corinthians 13:11-13

[11]Finally, brothers and sisters, farewell. Be restored; listen to
my appeal; agree with one another; live in peace; and the God of
love and peace will be with you. [12]Greet one another with a holy
kiss. All the saints greet you.
[13]The grace of the Lord Jesus Christ, the love of God, and the
communion of the Holy Spirit be with all of you.

Matthew 28:16-20

[16]Now the eleven disciples went to Galilee, to the mountain
to which Jesus had directed them. [17]When they saw him, they
worshiped him, but they doubted. [18]And Jesus came and said to
them, "All authority in heaven and on earth has been given to
me. [19]Go therefore and make disciples of all nations, baptizing
them in the name of the Father and of the Son and of the Holy
Spirit [20]and teaching them to obey everything that I have commanded you. And remember, I am with you always, to the end of
the age."

CEB

Psalm 8 (G25, N624, P162/163, SH6, UM743)

[1]LORD, our Lord, how majestic
is your name throughout the earth!
You made your glory higher than heaven!
[2]From the mouths of nursing babies
you have laid a strong foundation
because of your foes,
in order to stop vengeful enemies.
[3]When I look up at your skies,
at what your fingers made—
the moon and the stars
that you set firmly in place—
4 what are human beings
that you think about them;
what are human beings
that you pay attention to them?
[5]You've made them only slightly less than divine,
crowning them with glory and grandeur.
[6]You've let them rule over your handiwork,
putting everything under their feet—
7 all sheep and all cattle,
the wild animals too,
8 the birds in the sky,
the fish of the ocean,
everything that travels the pathways of the sea.
[9]LORD, our Lord, how majestic is your name throughout the earth!

---

2 Corinthians 13:11-13

[11]Finally, brothers and sisters, good-bye. Put things in order,
respond to my encouragement, be in harmony with each other,
and live in peace—and the God of love and peace will be with
you.
[12]Say hello to each other with a holy kiss. All of God's people
say hello to you.
[13]The grace of the Lord Jesus Christ, the love of God, and the
fellowship of the Holy Spirit be with you all.

Matthew 28:16-20

[16]Now the eleven disciples went to Galilee, to the mountain
where Jesus told them to go. [17]When they saw him, they worshipped him, but some doubted. [18]Jesus came near and spoke
to them, "I've received all authority in heaven and on earth.
[19]Therefore, go and make disciples of all nations, baptizing them
in the name of the Father and of the Son and of the Holy Spirit,
[20]teaching them to obey everything that I've commanded you.
Look, I myself will be with you every day until the end of this
present age."

Primary Hymns and Songs for the Day

"All Creatures of Our God and King" 2420288 (Gen, Pss, Trinity) (O)
C22, CG307, E400, EL835, G15, GR34, N17, P455, SH16, UM62, VU217 (Fr.)
H-3 Hbl-44; Chr-21; Desc-66; Org-73
S-1 #198-204. Various treatments
"Doxology" 5465879 (Gen, Pss, Trinity)
"Lord, You Give the Great Commission" 230673 (2 Cor, Matt) (O) or (C)
C459, CG651/CG653, E528, EL579, G298, GR463, P429, S2176, UM584, VU512
H-3 Hbl-61; Chr-132; Org-2
S-1 #4-5. Instrumental and vocal desc.
"How Majestic Is Your Name" 26007 (Pss)
C63, CG326, G613, S2023, ZS26
"Come, Join the Dance of Trinity" OL-06029 (Gen, Matt, Trinity)
EL412, WS3017
"We Shall Overcome" (PD-TO) (2 Cor)
C630, G379, N570, UM533 (PD-TO), Z127, ZS106
"Go Ye, Go Ye into the World" (Matt)
S2239
"Go, Make of All Disciples" (Matt) (C)
GR452, UM571
H-3 Hbl-74; Chr-123; Desc-64; Org-71
S-1 #9-197. Various treatments
"Enviado Soy de Dios" ("Sent Out in Jesus' Name") 6290823 (Matt) (C)
EL538, G747, S2184, SH718

Additional Hymn Suggestions

"Crashing Waters at Creation" (Gen)
EL455, G476, N326, VU449
"Out of Deep, Unordered Water" (Gen)
G484, P494, VU453
"For the Beauty of the Earth" 43200 (Gen)
C56, CG341, E416, EL879, G14, GR82, P473, N28, SH21, UM92 (PD), VU226
"Morning Has Broken" (Gen)
C53, CG27, E8, EL556, G664, SH465, UM145, VU409
"All Things Bright and Beautiful" (Gen)
C61, CG23, E405, G20, GR20, N31, P267, SH1, UM147 (PD), VU291
"God Who Stretched the Spangled Heavens" (Gen)
C651, CG21, E580, EL771, G24, N556, P268, UM150
"This Is the Day the Lord Hath Made" (Gen)
E50, G681, GR448, P230, UM658 (PD), Z243
"O God, We Bear the Imprint of Your Face" (Gen)
C681, G759, N585, P385
"Mothering God, You Gave Me Birth" (Gen, Trinity)
C83, EL735, G7, N467, S2050, VU320
"From All That Dwell Below the Skies" (Gen, Pss)
C49, CG330, E380, G327, GR76, N27, P229, UM101 (PD)
"I Sing the Almighty Power of God" 738058 (Gen, Pss)
C64, CG19, E398, G32, GR4, N12, P288, SH15, UM152, VU231
+"Father, We Praise Thee" (Pss, Trinity)
E1, EL558 (PD), N90, P459, UM680
+"O Love, How Deep" (Pss, Matt, Trinity)
E448/449, EL322, G618, GR95, N209, P83, SH115, UM267, VU348
"Sweet, Sweet Spirit" (2 Cor)
C261, CG241, G408, GR361, N293, P398, SH410, UM334
+"Shalom to You" 114122 (2 Cor)
C436, UM666
"How Clear Is Our Vocation, Lord" (2 Cor)
EL580, G432, P419, VU504
"God, Whose Giving Knows No Ending" (2 Cor, Matt)
C606, CG671, G716, N565, P422
"Lord, You Give the Great Commission" 230673 (2 Cor, Matt)
C459, CG651/CG653, E528, EL579, G298, GR463, P429, S2176, UM584, VU512
+*"O-So-So"* ("Come Now, O Prince of Peace") (2 Cor, Matt, Trinity)
EL247, G103, S2232, SH235
"The Church of Christ in Every Age" (Matt)
C475, EL729, G320, N306, P421, UM589, VU601
"Guide My Feet" OL-LMGM2537 (Matt)
CG637, G741, GR326, N497, P354, S2208, SH54, ZS141
"Go to the World" (Matt)
CG481, G295, SH720, VU420, WS3158
+"Holy, Holy, Holy! Lord God Almighty" 1156 (Trinity)
C4, CG1, E362, EL413, G1, GR23, N277, P138, SH450, UM64/65, VU315
+"Holy God, We Praise Thy Name" 114555 (Trinity)
CG9, E366, EL414 (PD), G4, GR2, N276, P460, SH431, UM79, VU894 (Fr.)
+"Maker, in Whom We Live" (PD) (Trinity)
GR25, UM88 (PD), VU321
+"Praise God for This Holy Ground" (Trinity)
G405, WS3009

Additional Contemporary and Modern Suggestions

"Thou Art Worthy" 14789 (Gen)
C114, S2041
"Veni Sancte Spiritus" ("Holy Spirit, Come to Us") OL-TaizeVN57 (Gen)
EL406, G281, S2118
"Come, Holy Spirit" 3383953 (Gen)
WS3092 (*See also* SH223, WS3091)
"Ah, Lord God" 17896 (Gen, Trinity)
"For Us" 7119349 (Gen, Trinity)
+"Beautiful Things" 5665521 (Gen)
+"Say So" 4944016 (Gen, Matt)
"How Great Is Our God" 4348399 (Gen, Pss, Trinity)
CG322, GR31, SH458, WS3003
"Sing the Praise of God Our Maker" OL-80079 (Gen, Pss, Trinity)
WS3013
"Across the Lands" 3709898 (Gen, Pss)
SH654, WS3032
"God of Wonders" 3118757 (Gen, Pss)
SH9, WS3034
"Majestic" 4573308 (Pss)
+"Friend of God" 3991651 (Pss)
+"You Have Saved Us" 5548514 (Pss)
"Make Me a Channel of Your Peace" OL-80478 (2 Cor)
G753, S2171, SH616 VU684
"Make Me a Channel of Your Peace" 6399315 (2 Cor)
"Canto de Esperanza" ("Song of Hope") 5193990 (2 Cor)
G765, P432, S2186, SH721, VU424
"They'll Know We Are Christians" 26997 (2 Cor, Trinity)
C494, CG272, G300, S2223, SH232
+"The Blessing" 7147007 (2 Cor, Matt)
+"Called Me Higher" 5887880 (Matt)
+"Won't Stop Now" 7111932 (Matt)
+"Song for the Nations" 20340 (Matt)
"Rising" 4662460 (Matt)
"A New Hallelujah" 5285860 (Matt)
"Celebrate Jesus" 16859 (Matt)
"Lord God Almighty" (Matt, Trinity)
S2006
"Holy, Holy" 18792 (Trinity)
P140, S2039
"Because We Believe" 2133379 (Trinity)
+"Trinity Song" 7068847 (Trinity)

Solo/Ensemble Suggestions
"This Is My Father's World" (Gen)
V-6 p. 42
"In the Image of God" (Gen)
V-8 p. 362
+"How Real!" (Gen)
V-8 p. 376
"Make Me a Channel of Your Peace" (2 Cor)
V-3 (2) p. 25
V-3 (3) p. 28
"Alleluia" (Trinity)
V-8 p. 358
"In the Beginning" (Gen)
arr. David Sims; AEC-3 p. 20
2-part, piano (https://bit.ly/AEC-3)
"As You Go on Your Way" (Matt)
James Engel; AEC-2 p. 19
Unison, organ (https://bit.ly/AEC-2)

+Hymn Anthem
"For the Beauty of the Earth" 43200 (Gen)
C56, CG341, EL879, G14, GR82, P473, N28, SH21, UM92 (PD)
Introduction: Keyboard (organ) plays refrain one time. Go directly into stanza 1 with no *Ritard* or extra beats added.
Stanza 1: All voices unison. Keyboard plays hymn harmonization. *Mezzo forte.*
Stanza 2: S/A only, unison. Keyboard plays A, T, and B parts, but up one octave. *Mezzo piano.*
Stanza 3: All voices, in four parts *a cappella* (or S and B parts only, accompanied by full setting). One light soprano soloist sings descant above, such as S-1, #93. *Mezzo forte.*
Stanza 4: T/B only, unison. Keyboard plays S-1, #94 or another harmonization. *Mezzo piano.*
Stanza 5: All voices, in four parts, *a cappella* (or unison, accompanied). *Mezzo forte.*
Stanza 6: All voices unison. Some sopranos sing a descant S-1, #95. Keyboard plays S-1, #96. *Mezzo forte.*

Other Suggestions
Visuals: Symbols of the Trinity, 3-wick candle
O Wind, light/dark, sky (evening/morning)
P Majesty, earth, infants, sky/stars, people, sheep/ox
E Waving, circle (unity), dove/branch, kiss/parting
G Jesus, eleven men, Christ candle, worship, globe, baptism
Introit: C278, EL530, G311, N72, P465, UM552, VU362. "Here, O Lord, Your Servants Gather" (2 Cor)
Opening Prayer: N826 (Gen) or N830 (Trinity)
Opening Prayer: WSL64. "God of all creation" (Gen)
Canticle: UM80. "Canticle of the Holy Trinity" (Trinity)
Litany: CG11. "God the Trinity" (Trinity)
Litany: WSL48. "O Lord, our God, creator" (Gen)
+Call to Prayer: WS3146. "O Breath of Life" OL-90731 Gen)
Prayer: N864 or WSL69 (Pss)
+Prayer: UM76. Trinity Sunday (Trinity)
Offertory Prayer: WSL109. "O great and holy God" (Pss)
+Response: VU538. "For the Gift of Creation" (Gen)
Blessing: WSL178. "May the God who made" (Gen)
+Sung Benediction: C437, SH722, UM665, VU964. "Go Now in Peace" 194317 (2 Cor)
Sung Benediction: WS3183. "As We Go" (Matt)
Theme Ideas: Call of God, Creation, Discipleship / Following God, God: Glory of God, Peace, Praise

Notes

NRSVue

Genesis 12:1-9

1Now the LORD said to Abram, "Go from your country and your kindred and your father's house to the land that I will show you. 2I will make of you a great nation, and I will bless you and make your name great, so that you will be a blessing. 3I will bless those who bless you, and the one who curses you I will curse, and in you all the families of the earth shall be blessed."

4So Abram went, as the LORD had told him, and Lot went with him. Abram was seventy-five years old when he departed from Haran. 5Abram took his wife Sarai and his brother's son Lot and all the possessions that they had gathered and the persons whom they had acquired in Haran, and they set forth to go to the land of Canaan. When they had come to the land of Canaan, 6Abram passed through the land to the place at Shechem, to the oak of Moreh. At that time the Canaanites were in the land. 7Then the LORD appeared to Abram and said, "To your offspring I will give this land." So he built there an altar to the LORD, who had appeared to him. 8From there he moved on to the hill country on the east of Bethel and pitched his tent, with Bethel on the west and Ai on the east, and there he built an altar to the Lord and invoked the name of the LORD. 9And Abram journeyed on by stages toward the Negeb.

Psalm 33:1-12 (G40, N643, P185, SH4, UM767)

1Rejoice in the LORD, O you righteous.
Praise befits the upright.
2Praise the LORD with the lyre;
make melody to him with the harp of ten strings.
3Sing to him a new song;
play skillfully on the strings, with loud shouts.
4For the word of the LORD is upright,
and all his work is done in faithfulness.
5He loves righteousness and justice;
the earth is full of the steadfast love of the LORD.
6By the word of the LORD the heavens were made
and all their host by the breath of his mouth.
7He gathered the waters of the sea as in a bottle;
he put the deeps in storehouses.
8Let all the earth fear the LORD;
let all the inhabitants of the world stand in awe of him,
9for he spoke, and it came to be;
he commanded, and it stood firm.
10The LORD brings the counsel of the nations to nothing;
he frustrates the plans of the peoples.
11The counsel of the LORD stands forever,
the thoughts of his heart to all generations.
12Happy is the nation whose God is the LORD,
the people whom he has chosen as his heritage.

CEB

Genesis 12:1-9

1The LORD said to Abram, "Leave your land, your family, and your father's household for the land that I will show you. 2I will make of you a great nation and will bless you. I will make your name respected, and you will be a blessing.

3I will bless those who bless you,
those who curse you I will curse;
all the families of the earth
will be blessed because of you."

4Abram left just as the LORD told him, and Lot went with him. Now Abram was 75 years old when he left Haran. 5Abram took his wife Sarai, his nephew Lot, all of their possessions, and those who became members of their household in Haran; and they set out for the land of Canaan. When they arrived in Canaan, 6Abram traveled through the land as far as the sacred place at Shechem, at the oak of Moreh. The Canaanites lived in the land at that time. 7The LORD appeared to Abram and said, "I give this land to your descendants," so Abram built an altar there to the LORD who appeared to him. 8From there he traveled toward the mountains east of Bethel, and pitched his tent with Bethel on the west and Ai on the east. There he built an altar to the LORD and worshipped in the LORD's name. 9Then Abram set out toward the arid southern plain, making and breaking camp as he went.

Psalm 33:1-12 (G40, N643, P185, SH4, UM767)

1All you who are righteous,
shout joyfully to the LORD!
It's right for those who do right to praise God.
2Give thanks to the LORD with the lyre!
Sing praises to him with the ten-stringed harp!
3Sing to him a new song!
Play your best with joyful shouts!
4Because the LORD's word is right,
his every act is done in good faith.
5He loves righteousness and justice;
the LORD's faithful love fills the whole earth.
6The skies were made by the LORD's word,
all their starry multitude by the breath of his mouth.
7He gathered the ocean waters into a heap;
he put the deep seas into storerooms.
8All the earth honors the LORD;
all the earth's inhabitants stand in awe of him.
9Because when he spoke, it happened!
When he commanded, there it was!
10The LORD overrules what the nations plan;
he frustrates what the peoples intend to do.
11But the LORD's plan stands forever;
what he intends to do lasts from one generation to the next.
12The nation whose God is the LORD,
the people whom God has chosen as his possession,
is truly happy!

NRSVue

Romans 4:13-25

[13]For the promise that he would inherit the world did not come to Abraham or to his descendants through the law but through the righteousness of faith. [14]For if it is the adherents of the law who are to be the heirs, faith is null and the promise is void. [15]For the law brings wrath, but where there is no law, neither is there transgression.

[16]For this reason the promise depends on faith, in order that it may rest on grace, so that it may be guaranteed to all his descendants, not only to the adherents of the law but also to those who share the faith of Abraham (who is the father of all of us, [17]as it is written, "I have made you the father of many nations"), in the presence of the God in whom he believed, who gives life to the dead and calls into existence the things that do not exist. [18]Hoping against hope, he believed that he would become "the father of many nations," according to what was said, "So shall your descendants be." [19]He did not weaken in faith when he considered his own body, which was already as good as dead (for he was about a hundred years old), and the barrenness of Sarah's womb. [20]No distrust made him waver concerning the promise of God, but he grew strong in his faith as he gave glory to God, [21]being fully convinced that God was able to do what he had promised. [22]Therefore "it was reckoned to him as righteousness." [23]Now the words, "it was reckoned to him," were written not for his sake alone [24]but for ours also. It will be reckoned to us who believe in him who raised Jesus our Lord from the dead, [25]who was handed over for our trespasses and was raised for our justification.

Matthew 9:9-13, 18-26

[9]As Jesus was walking along, he saw a man called Matthew sitting at the tax-collection station, and he said to him, "Follow me." And he got up and followed him.

[10]And as he sat at dinner in the house, many tax collectors and sinners came and were sitting with Jesus and his disciples. [11]When the Pharisees saw this, they said to his disciples, "Why does your teacher eat with tax collectors and sinners?" [12]But when he heard this, he said, "Those who are well have no need of a physician, but those who are sick. [13]Go and learn what this means, 'I desire mercy, not sacrifice.' For I have not come to call the righteous but sinners." . . .

[18]While he was saying these things to them, suddenly a leader came in and knelt before him, saying, "My daughter has just died, but come and lay your hand on her, and she will live." [19]And Jesus got up and followed him, with his disciples. [20]Then suddenly a woman who had been suffering from a flow of blood for twelve years came up behind him and touched the fringe of his cloak, [21]for she was saying to herself, "If I only touch his cloak, I will be made well." [22]Jesus turned, and seeing her he said, "Take heart, daughter; your faith has made you well." And the woman was made well from that moment. [23]When Jesus came to the leader's house and saw the flute players and the crowd making a commotion, [24]he said, "Go away, for the girl is not dead but sleeping." And they laughed at him. [25]But when the crowd had been put outside, he went in and took her by the hand, and the girl got up. [26]And the report of this spread through all of that district.

CEB

Romans 4:13-25

[13]The promise to Abraham and to his descendants, that he would inherit the world, didn't come through the Law but through the righteousness that comes from faith. [14]If they inherit because of the Law, then faith has no effect and the promise has been canceled. [15]The Law brings about wrath. But when there isn't any law, there isn't any violation of the law. [16]That's why the inheritance comes through faith, so that it will be on the basis of God's grace. In that way, the promise is secure for all of Abraham's descendants, not just for those who are related by Law but also for those who are related by the faith of Abraham, who is the father of all of us. [17]As it is written: *I have appointed you to be the father of many nations.* So Abraham is our father in the eyes of God in whom he had faith, the God who gives life to the dead and calls things that don't exist into existence. [18]When it was beyond hope, he had faith in the hope that he would become the father of many nations, in keeping with the promise God spoke to him: That's how many descendants you will have. [19]Without losing faith, Abraham, who was nearly 100 years old, took into account his own body, which was as good as dead, and Sarah's womb, which was dead. [20]He didn't hesitate with a lack of faith in God's promise, but he grew strong in faith and gave glory to God. [21]He was fully convinced that God was able to do what he promised. [22]Therefore, it was credited to him as righteousness.

[23]But the scripture that says it was credited to him wasn't written only for Abraham's sake. [24]It was written also for our sake, because it is going to be credited to us too. It will be credited to those of us who have faith in the one who raised Jesus our Lord from the dead. [25]He was handed over because of our mistakes, and he was raised to meet the requirements of righteousness for us.

Matthew 9:9-13, 18-26

[9]As Jesus continued on from there, he saw a man named Matthew sitting at a kiosk for collecting taxes. He said to him, "Follow me," and he got up and followed him. [10]As Jesus sat down to eat in Matthew's house, many tax collectors and sinners joined Jesus and his disciples at the table.

[11]But when the Pharisees saw this, they said to his disciples, "Why does your teacher eat with tax collectors and sinners?"

[12]When Jesus heard it, he said, "Healthy people don't need a doctor, but sick people do. [13]Go and learn what this means: I want mercy and not sacrifice. I didn't come to call righteous people, but sinners." . . .

[18]While Jesus was speaking to them, a ruler came and knelt in front of him, saying, "My daughter has just died. But come and place your hand on her, and she'll live." [19]So Jesus and his disciples got up and went with him. [20]Then a woman who had been bleeding for twelve years came up behind Jesus and touched the hem of his clothes. [21]She thought, If I only touch his robe I'll be healed.

[22]When Jesus turned and saw her, he said, "Be encouraged, daughter. Your faith has healed you." And the woman was healed from that time on.

[23]When Jesus went into the ruler's house, he saw the flute players and the distressed crowd. [24]He said, "Go away, because the little girl isn't dead but is asleep"; but they laughed at him. [25]After he had sent the crowd away, Jesus went in and touched her hand, and the little girl rose up. [26]News about this spread throughout that whole region.

Primary Hymns and Songs for the Day
"Lift Every Voice and Sing" 7071034 (Pss) (O)
C631, CG638, E599, EL841, G339, GR408, N593, P563, SH36, UM519, Z32 (PD), Z210, ZS113
H-3 Chr-128
"Lead Me, Lord" (Gen)
C593, GR332, N774, UM473 (PD), VU662
"Lord of the Dance" 78529 (Matt)
G157, P302, UM261, VU352
H-3 Chr-106; Org-81
"I Come with Joy" (Matt, Comm.)
C420, CG456, E304, EL482, G515, N349, P507, SH682, UM617, VU477
H-3 Hbl-70; Chr-105; Org-30
S-2 #52. Choral and keyboard arrangement
"Trust and Obey" (Gen, Matt) (C)
C556, CG509, GR334, SH636, UM467 (PD)
H-3 Chr-202
S-1 #336. Harmonization

Additional Hymn Suggestions
"To Abraham and Sarah" (Gen)
CG251, G51, VU634
"The God of Abraham Praise" 484742 (Gen, Rom)
C24, CG45, E401, EL831, G49, GR16, N24, P488, SH50, UM116 (PD), VU255
+"Lead On, O King Eternal" (Gen)
C632, CG63, E555, EL805, G269, GR478, N573, P447/448, UM580
+"Here I Am, Lord" OL-80670 (Gen)
C452, CG482, EL574, G69, GR589, P525, SH608, UM593, VU509
"God of the Ages" (Gen)
C725, CG62, E718, G331, GR59, N592, P262, UM698 (PD)
"God Made from One Blood" (Gen)
C500, CG686, N427, S2170, VU554
"Deep in the Shadows of the Past" (Gen)
G50, N320, P330, S2246
+"Give Me the Faith Which Can Remove" (Gen, Rom, Matt)
GR583, UM650 (PD)
"Rain Down" (Pss)
CG388, G48
"We Will Go Out with Joy" (Pss)
G539
"Praise the Lord Who Reigns Above" (Pss)
CG334, GR10, UM96 (PD)
"La Palabra Del Señor Es Recta" ("Righteous and Just Is the Word of the Lord") (Pss)
G40, UM107, SH4
"Cantemos al Señor" ("Let's Sing unto the Lord") (Pss)
C60, EL555, G669, N39, SH432, UM149
"Come Sing, O Church, in Joy!" (Rom)
G305, P430
"Alleluia, Alleluia" 32376 (Rom)
CG196, E178, G240, P106, SH189, UM162, VU179
"O Love, How Deep" (Rom, Matt)
E448/449, EL322, G618, GR95, N209, P83, SH115, UM267, VU348
"Standing on the Promises" (Rom)
C552, CG625, G838, GR434, SH45, UM374 (PD)
"See How Great a Flame Aspires" (Rom)
GR465, UM541
"Faith of Our Fathers" 7029079 Rom)
C635, CG645, EL812/813, N381, UM710 (PD), VU580
"There Are Some Things I May Not Know" (Rom)
N405, S2147, Z201 (PD), ZS172
"We Walk by Faith" 2591911 (Rom)
CG634, E209, EL635, G817, N256, P399, S2196, SH660
"Faith Is Patience in the Night" (Rom)
S2211
"In the Singing" (Rom, Comm.)
EL466, G533, S2255
"When Jesus the Healer Passed Through Galilee" (Matt)
UM263, VU358
"O Christ, the Healer" 1730268 (Rom, Matt)
C503. EL610, G793, N175, P380, UM265
"Heal Us, Emmanuel, Hear Our Prayer" (Matt)
UM266 (PD)
"Woman in the Night" (Matt)
C188, G161, UM274
"What Does the Lord Require" 287413 (Matt)
C659, E605, P405, UM441
+"Lord, Whose Love Through Humble Service" (Matt)
C461, CG650, E610, EL712, GR454, P427, SH239, UM581
+"Rescue the Perishing" 34549 (Matt)
CG480, GR457, UM591 (PD)
"Draw Us in the Spirit's Tether" (Matt, Comm.)
C392, EL470, G529, N337, P504, UM632, VU479
"Come and See" (*"Kyrie"*) (Matt)
S2127
"Would I Have Answered When You Called" (Matt)
S2137
+"Gracious Creator of Sea and of Land" (Matt)
WS3161
"Come, Sinners, to the Gospel Feast" 4047140 (Comm.)
UM616 (PD)
"My Hope Is Built" (PD) (Pss, Rom) (C)
C537, CG590, EL596/597, G353, GR102, N403, P379, SH324, UM368 (PD), ZS182

Additional Contemporary and Modern Suggestions
+"Promises" 7149439 (Gen)
+"No Outsiders" 7101035 (Gen, Rom)
"El-Shaddai" 26856 (Gen, Matt)
UM123, S-2 #54 Verses for Vocal Solo
+"Step by Step" 696994 (Gen, Matt)
CG495, G743, GR671, WS3004
"Clap Your Hands" 806674 (Pss)
S2028, ZS10
"Awesome God" 41099 (Pss)
G616, S2040, ZS7
"As It Is in Heaven" 4669748 (Pss)
"Our God Saves" 4972837 (Pss)
"Our Love Is Loud" 3560817 (Pss)
+"Your Spirit" 7091513 (Pss)
+"Our God Saves" 4972837 (Pss)
+"All the Poor and Powerless" 5881130 (Pss)
+"The Kingdom Is Yours" 7109354 (Pss, Rom)
+"Never Runs Out" 7193998 (Pss, Rom)
"Someone Asked the Question" 1640279 (Pss, Rom)
N523, S2144
"Grace Like Rain" 3689877 (Rom)
"Sing Alleluia to the Lord" NO- SS (Rom, Comm.)
C32, S2258, SH685
"Here Is Bread, Here Is Wine" 983717 (Rom, Comm.)
EL483, S2266
"Lord, Have Mercy" OL-17490 (Rom, Matt)
C299, G576, S2277
+"Who You Say I Am" 7102401 (Rom, Matt)
+"Won't Stop Now" 7111932 (Rom, Matt)
+"Called Me Higher" 5887880 (Matt)
+"From the Inside Out" 4705176 (Matt)
+"You're Worthy of My Praise" 487976 (Matt)
"Something Beautiful" 18060 (Matt)
UM394

"O Lord, You're Beautiful" 14514 (Matt)
S2064
"Cry of My Heart" 844980 (Matt)
S2165
"What Does the Lord Require of You" 456859 (Matt)
C661, CG690, G70, S2174, VU701
"Somlandela" ("We Will Follow") (PD-TO) (Matt)
WS3160
"As We Go" 5043277 (Matt)
WS3183
"I Will Never Be (the Same Again)" 1874911 (Matt)
"Jesus, Lover of My Soul" 1198817 (Matt)
"From Ashes to Beauty" 5288953 (Matt)
"Freedom in the Spirit" 7127886 (Matt)

Solo/Ensemble Suggestions

"Great Is Thy Faithfulness" (Gen, Matt)
V-8 p. 48
+"Make a Joyful Noise"
V-3 (5) p. 44
"Amazing Grace" (Rom)
V-8 p. 56
"Redeeming Grace" (Rom)
V-4 p. 47
+"Alleluia! Give Thanks to the Risen Lord" (Rom)
Arr. Joel Raney; Hope C6192
SATB, piano, opt. trumpet (https://bit.ly/H-6192)
+"Jesus, Lover of My Soul" (Matt)
Brian L. Hanson; Choristers Guild CGA1337
SATB, piano (https://bit.ly/C-1337)

+Hymn Anthem

"Cantemos al Señor" ("Let's Sing unto the Lord") (Pss)
C60, EL555, G669, N39, SH432, UM149
This anthem is best performed with improvised piano and guitar accompaniment. Add maracas, claves, and other percussion instruments for a festive rendition. Adapt the suggestions here to your choir.
Introduction: Guitar and piano.
Stanza 1: Soloist sings in Spanish.
Refrain: All voices, unison, in Spanish.
Stanza 1: All voices in English.
Refrain: All voices in Spanish.
Stanza 2: Soloist sings in Spanish.
Refrain: All voices, including congregation in Spanish.
Stanza 2: All voices in English.
Refrain: All voices, including congregation in Spanish.
Repeat once and take the final ending.

Other Suggestions

Visuals:
O Elderly man/woman, altar, tent
P Harp, scales of justice, creation, water/bottle/storehouse, UN, 33:1b,3a,12a
E Abraham/old man, risen Christ
G Tax forms, dinner, medical bag, woman/robe/girl
A celebration of music ministry may be celebrated on this day in relationship to the Psalm.
+Introit: S2101, stanza 4. "Two Fishermen" (Gen, Matt)
Response: C299, EL152, G576, S2275/2277, WS3133. "Lord, Have Mercy" (Matt)
Alternate Lessons (see page 4): Hos. 5:15-6:6, Ps. 50:7-15
Theme Ideas: Call of God, Covenant, Discipleship / Following God, Faith, Healing, Praise

Notes

NRSVue

Genesis 18:1-15, (21:1-7)

1The LORD appeared to Abraham by the oaks of Mamre, as he sat at the entrance of his tent in the heat of the day. 2He looked up and saw three men standing near him. When he saw them, he ran from the tent entrance to meet them and bowed down to the ground. 3He said, "My lord, if I find favor with you, do not pass by your servant. 4Let a little water be brought, and wash your feet, and rest yourselves under the tree. 5Let me bring a little bread, that you may refresh yourselves, and after that you may pass on—since you have come to your servant." So they said, "Do as you have said." 6And Abraham hastened into the tent to Sarah, and said, "Make ready quickly three measures of choice flour, knead it, and make cakes." 7Abraham ran to the herd, and took a calf, tender and good, and gave it to the servant, who hastened to prepare it. 8Then he took curds and milk and the calf that he had prepared and set it before them, and he stood by them under the tree while they ate.

9They said to him, "Where is your wife Sarah?" And he said, "There, in the tent." 10Then one said, "I will surely return to you in due season, and your wife Sarah shall have a son." And Sarah was listening at the tent entrance behind him. 11Now Abraham and Sarah were old, advanced in age; it had ceased to be with Sarah after the manner of women. 12So Sarah laughed to herself, saying, "After I have grown old, and my husband is old, shall I be fruitful?" 13The LORD said to Abraham, "Why did Sarah laugh and say, 'Shall I indeed bear a child, now that I am old?' 14Is anything too wonderful for the LORD? At the set time I will return to you, in due season, and Sarah shall have a son." 15But Sarah denied, saying, "I did not laugh," for she was afraid. He said, "Yes, you did laugh." . . .

21 The LORD dealt with Sarah as he had said, and the LORD did for Sarah as he had promised. 2Sarah conceived and bore Abraham a son in his old age, at the time of which God had spoken to him. 3Abraham gave the name Isaac to his son whom Sarah bore him. 4And Abraham circumcised his son Isaac when he was eight days old, as God had commanded him. 5Abraham was a hundred years old when his son Isaac was born to him. 6Now Sarah said, "God has brought laughter for me; everyone who hears will laugh with me." 7And she said, "Who would ever have said to Abraham that Sarah would nurse children? Yet I have borne him a son in his old age."

Psalm 116:1-2, 12-19 (G655, N699, P228, SH344, UM837)

1I love the LORD because he has heard
my voice and my supplications.
2Because he inclined his ear to me,
therefore I will call on him as long as I live.
. . . .
12What shall I return to the LORD
for all his bounty to me?
13I will lift up the cup of salvation
and call on the name of the LORD;
14I will pay my vows to the LORD
in the presence of all his people.
15Precious in the sight of the LORD
is the death of his faithful ones.
16O LORD, I am your servant;
I am your servant, the child of your serving girl.
You have loosed my bonds.
17I will offer to you a thanksgiving sacrifice
and call on the name of the LORD.
18I will pay my vows to the LORD
in the presence of all his people,
19in the courts of the house of the LORD,
in your midst, O Jerusalem.
Praise the LORD!

CEB

Genesis 18:1-15, (21:1-7)

1The LORD appeared to Abraham at the oaks of Mamre while he sat at the entrance of his tent in the day's heat. 2He looked up and suddenly saw three men standing near him. As soon as he saw them, he ran from his tent entrance to greet them and bowed deeply. 3He said, "Sirs, if you would be so kind, don't just pass by your servant. 4Let a little water be brought so you may wash your feet and refresh yourselves under the tree. 5Let me offer you a little bread so you will feel stronger, and after that you may leave your servant and go on your way—since you have visited your servant."

They responded, "Fine. Do just as you have said."

6So Abraham hurried to Sarah at his tent and said, "Hurry! Knead three seahs of the finest flour and make some baked goods!" 7Abraham ran to the cattle, took a healthy young calf, and gave it to a young servant, who prepared it quickly. 8Then Abraham took butter, milk, and the calf that had been prepared, put the food in front of them, and stood under the tree near them as they ate.

9They said to him, "Where's your wife Sarah?"

And he said, "Right here in the tent."

10Then one of the men said, "I will definitely return to you about this time next year. Then your wife Sarah will have a son!"

Sarah was listening at the tent door behind him. 11Now Abraham and Sarah were both very old. Sarah was no longer menstruating. 12So Sarah laughed to herself, thinking, I'm no longer able to have children and my husband's old.

13The LORD said to Abraham, "Why did Sarah laugh and say, 'Me give birth? At my age?' 14Is anything too difficult for the LORD? When I return to you about this time next year, Sarah will have a son."

15Sarah lied and said, "I didn't laugh," because she was frightened.

But he said, "No, you laughed." . . .

21 The LORD was attentive to Sarah just as he had said, and the LORD carried out just what he had promised her. 2She became pregnant and gave birth to a son for Abraham when he was old, at the very time God had told him. 3Abraham named his son—the one Sarah bore him—Isaac. 4Abraham circumcised his son Isaac when he was eight days old just as God had commanded him. 5Abraham was 100 years old when his son Isaac was born. 6Sarah said, "God has given me laughter. Everyone who hears about it will laugh with me." 7She said, "Who could have told Abraham that Sarah would nurse sons? But now I've given birth to a son when he was old!"

Psalm 116:1-2, 12-19 (G655, N699, P228, SH344, UM837)

1I love the LORD because he hears
my requests for mercy.
2I'll call out to him as long as I live,
because he listens closely to me. . . .
12What can I give back to the LORD
for all the good things he has done for me?
13I'll lift up the cup of salvation.
I'll call on the LORD's name.
14I'll keep the promises I made to the LORD
in the presence of all God's people.
15The death of the Lord's faithful
is a costly loss in his eyes.
16Oh yes, LORD, I am definitely your servant!
I am your servant and the son of your female servant—
you've freed me from my chains.
17So I'll offer a sacrifice of thanksgiving to you,
and I'll call on the LORD's name.
18I'll keep the promises I made to the LORD
in the presence of all God's people,
19in the courtyards of the LORD's house,
which is in the center of Jerusalem.
Praise the LORD!

NRSVue

Romans 5:1-8

[1]Therefore, since we are justified by faith, we have peace with God through our Lord Jesus Christ, [2]through whom we have obtained access to this grace in which we stand, and we boast in our hope of sharing the glory of God. [3]And not only that, but we also boast in our afflictions, knowing that affliction produces endurance, [4]and endurance produces character, and character produces hope, [5]and hope does not put us to shame, because God's love has been poured into our hearts through the Holy Spirit that has been given to us.

[6]For while we were still weak, at the right time Christ died for the ungodly. [7]Indeed, rarely will anyone die for a righteous person—though perhaps for a good person someone might actually dare to die. [8]But God proves his love for us in that while we still were sinners Christ died for us.

Matthew 9:35–10:8, (9-23)

[35]Then Jesus went about all the cities and villages, teaching in their synagogues and proclaiming the good news of the kingdom and curing every disease and every sickness. [36]When he saw the crowds, he had compassion for them because they were harassed and helpless, like sheep without a shepherd. [37]Then he said to his disciples, "The harvest is plentiful, but the laborers are few; [38]therefore ask the Lord of the harvest to send out laborers into his harvest."

10 Then Jesus summoned his twelve disciples and gave them authority over unclean spirits, to cast them out, and to cure every disease and every sickness. [2]These are the names of the twelve apostles: first, Simon, also known as Peter, and his brother Andrew; James son of Zebedee and his brother John; [3]Philip and Bartholomew; Thomas and Matthew the tax collector; James son of Alphaeus and Thaddaeus; [4]Simon the Cananaean and Judas Iscariot, the one who betrayed him.

[5]These twelve Jesus sent out with the following instructions: "Do not take a road leading to gentiles, and do not enter a Samaritan town, [6]but go rather to the lost sheep of the house of Israel. [7]As you go, proclaim the good news, 'The kingdom of heaven has come near.' [8]Cure the sick; raise the dead; cleanse those with a skin disease; cast out demons. You received without payment; give without payment. [9]Take no gold, or silver, or copper in your belts, [10]no bag for your journey, or two tunics, or sandals, or a staff, for laborers deserve their food. [11]Whatever town or village you enter, find out who in it is worthy, and stay there until you leave. [12]As you enter the house, greet it. [13]If the house is worthy, let your peace come upon it, but if it is not worthy, let your peace return to you. [14]If anyone will not welcome you or listen to your words, shake off the dust from your feet as you leave that house or town. [15]Truly I tell you, it will be more tolerable for the land of Sodom and Gomorrah on the day of judgment than for that town.

[16]"I am sending you out like sheep into the midst of wolves, so be wise as serpents and innocent as doves. [17]Beware of them, for they will hand you over to councils and flog you in their synagogues, [18]and you will be dragged before governors and kings because of me, as a testimony to them and the gentiles. [19]When they hand you over, do not worry about how you are to speak or what you are to say, for what you are to say will be given to you at that time, [20]for it is not you who speak, but the Spirit of your Father speaking through you. [21]Sibling will betray sibling to death, and a father his child, and children will rise against parents and have them put to death, [22]and you will be hated by all because of my name. But the one who endures to the end will be saved. [23]When they persecute you in this town, flee to the next, for truly I tell you, you will not have finished going through all the towns of Israel before the Son of Man comes."

CEB

Romans 5:1-8

[1]Therefore, since we have been made righteous through his faithfulness, we have peace with God through our Lord Jesus Christ. [2]We have access by faith into this grace in which we stand through him, and we boast in the hope of God's glory. [3]But not only that! We even take pride in our problems, because we know that trouble produces endurance, [4]endurance produces character, and character produces hope. [5]This hope doesn't put us to shame, because the love of God has been poured out in our hearts through the Holy Spirit, who has been given to us.

[6]While we were still weak, at the right moment, Christ died for ungodly people. [7]It isn't often that someone will die for a righteous person, though maybe someone might dare to die for a good person. [8]But God shows his love for us, because while we were still sinners Christ died for us.

Matthew 9:35–10:8, (9-23)

[35]Jesus traveled among all the cities and villages, teaching in their synagogues, announcing the good news of the kingdom, and healing every disease and every sickness. [36]Now when Jesus saw the crowds, he had compassion for them because they were troubled and helpless, like sheep without a shepherd. [37]Then he said to his disciples, "The size of the harvest is bigger than you can imagine, but there are few workers. [38]Therefore, plead with the Lord of the harvest to send out workers for his harvest."

10 He called his twelve disciples and gave them authority over unclean spirits to throw them out and to heal every disease and every sickness. [2]Here are the names of the twelve apostles: first, Simon, who is called Peter; and Andrew his brother; James the son of Zebedee; and John his brother; [3]Philip; and Bartholomew; Thomas; and Matthew the tax collector; James the son of Alphaeus; and Thaddaeus; [4]Simon the Cananaean; and Judas, who betrayed Jesus.

[5]Jesus sent these twelve out and commanded them, "Don't go among the Gentiles or into a Samaritan city. [6]Go instead to the lost sheep, the people of Israel. [7]As you go, make this announcement: 'The kingdom of heaven has come near.' [8]Heal the sick, raise the dead, cleanse those with skin diseases, and throw out demons. You received without having to pay. Therefore, give without demanding payment. [9]Workers deserve to be fed, so don't gather gold or silver or copper coins for your money belts to take on your trips. [10]Don't take a backpack for the road or two shirts or sandals or a walking stick. [11]Whatever city or village you go into, find somebody in it who is worthy and stay there until you go on your way. [12]When you go into a house, say, 'Peace!' [13]If the house is worthy, give it your blessing of peace. But if the house isn't worthy, take back your blessing. [14]If anyone refuses to welcome you or listen to your words, shake the dust off your feet as you leave that house or city. [15]I assure you that it will be more bearable for the land of Sodom and Gomorrah on Judgment Day than it will be for that city.

[16]"Look, I'm sending you as sheep among wolves. Therefore, be wise as snakes and innocent as doves. [17]Watch out for people—because they will hand you over to councils and they will beat you in their synagogues. [18]They will haul you in front of governors and even kings because of me so that you may give your testimony to them and to the Gentiles. [19]Whenever they hand you over, don't worry about how to speak or what you will say, because what you can say will be given to you at that moment. [20]You aren't doing the talking, but the Spirit of my Father is doing the talking through you. [21]Brothers and sisters will hand each other over to be executed. A father will turn his child in. Children will defy their parents and have them executed. [22]Everyone will hate you on account of my name. But whoever stands firm until the end will be saved. [23]Whenever they harass you in one city, escape to the next, because I assure that you will not go through all the cities of Israel before the Human One comes."

Primary Hymns and Songs for the Day

"The God of Abraham Praise" 484742 (Gen, Rom) (O)
C24, CG45, E401, EL831, G49, GR16, N24, P488, SH50, UM116 (PD), VU255
H-3 Hbl-62, 95; Chr-59; Org-77
S-1 #211. Harmonization
"I Love the Lord" 1168957 (Pss)
CG613, G799, P362, N511, SH343, VU617, WS3142, ZS176
"O Love That Wilt Not Let Me Go" (Gen, Rom)
C540, CG631, G833, GR92, N485, P384, SH314, UM480 (PD), VU658
H-3 Chr-146; Org-142
"Where Cross the Crowded Ways of Life" 2961345 (Matt)
C665, CG657, E609, EL719, G343, N543, P408, UM427 (PD), VU681
H-3 Chr-178, 180; Org-44
S-1 #141-3 Various treatments
"Go to the World" (Matt) (C)
CG481, G295, SH720, VU420, WS3158
H-3 Hbl-58; Chr-65; Org-152
S-1 #314-318. Various treatments
"The Summons" ("Will You Come and Follow Me") 4668756 (Matt) (C)
CG473, EL798, G726, S2130, SH598, VU567
H-3 Chr-220

Additional Hymn Suggestions

+"O God Beyond All Praising" (Pss)
CG366, EL880, S2009, VU256
"Come, Holy Spirit, Heavenly Dove" (Rom)
C248, E510, G279, GR290, N281, P126
"In the Cross of Christ I Glory" 36499 (Rom)
C207, CG183, E441/442, EL324, G213, GR239, N193, P84, UM295 (PD)
"When I Survey the Wondrous Cross" 27893 (Rom)
C195, CG186, EL803, G223, GR221, N224, P101, SH163/164, UM298 (PD)
"When I Survey the Wondrous Cross" 721333 (Rom)
E474, G224, P100, UM299 (PD), VU149 (Fr.)
"Open My Eyes, That I May See" 68003 (Rom)
C586, CG395, G451, GR311, P324, SH583, UM454, VU371
+"Living for Jesus" (Rom)
C610, GR595, S2149
+"Here Is Bread, Here Is Wine" 983717 (Rom, Comm.)
EL483, S2266
"O For a Thousand Tongues to Sing" 1369 (Rom, Matt)
C5, CG332, E493, EL886, G610, GR1, N42, P466, SH439, UM57 (PD), VU326 (*See also* WS3001)
+"O Zion, Haste" (Rom, Matt)
C482, CG479, E539, EL668, GR451, UM573 (PD)
"Rescue the Perishing" 34549 (Rom, Matt)
CG480, GR457, UM591 (PD)
"To God Be the Glory" (Matt)
C72, CG349, G634, GR531, P485, SH545, UM98 (PD)
"Come, Labor On" (Matt)
E541, G719, N532, P415
"Jesus Shall Reign" 1510 (Matt)
C95, CG158, E544, EL434, G265, GR282, N300, P423, SH209, UM157 (PD), VU330
+"Christ for the World We Sing" (Matt)
E537, GR450, UM568 (PD)
+"We've a Story to Tell to the Nations" (Matt)
C484, CG427, GR458, UM569 (PD)
+"Pass It On" (Matt)
C477, UM572, VU289
+"Lord, Whose Love Through Humble Service" (Matt)
C461, CG650, E610, EL712, GR454, P427, SH239, UM581
"Lord, You Give the Great Commission" 230673 (Matt) (C)
C459, CG651/CG653, E528, EL579, G298, GR463, P429, S2176, UM584, VU512
+"Here I Am, Lord" OL-80670 (Matt)
C452, CG482, EL574, G69, GR589, P525, SH608, UM593, VU509
"Together We Serve" (Matt)
G767, S2175
"Enviado Soy de Dios" ("Sent Out in Jesus' Name") 6290823 (Matt)
EL538, G747, S2184, SH718
"Gather Us In" OL-00031 (Matt) (O)
C284, EL532, G401, S2236, SH393
"We All Are One in Mission" 3176809 (Matt)
CG269, EL576, G733, P435, S2243, ZS99
"In Remembrance of Me" 25156 (Matt, Comm.)
C403, CG462, G521, S2254, SH667, ZS203

Additional Contemporary and Modern Suggestions

"Daughter of God" 4509781 (Gen)
+"Promises" 6454250 (Gen)
+"Not in a Hurry" 7047889 (Gen)
+"Be Still" 7116946 (Gen)
+"Won't Stop Now" 7111932 (Gen, Rom)
+"Presence" 7116947 (Gen, Rom)
"Hungry" ("Falling on My Knees") 2650364 (Gen, Pss)
WS3099
"I Will Call upon the Lord" 11263 (Pss)
G621, S2002
"I Love You, Lord" 25266 (Pss)
CG362, G627, S2068, SH417, ZS40
+"Chain Breaker" 7060031 (Pss)
+"Freedom" 7078151 (Pss)
"Because of Your Love" 4662501 (Pss)
"You Are" 4387343 (Pss)
"Beautiful Savior" 2492216 (Pss)
"I Could Sing of Your Love Forever" 1043199 (Pss, Rom)
"I Stand Amazed" 769450 (Pss, Rom)
"I Will Not Forget You" 2694306 (Ps, Rom, Matt)
"O How He Loves You and Me" 15850 (Rom)
CG600, S2108, SH535, ZS208
"Something Beautiful" 18060 (Rom)
UM394
"O Lord, Your Tenderness" 38136 (Rom)
S2143
"God Is Good All the Time" OL-88288 (Rom)
WS3026, ZS18
"You Are My King" ("Amazing Love") 2456623 (Rom)
SH539, WS3102
+"My Worth Is Not in What I Own" 7024758 (Rom)
+"Never Runs Out" 7193998 (Rom)
+"Love Moves You" ("Love Alone") 5775514 (Rom)
"God Is Good All the Time" 1729073 (Rom)
"I Will Boast" 4662350 (Rom)
"Grace Like Rain" 3689877 (Rom)
"O For a Thousand Tongues to Sing" 4048754 (Rom, Matt)
WS3001
"The King of Glory Comes" OL-81352 (Matt)
CG177, S2091, SH206
"I'm Gonna Live So God Can Use Me" (Matt)
C614, G700, GR615, P369, S2153, SH632, VU575
+"The Kingdom Is Yours" 7109354 (Matt)

Solo/Ensemble Suggestions

+"Man of Your Word" 7148536 (Gen)
V-9 p. 71
+"Great Things" 7111321 (Pss)
V-9 p. 36

"Redeeming Grace" (Rom)
V-4 p. 47
+"Oh, What Love!" (Rom)
V-8 p. 144
"Reach Out to Your Neighbor" (Matt)
V-8 p. 372
+"I Love the Lord" (Pss)
Arr. Cliff Duren; Lillenas 9780834187320
SATB, piano, soprano soloist (https://bit.ly/L-87320)
+"The Summons" (Matt)
Arr. Gary Daigle; GIA Publications G-9837
SATB, piano, opt. instruments (https://bit.ly/G-9837)

+Hymn Anthem

"Hymns of the Cross" (Phil) using
"When I Survey the Wondrous Cross"
C195, CG186, EL803, G223, GR221, N224, P101, SH163/164, UM298 (PD)
"Jesus, Keep Me Near the Cross"
C587, CG642, EL335, GR241, N197, UM301 (PD), VU142, Z19
"In the Cross of Christ I Glory"
C207, CG183, E441/442, EL324, G213, GR239, N193, P84, UM295 (PD)

Each stanza should be a bit louder than the one before it.

Introduction: If next stanza is not sung *a cappella*, the keyboard may introduce it by playing the first three and last measures of "When I Survey." *Mezzo piano.*

"When I Survey," stanza 1: Choir sings in four parts or unison, *a cappella* or accompanied.

"When I Survey," stanza 3: Choir sing in four parts or unison, accompanied. One soprano may sing a descant (S-1, #155) on an "ah" vowel.

"Jesus, Keep Me," stanza 1: S/A sing parts or unison. Keyboard plays hymnal setting.

"Jesus, Keep Me," stanza 4: T/B begin this stanza, unison. Keyboard plays hymnal setting. At the refrain, S/A may join and all sing parts or unison, *a cappella* or accompanied.

Interlude: Keyboard plays first four and last four measures of "In the Cross."

"In the Cross," stanza 5: All voices unison, *forte.* Keyboard plays S-1, #277 or another harmonization. Some sopranos may sing a descant (S-1, #276).

Other Suggestions

Visuals:

O Oaks, tent, noon, three men eating, old man/woman/laugh
P Prayer, raised cup, recent dead, open manacles, praise
E Crucifix, suffering, pouring
G Jesus, lost/helpless, one sheep, harvest, few working, prayer, twelve disciples, Matt 10:7b, 8b

+Introit: S2101, stanza 4. "Two Fishermen" (Matt)
Opening Prayer: N831 (Gen, Matt)
Response: GR524 (PD), N500, UM418, Z205, stanzas 3-4. "We Are Climbing Jacob's Ladder" (Rom, Matt)
+Call to Prayer: C351, UM641, WS3093, refrain. "Fill My Cup, Lord" 15946 (Pss)
Prayer: WSL19. "God of wilderness" (Gen)
+Prayer: UM570. Prayer of Ignatius of Loyola (Matt)
Benediction: WSL161. "Sisters and brothers" (Matt)
Alternate Lessons (see page 4): Exod. 19:2-8a; Ps. 100
Theme Ideas: Call of God, Children / Family of God, Cross, Discipleship / Following God, Faith, God: Love of God, Grace

Notes

NRSVue

Genesis 21:8-21

[8]The child grew and was weaned, and Abraham made a great feast on the day that Isaac was weaned. [9]But Sarah saw the son of Hagar the Egyptian, whom she had borne to Abraham, playing with her son Isaac. [10]So she said to Abraham, "Cast out this slave woman with her son, for the son of this slave woman shall not inherit along with my son Isaac." [11]The matter was very distressing to Abraham on account of his son. [12]But God said to Abraham, "Do not be distressed because of the boy and because of your slave woman; whatever Sarah says to you, do as she tells you, for it is through Isaac that offspring shall be named for you. [13]As for the son of the slave woman, I will make a nation of him also, because he is your offspring." [14]So Abraham rose early in the morning and took bread and a skin of water and gave it to Hagar, putting it on her shoulder, along with the child, and sent her away. And she departed and wandered about in the wilderness of Beer-sheba.

[15]When the water in the skin was gone, she cast the child under one of the bushes. [16]Then she went and sat down opposite him a good way off, about the distance of a bowshot, for she said, "Do not let me look on the death of the child." And as she sat opposite him, she lifted up her voice and wept. [17]And God heard the voice of the boy, and the angel of God called to Hagar from heaven and said to her, "What troubles you, Hagar? Do not be afraid, for God has heard the voice of the boy where he is. [18]Come, lift up the boy and hold him fast with your hand, for I will make a great nation of him." [19]Then God opened her eyes, and she saw a well of water. She went and filled the skin with water and gave the boy a drink.

[20]God was with the boy, and he grew up; he lived in the wilderness and became an expert with the bow. [21]He lived in the wilderness of Paran, and his mother got a wife for him from the land of Egypt.

Psalm 86:1-10, 16-17 (G844, N677)

[1]Incline your ear, O LORD, and answer me,
  for I am poor and needy.
[2]Preserve my life, for I am devoted to you;
  save your servant who trusts in you.
You are my God; [3]be gracious to me, O Lord,
  for to you do I cry all day long.
[4]Gladden the soul of your servant,
  for to you, O Lord, I lift up my soul.
[5]For you, O Lord, are good and forgiving,
  abounding in steadfast love to all who call on you.
[6]Give ear, O LORD, to my prayer;
  listen to my cry of supplication.
[7]In the day of my trouble I call on you,
  for you will answer me.
[8]There is none like you among the gods, O Lord,
  nor are there any works like yours.
[9]All the nations you have made shall come
  and bow down before you, O Lord,
  and shall glorify your name.
[10]For you are great and do wondrous things;
  you alone are God.

. . . .

[16]Turn to me and be gracious to me;
  give your strength to your servant;
  save the child of your maidservant.
[17]Show me a sign of your favor,
  so that those who hate me may see it and be put to shame,
  because you, LORD, have helped me and comforted me.

CEB

Genesis 21:8-21

[8]The boy grew and stopped nursing. On the day he stopped nursing, Abraham prepared a huge banquet. [9]Sarah saw Hagar's son laughing, the one Hagar the Egyptian had borne to Abraham. [10]So she said to Abraham, "Send this servant away with her son! This servant's son won't share the inheritance with my son Isaac."

[11]This upset Abraham terribly because the boy was his son. [12]God said to Abraham, "Don't be upset about the boy and your servant. Do everything Sarah tells you to do because your descendants will be traced through Isaac. [13]But I will make of your servant's son a great nation too, because he is also your descendant." [14]Abraham got up early in the morning, took some bread and a flask of water, and gave it to Hagar. He put the boy in her shoulder sling and sent her away.

She left and wandered through the desert near Beer-sheba. [15]Finally the water in the flask ran out, and she put the boy down under one of the desert shrubs. [16]She walked away from him about as far as a bow shot and sat down, telling herself, I can't bear to see the boy die. She sat at a distance, cried out in grief, and wept.

[17]God heard the boy's cries, and God's messenger called to Hagar from heaven and said to her, "Hagar! What's wrong? Don't be afraid. God has heard the boy's cries over there. [18]Get up, pick up the boy, and take him by the hand because I will make of him a great nation." [19]Then God opened her eyes, and she saw a well. She went over, filled the water flask, and gave the boy a drink. [20]God remained with the boy; he grew up, lived in the desert, and became an expert archer. [21]He lived in the Paran desert, and his mother found him an Egyptian wife.

Psalm 86:1-10, 16-17 (G844, N677)

[1]LORD, listen closely to me and answer me,
  because I am poor and in need.
[2]Guard my life because I am faithful.
  Save your servant who trusts in you—you! My God!
[3]Have mercy on me, Lord,
  because I cry out to you all day long.
[4]Make your servant's life happy again
  because, my Lord, I offer my life to you,
5 because, my Lord, you are good and forgiving,
  full of faithful love for all those who cry out to you.
[6]Listen closely to my prayer, LORD;
  pay close attention to the sound of my requests for mercy.
[7]Whenever I am in trouble, I cry out to you,
  because you will answer me.
[8]My Lord! There is no one like you among the gods!
  There is nothing that can compare to your works!
[9]All the nations that you've made will come
    and bow down before you, Lord;
  they will glorify your name,
10 because you are awesome
  and a wonder-worker.
    You are God. Just you.

. . . .

[16]Come back to me! Have mercy on me!
  Give your servant your strength;
  save this child of your servant!
[17]Show me a sign of your goodness
  so that those who hate me will see it and be put to shame—
    show a sign that you, LORD,
    have helped me and comforted me.

NRSVue

Romans 6:1b-11

1bShould we continue in sin in order that grace may increase? 2By no means! How can we who died to sin go on living in it? 3Do you not know that all of us who were baptized into Christ Jesus were baptized into his death? 4Therefore we were buried with him by baptism into death, so that, just as Christ was raised from the dead by the glory of the Father, so we also might walk in newness of life.

5For if we have been united with him in a death like his, we will certainly be united with him in a resurrection like his. 6We know that our old self was crucified with him so that the body of sin might be destroyed, so we might no longer be enslaved to sin. 7For whoever has died is freed from sin. 8But if we died with Christ, we believe that we will also live with him. 9We know that Christ, being raised from the dead, will never die again; death no longer has dominion over him. 10The death he died, he died to sin once for all, but the life he lives, he lives to God. 11So you also must consider yourselves dead to sin and alive to God in Christ Jesus.

Matthew 10:24-39

24"A disciple is not above the teacher nor a slave above the master; 25it is enough for the disciple to be like the teacher and the slave like the master. If they have called the master of the house Beelzebul, how much more will they malign those of his household!

26"So have no fear of them, for nothing is covered up that will not be uncovered and nothing secret that will not become known. 27What I say to you in the dark, tell in the light, and what you hear whispered, proclaim from the housetops. 28Do not fear those who kill the body but cannot kill the soul; rather, fear the one who can destroy both soul and body in hell. 29Are not two sparrows sold for a penny? Yet not one of them will fall to the ground apart from your Father. 30And even the hairs of your head are all counted. 31So do not be afraid; you are of more value than many sparrows.

32"Everyone, therefore, who acknowledges me before others, I also will acknowledge before my Father in heaven, 33but whoever denies me before others, I also will deny before my Father in heaven.

34"Do not think that I have come to bring peace to the earth; I have not come to bring peace but a sword.

35 For I have come to set a man against his father,
and a daughter against her mother,
and a daughter-in-law against her mother-in-law,
36 and one's foes will be members of one's own household.

37"Whoever loves father or mother more than me is not worthy of me, and whoever loves son or daughter more than me is not worthy of me, 38and whoever does not take up the cross and follow me is not worthy of me. 39Those who find their life will lose it, and those who lose their life for my sake will find it."

CEB

Romans 6:1b-11

1bShould we continue sinning so grace will multiply? 2Absolutely not! All of us died to sin. How can we still live in it? 3Or don't you know that all who were baptized into Christ Jesus were baptized into his death? 4Therefore, we were buried together with him through baptism into his death, so that just as Christ was raised from the dead through the glory of the Father, we too can walk in newness of life. 5If we were united together in a death like his, we will also be united together in a resurrection like his. 6This is what we know: the person that we used to be was crucified with him in order to get rid of the corpse that had been controlled by sin. That way we wouldn't be slaves to sin anymore, 7because a person who has died has been freed from sin's power. 8But if we died with Christ, we have faith that we will also live with him. 9We know that Christ has been raised from the dead and he will never die again. Death no longer has power over him. 10He died to sin once and for all with his death, but he lives for God with his life. 11In the same way, you also should consider yourselves dead to sin but alive for God in Christ Jesus.

Matthew 10:24-39

24"Disciples aren't greater than their teacher, and slaves aren't greater than their master. 25It's enough for disciples to be like their teacher and slaves like their master. If they have called the head of the house Beelzebul, it's certain that they will call the members of his household by even worse names.

26"Therefore, don't be afraid of those people because nothing is hidden that won't be revealed, and nothing secret that won't be brought out into the open. 27What I say to you in the darkness, tell in the light; and what you hear whispered, announce from the rooftops. 28Don't be afraid of those who kill the body but can't kill the soul. Instead, be afraid of the one who can destroy both body and soul in hell. 29Aren't two sparrows sold for a small coin? But not one of them will fall to the ground without your Father knowing about it already. 30Even the hairs of your head are all counted. 31Don't be afraid. You are worth more than many sparrows.

32"Therefore, everyone who acknowledges me before people, I also will acknowledge before my Father who is in heaven. 33But everyone who denies me before people, I also will deny before my Father who is in heaven.

34"Don't think that I've come to bring peace to the earth. I haven't come to bring peace but a sword. 35I've come to turn a man *against his father, a daughter against her mother, and a daughter-in-law against her mother-in-law.* 36*People's enemies are members of their own households.*

37"Those who love father or mother more than me aren't worthy of me. Those who love son or daughter more than me aren't worthy of me. 38Those who don't pick up their crosses and follow me aren't worthy of me. 39Those who find their lives will lose them, and those who lose their lives because of me will find them."

Primary Hymns and Songs for the Day
"At the Name of Jesus" (Rom) (O)
CG424, E435, EL416, G264, GR105, P148, SH657, UM168, VU335
"We Know That Christ Is Raised" OL-40344 (Rom, Baptism) (O)
E296, EL449, G485, P495, UM610, VU448
H-3 Hbl-100; Chr-214; Desc- ; Org-37
S-1 #118-127. Various treatments
"Give to the Winds Thy Fears" (PD) (Gen, Matt)
CG55, G815, GR366, N404, P286, UM129 (PD), VU636
H-3 Chr-71; Desc-39; Org-39
S-1 #129. Desc.
"Children of the Heavenly Father" (Gen, Matt, Father's Day)
CG69, EL781, GR56, N487, SH42, UM141
H-3 Chr-46; Desc-102
S-2 #180-185. Various treatments.
"Take Up Thy Cross" 2154808 (Matt) (C)
E675, EL667, G718, GR220, N204, P393, SH605, UM415, VU561
"I Have Decided to Follow Jesus" (Matt) (C)
C344, CG497, GR603, S2129, SH610

Additional Hymn Suggestions
"The God of Abraham Praise" 484742 (Gen)
C24, CG45, E401, EL831, G49, GR16, N24, P488, SH50, UM116 (PD), VU255
"Great Is Thy Faithfulness" 18723 (Gen)
C86, CG48, EL733, G39, GR44, N423, P276, SH48, UM140, VU288
+"Nobody Knows the Trouble I See" (Gen)
UM520, Z170 (PD)
+"All Who Hunger" (Gen)
C419, CG303, EL461, G509, S2126, VU460
+"Why Stand So Far Away, My God?" OL-30234 (Gen)
C671, G786, S2180
+"How Long, O Lord" 3317053 (Gen)
G777, S2209
"I Need Thee Every Hour" (Gen, Pss)
C578, CG404, G735, GR340, N517, UM397, VU671
"O Master, Let Me Walk with Thee" 158243 (Gen, Pss) (C)
C602, CG660, E659/660, EL818, G738, GR596, N503, P357, SH612, UM430 (PD), VU560
+"Out of the Depths I Cry to You" OL-03328 (Gen, Pss)
EL600, G424, N483, P240, SH513, UM515
+"By Gracious Powers" (Gen, Pss)
E695/696, EL626, G818, N413, P342, UM517
+"Lift Every Voice and Sing" 7071034 (Gen, Pss)
C631, CG638, E599, EL841, G339, GR408, N593, P563, SH36, UM519, Z32 (PD), Z210, ZS113
+"Be Still, My Soul" (Gen, Matt)
C566, CG57, G819, GR346, N488, SH330, UM534, VU652
"His Eye Is on the Sparrow" 77692 (Gen, Matt)
C82, G661, GR380, N475, S2146, SH322, Z33 (PD)
"Christ Is Alive" (Rom)
CG205, E182, EL389, G246, P108, UM318, VU158
"Just a Closer Walk with Thee" (Rom)
C557, EL697, G835, S2158, SH584, Z46 (PD)
"Baptized in Water" 5853694 (Rom, Baptism)
CG449, E294, EL456, G482, P492, S2248, SH666
"It Is Well with My Soul" 25376 (Rom, Matt)
C561, CG573, EL785, G840, GR344, N438, SH305, UM377 (PD), Z20
"Blessed Quietness" (Rom, Matt)
C267, CG244, N284 (PD), S2142, Z206
"Living for Jesus" (Rom, Matt)
C610, GR595, S2149
"God Will Take Care of You" 93645 (Matt)
GR358, N460, SH289, UM130 (PD)
"Where He Leads Me" (Matt)
C346, GR516, UM338 (PD), Z42
+"Dear Lord, Lead Me Day by Day" (Matt)
UM411, VU568
"Must Jesus Bear the Cross Alone" (Matt)
CG505, GR598, UM424 (PD)
"Leave It There" (Matt)
GR369, UM522, Z23 (PD)
"And Are We Yet Alive" (Matt)
GR386, UM553 (PD)
+"God of Grace and God of Glory" 43107 (Matt)
C464, CG285, E594/595, EL705, G307, GR45, N436, P420, SH250, UM577, VU686
"Swiftly Pass the Clouds of Glory" (Matt)
G190, P73, S2102
"You, Lord, Are Both Lamb and Shepherd" (Matt)
G274, SH210, VU210, WS3043
"Loving Spirit" 3379424 (Father's Day)
C244, EL397, G293, P323, S2123, VU387

Additional Contemporary and Modern Suggestions
"Hungry" ("Falling on My Knees") 2650364 (Gen)
WS3099
"Daughter of God" 4509781 (Gen)
+"Daughters of Zion" 7133716 (Gen)
+"The Kingdom Is Yours" 7109354 (Gen)
+"You Are My Strength" 4869940 (Gen)
+"Another in the Fire" 7124907 (Gen, Rom)
+"Great Things" 7111321 (Gen, Rom)
+"Better Than A Hallelujah" 5622564 (Gen, Pss)
"Came to My Rescue" 4705190 (Gen, Pss)
"I Will Call upon the Lord" 11263 (Pss)
G621, S2002
"We Will Glorify" 19038 (Pss)
CG360, S2087
"Glorify Thy Name" 1383 (Pss)
CG8, S2016, SH427
"Lord, Listen to Your Children" 659072 (Pss)
EL752, S2207
"I Exalt You" 17803 (Pss)
"Grace Alone" 2335524 (Rom)
CG43, S2162, ZS100
"God Is Good All the Time" OL-88288 (Rom)
"God Is Good All the Time" 1729073 (Rom)
"Amazing Grace" ("My Chains Are Gone") 4768151 (Rom)
GR574, WS3104
"We Fall Down" 2437367 (Rom)
G368, WS3187
"Salvation Is Here" 4451327 (Rom)
"Grace Like Rain" 3689877 (Rom)
+"Love Moves You" ("Love Alone") 5775514 (Rom)
+"His Mercy Is More" 7065053 (Rom)
+"Chain Breaker" 7060031 (Rom)
+"Freedom" 7078151 (Rom)
+"Living Hope" 7106807 (Rom)
+"Say So" 4944016
+"Stronger" 5060810 (Rom)
+"Won't Stop Now" 7111932 (Rom, Matt)
"I've Got Peace Like a River" (PD) (Rom, Matt)
C530, G623, N478, P368, S2145, SH276, VU577
"Somlandela" ("We Will Follow") (PD-TO) (Matt)
WS3160
"Let It Be Said of Us" 1855882 (Matt)
"Every Move I Make" 1595726 (Matt)
"Everyday" 2798154 (Matt)
"One Way" 4222082 (Matt)
"Take Up Our Cross" 5358955 (Matt)

+"New Wine" 7102397 (Matt)
+"Wesley Prayer" ("Fire") 7118633 (Matt)
"The Family Prayer Song" 1680466 (Father's Day)
S2188

Solo/Ensemble Suggestions

"Lost in the Night" (Gen, Pss)
V-5 (1) p. 18
+"I Couldn't Hear Nobody Pray" (Gen, Pss)
V-7 p. 40/43
+"Nobody Knows the Trouble I've Seen" (Gen, Pss)
V-7 p. 64/68
"His Eye Is on the Sparrow" (Gen, Matt)
V-8 p. 166
+"And Can It Be That I Should Gain" (Rom)
V-1 p. 29
"Waterlife" (Rom, Baptism)
V-5 (3) p. 17
+"Love Moved First" (Rom)
V-9 p. 56
"Lead Me to Calvary" (Matt)
V-8 p. 226
+"A Better Resurrection" (Rom, Matt)
Maxwell/Sorenson; Shawnee Press HL 00401276
SATB, piano, opt. violin/cello (https://bit.ly/HL-1276)
"What Grace Is Mine" (Rom, Matt)
Getty/arr. Lloyd Larson; Hope C6131
SATB, piano (https://bit.ly/Hope-C6131)

+Hymn Anthem

"Children of the Heavenly Father" (Gen, Matt)
CG69, EL781, GR56, N487, SH42, UM141
Stanza 1: Female soloist sings Stanza 1 *a cappella* (or accompanied).
Stanza 2: Male soloist sings melody. Keyboard (organ) plays lower three parts one octave higher than written. Hold repeated notes, creating a sustained accompaniment.
Stanza 3: All voices, unison. Keyboard plays lower three parts as written, sustaining repeated notes. *Mezzo piano.*
Stanza 4: All voices in four parts (or unison), *a cappella* (or accompanied). *Mezzo forte. Molto ritard* in last measures.

Other Suggestions

Visuals:
O Toddler/woman, bread/waterbag, wilderness, well, bow
P Praying hands, people bowing, Ps. 86:9
E Baptism, crucifix, open manacles
G Cross for each, light, housetop, two sparrows/penny, hair, sword
+Introit or Response: C593, GR332, N774, UM473 (PD), VU662. "Lead Me, Lord" (Gen, Matt)
+Introit: S2101, stanza 4. "Two Fishermen" (Matt)
Litany: WSL49. "For rebirth and resilience" (Gen, Pss, Matt)
+Canticle: UM516. "Canticle of Redemption" (Gen, Pss)
Affirmation of Faith: WSL82. "We are children of God" (Rom)
Response: EL814, G698, SH620, WS3119. "Take, O Take Me As I Am" (Rom)
Prayer: UM531 (Gen)
Response: CG399, EL751, G471, S2200, SH311/517. "O Lord, Hear My Prayer" (Pss)
Prayer: WSL201. "God our Creator" (Father's Day)
Prayer of Thanksgiving: WSL62 (Father's Day)
Alternate Lessons (see page 4): Jer. 20:7-13; Ps. 69:7-10 (11-15), 16-18
Theme Ideas: Baptism, Discipleship / Following God, God: Providence / God our Help, Grace

Notes

NRSVue

Genesis 22:1-14

1After these things God tested Abraham. He said to him, "Abraham!" And he said, "Here I am." 2He said, "Take your son, your only son Isaac, whom you love, and go to the land of Moriah and offer him there as a burnt offering on one of the mountains that I shall show you." 3So Abraham rose early in the morning, saddled his donkey, and took two of his young men with him and his son Isaac; he cut the wood for the burnt offering and set out and went to the place in the distance that God had shown him. 4On the third day Abraham looked up and saw the place far away. 5Then Abraham said to his young men, "Stay here with the donkey; the boy and I will go over there; we will worship, and then we will come back to you." 6Abraham took the wood of the burnt offering and laid it on his son Isaac, and he himself carried the fire and the knife. And the two of them walked on together. 7Isaac said to his father Abraham, "Father!" And he said, "Here I am, my son." He said, "The fire and the wood are here, but where is the lamb for a burnt offering?" 8Abraham said, "God himself will provide the lamb for a burnt offering, my son." And the two of them walked on together.

9When they came to the place that God had shown him, Abraham built an altar there and laid the wood in order. He bound his son Isaac and laid him on the altar on top of the wood. 10Then Abraham reached out his hand and took the knife to kill his son. 11But the angel of the LORD called to him from heaven and said, "Abraham, Abraham!" And he said, "Here I am." 12He said, "Do not lay your hand on the boy or do anything to him, for now I know that you fear God, since you have not withheld your son, your only son, from me." 13And Abraham looked up and saw a ram, caught in a thicket by its horns. Abraham went and took the ram and offered it up as a burnt offering instead of his son. 14So Abraham called that place "The LORD will provide," as it is said to this day, "On the mount of the LORD it shall be provided."

Psalm 13 (G777, N626, SH518, UM746)

1How long, O LORD? Will you forget me forever?
    How long will you hide your face from me?
2How long must I bear pain in my soul
    and have sorrow in my heart all day long?
How long shall my enemy be exalted over me?
3Consider and answer me, O LORD my God!
    Give light to my eyes, or I will sleep the sleep of death,
4and my enemy will say, "I have prevailed";
    my foes will rejoice because I am shaken.
5But I trusted in your steadfast love;
    my heart shall rejoice in your salvation.
6I will sing to the LORD
    because he has dealt bountifully with me.

CEB

Genesis 22:1-14

1After these events, God tested Abraham and said to him, "Abraham!"

Abraham answered, "I'm here."

2God said, "Take your son, your only son whom you love, Isaac, and go to the land of Moriah. Offer him up as an entirely burned offering there on one of the mountains that I will show you." 3Abraham got up early in the morning, harnessed his donkey, and took two of his young men with him, together with his son Isaac. He split the wood for the entirely burned offering, set out, and went to the place God had described to him.

4On the third day, Abraham looked up and saw the place at a distance. 5Abraham said to his servants, "Stay here with the donkey. The boy and I will walk up there, worship, and then come back to you."

6Abraham took the wood for the entirely burned offering and laid it on his son Isaac. He took the fire and the knife in his hand, and the two of them walked on together. 7Isaac said to his father Abraham, "My father?"

Abraham said, "I'm here, my son."

Isaac said, "Here is the fire and the wood, but where is the lamb for the entirely burned offering?"

8Abraham said, "The lamb for the entirely burned offering? God will see to it, my son." The two of them walked on together.

9They arrived at the place God had described to him. Abraham built an altar there and arranged the wood on it. He tied up his son Isaac and laid him on the altar on top of the wood. 10Then Abraham stretched out his hand and took the knife to kill his son as a sacrifice. 11But the LORD's messenger called out to Abraham from heaven, "Abraham? Abraham?"

Abraham said, "I'm here."

12The messenger said, "Don't stretch out your hand against the young man, and don't do anything to him. I now know that you revere God and didn't hold back your son, your only son, from me." 13Abraham looked up and saw a single ram caught by its horns in the dense underbrush. Abraham went over, took the ram, and offered it as an entirely burned offering instead of his son. 14Abraham named that place "the LORD sees." That is the reason people today say, "On this mountain the LORD is seen."

Psalm 13 (G777, N626, SH518, UM746)

1How long will you forget me, LORD? Forever?
    How long will you hide your face from me?
2How long will I be left to my own wits,
    agony filling my heart? Daily?
How long will my enemy keep defeating me?
3Look at me!
    Answer me, LORD my God!
Restore sight to my eyes!
    Otherwise, I'll sleep the sleep of death,
4   and my enemy will say, "I won!"
        My foes will rejoice over my downfall.
5But I have trusted in your faithful love.
    My heart will rejoice in your salvation.
6Yes, I will sing to the LORD
    because he has been good to me.

NRSVue

Romans 6:12-23
[12]Therefore do not let sin reign in your mortal bodies, so that
you obey their desires. [13]No longer present your members to
sin as instruments of unrighteousness, but present yourselves
to God as those who have been brought from death to life, and
present your members to God as instruments of righteousness.
[14]For sin will have no dominion over you, since you are not
under law but under grace.
[15]What then? Should we sin because we are not under law
but under grace? By no means! [16]Do you not know that, if you
present yourselves to anyone as obedient slaves, you are slaves of
the one whom you obey, either of sin, which leads to death, or of
obedience, which leads to righteousness? [17]But thanks be to God
that you who were slaves of sin have become obedient from the
heart to the form of teaching to which you were entrusted [18]and
that you, having been set free from sin, have become enslaved
to righteousness. [19]I am speaking in human terms because of
your limitations. For just as you once presented your members as
slaves to impurity and lawlessness, leading to even more lawlessness, so now present your members as slaves to righteousness,
leading to sanctification.
[20]When you were slaves of sin, you were free in regard to
righteousness. [21]So what fruit did you then gain from the things
of which you now are ashamed? The end of those things is
death. [22]But now that you have been freed from sin and enslaved
to God, the fruit you have leads to sanctification, and the end
is eternal life. [23]For the wages of sin is death, but the free gift of
God is eternal life in Christ Jesus our Lord.

Matthew 10:40-42
[40]"Whoever welcomes you welcomes me, and whoever welcomes me welcomes the one who sent me. [41]Whoever welcomes
a prophet in the name of a prophet will receive a prophet's
reward, and whoever welcomes a righteous person in the name
of a righteous person will receive the reward of the righteous,
[42]and whoever gives even a cup of cold water to one of these
little ones in the name of a disciple—truly I tell you, none of
these will lose their reward."

CEB

Romans 6:12-23
[12]So then, don't let sin rule your body, so that you do what it
wants. [13]Don't offer parts of your body to sin, to be used as weapons to do wrong. Instead, present yourselves to God as people
who have been brought back to life from the dead, and offer all
the parts of your body to God to be used as weapons to do right.
[14]Sin will have no power over you, because you aren't under Law
but under grace.
[15]So what? Should we sin because we aren't under Law but
under grace? Absolutely not! [16]Don't you know that if you offer
yourselves to someone as obedient slaves, that you are slaves of
the one whom you obey? That's true whether you serve as slaves
of sin, which leads to death, or as slaves of the kind of obedience
that leads to righteousness. [17]But thank God that although you
used to be slaves of sin, you gave wholehearted obedience to the
teaching that was handed down to you, which provides a pattern.
[18]Now that you have been set free from sin, you have become
slaves of righteousness. [19](I'm speaking with ordinary metaphors
because of your limitations.) Once, you offered the parts of your
body to be used as slaves to impurity and to lawless behavior that
leads to still more lawless behavior. Now, you should present the
parts of your body as slaves to righteousness, which makes your
lives holy. [20]When you were slaves of sin, you were free from the
control of righteousness. [21]What consequences did you get from
doing things that you are now ashamed of? The outcome of
those things is death. [22]But now that you have been set free from
sin and become slaves to God, you have the consequence of a
holy life, and the outcome is eternal life. [23]The wages that sin
pays are death, but God's gift is eternal life in Christ Jesus our
Lord.

Matthew 10:40-42
[40]"Those who receive you are also receiving me, and those
who receive me are receiving the one who sent me. [41]Those who
receive a prophet as a prophet will receive a prophet's reward.
Those who receive a righteous person as a righteous person will
receive a righteous person's reward. [42]I assure you that everybody
who gives even a cup of cold water to these little ones because
they are my disciples will certainly be rewarded."

Primary Hymns and Songs for the Day

"The God of Abraham Praise" 484742 (Gen) (O)
C24, CG45, E401, EL831, G49, GR16, N24, P488, SH50, UM116 (PD), VU255
"Breathe on Me, Breath of God" 99481 (Rom)
C254, CG235, E508, G286, GR304, N292, P316, SH224/273, UM420 (PD), VU382 (Fr.)
H-3 Hbl-49; Chr-45; Desc-101; Org-166
"Living for Jesus" (Rom, Matt)
C610, GR595, S2149
"Baptized in Water" 5853694 (Rom, Baptism)
CG449, E294, EL456, G482, P492, S2248, SH666
"Welcome" OL-232386 (Matt)
WS3152 (*See also* EL641, G301)
"Let Us Build a House Where Love Can Dwell" (Matt)
EL641, G301, SH228 (*See also* WS3152)
"The Spirit Sends Us Forth to Serve" (Matt) (C)
CG520, EL551, S2241
H-3 Hbl-129; Chr-106; Desc-65; Org-72
S-2 #105. Flute/violin desc.
#106. Harm.

Additional Hymn Suggestions

"God of Our Life" (Gen)
C713, G686, N366, P275
"Here I Am, Lord" OL-80670 (Gen)
C452, CG482, EL574, G69, GR589, P525, SH608, UM593, VU509
"We Walk by Faith" 2591911 (Gen)
CG634, E209, EL635, G817, N256, P399, S2196, SH660
"Why Stand So Far Away, My God?" OL-30234 (Gen, Pss)
C671, G786, S2180
"By Gracious Powers" (Gen, Pss)
E695/696, EL626, G818, N413, P342, UM517
"Ye Servants of God" 90765 (Rom)
C110, CG420, E535, EL825 (PD), G299, GR40, N305, P477, UM181 (PD), VU342
"And Can It Be that I Should Gain" 25280 (Rom)
CG605, GR569, SH540, UM363 (PD)
"Grace Greater Than Our Sin" (Rom)
CG586, GR558, UM365
"I Stand Amazed in the Presence" (Rom)
CG576, GR122, SH537, UM371 (PD)
"Amazing Grace" 22025 (Rom)
C546, CG587, E671, EL779, G649, GR572, N547/548, P280, SH523, UM378 (PD), VU266 (Fr.), Z211
"O Jesus, I Have Promised" 40454 (Rom)
C612, E655, EL810, G724/725, GR592, N493, P388/389, SH623, UM396 (PD), VU120
"Take My Life, and Let It Be" 1390 (Rom)
C609, CG490, E707, EL583/EL685, G697, GR586, P391, N448, SH627/628, UM399 (PD), VU506
"O For a Heart to Praise My God" (Rom)
GR314, UM417 (PD)
"I Am Thine, O Lord" (Rom)
C601, CG504, GR591, N455, UM419 (PD)
"Make Me a Captive, Lord" 1228206 (Rom)
GR587, P378, SH639, UM421
"Trust and Obey" (Rom)
C556, CG509, GR334, SH636, UM467 (PD)
"Depth of Mercy" 1320726 (Rom)
GR234, UM355
"Depth of Mercy" 5412781 (Rom)
WS3097
"Where Cross the Crowded Ways of Life" 2961345 (Rom, Matt)
C665, CG657, E609, EL719, G343, N543, P408, UM427 (PD), VU681
"Jesu, Jesu" 3049039 (Rom, Matt)
C600, CG656, E602, EL708, G203, N498, P367, SH155, UM432, VU593, S-1 #63. Vocal part
"There's a Spirit in the Air" (Matt)
C257, N294, P433, UM192, VU582
"O Master, Let Me Walk with Thee" 158243 (Matt)
C602, CG660, E659/E660, EL818, G738, GR596, N503, P357, SH612, UM430 (PD), VU560
"Cuando el Pobre" ("When the Poor Ones") OL-97385 (Matt)
C662, EL725, G762, P407, SH240, UM434, VU702
"You Satisfy the Hungry Heart" 84788 (Matt, Comm.)
C429, CG468, EL484, G523, P521, SH672, UM629, VU478
"God Made from One Blood" (Matt)
C500, CG686, N427, S2170, VU554
"Together We Serve" (Matt)
G767, S2175
"In Remembrance of Me" 25156 (Matt, Comm.)
C403, CG462, G521, S2254, SH667, ZS203
"As We Gather at Your Table" (Matt, Comm.)
EL522, N332, S2268, SH411, VU457
+"A Place at the Table" (Matt, Comm.)
G769, WS3149
"This Is My Song" (Independence Day)
C722, CG697, EL887, G340, N591, UM437

Additional Contemporary and Modern Suggestions

+"Another in the Fire" 7124907 (Gen)
+"Love Came Down" 5148938 (Gen)
+"Not in a Hurry" 7047889 (Gen, Rom)
+"You Are My Strength" 4869940 (Gen, Rom)
"We Fall Down" 2437367 (Gen, Rom)
G368, WS3187
"Hungry" ("Falling on My Knees") 2650364 (Gen, Pss)
WS3099
"Your Love, Oh Lord" 1894255 (Gen, Pss)
"I Will Call upon the Lord" 11263 (Pss)
G621, S2002
"Someone Asked the Question" 1640279 (Pss)
N523, S2144
"The Steadfast Love of the Lord" 21590 (Pss)
+"Lord, Listen to Your Children" 659072 (Pss)
EL752, S2207
"Forever" 3148428 (Pss)
CG53, WS3023
"How Great Are You, Lord" 2888576 (Pss, Rom)
"There's a Song" 2041825 (Rom)
S2141
"Grace Alone" 2335524 (Rom)
CG43, S2162, ZS100
"In the Lord I'll Be Ever Thankful" OL-00118 (Rom)
G654, S2195, SH316
"I Am Crucified with Christ" 2652874 (Rom)
"Amazing Grace" ("My Chains Are Gone") 4768151 (Rom)
GR574, WS3104
"Grace Like Rain" 3689877 (Rom)
+"Chain Breaker" 7060031 (Rom)
+"Freedom" 7078151
+"Great Things" 7111321
+"His Mercy Is More" 7065053 (Rom)
+"Living Hope" 7106807
+"Say So" 4944016
+"Yet Not I but Through Christ in Me" 7121852 (Rom)
+"God Is Love" 7136019 (Rom, Matt)
+"The Kingdom Is Yours" 7109354 (Matt)
+"Come to the Table" 7130008
+"No Outsiders" 7101035
"Make Me a Servant" 33131 (Matt)
CG651, S2176
"People Need the Lord" 18084 (Matt)
S2244

Solo/Ensemble Suggestions

+"Truth Be Told" 7138590 (Gen, Rom, Matt)
V-9 p. 118
"Grace Greater Than Our Sin" (Rom)
V-8 p. 180
"Take My Life" ("Consecration") (Rom)
V-8 p. 262
"Reach Out to Your Neighbor" (Matt)
V-8 p. 372
"By Gracious Powers" (Gen, Pss)
John Ferguson; Augsburg 9780800675493
SATB, organ, opt. flute, congregation (https://bit.ly/A-75493)
"Whoever Welcome You Welcomes Me" (Matt)
Larry E. Schultz; Choristers Guild CGA1067
Unison/2-part, piano, opt. flute (https://bit.ly/CGA1067)

+Hymn Anthem

"Out of the Depths I Cry to You" OL-03328 (Pss)
EL600, G424 (PD), P240, SH513, UM515

Divide the hymn into two sections. Section 1 goes to measure 10, "in spite of my rebelling." Section 2 follows.

The harmonization by J.S. Bach in G424 is public domain and may be best for this purpose.

Introduction: Handbells (half notes, open 5th, E &B) and finger cymbals (first beat of each measure) play 4 measures. *Mezzo forte.*

Stanza 1: T/B sing melody with a full tone, but never above *mezzo forte.* Accompany with handbells and finger cymbals through section 1. Keyboard (organ) accompanies section 2. *Mezzo forte.*

Stanza 2: *Mezzo forte.*
Option 1: Basses sing melody. T/A sing their parts, but never so loud as to cover the bass melody. *A cappella* (or accompanied by keyboard playing tenor and alto parts only).
Option 2: T/B sing melody; keyboard plays tenor and alto parts only.

Stanza 3: All voices, unison, with conviction. Keyboard plays full accompaniment. *Forte.*

Stanza 4: All voices, SATB or unison. Accompany with finger cymbals only through section 1, then *a cappella* in section 2. (Use keyboard playing full accompaniment if necessary.) In contrast to the conviction of stanza three, this stanza is more introspective. *Mezzo forte.*

Ending: As choir sings last notes, handbells and finger cymbals repeat the introduction, adding a final chord. *Mezzo piano.*

Other Suggestions

Visuals:
O Gen. 22:1c, mountain, dawn, donkey, man/boy, wood/knife, altar, angel, ram
P Praying hands, eyes/sleep, joy, singing
E Baptism, manacles, Rom 6:23
G Welcome, cup of water offered

Greeting: N819 (Gen, Pss) or N816 (Matt) or N824 (Rom)
+Prayer: UM531. "For Overcoming Adversity" (Gen)
Response: CG399, EL751, G471, S2200, SH311/517. "O Lord, Hear My Prayer" (Pss)
Prayer: WSL203. "God of all nations" (Independence Day)
Alternate Lessons (see page 4): Jer. 28:5-9; Ps. 89:1-4, 15-18
Theme Ideas: Covenant, Faith, Grace, Inclusion, Lament, Sin and Forgiveness, Welcome

Notes

NRSVue

Genesis 24:34-38, 42-49, 58-67

34So he said, "I am Abraham's servant. 35The LORD has greatly blessed my master, and he has become wealthy; he has given him flocks and herds, silver and gold, male and female slaves, camels and donkeys. 36And Sarah my master's wife bore a son to my master when she was old, and he has given him all that he has. 37My master made me swear, saying, 'You shall not take a wife for my son from the daughters of the Canaanites in whose land I live, 38but you shall go to my father's house, to my kindred, and get a wife for my son.' . . .

42"I came today to the spring, and said, 'O LORD, God of my master Abraham, if now you will only make successful the way I am going! 43I am standing here by the spring of water; let the young woman who comes out to draw, to whom I shall say, "Please give me a little water from your jar to drink," 44and who will say to me, "Drink, and I will draw for your camels also"—let her be the woman whom the LORD has appointed for my master's son.'

45"Before I had finished speaking in my heart, there was Rebekah coming out with her water jar on her shoulder, and she went down to the spring and drew. I said to her, 'Please let me drink.' 46She quickly let down her jar from her shoulder and said, 'Drink, and I will also water your camels.' So I drank, and she also watered the camels. 47Then I asked her, 'Whose daughter are you?' She said, 'The daughter of Bethuel, Nahor's son, whom Milcah bore to him.' So I put the ring on her nose and the bracelets on her arms. 48Then I bowed my head and worshiped the LORD and blessed the LORD, the God of my master Abraham, who had led me by the right way to obtain the daughter of my master's kinsman for his son. 49Now then, if you will deal loyally and truly with my master, tell me; and if not, tell me, so that I may turn either to the right hand or to the left." . . .

58And they called Rebekah and said to her, "Will you go with this man?" She said, "I will." 59So they sent away their sister Rebekah and her nurse along with Abraham's servant and his men. 60And they blessed Rebekah and said to her,

"May you, our sister, become
thousands of myriads;
may your offspring gain possession
of the gates of their foes."

61Then Rebekah and her maids rose up, mounted the camels, and followed the man, and the servant took Rebekah and went his way.

62Now Isaac had come from Beer-lahai-roi and was settled in the Negeb. 63Isaac went out in the evening to walk in the field, and, looking up, he saw camels coming. 64And Rebekah looked up, and when she saw Isaac, she slipped quickly from the camel 65and said to the servant, "Who is the man over there, walking in the field to meet us?" The servant said, "It is my master." So she took her veil and covered herself. 66And the servant told Isaac all the things that he had done. 67Then Isaac brought her into his mother Sarah's tent. He took Rebekah, and she became his wife, and he loved her. So Isaac was comforted after his mother's death.

CEB

Genesis 24:34-38, 42-49, 58-67

34The man said, "I am Abraham's servant." 35The LORD has richly blessed my master, has made him a great man, and has given him flocks, cattle, silver, gold, men servants, women servants, camels, and donkeys. 36My master's wife Sarah gave birth to a son for my master in her old age, and he's given him everything he owns. 37My master made me give him my word: 'Don't choose a wife for my son from the Canaanite women, in whose land I'm living. 38No, instead, go to my father's household and to my relatives and choose a wife for my son.' . . .

42"Today I arrived at the spring, and I said, 'LORD, God of my master Abraham, if you wish to make the trip I'm taking successful, 43when I'm standing by the spring and the young woman who comes out to draw water and to whom I say, "Please give me a little drink of water from your jar," 44and she responds to me, "Drink, and I will draw water for your camels too," may she be the woman the LORD has selected for my master's son.' 45Before I finished saying this to myself, Rebekah came out with her water jar on her shoulder and went down to the spring to draw water. And I said to her, 'Please give me something to drink.' 46She immediately lowered her water jar and said, 'Drink, and I will give your camels something to drink too.' So I drank and she also gave water to the camels. 47Then I asked her, 'Whose daughter are you?' And she said, 'The daughter of Bethuel, Nahor's son whom Milcah bore him.' I put a ring in her nose and bracelets on her arms. 48I bowed and worshipped the LORD and blessed the LORD, the God of my master Abraham, who led me in the right direction to choose the granddaughter of my master's brother for his son. 49Now if you're loyal and faithful to my master, tell me. If not, tell me so I will know where I stand either way." . . .

58They called Rebekah and said to her, "Will you go with this man?"

She said, "I will go."

59So they sent off their sister Rebekah, her nurse, Abraham's servant, and his men. 60And they blessed Rebekah, saying to her,

"May you, our sister, become
thousands of ten thousand;
may your children possess
their enemies' cities."

61Rebekah and her young women got up, mounted the camels, and followed the man. So the servant took Rebekah and left.

62Now Isaac had come from the region of Beer-lahai-roi and had settled in the arid southern plain. 63One evening, Isaac went out to inspect the pasture, and while staring he saw camels approaching. 64Rebekah stared at Isaac. She got down from the camel 65and said to the servant, "Who is this man walking through the pasture to meet us?"

The servant said, "He's my master." So she took her headscarf and covered herself. 66The servant told Isaac everything that had happened. 67Isaac brought Rebekah into his mother Sarah's tent. He married Rebekah and loved her. So Isaac found comfort after his mother's death.

NRSVue

Psalm 45:10-17 (G333, N650)

[10]Hear, O daughter, consider and incline your ear;
forget your people and your father's house,
[11] and the king will desire your beauty.
Since he is your lord, bow to him;
[12] Daughter Tyre will seek your favor with gifts,
the richest of the people [13]with all kinds of wealth.
The princess is decked in her chamber with gold-woven robes;
[14] in many-colored robes she is led to the king;
behind her the virgins, her companions, follow.
[15]With joy and gladness they are led along
as they enter the palace of the king.
[16]In the place of ancestors you, O king, shall have sons;
you will make them princes in all the earth.
[17]I will cause your name to be celebrated in all generations;
therefore the peoples will praise you forever and ever.

Romans 7:15-25a

[15]I do not understand my own actions. For I do not do what I
want, but I do the very thing I hate. [16]Now if I do what I do not
want, I agree that the law is good. [17]But in fact it is no longer I
who do it but sin that dwells within me. [18]For I know that the
good does not dwell within me, that is, in my flesh. For the
desire to do the good lies close at hand, but not the ability. [19]For
I do not do the good I want, but the evil I do not want is what I
do. [20]Now if I do what I do not want, it is no longer I who do it
but sin that dwells within me.
[21]So I find it to be a law that, when I want to do what is good,
evil lies close at hand. [22]For I delight in the law of God in my
inmost self, [23]but I see in my members another law at war with
the law of my mind, making me captive to the law of sin that
dwells in my members. [24]Wretched person that I am! Who will
rescue me from this body of death? [25a]Thanks be to God through
Jesus Christ our Lord!

Matthew 11:16-19, 25-30

[16]"But to what will I compare this generation? It is like children sitting in the marketplaces and calling to one another,
[17]'We played the flute for you, and you did not dance;
we wailed, and you did not mourn.'
[18]"For John came neither eating nor drinking, and they say, 'He
has a demon'; [19]the Son of Man came eating and drinking, and
they say, 'Look, a glutton and a drunkard, a friend of tax collectors and sinners!' Yet wisdom is vindicated by her deeds." . . .
[25]At that time Jesus said, "I thank you, Father, Lord of heaven
and earth, because you have hidden these things from the wise
and the intelligent and have revealed them to infants; [26]yes,
Father, for such was your gracious will. [27]All things have been
handed over to me by my Father, and no one knows the Son
except the Father, and no one knows the Father except the Son
and anyone to whom the Son chooses to reveal him.
[28]"Come to me, all you who are weary and are carrying heavy
burdens, and I will give you rest. [29]Take my yoke upon you, and
learn from me, for I am gentle and humble in heart, and you
will find rest for your souls. [30]For my yoke is easy, and my burden
is light."

CEB

Psalm 45:10-17 (G333, N650)

[10]Listen, daughter; pay attention, and listen closely!
Forget your people and your father's house.
[11]Let the king desire your beauty.
Because he is your master, bow down to him now.
[12]The city of Tyre, the wealthiest of all,
will seek your favor with gifts, [13]with riches of every sort
for the royal princess, dressed in pearls,
her robe embroidered with gold.
[14]In robes of many colors, she is led to the king.
Her attendants, the young women servants following her,
are presented to you as well.
[15]As they enter the king's palace,
they are led in with celebration and joy.
[16]Your sons, great king, will succeed your fathers;
you will appoint them as princes throughout the land.
[17]I will perpetuate your name from one generation to the next
so the peoples will praise you forever and always.

Romans 7:15-25a

[15]I don't know what I'm doing, because I don't do what I want
to do. Instead, I do the thing that I hate. [16]But if I'm doing the
thing that I don't want to do, I'm agreeing that the Law is right.
[17]But now I'm not the one doing it anymore. Instead, it's sin
that lives in me. [18]I know that good doesn't live in me—that is,
in my body. The desire to do good is inside of me, but I can't do
it. [19]I don't do the good that I want to do, but I do the evil that I
don't want to do. [20]But if I do the very thing that I don't want to
do, then I'm not the one doing it anymore. Instead, it is sin that
lives in me that is doing it.
[21]So I find that, as a rule, when I want to do what is good,
evil is right there with me. [22]I gladly agree with the Law on the
inside, [23]but I see a different law at work in my body. It wages a
war against the law of my mind and takes me prisoner with the
law of sin that is in my body. [24]I'm a miserable human being.
Who will deliver me from this dead corpse? [25a]Thank God
through Jesus Christ our Lord!

Matthew 11:16-19, 25-30

[16]"To what will I compare this generation? It is like a child
sitting in the marketplaces calling out to others, [17]'We played the
flute for you and you didn't dance. We sang a funeral song and
you didn't mourn.' [18]For John came neither eating nor drinking,
and they say, 'He has a demon.' [19]Yet the Human One came eating and drinking, and they say, 'Look, a glutton and a drunk, a
friend of tax collectors and sinners.' But wisdom is proved to be
right by her works." . . .
[25]At that time Jesus said, "I praise you, Father, Lord of heaven
and earth, because you've hidden these things from the wise and
intelligent and have shown them to babies. [26]Indeed, Father, this
brings you happiness.
[27]"My Father has handed all things over to me. No one knows
the Son except the Father. And nobody knows the Father except
the Son and anyone to whom the Son wants to reveal him.
[28]"Come to me, all you who are struggling hard and carrying
heavy loads, and I will give you rest. [29]Put on my yoke, and learn
from me. I'm gentle and humble. And you will find rest for yourselves. [30] My yoke is easy to bear, and my burden is light."

Primary Hymns and Songs for the Day

"Love Divine, All Loves Excelling" 40306 (Rom) (O)
C517, CG281, E657, EL631, G366, GR88, N43, P376, SH353/354, UM384 (PD), VU333
H-3 Chr-134; Desc-18; Org-13
S-1 #41-42. Desc. and harm.
"Lord, I Want to Be a Christian" 3184437 (Rom)
C589, CG507, G729, GR611, N454, P372 (PD), SH621, UM402, Z76 (PD-TO)
H-3 Chr-130
"Come, Thou Fount of Every Blessing" (Rom, Matt, Comm.)
C16, CG295, E686, EL807, G475, GR37, N459, P356, SH394, UM400 (PD), VU559
H-3 Chr-57; Desc-79; Org-96
S-1 #244. Desc.
"Just a Closer Walk with Thee" (Rom, Matt)
C557, EL697, G835, S2158, SH584, Z46 (PD)
"How Firm a Foundation" 107816 (Rom, Matt) (C)
C618, CG425, E636, EL796, G463, GR46, N407, P361, SH291, UM529 (PD), VU660
H-3 Hbl-27, 69; Chr-102; Desc-41; Org-41
S-1 #133. Harm.
#134. Performance note

Additional Hymn Suggestions

"O God, in a Mysterious Way" (PD) (Gen)
CG39, E677, G30, GR51N412, P270, SH47
+"Great Is Thy Faithfulness" 18723 (Gen)
C86, CG48, EL733, G39, GR44, N423, P276, SH48, UM140, VU288
"When Love Is Found" (Gen, Pss, Comm.)
C499, CG524, N362, SH279, UM643, VU489
+"What Feast of Love" (Pss, Comm.)
EL487, WS3170
"To God Be the Glory" (Rom)
C72, CG349, G634, GR531, P485, SH545, UM98 (PD)
"Jesu, Thy Boundless Love to Me" (Rom)
G703, GR133, P366, UM183, VU631
+"Pass Me Not, O Gentle Savior" 41594 (Rom)
GR527, N551, UM351 (PD), VU665
+"It's Me, It's Me, O Lord" (Rom)
C579, GR444, N519, UM352, Z110 (PD), ZS149
"Make Me a Captive, Lord" 1228206 (Rom)
GR587, P378, SH639, UM421
"Spirit of God, Descend upon My Heart" 2083 (Rom)
C265, CG243, EL800, G688, GR294, N290, P326, SH277, UM500 (PD), VU378
"Blessed Jesus, At Thy Word" (Rom)
E440, EL520, G395, N74, P454, UM596 (PD), VU500
+"Before I Take the Body of My Lord" (Rom)
C391, G428, VU462
"O Love, How Deep" (Rom, Matt)
E448/449, EL322, G618, GR95, N209, P83, SH115, UM267, VU348
"Come, Ye Sinners, Poor and Needy" (Rom, Matt)
CG471, G415, GR502, UM340, ZS186
+"Come, O Thou Traveler Unknown" (Rom, Matt)
E638/639, GR577, SH24, UM386
"Soldiers of Christ, Arise" (Rom, Matt)
E548, GR471, UM513
+"I Heard the Voice of Jesus Say" (Matt)
CG577, E692, EL611, G182, N489, SH127, VU626
"Jesus Loves Me" (Matt)
C113, CG603, EL595 (PD), G188, GR155, N327, P304, SH570, UM191, VU365, Z17
+"Only Trust Him" (Matt)
See especially stanza 1.
CG475, GR506, UM337 (PD)
"Softly and Tenderly, Jesus Is Calling" (Matt)
C340, CG474, EL608 (PD), G418, GR504, N449, SH601, UM348
"Be Thou My Vision" 5021907 (Matt)
C595, CG71, E488, EL793, G450, GR49, N451, P339, SH640, UM451, VU642
"Near to the Heart of God" (Matt)
C581, CG383, G824, GR357, P527, UM472 (PD)
"O Love That Wilt Not Let Me Go" (Matt)
C540, CG631, G833, GR92, N485, P384, SH314, UM480 (PD), VU658
"What a Friend We Have in Jesus" (Matt)
C585, CG409, EL742, G465, GR116, N506, P403, SH585/586, UM526 (PD), VU661
"Give Me the Faith Which Can Remove" (Matt)
GR583, UM650 (PD)
"Blessed Quietness" (Matt)
C267, CG244, N284 (PD), S2142, Z206
"Living for Jesus" (Matt)
C610, GR595, S2149
"Feed Us, Lord" 4636207 (Matt, Comm.)
G501, WS3167

Additional Contemporary and Modern Suggestions

"Daughter of God" 4509781 (Gen)
+"Promises" 7149439 (Gen)
+"Who You Say You Are" 7130503 (Gen)
+"Do It Again" 7067555 (Gen)
+"Trinity Song" 7068847 (Gen, Matt)
"I Could Sing of Your Love Forever" 1043199 (Pss, Matt)
"I Will Celebrate" 21239 (Pss)
"I Love You, Lord" 25266 (Pss)
CG362, G627, S2068, SH417, ZS40
"Tino tenda, Jesu" ("Thank You, Jesus") OL-94999 (Rom)
S2081
"In the Lord I'll Be Ever Thankful" OL-00118 (Rom)
G654, S2195, SH316
"My Tribute" 11218 (Rom)
C39, CG574, GR580, N14, SH434, UM99; V-8 p. 5. Vocal Solo
"Thy Word Is a Lamp" 14301 (Rom)
C326, CG38, G458, UM601
+"Confession" (Rom)
WS3138
+"Nothing Else" 7123436 (Rom)
+"Run to the Father" 7133494 (Rom)
+"All the Poor and Powerless" 5881130 (Rom)
+"Love Moves You" ("Love Alone") 5775514 (Rom)
+"All of Me" 6290160 (Rom)
"Counting on God" 5064366 (Rom)
"Foundation" 7061516 (Rom, Matt)
"Give Thanks" 20285 (Rom, Matt)
C528, CG373, G647, S2036, SH489, ZS127
"Fill My Cup, Lord" 15946 (Matt, Comm.)
UM641 *(refrain only)*
C351, UM641 *(refrain only)*, WS3093
"Come to the Table of Grace" 7034746 (Matt, Comm.)
G507, WS3168
"Holy and Anointed One" 164361 (Matt)
"Jesus I Trust in You" 4510828 (Matt)
"My Redeemer Lives" 2397964 (Matt)
+"Come to the Table" 7130008 (Matt)
+"Freedom" 7078151 (Matt)
+"Springtime" 7146308
+"The Kingdom Is Yours" 7109354

Solo/Ensemble Suggestions

"Bridal Prayer" (Gen, Pss)
V-8 p. 104
"Just a Closer Walk with Thee" (Rom, Matt)
V-5 (2) p. 31
V-8 p. 323
"He Shall Feed His Flock" from Messiah (Matt)
V-2
V-8 p. 334
"A Song of Trust" (Matt)
V-4 p. 20
"I Will Sing of Thy Great Mercies" (Matt)
V-4 p. 43
"Come, Ye Sinners" (Rom, Matt)
arr. David Ashley White; AEC-2 p. 38
2-part, keyboard, oboe (https://bit.ly/AEC-2)
"How Firm a Foundation" (Rom, Matt)
Arr. Tom Trenney; MorningStar MSM-50-5180
SATB, organ, opt. congregation (https://bit.ly/50-5180)

+Hymn Anthem

"Jesus Loves Me" (Matt)
C113, CG603, EL595 (PD), G188, GR155, N327, P304, SH570, UM191, VU365, Z17

Invite someone from your choir, church, or community to teach all singers how to "sign" the refrain using the international sign language for the deaf. Children and youth are especially intrigued with signing and will learn it quickly. The experienced signer(s) may sign all the text with the choir (or small group) signing the refrain.

Introduction: Guitar (or improvised piano) gives a simple introduction.

Stanza 1 and Refrain: All children (or a soloist) sing melody. Accompany as in introduction.

Stanza 2: T/B sing melody. S/A sing alto part. Accompany with keyboard and/or guitar. *Mezzo forte.*

Refrain: T/B continue melody. S/A continue alto part. Some S sing tenor part one octave higher. *Mezzo forte.*

Stanza 3 and refrain: Adults sing four parts (or any combination), children and youth sing melody. Accompany with keyboard playing full setting. *Forte,* declamatory.

Ending: Guitar and/or keyboard play hymn once more. All who are able sign Stanza 1 and refrain. You may choose to sign without accompaniment so that the beauty of the signing is seen and "heard" in silence.

Other Suggestions

See June 28 for Independence Day Suggestions.

Visuals:

O Spring, water jar, nose ring, bracelets, ring
P Many-colored/gold robes, joy, bride/maids
E Open Bible, manacles (closed/open), Christ
G Children playing, marketplace, flute, John, Jesus, eating/drinking, infants, burdens, yoke

Celebrate marriage covenant renewal. (Gen)
Additional Hymn Suggestions: N361-N364 (Gen, Pss)
Call to Worship: WSL65. "Jesus said Come unto me" (Matt)
Canticle: UM646. "Canticle of Love" (Gen, Pss)
Call to Prayer: WS3094. "Come to Me" (Matt)
+Sung Confession: WS3138. "Confession" (Rom)
Response: WS3110, verses 4-5 "By Grace We Have Been Saved" OL-00706 (Rom)
+Prayer: UM360. Freedom in Christ (Rom)
Prayer: UM423. Finding Rest in God (Matt)
Alternate Lessons (see page 4): Zech. 9:9-12; Ps. 145:8-14
Theme Ideas: Assurance, Children / Family of God, Comfort, Covenant, Love, Sin and Forgiveness

Notes

NRSVue

Genesis 25:19-34

19 These are the descendants of Isaac, Abraham's son:
Abraham was the father of Isaac, 20 and Isaac was forty years old
when he married Rebekah, daughter of Bethuel the Aramean of
Paddan-aram, sister of Laban the Aramean. 21 Isaac prayed to the
LORD for his wife because she was barren, and the LORD granted
his prayer, and his wife Rebekah conceived. 22 The children
struggled together within her, and she said, 'If it is to be this way,
why do I live?' So she went to inquire of the LORD. 23 And the
LORD said to her,

"Two nations are in your womb,
    and two peoples born of you shall be divided;
the one shall be stronger than the other;
    the elder shall serve the younger."

24 When her time to give birth was at hand, there were twins
in her womb. 25 The first came out red, all his body like a hairy
mantle, so they named him Esau. 26 Afterward his brother came
out, with his hand gripping Esau's heel, so he was named Jacob.
Isaac was sixty years old when she bore them.

27 When the boys grew up, Esau was a skillful hunter, a man
of the field, while Jacob was a quiet man, living in tents. 28 Isaac
loved Esau because he was fond of game, but Rebekah loved
Jacob.

29 Once when Jacob was cooking a stew, Esau came in from
the field, and he was famished. 30 Esau said to Jacob, "Let me
eat some of that red stuff, for I am famished!" (Therefore he
was called Edom.) 31 Jacob said, "First sell me your birthright."
32 Esau said, "I am about to die; of what use is a birthright to me?"
33 Jacob said, "Swear to me first." So he swore to him and sold
his birthright to Jacob. 34 Then Jacob gave Esau bread and lentil
stew, and he ate and drank,and rose and went his way. Thus Esau
despised his birthright.

Psalm 119:105-112 (G64, N701, UM840)

105 Your word is a lamp to my feet
    and a light to my path.
106 I have sworn an oath and confirmed it,
    to observe your righteous ordinances.
107 I am severely afflicted;
    give me life, O LORD, according to your word.
108 Accept my offerings of praise, O LORD,
    and teach me your ordinances.
109 I hold my life in my hand continually,
    but I do not forget your law.
110 The wicked have laid a snare for me,
    but I do not stray from your precepts.
111 Your decrees are my heritage forever;
    they are the joy of my heart.
112 I incline my heart to perform your statutes
    forever, to the end.

CEB

Genesis 25:19-34

19 These are the descendants of Isaac, Abraham's son. Abraham became the father of Isaac. 20 Isaac was 40 years old when
he married Rebekah the daughter of Bethuel the Aramean and
the sister of Laban the Aramean, from Paddan-aram. 21 Isaac
prayed to the LORD for his wife, since she was unable to have
children. The LORD was moved by his prayer, and his wife
Rebekah became pregnant. 22 But the boys pushed against each
other inside of her, and she said, "If this is what it's like, why did
it happen to me?"

So she went to ask the LORD. 23 And the LORD said to her,

"Two nations are in your womb;
    two different peoples will emerge from your body.
One people will be stronger than the other;
    the older will serve the younger."

24 When she reached the end of her pregnancy, she discovered
that she had twins. 25 The first came out red all over, clothed
with hair, and she named him Esau. 26 Immediately afterward,
his brother came out gripping Esau's heel, and she named him
Jacob. Isaac was 60 years old when they were born.

27 When the young men grew up, Esau became an outdoors-
man who knew how to hunt, and Jacob became a quiet man who
stayed at home. 28 Isaac loved Esau because he enjoyed eating
game, but Rebekah loved Jacob. 29 Once when Jacob was boiling
stew, Esau came in from the field hungry 30 and said to Jacob,
"I'm starving! Let me devour some of this red stuff." That's why
his name is Edom.

31 Jacob said, "Sell me your birthright today."

32 Esau said, "Since I'm going to die anyway, what good is my
birthright to me?"

33 Jacob said, "Give me your word today." And he did. He sold
his birthright to Jacob. 34 So Jacob gave Esau bread and lentil
stew. He ate, drank, got up, and left, showing just how little he
thought of his birthright.

Psalm 119:105-112 (G64, N701, UM840)

105 Your word is a lamp before my feet
    and a light for my journey.
106 I have sworn, and I fully mean it:
    I will keep your righteous rules.
107 I have been suffering so much—
    LORD, make me live again according to your promise.
108 Please, LORD, accept my spontaneous gifts of praise.
    Teach me your rules!
109 Though my life is constantly in danger,
    I won't forget your Instruction.
110 Though the wicked have set a trap for me,
    I won't stray from your precepts.
111 Your laws are my possession forever
    because they are my heart's joy.
112 I have decided to keep your statutes forever, every last one.

NRSVue

Romans 8:1-11

1Therefore there is now no condemnation for those who are in Christ Jesus. 2For the law of the Spirit of life in Christ Jesus has set you free from the law of sin and of death. 3For God has done what the law, weakened by the flesh, could not do: by sending his own Son in the likeness of sinful flesh and to deal with sin, he condemned sin in the flesh, 4so that the just requirement of the law might be fulfilled in us, who walk not according to the flesh but according to the Spirit. 5For those who live according to the flesh set their minds on the things of the flesh, but those who live according to the Spirit set their minds on the things of the Spirit. 6To set the mind on the flesh is death, but to set the mind on the Spirit is life and peace. 7For this reason the mind that is set on the flesh is hostile to God; it does not submit to God's law—indeed, it cannot, 8and those who are in the flesh cannot please God.

9But you are not in the flesh; you are in the Spirit, since the Spirit of God dwells in you. Anyone who does not have the Spirit of Christ does not belong to him. 10But if Christ is in you, then the body is dead because of sin, but the Spirit is life because of righteousness. 11If the Spirit of him who raised Jesus from the dead dwells in you, he who raised Christ Jesus from the dead will give life to your mortal bodies also through his Spirit that dwells in you.

Matthew 13:1-9, 18-23

1That same day Jesus went out of the house and sat beside the sea. 2Such great crowds gathered around him that he got into a boat and sat there, while the whole crowd stood on the beach. 3And he told them many things in parables, saying: "Listen! A sower went out to sow. 4And as he sowed, some seeds fell on a path, and the birds came and ate them up. 5Other seeds fell on rocky ground, where they did not have much soil, and they sprang up quickly, since they had no depth of soil. 6But when the sun rose, they were scorched, and since they had no root, they withered away. 7Other seeds fell among thorns, and the thorns grew up and choked them. 8Other seeds fell on good soil and brought forth grain, some a hundredfold, some sixty, some thirty. 9If you have ears, hear!" . . .

18"Hear, then, the parable of the sower. 19When anyone hears the word of the kingdom and does not understand it, the evil one comes and snatches away what is sown in the heart; this is what was sown on the path. 20As for what was sown on rocky ground, this is the one who hears the word and immediately receives it with joy, 21yet such a person has no root but endures only for a while, and when trouble or persecution arises on account of the word, that person immediately falls away. 22As for what was sown among thorns, this is the one who hears the word, but the cares of this age and the lure of wealth choke the word, and it yields nothing. 23But as for what was sown on good soil, this is the one who hears the word and understands it, who indeed bears fruit and yields in one case a hundredfold, in another sixty, and in another thirty."

CEB

Romans 8:1-11

1So now there isn't any condemnation for those who are in Christ Jesus. 2The law of the Spirit of life in Christ Jesus has set you free from the law of sin and death. 3God has done what was impossible for the Law, since it was weak because of selfishness. God condemned sin in the body by sending his own Son to deal with sin in the same body as humans, who are controlled by sin. 4He did this so that the righteous requirement of the Law might be fulfilled in us. Now the way we live is based on the Spirit, not based on selfishness. 5People whose lives are based on selfishness think about selfish things, but people whose lives are based on the Spirit think about things that are related to the Spirit. 6The attitude that comes from selfishness leads to death, but the attitude that comes from the Spirit leads to life and peace. 7So the attitude that comes from selfishness is hostile to God. It doesn't submit to God's Law, because it can't. 8People who are self-centered aren't able to please God.

9But you aren't self-centered. Instead you are in the Spirit, if in fact God's Spirit lives in you. If anyone doesn't have the Spirit of Christ, they don't belong to him. 10If Christ is in you, the Spirit is your life because of God's righteousness, but the body is dead because of sin. 11If the Spirit of the one who raised Jesus from the dead lives in you, the one who raised Christ from the dead will give life to your human bodies also, through his Spirit that lives in you.

Matthew 13:1-9, 18-23

1That day Jesus went out of the house and sat down beside the lake. 2Such large crowds gathered around him that he climbed into a boat and sat down. The whole crowd was standing on the shore.

3He said many things to them in parables: "A farmer went out to scatter seed. 4As he was scattering seed, some fell on the path, and birds came and ate it. 5Other seed fell on rocky ground where the soil was shallow. They sprouted immediately because the soil wasn't deep. 6But when the sun came up, it scorched the plants, and they dried up because they had no roots. 7Other seed fell among thorny plants. The thorny plants grew and choked them. 8Other seed fell on good soil and bore fruit, in one case a yield of one hundred to one, in another case a yield of sixty to one, and in another case a yield of thirty to one. 9Everyone who has ears should pay attention." . . .

18"Consider then the parable of the farmer. 19Whenever people hear the word about the kingdom and don't understand it, the evil one comes and carries off what was planted in their hearts. This is the seed that was sown on the path. 20As for the seed that was spread on rocky ground, this refers to people who hear the word and immediately receive it joyfully. 21Because they have no roots, they last for only a little while. When they experience distress or abuse because of the word, they immediately fall away. 22As for the seed that was spread among thorny plants, this refers to those who hear the word, but the worries of this life and the false appeal of wealth choke the word, and it bears no fruit. 23As for what was planted on good soil, this refers to those who hear and understand, and bear fruit and produce—in one case a yield of one hundred to one, in another case a yield of sixty to one, and in another case a yield of thirty to one."

Primary Hymns and Songs for the Day

"O Spirit of the Living God" (PD) (Rom) (O)
N263, SH222, UM539
H-3 Hbl-44; Chr-21; Desc-40; Org-40
S-1 #131-132. Intro. and desc.
"Spirit of the Living God" 23488 (Rom)
C259, CG233, G288, GR299, N283, P322, SH555, UM393, VU376, Z226, S-1 #212 Vocal desc. idea
H-3 Chr-176
S-1 #212. Vocal descant idea
"Thy Word Is a Lamp" 14301 (Pss, Matt)
C326, CG38, G458, UM601
"O Blessed Spring" (Matt)
EL447, S2076, VU632
H-3 Chr-200; Org-45
"Hymn of Promise" 126529 (Matt) (C)
C638, CG545, G250, N433, UM707, VU703
H-3 Chr-112; Org-117
S-1 #270. Desc.

Additional Hymn Suggestions

"The God of Abraham Praise" 484742 (Gen)
C24, CG45, E401, EL831, G49, GR16, N24, P488, SH50, UM116 (PD), VU255
"Where Cross the Crowded Ways of Life" 2961345 (Gen)
C665, CG657, E609, EL719, G343, N543, P408, UM427 (PD), VU681
"For the Healing of the Nations" 1510804 (Gen)
C668, CG698, G346, N576, UM428, VU678
"Come Down, O Love Divine" 761678 (Gen, Rom)
C582, E516, EL804, G282, GR293, N289, P313, UM475 (PD), VU367
"Out of the Depths" (Gen)
C510, N554, S2136, VU611
"God Made from One Blood" (Gen)
C500, CG686, N427, S2170, VU554
"Lead Me, Lord" (Pss)
C593, GR332, N774, UM473 (PD), VU662
"Blessed Jesus, at Thy Word" (Pss, Matt)
E440, EL520, G395, N74, P454, UM596 (PD), VU500
"O Word of God Incarnate" 2786410 (Pss, Matt)
C322, E632, EL514, G459, GR1126, N315, P327, UM598 (PD), VU499
"Wonderful Words of Life" 47392 (Pss, Matt)
C323, CG163, GR429, N319, SH549, UM600 (PD)
"Be Thou My Vision" 5021907 (Pss, Rom)
C595, CG71, E488, EL793, G450, GR49, N451, P339, SH640, UM451, VU642
"Just a Closer Walk with Thee" (Pss, Rom)
C557, EL697, G835, S2158, SH584, Z46 (PD)
"Christ Beside Me" (Pss, Rom)
G702, S2166
"Lead Me, Guide Me" (Pss, Rom)
C583, CG403, EL768, G740, S2214, SH582, ZS173
"Spirit Divine, Attend Our Prayers" (Rom)
E509, G407, P325, SH571, VU385
"O For a Thousand Tongues to Sing" 1369 (Rom)
C5, CG332, E493, EL886, G610, GR1, N42, P466, SH439, UM57 (PD), VU326 (*See also* WS3001)
"To God Be the Glory" (Rom)
C72, CG349, G634, GR531, P485, SH545, UM98 (PD)
"Alas! and Did My Savior Bleed" 106123 (Rom)
CG182, EL337, G212, GR231, N200, P78, UM294 (PD)
"Alas! and Did My Savior Bleed" 29499 (Rom)
C204, CG595, GR564, N199, SH172, UM359 (PD), Z8, ZS67
"Spirit of Faith, Come Down" (Rom)
GR289, UM332 (PD)
"And Can It Be that I Should Gain" 25280 (Rom)
CG605, GR569, SH540, UM363 (PD)
"Every Time I Feel the Spirit" (PD-TO) (Rom)
C592, G66, GR446, N282, P315, UM404, Z121 (PD)
"Breathe on Me, Breath of God" 99481 (Rom, Matt)
C254, CG235, E508, G286, GR304, N292, P316, SH224/273, UM420 (PD), VU382 (Fr.)
"Holy Spirit, Truth Divine" 300431 (Rom, Matt)
C241, EL398, GR320, N63, P321, UM465, VU368
"Creating God, Your Fingers Trace" (Matt)
C335, E394/395, EL684, N462, P134, UM109, VU265
"Father, We Thank You" (Matt)
E302/E303, EL478, GR394, SH686, UM563/565
"Give Me the Faith Which Can Remove" (Matt)
GR583, UM650 (PD)
"Lord, Dismiss Us With Thy Blessing" 4529091 (Matt)
C439, E344, EL545, G546, GR686, N77, P538, UM671 (PD), VU425
"Come, Ye Thankful People, Come" 50200 (Matt)
C718, CG372, E290, EL693, G367, GR83, N422, P551, SH355, UM694 (PD), VU516
"Come, We That Love the Lord" 84159 (Matt) (O)
CG549, E392, GR38, N379, UM732, VU715
"Marching to Zion" 144398 (Matt) (O)
C707, CG550, EL625, GR626, N382, UM733, VU714, Z3
"Mothering God, You Gave Me Birth" (Matt, Comm.)
C83, EL735, G7, N467, S2050, VU320
"When God Restored Our Common Life" OL-00642 (Matt)
G74, S2182
"Bring Forth the Kingdom" (Matt)
N181, S2190, SH130
"Come to Tend God's Garden" (Matt)
N586
"Christ will Come Again" (Matt)
N608

Additional Contemporary and Modern Suggestions

"The Family Prayer Song" 1680466 (Gen)
S2188
"A Wilderness Wandering People" 7068566 (Gen)
WS3113
"Daughter of God" 4509781 (Gen)
"Jesus, the Light of the World" 6363190 (Pss)
WS3056 (*See also* CG129, G127, GR214, N160, SH103, ZS62)
"God Is the Strength of My Heart" 80919 (Pss)
"In the Secret" 1810119 (Pss)
"Knowing You" 1045238 (Pss)
"Holy and Anointed One" 164361 (Pss)
"Show Me Your Ways" 1675024 (Pss)
"Ancient Words" 2986399 (Pss)
"My Life Is in You, Lord" 17315 (Pss, Rom, Matt)
S2032
"Cry of My Heart" 844980 (Pss, Rom, Matt)
S2165
"More Precious than Silver" 11335 (Pss, Rom, Matt)
S2065
"To Know You More" 1767420 (Pss, Rom, Matt)
S2161
"Step by Step" 696994 (Pss, Rom, Matt)
CG495, G743, GR671, WS3004
"Breathe" 1874117 (Pss, Rom, Matt)
WS3112, ZS47
+"Word of God, Speak" 3912788 (Pss, Matt)
+"Springtime" 7146308 (Pss, Matt)
+"Chain Breaker" 7060031 (Rom)
+"Freedom" 7078151 (Rom)
+"Great Things" 7111321 (Rom)
+"Living Hope" 7106807 (Rom)
+"Say So" 4944016 (Rom)
+"Stronger" 5060810 (Rom)

"My Tribute" 11218 (Rom)
C39, CG574, GR580, N14, SH434, UM99; V-8 p. 5. Vocal Solo
"Spirit Song" 27824 (Rom)
C352, SH409, UM347
"O For a Thousand Tongues to Sing" 4048754 (Rom)
WS3001
"Redemption" (Rom)
WS3111
+"New Wine" 7102397 (Matt)

Solo/Ensemble Suggestions

+"How I Love Your Word" (Pss)
V-3 (5) p. 9
"Just a Closer Walk with Thee" (Pss, Rom, Matt)
V-5 (2) p. 31
V-8 p. 323
+"Great Things" 7111321 (Rom)
V-9 p. 36
"Your Word, Oh Lord" (Pss)
Donald McCullough; Hinshaw HMC1928
SAB, piano (https://bit.ly/H-1928)
+"O Word of God Incarnate" (Pss, Matt)
Arr. Brenda Portman; Augsburg 9781506495354
Unison, piano (https://bit.ly/Aug-95354)

+Hymn Anthem

"Hymn of Promise" 126529 (Matt) (C)
C638, CG545, G250, N433, UM707, VU703
Introduction: Keyboard (piano) plays System 1 bass clef notes but up two octaves. Omit first two "C's" in the pickup measure. Play twice.
Stanza 1: Soloist sings stanza 1. Keyboard continues playing bass clef up two octaves throughout. Use sustain pedal to give ethereal effect. Play last two measures as written.
Interlude: Keyboard plays System 4 ("unrevealed until . . .") as written.
Stanza 2: All voices, unison. Keyboard plays setting as written.
Interlude: Keyboard plays System 4 as written.
Stanza 3: All voices, unison, *mezzo forte.* Some sopranos sing a descant, such as S-1, #270. Keep it strong and definite. *Decrescendo* and *ritard* last measures.
Ending: Repeat System 4 with voices and keyboard, *mezzo piano.*

Other Suggestions

Visuals:
O Wedding, prayer, newborn twins, birth certificate
P Open Bible, lamp, path, open hand, snare, Ps. 119:11
E Open manacles, Spirit symbols, open/closed Bibles
G Boat/sea, sower/seed, birds/sun/thorns, soil/grain
Matthew as drama can be enacted by one sower or a dozen persons, acting as sower, seeds, birds, and thorns.
Prayer of Confession: WSL92. "God of truth" (Matt)
Affirmation of Faith: WSL78. "God loves us" (Matt)
Sung Blessing: WS3159. "Let Our Earth Be Peaceful" (Matt)
Alternate Lessons (see page 4): Isa. 55:10-13; Ps. 65: (1-8), 9-13
Theme Ideas: Children / Family of God, Conflict, God: Kingdom of God, God: Word of God, Growth, Holy Spirit, Jesus: Mind of Christ

Notes

NRSVue

Genesis 28:10-19a

10 Jacob left Beer-sheba and went toward Haran. 11 He came to
a certain place and stayed there for the night, because the sun
had set. Taking one of the stones of the place, he put it under
his head and lay down in that place. 12 And he dreamed that
there was a stairway set up on the earth, the top of it reaching
to heaven, and the angels of God were ascending and descending on it. 13 And the LORD stood beside him and said, "I am the
LORD, the God of Abraham your father and the God of Isaac;
the land on which you lie I will give to you and to your offspring,
14 and your offspring shall be like the dust of the earth, and
you shall spread abroad to the west and to the east and to the
north and to the south, and all the families of the earth shall
be blessed in you and in your offspring. 15 Know that I am with
you and will keep you wherever you go and will bring you back
to this land, for I will not leave you until I have done what I
have promised you." 16 Then Jacob woke from his sleep and said,
"Surely the LORD is in this place—and I did not know it!" 17 And
he was afraid and said, "How awesome is this place! This is none
other than the house of God, and this is the gate of heaven."
18 So Jacob rose early in the morning, and he took the stone
that he had put under his head and set it up for a pillar and
poured oil on the top of it. 19a He called that place Bethel.

Psalm 139:1-12, 23-24 (G28/29/426, N715, P248, UM854)

1 O LORD, you have searched me and known me.
2 You know when I sit down and when I rise up;
you discern my thoughts from far away.
3 You search out my path and my lying down
and are acquainted with all my ways.
4 Even before a word is on my tongue,
O LORD, you know it completely.
5 You hem me in, behind and before,
and lay your hand upon me.
6 Such knowledge is too wonderful for me;
it is so high that I cannot attain it.
7 Where can I go from your spirit?
Or where can I flee from your presence?
8 If I ascend to heaven, you are there;
if I make my bed in Sheol, you are there.
9 If I take the wings of the morning
and settle at the farthest limits of the sea,
10 even there your hand shall lead me,
and your right hand shall hold me fast.
11 If I say, "Surely the darkness shall cover me,
and night wraps itself around me,"
12 even the darkness is not dark to you;
the night is as bright as the day,
for darkness is as light to you.

. . . .

23 Search me, O God, and know my heart;
test me and know my thoughts.
24 See if there is any wicked way in me,
and lead me in the way everlasting.

CEB

Genesis 28:10-19a

10 Jacob left Beer-sheba and set out for Haran. 11 He reached
a certain place and spent the night there. When the sun had
set, he took one of the stones at that place and put it near his
head. Then he lay down there. 12 He dreamed and saw a raised
staircase, its foundation on earth and its top touching the sky,
and God's messengers were ascending and descending on it.
13 Suddenly the LORD was standing on it and saying, "I am the
LORD, the God of your father Abraham and the God of Isaac. I
will give you and your descendants the land on which you are
lying. 14 Your descendants will become like the dust of the earth;
you will spread out to the west, east, north, and south. Every family of earth will be blessed because of you and your descendants.
15 I am with you now, I will protect you everywhere you go, and I
will bring you back to this land. I will not leave you until I have
done everything that I have promised you."
16 When Jacob woke from his sleep, he thought to himself, The
LORD is definitely in this place, but I didn't know it. 17 He was terrified and thought, This sacred place is awesome. It's none other
than God's house and the entrance to heaven. 18 After Jacob got
up early in the morning, he took the stone that he had put near
his head, set it up as a sacred pillar, and poured oil on the top of
it. 19a He named that sacred place Bethel.

Psalm 139:1-12, 23-24 (G28/29/426, N715, P248, UM854)

1 LORD, you have examined me.
You know me.
2 You know when I sit down and when I stand up.
Even from far away, you comprehend my plans.
3 You study my traveling and resting.
You are thoroughly familiar with all my ways.
4 There isn't a word on my tongue, LORD,
that you don't already know completely.
5 You surround me—front and back.
You put your hand on me.
6 That kind of knowledge is too much for me;
it's so high above me that I can't fathom it.
7 Where could I go to get away from your spirit?
Where could I go to escape your presence?
8 If I went up to heaven, you would be there.
If I went down to the grave, you would be there too!
9 If I could fly on the wings of dawn,
stopping to rest only on the far side of the ocean—
10 even there your hand would guide me;
even there your strong hand would hold me tight!
11 If I said, "The darkness will definitely hide me;
the light will become night around me,"
12 even then the darkness isn't too dark for you!
Nighttime would shine bright as day,
because darkness is the same as light to you!

. . . .

23 Examine me, God! Look at my heart!
Put me to the test! Know my anxious thoughts!
24 Look to see if there is any idolatrous way in me,
then lead me on the eternal path!

NRSVue

Romans 8:12-25

12So then, brothers and sisters, we are obligated, not to the flesh, to live according to the flesh—13for if you live according to the flesh, you will die, but if by the Spirit you put to death the deeds of the body, you will live. 14For all who are led by the Spirit of God are children of God. 15For you did not receive a spirit of slavery to fall back into fear, but you have received a spirit of adoption. When we cry, "Abba! Father!" 16it is that very Spirit bearing witness with our spirit that we are children of God, 17and if children, then heirs: heirs of God and joint heirs with Christ, if we in fact suffer with him so that we may also be glorified with him.

18I consider that the sufferings of this present time are not worth comparing with the glory about to be revealed to us. 19For the creation waits with eager longing for the revealing of the children of God, 20for the creation was subjected to futility, not of its own will, but by the will of the one who subjected it, in hope 21that the creation itself will be set free from its enslavement to decay and will obtain the freedom of the glory of the children of God. 22We know that the whole creation has been groaning together as it suffers together the pains of labor, 23and not only the creation, but we ourselves, who have the first fruits of the Spirit, groan inwardly while we wait for adoption, the redemption of our bodies. 24For in hope we were saved. Now hope that is seen is not hope, for who hopes for what one already sees? 25But if we hope for what we do not see, we wait for it with patience.

Matthew 13:24-30, 36-43

24He put before them another parable: "The kingdom of heaven may be compared to someone who sowed good seed in his field, 25but while everybody was asleep, an enemy came and sowed weeds among the wheat and then went away. 26So when the plants came up and bore grain, then the weeds appeared as well. 27And the slaves of the householder came and said to him, 'Master, did you not sow good seed in your field? Where, then, did these weeds come from?' 28He answered, 'An enemy has done this.' The slaves said to him, 'Then do you want us to go and gather them?' 29But he replied, 'No, for in gathering the weeds you would uproot the wheat along with them. 30Let both of them grow together until the harvest, and at harvest time I will tell the reapers, Collect the weeds first and bind them in bundles to be burned, but gather the wheat into my barn.' " . . .

36Then he left the crowds and went into the house. And his disciples approached him, saying, "Explain to us the parable of the weeds of the field." 37He answered, "The one who sows the good seed is the Son of Man; 38the field is the world, and the good seed are the children of the kingdom; the weeds are the children of the evil one, 39and the enemy who sowed them is the devil; the harvest is the end of the age, and the reapers are angels. 40Just as the weeds are collected and burned up with fire, so will it be at the end of the age. 41The Son of Man will send his angels, and they will collect out of his kingdom all causes of sin and all evildoers, 42and they will throw them into the furnace of fire, where there will be weeping and gnashing of teeth. 43Then the righteous will shine like the sun in the kingdom of their Father. Let anyone with ears listen!"

CEB

Romans 8:12-25

12So then, brothers and sisters, we have an obligation, but it isn't an obligation to ourselves to live our lives on the basis of selfishness. 13If you live on the basis of selfishness, you are going to die. But if you put to death the actions of the body with the Spirit, you will live. 14All who are led by God's Spirit are God's sons and daughters. 15You didn't receive a spirit of slavery to lead you back again into fear, but you received a Spirit that shows you are adopted as his children. With this Spirit, we cry, "Abba, Father." 16The same Spirit agrees with our spirit, that we are God's children. 17But if we are children, we are also heirs. We are God's heirs and fellow heirs with Christ, if we really suffer with him so that we can also be glorified with him.

18I believe that the present suffering is nothing compared to the coming glory that is going to be revealed to us. 19The whole creation waits breathless with anticipation for the revelation of God's sons and daughters. 20Creation was subjected to frustration, not by its own choice—it was the choice of the one who subjected it—but in the hope 21that the creation itself will be set free from slavery to decay and brought into the glorious freedom of God's children. 22We know that the whole creation is groaning together and suffering labor pains up until now. 23And it's not only the creation. We ourselves who have the Spirit as the first crop of the harvest also groan inside as we wait to be adopted and for our bodies to be set free. 24We were saved in hope. If we see what we hope for, that isn't hope. Who hopes for what they already see? 25But if we hope for what we don't see, we wait for it with patience.

Matthew 13:24-30, 36-43

24Jesus told them another parable: "The kingdom of heaven is like someone who planted good seed in his field. 25While people were sleeping, an enemy came and planted weeds among the wheat and went away. 26When the stalks sprouted and bore grain, then the weeds also appeared.

27"The servants of the landowner came and said to him, 'Master, didn't you plant good seed in your field? Then how is it that it has weeds?'

28"'An enemy has done this,' he answered.

"The servants said to him, 'Do you want us to go and gather them?'

29"But the landowner said, 'No, because if you gather the weeds, you'll pull up the wheat along with them. 30Let both grow side by side until the harvest. And at harvesttime I'll say to the harvesters, "First gather the weeds and tie them together in bundles to be burned. But bring the wheat into my barn." ' " . . .

36Jesus left the crowds and went into the house. His disciples came to him and said, "Explain to us the parable of the weeds in the field."

37Jesus replied, "The one who plants the good seed is the Human One. 38The field is the world. And the good seeds are the followers of the kingdom. But the weeds are the followers of the evil one. 39The enemy who planted them is the devil. The harvest is the end of the present age. The harvesters are the angels. 40Just as people gather weeds and burn them in the fire, so it will be at the end of the present age. 41The Human One will send his angels, and they will gather out of his kingdom all things that cause people to fall away and all people who sin. 42He will throw them into a burning furnace. People there will be weeping and grinding their teeth. 43Then the righteous will shine like the sun in their Father's kingdom. Those who have ears should hear."

Primary Hymns and Songs for the Day

"Come, Ye Thankful People, Come" 50200 (Matt) (O)
C718, CG372, E290, EL693, G367, GR83, N422, P551, SH355, UM694 (PD), VU516
H-3 Hbl-54; Chr-58; Desc-94; Org-137
S-1 #302-303. Harm. with desc.
"We Are Climbing Jacob's Ladder" (Gen)
GR524 (PD), N500, UM418, Z205
H-3 Chr-205
S-1 #187. Choral arr.
"Nearer, My God, to Thee" (Gen)
C577, GR345, N606, UM528 (PD), VU497 (Fr.)
"Bring Forth the Kingdom" (Matt)
N181, S2190, SH130
"Love Divine, All Loves Excelling" 40306 (Rom) (C)
C517, CG281, E657, EL631, G366, GR88, N43, P376, SH353/354, UM384 (PD), VU333

Additional Hymn Suggestions

+"Immortal, Invisible, God Only Wise" 124466 (Gen)
C66, CG58, E423, EL834, G12, GR7, N1, P263, UM103 (PD), VU264 (*See also* ZS4)
+"O God Our Help in Ages Past" (Gen)
C67, CG566, E680, EL632, G687, GR15, N25, P210, SH41, UM117 (PD), VU806
"Guide Me, O Thou Great Jehovah" 1448 (Gen)
C622, CG33, E690, EL618, G65, GR47, N18, P281, SH51, UM127 (PD), VU651 (Fr.)
+"Great Is Thy Faithfulness" 18723 (Gen)
C86, CG48, EL733, G39, GR44, N423, P276, SH48, UM140, VU288
+"Come, O Thou Traveler Unknown" (Gen)
E638/639, GR577, SH24, UM386
+"Swing Low, Sweet Chariot" (Gen)
C643, G825, GR630, UM703, Z104 (PD)
"Touch the Earth Lightly" (Gen)
C693, EL739, G713, N569, VU307, WS3129
"Lead Me, Guide Me" (Gen, Pss)
C583, CG403, EL768, G740, S2214, SH582, ZS173
+"Lead On, O Cloud of Presence" (Gen, Pss)
C633, S2234, VU421
"Señor, tú ves mi corazón" ("Lord, See My Heart") (Pss)
SH56
"Gather Us In" OL-00031 (Pss, Matt)
C284, EL532, G401, S2236, SH393
"Hope of the World" 643002 (Rom)
C538, E472, G734, N46, P360, UM178, VU215
"Spirit of Faith, Come Down" (Rom)
GR289, UM332 (PD)
"How Can We Sinners Know" (Rom)
GR533, UM372 (PD)
"O Come and Dwell in Me" (Rom)
GR298, UM388 (PD)
"Every Time I Feel the Spirit" (PD-TO) (Rom)
C592, G66, GR446, N282, P315, UM404, Z121 (PD)
"For the Healing of the Nations" 1510804 (Rom, Matt)
C668, CG698, G346, N576, UM428, VU678
"We Shall Overcome" (PD-TO) (Rom)
C630, G379, N570, UM533 (PD-TO), Z127, ZS106
"The Church's One Foundation" 1607188 (Rom)
C272, CG246, E525, EL654, G321, GR388/646, N386, P442, SH233, UM545/546, VU332 (Fr.)
"Santo" ("Holy") (Rom)
EL762, G594, SH39, S2019
"O Holy Spirit, Root of Life" (Rom)
C251, EL399, N57, S2121, VU379
"Baptized in Water" 5853694 (Rom, Baptism)
CG449, E294, EL456, G482, P492, S2248, SH666
"Live Into Hope" (Rom)
G772, P332, VU699
"Father, We Thank You" (Matt)
E302/E303, EL478, GR394, SH686, UM563/565
+"We've a Story to Tell to the Nations" (Matt)
C484, CG427, GR458, UM569 (PD)
+"Hymn of Promise" 126529 (Matt)
C638, CG545, G250, N433, UM707, VU703
+"My Lord, What a Morning" (PD-TO) (Matt)
C708, EL438, G352, P449, SH356, UM719, VU708, Z145
+"O Day of God, Draw Nigh" (PD) (Matt)
C700, E601, N611, P452, UM730 (PD), VU688/689 (Fr.)
"God the Sculptor of the Mountains" (Matt)
EL736, G5, S2060
"We All Are One in Mission" 3176809 (Matt)
CG269, EL576, G733, P435, S2243, ZS99
"Come to Tend God's Garden" (Matt)
N586
"Christ will Come Again" (Matt)
N608

Additional Contemporary and Modern Suggestions

"Surely the Presence of the Lord" 7909 (Gen)
C263, GR306, UM328; S-2 #200. Stanzas for soloist
"Holy Ground" 21198 (Gen)
C112, G406, S2272
"Shout to the North" 1562261 (Gen)
G319, WS3042
"In God Alone" OL-87508 (Gen)
"There's a Spirit of Love in This Place" OL-38821 (Gen)
WS3148, ZS103
+"Light of the World" 73342 (Gen, Pss)
S2204
"God Will Make a Way" 458620 (Gen, Pss)
SH57
"Lead Me, Lord" 1609045 (Gen, Pss)
"He Knows My Name" 2151368 (Gen, Pss)
+"I Have a Hope" 5087587 (Gen, Pss)
+"Shine on Us" 1754646 (Gen, Pss)
+"Do It Again" 7067555 (Gen, Pss)
+"Made a Way" 7071768 (Gen, Pss)
+"Nothing to Fear" 7133723 (Gen, Pss)
+"Tremble" 7065049 (Gen, Pss)
+"Way Maker" 7115744 (Gen, Pss)
+"Called Me Higher" 5887880 (Gen, Pss)
+"Won't Stop Now" 7111932 (Gen, Pss)
+"Love Came Down" 5148938 (Gen, Rom)
+"Wesley Prayer" ("Fire") 7118633 (Gen, Rom)
"I Will Never Be" 1874911 (Gen, Matt)
"God of Wonders" 3118757 (Pss)
SH9, WS3034
"The Potter's Hand" 2449771 (Pss)
"These Hands" 3251827 (Pss)
+"Wonderfully Made" 5768239 (Pss)
"Song of Hope" ("Heaven Come Down") 5111477 (Rom)
+"Is He Worthy?" 7108951 (Rom)
+"No Outsiders" 7101035 (Rom)
"Spirit of the Living God" 23488 (Rom)
C259, CG233, G288, GR299, N283, P322, SH555, UM393, VU376, Z226, S-1 #212 Vocal desc. idea
"Santo" ("Holy") (Rom)
EL762, G594, SH39, S2019
"Holy, Holy" 18792 (Rom)
P140, S2039
"Come, Holy Spirit" 3383953 (Rom)
WS3092 (*See also* SH223, WS3091)
+"New Wine" 7102397 (Rom, Matt)
+"Start a Fire" 7017142 (Rom, Matt)

"On Eagle's Wings" OL-80468 (Matt)
C77, CG51, EL787, G43, N775, SH318, UM143, VU807/808, S-2 #143. Stanzas for soloist
+"Springtime" 7146308 (Matt)
+"Refiner's Fire" 426298 (Matt)

Solo/Ensemble Suggestions

+"God Will Make a Way" (with "He Leadeth Me") (Gen, Pss)
V-3 (2) p. 9
"Sing a Song of Joy" (Gen, Pss)
V-4 p. 2
+"A Contrite Heart" (Pss)
V-4 p. 10
"Borning Cry" (Pss)
V-5 (1) p. 10
"I Am His, and He Is Mine" (Gen, Rom)
V-8 p. 348
"Then Shall the Righteous Shine Forth" (Matt 13:43)
V-8 p. 274
+"Is He Worthy" (Rom)
Arr. Lloyd Larson; Hope C6378
SATB, piano, opt. instruments (https://bit.ly/C-6378)
"The Gate of Heaven" (Gen)
Craig Courtney; Beckenhorst BP1979
SATB, piano, cello or violin (https://bit.ly/BP1979)

+Hymn Anthem

"The Kingdom of God" OL-22800 and OL-22799 (Matt)
UM275
This hymn may be reproduced for your choir with OneLicense.
Treat this hymn simply. Handbells might be added in a creative manner. Keyboard (organ) plays the hymnal setting throughout.
Introduction: Flute, recorder, or keyboard plays melody once. Play freely, without rhythmic restraint.
Stanza 1 and Refrain: Soloist.
Stanza 2: Soloist.
Refrain: All voices.
Stanza 3: Soloist with flute or recorder.
Refrain: All voices with flute or recorder.
Stanza 4: All voices.
Refrain: All voices.
Ending: Same as introduction.

Other Suggestions

Visuals:
O Night, stone, ladder, angels, dust, gate, oil
P Sit/stand, path, bed, hand, wings, sea, light/dark
E Children, fear, adoption papers, will, fruit, labor
G Seed, bundle of weeds/wheat, scythe, harvest/field, angels, fire, Matt 13: 43, sun
+Introit: C593, GR332, N774, UM473 (PD), VU662. "Lead Me, Lord" (Gen, Pss)
Call to Worship: N774 (Pss)
Opening Prayer: N828 or N831 (Rom, Matt)
Confession and Assurance: N835 and N841 (Matt, Rom)
Affirmation of Faith: WSL78. "God loves us" (Matt)
Litany: WSL58. "Worriers of the world, unite" (Gen, Rom)
Canticle: UM205. "Canticle of Light and Darkness" (Pss)
Prayer: WSL64. "God of all creation" (Rom)
Alternate Lessons (see page 4): Wisd. of Sol. 12:13, 16-19 or Isa. 44:6-8; Ps. 86:11-17
Theme Ideas: Children / Family of God, God: Faithfulness, God: Kingdom of God, God: Presence, Growth, Holy Spirit, Hope

Notes

NRSVue

Genesis 29:15-28

15Then Laban said to Jacob, "Because you are my kinsman,
should you therefore serve me for nothing? Tell me, what shall
your wages be?" 16Now Laban had two daughters; the name of
the elder was Leah, and the name of the younger was Rachel.
17Leah's eyes were weak, but Rachel was graceful and beautiful.
18Jacob loved Rachel, so he said, "I will serve you seven years for
your younger daughter Rachel." 19Laban said, "It is better that
I give her to you than that I should give her to any other man;
stay with me." 20So Jacob served seven years for Rachel, and they
seemed to him but a few days because of his love for her.
21Then Jacob said to Laban, "Give me my wife that I may go in
to her, for my time is completed." 22So Laban gathered together
all the people of the place and made a feast. 23But in the evening
he took his daughter Leah and brought her to Jacob, and he
went in to her. 24(Laban gave his maid Zilpah to his daughter
Leah to be her maid.) 25When morning came, it was Leah! And
Jacob said to Laban, "What is this you have done to me? Did
I not serve with you for Rachel? Why then have you deceived
me?" 26Laban said, "This is not done in our country—giving
the younger before the firstborn. 27Complete the week of this
one, and we will give you the other also in return for serving me
another seven years." 28Jacob did so and completed her week;
then Laban gave him his daughter Rachel as a wife.

Psalm 105:1-11, 45b (G59, N691, UM828)

1O give thanks to the LORD; call on his name;
  make known his deeds among the peoples.
2Sing to him, sing praises to him;
  tell of all his wonderful works.
3Glory in his holy name;
  let the hearts of those who seek the LORD rejoice.
4Seek the LORD and his strength;
  seek his presence continually.
5Remember the wonderful works he has done,
  his miracles and the judgments he uttered,
6O offspring of his servant Abraham,
  children of Jacob, his chosen ones.
7He is the LORD our God;
  his judgments are in all the earth.
8He is mindful of his covenant forever,
  of the word that he commanded for a thousand generations,
9the covenant that he made with Abraham,
  his sworn promise to Isaac,
10which he confirmed to Jacob as a statute,
  to Israel as an everlasting covenant,
11saying, "To you I will give the land of Canaan
  as your portion for an inheritance."

. . . .

45bPraise the LORD!

CEB

Genesis 29:15-28

15Laban said to Jacob, "You shouldn't have to work for free
just because you are my relative. Tell me what you would like to
be paid."
16Now Laban had two daughters: the older was named Leah
and the younger Rachel. 17Leah had delicate eyes, but Rachel
had a beautiful figure and was good-looking. 18Jacob loved
Rachel and said, "I will work for you for seven years for Rachel,
your younger daughter."
19Laban said, "I'd rather give her to you than to another man.
Stay with me."
20Jacob worked for Rachel for seven years, but it seemed like
a few days because he loved her. 21Jacob said to Laban, "The
time has come. Give me my wife so that I may sleep with her."
22So Laban invited all the people of that place and prepared a
banquet. 23However, in the evening, he took his daughter Leah
and brought her to Jacob, and he slept with her. 24Laban had
given his servant Zilpah to his daughter Leah as her servant. 25In
the morning, there she was—Leah! Jacob said to Laban, "What
have you done to me? Didn't I work for you to have Rachel? Why
did you betray me?"
26Laban said, "Where we live, we don't give the younger
woman before the oldest. 27Complete the celebratory week with
this woman. Then I will give you this other woman too for your
work, if you work for me seven more years." 28So that is what
Jacob did. He completed the celebratory week with this woman,
and then Laban gave him his daughter Rachel as his wife.

Psalm 105:1-11, 45b (G59, N691, UM828)

1Give thanks to the LORD;
  call upon his name;
  make his deeds known to all people!
2Sing to God;
  sing praises to the Lord;
  dwell on all his wondrous works!
3Give praise to God's holy name!
  Let the hearts rejoice of all those seeking the LORD!
4Pursue the LORD and his strength;
  seek his face always!
5Remember the wondrous works he has done,
  all his marvelous works, and the justice he declared—
6 you who are the offspring of Abraham, his servant,
    and the children of Jacob, his chosen ones.
7The LORD—he is our God.
  His justice is everywhere throughout the whole world.
8God remembers his covenant forever,
  the word he commanded to a thousand generations,
9 which he made with Abraham,
    the solemn pledge he swore to Isaac.
10God set it up as binding law for Jacob,
  as an eternal covenant for Israel,
11 promising, "I hereby give you the land of Canaan
  as your allotted inheritance."

. . . .

45bPraise the LORD!

NRSVue

Romans 8:26-39

[26]Likewise the Spirit helps us in our weakness, for we do not
know how to pray as we ought, but that very Spirit intercedes
with groanings too deep for words. [27]And God, who searches
hearts, knows what is the mind of the Spirit, because the Spirit
intercedes for the saints according to the will of God.
[28]We know that all things work together for good for those
who love God, who are called according to his purpose. [29]For
those whom he foreknew he also predestined to be conformed
to the image of his Son, in order that he might be the firstborn
within a large family. [30]And those whom he predestined he also
called, and those whom he called he also justified, and those
whom he justified he also glorified.
[31]What then are we to say about these things? If God is for us,
who is against us? [32]He who did not withhold his own Son but
gave him up for all of us, how will he not with him also give us
everything else? [33]Who will bring any charge against God's elect?
It is God who justifies. [34]Who is to condemn? It is Christ Jesus
who died, or rather, who was raised, who is also at the right hand
of God, who also intercedes for us. [35]Who will separate us from
the love of Christ? Will affliction or distress or persecution or
famine or nakedness or peril or sword? [36]As it is written,

"For your sake we are being killed all day long;
we are accounted as sheep to be slaughtered."

[37]No, in all these things we are more than victorious through
him who loved us. [38]For I am convinced that neither death, nor
life, nor angels, nor rulers, nor things present, nor things to
come, nor powers, [39]nor height, nor depth, nor anything else in
all creation will be able to separate us from the love of God in
Christ Jesus our Lord.

Matthew 13:31-33, 44-52

[31]He put before them another parable: "The kingdom of
heaven is like a mustard seed that someone took and sowed
in his field; [32]it is the smallest of all the seeds, but when it has
grown it is the greatest of shrubs and becomes a tree, so that the
birds of the air come and make nests in its branches." [33]He told
them another parable: "The kingdom of heaven is like yeast that
a woman took and mixed in with three measures of flour until
all of it was leavened." . . .
[44]"The kingdom of heaven is like treasure hidden in a field,
which a man found and reburied; then in his joy he goes and
sells all that he has and buys that field.
[45]"Again, the kingdom of heaven is like a merchant in search
of fine pearls; [46]on finding one pearl of great value, he went and
sold all that he had and bought it.
[47]"Again, the kingdom of heaven is like a net that was thrown
into the sea and caught fish of every kind; [48]when it was full,
they drew it ashore, sat down, and put the good into baskets
but threw out the bad. [49]So it will be at the end of the age. The
angels will come out and separate the evil from the righteous
[50]and throw them into the furnace of fire, where there will be
weeping and gnashing of teeth.
[51]"Have you understood all this?" They answered, "Yes." [52]And
he said to them, "Therefore every scribe who has become a disciple in the kingdom of heaven is like the master of a household
who brings out of his treasure what is new and what is old."

CEB

Romans 8:26-39

[26]In the same way, the Spirit comes to help our weakness. We
don't know what we should pray, but the Spirit himself pleads
our case with unexpressed groans. [27]The one who searches
hearts knows how the Spirit thinks, because he pleads for the
saints, consistent with God's will. [28]We know that God works all
things together for good for the ones who love God, for those
who are called according to his purpose. [29]We know this because
God knew them in advance, and he decided in advance that
they would be conformed to the image of his Son. That way his
Son would be the first of many brothers and sisters. [30]Those who
God decided in advance would be conformed to his Son, he also
called. Those whom he called, he also made righteous. Those
whom he made righteous, he also glorified.
[31]So what are we going to say about these things? If God is for
us, who is against us? [32]He didn't spare his own Son but gave him
up for us all. Won't he also freely give us all things with him?
[33]Who will bring a charge against God's elect people? It is God
who acquits them. [34]Who is going to convict them? It is Christ
Jesus who died, even more, who was raised, and who also is at
God's right side. It is Christ Jesus who also pleads our case for us.
[35]Who will separate us from Christ's love? Will we be separated
by trouble, or distress, or harassment, or famine, or nakedness,
or danger, or sword? [36]As it is written,

We are being put to death all day long for your sake.
We are treated like sheep for slaughter.

[37]But in all these things we win a sweeping victory through the
one who loved us. [38]I'm convinced that nothing can separate us
from God's love in Christ Jesus our Lord: not death or life, not
angels or rulers, not present things or future things, not powers
[39]or height or depth, or any other thing that is created.

Matthew 13:31-33, 44-52

[31]He told another parable to them: "The kingdom of heaven
is like a mustard seed that someone took and planted in his
field. [32]It's the smallest of all seeds. But when it's grown, it's the
largest of all vegetable plants. It becomes a tree so that the birds
in the sky come and nest in its branches."
[33]He told them another parable: "The kingdom of heaven is
like yeast, which a woman took and hid in a bushel of wheat flour
until the yeast had worked its way through all the dough." . . .
[44]"The kingdom of heaven is like a treasure that somebody
hid in a field, which someone else found and covered up. Full of
joy, the finder sold everything and bought that field.
[45]"Again, the kingdom of heaven is like a merchant in search
of fine pearls. [46]When he found one very precious pearl, he went
and sold all that he owned and bought it.
[47]"Again, the kingdom of heaven is like a net that people
threw into the lake and gathered all kinds of fish. [48]When it was
full, they pulled it to the shore, where they sat down and put the
good fish together into containers. But the bad fish they threw
away. [49]That's the way it will be at the end of the present age.
The angels will go out and separate the evil people from the
righteous people, [50]and will throw the evil ones into a burning
furnace. People there will be weeping and grinding their teeth.
[51]"Have you understood all these things?" Jesus asked.
They said to him, "Yes."
[52]Then he said to them, "Therefore, every legal expert who
has been trained as a disciple for the kingdom of heaven is like
the head of a household who brings old and new things out of
their treasure chest."

Primary Hymns and Songs for the Day
"I Love Thy Kingdom, Lord" (Matt) (O)
C274, CG262, E524, G310, GR396, N312, P441, UM540 (PD)
H-3 Hbl-53; Chr-167; Desc-97; Org-147
S-1 #311. Desc. and harm.
"Bring Forth the Kingdom" (Matt)
N181, S2190, SH130
"Seek Ye First" 1352 (Matt)
C354, CG436, E711, G175, GR341, P333, SH126, UM405, VU356
"O Day of God, Draw Nigh" (PD) (Matt, Pss) (C)
C700, E601, N611, P452, UM730 (PD), VU688/689 (Fr.)
H-3 Hbl-79; Chr-141; Desc-95; Org-143
S-1 #306-308. Various treatments

Additional Hymn Suggestions
+"Guide Me, O Thou Great Jehovah" 1448 (Gen)
C622, CG33, E690, EL618, G65, GR47, N18, P281, SH51, UM127 (PD), VU651 (Fr.)
"Where Cross the Crowded Ways of Life" 2961345 (Gen)
C665, CG657, E609, EL719, G343, N543, P408, UM427 (PD), VU681
+"O God, Our Help in Ages Past" 43152 (Gen, Pss)
C67, CG566, E680, EL632, G687, GR15, N25, P210, SH41, UM117 (PD), VU806
"O God, in a Mysterious Way" (PD) (Gen, Rom)
CG39, E677, G30, GR51N412, P270, SH47
+"Give to the Winds Thy Fears" (PD) (Gen, Rom)
CG55, G815, GR366, N404, P286, UM129 (PD), VU636
+"God the Sculptor of the Mountains" (Gen, Matt)
EL736, G5, S2060
"Depth of Mercy" 1320726 (Rom)
GR234, UM355
"O Love That Wilt Not Let Me Go" (Rom)
C540, CG631, G833, GR92, N485, P384, SH314, UM480 (PD), VU658
"Prayer Is the Soul's Sincere Desire" (Rom)
CG391, GR438, N508, UM492
"Like the Murmur of the Dove's Song" (Rom)
C245, CG233, E513, EL403, G285, N270, P314, SH407, UM544, VU205
"Blest Be the Dear Uniting Love" (Rom)
GR389, UM566 (PD)
"O Holy Spirit, Root of Life" (Rom)
C251, EL399, N57, S2121, VU379
"Since Jesus Came into My Heart" (Rom)
CG614, GR552, S2140
"God, How Can We Forgive" OL-04799 (Rom)
G445, S2169
"Nothing Can Ever" (*"Nunca nada podrá"*) (Rom)
SH139
"Fight the Good Fight" (Rom)
E552, G846, GR473, P307 (PD), VU674
+"Give Me the Faith Which Can Remove" (Rom, Matt)
GR583, UM650 (PD)
+"I Want Jesus to Walk with Me" (Matt)
C627, CG635, EL325, G775, GR368, N490, P363, SH135, UM521 (PD-TO), Z95, ZS69
"Jesus, Priceless Treasure" (Matt)
E701, EL775, G830, GR114, N480 P365, UM532 (PD), VU667 / VU668 (Fr.)
+"We've a Story to Tell to the Nations" (Matt)
C484, CG427, GR458, UM569 (PD)
+"Here I Am, Lord" OL-80670 (Matt)
C452, CG482, EL574, G69, GR589, P525, SH608, UM593, VU509
"Come, Ye Thankful People, Come" 50200 (Matt)
C718, CG372, E290, EL693, G367, GR83, N422, P551, SH355, UM694 (PD), VU516
"Bring Forth the Kingdom" (Matt)
N181, S2190, SH130
"We All Are One in Mission" 3176809 (Matt)
CG269, EL576, G733, P435, S2243, ZS99
"Enter in the Realm of God" (Matt)
N615

Additional Contemporary and Modern Suggestions
"Your Love, Oh Lord" 1894255 (Gen, Pss)
"You Never Let Go" 4674166 (Gen, Rom)
"How Great Is Our God" 4348399 (Pss)
CG322, GR31, SH458, WS3003
+"You Are Good" 3383788 (Pss)
SH455, WS3014
"In the Lord I'll Be Ever Thankful" OL-00118 (Pss)
G654, S2195, SH316
+"Rise" 7036613 (Pss, Rom)
+"You Keep Hope Alive" 7125876 (Pss, Rom)
+"God, You're So Good" 7105729 (Pss, Rom)
+"Goodness of God" 7117726 (Pss, Rom)
+"Never Runs Out" 7193998 (Pss, Rom)
+"Today" 5775617 (Pss, Rom)
+"How He Loves" 5032549 (Rom)
+"At the Cross" 4591816 (Rom)
+"Promises" 6454250 (Rom)
"Love Moves You" ("Love Alone") 5775514 (Rom)
"Think about His Love" 16299 (Rom)
"No Greater Love" 930887 (Rom)
"The Power of Your Love" 917491 (Rom)
"I Could Sing of Your Love Forever" 1043199 (Rom)
"Show Me Your Ways" 1675024 (Rom)
"Good to Me" 313480 (Rom)
"The Happy Song" 1043209 (Rom)
"I'm Goin'a Sing When the Spirit Says Sing" (Rom)
GR330, UM333, Z81 (PD)
"There's a Song" 2041825 (Rom)
S2141
"Change My Heart, O God" 1565 (Rom)
EL801, G695, S2152, SH507, ZS178
"Cry of My Heart" 844980 (Rom)
S2165
"In His Time" 25981 (Rom)
S2203
"Hallelujah" ("Your Love Is Amazing") 3091812 (Rom)
WS3027
"Shout to the North" 1562261 (Rom)
G319, WS3042
"Come, Holy Spirit" 3383953 (Rom)
WS3092 (*See also* SH223, WS3091)
+"In Christ Alone" 3350395 (Rom)
CG569, GR106, SH656, WS3105
"Your Grace Is Enough" 4477026 (Rom)
WS3106
+"Come, Now Is the Time to Worship" 2430948 (Rom)
GR669, SH396, WS3176
"You Are My All in All" 825356 (Rom, Matt)
CG571, G519, SH335, WS3040, ZS184
+"Won't Stop Now" 7111932 (Rom, Matt)
+"Called Me Higher" 5887880 (Rom, Matt)
+"New Wine" 7102397 (Rom, Matt)
+"Start a Fire" 7017142 (Rom, Matt)
+"From Ashes to Beauty" 5288953 (Rom, Matt)
"More Precious than Silver" 11335 (Matt)
S2065
"Fill My Cup, Lord" 15946 (Matt) (Stanzas 2-3)
C351, UM641 (*refrain only*), WS3093
"When It's All Been Said and Done" 2788353 (Matt)

"Forever Reign" 5639997 (Matt)
+"Jesus at the Center" 6115180 (Matt)
+"Graves Into Gardens" 7138219 (Matt)
+"Say So" 4944016

Solo/Ensemble Suggestions

"If God Be For Us" (Rom)
V-2
+"It Won't Stop" (Rom)
V-8 p. 70
"Who Shall Separate Us?" (Rom)
V-8 p. 265
+"Graves Into Gardens" 7138219 (Rom)
V-9 p. 15
+"I Want Jesus to Walk with Me" (Matt)
V-7 p. 50/54
V-8 p. 187
+"All My Hope" (Rom)
Arr. David Angerman; Praise Song HL-00293368
SATB, piano (https://bit.ly/PS-3368)
+"Seek Ye First" (Matt)
Arr. Lloyd Larson; Hope C5589
SATB, piano (https://bit.ly/C-5589)

+Hymn Anthem

"Lord God, Your Love Has Called Us Here" 1517065 (Gen)
EL358. P353, UM579

Introduction: Keyboard (organ) plays first four measures of hymnal setting and then last four measures.

Stanza 1: Sing the S, T, and B parts only. Add a few lower voices to the S part, one octave lower, and add a vew upper voices to the T part, one ocatve higher. Omit the A part. (Or choir sings the hymnal setting in four parts or unison, a cappella or accompanied.) *Mezzo forte.*

Stanza 2: T/B sing melody. Keyboard plays S-1, #58 or another harmonization. *Mezzo piano.*

Stanza 3: S/A sing melody. Keyboard plays S-1, #59 or another harmonization. *Mezzo forte.*

Stanza 4: All voices, unison. Keyboard plays S-1, #60 or another harmonization. Begin stanza piano and let it build to a strong *forte* by the end.

Stanza 5: Full of power and faith. All voices, unison. Keyboard plays hymnal setting. Some sopranos may sing the Supp. #57 or another descant.

Other Suggestions

Visuals:

O Young lovers, "7," feast, engagement
P Singing, hearts, covenant, praise
E Prayer, Spirit, heart, Rom. 8:28, 31, 38, Jesus, newborn, cross, disaster, love
G Mustard seed/shrub, birds/nest, yeast/flour, treasure, pearl, net/fish/baskets, fire, new/old

+Introit: S2101, stanza 4. "Two Fishermen" (Matt)
Canticle: UM406. "Canticle of Prayer" (Rom)
Call to Prayer: N521. "In Solitude" (Rom)
Call to Prayer: SH223, WS3091. "Come, Holy Spirit" (Rom)
Prayer: S2201. "Prayers of the People" (Rom, Matt)
Affirmation of Faith: UM887 (Rom)
Affirmation of Faith: WSL76 or WSL77 (Rom)
Theme Ideas: Children / Family of God, Conflict, Discipleship / Following God, God: Kingdom of God, God: Love of God, God: Providence / God our Help, Growth, Holy Spirit, Love

Notes

NRSVue

Genesis 32:22-31

22The same night he got up and took his two wives, his two
maids, and his eleven children and crossed the ford of the
Jabbok. 23He took them and sent them across the stream, and
likewise everything that he had. 24Jacob was left alone, and a
man wrestled with him until daybreak. 25When the man saw
that he did not prevail against Jacob, he struck him on the hip
socket, and Jacob's hip was put out of joint as he wrestled with
him. 26Then he said, "Let me go, for the day is breaking." But
Jacob said, "I will not let you go, unless you bless me." 27So he
said to him, "What is your name?" And he said, "Jacob." 28Then
the man said, "You shall no longer be called Jacob, but Israel, for
you have striven with God and with humans and have prevailed."
29Then Jacob asked him, "Please tell me your name." But he said,
"Why is it that you ask my name?" And there he blessed him. 30So
Jacob called the place Peniel, saying, "For I have seen God face
to face, yet my life is preserved." 31The sun rose upon him as he
passed Penuel, limping because of his hip.

Psalm 17:1-7, 15 (G211, N629, UM749)

1Hear a just cause, O LORD; attend to my cry;
give ear to my prayer from lips free of deceit.
2From you let my vindication come;
let your eyes see the right.
3If you try my heart, if you visit me by night,
if you test me, you will find no wickedness in me;
my mouth does not transgress.
4As for what others do, by the word of your lips
I have avoided the ways of the violent.
5My steps have held fast to your paths;
my feet have not slipped.
6I call upon you, for you will answer me, O God;
incline your ear to me; hear my words.
7Wondrously show your steadfast love,
O savior of those who seek refuge
from their adversaries at your right hand.

. . . .

15As for me, I shall behold your face in righteousness;
when I awake I shall be satisfied, beholding your likeness.

CEB

Genesis 32:22-31

22Jacob got up during the night, took his two wives, his two
women servants, and his eleven sons, and crossed the Jabbok River's shallow water. 23He took them and everything that
belonged to him, and he helped them cross the river. 24But
Jacob stayed apart by himself, and a man wrestled with him until
dawn broke. 25When the man saw that he couldn't defeat Jacob,
he grabbed Jacob's thigh and tore a muscle in Jacob's thigh as
he wrestled with him. 26The man said, "Let me go because the
dawn is breaking."

But Jacob said, "I won't let you go until you bless me."

27He said to Jacob, "What's your name?" and he said, "Jacob."
28Then he said, "Your name won't be Jacob any longer, but
Israel, because you struggled with God and with men and won."

29Jacob also asked and said, "Tell me your name."

But he said, "Why do you ask for my name?" and he blessed
Jacob there. 30Jacob named the place Peniel, "because I've seen
God face-to-face, and my life has been saved." 31The sun rose as
Jacob passed Penuel, limping because of his thigh.

Psalm 17:1-7, 15 (G211, N629, UM749)

1Listen to what's right, LORD;
pay attention to my cry!
Listen closely to my prayer;
it's spoken by lips that don't lie!
2My justice comes from you;
let your eyes see what is right!
3You have examined my heart,
testing me at night.
You've looked me over closely,
but haven't found anything wrong.
My mouth doesn't sin.
4But these other people's deeds?
I have avoided such violent ways
by the command from your lips.
5My steps are set firmly on your paths;
my feet haven't slipped.
6I cry out to you because you answer me.
So tilt your ears toward me now—
listen to what I'm saying!
7Manifest your faithful love in amazing ways
because you are the one
who saves those who take refuge in you,
saving them from their attackers
by your strong hand.

. . . .

15But me? I will see your face in righteousness;
when I awake, I will be filled full by seeing your image.

NRSVue

Romans 9:1-5

[1]I am speaking the truth in Christ—I am not lying; my conscience confirms it by the Holy Spirit—[2]I have great sorrow and unceasing anguish in my heart. [3]For I could wish that I myself were accursed and cut off from Christ for the sake of my own brothers and sisters, my own flesh and blood. [4]They are Israelites, and to them belong the adoption, the glory, the covenants, the giving of the law, the worship, and the promises; [5]to them belong the patriarchs, and from them, according to the flesh, comes the Christ, who is over all, God blessed forever. Amen.

Matthew 14:13-21

[13]Now when Jesus heard this, he withdrew from there in a boat to a deserted place by himself. But when the crowds heard it, they followed him on foot from the towns. [14]When he went ashore, he saw a great crowd, and he had compassion for them and cured their sick. [15]When it was evening, the disciples came to him and said, "This is a deserted place, and the hour is now late; send the crowds away so that they may go into the villages and buy food for themselves." [16]Jesus said to them, "They need not go away; you give them something to eat." [17]They replied, "We have nothing here but five loaves and two fish." [18]And he said, "Bring them here to me." [19]Then he ordered the crowds to sit down on the grass. Taking the five loaves and the two fish, he looked up to heaven and blessed and broke the loaves and gave them to the disciples, and the disciples gave them to the crowds. [20]And all ate and were filled, and they took up what was left over of the broken pieces, twelve baskets full. [21]And those who ate were about five thousand men, besides women and children.

CEB

Romans 9:1-5

[1]I'm speaking the truth in Christ—I'm not lying, as my conscience assures me with the Holy Spirit: [2]I have great sadness and constant pain in my heart. [3]I wish I could be cursed, cut off from Christ if it helped my brothers and sisters, who are my flesh-and-blood relatives. [4]They are Israelites. The adoption as God's children, the glory, the covenants, the giving of the Law, the worship, and the promises belong to them. [5]The Jewish ancestors are theirs, and the Christ descended from those ancestors. He is the one who rules over all things, who is God, and who is blessed forever. Amen.

Matthew 14:13-21

[13]When Jesus heard about John, he withdrew in a boat to a deserted place by himself. When the crowds learned this, they followed him on foot from the cities. [14]When Jesus arrived and saw a large crowd, he had compassion for them and healed those who were sick. [15]That evening his disciples came and said to him, "This is an isolated place and it's getting late. Send the crowds away so they can go into the villages and buy food for themselves."

[16]But Jesus said to them, "There's no need to send them away. You give them something to eat."

[17]They replied, "We have nothing here except five loaves of bread and two fish."

[18]He said, "Bring them here to me." [19]He ordered the crowds to sit down on the grass. He took the five loaves of bread and the two fish, looked up to heaven, blessed them and broke the loaves apart and gave them to his disciples. Then the disciples gave them to the crowds. [20]Everyone ate until they were full, and they filled twelve baskets with the leftovers. [21]About five thousand men plus women and children had eaten.

Primary Hymns and Songs for the Day

"Holy God, We Praise Thy Name" 114555 (Rom) (O)
C G9, E366, EL414 (PD), G4, GR2, N276, P460, SH431, UM79, VU894 (Fr.)
H-3 Chr-78, 98; Desc-48; Org-48
S-1 #151-153. Harmonization and descants

"Come, O Thou Traveler Unknown" (Gen) (O)
E638/639, GR577, SH24, UM386
S-2 #33-37. Various treatments

"O Love That Wilt Not Let Me Go" (Gen)
C540, CG631, G833, GR92, N485, P384, SH314, UM480 (PD), VU658
H-3 Chr-146; Org-142

"Break Thou the Bread of Life" (Matt, Comm.)
C321, CG35, EL515, G460, GR430, N321, P329, SH552, UM599 (PD), VU501
H-3 Chr-44; Org-15

"Where Cross the Crowded Ways of Life" 2961345 (Matt) (C)
C665, CG657, E609, EL719, G343, N543, P408, UM427 (PD), VU681
H-3 Chr-178, 180; Org-44
S-1 #141-3 Various treatments

Additional Hymn Suggestions

"The God of Abraham Praise" 484742 (Gen)
C24, CG45, E401, EL831, G49, GR16, N24, P488, SH50, UM116 (PD), VU255

+"Guide Me, O Thou Great Jehovah" 1448 (Gen)
C622, CG33, E690, EL618, G65, GR47, N18, P281, SH51, UM127 (PD), VU651 (Fr.)

+"Swing Low, Sweet Chariot" (Gen)
C643, G825, GR630, UM703, Z104 (PD)

"Oh, I Know the Lord's Laid His Hands on Me" (PD) (Gen)
S2139 (PD), Z166

"God Be with You till We Meet Again" (Gen, Matt)
C434, CG523, EL536, G541, GR688, N81, UM672 (PD), VU422, Z37

"God Be with You Till We Meet Again" (Gen, Matt)
G542, P540, UM673 (PD), VU423

+"We Cannot Measure How You Heal" 4751065 (Gen, Matt)
CG540, G797, SH341, VU613, WS3139

+"God Be with You" (Gen, Matt)
C435, N809, Z203, ZS215

"All My Hope Is Firmly Grounded" 3594474 (Pss, Rom)
C88, E665, EL757, GR68, N408, UM132, VU654/655

"Open Your Ears" (Jer)
E536, EL519, G453, VU272

"If Thou But Suffer God to Guide Thee" 564215 (Rom)
C565, CG76, E635, EL769, G816, GR75, N410, P282, SH326, UM142 (PD), VU285 (Fr.) and VU286

"Standing on the Promises" (Rom)
C552, CG625, G838, GR434, SH45, UM374 (PD)

"Holy Spirit, Truth Divine" 300431 (Rom)
C241, EL398, GR320, N63, P321, UM465, VU368

"The Church of Christ in Every Age" (Rom)
C475, EL729, G320, N306, P421, UM589, VU601

"Deep in the Shadows of the Past" (Rom)
G50, N320, P330, S2246

+"Heal Me, Hands of Jesus" (Matt)
C504, CG541, UM262, VU621

"Softly and Tenderly, Jesus Is Calling" (Matt)
C340, CG474, EL608 (PD), G418, GR504, N449, SH601, UM348

"Dear Lord and Father of Mankind" 106185 (Matt)
(Alternate Text: "Dear God, Embracing Humankind")
C594, CG413, E652/563, G169, GR499, N502, P345, UM358 (PD), VU608

+"Precious Lord, Take My Hand" 7205306 (Matt)
C628, CG400, EL773, G834, N472, P404, SH336, UM474, VU670, Z179

"For the Bread Which You Have Broken" (Matt, Comm.)
C411, E340/341, EL494, G516, P508/509, UM614/615, VU470

"Let Us Break Bread Together" (Matt, Comm.)
C425, CG461, EL471 (PD), G525, GR418, N330, P513, SH674, UM618, VU480, Z88 (PD)

"Bread of the World" (Matt, Comm.)
C387, E301, G499, GR412, N346, P502, UM624, VU461

"All Who Hunger" (Matt)
C419, CG303, EL461, G509, S2126, VU460

+"In Remembrance of Me" 25156 (Matt, Comm.)
C403, CG462, G521, S2254, SH667, ZS203

"Come, Share the Lord" (Matt, Comm.)
C408, CG459, G510, S2269, VU469

"A Place at the Table" (Matt, Comm.)
G769, WS3149

+"Feed Us, Lord" 4636207 (Matt, Comm.)
G501, WS3167

Additional Contemporary and Modern Suggestions

"Surely the Presence of the Lord" 7909 (Gen)
C263, GR306, UM328; S-2 #200. Stanzas for soloist

"Spirit of the Living God" 23488 (Gen)
C259, CG233, G288, GR299, N283, P322, SH555, UM393, VU376, Z226, S-1 #212 Vocal desc. idea

"Seek Ye First" 1352 (Gen)
C354, CG436, E711, G175, GR341, P333, SH126, UM405, VU356

"Holy Ground" 21198 (Gen)
C112, G406, S2272

"There's a Spirit of Love in This Place" OL-38821 (Gen)
WS3148, ZS103

"Just Let Me Say" 1406413 (Gen)
+"God, You're So Good" 7105729 (Gen)
+"Wesley Prayer" ("Fire") 7118633 (Gen)
+"The Blessing" 7147007 (Gen)
+"In the Silence" 6182357 (Gen, Pss)
"He Knows My Name" 2151368 (Gen, Pss)
"The Steadfast Love of the Lord" 21590 (Gen, Pss)
"Your Love, Oh Lord" 1894255 (Gen, Pss)
"How Great Is Our God" 4348399 (Gen, Pss)
CG322, GR31, SH458, WS3003

"I Will Call upon the Lord" 11263 (Pss)
G621, S2002

"O Lord, Hear My Prayer" (Pss)
CG399, EL751, G471, S2200, SH311/517

"Came to My Rescue" 4705190 (Pss)
"Forever" 3148428 (Pss, Rom)
CG53, WS3023

"Jesus, Name above All Names" 21291 (Rom)
S2071, ZS27

+"King of Kings" 7127647 (Rom)
"Spirit Song" 27824 (Matt, Comm.)
C352, SH409, UM347

"Jesu, Tawa Pano" ("Jesus, We Are Here") OL-17487 (Matt)
EL529, G392, S2273, SH611, ZS148

"You Who Are Thirsty" 814453 (Matt, Comm.)
S2132

"There Will Be Bread" 4512352 (Matt, Comm.)
"You Are" 4387343 (Matt)
+"Way Maker" 7115744 (Matt)
+"Come to the Table" 7130008 (Matt, Comm.)
+"Springtime" 7146308 (Matt, Comm.)
+"We Remember We Believe" 5767711 (Matt, Comm.)

Solo/Ensemble Suggestions
+"Refuge and Strength" (Pss)
V-3 (5) p. 14
"A Contrite Heart" (Pss)
V-4 p. 10
+"Lord, Listen to Your Children" (Pss)
V-8 p. 168
"Softly and Tenderly" (Matt)
V-5 (3) p. 52
"Let Us Break Bread Together" (Matt, Comm.)
V-6 p. 38
+"God So Loved" 7169675 (Matt, Comm.)
V-9 p. 28
+"He Breaks the Bread, He Pours the Wine" (Matt, Comm.)
V-10 p. 43
"God Bestows on Each One a Name" (Gen)
Fred Gramann; E.C. Schirmer 7330
SATB a cappella (https://bit.ly/ECS-7330)
+"All Who Hunger, Gather Gladly" (Matt)
David M. Cherwien, Morningstar MSM- 50-8322
SAB, organ, opt. C-instrument (https://bit.ly/MSM-50-8322)

+Hymn Anthem
"Break Thou the Bread" (Matt, Comm.)
"Break Thou the Bread of Life"
C321, CG35, EL515, G460, GR430, N321, P329, SH552, UM599 (PD), VU501
"Here, O My Lord, I See Thee" 136265
GR411, UM623 (PD)
This arrangement assumes that both hymns are in the same key.
Introduction: Keyboard (organ) plays "Break Thou the Bread of Life," last four measures.
"Break Thou the Bread of Life," Stanza 1: Soloist.
"Here, O My Lord, I See Thee," Stanza 1: All voices, unison. *Mezzo forte.*
"Here, O My Lord, I See Thee," Stanza 2: All voices in four parts or unison, *a cappella* or accompanied.
"Break Thou the Bread of Life," Stanza 2: Soloist.
"Here, O My Lord, I See Thee," Stanza 5: All voices, unison. *Forte.* Some sopranos may sing a descant, such as S-1, #265.

Other Suggestions
Visuals:
O River ford, wrestling, hip, cane, Gen. 32:26b, name
P Prayer, heart, night, feet/path, listening
E Broken heart, salvation history, Christ
G Boat, healing, loaves, two fish, twelve baskets, 5,000
Opening Prayer: N818 (Gen)
Response: EL752, S2207. "Lord, Listen to Your Children" 659072 (Pss)
Prayer: UM477. For Illumination (Gen)
+Prayer Response: CG399, EL751, G471, S2200, SH311/517. "O Lord, Hear My Prayer" (Pss)
Poem: UM387. Come, O Thou Traveler Unknown (Gen)
Prayer: WSL55. "Almighty God, you sustained" (Matt)
Offertory Prayer: WSL134. "Loving Father" (Matt)
Sung Communion: WS3171. "Communion Setting" (Matt)
Response: C411, E340/341, EL494, G516, P508/509, UM614/615, VU470. "For the Bread Which You Have Broken" (Matt, Comm.)
Benediction: WSL167. "Go! Never stop going out" (Matt)
Alternate Lessons (see page 4): Isa. 55:1-5; Ps. 145:8-9, 14-21
Theme Ideas: Bread of Life, Communion, God: Hunger / Thirst for God, God: Love of God, God: Presence

Notes

NRSVue

Genesis 37:1-4, 12-28

[1]Jacob settled in the land where his father had lived as an alien, the land of Canaan. [2]These are the descendants of Jacob.

Joseph, being seventeen years old, was shepherding the flock with his brothers; he was a helper to the sons of Bilhah and Zilpah, his father's wives, and Joseph brought a bad report of them to their father. [3]Now Israel loved Joseph more than any other of his children because he was the son of his old age, and he made him an ornamented robe. [4]But when his brothers saw that their father loved him more than all his brothers, they hated him and could not speak peaceably to him. . . .

[12]Now his brothers went to pasture their father's flock near Shechem. [13]And Israel said to Joseph, "Are not your brothers pasturing the flock at Shechem? Come, I will send you to them." He answered, "Here I am." [14]So he said to him, "Go now, see if it is well with your brothers and with the flock, and bring word back to me." So he sent him from the valley of Hebron.

He came to Shechem, [15]and a man found him wandering in the fields; the man asked him, "What are you seeking?" [16]"I am seeking my brothers," he said; "tell me, please, where they are pasturing the flock." [17]The man said, "They have gone away, for I heard them say, 'Let us go to Dothan.'" So Joseph went after his brothers and found them at Dothan. [18]They saw him from a distance, and before he came near to them they conspired to kill him. [19]They said to one another, "Here comes this dreamer. [20]Come now, let us kill him and throw him into one of the pits; then we shall say that a wild animal has devoured him, and we shall see what will become of his dreams." [21]But when Reuben heard it, he delivered him out of their hands, saying, "Let us not take his life." [22]Reuben said to them, "Shed no blood; throw him into this pit here in the wilderness, but lay no hand on him"—that he might rescue him out of their hand and restore him to his father. [23]So when Joseph came to his brothers, they stripped him of his robe, the ornamented robe that he wore, [24]and they took him and threw him into a pit. The pit was empty; there was no water in it.

[25]Then they sat down to eat, and looking up they saw a caravan of Ishmaelites coming from Gilead, with their camels carrying gum, balm, and resin, on their way to carry it down to Egypt. [26]Then Judah said to his brothers, "What profit is it if we kill our brother and conceal his blood? [27]Come, let us sell him to the Ishmaelites and not lay our hands on him, for he is our brother, our own flesh." And his brothers agreed. [28]When some Midianite traders passed by, they drew Joseph up, lifting him out of the pit, and sold him to the Ishmaelites for twenty pieces of silver. And they took Joseph to Egypt.

Psalm 105:1-6, 16-22, 45b (G59, N691, UM828)

[1]O give thanks to the LORD; call on his name;
make known his deeds among the peoples.
[2]Sing to him, sing praises to him;
tell of all his wonderful works.
[3]Glory in his holy name;
let the hearts of those who seek the LORD rejoice.
[4]Seek the LORD and his strength;
seek his presence continually.
[5]Remember the wonderful works he has done,
his miracles and the judgments he has uttered,
[6]O offspring of his servant Abraham,
children of Jacob, his chosen ones.

. . . .

CEB

Genesis 37:1-4, 12-28

[1]Jacob lived in the land of Canaan where his father was an immigrant. [2]This is the account of Jacob's descendants. Joseph was 17 years old and tended the flock with his brothers. While he was helping the sons of Bilhah and Zilpah, his father's wives, Joseph told their father unflattering things about them. [3]Now Israel loved Joseph more than any of his other sons because he was born when Jacob was old. Jacob had made for him a long robe. [4]When his brothers saw that their father loved him more than any of his brothers, they hated him and couldn't even talk nicely to him. . . .

[12]Joseph's brothers went to tend their father's flocks near Shechem. [13]Israel said to Joseph, "Aren't your brothers tending the sheep near Shechem? Come, I'll send you to them."

And he said, "I'm ready."

[14]Jacob said to him, "Go! Find out how your brothers are and how the flock is, and report back to me."

So Jacob sent him from the Hebron Valley. When he approached Shechem, [15]a man found him wandering in the field and asked him, "What are you looking for?"

[16]Joseph said, "I'm looking for my brothers. Tell me, where are they tending the sheep?"

[17]The man said, "They left here. I heard them saying, 'Let's go to Dothan.'" So Joseph went after his brothers and found them in Dothan.

[18]They saw Joseph in the distance before he got close to them, and they plotted to kill him. [19]The brothers said to each other, "Here comes the big dreamer. [20]Come on now, let's kill him and throw him into one of the cisterns, and we'll say a wild animal devoured him. Then we will see what becomes of his dreams!"

[21]When Reuben heard what they said, he saved him from them, telling them, "Let's not take his life." [22]Reuben said to them, "Don't spill his blood! Throw him into this desert cistern, but don't lay a hand on him." He intended to save Joseph from them and take him back to his father.

[23]When Joseph reached his brothers, they stripped off Joseph's long robe, [24]took him, and threw him into the cistern, an empty cistern with no water in it. [25]When they sat down to eat, they looked up and saw a caravan of Ishmaelites coming from Gilead, with camels carrying sweet resin, medicinal resin, and fragrant resin on their way down to Egypt. [26]Judah said to his brothers, "What do we gain if we kill our brother and hide his blood? [27]Come on, let's sell him to the Ishmaelites. Let's not harm him because he's our brother; he's family." His brothers agreed. [28]When some Midianite traders passed by, they pulled Joseph up out of the cistern. They sold him to the Ishmaelites for twenty pieces of silver, and they brought Joseph to Egypt.

Psalm 105:1-6, 16-22, 45b (G59, N691, UM828)

[1]Give thanks to the LORD;
call upon his name;
make his deeds known to all people!
[2]Sing to God;
sing praises to the Lord;
dwell on all his wondrous works!
[3]Give praise to God's holy name!
Let the hearts rejoice of all those seeking the LORD!
[4]Pursue the LORD and his strength;
seek his face always!
[5]Remember the wondrous works he has done,
all his marvelous works, and the justice he declared—
6 you who are the offspring of Abraham, his servant,
and the children of Jacob, his chosen ones.

. . . .

NRSVue

Psalm 105:1-6, 16-22, 45b (continued)

16When he summoned famine against the land
 and cut off every supply of bread,
17he had sent a man ahead of them,
 Joseph, who has been sold as a slave.
18His feet were hurt with fetters;
 his neck was put in a collar of iron;
19until what he had said came to pass,
 the word of the LORD kept testing him.
20The king sent and released him;
 the ruler of the peoples set him free.
21He made him lord of his house
 and ruler of all his possessions,
22to instruct his officials at his pleasure
 and to teach his elders wisdom.

. . . .

45bPraise the LORD!

Romans 10:5-15

5Moses writes concerning the righteousness that comes from
the law, that "the person who does these things will live by
them." 6But the righteousness that comes from faith says, "Do
not say in your heart, 'Who will ascend into heaven?'" (that is,
to bring Christ down) 7"or 'Who will descend into the abyss?'"
(that is, to bring Christ up from the dead). 8But what does it say?

"The word is near you,
 In your mouth and in your heart"

(that is, the word of faith that we proclaim), 9because if you
confess with your mouth that Jesus is Lord and believe in your
heart that God raised him from the dead, you will be saved. 10For
one believes with the heart, leading to righteousness, and one
confesses with the mouth, leading to salvation. 11The scripture
says, "No one who believes in him will be put to shame." 12For
there is no distinction between Jew and Greek; the same Lord is
Lord of all and is generous to all who call on him. 13For "everyone who calls on the name of the Lord shall be saved."

14But how are they to call on one in whom they have not
believed? And how are they to believe in one of whom they have
never heard? And how are they to hear without someone to
proclaim him? 15And how are they to proclaim him unless they
are sent? As it is written, "How beautiful are the feet of those
who bring good news!"

Matthew 14:22-33

22Immediately he made the disciples get into a boat and go
on ahead to the other side, while he dismissed the crowds. 23And
after he had dismissed the crowds, he went up the mountain by
himself to pray. When evening came, he was there alone, 24but
by this time the boat, battered by the waves, was far from the
land, for the wind was against them. 25And early in the morning he came walking toward them on the sea. 26But when the
disciples saw him walking on the sea, they were terrified, saying,
"It is a ghost!" And they cried out in fear. 27But immediately Jesus
spoke to them and said, "Take heart, it is I; do not be afraid."

28Peter answered him, "Lord, if it is you, command me to
come to you on the water." 29He said, "Come." So Peter got out
of the boat, started walking on the water, and came toward Jesus.
30But when he noticed the strong wind, he became frightened,
and, beginning to sink, he cried out, "Lord, save me!" 31Jesus
immediately reached out his hand and caught him, saying to
him, "You of little faith, why did you doubt?" 32When they got
into the boat, the wind ceased. 33And those in the boat worshiped him, saying, "Truly you are the Son of God."

CEB

Psalm 105:1-6, 16-22, 45b (continued)

16When God called for a famine in the land,
 destroying every source of food,
17 he sent a man ahead of them,
 who was sold as a slave: it was Joseph.
18Joseph's feet hurt in his shackles;
 his neck was in an iron collar,
19 until what he predicted actually happened,
 until what the LORD had said proved him true.
20The king sent for Joseph and set him free;
 the ruler of many people released him.
21The king made Joseph master of his house and ruler over
 everything he owned,
22 to make sure his princes acted according to his will,
 and to teach wisdom to his advisors.

. . . .

45bPraise the LORD!

Romans 10:5-15

5Moses writes about the righteousness that comes from the
Law: *The person who does these things will live by them.* 6But the
righteousness that comes from faith talks like this: *Don't say in
your heart, "Who will go up into heaven?"* (that is, to bring Christ
down) 7or *"Who will go down into the region below?"* (that is, to
bring Christ up from the dead). 8But what does it say? *The word
is near you, in your mouth and in your heart* (that is, the message of
faith that we preach). 9Because if you confess with your mouth
"Jesus is Lord" and in your heart you have faith that God raised
him from the dead, you will be saved. 10Trusting with the heart
leads to righteousness, and confessing with the mouth leads to
salvation. 11The scripture says, *All who have faith in him won't be
put to shame.* 12There is no distinction between Jew and Greek,
because the same Lord is Lord of all, who gives richly to all who
call on him. 13*All who call on the Lord's name will be saved.*

14So how can they call on someone they don't have faith in?
And how can they have faith in someone they haven't heard of?
And how can they hear without a preacher? 15And how can they
preach unless they are sent? As it is written, *How beautiful are the
feet of those who announce the good news.*

Matthew 14:22-33

22Right then, Jesus made the disciples get into the boat and
go ahead to the other side of the lake while he dismissed the
crowds. 23When he sent them away, he went up onto a mountain
by himself to pray. Evening came and he was alone. 24Meanwhile,
the boat, fighting a strong headwind, was being battered by the
waves and was already far away from land. 25Very early in the
morning he came to his disciples, walking on the lake. 26When
the disciples saw him walking on the lake, they were terrified
and said, "It's a ghost!" They were so frightened they screamed.

27Just then Jesus spoke to them, "Be encouraged! It's me.
Don't be afraid."

28Peter replied, "Lord, if it's you, order me to come to you on
the water."

29And Jesus said, "Come."

Then Peter got out of the boat and was walking on the water
toward Jesus. 30But when Peter saw the strong wind, he became
frightened. As he began to sink, he shouted, "Lord, rescue me!"

31Jesus immediately reached out and grabbed him, saying,
"You man of weak faith! Why did you begin to have doubts?"
32When they got into the boat, the wind settled down.

33Then those in the boat worshipped Jesus and said, "You
must be God's Son!"

Primary Hymns and Songs for the Day

"How Firm a Foundation" 107816 (Rom, Matt) (O)
C618, CG425, E636, EL796, G463, GR46, N407, P361, SH291, UM529 (PD), VU660
H-3 Hbl-14, 19, 27; Chr-102; Desc-41; Org-41
S-1 #133. Harmonization
#134. Performance note

"Stand By Me" (Matt) (O)
C629, GR352, UM512, Z41 (PD-TO), ZS164
H-3 Chr-177

"Children of the Heavenly Father" (Gen, Pss)
CG69, EL781, GR56, N487, SH42, UM141
H-3 Chr-46; Desc-102
S-2 #180-185. Various treatments

"Santo" ("Holy") (Rom)
EL762, G594, SH39, S2019

"Here I Am, Lord" OL-80670 (Gen, Matt, Rom) (C)
C452, CG482, EL574, G69, GR589, P525, SH608, UM593, VU509
H-3 Chr-97; Org-54

Additional Hymn Suggestions

+"Where Cross the Crowded Ways of Life" 2961345 (Gen)
C665, CG657, E609, EL719, G343, N543, P408, UM427 (PD), VU681

+"For the Healing of the Nations" 1510804 (Gen)
C668, CG698, G346, N576, UM428, VU678

"We Shall Overcome" (PD-TO) (Gen)
C630, G379, N570, UM533 (PD-TO), Z127, ZS106

+"We'll Understand It Better By and By" (Gen, Matt)
GR370, N444, UM525 (PD), Z55, ZS168

"To God Be the Glory" (Rom)
C72, CG349, G634, GR531, P485, SH545, UM98 (PD)

"I Love to Tell the Story" (Rom)
C480, CG581, EL661, G462, GR160, N522, SH569, UM156 (PD), VU343

"At the Name of Jesus" (Rom)
CG424, E435, EL416, G264, GR105, P148, SH657, UM168, VU335

+"Forward through the Ages" (PD) (Rom)
N377, UM555 (PD)

"Only Trust Him" (Rom)
See especially stanza 1.
CG475, GR506, UM337 (PD)

"Just As I Am" (Rom)
C339, CG500, E693, EL592, G442, GR509, N207, P370, SH500, UM357 (PD), VU508, Z208

"O For a Heart to Praise My God" (Rom)
GR314, UM417 (PD)

"In Christ There Is No East or West" 2608952 (UMH ONLY St. 3 OL-13651) (Rom)
C687, CG273, E529, EL650 (PD), G317/318, GR392, N394/395, P439/440, UM548, VU606, Z65 (PD)

"We've a Story to Tell to the Nations" (Rom) (C)
C484, CG427, GR458, UM569 (PD)

"I Know Whom I Have Believed" (Rom)
CG588, GR571, SH529, UM714 (PD)

"Since Jesus Came into My Heart" (Rom)
CG614, GR552, S2140

"A Place at the Table" (Rom, Comm.)
G769, WS3149

"We Walk by Faith" 2591911 (Rom, Matt)
CG634, E209, EL635, G817, N256, P399, S2196, SH660

"Take, O Take Me as I Am" 4562041 (Rom, Matt)
EL814, G698, SH620, WS3119

+"O God Our Help in Ages Past" (Matt)
C67, CG566, E680, EL632, G687, GR15, N25, P210, SH41, UM117 (PD), VU806

"Give to the Winds Thy Fears" (PD) (Matt)
CG55, G815, GR366, N404, P286, UM129 (PD), VU636

"I Sing the Almighty Power of God" 738058 (Matt)
C64, CG19, E398, G32, GR4, N12, P288, SH15, UM152, VU231

"O Sing a Song of Bethlehem" 2798408 (Matt)
CG164, G159, N51, P308, UM179 (PD)

"Tell Me the Stories of Jesus" 2627445 (Matt)
C190, GR159, UM277 (PD), VU357

"Dear Lord and Father of Mankind" 106185 (Matt)
(Alternate Text: "Dear God, Embracing Humankind")
C594, CG413, E652/563, G169, GR499, N502, P345, UM358 (PD), VU608

"My Hope Is Built" (PD) (Matt)
C537, CG590, EL596/597, G353, GR102, N403, P379, SH324, UM368 (PD), ZS182

"Precious Lord, Take My Hand" 7205306 (Matt)
C628, CG400, EL773, G834, N472, P404, SH336, UM474, VU670, Z179

"Lonely the Boat" (Matt)
G185, P373, UM476

"Jesus, Lover of My Soul" (Matt)
C542, CG406, E699, G440, GR120, N546, P303, SH542/543, UM479, VU669

+"I Want Jesus to Walk with Me" (Matt)
C627, CG635, EL325, G775, GR368, N490, P363, SH135, UM521 (PD-TO), Z95, ZS69

"Wade in the Water" OL-246943 (Matt)
C371, EL459 (PD), S2107, Z129 (PD), ZS189

"My Life Flows On" (Matt)
C619, CG592, EL763, G821, N476, S2212, VU716

"Love Lifted Me" (Matt)
CG618, GR89, WS3101, Z71 (PD)

Additional Contemporary and Modern Suggestions

+"Daughters of Zion" (Gen)
+"You Keep Hope Alive" 7125876 (Gen, Pss)
+"Let Justice Roll" ("Like a River") 4974842 (Gen, Rom)
+"Alpha and Omega" 4654148 (Pss)
"Give Thanks" 20285 (Pss)
C528, CG373, G647, S2036, SH489, ZS127
"Someone Asked the Question" 1640279 (Pss)
N523, S2144
"In the Lord I'll Be Ever Thankful" OL-00118 (Pss)
G654, S2195, SH316
"How Great Is Our God" 4348399 (Pss)
CG322, GR31, SH458, WS3003
"Step by Step" 696994 (Pss, Matt)
CG495, G743, GR671, WS3004
"Forever" 3148428 (Pss, Matt)
CG53, WS3023
"How Can I Keep from Singing" 4822372 (Pss, Matt)
"Came to My Rescue" 4705190 (Pss, Matt)
"He Is Lord" 1515225 (Rom)
C117, CG208, GR268, SH657, UM177, Z233
"One Bread, One Body" OL-80673 (Rom, Comm.)
C393, EL496, G530, SH678, UM620, VU467
"God Is Good All the Time" 1729073 (Rom)
"The Heavens Shall Declare" 904033 (Rom)
"We Will Dance" 1034438 (Rom)
+"Beautiful Things" 5665521 (Rom)
+"No Outsiders" 7101035 (Rom)
+"The Kingdom Is Yours" 7109354 (Rom)
"I Will Call upon the Lord" 11263 (Rom, Matt)
G621, S2002
+"Light of the World" 73342 (Matt)
S2204
"Cares Chorus" 25974 (Matt)
S2215

+"In Christ Alone" 3350395 (Matt)
CG569, GR106, SH656, WS3105
"You Never Let Go" 4674166 (Matt)
"Foundation" 7061516 (Matt)
"Freedom in the Spirit" 7127886 (Matt)
+"How Can I Keep from Singing" 4822372 (Matt)
"Famous For" ("I Believe") 7096220 (Matt)
V-9, p. 22. Vocal Solo

Solo/Ensemble Suggestions

+"Help Us Accept Each Other" (Gen)
V-8 p. 343
+"Truth Be Told" 7138590 (Gen, Rom, Matt)
V-9 p. 118
"Wade in the Water" (Matt, Baptism)
V-5 (2) p. 46
+"I Will Fear No More" (Matt)
V-9 p. 42
+"Peace Be Still" (Matt)
V-9 p. 64
+" Come to Jesus" (Matt)
Rice/Hayes; Hope C6005
SAB, piano (https://bit.ly/C-6005)
"O Lord Increase My Faith" (Matt)
Orlando Gibbons; E.C. Schirmer 375
SATB *a cappella* (https://bit.ly/ECS375)

+Hymn Anthem

"I Know Whom I Have Believed" (Rom)
CG588, GR571, SH529, UM714 (PD)
These three duet ideas may used according to your resources.
1: S/A soloists singing the soprano and alto parts.
2: T/B soloist singing the melody and S/A soloist singing the alto part.
3: S/A soloist singing the melody and a T/B soloist singing singing the tenor part.
Keyboard plays full accompaniment throughout.
Introduction: Keyboard (piano) plays refrain. *Mezzo forte.*
Stanza 1: All voices, unison. *Mezzo forte.*
Refrain: SATB or unison. *Forte.*
Stanza 2 and Refrain: Duet (choose one of the ideas above). *Mezzo forte.*
Stanza 3: Duet. *Mezzo forte.*
Refrain: All voices, unison. *Crescendo* during the refrain to *forte.*
Stanza 4 and Refrain: SATB or unison. *Forte* with *ritard* at the end.

Other Suggestions

Visuals:
O Staff, colorful robe, pit, caravan, twenty coins, Egypt
P Singing, hearts, famine, open manacles, iron collar
E Christ, heart, speaking, Rom. 10:8b, 13, 15b, feet
G Boat, mountain, prayer, storm/sea, Jesus/Peter/water, Matt 14:30b, 31b, 33b
Greeting: N822 (Pss)
Opening Prayer: N828 (Matt)
Medley: "Take This Moment, Sign, and Space" (WS3118) and "Take, O Take Me As I Am" (EL814, G698, SH620, WS3119) (Gen, Matt)
Sung Confession: WS3138. "Confession" (Gen, Rom)
Call to Prayer: UM499. "Serenity" (Matt)
Blessing: N876 (Matt)
Alternate Lessons (see page 4): 1 Kgs. 19:9-18; Ps. 85:8-13
Theme Ideas: Children / Family of God, Conflict, Doubt, Faith, God: Providence / God our Help, Inclusion

Notes

NRSVue

Genesis 45:1-15

[1]Then Joseph could no longer control himself before all those who stood by him, and he cried out, "Send everyone away from me." So no one stayed with him when Joseph made himself known to his brothers. [2]And he wept so loudly that the Egyptians heard it, and the household of Pharaoh heard it. [3]Joseph said to his brothers, "I am Joseph. Is my father still alive?" But his brothers could not answer him, so dismayed were they at his presence.

[4]Then Joseph said to his brothers, "Come closer to me." And they came closer. He said, "I am your brother, Joseph, whom you sold into Egypt. [5]And now do not be distressed or angry with yourselves because you sold me here, for God sent me before you to preserve life. [6]For the famine has been in the land these two years, and there are five more years in which there will be neither plowing nor harvest. [7]God sent me before you to preserve for you a remnant on earth and to keep alive for you many survivors. [8]So it was not you who sent me here but God; he has made me a father to Pharaoh and lord of all his house and ruler over all the land of Egypt. [9]Hurry and go up to my father and say to him, 'Thus says your son Joseph, God has made me lord of all Egypt; come down to me; do not delay. [10]You shall settle in the land of Goshen, and you shall be near me, you and your children and your children's children, as well as your flocks, your herds, and all that you have. [11]I will provide for you there, since there are five more years of famine to come, so that you and your household and all that you have will not come to poverty.' [12]And now your eyes and the eyes of my brother Benjamin see that it is my own mouth that speaks to you. [13]You must tell my father how greatly I am honored in Egypt and all that you have seen. Hurry and bring my father down here." [14]Then he fell upon his brother Benjamin's neck and wept, while Benjamin wept upon his neck. [15]And he kissed all his brothers and wept upon them, and after that his brothers talked with him.

Psalm 133 (G397/398, N712, P241, UM850)

[1]How very good and pleasant it is
when kindred live together in unity!
[2]It is like the precious oil on the head,
running down upon the beard,
on the beard of Aaron,
running down over the collar of his robes.
[3]It is like the dew of Hermon,
which falls on the mountains of Zion.
For there the LORD ordained his blessing,
life forevermore.

CEB

Genesis 45:1-15

[1]Joseph could no longer control himself in front of all his attendants, so he declared, "Everyone, leave now!" So no one stayed with him when he revealed his identity to his brothers. [2]He wept so loudly that the Egyptians and Pharaoh's household heard him. [3]Joseph said to his brothers, "I'm Joseph! Is my father really still alive?" His brothers couldn't respond because they were terrified before him.

[4]Joseph said to his brothers, "Come closer to me," and they moved closer. He said, "I'm your brother Joseph! The one you sold to Egypt. [5]Now, don't be upset and don't be angry with yourselves that you sold me here. Actually, God sent me before you to save lives. [6]We've already had two years of famine in the land, and there are five years left without planting or harvesting. [7]God sent me before you to make sure you'd survive and to rescue your lives in this amazing way. [8]You didn't send me here; it was God who made me a father to Pharaoh, master of his entire household, and ruler of the whole land of Egypt.

[9]"Hurry! Go back to your father. Tell him this is what your son Joseph says: 'God has made me master of all of Egypt. Come down to me. Don't delay. [10]You may live in the land of Goshen, so you will be near me, your children, your grandchildren, your flocks, your herds, and everyone with you. [11]I will support you there, so you, your household, and everyone with you won't starve, since the famine will still last five years.' [12]You and my brother Benjamin have seen with your own eyes that I'm speaking to you. [13]Tell my father about my power in Egypt and about everything you've seen. Hurry and bring my father down here." [14]He threw his arms around his brother Benjamin's neck and wept, and Benjamin wept on his shoulder. [15]He kissed all of his brothers and wept, embracing them. After that, his brothers were finally able to talk to him.

Psalm 133 (G397/398, N712, P241, UM850)

[1]Look at how good and pleasing it is
when families live together as one!
[2]It is like expensive oil poured over the head,
running down onto the beard—
Aaron's beard!—
which extended over the collar of his robes.
[3]It is like the dew on Mount Hermon
streaming down onto the mountains of Zion,
because it is there that the LORD has commanded the blessing:
everlasting life.

NRSVue

Romans 11:1-2a, 29-32

[1]I ask, then, has God rejected his people? By no means! I myself am an Israelite, a descendant of Abraham, a member of the tribe of Benjamin. [2a]God has not rejected his people whom he foreknew. . . .

[29]for the gifts and the calling of God are irrevocable. [30]Just as you were once disobedient to God but have now received mercy because of their disobedience, [31]so also they have now been disobedient in order that, by the mercy shown to you, they also may now receive mercy. [32]For God has imprisoned all in disobedience so that he may be merciful to all.

Matthew 15:(10-20), 21-28

[10]Then he called the crowd to him and said to them, "Listen and understand: [11]it is not what goes into the mouth that defiles a person, but it is what comes out of the mouth that defiles." [12]Then the disciples approached and said to him, "Do you know that the Pharisees took offense when they heard what you said?" [13]He answered, "Every plant that my heavenly Father has not planted will be uprooted. [14]Let them alone; they are blind guides of the blind. And if one blind person guides another, both will fall into a pit." [15]But Peter said to him, "Explain this parable to us." [16]Then he said, "Are you also still without understanding? [17]Do you not see that whatever goes into the mouth enters the stomach and goes out into the sewer? [18]But what comes out of the mouth proceeds from the heart, and this is what defiles. [19]For out of the heart come evil intentions, murder, adultery, sexual immorality, theft, false witness, slander. [20]These are what defile a person, but to eat with unwashed hands does not defile."

[21]Jesus left that place and went away to the district of Tyre and Sidon. [22]Just then a Canaanite woman from that region came out and started shouting, "Have mercy on me, Lord, Son of David; my daughter is tormented by a demon." [23]But he did not answer her at all. And his disciples came and urged him, saying, "Send her away, for she keeps shouting after us." [24]He answered, "I was sent only to the lost sheep of the house of Israel." [25]But she came and knelt before him, saying, "Lord, help me." [26]He answered, "It is not fair to take the children's food and throw it to the dogs." [27]She said, "Yes, Lord, yet even the dogs eat the crumbs that fall from their masters' table." [28]Then Jesus answered her, "Woman, great is your faith! Let it be done for you as you wish." And her daughter was healed from that moment.

CEB

Romans 11:1-2a, 29-32

[1]I ask you, has God rejected his people? Absolutely not! I'm an Israelite, a descendant of Abraham, from the tribe of Benjamin. [2a]God hasn't rejected his people, whom he knew in advance. . . .

[29]God's gifts and calling can't be taken back. [30]Once you were disobedient to God, but now you have mercy because they were disobedient. [31]In the same way, they have also been disobedient because of the mercy that you received, so now they can receive mercy too. [32]God has locked up all people in disobedience, in order to have mercy on all of them.

Matthew 15:(10-20), 21-28

[10]Jesus called the crowd near and said to them, "Listen and understand. [11]It's not what goes into the mouth that contaminates a person in God's sight. It's what comes out of the mouth that contaminates the person."

[12]Then the disciples came and said to him, "Do you know that the Pharisees were offended by what you just said?"

[13]Jesus replied, "Every plant that my heavenly Father didn't plant will be pulled up. [14]Leave the Pharisees alone. They are blind people who are guides to blind people. But if a blind person leads another blind person, they will both fall into a ditch."

[15]Then Peter spoke up, "Explain this riddle to us."

[16]Jesus said, "Don't you understand yet? [17]Don't you know that everything that goes into the mouth enters the stomach and goes out into the sewer? [18]But what goes out of the mouth comes from the heart. And that's what contaminates a person in God's sight. [19]Out of the heart come evil thoughts, murders, adultery, sexual sins, thefts, false testimonies, and insults. [20]These contaminate a person in God's sight. But eating without washing hands doesn't contaminate in God's sight."

[21]From there, Jesus went to the regions of Tyre and Sidon. [22]A Canaanite woman from those territories came out and shouted, "Show me mercy, Son of David. My daughter is suffering terribly from demon possession." [23]But he didn't respond to her at all.

His disciples came and urged him, "Send her away; she keeps shouting out after us."

[24]Jesus replied, "I've been sent only to the lost sheep, the people of Israel."

[25]But she knelt before him and said, "Lord, help me."

[26]He replied, "It is not good to take the children's bread and toss it to dogs."

[27]She said, "Yes, Lord. But even the dogs eat the crumbs that fall off their masters' table."

[28]Jesus answered, "Woman, you have great faith. It will be just as you wish." And right then her daughter was healed.

Primary Hymns and Songs for the Day

"My Faith Looks Up to Thee" 43334 (Matt) (O)
C576, CG407, E691, EL759, G829, GR351, P383, UM452 (PD), VU663, Z215
H-3 Hbl-77; Chr-138; Org-108
S-2 #142. Flute/violin desc.

"And Are We Yet Alive" (Gen, Pss) (O)
GR386, UM553 (PD)

"Where Charity and Love Prevail" 40313 (Gen, Pss)
SH271, UM549
H-3 Hbl-71, 104; Chr-219; Desc-95; Org-143
S-2 #162. Harmonization
E581, CG264, EL359, G316, N396

"This Is a Day of New Beginnings" (Gen, Matt) (C)
C518, N417, UM383
H-3 Chr-196

"In Christ There Is No East or West" 2608952 (Pss, Rom) (C)
CG273, E529, EL650 (PD), G317, N394, P440, UM548, VU606, Z65 (PD)
H-3 Chr-111; Desc-74; Org-88
S-1 #231-233. Various hristian
C687, G318, GR392, N395, P439
H-3 Hbl-104; Chr-219; Desc-95; Org-143
S-2 #162. Harmonization
SH226

Additional Hymn Suggestions

"Great Is Thy Faithfulness" 18723 (Gen) (O)
C86, CG48, EL733, G39, GR44, N423, P276, SH48, UM140, VU288

"Forgive Our Sins as We Forgive" (Gen)
CG694 E674, EL605, G444, GR442, P347, SH504, UM390, VU364

"Perdón, Señor" ("Forgive Us, Lord") 3409466 (Gen)
G431, S2134, SH505

"Come, Share the Lord" (Gen, Comm.)
C408, CG459, G510, S2269, VU469

"All Praise to Our Redeeming Lord" (Gen, Pss)
GR387, UM554

"Help Us Accept Each Other" 133756 (Gen, Pss)
C487, G754, N388, P358, UM560

"Draw Us in the Spirit's Tether" (Gen, Pss, Comm.)
C392, EL470, G529, N337, P504, UM632, VU479

"God Made from One Blood" (Gen, Pss)
C500, CG686, N427, S2170, VU554

"When God Restored Our Common Life" OL-00642 (Gen, Matt)
G74, S2182

"Mirad cuán bueno y cuán delicioso" ("Behold, How Good and Delightful") (Pss)
SH234

"How Clear Is Our Vocation, Lord" (Rom)
EL580, G432, P419, VU504

"I Greet Thee, Who My Sure Redeemer Art" (Rom)
G624, GR41, N251, P457, VU393

"There's a Wideness in God's Mercy" 3063417 (Rom, Matt)
C73, CG41, E469/470, EL587/588, G435, GR64, N23, P298, SH526, UM121, VU271

"Depth of Mercy" 1320726 (Rom, Matt)
GR234, UM355

"And Can It Be that I Should Gain" 25280 (Rom, Matt)
CG605, GR569, SH540, UM363 (PD)

"Standing on the Promises" (Rom, Matt)
C552, CG625, G838, GR434, SH45, UM374 (PD)

"O Spirit of the Living God" (PD) (Rom, Matt)
N263, SH222, UM539

"Christ for the World We Sing" (Rom, Matt)
E537, GR450, UM568 (PD)

"O For a Thousand Tongues to Sing" 1369 (Matt)
C5, CG332, E493, EL886, G610, GR1, N42, P466, SH439, UM57 (PD), VU326 (*See also* WS3001)

"All Hail the Power of Jesus' Name" 196858 (Matt)
C91/C92, CG339/340, E450/451, EL634, G263, GR279/280, N304, P142/143, SH207, UM154/155, VU334

"Jesus Shall Reign" 1510 (Rom, Matt)
C95, CG158, E544, EL434, G265, GR282, N300, P423, SH209, UM157 (PD), VU330

"My Hope Is Built" (PD) (Matt)
C537, CG590, EL596/597, G353, GR102, N403, P379, SH324, UM368 (PD), ZS182

"Lord, I Want to Be a Christian" 3184437 (Matt)
C589, CG507, G729, GR611, N454, P372 (PD), SH621, UM402, Z76 (PD-TO)

"We Walk by Faith" 2591911 (Matt)
CG634, E209, EL635, G817, N256, P399, S2196, SH660

"Healer of Our Every Ill" OL-00115 (Matt)
C506, EL612, G795, S2213, SH339, VU619

"Lord, Have Mercy" OL-17490 (Matt)
C299, G576, S2277

Additional Contemporary and Modern Suggestions

"Something Beautiful" 18060 (Gen)
UM394

"Make Me a Channel of Your Peace" OL-80478 (Gen)
G753, S2171, SH616 VU684

"Make Me a Channel of Your Peace" 6399315 (Gen)
+"Beauty for Ashes" 4414735 (Gen)
+"Promises" 7149439 (Gen)
+"Who You Say You Are" 7130503 (Gen)
+"Do It Again" 7067555 (Gen)

"Make Us One" 695737 (Gen, Pss)
S2224, ZS93

"Let It Be Said of Us" 1855882 (Gen, Pss)
+"Let Justice Roll" ("Like a River") 4974842 (Gen, Pss)
+"Good Grace" 7122177 (Gen, Pss)

"People Need the Lord" 18084 (Gen, Matt)
S2244

"Mighty to Save" 4591782 (Gen, Matt)
WS3038

"Your Grace Is Enough" 4477026 (Gen, Matt)
WS3106

"Live in Charity" (*"Ubi Caritas"*) OL-00798 (Pss)
C523, EL642, G205, S2179

"O Look and Wonder" (*"¡Miren Qué Bueno!"*) (Pss, Rom)
C292, EL649, G397, S2231, SH230, VU856

"Oh, I Know the Lord's Laid His Hands on Me" (PD) (Matt)
S2139 (PD), Z166

"I'm So Glad Jesus Lifted Me" (PD) (Matt)
C529, EL860 (PD), N474, S2151

"Lord, Listen to Your Children Praying" 22829 (Matt)
C305, CG389, G469, S2193, SH577, VU400, ZS156

"O For a Thousand Tongues to Sing" 4048754 (Matt)
WS3001

"Come, Emmanuel" 3999938 (Matt)
WS3130

"You Hear" 6005063 (Matt)
+"Way Maker" 7115744 (Matt)
+"Daughters of Zion" 7133716 (Matt)
+"The Kingdom Is Yours" 7109354 (Matt)

Solo/Ensemble Suggestions

"Make Me a Channel of Your Peace" (Gen)
V-3 (2) p. 25
V-3 (3) p. 28

"Help Us Accept Each Other" (Gen, Pss)
V-8 p. 343

"I Heard About a Man" (Matt)
V-8 p. 72
"Christ Has Broken Down the Wall" (Gen, Matt)
Mark Miller, Choristers Guild CGA-1224
SATB, piano (https://bit.ly/CGA-1224)
"Hine Mah Tov" (Pss)
Simon Sargon; Transcontinental Music 00191235
SATB, keyboard, flute (https://bit.ly/S-91235)

+Hymn Anthem
"Silence, Frenzied, Unclean Spirit" (Matt)
C186, G180/G181, N176, UM264, VU620
This text is set to reflect the drama of the biblical narratives. It should be performed in a dramatic style, musically expressing the pain of the demonic possession and the release of Christ's healing. It may be performed rather slowly, with *rubato* and *accelerando* at the director's discretion. This anthem uses the tune AUTHORITY, but the tune EBENEZER (G181) could be adapted as well.
Intro: Find the accompaniment chord on beat 3 and 4 of measure 2. Play four times on the piano, with deliberate accent and *fortissimo.* Sustain the last chord.
Stanza 1: T/B soloist sings the first four measures, *piano,* beginning as the introduction begins to fade away. Soloist should sing with confidence, but not giving in to the pounding of the keyboard chords that preceded.
Keyboard then plays the chord found on beat 1 of measure 5, as before. As these chords die away, soloist sings measures 5-8.
S/A soloist completes the stanza, accompanied by the keyboard playing the full accompaniment. Pause briefly before the text "stunned and hushed." *Mezzo forte.*
Stanza 2: All voices, unison, but never above *mezzo forte.* Keyboard plays full accompaniment. Continue in the dramatic style with subtle changes in the dynamics and tempo.
Stanza 3: All voices, unison, with a gradual *crescendo* throughout. In the first eight measures, keyboard plays only the chords on the first and third beats of each measure. measures 9-12 are played as written. In measures 13-16, double the bass notes an octave below. The final four measures are sung with power and conviction. End *forte.*
Ending: As the choir sings and holds the word "whole," the keyboard plays the same four chords as the intro, but this time getting softer with each chord. End *piano.* The choir holds their last note during this ending, getting softer, also ending *piano.*

Other Suggestions
Visuals:
O Weeping, remnant, famine, Gen. 45:5c, 8, men hugging
P Unity, Ps. 133:1, oil, robe, dew, mountain
E No/yes, Rom. 11:29, 32, gifts, calling, prison/manacles
G Woman shouting, Jesus, dogs/crumbs, girl healed
Greeting: N824 (Pss)
Call to Prayer: CG576, GR122, SH537, UM371 (PD), stanza 1. "I Stand Amazed" (Matt)
Prayer of Confession: WSL93. "Renewing God" (Gen, Matt)
+Response: EL152, S2275, WS3133. *"Kyrie"* (Gen, Matt)
Prayer: C483. For a Renewed Sense of Compassion (Gen)
Litany of Thanksgiving: WSL175. "Thank you, Jesus" (Matt)
Alternate Lessons (see page 4): Isa. 56:1, 6-8; Ps. 67
Theme Ideas: Children / Family of God, Conflict, Grace, Healing, Reconciliation, Sin and Forgiveness, Unity

Notes

NRSVue

Exodus 1:8–2:10

[8]Now a new king arose over Egypt who did not know Joseph. [9]He said to his people, “Look, the Israelite people are more numerous and more powerful than we. [10]Come, let us deal shrewdly with them, or they will increase and, in the event of war, join our enemies and fight against us and escape from the land.” [11]Therefore they set taskmasters over them to oppress them with forced labor. They built supply cities, Pithom and Rameses, for Pharaoh. [12]But the more they were oppressed, the more they multiplied and spread, so that the Egyptians came to dread the Israelites. [13]The Egyptians subjected the Israelites to hard servitude [14]and made their lives bitter with hard servitude in mortar and bricks and in every kind of field labor. They were ruthless in all the tasks that they imposed on them.

[15]The king of Egypt said to the Hebrew midwives, one of whom was named Shiphrah and the other Puah, [16]“When you act as midwives to the Hebrew women and see them on the birthstool, if it is a son, kill him, but if it is a daughter, she shall live.” [17]But the midwives feared God; they did not do as the king of Egypt commanded them, but they let the boys live. [18]So the king of Egypt summoned the midwives and said to them, “Why have you done this and allowed the boys to live?” [19]The midwives said to Pharaoh, “Because the Hebrew women are not like the Egyptian women, for they are vigorous and give birth before the midwife comes to them.” [20]So God dealt well with the midwives, and the people multiplied and became very strong. [21]And because the midwives feared God, he gave them families. [22]Then Pharaoh commanded all his people, “Every son that is born to the Hebrews you shall throw into the Nile, but you shall let every daughter live.”

2 Now a man from the house of Levi went and married a Levite woman. [2]The woman conceived and bore a son, and when she saw that he was a fine baby, she hid him three months. [3]When she could hide him no longer she got a papyrus basket for him and plastered it with bitumen and pitch; she put the child in it and placed it among the reeds on the bank of the river. [4]His sister stood at a distance, to see what would happen to him.

[5]The daughter of Pharaoh came down to bathe at the river, while her attendants walked beside the river. She saw the basket among the reeds and sent her maid to bring it. [6]When she opened it, she saw the child. He was crying, and she took pity on him. “This must be one of the Hebrews’ children,” she said. [7]Then his sister said to Pharaoh’s daughter, “Shall I go and get you a nurse from the Hebrew women to nurse the child for you?” [8]Pharaoh’s daughter said to her, “Yes.” So the girl went and called the child’s mother. [9]Pharaoh’s daughter said to her, “Take this child and nurse it for me, and I will give you your wages.” So the woman took the child and nursed it. [10]When the child grew up, she brought him to Pharaoh’s daughter, and he became her son. She named him Moses, “because,” she said, “I drew him out of the water.”

CEB

Exodus 1:8–2:10

[8]Now a new king came to power in Egypt who didn’t know Joseph. [9]He said to his people, “The Israelite people are now larger in number and stronger than we are. [10]Come on, let’s be smart and deal with them. Otherwise, they will only grow in number. And if war breaks out, they will join our enemies, fight against us, and then escape from the land.” [11]As a result, the Egyptians put foremen of forced work gangs over the Israelites to harass them with hard work. They had to build storage cities named Pithom and Rameses for Pharaoh. [12]But the more they were oppressed, the more they grew and spread, so much so that the Egyptians started to look at the Israelites with disgust and dread. [13]So the Egyptians enslaved the Israelites. [14]They made their lives miserable with hard labor, making mortar and bricks, doing field work, and by forcing them to do all kinds of other cruel work.

[15]The king of Egypt spoke to two Hebrew midwives named Shiphrah and Puah: [16]“When you are helping the Hebrew women give birth and you see the baby being born, if it’s a boy, kill him. But if it’s a girl, you can let her live.” [17]Now the two midwives respected God so they didn’t obey the Egyptian king’s order. Instead, they let the baby boys live.

[18]So the king of Egypt called the two midwives and said to them, “Why are you doing this? Why are you letting the baby boys live?”

[19]The two midwives said to Pharaoh, “Because Hebrew women aren’t like Egyptian women. They’re much stronger and give birth before any midwives can get to them.” [20]So God treated the midwives well, and the people kept on multiplying and became very strong. [21]And because the midwives respected God, God gave them households of their own.

[22]Then Pharaoh gave an order to all his people: “Throw every baby boy born to the Hebrews into the Nile River, but you can let all the girls live.”

2 Now a man from Levi’s household married a Levite woman. [2]The woman became pregnant and gave birth to a son. She saw that the baby was healthy and beautiful, so she hid him for three months. [3]When she couldn’t hide him any longer, she took a reed basket and sealed it up with black tar. She put the child in the basket and set the basket among the reeds at the riverbank. [4]The baby’s older sister stood watch nearby to see what would happen to him.

[5]Pharaoh’s daughter came down to bathe in the river, while her women servants walked along beside the river. She saw the basket among the reeds, and she sent one of her servants to bring it to her. [6]When she opened it, she saw the child. The boy was crying, and she felt sorry for him. She said, “This must be one of the Hebrews’ children.”

[7]Then the baby’s sister said to Pharaoh’s daughter, “Would you like me to go and find one of the Hebrew women to nurse the child for you?”

[8]Pharaoh’s daughter agreed, “Yes, do that.” So the girl went and called the child’s mother. [9]Pharaoh’s daughter said to her, “Take this child and nurse it for me, and I’ll pay you for your work.” So the woman took the child and nursed it. [10]After the child had grown up, she brought him back to Pharaoh’s daughter, who adopted him as her son. She named him Moses, “because,” she said, “I pulled him out of the water.”

NRSVue

Psalm 124 (G330, N706, P236, UM846)

1If it had not been the LORD who was on our side
—let Israel now say—
2if it had not been the LORD who was on our side,
when our enemies attacked us,
3then they would have swallowed us up alive,
when their anger was kindled against us;
4then the flood would have swept us away;
the torrent would have gone over us;
5then over us would have gone
the raging waters.
6Blessed be the LORD,
who has not given us
as prey to their teeth.
7We have escaped like a bird
from the snare of the hunters;
the snare is broken,
and we have escaped.
8Our help is in the name of the LORD,
who made heaven and earth.

Romans 12:1-8

1I appeal to you therefore, brothers and sisters, on the basis
of God's mercy, to present your bodies as a living sacrifice, holy
and acceptable to God, which is your reasonable act of worship.
2Do not be conformed to this age, but be transformed by the
renewing of the mind, so that you may discern what is the will of
God—what is good and acceptable and perfect.
3For by the grace given to me I say to everyone among you not
to think of yourself more highly than you ought to think but to
think with sober judgment, each according to the measure of
faith that God has assigned. 4For as in one body we have many
members and not all the members have the same function, 5so
we, who are many, are one body in Christ, and individually we
are members one of another. 6We have gifts that differ according
to the grace given to us: prophecy, in proportion to faith; 7minis-
try, in ministering; the teacher, in teaching; 8the encourager, in
encouragement; the giver, in sincerity; the leader, in diligence;
the compassionate, in cheerfulness.

Matthew 16:13-20

13Now when Jesus came into the district of Caesarea Philippi,
he asked his disciples, "Who do people say that the Son of Man
is?" 14And they said, "Some say John the Baptist but others Elijah
and still others Jeremiah or one of the prophets." 15He said to
them, "But who do you say that I am?" 16Simon Peter answered,
"You are the Messiah, the Son of the living God." 17And Jesus
answered him, "Blessed are you, Simon son of Jonah! For flesh
and blood has not revealed this to you but my Father in heaven.
18And I tell you, you are Peter, and on this rock I will build my
church, and the gates of Hades will not prevail against it. 19I will
give you the keys of the kingdom of heaven, and whatever you
bind on earth will be bound in heaven, and whatever you loose
on earth will be loosed in heaven." 20Then he sternly ordered
the disciples not to tell anyone that he was the Messiah.

CEB

Psalm 124 (G330, N706, P236, UM846)

1If the LORD hadn't been for us—
let Israel now repeat!—
2 if the LORD hadn't been for us,
when those people attacked us
3then they would have swallowed us up whole
with their rage burning against us!
4Then the waters would have drowned us;
the torrent would have come over our necks;
5 then the raging waters would have come over our necks!
6Bless the LORD
because he didn't hand us over
like food for our enemies' teeth!
7We escaped like a bird from the hunters' trap;
the trap was broken so we escaped!
8Our help is in the name of the LORD,
the maker of heaven and earth.

Romans 12:1-8

1So, brothers and sisters, because of God's mercies, I encourage you to present your bodies as a living sacrifice that is holy
and pleasing to God. This is your appropriate priestly service.
2Don't be conformed to the patterns of this world, but be transformed by the renewing of your minds so that you can figure out
what God's will is—what is good and pleasing and mature.
3Because of the grace that God gave me, I can say to each
one of you: don't think of yourself more highly than you ought
to think. Instead, be reasonable since God has measured out
a portion of faith to each one of you. 4We have many parts in
one body, but the parts don't all have the same function. 5In
the same way, though there are many of us, we are one body in
Christ, and individually we belong to each other. 6We have different gifts that are consistent with God's grace that has been given
to us. If your gift is prophecy, you should prophesy in proportion
to your faith. 7If your gift is service, devote yourself to serving. If
your gift is teaching, devote yourself to teaching. 8If your gift is
encouragement, devote yourself to encouraging. The one giving
should do it with no strings attached. The leader should lead
with passion. The one showing mercy should be cheerful.

Matthew 16:13-20

13Now when Jesus came to the area of Caesarea Philippi, he
asked his disciples, "Who do people say the Human One is?"
14They replied, "Some say John the Baptist, others Elijah, and
still others Jeremiah or one of the other prophets."
15He said, "And what about you? Who do you say that I am?"
16Simon Peter said, "You are the Christ, the Son of the living
God."
17Then Jesus replied, "Happy are you, Simon son of Jonah,
because no human has shown this to you. Rather my Father who
is in heaven has shown you. 18I tell you that you are Peter. And
I'll build my church on this rock. The gates of the underworld
won't be able to stand against it. 19I'll give you the keys of the
kingdom of heaven. Anything you fasten on earth will be fas-
tened in heaven. Anything you loosen on earth will be loosened
in heaven." 20Then he ordered the disciples not to tell anybody
that he was the Christ.

Primary Hymns and Songs for the Day
"Guide Me, O Thou Great Jehovah" 1448 (Exod) (O)
C622, CG33, E690, EL618, G65, GR47, N18, P281, SH51, UM127 (PD), VU651 (Fr.)
H-3 Hbl-25, 51, 58; Chr-89; Desc-26; Org-23
S-1 #76-77. Desc. and harm.
"Forward through the Ages" (PD) (Matt, Rom) (O)
N377, UM555 (PD)
H-3 Hbl-59; Chr-156; Org-140
"Glorious Things of Thee Are Spoken" 99371 (Exod, Pss, Matt)
C709, CG282, E522/523, EL647, G81, GR395, N307, P446, UM731 (PD)
"I'm Gonna Live So God Can Use Me" (Rom)
C614, G700, GR615, P369, S2153, SH632, VU575
"Take My Life, and Let It Be" 1390 (Rom) (C)
C609, CG490, G697, GR586, P391, SH627
H-3 Chr-34, 177; Desc-51; Org-53
S-2 #78-80. Various treatments
E707, EL583/EL685, N448, SH628, UM399 (PD), VU506

Additional Hymn Suggestions
"O God Our Help in Ages Past" (Exod)
C67, CG566, E680, EL632, G687, GR15, N25, P210, SH41, UM117 (PD), VU806
"God Will Take Care of You" 93645 (Exod)
GR358, N460, SH289, UM130 (PD)
"Amazing Grace" 22025 (Exod)
C546, CG587, E671, EL779, G649, GR572, N547/548, P280, SH523, UM378 (PD), VU266 (Fr.), Z211
"Spirit, Spirit of Gentleness" (Exod)
C249, EL396, G291, N286, P319, S2120, VU375 (Fr.)
"Why Stand So Far Away, My God?" OL-30234 (Exod)
C671, G786, S2180
+"Sing Praise to God Who Reigns Above" 7061649 (Exod, Pss)
C6, CG315, E408, EL871, G645, GR5, N6, P483, UM126 (PD), VU216
"Deep in the Shadows of the Past" (Exod, Pss)
G50, N320, P330, S2246
"Come, Thou Fount of Every Blessing" (Exod, Rom)
C16, CG295, E686, EL807, G475, GR37, N459, P356, SH394, UM400 (PD), VU559
"All My Hope Is Firmly Grounded" 3594474 (Pss)
C88, E665, EL757, GR68, N408, UM132, VU654/655
"Rock of Ages, Cleft for Me" (Pss, Matt)
C214, EL623, G438, GR242, N596, SH301, UM361 (PD)
"I Am Thine, O Lord" (Rom)
C601, CG504, GR591, N455, UM419 (PD)
"I Love Thy Kingdom, Lord" (Rom)
C274, CG262, G310, GR396, N312, P441, UM540 (PD)
"Onward, Christian Soldiers" (Rom)
CG261, E562, GR472, UM575 (PD)
"I Come with Joy" (Rom, Comm.)
C420, CG456, E304, EL482, G515, N349, P507, SH682, UM617, VU477
"Draw Us in the Spirit's Tether" (Rom, Comm.)
C392, EL470, G529, N337, P504, UM632, VU479
"Living for Jesus" (Rom)
C610, GR595, S2149
"Somos el Cuerpo de Cristo" ("We Are the Body of Christ") (1 Cor)
G768, SH229
"One Is the Body" 1099301 (Rom, Comm.)
WS3156
"Father, We Thank You" (Rom, Matt, Comm.)
E302/E303, EL478, GR394, SH686, UM563/565
"A Charge to Keep I Have" 118850 (Rom, Matt)
CG623, GR456, SH634, UM413 (PD)
"The Church's One Foundation" 1607188 (Rom, Matt)
C272, CG246, E525, EL654, G321, GR388/646, N386, P442, SH233, UM545/546, VU332 (Fr.)
"Christ, from Whom All Blessings Flow" (Rom, Matt)
GR399, UM550 (PD)
"Christ Is Made the Sure Foundation" 7036287 (Rom, Matt)
C275, CG248, E518, EL645, G394, GR101, N400, P416/417, SH225, UM559 (PD), VU325
"The Church of Christ, in Every Age" (Rom, Matt)
C475, EL729, G320, N306, P421, UM589, VU601
"Here I Am, Lord" OL-80670 (Rom, Matt)
C452, CG482, EL574, G69, GR589, P525, SH608, UM593, VU509
+"We Would Be Building" (Rom, Matt)
N607
"Jesus, the Very Thought of Thee" (Matt)
C102, CG386, E642, EL754, G629, GR127, N507, P310, UM175 (PD)
"My Hope Is Built" (PD) (Matt)
C537, CG590, EL596/597, G353, GR102, N403, P379, SH324, UM368 (PD), ZS182
"Christ for the World We Sing" (Matt)
E537, GR450, UM568 (PD)
"I'm So Glad Jesus Lifted Me" (PD) (Matt)
C529, EL860 (PD), N474, S2151

Additional Contemporary and Modern Suggestions
"Freedom Is Coming" 4194244 (Exod)
G359, S2192, SH29, ZS110
+"O Freedom" OL-68414 (Exod)
S2194 (PD-TO), Z102, ZS109
"Daughter of God" 4509781 (Exod)
"Grace Like Rain" 3689877 (Exod)
+"Promises" 7149439 (Exod, Pss)
+"Do It Again" 7067555 (Exod, Pss)
+"Who You Say You Are" 7130503 (Exod, Pss, Matt)
"If It Had Not Been for the Lord" 167076 (Pss)
S2053
+"Blessed Be the Name" 34525 (Pss)
CG350, GR67, UM63
+"Blessed Be Your Name" 3798438 (Pss)
SH449, WS3002
+"Surrounded" ("Fight My Battles") 7098758 (Pss)
+"Who You Say I Am" 7102401 (Pss)
+"No Outsiders" 7101035 (Pss, Rom)
+"Love Came Down" 5148938 (Pss, Rom)
+"My Life Is in You, Lord" 17315 (Pss, Rom)
S2032
"One Bread, One Body" OL-80673 (Rom, Comm.)
C393, EL496, G530, SH678, UM620, VU467
"Take Our Bread" (Rom, Comm.)
C413, UM640
"We Bring the Sacrifice of Praise" 9990 (Rom)
S2031, ZS213
"Grace Alone" 2335524 (Rom)
CG43, S2162, ZS100
"Sanctuary" 24140 (Rom)
G701, S2164, SH265, ZS165
"Bind Us Together" 1228 (Rom)
S2226
"Redemption" (Rom)
WS3111
+"Refresh My Heart" 917518 (Rom)
+"New Wine" 7102397 (Rom)
+"Wesley Prayer" ("Fire") 7118633 (Rom)
"All of Me" 6290160 (Rom)
"I Stand Amazed" 769450 (Rom)
"Take This Life" 2563365 (Rom)
"These Hands" 3251827 (Rom)
"There Will Be Bread" 4512352 (Rom, Comm.)
"Foundation" 7061516 (Rom, Matt)

"Amazing Grace" ("My Chains Are Gone") 4768151 (Matt)
GR574, WS3104
+"The Way" 7089024 (Matt)
+"Won't Stop Now" 7111932 (Matt)
+"His Mercy Is More" 7065053(Matt)
+"You've Always Been" 7115283 (Matt)
+"Who You Are to Me" 7153627 (Matt)
V-9, p. 124. Vocal Solo

Solo/Ensemble Suggestions
+"The Coventry Carol" (Exod)
V-3 (4) p. 44
+"Great Is Thy Faithfulness" (Exod, Pss)
V-8 p. 48
+"One Bread, One Body" (Rom)
V-3 (2) p. 40
"Take My Life" ("Consecration") (Rom)
V-8 p. 262
"Take My Life, and Let It Be" (Rom)
Arr. Mark Sedio; AEC-2 p. 76
SATB, piano, flute, percussion, opt. guitar (https://bit.ly/AEC-2-76)
+"Ceaseless Praise" (Rom)
Arr. Joshua Metzger; Celebrating Grace 810067
SATB, piano, opt. percussion (https://bit.ly/CG-0067)
"As This Broken Bread" (Rom, Matt, Comm.)
Wayne Wold; AEC-1 p. 5
2-part mixed, organ (https://bit.ly/AEC-1-5)

+Hymn Anthem
"Guide Me, O Thou Great Jehovah" 1448 (Exod) (O)
C622, CG33, E690, EL618, G65, GR47, N18, P281, SH51, UM127 (PD), VU651 (Fr.)
Stanza 1: A tenor soloist sings measures 1-4. Hold last note ("land") while soprano soloist sings measures 5-8. Both sing measures 9-14, soprano on melody, tenor on tenor part. *A cappella* (or accompany with keyboard).
Stanza 2: Full choir sings four parts (or unison). One soprano (or flute) can sing a descant (S-1, #76. Stanza 2 words will have to be written in.) *A cappella* (or accompany with keyboard). *Mezzo forte.*
Stanza 3: All voices sing melody. Keyboard plays S-1, #77 or another harmonization. Full, *forte.*

Other Suggestions
Visuals:
O Bricks/mortar, birthstool, newborn, basket/reeds/river
P Enemies, flood/torrent/water, bird/broken snare, Ps. 124:8
E Transformer, dance, offering plate, seven gifts
G Jesus teaching, Peter, large rock/keys, Matt. 16:15, 16
Greeting: WSL192. "All your gifts are welcome" (Rom)
+Call to Prayer: EL406, G281, S2118. "Holy Spirit, Come to Us" (Rom)
Prayer: UM607. A Covenant Prayer (Rom)
Reading: N574. "In Egypt Under Pharaoh" (Exod)
Offering Prayer: N844 (Rom)
Alternate Lessons (see page 4): Isa. 51:1-6; Ps. 138
+Sung Benediction: S2101, stanza 4. "Two Fishermen" (Rom)
Theme Ideas: Discipleship / Following God, God: Faithfulness, God: Providence / God our Help, Humility, Jesus: Body of Christ, Spiritual Gifts, Unity

Notes

NRSVue

Exodus 3:1-15

Moses was keeping the flock of his father-in-law Jethro, the
priest of Midian; he led his flock beyond the wilderness and
came to Mount Horeb, the mountain of God. [2]There the angel
of the Lord appeared to him in a flame of fire out of a bush;
he looked, and the bush was blazing, yet it was not consumed.
[3]Then Moses said, "I must turn aside and look at this great
sight and see why the bush is not burned up." [4]When the Lord
saw that he had turned aside to see, God called to him out of
the bush, "Moses, Moses!" And he said, "Here I am." [5]Then he
said, "Come no closer! Remove the sandals from your feet, for
the place on which you are standing is holy ground." [6]He said
further, "I am the God of your father, the God of Abraham, the
God of Isaac, and the God of Jacob." And Moses hid his face, for
he was afraid to look at God.

[7]Then the Lord said, "I have observed the misery of my people who are in Egypt; I have heard their cry on account of their
taskmasters. Indeed, I know their sufferings, [8]and I have come
down to deliver them from the Egyptians and to bring them up
out of that land to a good and spacious land, to a land flowing
with milk and honey, to the country of the Canaanites, the Hittites, the Amorites, the Perizzites, the Hivites, and the Jebusites.
[9]The cry of the Israelites has now come to me; I have also seen
how the Egyptians oppress them. [10]Now go, I am sending you to
Pharaoh to bring my people, the Israelites, out of Egypt." [11]But
Moses said to God, "Who am I that I should go to Pharaoh and
bring the Israelites out of Egypt?" [12]He said, "I will be with you,
and this shall be the sign for you that it is I who sent you: when
you have brought the people out of Egypt, you shall serve God
on this mountain."

[13]But Moses said to God, "If I come to the Israelites and say to
them, 'The God of your ancestors has sent me to you,' and they
ask me, 'What is his name?' what shall I say to them?" [14]God said
to Moses, "I am who I am." He said further, "Thus you shall say
to the Israelites, 'I am has sent me to you.' " [15]God also said to
Moses, "Thus you shall say to the Israelites, 'The Lord, the God
of your ancestors, the God of Abraham, the God of Isaac, and
the God of Jacob, has sent me to you':

This is my name forever,
and this my title for all generations."

Psalm 105:1-6, 23-26, 45c (G59, N691, UM828)

O give thanks to the Lord; call on his name;
make known his deeds among the peoples.
[2]Sing to him, sing praises to him;
tell of all his wonderful works.
[3]Glory in his holy name;
let the hearts of those who seek the Lord rejoice.
[4]Seek the Lord and his strength;
seek his presence continually.
[5]Remember the wonderful works he has done,
his miracles and the judgments he has uttered,
[6]O offspring of his servant Abraham,
children of Jacob, his chosen ones.

. . . .

[23]Then Israel came to Egypt;
Jacob lived as an alien in the land of Ham.
[24]And the Lord made his people very fruitful
and made them stronger than their foes,
[25]whose hearts he then turned to hate his people,
to deal craftily with his servants.
[26]He sent his servant Moses
and Aaron, whom he had chosen.

. . . .

Praise the Lord!

CEB

Exodus 3:1-15

Moses was taking care of the flock for his father-in-law Jethro,
Midian's priest. He led his flock out to the edge of the desert, and
he came to God's mountain called Horeb. [2]The Lord's messenger
appeared to him in a flame of fire in the middle of a bush. Moses
saw that the bush was in flames, but it didn't burn up. [3]Then
Moses said to himself, Let me check out this amazing sight and
find out why the bush isn't burning up.

[4]When the Lord saw that he was coming to look, God called to
him out of the bush, "Moses, Moses!"

Moses said, "I'm here."

[5]Then the Lord said, "Don't come any closer! Take off your
sandals, because you are standing on holy ground." [6]He continued, "I am the God of your father, Abraham's God, Isaac's God,
and Jacob's God." Moses hid his face because he was afraid to look
at God.

[7]Then the Lord said, "I've clearly seen my people oppressed
in Egypt. I've heard their cry of injustice because of their slave
masters. I know about their pain. [8]I've come down to rescue
them from the Egyptians in order to take them out of that land
and bring them to a good and broad land, a land that's full of
milk and honey, a place where the Canaanites, the Hittites, the
Amorites, the Perizzites, the Hivites, and the Jebusites all live.
[9]Now the Israelites' cries of injustice have reached me. I've seen
just how much the Egyptians have oppressed them. [10]So get going.
I'm sending you to Pharaoh to bring my people, the Israelites, out
of Egypt."

[11]But Moses said to God, "Who am I to go to Pharaoh and to
bring the Israelites out of Egypt?"

[12]God said, "I'll be with you. And this will show you that I'm the
one who sent you. After you bring the people out of Egypt, you
will come back here and worship God on this mountain."

[13]But Moses said to God, "If I now come to the Israelites and say
to them, 'The God of your ancestors has sent me to you,' they are
going to ask me, 'What's this God's name?' What am I supposed
to say to them?"

[14]God said to Moses, "I Am Who I Am. So say to the Israelites, 'I
Am has sent me to you.'" [15]God continued, "Say to the Israelites,
'The Lord, the God of your ancestors, Abraham's God, Isaac's
God, and Jacob's God, has sent me to you.' This is my name for-
ever; this is how all generations will remember me."

Psalm 105:1-6, 23-26, 45c (G59, N691, UM828)

Give thanks to the Lord;
call upon his name;
make his deeds known to all people!
[2] Sing to God;
sing praises to the Lord;
dwell on all his wondrous works!
[3] Give praise to God's holy name!
Let the hearts rejoice of all those seeking the Lord!
[4] Pursue the Lord and his strength;
seek his face always!
[5] Remember the wondrous works he has done,
all his marvelous works, and the justice he declared—
[6] you who are the offspring of Abraham, his servant,
and the children of Jacob, his chosen ones.

. . . .

[23] That's how Israel came to Egypt,
how Jacob became an immigrant in the land of Ham.
[24] God made his people very fruitful,
more powerful than their enemies,
[25] whose hearts God changed so they hated his people
and dealt shrewdly with his servants.
[26]God sent Moses his servant
and the one he chose, Aaron.

. . . .

Praise the Lord!

NRSVue

Romans 12:9-21

[9]Let love be genuine; hate what is evil; hold fast to what is
good; [10]love one another with mutual affection; outdo one
another in showing honor. [11]Do not lag in zeal; be ardent in
spirit; serve the Lord. [12]Rejoice in hope; be patient in affliction;
persevere in prayer. [13]Contribute to the needs of the saints; pursue hospitality to strangers.
[14]Bless those who persecute you; bless and do not curse them.
[15]Rejoice with those who rejoice; weep with those who weep.
[16]Live in harmony with one another; do not be arrogant, but
associate with the lowly; do not claim to be wiser than you are.
[17]Do not repay anyone evil for evil, but take thought for what is
noble in the sight of all. [18]If it is possible, so far as it depends on
you, live peaceably with all. [19]Beloved, never avenge yourselves,
but leave room for the wrath of God, for it is written, "Vengeance is mine; I will repay, says the Lord." [20]Instead, "if your
enemies are hungry, feed them; if they are thirsty, give them
something to drink, for by doing this you will heap burning
coals on their heads." [21]Do not be overcome by evil, but overcome evil with good.

Matthew 16:21-28

[21]From that time on, Jesus began to show his disciples that he
must go to Jerusalem and undergo great suffering at the hands
of the elders and chief priests and scribes and be killed and on
the third day be raised. [22]And Peter took him aside and began to
rebuke him, saying, "God forbid it, Lord! This must never happen to you." [23]But he turned and said to Peter, "Get behind me,
Satan! You are a hindrance to me, for you are setting your mind
not on divine things but on human things."
[24]Then Jesus told his disciples, "If any wish to come after me,
let them deny themselves and take up their cross and follow
me. [25]For those who want to save their life will lose it, and those
who lose their life for my sake will find it. [26]For what will it profit
them if they gain the whole world but forfeit their life? Or what
will they give in return for their life?
[27]"For the Son of Man is to come with his angels in the glory
of his Father, and then he will repay everyone for what has been
done. [28]Truly I tell you, there are some standing here who will
not taste death before they see the Son of Man coming in his
kingdom."

CEB

Romans 12:9-21

[9]Love should be shown without pretending. Hate evil, and
hold on to what is good. [10]Love each other like the members of
your family. Be the best at showing honor to each other. [11]Don't
hesitate to be enthusiastic—be on fire in the Spirit as you serve
the Lord! [12]Be happy in your hope, stand your ground when
you're in trouble, and devote yourselves to prayer. [13]Contribute
to the needs of God's people, and welcome strangers into your
home. [14]Bless people who harass you—bless and don't curse
them. [15]Be happy with those who are happy, and cry with those
who are crying. [16]Consider everyone as equal, and don't think
that you're better than anyone else. Instead, associate with
people who have no status. Don't think that you're so smart.
[17]Don't pay back anyone for their evil actions with evil actions,
but show respect for what everyone else believes is good.
[18]If possible, to the best of your ability, live at peace with
all people. [19]Don't try to get revenge for yourselves, my dear
friends, but leave room for God's wrath. It is written, Revenge
belongs to me; I will pay it back, says the Lord. [20]Instead, If your
enemy is hungry, feed him; if he is thirsty, give him a drink. By
doing this, you will pile burning coals of fire upon his head.
[21]Don't be defeated by evil, but defeat evil with good.

Matthew 16:21-28

[21]From that time Jesus began to show his disciples that he had
to go to Jerusalem and suffer many things from the elders, chief
priests, and legal experts, and that he had to be killed and raised
on the third day. [22]Then Peter took hold of Jesus and, scolding
him, began to correct him: "God forbid, Lord! This won't happen to you." [23]But he turned to Peter and said, "Get behind me,
Satan. You are a stone that could make me stumble, for you are
not thinking God's thoughts but human thoughts."
[24]Then Jesus said to his disciples, "All who want to come after
me must say no to themselves, take up their cross, and follow
me. [25]All who want to save their lives will lose them. But all who
lose their lives because of me will find them. [26]Why would people
gain the whole world but lose their lives? What will people give
in exchange for their lives? [27]For the Human One is about to
come with the majesty of his Father with his angels. And then he
will repay each one for what that person has done. [28]I assure you
that some standing here won't die before they see the Human
One coming in his kingdom."

Primary Hymns and Songs for the Day

"The God of Abraham Praise" 484742 (Exod) (O)
C24, CG45, E401, EL831, G49, GR16, N24, P488, SH50, UM116 (PD), VU255
H-3 Hbl-62, 95; Chr-59; Org-77
S-1 #211. Harm.

"Go Down, Moses" (Exod)
C663, E648, G52, GR403, N572, P334, SH28, UM448, Z112 (PD), Z212
H-3 Chr-215; Org-46

"The Servant Song" 72673 (Rom)
C490, CG289, EL659, G727, N539, S2222, SH264, VU595

"I Have Decided to Follow Jesus" (Matt)
C344, CG497, GR603, S2129, SH610

"Take Up Thy Cross" 2154808 (Matt) (C)
E675, EL667, G718, GR220, N204, P393, SH605, UM415, VU561

Additional Hymn Suggestions

"Holy, Holy, Holy! Lord God Almighty" 1156 (Exod)
C4, CG1, E362, EL413, G1, GR23, N277, P138, SH450, UM64/65, VU315

"Come, Ye Faithful, Raise the Strain" 355929 (Exod)
C215, CG218, E199/200, EL363, G234, GR253, N230, P115/114, UM315 (PD), VU165

"God of Grace and God of Glory" 43107 (Exod)
C464, CG285, E594/595, EL705, G307, GR45, N436, P420, SH250, UM577, VU686

"Deep in the Shadows of the Past" (Exod)
G50, N320, P330, S2246

"Praise God for This Holy Ground" (Exod)
G405, WS3009

"Allá en el monte Horebe la zarza ardía" ("There Was a Burning Bush upon Mount Horeb") (Exod, Pss)
SH35

"What Gift Can We Bring" 216549 (Exod, Pss)
CG533, N370, UM87

"Swiftly Pass the Clouds of Glory" (Exod, Matt)
G190, P73, S2102

"Guide Me, O Thou Great Jehovah" 1448 (Pss)
C622, CG33, E690, EL618, G65, GR47, N18, P281, SH51, UM127 (PD), VU651 (Fr.)

"This Is a Day of New Beginnings" 231043 (Rom)
C518, N417, UM383

"Forgive Our Sins as We Forgive" (Rom)
CG694 E674, EL605, G444, GR442, P347, SH504, UM390, VU364

"Cuando el Pobre" ("When the Poor Ones") OL-97385 (Rom)
C662, EL725, G762, P407, SH240, UM434, VU702

+"Where Charity and Love Prevail" 40313 (Rom)
CG264, E581, EL359, G316, N396, SH271, UM549

"Like the Murmur of the Dove's Song" (Rom)
C245, CG233, E513, EL403, G285, N270, P314, SH407, UM544, VU205

"The Church of Christ, in Every Age" (Rom)
C475, EL729, G320, N306, P421, UM589, VU601

"God, How Can We Forgive" OL-04799 (Rom)
G445, S2169

"Healer of Our Every Ill" OL-00115 (Rom)
C506, EL612, G795, S2213, SH339, VU619

"In Remembrance of Me" (Rom, Comm.)
C403, CG462, G521, S2254, SH667, ZS203

"Lord, I Want to Be a Christian" 3184437 (Rom, Matt)
C589, CG507, G729, GR611, N454, P372 (PD), SH621, UM402, Z76 (PD-TO)

"Holy Spirit, Truth Divine" 300431 (Rom, Matt)
C241, EL398, GR320, N63, P321, UM465, VU368

"Be Still, My Soul" (Rom, Matt)
C566, CG57, G819, GR346, N488, SH330, UM534, VU652

"Lord, Whose Love Through Humble Service" (Rom, Matt)
C461, CG650, E610, EL712, GR454, P427, SH239, UM581

"Beneath the Cross of Jesus" (Matt)
C197, CG184, E498, EL338, G216, GR248, N190, P92, SH166, UM297 (PD), VU135

"Where He Leads Me" (Matt)
C346, GR516, UM338 (PD), Z42

"Take My Life, and Let It Be" 1390 (Matt)
C609, CG490, E707, EL583/EL685, G697, GR586, P391, N448, SH627/628, UM399 (PD), VU506

"I Am Thine, O Lord" (Matt)
C601, CG504, GR591, N455, UM419 (PD)

"Must Jesus Bear the Cross Alone" (Matt)
CG505, GR598, UM424 (PD)

"More Love to Thee, O Christ" 36750 (Matt)
C527, CG365, G828, GR588, N456, P359, UM453 (PD)

"Nearer, My God, to Thee" (Matt)
C577, GR345, N606, UM528 (PD), VU497 (Fr.)

"And Are We Yet Alive" (Matt)
GR386, UM553 (PD)

"The Summons" ("Will You Come and Follow Me") 4668756 (Matt)
CG473, EL798, G726, S2130, SH598, VU567

"Living for Jesus" (Matt)
C610, GR595, S2149

Additional Contemporary and Modern Suggestions

+"Freedom Is Coming" 4194244 (Exod)
G359, S2192, SH29, ZS110

+"O Freedom" OL-68414 (Exod)
S2194 (PD-TO), Z102, ZS109

"Holy Ground" 21198 (Exod)
C112, G406, S2272

"Awesome in This Place" 847554 (Exod)

"Nobody" 7121827 (Exod)

+"Wesley Prayer" ("Fire") 7118633 (Exod)

+"Who You Say You Are" 7130503 (Exod)

+"Alpha and Omega" 4654148 (Pss)

"How Great Is Our God" 4348399 (Pss)
CG322, GR31, SH458, WS3003

"In the Lord I'll Be Ever Thankful" OL-00118 (Pss)
G654, S2195, SH316

"Goodness Is Stronger than Evil" OL-02636 (Rom)
EL721, G750, S2219

"Make Me a Channel of Your Peace" OL-80478 (Rom)
G753, S2171, SH616 VU684

"Make Me a Channel of Your Peace" 6399315 (Rom)

"Make Us One" 695737 (Rom)
S2224, ZS93

"They'll Know We Are Christians" 26997 (Rom)
C494, CG272, G300, S2223, SH232

"Bind Us Together" 1228 (Rom)
S2226

"Ubi Caritas" ("Live in Charity") OL-00798 (Rom)
C523, EL642, G205, S2179

"Rule of Life" (PD-TO) (Rom)
WS3117, ZS95

"There's a Spirit of Love in This Place" OL-38821 (Rom)
WS3148, ZS103

"O God in Whom We Live" (Rom)
WS3153

"Draw the Circle Wide" OL-117657 / OL-101422 (Rom)
WS3154

"Feed Us, Lord" 4636207 (Rom, Comm.)
G501, WS3167

+"You Keep Hope Alive" 7125876 (Rom)
V-9, p. 132. Vocal Solo

"Somlandela" ("We Will Follow") (PD-TO) (Matt)
WS3160

"Let It Be Said of Us" 1855882 (Matt)
"Every Move I Make" 1595726 (Matt)
"Everyday" 2798154 (Matt)
"Take Up Our Cross" 5358955 (Matt)
+"The Wonderful Cross" 3148435 (Matt)
+"New Wine" 7102397 (Matt)
+"Won't Stop Now" 7111932 (Matt)
+"Called Me Higher" 5887880 (Matt)

Solo/Ensemble Suggestions

"In Remembrance" (Rom, Comm.)
V-5 (2) p. 7
"May the Mind of Christ" (Rom)
V-8 p. 114
+"I Want Jesus to Walk with Me" (Matt)
V-7 p. 50/54
V-8 p. 187
"Nothing . . . Everything" (Matt)
V-8 p. 162
+"Go to the World" (Rom)
Karen Marrolli; MorningStar MSM 50-6223
SATB, piano (https://bit.ly/M-6223)
"Lord, Make Me an Instrument of Your Peace" (Rom)
Jody Lindh; Choristers Guild CGA612
SATB, keyboard (https://bit.ly/CGA-612)

+Hymn Anthem

"Forgive Our Sins as We Forgive" (Rom)
E674, EL605, G444, GR442, P347, SH504, UM390
Introduction: Cello, bassoon, or keyboard plays bass line.
Stanza 1: A male soloist sings the melody. The instrument that played the introduction plays the bass line again as accompaniment.
Stanza 2: S/A sing melody, T/B sing bass line. *A cappella* (or lightly accompanied on the keyboard). *Mezzo forte.*
Interlude: Keyboard plays hymnal setting. Choir sings melody on "ooh" for first four measures, changing to "ah" on the last four. Gradual *crescendo* during the entire interlude. Keyboard plays F# on the final chord, making the chord major. End *forte.*
Stanza 3: Choir sings SATB parts. A few higher voices may sing the Tenor line an octave higher. A few lower voices may sing the meloday down an octave. *A cappella* or accompanied with single instrument or keyboard. *Forte.*
Stanza 4: As stanza 1, with male soloist and single instrument or keyboard. *Mezzo forte.* If keyboard is used, the final chord may again be played as a major chord on the word "peace."

Other Suggestions

Visuals:
O Sandals, burning bush, mountain, milk/honey, 3:14
P Musical notes, singing
E Images of love overcoming hate, service to others
G Wooden cross on its side, self-denial, sandals
Introit: WS3047, stanza 1. "God Almighty, We Are Waiting" (Exod)
Canticle: UM646. "Canticle of Love" (Rom)
Prayer: WSL57. "Days pass and the years vanish" (Exod)
Prayer: UM392 (Exod, Matt)
Prayer: UM401 (Rom)
Offertory Prayer: WSL103. "Blessed God" (Rom)
Blessing: WSL165. "Go out into the world" (Rom)
Sung Benediction: WS3159. "Let Our Earth Be Peaceful" (Rom)
Theme Ideas: Compassion, C, Discipleship / Following God, God: Call of God / Listening, Love / Great Commandment

Notes

THEME INDEX

Assurance: 4/19/26, 5/17/26, 7/5/26

Baptism: 1/11/26, 4/19/26, 5/10/26, 6/21/26
Beatitudes/Blessings: 11/1/25, 2/1/26
Bread of Life: 11/27/25, 4/19/26, 8/2/26

Call of God: 10/5/25, 1/18/26, 1/25/26, 3/15/26, 5/14/26, 5/31/26, 6/7/26, 6/14/26
Children / Family of God: 12/28/25, 6/14/26, 7/5/26, 7/12/26, 7/19/26, 7/26/26, 8/9/26, 8/16/26
Comfort: 5/3/26, 7/5/26
Communion: 10/5/25, 4/2/26, 4/19/26 , 8/2/26
Compassion: 12/31/25, 8/30/26
Conflict: 7/12/26, 7/26/26, 8/9/26, 8/16/26
Courage: 11/9/25
Covenant: 10/19/25, 1/11/26, 2/22/26, 3/1/26, 4/3/26, 6/7/26, 6/28/26, 7/5/26
Creation: 5/31/26
Cross: 9/7/25, 11/23/25, 1/25/26, 2/1/26, 4/3/26, 6/14/26, 8/30/26

Discipleship / Following God: 9/7/25, 10/26/25, 11/2/25, 1/18/26, 1/25/26, 2/8/26, 4/26/26, 5/14/26, 5/17/26, 5/31/26, 6/7/26, 6/14/26, 6/21/26, 7/26/26, 8/23/26, 8/30/26
Doubt: 4/12/26, 8/9/26

Endurance: 11/16/25, 4/26/26

Faith: 10/5/25, 3/1/26, 3/8/26, 4/12/26, 5/14/26, 6/7/26, 6/14/26, 6/28/26, 8/9/26
Faithfulness: 9/21/25, 10/5/25, 10/12/25, 10/26/25, 11/2/25, 11/9/25, 2/1/26, 2/8/26

God
- **Call of God / Listening:** 8/30/26
- **Faithfulness:** 11/9/25, 5/10/26, 7/19/26, 8/23/26
- **Glory Of God:** 12/31/25, 1/11/26, 2/15/26, 3/29/26, 4/5/26, 5/24/26, 5/31/26
- **Hunger / Thirst for God:** 11/27/25, 2/1/26, 3/8/26, 5/24/26, 8/2/26
- **Kingdom of God:** 11/16/25, 7/12/26, 7/19/26, 7/26/26
- **Love of God:** 3/8/26, 6/14/26, 7/26/26, 8/2/26
- **Presence:** 7/19/26, 8/2/26
- **Providence / God our Help:** 9/28/25, 3/1/26, 5/3/26, 5/17/26, 6/21/26, 7/26/26, 8/9/26, 8/23/26, 4/2/26
- **Shepherd:** 9/14/25, 3/8/26, 3/15/26, 4/26/26
- **Wisdom:** 10/19/25, 1/6/26, 2/1/26, 2/8/26, 2/15/26
- **Word of God:** 10/19/25, 7/12/26

Grace: 9/14/25, 12/21/25, 12/24/25, 1/4/26, 1/6/26, 2/22/26, 4/19/26, 6/14/26, 6/21/26, 6/28/26, 8/16/26
Grief: 9/21/25, 10/5/25
Growth: 7/12/26, 7/19/26, 7/26/26

Healing: 10/12/25, 3/15/26, 3/22/26, 6/7/26, 8/16/26
Holy Spirit: 10/26/25, 1/11/26, 3/1/26, 4/12/26, 4/19/26, 4/26/26, 5/3/26, 5/10/26, 5/14/26, 5/17/26, 5/24/26, 7/12/26, 7/19/26, 7/26/26
Hope: 9/28/25, 10/19/25, 11/1/25, 12/14/25, 3/8/26, 4/12/26, 7/19/26
Humility: 10/26/25, 2/1/26, 8/23/26

Inclusion: 9/7/25, 1/11/26, 1/25/26, 4/5/26, 6/28/26, 8/9/26

Jesus
- **Body of Christ:** 8/23/26
- **Childhood:** 12/28/25, 1/6/26
- **Cornerstone:** 5/3/26
- **Crucifixion:** 3/29/26, 4/2/26, 4/3/26
- **Incarnation:** 12/21/25, 12/24/25
- **Jesus Our Savior:** 4/2/26, 4/3/26
- **Mind of Christ:** 11/27/25, 2/8/26, 3/22/26, 3/29/26, 4/5/26, 7/12/26
- **Return and Reign:** 11/23/25, 11/30/25, 12/7/25, 12/14/25
- **Temptation:** 2/22/26

Joy: 10/12/25, 10/26/25, 1/4/26
Justice: 11/23/25, 12/7/25, 12/14/25, 12/31/25, 1/6/26, 2/1/26, 2/8/26

Lament: 9/21/25, 10/5/25, 11/2/25, 12/28/25, 3/22/26, 3/29/26, 4/3/26, 5/3/26, 6/28/26
Light: 12/24/25, 1/4/26, 1/6/26, 1/11/26, 1/18/26, 1/25/26, 2/8/26, 3/15/26
Love: 10/19/25, 4/2/26, 5/10/26, 7/5/26, 7/26/26
Love / Great Commandment: 8/30/26

New Creation: 11/16/25, 12/31/25, 1/11/26, 3/22/26, 4/12/26

Patience: 12/14/25, 12/31/25, 2/18/26
Peace: 10/12/25, 11/23/25, 11/27/25, 11/30/25, 12/7/25, 1/4/26, 5/31/26
Praise: 10/12/25, 10/26/25, 11/1/25, 11/27/25, 12/24/25, 12/28/25, 2/15/26, 3/8/26, 3/29/26, 5/14/26, 5/31/26, 6/7/26
Prayer: 9/21/25, 10/19/25, 2/18/26
Preparation: 11/30/25, 12/7/25, 12/14/25

Reconciliation: 8/16/26
Redemption / Salvation: 9/14/25, 12/21/25, 12/28/25, 1/4/26, 2/8/26, 2/18/26
Repentance: 11/2/25, 2/18/26, 3/22/26
Resurrection: 11/9/25, 3/1/26, 3/22/26, 4/5/26, 4/12/26, 4/19/26, 5/14/26

Saints: 11/1/25, 11/9/25, 2/1/26
Servanthood / Service: 4/2/26
Sin and Forgiveness: 9/7/25, 9/14/25, 2/18/26, 2/22/26, 3/8/26, 6/28/26, 7/5/26, 8/16/26
Spiritual Gifts: 1/18/26, 5/24/26, 8/23/26
Stewardship: 9/28/25, 11/2/25, 11/27/25

Thanksgiving / Gratitude: 10/12/25, 11/16/25, 11/27/25, 3/29/26, 4/5/26

Unity: 10/12/25, 1/25/26, 4/26/26, 5/24/26, 8/16/26, 8/23/26

Vision: 11/2/25, 3/15/26

Waiting: 11/2/25, 11/9/25, 11/30/25, 12/7/25, 12/14/25, 1/18/26, 5/17/26
Welcome: 9/7/25

Old Testament

Genesis 1:1–2:4a 5/31/26
Genesis 2:15-17; 3:1-7 . . . . 2/22/26
Genesis 12:1-4a 3/1/26
Genesis 12:1-9 . . . . 6/7/26
Genesis 18:1-15, (21:1-7) 6/14/26
Genesis 21:8-21 . . . . 6/21/26
Genesis 22:1-14 . . . . 6/28/26
Genesis 24:34-38, 42-49, 58-67 . . . . 7/5/26
Genesis 25:19-34 . . . . 7/12/26
Genesis 28:10-19 a. 7/12/26
Genesis 29:15-28 . . . . 7/26/26
Genesis 32:22-31 . . . . 8/2/26
Genesis 37:1-4, 12-28. . . . . 8/9/26
Genesis 45:1-15 . . . . 8/16/26

Exodus 1:8–2:10 . . . . 8/23/26
Exodus 3:1-15 . . . . 8/30/26
Exodus 12:1-4 (5-10) 11-14. . . . . 4/2/26
Exodus 17:1-7 . . . . 3/8/26
Exodus 24:12-18 . . . . 2/15/26

Deuteronomy 26:1-11 . . . . 11/27/25

1 Samuel 16:1-13. . . . . 3/15/26

Psalm 8 . . . . 12/31/25
Psalm 8 . . . . 5/31/26
Psalm 13 . . . . 6/28/26
Psalm 14 . . . . 9/14/25
Psalm 15 . . . . 2/1/26
Psalm 16 . . . . 4/12/26
Psalm 17:1-7, 15 . . . . 8/2/26
Psalm 22 . . . . 4/3/26
Psalm 23 . . . . 3/15/26
Psalm 23 . . . . 4/26/26
Psalm 27:1, 4-9 . . . . 1/25/26
Psalm 29 . . . . 1/11/26
Psalm 31:1-5, 15-16 . . . . 5/3/26
Psalm 31:9-16 . . . . 3/29/26
Psalm 32 . . . . 2/22/26
Psalm 33:1-12 . . . . 6/7/26
Psalm 40:1-11 . . . . 1/18/26
Psalm 45:10-17 . . . . 7/5/26
Psalm 47 . . . . 5/14/26
Psalm 51:1-17 . . . . 2/18/26
Psalm 65 . . . . 10/26/25
Psalm 66:1-12 . . . . 10/12/25
Psalm 66:8-20 . . . . 5/10/26
Psalm 68:1-10 . . . . 5/17/26
Psalm 72:1-7, 10-14 . . . . 1/6/26
Psalm 72:1-7, 18-19 . . . . 12/7/25
Psalm 79:1-9 . . . . 9/21/25
Psalm 80:1-7, 17-19 . . . . 12/21/25
Psalm 86:1-10, 16-17 . . . . 6/21/26
Psalm 91:1-6, 14-16 . . . . 9/28/25
Psalm 95 . . . . 3/8/26
Psalm 96 . . . . 12/24/25
Psalm 99 . . . . 2/15/26
Psalm 100 . . . . 11/27/25
Psalm 104:24-34, 35b 5/24/26
Psalm 105:1-6, 16-22, 45b 8/9/26
Psalm 105:1-6, 23-26, 45c 8/30/26
Psalm 105:1-11, 45b 7/26/26
Psalm 112:1-9 (10) 2/8/26
Psalm 116:1-2, 12-19 . . . . 4/2/26
Psalm 116:1-2, 12-19 . . . . 6/14/26
Psalm 116:1-4, 12-19 . . . . 4/19/26
Psalm 118:1-2, 14-24 . . . . 4/5/26
Psalm 118:1-2, 19-29 . . . . 3/29/26
Psalm 119:97-104 . . . . 10/19/25
Psalm 119:105-112 . . . . 7/12/26
Psalm 119:137-144 . . . . 11/2/25
Psalm 121 . . . . 3/1/26
Psalm 122 . . . . 11/30/25
Psalm 124 . . . . 8/23/26
Psalm 130 . . . . 3/22/26
Psalm 133 . . . . 8/16/26
Psalm 137 . . . . 10/5/25
Psalm 139:1-6, 13-18 . . . . 9/7/25
Psalm 139:1-12, 23-24 . . . . 7/12/26
Psalm 145:1-5, 17-21 . . . . 11/9/25
Psalm 147:12-20 . . . . 1/4/26
Psalm 148 . . . . 12/28/25
Psalm 149 . . . . 11/1/25

Ecclesiastes 3:1-13 . . . . 12/31/25

Isaiah 2:1-5. . . . . 11/30/25
Isaiah 7:10-16. . . . . 12/21/25
Isaiah 9:1-4. . . . . 1/25/26
Isaiah 9:2-7. . . . . 12/24/25
Isaiah 11:1-10. . . . . 12/7/25
Isaiah 12. . . . . 11/16/25
Isaiah 35:1-10. . . . . 12/14/25
Isaiah 42:1-9. . . . . 1/11/26
Isaiah 49:1-7. . . . . 1/18/26
Isaiah 50:4-9a 3/29/26
Isaiah 52:13–53:12. . . . . 4/3/26
Isaiah 58:1-9a (9b -12) 2/8/26
Isaiah 60:1-6. . . . . 1/6/26
Isaiah 63:7-9. . . . . 12/28/25
Isaiah 65:17-25. . . . . 11/16/25

Jeremiah 18:1-11 . . . . 9/7/25
Jeremiah 4:11-12, 22-28 . . . . 9/14/25
Jeremiah 8:18-9:1 . . . . 9/21/25
Jeremiah 23:1-6 . . . . 11/23/25

Jeremiah 29:1, 4-7 . . . . 10/12/25
Jeremiah 31:7-14 . . . . 1/4/26
Jeremiah 31:27-34 . . . . 10/19/25
Jeremiah 32:1-3a, 6-15 . . . . 9/28/25

Lamentations 1:1-6 . . . . 10/5/25

Ezekiel 37:1-14 . . . . 3/22/26

Daniel 7:1-3, 15-18 . . . . 11/1/25

Joel 2:1-2, 12-17 . . . . 2/18/26
Joel 2:23-32 . . . . 10/26/25

Micah 6:1-8 . . . . 2/1/26

Habakkuk 1:1-4; 2:1-4 . . . . 11/2/25

Haggai 1:15b–2:9 . . . . 11/9/25

New Testament

Matthew 1:18-25 . . . . 12/21/25
Matthew 2:1-12 . . . . 1/6/26
Matthew 2:13-23 . . . . 12/28/25
Matthew 3:1-12 . . . . 12/7/25
Matthew 3:13-17 . . . . 1/11/26
Matthew 4:1-11 . . . . 2/22/26
Matthew 4:12-23 . . . . 1/25/26
Matthew 5:1-12 . . . . 2/1/26
Matthew 5:13-20 . . . . 2/8/26
Matthew 6:1-6, 16-21 . . . . 2/18/26
Matthew 9:9-13, 18-26 . . . . 6/7/26
Matthew 9:35-10:8, (9-23) 6/14/26
Matthew 10:24-39 . . . . 6/21/26
Matthew 10:40-42 . . . . 6/28/26
Matthew 11:2-11 . . . . 12/14/25
Matthew 11:16-19, 25-30 . . . . 7/5/26
Matthew 13:1-9, 18-23 . . . . 7/12/26
Matthew 13:24-30, 36-43 . . . . 7/12/26
Matthew 13:31-33, 44-52 . . . . 7/26/26
Matthew 14:13-21 . . . . 8/2/26
Matthew 14:22-33 . . . . 8/9/26
Matthew 15:(10-20), 21-28 . . . . 8/16/26
Matthew 16:13-20 . . . . 8/23/26
Matthew 16:21-28 . . . . 8/30/26
Matthew 17:1-9 . . . . 2/15/26
Matthew 21:1-11 . . . . 3/29/26
Matthew 24:36-44 . . . . 11/30/25
Matthew 25:31-46 . . . . 12/31/25
Matthew 26:14-27:66 (27:11-54) 3/29/26
Matthew 28:16-20 . . . . 5/31/26

Luke 1:46b-55 . . . . 12/14/25
Luke 1:68-79 . . . . 11/23/25
Luke 2:1-20 . . . . 12/24/25
Luke 6:20-31 . . . . 11/1/25
Luke 14:25-33 . . . . 9/7/25
Luke 15:1-10 . . . . 9/14/25
Luke 16:1-13 . . . . 9/21/25
Luke 16:19-31 . . . . 9/28/25
Luke 17:5-10 . . . . 10/5/25
Luke 17:11-19 . . . . 10/12/25
Luke 18:1-8 . . . . 10/19/25
Luke 18:9-14 . . . . 10/26/25
Luke 19:1-10 . . . . 11/2/25
Luke 20:27-38 . . . . 11/9/25
Luke 21:5-19 . . . . 11/16/25
Luke 23:33-43 . . . . 11/23/25
Luke 24:13-35 . . . . 4/19/26
Luke 24:44-53 . . . . 5/14/26

John 1: (1-9), 10-18 . . . . 1/4/26
John 1:29-42 . . . . 1/18/26
John 3:1-17 . . . . 3/1/26
John 4:5-42 . . . . 3/8/26
John 6:25-35 . . . . 11/27/25
John 7:37-39 . . . . 5/24/26
John 9:1-41 . . . . 3/15/26
John 10:1-10 . . . . 4/26/26
John 11:1-45 . . . . 3/22/26
John 13:1-17, 31b -35 . . . . 4/2/26
John 14:1-14 . . . . 5/3/26
John 14:15-21 . . . . 5/10/26
John 17:1-11 . . . . 5/17/26
John 18:1–19:42 . . . . 4/3/26
John 20:1-18 (or Matthew 28:1-10) 4/5/26
John 20:19-31 . . . . 4/12/26

Acts 1:1-11 . . . . 5/14/26
Acts 1:6-14 . . . . 5/17/26
Acts 2:1-21 . . . . 5/24/26
Acts 2:14a, 22-32 . . . . 4/12/26
Acts 2:14a, 36-41 . . . . 4/19/26
Acts 2:42-47 . . . . 4/26/26
Acts 7:55-60 . . . . 5/3/26
Acts 10:34-43 . . . . 1/11/26
Acts 10:34-43 . . . . 4/5/26
Acts 17:22-31 . . . . 5/10/26

Romans 1:1-7 . . . . 12/21/25
Romans 4:1-5, 13-17 . . . . 3/1/26
Romans 4:13-25 . . . . 6/7/26
Romans 5:1-8 . . . . 6/14/26
Romans 5:1-11 . . . . 3/8/26
Romans 5:12-19 . . . . 2/22/26
Romans 6:1b-11 . . . . 6/21/26
Romans 6:12-23 . . . . 6/28/26
Romans 7:15-25a 7/5/26
Romans 8:1-11 . . . . 7/12/26
Romans 8:6-11 . . . . 3/22/26

Romans 8:12-25 . . . . 7/12/26
Romans 8:26-39 . . . . 7/26/26
Romans 9:1-5 . . . . 8/2/26
Romans 10:5-15 . . . . 8/9/26
Romans 11:1-2a, 29-32 . . . . 8/16/26
Romans 12:1-8 . . . . 8/23/26
Romans 12:9-21 . . . . 8/30/26
Romans 13:11-14 . . . . 11/30/25
Romans 15:4-13 . . . . 12/7/25

1 Corinthians 1:1-9 . . . . 1/18/26
1 Corinthians 1:10-18 . . . . 1/25/26
1 Corinthians 1:18-31 . . . . 2/1/26
1 Corinthians 2:1-12 (13-16) 2/8/26
1 Corinthians 11:23-26 . . . . 4/2/26
1 Corinthians 12:3b-13 . . . . 5/24/26

2 Corinthians 13:11-13 . . . . 5/31/26
2 Corinthians 5:20 b–6:10 . . . . 2/18/26

Ephesians 1:3-14 . . . . 1/4/26
Ephesians 1:11-23 . . . . 11/1/25
Ephesians 1:15-23 . . . . 5/14/26
Ephesians 3:1-12 . . . . 1/6/26
Ephesians 5:8-14 . . . . 3/15/26

Philippians 2:5-11 . . . . 3/29/26
Philippians 4:4-9 . . . . 11/27/25

Colossians 1:11-20 . . . . 11/23/25
Colossians 3:1-4 . . . . 4/5/26

2 Thessalonians 1:1-4, 11-12 . . . . 11/2/25
2 Thessalonians 2:1-5, 13-17 . . . . 11/9/25
2 Thessalonians 3:6-13 . . . . 11/16/25

1 Timothy 1:12-17 . . . . 9/14/25
1 Timothy 2:1-7 . . . . 9/21/25
1 Timothy 6:6-19 . . . . 9/28/25

2 Timothy 1:1-14 . . . . 10/5/25
2 Timothy 2:8-15 . . . . 10/12/25
2 Timothy 3:14–4:5 . . . . 10/19/25
2 Timothy 4:6-8, 16-18 . . . . 10/26/25

Titus 2:11-14 . . . . 12/24/25

Philemon 1-21 . . . . 9/7/25

Hebrews 2:10-18 . . . . 12/28/25
Hebrews 10:16-25 . . . . 4/3/26

James 5:7-10 . . . . 12/14/25

1 Peter 1:3-9 . . . . 4/12/26
1 Peter 1:17-23 . . . . 4/19/26
1 Peter 2:2-10 . . . . 5/3/26
1 Peter 2:19-25 . . . . 4/26/26
1 Peter 3:13-22 . . . . 5/10/26
1 Peter 4:12-14; 5:6-11 . . . . 5/17/26

2 Peter 1:16-21 . . . . 2/15/26

Revelation 21:1-6a 12/31/25

WORSHIP PLANNING SHEET 1

Date: ____________________ Color: ________________________________

Preacher: ________________________________

Liturgist: ________________________________

Selected Scripture: ________________________________

Selected Hymns | No. | Placement

____

____

____

____

Psalter #____________________

Keyboard Selections

Title | Composer | Placement

____

____

____

Anthems

Title | Choir | Composer | Placement

____

____

Vocal Solos

Title | Singer | Composer | Placement

____

____

Other Ideas:

Acolytes: ________________________________

Head Usher: ________________________________

Altar Guild Contact: ________________________________

Other Participants: ________________________________

____

WORSHIP PLANNING SHEET 2

Date: ________________ Sunday: ________________ Color: ______________________________

Preacher: ____

Liturgist: ____

Opening Voluntary Composer

____

____

Hymn Tune Name No.

____

Opening Prayer: ____

Prayer for Illumination: ____

First Lesson: ____

Psalter: ____

Second Lesson: ____

Gospel Lesson: ____

Hymn Tune Name No.

____

Response to the Word: ____

Prayers of the People: ____

Offertory Composer

____

Communion Setting: ____

Communion Hymns Tune Name No.

____

____

Closing Hymn Tune Name No.

____

Benediction: ____

Closing Voluntary Composer

____

CONTEMPORARY WORSHIP PLANNING SHEET

Because of the diversity in orders of worship, you will want to adjust this planning sheet to meet the needs of your worship planning team. A common order used would consist of three to four opening praise choruses and lively hymns, a time of informal prayers of the congregation along with songs of prayer, reading of the primary scripture for the day, a drama or video to illustrate the day's theme, a message from the preacher, a testimony on the theme for the day (if a drama or video was not presented earlier), followed by closing songs appropriate to the mood of the service and the message. Any offering would usually be taken early in the service, and Holy Communion would normally take place following the message. Special music (solos, duets, instrumental music) can be used wherever it best expresses the theme of the service.

Date: ______________________ Sunday: ______________________

Thematic Emphasis or Topic: ______________________

Color: ______________________ Visual Focus: ______________________

Opening Songs:

____

____

Prayer Songs:

____

Scripture Selection(s):

____

Drama or Video:

____

Message Title:

____

Testimony: ______________________

Special Music:

____

Closing Songs:

____

Preacher: ______________________ Music Leader: ______________________

Worship Facilitator: ______________________ Prayer Leader: ______________________

NOTES

2025–2026 Lectionary Calendar

Lectionary verses and worship suggestions in this edition of *Prepare!* relate to the unshaded dates in the calendar below. Lectionary Year C: September 1, 2025–November 28, 2025; Lectionary Year A: December 1, 2025–August 31, 2026.

2025

JANUARY

S	M	T	W	T	F	S
			1	2	3	4
5	6	7	8	9	10	11
12	13	14	15	16	17	18
19	20	21	22	23	24	25
26	27	28	29	30	31	

FEBRUARY

S	M	T	W	T	F	S
						1
2	3	4	5	6	7	8
9	10	11	12	13	14	15
16	17	18	19	20	21	22
23	24	25	26	27	28	

MARCH

S	M	T	W	T	F	S
						1
2	3	4	5	6	7	8
9	10	11	12	13	14	15
16	17	18	19	20	21	22
23	24	25	26	27	28	29
30	31					

APRIL

S	M	T	W	T	F	S
		1	2	3	4	5
6	7	8	9	10	11	12
13	14	15	16	17	18	19
20	21	22	23	24	25	26
27	28	29	30			

MAY

S	M	T	W	T	F	S
				1	2	3
4	5	6	7	8	9	10
11	12	13	14	15	16	17
18	19	20	21	22	23	24
25	26	27	28	29	30	31

JUNE

S	M	T	W	T	F	S
1	2	3	4	5	6	7
8	9	10	11	12	13	14
15	16	17	18	19	20	21
22	23	24	25	26	27	28
29	30					

JULY

S	M	T	W	T	F	S
		1	2	3	4	5
6	7	8	9	10	11	12
13	14	15	16	17	18	19
20	21	22	23	24	25	26
27	28	29	30	31		

AUGUST

S	M	T	W	T	F	S
					1	2
3	4	5	6	7	8	9
10	11	12	13	14	15	16
17	18	19	20	21	22	23
24	25	26	27	28	29	30
31						

SEPTEMBER

S	M	T	W	T	F	S
	1	2	3	4	5	6
7	8	9	10	11	12	13
14	15	16	17	18	19	20
21	22	23	24	25	26	27
28	29	30				

OCTOBER

S	M	T	W	T	F	S
			1	2	3	4
5	6	7	8	9	10	11
12	13	14	15	16	17	18
19	20	21	22	23	24	25
26	27	28	29	30	31	

NOVEMBER

S	M	T	W	T	F	S
						1
2	3	4	5	6	7	8
9	10	11	12	13	14	15
16	17	18	19	20	21	22
23	24	25	26	27	28	29
30						

DECEMBER

S	M	T	W	T	F	S
	1	2	3	4	5	6
7	8	9	10	11	12	13
14	15	16	17	18	19	20
21	22	23	24	25	26	27
28	29	30	31			

2026

JANUARY

S	M	T	W	T	F	S
				1	2	3
4	5	6	7	8	9	10
11	12	13	14	15	16	17
18	19	20	21	22	23	24
25	26	27	28	29	30	31

FEBRUARY

S	M	T	W	T	F	S
1	2	3	4	5	6	7
8	9	10	11	12	13	14
15	16	17	18	19	20	21
22	23	24	25	26	27	28

MARCH

S	M	T	W	T	F	S
1	2	3	4	5	6	7
8	9	10	11	12	13	14
15	16	17	18	19	20	21
22	23	24	25	26	27	28
29	30	31				

APRIL

S	M	T	W	T	F	S
			1	2	3	4
5	6	7	8	9	10	11
12	13	14	15	16	17	18
19	20	21	22	23	24	25
26	27	28	29	30		

MAY

S	M	T	W	T	F	S
					1	2
3	4	5	6	7	8	9
10	11	12	13	14	15	16
17	18	19	20	21	22	23
24	25	26	27	28	29	30
31						

JUNE

S	M	T	W	T	F	S
	1	2	3	4	5	6
7	8	9	10	11	12	13
14	15	16	17	18	19	20
21	22	23	24	25	26	27
28	29	30				

JULY

S	M	T	W	T	F	S
			1	2	3	4
5	6	7	8	9	10	11
12	13	14	15	16	17	18
19	20	21	22	23	24	25
26	27	28	29	30	31	

AUGUST

S	M	T	W	T	F	S
						1
2	3	4	5	6	7	8
9	10	11	12	13	14	15
16	17	18	19	20	21	22
23	24	25	26	27	28	29
30	31					

SEPTEMBER

S	M	T	W	T	F	S
		1	2	3	4	5
6	7	8	9	10	11	12
13	14	15	16	17	18	19
20	21	22	23	24	25	26
27	28	29	30			

OCTOBER

S	M	T	W	T	F	S
				1	2	3
4	5	6	7	8	9	10
11	12	13	14	15	16	17
18	19	20	21	22	23	24
25	26	27	28	29	30	31

NOVEMBER

S	M	T	W	T	F	S
1	2	3	4	5	6	7
8	9	10	11	12	13	14
15	16	17	18	19	20	21
22	23	24	25	26	27	28
29	30					

DECEMBER

S	M	T	W	T	F	S
		1	2	3	4	5
6	7	8	9	10	11	12
13	14	15	16	17	18	19
20	21	22	23	24	25	26
27	28	29	30	31		